PENGUIN BOOKS

BLOOD AND POWER

A Ph.D. in American Civilization from Brown University,
Stephen Fox belongs to a small and respected group of inde-
pendent scholars who have chosen to write without univer-
sity affiliations. He is the author of *The Guardian of Boston:
William Monroe Trotter* and *John Muir and His Legacy: The
American Conservation Movement*. His most recent book, *The
Mirror Makers: A History of American Advertising and Its Crea-
tors*, received a front-page review in *The New York Times*.

BLOOD

AND

POWER

ORGANIZED CRIME IN
TWENTIETH-CENTURY AMERICA

STEPHEN FOX

PENGUIN BOOKS

PENGUIN BOOKS
Published by the Penguin Group
Penguin Books USA Inc.,
375 Hudson Street, New York, New York 10014, U.S.A.
Penguin Books Ltd, 27 Wrights Lane, London W8 5TZ, England
Penguin Books Australia Ltd, Ringwood, Victoria, Australia
Penguin Books Canada Ltd, 10 Alcorn Avenue,
Toronto, Ontario, Canada M4V 3B2
Penguin Books (N.Z.) Ltd, 182–190 Wairau Road,
Auckland 10, New Zealand

Penguin Books Ltd, Registered Offices:
Harmondsworth, Middlesex, England

First published in the United States of America by
William Morrow and Company, Inc., 1989
Published in Penguin Books 1990

3   5   7   9   10   8   6   4

LIBRARY OF CONGRESS CATALOGING IN PUBLICATION DATA
Fox, Stephen R.
Blood and power: organized crime in twentieth-century America/
Stephen Fox.
p.   cm.
Reprint. Originally published: New York: William Morrow, 1989.
ISBN 0 14 01.3438 7
1. Organized crime—United States—History—20th century.
2. Mafia—United States—History—20th century.   3. Criminal
justice, Administration of—United States—History—20th
century.
I. Title.
HV6446.F68   1990
364.1′06′0973—dc20   89–78361

Printed in the United States of America

For the Boston Public Library

PREFACE

This history of organized crime in the United States since the 1920s treats both cops and robbers because the American underworld has developed through mutual provocations between the two groups, each responding to the other's initiatives. Inevitably I have allotted much space here to Italian gangsters in New York and Chicago. The historical record plainly demands such an emphasis. At the same time, whenever appropriate, I have introduced gangsters of other ethnic backgrounds, in other places, because their stories have been relatively neglected. Even among different groups and different locales, though, certain patterns have stayed remarkably consistent.

Public perceptions of the underworld, especially of the Mafia, have passed through four distinct phases: a long period of denial; then tentative recognition after the Apalachin meeting, the Valachi hearings, and *The Godfather;* a second period of denial and romanticization; and, since around 1980, the current level of understanding, occasioned mainly by serious federal prosecutions and the publication of gangster memoirs. I have written this book from a perspective informed by the fourth phase, but I have attempted to treat the earlier phases without undue hindsight. As a historian, I am always struck by how partial and subjective our knowledge of an epoch must be, how we all must grope around and do what we can with fragments of information.

My general theme in this book is that any serious study of

American organized crime cannot avoid its ethnic aspects. Gangsters have always dealt in blood and power—blood in several senses of the word. Perhaps more so and longer so than in any other area of American life, ethnicity has mattered in the underworld, affecting methods, powers, associations, and job specialties. For many observers of the American scene nowadays, ethnicity has become a touchily delicate topic, to be discussed only with diplomatic throat-clearings and carefully balanced qualifying statements. Gangsters have never felt bound by such discretion, and I have tried here to follow their lead. Some readers may note that this book describes many Irish, Jewish, and Italian Americans in harsh terms, and many WASP Americans rather more favorably. I would ask such readers to bear in mind that I am usually treating racketeers in the first instance and racketbusters in the second. "I'm not talking about Italians," Joe Valachi said at his hearings in 1963. "I'm talking about criminals." A vital distinction, for both Valachi and this book.

—STEPHEN RUSSELL FOX

Cambridge, Massachusetts

CONTENTS

ONE

THE CAUSE OF IT ALL

Organized crime afflicted American life before the 1920s, but in small ways. Groups of crooks with entrepreneurial visions paid off the right cops and politicians, and in return controlled a neighborhood, or a section of a city, or at most an entire metropolis. But the enterprises under "protection"—mainly street crime, burglaries, prostitution, and gambling—were essentially restricted to certain places and people. Most good citizens could go their own way without being affected. A clear line divided the underworld from the upperworld. The gangs, confined by geography and relatively modest ambitions, did not operate on national or even regional scales. During occasional spasms of reform the cops and politicians, bribed or not, could still at their whim subdue the gangs for a while.

Beginning in the 1920s, all these circumstances worsened because of Prohibition, in ways nobody predicted or understood at the time. Gangsters have always operated in a shifting, layered, shadowy world. They leave inscrutable histories replete with accident and misdirection, the imponderables of personality, appearances that correspond to no realities, and many surprises. Thus at the outset, by an exquisite historical irony, WASP anxiety helped establish organized crime. An imagined alien conspiracy led to a real conspiracy. Fantasy produced its own twisted reality.

❦ ❦

From about the mid-1800s on, American life was modernized by three overlapping social revolutions. Industrialization turned a slower agrarian society powered by muscle and wind into a factory world racing on steam, electricity, and fossil fuels. Urbanization took farmers and others from their isolated, homogeneous island communities and deposited them in heterogeneous cities and towns. Immigration from abroad, in its ethnic diversity, challenged the easy domination by the British-descended Protestants who had originally settled their portion of North America and run things for two centuries.

To old-stock Americans of the late 1800s, society was cracking open and losing definition in alarming ways. It was called progress, and most people played along. But amid the blazing successes of technology and industry, the old WASPs detected a polity careening out of control, out of *their* control. Building the railroads, working the factories, crowding the cities, alien immigrants made an obvious scapegoat. How then to reimpose control? By wellborn efforts to reform corrupt politics; to extend the vote to women, with their well-known higher moral qualities; to restrict immigration; to encourage the eugenics of selective breeding and scientific racism. And in particular, to cap the most universal petcock, the drinking of alcohol, with its capacity for heedlessly releasing human energies and emotions.

During the first two decades of the twentieth century, as immigration peaked at an average of a million new Americans each year, Prohibition took hold, first in twenty-seven states acting individually, then on a national level by the Eighteenth Amendment. Historians have interpreted the movement for Prohibition in essentially three ways: as an assertion by Protestants against non-Protestants, by rural Americans against urban Americans, or by the middle class against the working class. Each interpretation is mostly true but incomplete.

The prohibitionists were overwhelmingly Protestants, especially Methodists, Baptists, Presbyterians, and Congregationalists. By contrast most Catholics and Jews were hostile or indifferent to the dry crusade. "The minute regulations and prohibitions of personal conduct which are found in what may be called the Puritan churches," said Monsignor John A. Ryan, a prominent Catholic, "make them 'the natural home' of the prohibition dogma." But this alignment on the issue broke down in the South. There both whites and blacks generally worshiped in Protestant churches, yet the whites embraced Prohibition and the blacks resisted it. Most southern states had already banned liquor before the Eighteenth Amendment was passed, largely because the potential wet vote by blacks was disenfranchised.

The prohibitionists drew their political strength from rural areas and states. In other ways, though, the rural-urban distinction does not hold. The leaders of the Prohibition party and the Anti-Saloon League, the two main dry lobbies, were actually more urban in origin and residence than the American norm of the day. And in California, the two principal urban centers disagreed on this as on most other issues: San Francisco was wet; Los Angeles was dry.

In general, the middle class voted dry while the working class voted wet. But here again a major exception presents itself: the *organized* wet forces drew their financial support and political clout from solidly middle-class commercial interests. Prohibition obviously threatened the liquor business, so saloonkeepers, liquor retailers, winegrowers, and brewers—men of at least middle-class incomes—gave the money that sustained wet lobbies.

The only wet-dry distinction that applies in each case is an ethnic one. WASPs supported Prohibition while non-WASPs opposed it. In the South the dry whites were overwhelmingly British-descended Protestants, worried about the drinking habits of the black Protestants. In California, dry Los Angeles was populated mostly by transplanted midwestern WASPs, while wet San Francisco had higher proportions of Irish, Italians, Chinese, and other non-WASPs. The wet liquor lobby consisted basically of Irish saloonkeepers in the Northeast, German brewers in the Midwest, and Italian winegrowers in California. Booze was one of the few major American businesses of the time not dominated by WASPs.

Prohibition therefore amounted to an ethnic experiment in social control, "to preserve this nation and the Anglo-Saxon type," as the journal of the Anti-Saloon League declared. In hindsight, it seems that what really drove the prohibitionists were the large, unidentifiable strains of modernization and diversity, of social upheaval and new ways of life: the side effects of "progress." But the problems the drys could see and identify at the time were crime, political corruption, saloons, and foreigners, all tied together in one alien bundle. Methodist Bishop James Cannon, a major dry leader, said that Italians, Sicilians, Poles, and Russian Jews—"the kind of dirty people that you find today on the sidewalks of New York"—gave him a stomachache. "We have been unable to assimilate such people in our national life," Cannon asserted. "Is it not about time," added a Congregational minister, William H. Hess, "for the real Americans to drive the low-down, grafting, Irish-Catholic rum-sellers and 'rummies' out of city politics?"

So it was done. The Eighteenth Amendment, banning the manufacture, sale, and transportation of alcoholic liquors, took effect in January 1920. "Having banished the beer glass and the whiskey bottle," noted the *American Hebrew,* "Puritan Alexanders are now longing for more worlds to conquer. Is the ice cream parlor next?"

There followed a brief pause, while people waited to see if Prohibition would work; and then a swelling flood of dubious booze purveyed by multiplying armies of rumrunners and bootleggers. The two terms were wonderfully flexible. A rumrunner might deal in any form of alcohol whatever. A bootlegger might be a wholesaler, retailer, manufacturer, sea captain, smuggler, trucker, or political fixer, or some combination of these roles. The WASP population contributed a few important bootleggers, such as Roy Olmstead of Seattle, the Shelton brothers of East St. Louis, and the Billingsley brothers of Oklahoma, Seattle, Detroit, and New York. But as the 1920s wore on and the business stabilized, the worst fantasies of the prohibitionists found confirmation as three non-WASP ethnic groups provided the most significant bootleggers.

❧ ❧

In June of 1922 the Harvard College class of 1912 gathered in Plymouth, Massachusetts, for its tenth reunion. The class secretary, Ralph Lowell of the Boston Lowells, later called his classmate Joe Kennedy "the Decennial Santa Claus" for his generosity to the celebrants. "Joe was our chief bootlegger," Lowell explained. "He arranged with his agents to have the stuff sent in right on the beach at Plymouth. It came ashore the way the Pilgrims did."

❧ ❧

However distorted and exaggerated, ethnic stereotypes usually derive from a hard kernel of truth. Layers of myth and overgeneralization come to surround the kernel, so that outsiders see only the stereotypes instead of the people themselves. But to reject the stereotypes in principle is to risk missing the essential truth inside them, and the clues to historical reality they may suggest. The popular association of drinking with Irish-Americans, for example, is borne out by comparative statistics on alcoholism among various groups. In the older industrial cities to which most Irish immigrants had gravitated, saloons stood at the center of community life as primary social institutions. The Irish saloonkeeper functioned in turn as confidant, social worker, referee, and political ward boss—and often as promoter of the gambling in the back room and the whores upstairs.

It made sense, then, that Irishmen were the first in the 1920s to recognize the large possibilities in slaking a parched America. Prohibition offered real opportunities to an ambitious young man like Thomas Jefferson McGinty of Cleveland. In his career upward he followed the same steps as many other roughnecks in other cities. He had first surfaced as a professional boxer, and had also used his fists in working for the *Cleveland Plain Dealer*'s circulation department. At that time, with many newspapers and no electronic media, the major dailies waged brutal struggles for turf and dominance. Newspapers hired gangs to intimidate news dealers and to fight the gangs hired by rival papers. When the circulation wars subsided, the gangs naturally went into associated lines of work.

Overtly a fight promoter, Tommy McGinty was Cleveland's biggest bootlegger in the early 1920s. With two members of his family he also ran a saloon, McGinty's, at 2077 West Twenty-fifth Street. They were indicted in 1924 by a federal grand jury, charged with operating "a gigantic wholesale and retail conspiracy." Tommy hid out for a couple of days, then pleaded not guilty after his arrest. He was convicted and served eighteen months in the Atlanta penitentiary. Upon his release he resumed bootlegging, with no further interference from the authorities—who presumably were paid off.

Tommy Banks of Minneapolis enjoyed a similarly unmolested success. Originally from a small town in southeastern Nebraska, he served overseas during the First World War and afterward migrated to Minneapolis. As a bellboy at the Dyckman Hotel he made up to $200 a day selling bootlegged whiskey to guests, and decided to shift from retailing to wholesaling. Only twenty-five years old, he quit his job and started moving legitimate brands in from Canada, where booze was still legal, and later from Chicago. According to his testimony years later in a tax case, he averaged $30,000 a year in profit, surely a gross understatement. He was asked why in those days he kept $300,000 in cash in a wardrobe chest. "Because I was in the bootleg business," he said. Wasn't he afraid of fire? "I never gave it a thought," Banks replied.

He was a notorious but unpublicized figure, an acknowledged leader of the Minneapolis underworld, with lines to other enterprises from his home in bootlegging. Small and balding, quietly dressed and well mannered, he showed no gangster flamboyance. The local police never arrested him. He paid two insignificant fines on minor federal liquor charges and otherwise went his own way. The Minneapolis newspapers did not print his name or photograph until a messy episode in 1945, when a man was murdered in his presence.

McGinty and Banks both made fortunes in bootlegging after starting from nothing. For Pete McDonough of San Francisco, the unexpected bonanza of Prohibition merely capped a lifetime of corrupt dealings. McDonough's father, a retired police sergeant, had in the 1890s opened a saloon at the corner of Clay and Kearny streets. It was a fully realized vision of Gilded Age elegance, with cupids on the ceiling, mahogany woodwork, and silver spittoons. Adjacent to the Hall of Justice, which housed the city jail and police courts, McDonough's was well patronized by lawyers with business next door. The McDonoughs started writing bail bonds for their clientele, then dealt directly with the courts and established the first bail-bond firm in the city. In collusion with Sheriff Tom Finn, his former partner and sometime political rival, Pete McDonough came to control the bailing process itself, with power over who went free and who stayed in jail. From that base he wielded enormous if diffusely defined leverage in city affairs. A temperance magazine described him, with little exaggeration, as "king of San Francisco's underworld, boss of the Barbary Coast, bail bond broker for criminals, unscrupulous politician and manipulator of police courts."

Prohibition thus offered McDonough just another racket to add to his other pursuits. Though his saloon was officially closed by the 1920s, Pete and his family still dealt booze on the side. In March 1923 they sold five gallons of whiskey to a federal

Prohibition agent; McDonough also told the man he had three or four boats bringing whiskey into San Francisco on a regular basis. McDonough and his nephew were indicted. A conviction seemed unlikely, given the prevailing climate of corruption in the city. The five gallons of evidence mysteriously disappeared from a clerk's office. A key government witness was pressured not to testify; the government removed a planted juror by a peremptory challenge. McDonough's nephew pleaded guilty and said his uncle had taken no part in the sale. The jury astonishingly still found McDonough guilty of selling whiskey and maintaining a nuisance.

He was sentenced to fifteen months in jail and a $1,000 fine. Friends submitted a pardon petition signed by the mayor, the district attorney, the city's two congressmen, four police judges, seventeen state legislators, and hundreds of other esteemed citizens. Nothing doing. Paroled after eight months behind bars, McDonough resumed his usual activities, perhaps surprised but not at all reformed.

Irish bootleggers were most numerous and powerful in those cities with the largest Irish populations. In Boston they typically sprang from the Irish redoubt of South Boston. Protected on three sides by the ocean, immured from the rest of Boston by the Fort Point Channel and railroad tracks, Southie was (and still remains) a separate country, ferociously proud and insular. In the 1920s four native sons, the Wallace brothers, dominated the small-time rackets in Southie. Billy, the oldest, ran a speakeasy at the corner of Old Colony Avenue and Dorchester Avenue. "Billy was the best and the toughest," an acquaintance recalled sixty years later. "Billy was independent from the others. He was the guy that *worked* for a living. The others would steal for their money."

Steve Wallace, the next oldest brother, boxed under the name Gustin, taken from a street in the neighborhood. The assortment of hooligans led by Steve and his brothers Frank and Jimmy was then called the Gustin gang. At first, around 1915, they were known as "tailboard thieves." When a truck stopped at an intersection they would approach from the rear, strip the most valuable cargo, and run off laden. Steve, only five feet five inches and 130 pounds, was a brawler, mean and reckless. Frank, more soft-spoken and genial, was the smart one, the organizer—though intelligence was a relative concept among the Gustins. Demeanor notwithstanding, Frank averaged an arrest every three months, for larceny, trespassing, gaming, assault and battery, breaking and entering, on and on, but hardly any convictions.

As bootleggers, the Gustins started at the bottom of the enterprise, landing booze at various points on South Boston's ample shoreline and delivering it to customers. Eventually they moved up to hijacking. In some way they obtained the gold badges shown by legitimate federal Prohibition agents. They would approach a rival gang's bootleg shipment, flash the badges, confiscate the booze, and sell it themselves. For a dozen years they roared up and down Southie, protected by local folkways and their own political influence. The Gustins' attorney in some of their court appearances was John W. McCormack, then a state legislator from South Boston, later a congressman and Speaker of the House of Representatives.

Next up the Irish bootlegging social ladder in Boston stood the substantial figure of Dan Carroll. One of eleven children born to Irish immigrants in Southie, he first took a traditional Irish route upward by joining the police force. But after the police strike of 1919—during which Governor Calvin Coolidge came to national attention by characteristically doing nothing—Carroll was discharged for belonging to the cops' union. "The Boston police strike made Calvin Coolidge President," people said later, "and Dan Carroll a millionaire." With loans from friends Carroll founded a trucking firm. Thirty-four years old as Prohibition began, he was ready.

Carroll's trucks met bootleg shipments as they came ashore at night, brought the booze to a warehouse on Atlantic Avenue, just across the channel from Southie, and then from the warehouse to other points. In daylight his trucks carried more conventional loads. As his power and money piled up, Carroll became the uncrowned king of the plush gangster hangouts in the Back Bay and Kenmore Square: the speaks and restaurants around "Gangster's Row" at the corner of Massachusetts Avenue and Boylston Street, the boxing matches at the Boston Arena and Mechanics Building, the Red Sox and other games at Fenway Park. Amid this welter of gamblers, hoodlums, and sportsmen, Carroll amused himself by managing prizefighters, including a few title contenders. He owned a nightclub, the Lambs Club, behind Fenway Park. In 1925 he was accused of selling liquor there, but at the trial the judge ordered an acquittal. "All the trouble we ever had there was outside the club," Carroll later explained. "Of course, once in a while somebody inside would get a smash in the mouth, but there wasn't any real trouble there."

Carroll was a big man in every sense—over two hundred pounds, with a broad, strong face, always carefully dressed and groomed, exuding vitality and personal power. He had connections with cops and businessmen, politicians and judges. In 1929 a bold reporter asked him about the rumors that his fortune was based on rackets. "Oh, I got a hand in everything that goes, to hear them tell it," he replied. "I don't bother to deny all these things. I just pay no attention to them." Well, exactly how *had* he come so far in nine years? "The breaks," said Dan Carroll. Just the breaks.

For Carroll and the Wallaces, bootlegging dangled chances otherwise not available to them. The case of Joseph P. Kennedy is more puzzling. He did not need to risk bootlegging; he was already well on his way. In Boston Irish society, status began with how long one's family had lived in America. Joe Kennedy, born in 1888, was already second generation, the grandson of immigrants. His father, P. J. Kennedy, owned saloons and liquor dealerships, prospering enough to raise his family in a four-story house on top of a hill overlooking the harbor in East Boston. As a schoolboy Joe left Eastie every day to attend Boston Latin, the elite school of the Yankees and other established families. "The Kennedys were a little different," a neighborhood boy said later. "They had money. And as a result, the other kids used to take advantage of the Kennedy wealth." With Joe away at Boston Latin, the neighborhood kids would tell the Kennedys' maid they had his permission to use his ball, bat, and glove; they would return the equipment before Joe came home.

All his adult life Kennedy was caught between two poles: a sentimental affection for his ethnic and family background, and a gargantuan, unquenchable ambition that pulled him away, always up and out, to distant, ever-receding heights. A classic American tension, in Kennedy this conflict was stoked by fires that burned harder, more dangerously than in most people. P. J. Kennedy had made a little money and wielded some influence in local Democratic politics, and there his ambition stopped. From his father, Joe absorbed the bedrock principle of ward politics and personalized relations, that of loyalty to persons over loyalty to measures or abstractions. "My father," Joe would say, "warned me not so much against the thief and the harlot as against the disloyal and the ungrateful." Again: "My father taught me, 'Be grateful and be loyal at whatever cost.' " Thus the public obeisance. But in reality, as Kennedy left a spoor of alienated former associates, he let no loyalties, nothing whatever, interfere with his ambitions.

As a young man, Kennedy made his initial forays by convincing the Yankees around him that, although an Irishman, he was a *good* Irishman. At Harvard he gave his father's occupation as "Importer." The college roommates he picked were two WASPs, one an All-American football star, the other from old Philadelphia money. After college, through his father's connections he became, at twenty-five, the president of a small East Boston bank. His real breaks, though, came from the protection and tutelage of two "swamp Yankees," Guy Currier and Galen Stone, rural New Englanders who had come down to Boston and displaced the fading Brahmins. Currier and Stone gave him entries and lessons at the highest levels of Boston finance and business. In May 1917, on the day his son John was born, Kennedy was elected a trustee of the Massachusetts Electric Companies, joining a board of Brahmins and swamp Yankees.

Kennedy's bootlegging, then, implied a nostalgic return to his roots, perhaps more necessary emotionally than financially. When Prohibition started, his father's company still had stocks of liquor on hand, now to command premium prices. Joe had similar ties in his wife's family: as mayor of Boston his father-in-law, John F. Fitzgerald, had obtained liquor licenses for three Fitzgerald brothers. ("Our present Mayor," a Protestant minister had said of Honey Fitz, "has the distinction of appointing more saloonkeepers and bartenders to public office than any previous mayor.") After 1920 the Fitzgeralds, James in particular, ran booze and speakeasies. Beyond these old bonds, possibly to compete with them, Joe also started bootlegging on his own. To this day, stories are told of a certain beach in Plymouth where Kennedy's imports would come ashore, and not just for his Harvard reunion; of his cutting deals in the office of a prominent rumrunner at 53 State Street in Boston; of Kennedy himself awaiting shipments on a dock, striding around, looking worried. Later his bootlegging interests were handled by an associate named Ted O'Leary, a large, pink-faced man who resembled a bouncer. They would obliquely refer to liquor deals as "ice cream," a jocularity that persisted in Kennedy circles long after Prohibition.

Chicago's two main Irish bootleggers were Dion O'Banion and Roger Touhy. O'Banion, born in 1892 to immigrant parents, grew up in a tenement in Little Hell, a rough Irish neighborhood on the North Side, adjacent to an encroaching section of Sicilians. Though he spent four years as a chorister and altar boy at Holy Name Cathedral, young Dion also ran with a juvenile gang, the Market Streeters. They were hired as sluggers in a newspaper circulation war by the *Chicago Herald-Examiner*. In his late teens he served two brief sentences for burglary and assault, his only times in jail.

Well established as a thug at the outset of Prohibition, O'Banion in the early 1920s was the most visible, powerful hoodlum in Chicago. His gang included a few Italians and Jews as well as Irishmen. They hijacked the bootleg shipments of lesser gangs, which brought them easy money but many enemies. As a hobby O'Banion ran a florist shop, arranging flowers with a good eye and dexterous hand. "O'Banion was clever, good-humored and, in the main, well balanced," noted an observer. "He was stockily built, blue eyed, could sing a song well and had a genuinely pleasant smile." His fine home on Pine Grove Avenue was furnished in expensive taste, with paintings and etchings on the wall. A testimonial dinner for O'Banion in 1924 was attended by the police department's chief of detectives, twenty other high-ranking cops, and ten city officials. The chief of detectives later said he "thought the party was given for someone else."

According to his discreet memoirs, Roger Touhy never considered any rackets until Prohibition. One of seven children, his father a Chicago cop, Roger worked as a telegraph operator, then a car dealer. As he told the story, he got into bootlegging because he had trucks to rent. A beer distributor and saloonkeeper named Matt Kolb offered him a partnership for $10,000 to brew their own merchandise. "I set out to make a superior product," Touhy recalled. Operating in the suburbs north and west of Chicago, at their peak Touhy and his brothers had ten fermenting plants, a half-dozen tank trucks, and a weekly volume of a thousand barrels. Each barrel of beer cost under five dollars to produce and sold for fifty-five dollars to saloons and nightclubs. "Clergymen, bankers, mayors, U.S. senators, newspaper publishers, blue-nose reformers and the guy in the corner grocery all drank our beer," Touhy noted. "There wasn't any stigma to selling beer. It was a great public service."

But the Terrible Touhys paid in other ways. Brother Jim was killed in a roadhouse shooting. Brother Joseph killed the murderer and served four years in jail for his vengeance. Later Joseph and brother John were both killed in beer wars among bootleggers. Roger was left as leader of the gang. The hijackings and territory struggles went on.

In New York the Irish bootleggers came mostly from the Irish neighborhoods of the Lower West Side. Larry Fay grew up in Hell's Kitchen west of Eighth Avenue, dabbled as a young man in street gangs and minor crimes, but until Prohibition he made a legitimate living as a cabbie. In 1920 he drove a fare to Montreal and brought some whiskey back to sell, making a profit of $180. From that modest beginning he expanded quickly. Out at sea, his men met boats from Canada and Bermuda and whisked the cargoes to a warehouse in Hoboken, across the Hudson River from Manhattan. With his profits Fay bought a fleet of taxicabs, fancy cars with nickel trim, musical horns, and trademark black swastikas on the sides. "He always had a yen to be respectable," an associate said later.

Big Bill Dwyer made his name and fortune by organizing Rum Row. He was reared near the Chelsea docks on the West Side and first labored as a stevedore. Having worked around boats his whole life, he knew how to handle himself in later marine endeavors. Thirty-seven years old at the start of Prohibition, he was one of the oldest major bootleggers. This relative maturity may have given him the credibility to move among his several worlds: the wealthy, anonymous investors who bankrolled him; the cops, customs officials and coastguardsmen he bribed; and the sailors, truckers, and mechanics who did the work.

On one side of the transaction, legitimate liquor dealers in Europe, Canada, and Central America were ready to sell, without overmuch curiosity about who bought. On the other side, the market around New York was vast and thirsty. Dwyer had merely to connect the two. The crucial link turned out to be St. Pierre, a small island twenty miles south of Newfoundland. A lingering vestige of the French empire in North America, St. Pierre was free of even the modest legal constraints imposed elsewhere by Canadian authorities. "Now if you are never in St. Pierre," explained Jack O'Hearts in a Damon Runyon story, "I wish to say you miss nothing much, because what is it but a little squirt of a burg sort of huddled up alongside some big rocks off Newfoundland, and very hard to get to, any way you go ... although of course it is very useful to parties in our line of business. It does not look like much, and it belongs to France, and nearly all the citizens speak French." Here shipments of booze came in, were reloaded, and set off for vague destinations with little incriminating paperwork.

In the case of Dwyer's boats, they headed for Rum Row, a shifting anchorage off New York, beyond the three-mile limit—later extended to twelve miles—where bootleg shipments were safe from the Coast Guard patrols. If a particular Coast Guard crew had been bribed, it would ignore any boat with a dory carried on the stern, the mark of a Dwyer shipment. His speedboats, powered by surplus Liberty airplane engines, ran out to Rum Row from berths in Brooklyn and the Bronx. They sped in twenty thousand cases a week, mostly whiskey, to various points in New York and New Jersey. Once a Coast Guard cutter itself brought in seven hundred cases for Dwyer, landing them on a dock near Canal Street in Manhattan.

Dwyer dominated bootlegging in New York until 1923, when Owney Madden got out of Sing Sing. Unlike Fay and Dwyer, Madden was a career criminal, arrested forty-four times before Prohibition. Born of Irish parents in Leeds, England, in 1892, he was brought to Hell's Kitchen as a boy. He joined the Gopher gang, a collection of bruisers, pickpockets, and boxcar bandits that roamed the West Side between Fourteenth and Forty-second streets. "Wildest bunch of roosters you ever saw," Madden later recalled fondly. In 1915 he was convicted of causing the murder of Little Patsy Doyle, with whom he had been feuding for leadership of the Gophers. Sent away for eight years, he missed the onset of Prohibition.

He came back primed, lean and hard. In profile he resembled a falcon or a buzzard. He had sleek black hair, piercing blue eyes, etched lines in his face, and a chalky complexion. He strutted like a priapic cock, truculent and bristling. Big Bill Dwyer sensibly took him in as a partner. Together they owned the Phenix Cereal Beverage Company on Tenth Avenue, the largest brewery in Manhattan. It turned out eight hundred thousand half barrels of beer annually. Each half barrel, costing $2.50 or less to produce, was sold to distributors for $12, then to speakeasies for $18. The owners of the brewery drew a profit of over $7 million a year. "Madden's No. 1 Brew" was considered the best domestic beer in New York.

For the rest of Prohibition Madden controlled midtown Manhattan, a distinct step up from the Lower West Side of his youth. George Raft, then a nightclub dancer, occasionally helped Madden move some booze. "Sure, I admired Owney Madden," he later allowed. "He was a big hero in our neighborhood. He ran things in New York and even the mayor and the governor of New York liked him." Easing into an elder statesman's role, Madden gave jobs to ex-cons and lectured young hotheads about avoiding unnecessary violence. "You just had to ask Owney for anything you wanted," recalled Ed Sullivan, then a Broadway columnist, "and you'd get it—protection, special favors, and that kind of stuff. It was like knowing the mayor to know Madden."

❦ ❦

At Senate hearings on organized crime in 1951, Senator Estes Kefauver asked a witness, Moe Dalitz of Cleveland, about his ample investments. "Now, to get your investments started off," Kefauver asked, "you did get yourself a pretty good little nest egg out of rumrunning, didn't you?"

"Well," Dalitz replied, "I didn't inherit any money, Senator."

❦ ❦

Most American Jews greeted the arrival of Prohibition with a shrug. Jews traditionally drank small, often sacramental quantities of wine and brandy in their synagogues and homes. Even under Prohibition, every adult Jew was allowed a gallon of sacramental wine each year. But Jewish cultural taboos discouraged drinking to excess, and Jews as a group had quite low rates of alcoholism. Jewish leaders had taken little part in the rancorous debates over Prohibition: to them it was merely a crusade by the *goyim*, irrelevant to matters closer at hand. "Prohibition is an Anglo-Saxon–Protestant issue," noted Louis Wolsey, a prominent Reform rabbi, "that we Jews ought to keep out of."

Lacking significant cultural ties with liquor, some Jews nonetheless seized on the financial chances offered by Prohibition. Big-time Jewish bootlegging started with the Bronfman brothers in Canada. Their family had emigrated in 1889 from Bessarabia in Russia to Saskatchewan. Of the four sons, Sam and Harry were the most forceful. At first the Bronfmans ran hotels in Saskatchewan and Manitoba—hotels known to some as brothels. ("If they were," Sam said later, "then they were the best in the West!") Partly to supply these hotels, the Bronfmans became importers, then manufacturers, of liquor. When America went dry, their products went south. "We used to drive north and south with liquor we weren't supposed to have," an employee later recalled. "The Bronfmans would fill in certificates for us with the amount of liquor listed. . . . The permits were signed by Harry and were all quite legal. The booze was good enough, but it all came out of the same barrel, even if it had half a dozen different labels."

Bootlegging from Canada included its own corruptions and dangers. A Bronfman brother-in-law was killed in 1922. Another brother-in-law was charged with selling whiskey to a Prohibition agent; in getting him off, Harry in turn was accused of jury tampering, but acquitted at his second trial. The family business, though, kept growing. The Bronfmans moved to Montreal in 1924 and opened their first distillery. With Harry in charge of production, Sam went on the road to the United States, arranging deals with bootleggers. "We loaded a carload of goods, got our cash, and shipped it," Sam explained. "We shipped a lot of goods. Of course, we knew where it went, but we had no legal proof."

By 1928 the Bronfmans had done well enough to buy Joseph E. Seagram and Sons, an old Canadian distillery firm. Thereafter the Bronfman products were sold under that respected name. As corporate headquarters, the Bronfmans built a bizarre miniature feudal castle at 1430 Peel Street in Montreal. Here American bootleggers were welcomed, with a special office of their own for conducting business. "The attitude was," Harry's son Gerald said later, "that as long as the government knew what we were doing, what difference did it make? We didn't have to decide who we should sell to. As long as there was somebody who was going to pay, why not sell it?" The Canadian government, under American pressure, finally took belated steps against this trade in 1930—too late to have much effect.

Jewish bootlegging in the United States was centered on New York City. With a diverse Jewish population of over 1.6 million, the city was home in the 1920s to some 46 percent of all American Jews. New York's underworld included many Jewish gangsters, notably Arnold Rothstein, the most ubiquitously influential American criminal of his time. He had no gang, just a name: the Big

Fellow or the Man Uptown or the Brain. Instead of muscle and guns, he dealt in cash and advice. With his initial base in gambling, Rothstein made enough money to extend big loans for purposes—like bootlegging—not recognized by any bank. He sprang from and lived in rarefied worlds that his scrabbling borrowers might not approach, a fact not lost on them. "The mobsters hated him, but because he had cash to loan when they needed it, they had to go to him," recalled Nils Granlund, a Broadway figure. "He had something to do with every speakeasy, he financed rumrunners and the hijackers who took it from them."

For Rothstein, a life in crime was a choice, not a matter of sociological determinism. Two generations removed from the pogroms of Bessarabia, he had grown up comfortably in the Orthodox Jewish community of Manhattan's Upper West Side. His father, Abraham, up from the Lower East Side, became rich in dry goods and cotton converting. Intensely religious, the father mediated community squabbles and was called Abe the Just. His younger son, Arnold, avoided smoking and drinking but could not resist cards and dice. "I didn't go to school much," he said later, "but I used to gamble a lot and lose." Around 1910, Arnold—then in his late twenties—opened his own gambling house on Forty-sixth Street, complete with a roulette wheel and faro bank.

Here, and at his other joints, Rothstein's wondrously varied acquaintances would mingle and deal. They included Broadway gamblers such as Nicky Arnstein, Tim Murphy, Nigger Nate Raymond, and Nick the Greek; wealthy businessmen like Harry Sinclair, Percy Hill, Julius Fleischmann, and Charles Gates; sportsmen like Charles Stoneham and John McGraw of the New York Giants; and the cops and politicians Rothstein had to grease to stay open. According to papers later found among his effects, Rothstein bribed the Chicago White Sox players who threw the 1919 World Series. Rothstein also paid bail bonds, helped fence stolen goods, financed dope deals and fraudulent securities offices, and bought judges, hotels, and racehorses. No interested parties could ignore his power. In his own way, Rothstein was a mediator too, like Abe the Just.

Withal Arnold Rothstein craved respectability. He loaned money to legitimate businesses and did favors for public figures. Out on the town, he liked to be acknowledged. "My husband," said his wife, Carolyn, "would rather be noticed by a famous person than make fifty thousand dollars." But many of his prominent friends would slight him in public. And despite the opulent appearances he maintained, his life amounted to a grinding, endless cash-flow problem. He brayed his betting coups—such as winning $800,000 on a horse at Aqueduct in 1921—and concealed his losses. Every day he had to balance accounts, always waiting for a phone call, driving secondhand cars, eating in modest restaurants. "I never kept more than two maids," his wife lamented. Clinging to his old ties with the upperworld, he stumbled inexorably down, further and further, pulled by vanity and greed. "At the end," according to Carolyn Rothstein, "he had reached the point where his associates were mostly of the underworld."

Once into rackets, even relatively honest men found themselves mired in enticing quicksand. Mannie Kessler, the most celebrated Jewish bootlegger in New York in the early 1920s, had been a legitimate liquor dealer for fifteen years before Prohibition. His home boasted expensive rugs, tapestries, Japanese bronzes, and thousands of books, many of which he had actually read. As Kessler told the story after he was caught the first time, he had been pushed into bootlegging by corrupt circumstances. Just before the start of Prohibition, he had bought a thousand cases of whiskey to sell to hospitals and drugstores for medicinal purposes. "But pretty soon crooked drugstores began to appear and I *had* to sell to them," said Kessler. "Before very long I discovered that the government Prohibition officials in our district were crooked. You never saw such a gang."

Presumably without much resistance, Kessler started bootlegging too. From Rum Row he brought in five thousand cases at a time, including one large cargo worth $850,000. His first conviction sent him to Atlanta for two years, where he bribed the warden, spent evenings outside the prison, and whiled away days playing poker in rooms above the warden's garage. Out of jail and back in New York, he promised to behave. "Why, there's money in Prohibition for crooks," he said piously. "Bootlegging is an easy game. Criminals go into it because they can make money in it without blowing safes or using revolvers." But soon he was in trouble again, and again, and again. In 1931 a federal prosecutor estimated Kessler's Prohibition profits at $10 million.

Middle class and middle aged, Rothstein and Kessler were not typical of New York's Jewish bootleggers. Most were in their twenties, first or second generation, from poor neighborhoods and with early records in street gangs and petty crimes. The older German Jewish immigrants had moved uptown without a real criminal phase in their histories. Jewish crime in the early 1900s was dominated by Russian and eastern European immigrants on the Lower East Side. They favored such property crimes as burglary, picking pockets, fencing, arson, and horse poisoning, usually for extortion. "The heavy concentration of property crimes among Jews," the *American Hebrew* explained in 1908, "is only another way of saying that they are most occupied in mercantile pursuits." In New York County, Jews accounted for 15.9 percent of all felony arraignments in 1900 and 25.4 percent in 1915. About 80 percent of these were for property crimes. Prohibition then presented ordinary Jewish criminals with an especially lucrative form of property crime.

Meyer Lansky, born in Poland, came to the Lower East Side with his mother as a boy. He watched the gamblers shooting craps on Delancey Street and by the age of twelve had started shooting with them. Out of school and into the streets after the eighth grade, beset by Irish and Italian street gangs, he joined up with Bugsy Siegel: "He was young but very brave," Lansky recalled. "He liked guns." The new "Bug and Meyer gang" then acquired a mentor, the best in New York. "Rothstein had the most remarkable brain," Lansky said later. "We all admired him. He was always totally honest with us and he taught us a great deal. We got on well right from the beginning—like me he was a gambler from the cradle." Perhaps through Rothstein, Lansky started bootlegging with the Bronfman brothers. Sam Bronfman came to New York and courted Lansky with fancy dinners, and Lansky in turn arranged tickets for Bronfman to the Dempsey-Firpo fight in New York in 1923. The two men embarked on a durable partnership. In 1925 Lansky and Siegel were still young, only twenty-three and nineteen, with notable careers ahead of them.

Dutch Schultz was a bigger man at the time, but briefly. A rare German Jew among New York's bootleggers, he had grown up in the Bronx, the son of a saloonkeeper and livery stable owner. In his teens he ran with the Bergen gang, in the neighborhood around Third Avenue and 149th Street in the Bronx. At seventeen he was convicted of burglary and served fifteen months, his only time in jail. During Prohibition he tended bar and worked as a gunman for Legs Diamond but showed no particular aptitude until the late 1920s, when he bought into two Bronx speakeasies. At first his beer came from breweries in Yonkers and across the river in Union City, New Jersey. As he prospered he could buy from the West Side powers in midtown Manhattan, Owney Madden and Big Bill Dwyer, more reliable sources. By 1931 Schultz had seventeen garages and beer drops scattered through the Bronx. Later that year he ordered the murder of Legs Diamond, once his boss, then his rival.

As the undisputed beer baron of the Bronx, Schultz traded on fear, not respect or affection. "Like anyone else who ever knew him I disliked him intensely," the bank robber Willie Sutton recalled. "He was a vicious, pathologically suspicious killer who kept his people in line through sheer terror." Schultz had no special presence: a bland, round face with a broken nose, of medium height and sallow coloring, and an abrupt, jittery manner. One night George Raft was sitting in a Third Avenue speak, with Schultz at the next table. When a raid was announced, Schultz hid three guns under Raft's coat. After the cops searched Schultz, found nothing, and departed, Schultz retrieved his guns and did not thank Raft for the favor. "He seemed to have no more warmth or need for human companionship than a machine," said Polly Adler, whose whorehouse Schultz patronized, "yet I think he knew that no one liked him and tried to con himself into believing it didn't matter, that money and power were what counted."

Schultz was so detested that his gang necessarily operated by itself, within the Bronx, connected to other gangs by business arrangements but not by partnerships. As such the Schultz mob was an anachronism by the latter years of Prohibition. By then the richest gangs were linking various cities and counties, even running across state lines and legal jurisdictions. Among New York's Jewish bootleggers, Waxey Gordon in particular recognized this change and exploited it. The son of Polish immigrants, he started humbly as a pickpocket on the Lower East Side. As a slugger for Dopey Benny Fein's gang he gambled, committed burglaries, and broke strikes. With other gangs he also dealt cocaine; all this before Prohibition.

A loan from Arnold Rothstein started Gordon in bootlegging

with his associates Max Greenberg and Max Hassel. At their purported real-estate office in the Knickerbocker Hotel at Forty-second Street and Broadway, they coordinated shipments from St. Pierre with an arcane system of maps, codes, passwords, and radio signals. The former pickpocket had his own kind of imaginative, entrepreneurial daring. Gordon acquired interests in breweries and distilleries, mostly in northeast New Jersey, but others as distant as Lancaster, Pennsylvania, and Elmira, New York. The operation in Elmira was spread through several buildings connected by hoses laid through the city's sewer system. One large still burbled away within three blocks of Elmira's police headquarters.

Gordon's holdings eventually extended to at least thirteen breweries and distilleries in three states. He probably made and distributed more illegal beer than anyone else on the East Coast. In 1930 he was declared Public Enemy Number One in New York; that year his income, so far as government accountants could tell, exceeded $1.4 million. He split his time between an Upper West Side apartment—ten rooms, four baths, four servants—and his summer home on the Jersey shore. "He is an able business man," an observer conceded, "and his outstanding characteristic is greed."

Gordon's most dangerous partner was Longy Zwillman, the biggest man in Newark. Zwillman grew up in Newark's Third Ward, a tough Jewish neighborhood. As a teenager he worked briefly as a huckster, selling fruits and vegetables from a wagon, but with his boyhood friends Doc Stacher and Niggy Rutkin he also ran with the Ramblers, a street gang that hung around Pop Handler's saloon. Bootlegging and hijacking made Zwillman rich enough to regard himself as a philanthropist. "I had the biggest political club in Newark," he later said proudly. "I was living out in my old neighborhood, which is the ghetto, a very poor neighborhood, and everybody needed help, everybody needed jobs, and we were making a little money, so we started a club and got everybody into it." Of course the club also provided him with a headquarters and respectable front. Zwillman's specialty as a bootlegger was enforcement, the threat and execution of violence. For these services Waxey Gordon gave Zwillman a cut of the entire take and a brewery of his own.

In 1930, probably for similar reasons, Zwillman acquired a 50 percent interest in the Reinfeld syndicate, a huge bootlegging operation that sprawled all over New Jersey. Joe Reinfeld, a naturalized Polish immigrant, had pleaded guilty to a minor liquor offense in 1920 but had escaped two more serious indictments in the years since. Also from Newark, he brought Niggy Rutkin into his syndicate in 1927. Rutkin on his own had been selling booze unmolested ("I was stopped a few times by policemen going from Newark to New York City, and all they wanted was a couple of bottles of good liquor"). Dealing with Canadian and European outlets, moving his product through St. Pierre, Reinfeld had problems only when his booze reached New Jersey. "They had no difficulty bringing in liquor," Rutkin recalled, "but they didn't have the outlets to sell it. I did." The addition of Zwillman and Doc Stacher, with their muscle, then added the final specialists to the Reinfeld syndicate.

In purely technical terms, it was a beautiful system. Reinfeld did the buying, mostly from the Bronfmans in Montreal, sometimes averaging twenty-two thousand cases a month. Reinfeld also paid off the Coast Guard and local lawmen. At first a customer would buy a receipt in Newark, take a boat out beyond the twelve-mile limit, exchange the receipt for merchandise, and bring it back himself; thus no risk to the syndicate. Later, with Rutkin's help, the syndicate made landings—but never during the summer, with its long hours of daylight and curious vacationers on the beaches and waterfronts. Depending on how attentive the unbribed lawmen were, the Reinfeld gang smuggled into Monmouth County in the north, or Delaware Bay down south, or up the Delaware River toward Philadelphia.

One operation off the coast of Deal, New Jersey, may suggest the gang's cleverness. On a rough night in winter, with the Coast Guard reluctant to patrol, a Reinfeld ship with its cargo in copper-lined tanks would look for a red light on the top floor of an oceanfront house. Spotting the light, the ship would anchor a hundred yards offshore. A small boat would bring out a hose, rubber on the outside and linen on the inside. Then twenty-five thousand gallons of Canadian whiskey would be pumped into oaken tanks in three houses on shore. "That was much simpler than bringing little barrels," Rutkin pointed out. "It saved a lot of work and it was very efficient."

Outside the New York area, Jewish bootleggers were most active in Boston, Cleveland, Detroit, and Philadelphia. Boston's Charlie Solomon functioned as a counterpart to Arnold Rothstein in his background, general smoothness, and omnipresent influence. Born in Russia in 1884, Solomon had been brought to Boston as a small boy and later spoke unaccented English. He grew up middle class in the multi-ethnic West End; his father owned a theater. His three brothers all went straight, and Charlie for a time worked as a counterman in an uncle's restaurant. But by his twenties he was involved in prostitution, fencing, and bail bonding. He was notorious for smuggling narcotics, mainly cocaine and morphine.

In the 1920s Solomon and his sometime partner Dan Carroll ran the Boston underworld. As a bootlegger Solomon dealt with the Bronfmans in Canada and with associates in New York and Chicago. Protected by his high-level contacts in Boston, he was never indicted there on liquor charges. At his trial in a drug case in 1922, he was represented by Grenville MacFarland, editor and general counsel of the *Boston American*. (An irony: the *American* had recently been crusading against narcotics abuse.) Solomon was acquitted but then convicted in a second trial for frightening a witness into perjury in the first case. "He has a certain amount of petty political influence," the United States attorney in Boston noted, "and I suppose that applications for his parole will be made." Solomon was sentenced to five years in Atlanta, of which he served thirteen months. While he was away, two of Boston's congressmen—George H. Tinkham and James A. Gallivan—asked that he be transferred to a jail near Boston. Gallivan, from South Boston, said he made the suggestion at the request of "some good friends of mine." Once back home, Solomon cruised through the rest of Prohibition with no further legal difficulties.

Below Solomon operated a second tier of Jewish bootleggers in Boston: Hyman Abrams, Max Fox, Joe Linsey, and Lou Fox. Of these, Joe Linsey became the most prominent later on. Born in Russia, raised in Boston, he had been only nine when his father died. The boy went to work delivering groceries and later was apprenticed as a meatcutter. Twenty-one years old at the start of Prohibition, he bootlegged with Solomon and others from a front, the National Realty Company, at 43 Tremont Street. All but inevitably, Linsey also bought from the Bronfmans. He was caught once and served a year in jail, but two later bootlegging indictments were quashed.

The bootleggers in Cleveland and Detroit enjoyed the advantage of easy water access to Canadian sources—fifty miles across Lake Erie from Cleveland, and half a mile across the Detroit River from Detroit. In Cleveland, booze flowed through the discreet and enduring partnership of Moe Dalitz, Sam Tucker, Lou Rothkopf, and Morris Kleinman. All had been born within a few years of the turn of the century: Tucker in Lithuania, and then an immigrant at fifteen, the other three in the United States of immigrant parents. The four partners moved so much liquor across Lake Erie that it was known as "the Jewish Lake." Later, when Canadian authorities stiffened, Dalitz and his associates shipped the imports first to Galveston, Texas, and then by rail to Cleveland. They worked so carefully, so shrewdly, that they had no significant criminal records until years afterward. (Called before the Kefauver committee in 1951, Dalitz explained why he had dodged the committee's subpoena: "I, frankly, was just alarmed at the whole thing and all the publicity; I have never had any publicity in the past.")

The Detroit River, stretching thirty miles from Lake St. Clair in the north to Lake Erie in the south, amounted to a long, multiply perforated border between Canadian liquor dealers and American bootleggers. Probably more Canadian contraband came through there than any other entry point. In other cities with major Jewish bootleggers, Jews constituted at least 10.4 percent of the population. Detroit had only fifty thousand Jews, merely 5 percent of the whole city. But the Purple Gang dominated most of the bootlegging in Detroit through the individual force and personalities of its leaders.

The Purple Gang arose from two street gangs in the Hastings Street neighborhood on Detroit's East Side, the Oakland Sugar House Gang and another group led by Sammy Purple Cohen. In the early 1920s they combined as the Purple Gang under the three Bernstein brothers. From their start in shoplifting and extortion they went into distilling and brewing liquor, then into importing it from Canada. Abe Bernstein was the brains of the enterprise. "He was small and dapper," it was said, "with the soft hands of a woman and a quiet way of speaking." The Purples were prominent around town, living in fancy houses and often seen in public, "gamblers and big spenders," according to the jazzman Mezz Mezzrow, "flashy good-natured Jews, dressed in loud checked suits and open-necked sports shirts."

In its business affairs, though, the Purple Gang was brutal.

Aside from bootlegging, it also dealt in gambling, insurance frauds, narcotics, kidnappings, and contract murders. Secure in their eminence, the Purples often performed sloppy work and did not care whom they doublecrossed. When a St. Louis gang in 1926 tried to muscle into Detroit's gambling, the Purples visited three of the intruders and killed them with machine guns. A few years later, the Purple Gang suspected its bootlegging associates in the "Little Jewish Navy" of hijacking a $110,000 liquor shipment intended for an American Legion convention in Detroit. The Purples confronted the culprits at the Collingwood Manor apartments and—in the "Collingwood Massacre"—shot three of them. Three members of the Purple Gang, including Abe Bernstein's brother Raymond, were convicted of this indiscretion and given life sentences.

In Philadelphia the most prominent bootlegger was Boo-Boo Hoff, up from a Jewish neighborhood in South Philly. He had started as a newsboy, clerked in a cigar store, managed boxers, and promoted prizefights. With his partner Charley Schwartz he ran gambling houses, one of which fronted as a political club in the Fifth Ward. As bootleggers they specialized in the diversion of industrial alcohol, which could still be legally manufactured, into illegal potable forms. In the single year of 1926, their Quaker Industrial Alcohol Company produced nearly 1.5 million gallons, to be consumed in questionable ways. Hoff and Schwartz conducted their various scams from the respectably named Franklin Mortgage and Investment Company, with its office in the Bankers Trust Building at Walnut and Juniper streets, the heart of the business section. One of the Franklin company's incorporators was Benjamin M. Golder, an attorney and (after 1924) a member of Congress.

Philadelphia's bootleggers were so brazenly unchecked that in August 1928 Judge Edwin O. Lewis convened a special grand jury to investigate matters. The grand jury sat for seven months, through 179 sessions and 748 witnesses. It discovered 1,170 saloons and cafés and thousands of speakeasies, "maintained openly and notoriously to the certain knowledge of the citizens." The grand jury estimated that city policemen were receiving $2 million a year in graft. Cops with annual salaries of $2,500 or less were found to have bank accounts ranging from $5,000 to almost $20,000, with no other sources of income. As for Boo-Boo

Hoff, the grand jury declared him "unquestionably" a leading bootlegger—but so protected behind agents and dummies that he could not be indicted. "I recognize," Judge Lewis conceded, "that the public may not be fully satisfied."

❧ ❧

Chicago, St. Valentine's Day, 1929. Seven men were lined up against a garage wall. Over a thousand machine-gun bullets were fired at them. Heads and legs were nearly severed from bodies. A pool of blood formed, forty feet wide.

The cops asked Bugs Moran about it. "Only the Capone gang kills like that," said Moran.

❧ ❧

After the Irish and Jewish immigrants came the Italians. From 1900 to 1920 over 3 million Italian immigrants arrived in America, more during that period than from any other country. Some 90 percent of these new Americans were from southern Italy and Sicily, mostly from peasant and working-class backgrounds. In the old country their lives were bounded by tight, concentric circles of family, village, church, and an ancient, bitterly earned suspicion of distant laws and lawmen. In the new country these immigrants tried to recreate the familiar contexts in American tenements and neighborhoods. The prize of old-time internal cohesion was bought at the cost of relative isolation from newer American surroundings.

In New York and elsewhere, Italian boys and adolescents clumped in street gangs for protection from gangs in the next neighborhood or crosstown. Seldom committing really serious crimes, the youth gangs mainly fought each other in characteristic styles. "The most vicious of all the gangs were easily the Italians," recalled Daniel Fuchs, a reformed member of a Jewish street gang in Brooklyn (and later a noted screenwriter and novelist). "They were severe in their methods, seldom willing to fight with their fists or with stones, but resorting unethically to knives and guns. After all, the Irish could be said to fight almost for the fun of it; while the Jews always fought in self-defense. But the Italians went out definitely to maim or kill." Arthur A. Carey, a New York homicide cop, described the Sullivan firearms law in 1930 as an effort "to restore the supremacy of the Irish gangs, who fought with their fists and clubs, by outlawing the weapons of the Jewish and Italian gangs, who used guns, stilettoes and bombs." Fuchs as a Jew and Carey as an Irishman might have disagreed about the hazards presented by Jewish gangs, but they agreed about the Italians.

The Italian street gang members who then graduated to real crimes brought along their old habits. From 1900 to 1914, about half the felony arrests of Italians in New York involved violent crimes—compared with 12 percent for Jewish felony arrests. Italian criminals favored murders, bombings, and kidnappings. Many killings and maimings were related to extortion plots attributed to the Black Hand, a loosely structured, even free-lance enterprise that mainly preyed on fellow Italians. Probably the Black Hand never existed as an organization, strictly defined, but the crimes committed in its name gave it a fearsome cachet in Italian neighborhoods.

From such backgrounds arose the Italian bootleggers. They were typically immigrants and career criminals, in trouble before Prohibition. Isolated by internal pride and external hostility, they generally lacked the ties with cops and politicians enjoyed by Irish bootleggers. Compared with Jewish bootleggers, the Italians were usually less sophisticated and less well connected to foreign sources. What the Italian bootleggers had, though, was their reputation for deadly, unpredictable violence and scaring people not easily frightened. That fear by itself gave them power.

Tony Cornero and his family, legendary California bootleggers, were a gang unto themselves. His brothers, Frank and Pico, and sister, Esther, all acquired criminal records in family enterprises. Born in Italy around the turn of the century, they were brought to America by their mother in 1904. After she remarried, they grew up in San Francisco. At sixteen Tony pleaded guilty to robbery and spent ten months in reform school, a sojourn that left him unreformed. Over the next decade he moved to southern California and piled up ten arrests, including three for bootlegging and three related to murder. "Southern California has been a favored spot for the smuggling of liquor," according to the top Prohibition agent in the region, "and the prime movers in these operations have been the Cornero family. . . . It is common knowledge that they have made a fortune in these illegal operations."

A stocky man with a granite face and hard eyes, usually seen in a broad-brimmed stetson hat, Tony Cornero was exceptionally bright and resourceful. "A very smart, able, practical man," as one of his many prosecutors remembered him, "and he was very ingenious, and I'd say gutsy." Indicted again on a bootlegging charge late in 1926, Cornero caught a train for Seattle. With the feds closing in, he jumped from the train in northern California and hired an airplane to fly him to a point near Portland, Oregon. There he caught the same train again, leaped from it again near Seattle, and finally made it to safety in Canada.

Cornero stayed away for three years, showing up at various places in Europe and South America, never without spending money. At Hamburg, Germany, in the fall of 1927, he paid $170,000 for a 450-ton steel ship. Cornero loaded it with over $3 million worth of booze—100,000 gallons of alcohol, 419 barrels of whiskey, and more—and sent it off bound for California through the Panama Canal. (The German crew, hoping for a reward, turned it over to authorities in New Orleans.) In 1929, perhaps homesick, perhaps weary of the chase, Cornero returned to California and surrendered. He served a two-year sentence. Meantime his family did not retire from the trade. As late as 1932, Frank Cornero was arrested for sending shortwave signals to rumrunning boats off the California coast.

Kansas City's bootleggers were rooted in Little Italy, a tight little neighborhood on the city's North Side, squeezed between Irish and black areas. Of the fifteen thousand residents of Little Italy, some 85 percent were Sicilians. The Black Hand was active there before Prohibition, with forty unsolved murders between 1906 and 1916. These gangsters then went into bootlegging. Most were "Greenies" like Joe Di Giovanni and James Balestrere, immigrants whose English and acculturation to America remained rudimentary. When Balestrere was asked why his family had brought him as a teenager from Milwaukee to Kansas City, he said, "My brother-in-law, he was a contractor here, stonemason, building foundation here, and my mother had come here because my sister was going to have a baby, and so when they come back, she like Kansas City better than Milwaukee, so we come here."

Johnny Lazia, the bigshot of the North Side, was a quite different personality. He had a conventional criminal background: the son of an immigrant laborer, out of school after the eighth grade, arrested seven times by the age of eighteen. In 1917 he was sentenced to twelve years in the state penitentiary for a holdup. But he was already well connected. Local politicians intervened for him, and Lazia was paroled after serving only eight months and seven days. Back in Little Italy, he acted like a reformed man. Nicknamed Brother John, he sold real estate, lent money, gave to charities, and tried to keep wayward youths out of jail. He smiled a lot and told funny stories in passable English. In his rimless glasses, carrying gloves and a cane, he did not resemble a gangster. Behind this amiable facade, though, he controlled the North Side's bootlegging and rackets. In 1928 he challenged Mike Ross, an Irishman, for political leadership of the North Side. After Ross's men were kidnapped, beaten, and shot at, Lazia took over and was allied with Tom Pendergast, the omnipotent boss of Kansas City.

In Boston the North End, formerly an Irish and Jewish neighborhood, was mostly Italian by the 1920s. Amid the narrow, winding streets and old brick buildings crammed with Italian groceries and restaurants, a small criminal group plied its minor rackets. Bootlegging was at first conducted on a household scale, with the traditional homemade Italian wine—"Dago red"—simply produced in greater volume for sale outside the home. As Prohibition wore on, a few Italian gangsters moved up to more ambitious rumrunning and became, in their way, local heroes. "When I was a kid, we all knew what a big-time crook was, and most of us looked up to them," a thief named Jimmy Costa recalled of his North End boyhood in the 1920s. "These racket guys would drive up in those big touring cars filled with pretty girls and all the money they wanted. I remember one of them giving us kids five bucks each just to stand and watch his car while he and the girls went to eat at a restaurant. Jesus, five bucks was almost as much as my father made in a week."

Philip Buccola and Joe Lombardo, native Sicilians who had immigrated first to New York and then to Boston, dominated North End rackets and bootlegging. Buccola ecumenically married an Irish woman in Boston and had an Irish partner, Dan Carroll, in managing boxers and criminal endeavors. The Italians feuded, however, with the rowdy Gustin gang from South Boston. Occasionally the Gustins and Italians would careen through the North End in open cars, shooting at each other. And at one point Buccola and Carroll squabbled, perhaps over money. Buccola was planning to have Carroll killed until Charlie Solomon interceded and saved his life, no doubt after Carroll had made amends.

Joe Lombardo was more in the mold of Johnny Lazia, genteel on the outside. He left school after the fourth or fifth grade and later supposedly worked as a salesman of ladies' garments. His chauffeur's nephew remembered Lombardo as conservatively dressed, like a banker, and clean smelling, as though he always had just stepped from a shower. After one of his arrests, an examining doctor concluded: "His cultural and social interests on a middle class level. Intellectual status is fully up to average. Conversation and appearance that of a fairly well educated man. Adapts himself to his present situation without emotional stress. Friendly and of excellent poise." Again appearances were deceptive, hiding an agile criminal mind and a flaring use of violence. As Buccola managed boxers, Lombardo ran a restaurant— respectable fronts that concealed a great deal.

During Prohibition the Italian gangsters in Kansas City and Boston fought with non-Italian gangs but avoided the inefficiencies of blood feuds among themselves. Internal quarrels were smothered before reaching a killing point. In other cities, especially Detroit, New York, and Chicago, Italians were as likely to murder each other as to eliminate Irish and Jewish rivals. Italian feuds were arrayed across subtle, all but invisible lines of geography, family, or remembered grudges. Social forces in America conspired to blur these lines, so they were clung to even more tenaciously in the new country: Neapolitans against Sicilians, or Sicilians from one town against Sicilians from another town. "Gentile is a Sicilian," Sam Perrone of Detroit said of an associate. "Of course, theirs is a different town. He's from a different town than I come from." They were Italians, but Sicilians, but from a certain Sicilian town. In peasant culture, the smallest unit meant the most.

In Detroit, at the outset of Prohibition, it came down to families. The Italian bootleggers settled into two warring factions grouped around the Giannola and Vitale families. Quickly, by the end of 1920, all the leaders of both families had been killed. The survivors declared peace and carved up among themselves those bootlegging areas of Detroit not controlled by the Purple Gang. The new arrangement, called the Pascuzzi Combine, was negotiated and then administered by Samuel Catalonette, a man of evident diplomatic gifts. Anthony D'Anna, one of the Giannolas, had lost his father and two uncles in the feud. John Vitale, who had killed D'Anna's father, was also murdered. After the peace,

D'Anna then engaged in rackets with remnants from both factions. In America, lucrative enterprise might run thicker than blood.

Yet the old home ties persisted. After Catalonette's peaceful death in 1930, Joe Zerilli took his place at the top—a position he held on to for decades. Zerilli and his aide Black Bill Tocco had come from the same town of Terrasini in Sicily. Two of their top men, both imported from St. Louis, were Pete Licavoli and Scarface Joe Bommarito, both born in America of immigrants from Terrasini. After killing one more Sicilian pretender, Chet La Mare, in 1931, this leadership group could concentrate on bootlegging and fighting the Purples. The Italian and Jewish rumrunners in Detroit plinked away at each other all through Prohibition. "Any time an Italian was killed, they pulled in the Purples," a Detroit police reporter noted, "and any time they killed a Purple, they pulled in the Italians." The Italians kept to themselves and were less prominent around town than the Purples, but they moved almost as much booze across the Detroit River.

New York City contributed the most significant Italian bootleggers—significant both at the time and for the future of organized crime in America. Always ranging more widely, gobbling more territory, and assuming more power, they had only ethnic identity in common with the city's older Italian street gangs. Before 1920, Italian gangsters marauded through neighborhoods on the Lower East Side and, uptown, in Italian Harlem around 108th Street. Paul Vaccarelli's ferocious Five Points gang pushed as far west as the Bowery. Ciro Terranova's gang eventually moved up from Italian Harlem to the Bronx and opened a "political club" as headquarters. Across the street in the Bronx, working in a drugstore after school, young Charles Siragusa watched them, appalled and fascinated. (Later, as a federal narcotics agent, Siragusa became a dread enemy of the Mafia.) Parking their big, shiny-black touring cars anywhere they pleased, dressed always in blue pinstriped suits and gray fedoras with three-inch brims, spilling out of their club and taking over the sidewalk, occasionally littering the gutter with bloody corpses, Terranova's men swaggered and bragged about murders and other exploits. "It was then I swore that someday I would fight them and win," Siragusa recalled. "My hatred for the hoodlums turned to contempt."

Mean and tough as they were, after 1920 these older gangsters were brushed aside by younger, more ambitious men. Joe Bonanno, born in Sicily in 1905, entered the United States illegally in 1924 with the help of his cousin Stefano Magaddino. Settled among Italians in the Williamsburg section of Brooklyn, Bonanno started bootlegging whiskey from homemade stills. "I thought it was too good to be true," he said later. "I didn't consider it wrong. It seemed fairly safe in that the police didn't bother you. There was plenty of business for everyone. The profits were tremendous. And let's face it, especially for a young man, it was a lot of fun." Suddenly enjoying the promise of America, Bonanno liked it all: the big Hudson automobile he bought, with its floor compartments for gallon cans of whiskey; the newly found glamor of nightclubs, theaters, and prizefights; the quick, life-enhancing thrill of occasional dangers that left a man feeling vividly, gratefully alive.

As elsewhere, the many independent Italian bootleggers were gradually consolidated through murders and mergers into fewer, larger gangs. A predictable phase in the history of any American enterprise, by the late 1920s this winnowing had produced five Italian, overwhelmingly Sicilian gangs in New York. An organization led by Gaetano Reina, Gaetano Gagliano, and Tommy Lucchese inflicted itself on the Bronx. Another under Joe Profaci and Giuseppe Magliocco operated in Staten Island and Brooklyn. A third, under Alfred Mineo and including Carlo Gambino, Albert Anastasia, and Vincent Mangano, had interests in Manhattan and Brooklyn.

In the fourth gang, Joe Bonanno attached himself as apprentice to Salvatore Maranzano, a recent immigrant from his own Castellammarese region west of Palermo. "I felt honored and privileged just to be near him," Bonanno remembered. "I suppose it was like falling in love, only it was between men. When I was around Maranzano, I felt more alive, more alert, more called upon to fulfill my potential." Their gang, mainly composed of fellow Castellammarese, was spread across Manhattan and Brooklyn, with interests elsewhere. Bonanno got the job of supervising Maranzano's whiskey stills in Pennsylvania and upstate New York. Now moving beyond his Williamsburg neighborhood, Bonanno carried a pistol, bought supplies, paid bails, and guarded against hijackings and suspicious fires. "Those were the flush times,"

Bonanno recalled. "I was much like a squire in the service of a knight."

The fifth and most powerful gang, also in Manhattan and Brooklyn, was led by Joe the Boss Masseria. He too was a Sicilian immigrant, but his group included men from Naples (Vito Genovese and Joe Adonis) and the southernmost Italian province of Calabria (Frank Costello and Willie Moretti), as well as Sicilians like Charlie Lucky Luciano. Rising to dominance in the early 1920s, Masseria had shown astounding gifts for dodging bullets and escaping ambushes at close range. Agile and fortunate, he seemed unkillable. With success he relaxed and gluttonously grew fat. The Castellammarese gangsters called him "the Chinese" because his chubby cheeks turned his eyes into slits. "I couldn't help comparing my beloved Maranzano with the oaf Masseria," Bonanno noted, not without bias. "Masseria was vulgar, sloppy and puffy. Maranzano was refined, taut and intellectual."

Two of Masseria's bootleggers eventually became the most influential American gangsters of their time. Frank Costello and Charlie Lucky Luciano had both been brought to America as small boys, and they were more Americanized than most contemporary Italian gangsters. To exceptional degrees, they moved among and were trusted by non-Italian criminals, a key to their ultimate power and generalized authority. Costello was even married by a Protestant minister to a Jewish woman. "All of his close associates were Jewish or Irish," recalled a cop who tailed Costello in the 1920s. "You'd never see him with Italians. We had no idea he was involved with them." Luciano for his part had a special, unspoken rapport with Meyer Lansky. "They were more than brothers, they were like lovers," according to Bugsy Siegel. "They would just look at each other and you would know that a few minutes later one would say what the other was thinking. I never heard them argue."

"Other kids are brought up nice and sent to Harvard and Yale," Costello said in old age. "Me? I was brought up like a mushroom." He was born in 1891, the youngest of six children, to poor farmers in the town of Lauropoli, near the Ionian Sea. He was christened Francesco Castiglia. His earliest Calabrese memories were of sweet tomatoes and pita bread. At the age of four he was placed in the Italian procession to America, bedded down for the sea voyage on a blanket in a big iron cooking pot. Settled on 108th Street, the family squeezed a living from a tiny grocery store. As the youngest child, Francesco was left to himself and walked the streets alone for hours at a time. Years later he told his psychiatrist he had hated his father for being too humble, too willing to settle for the dirt and poverty of Italian Harlem. Out of school after the fifth grade, he had two minor arrests, then served ten months in 1915 for illegal possession of a pistol—his only time in jail until thirty-seven years later. At some point he started calling himself Frank Costello, an Irish version of his own name.

As a rumrunner Costello summed up the history of New York bootlegging: tutored and financed by Arnold Rothstein, early deals with Mannie Kessler, purchases from Sam Bronfman by way of St. Pierre, later deals with Big Bill Dwyer, and finally his own complex operation from an office at 405 Lexington Avenue. No one could have come that far without, at times, playing it rough. "If you're writing a book about how nice a guy Frank was," one crony told a writer a half century later, "don't put too much in there about the Twenties." According to Kessler, Costello robbed him of a thousand cases of whiskey and then turned him in, sending him to Atlanta for two years; yet after another bootlegger squealed about a Costello boat seized near Freeport, Long Island, Costello had the man killed. Costello was seen at other points on Long Island—Montauk, Huntington, Oyster Bay—supervising the transfer of booze from speedboats to his trucks. He then arranged the protection of those trucks from hijackers, the most dangerous part of the enterprise. His reputation was so strong that, as Costello told the story, Joe Kennedy of Boston asked him to help bring in shipments from Rum Row. Costello and Kennedy then became partners in bootlegging. "You had the sense," a friend of Costello's said later, "that they were close during Prohibition and then something happened. Frank said that he helped Kennedy become wealthy." (Owney Madden also later claimed a bootlegging partnership with Kennedy.)

Lucky Luciano, six years younger than Costello, outranked him in Masseria's hierarchy. Luciano had the advantage of Sicilian birth, in a small town near Palermo. The third of five children, he alone among his siblings became a criminal. Growing up on the Lower East Side around Tenth Street and First Avenue, he went his own way, into the streets. By the age of fourteen he had left school, begun a sex life, and started smoking opium. "I used to hit the pipe joints in Chinatown when I was a kid, we all did it," he recalled. "I liked it, the stuff did funny things to my head." His first arrest, at eighteen, was for heroin possession. But he mainly dealt drugs instead of using them. In a group of Sicilians he looked tall and thin, at five feet ten inches and 140 pounds; he could speak some Sicilian but usually preferred American street slang. "An aggressive, egocentric, antisocial type who has more or less adopted the criminal habits," a prison psychiatrist concluded later. "He evidences no mental abnormalities. He is of bright intelligence, mental age 15.5 years on the Stanford-Binet test. . . . He is rather a sociopath than a psychopath, more a product of the street influences than any inherent personality defect."

During Prohibition Luciano was arrested for bootlegging, gun possession, felonious assault, armed robbery, grand larceny, and gambling. None of these charges led to convictions. In 1923, arrested for selling heroin, he flipped and told the feds about a trunkful of drugs in a basement on Mulberry Street. The government therefore dropped the main charges against him. Luciano then provided more information about his competitors in narcotics, helping remove them and enhancing his own position in the field. (Presumably he informed on no Sicilians.) Luciano was the rising star in the Masseria gang, second in command to Joe the Boss himself. Given his easy way with non-Italians, he was Masseria's liaison to Arnold Rothstein—and so became yet another of Rothstein's eager students.

In 1930 Luciano led a generational revolt against the bosses of New York's Italian gangs. During a nineteen-month period in 1930–31, Gaetano Reina, Alfred Mineo, Salvatore Maranzano, and even the unkillable Masseria were all murdered. After negotiations and peace treaties, Gaetano Gagliano, Vincent Mangano, Joe Bonanno, and Luciano took their places as gang leaders. Along with Joe Profaci, the only survivor from the original group, they constituted a new, younger, more American generation of bosses, less tied to the old country. Mangano at forty-four was the oldest, with the others averaging in their early thirties. By general consent, Luciano was the acknowledged first among equals.

Meantime, out in Chicago, the most famous bootlegger of all had, after a dozen years of terrible crimes, just been convicted of income tax evasion. Al Capone was the only Italian gangster who could match the power of the New Yorkers, and his fortuitous removal at this critical point helped establish the national authority of the five New York gangs. Actually Capone always had more reputation than influence. He was a big buffoon, laughing and stupid, chuckleheaded even before syphilis got him, a thrashing, flailing rogue elephant whom even his friends gave a wide berth. "No one was close to Al," said one of his men. Capone owed his celebrity to the accidents of media. Because bootlegging in Chicago was wondrously disorganized and competitive, it caused many gang murders, an average of one a week—more than anywhere else. The guns and blood brought the city consistent national attention. Blooming and preening and capering in this spotlight, Capone loved the publicity and welcomed inquiring journalists who would feed his legend. They took his maunderings and turned them into sentences and paragraphs, using words of which Capone had never heard. Thus he was made to seem crafty, even intelligent.

Capone—"whose surname, in Italian, means a castrated male chicken," Joe Bonanno noted with contempt—was born in Brooklyn of Neapolitan immigrants. He quit school after hitting his sixth-grade teacher. Growing up around Broadway and Flushing Avenue in Williamsburg, he impressed nobody. "He is remembered as something of a nonentity, affable, soft of speech and even mediocre in everything but dancing," Daniel Fuchs recalled. "When this Brooklyn boy made good in the world, the surprise was general among his old friends and acquaintances." In the Five Points gang Capone displayed some aptitude for personal violence. Johnny Torrio, also a Neapolitan and a Five Points alumnus, had moved to Chicago and needed an enforcer. Twenty-one years old, Capone arrived in 1920.

Torrio did the thinking, Capone provided the muscle, and they ascended quickly in the anarchistic carnival of Chicago gangdom. Their bootlegging was founded on breweries, formerly legitimate, which they took over and ran illegally. Later they dealt booze with Detroit's Purple Gang and others around the country. Torrio and Capone also built substantial empires in prostitution and gambling. A minor genius in his field, Torrio moved their operations to suburbs like Cicero and Burnham with tiny municipal governments that could be easily manipulated. They were lucky too. Torrio and Capone happily stood aside while Dion O'Banion and his men and the Genna family of Sicilians killed each other off. After Little Hymie Weiss, O'Banion's successor, tried three times to murder Capone, he was killed in turn. Torrio then left Chicago after conviction in a brewery case and being wounded in an ambush. Capone fortunately had someone else to do his thinking in a Russian Jewish immigrant named Greasy Thumb Guzik, his accountant and "business manager."

The St. Valentine's Day Massacre, aimed at Bugs Moran's gang, marked both the high point of Capone's power and the catalyst for his downfall. The murders were so gruesome, the public so offended, that federal tax investigators were ordered to get Capone. It took them two years, but they finally assembled the evidence and witnesses. Convicted in the fall of 1931, Capone was led away, his mind already fading in and out. His gang and his legend went on, but his own time was up.

❧ ❧

Across the line, chasing the bootleggers, was Mabel Walker Willebrandt, an assistant attorney general of the United States. She could not have had less in common with her quarry, and they could not begin to comprehend each other. She had been born in a sod dugout on the plains of southwestern Kansas, a WASP on her mother's side and a second-generation German Protestant on her father's. After spending her childhood on farms she moved to Kansas City and, following her marriage, to Los Angeles. There she went to law school and did political work for progressive and feminist causes. Not a prohibitionist before Prohibition, she drank liquor "in moderation, of course," she made clear. But political women in general were identified with Prohibition; woman suffrage and Prohibition were achieved by the same political forces, and both measures were intended to cleanse politics and renew WASP control. So when the Republicans regained the White House in 1920, it made sense to put a feminist in charge of Prohibition enforcement.

Willebrandt was a small, taut woman, crisp and understated in public, demanding in private of herself and her associates. In her diary she left hints of a nativist suspicion of other ethnic groups. "There is something deeply pathetic," she wrote of Samuel Gompers, "in the figure of this squat little English Jew." Essentially, though, she was driven by a good lawyer's respect for the law and her own very Protestant conscience. She believed she had a particular relationship with God, a private, personal understanding just between God and herself. "For all of my life I have had the most uncanny feeling," she wrote her parents at Christmastime in 1923, "against which I have often struggled, that seems always to say to me, 'You are marked to step into a crisis some time, as the instrument of God.' It seems that it may mean danger or disgrace, or in some way cause me agony of heart, but I can't escape it. With recurring frequency I have had the feeling so often all my life, since I was a very little girl. Lately I've quit fighting it." Evidently she saw herself as "the instrument of God" in trying to impose Prohibition on a resistant American public. In that faith she found the strength to persist, but it also gave her a fanatical edge.

At the Justice Department, she was only the second female assistant attorney general—another woman had served briefly in 1920—and the first to hold the position for an extended time. At meetings she was usually the only woman of authority in the room. ("It was a *stag* party," she noted of a dinner given by the solicitor general, "I the only doe!") She was young as well, just thirty-two when she took the job in 1921. Surrounded by older, skeptical men, she often could not get their attention. She had no respect for Attorney General Harry Daugherty ("manifestly utterly unqualified as a Law Enforcement Executive") or for Secretary of the Treasury Andrew Mellon, in whose department a separate Prohibition Bureau was incongruously lodged.

The Prohibition Bureau's agents, underpaid and easily bribed, were not civil service employees until 1927. One in twelve was dismissed for corruption, and many others quit to become bootleggers. The top men at the Prohibition Bureau, Roy Haynes and then Lincoln Andrews, did not impress Willebrandt either. "At first we had a regime of preachers under Commissioner Haynes," she concluded in 1926, "with a politician in sheep's clothing creeping in here and there. Weak and ineffectual as his regime was, it was never as bad as General Andrews has given us in the past year. After the preacher regime we have had an army officer regime, which has been a hopeless failure." No doubt Haynes and Andrews had their own impressions of Mabel Willebrandt.

Granted these personal and administrative obstacles, the problem of enforcing Prohibition came down to the overriding fact that people still wanted to drink. Folklore to the contrary, Americans did not drink *more* during Prohibition. To the extent that mass drinking levels may be estimated from such evidence as arrests for drunkenness, the incidence of alcoholism, and federal

excise taxes on alcohol before and after Prohibition, it appears
that drinking was actually reduced during the dry years, perhaps
by half. That still left a demand sufficient to frustrate enforcement
agencies and make bootleggers rich. For a typical consumer,
Prohibition meant higher retail prices—up 150 to 600 percent
from before 1920—and a general uncertainty about the true
nature of the product. "One can never be quite sure what will
happen to you after a New York cocktail," a British visitor
observed in 1927. Only people of wealth could afford to buy real
booze. The rest took their chances. "You used to have to stand up
while a rich man talked to you," said one bootlegger; "but now if
he knew you'd got the stuff, he would invite you to lie down on his
parlor sofa."

A nice twist: Prohibition had been forced on working-class
drinkers by middle-class moralists. And now one had to be middle
class, at least, to get a good drink, and powerful enough not to
worry about raids. When Al Smith was governor of New York, a
caller could always be well served at the Governor's Mansion in
Albany. Smith's friend John J. Raskob, a prominent Democrat
and a top executive at both Du Pont and General Motors, gave
him a special Christmas present in 1930: a traveling bag with a
secret compartment in the bottom to hide a bottle. Raskob, who
led the movement to repeal the Eighteenth Amendment, liked to
twit Alfred Sloan, his boss at GM, and Walter Chrysler about their
rich men's hypocrisies. "I am having a lot of fun taking a crack at
you and Alfred every now and then," Raskob told Chrysler,
"about denying the working man his glass of beer with your
lockers filled with vintage champagnes, rare old wines and selected brands of old whiskeys, liqueurs etc."

It depended on the particular ox being gored. George Read
Nutter was an old-fashioned Boston reformer, the main force
behind the city's hopeful Good Government Association. By the
1920s Nutter had become a patrician at bay, beset by the Irish
voters controlling his Boston and the Jewish students attending
his Harvard. To his credit, though, Nutter could still appreciate
the contradictions of his own Brahmin caste. In 1923 he attended
a stag dinner at the home of a senior probate judge. "As there was
an abundance (as usual at dinner now!) of things to drink," he
wrote in his diary, "I happened to remark upon the incongruity of
a judge who enjoyed his glass at dinner and the next day
sentenced a bootlegger." But then the judge was of a separate

class and ethnic group from the bootlegger. That made it different. A few years later, at a dinner of the Beacon Society at the Algonquin Club, "I was surprised at the way liquor was served," Nutter wrote. "This was at a leading club in town—at a dinner of a society that prides itself on its selected membership. I must confess the way this law is flouted is very startling." As time passed, drinking became more public, and the Eighteenth Amendment more of a dead letter.

Mabel Willebrandt, at least, did not give up. Local enforcement agencies, over which she had no authority, were notoriously sluggish and corruptible. New York in 1921 passed a state law to enforce Prohibition. In three years 6,904 cases were brought under it, leading to only 20 convictions. However, Willebrandt could still badger the United States attorneys in federal districts around the country. Many of them displeased her. She was especially disappointed by John T. Williams of San Francisco (his "drunkenness on duty, his consorting with underworld characters in San Francisco, and his assertion of entrenched political protection"), Robert O. Harris of Boston ("violent and outspoken opposition to the 18th amendment and all it typified . . . utterly uncooperative and unqualified to be in charge"), and Walter Van Riper, an assistant U.S. attorney in New Jersey who was thought to be swayed by the wet Senator Walter Edge ("If I dethrone Edge in New Jersey, I shall not have lived in vain").

Large hopes were raised by the appointment, early in 1925, of Emory R. Buckner as the U.S. attorney for New York. A senior partner in Elihu Root's law firm, Buckner was far more capable and accomplished than most of his peers in the federal system. Like Willebrandt, Buckner came from a different planet than did the bootleggers. Born on the family farm in Iowa, the son of a circuit-riding Methodist preacher, he grew up in small-town Nebraska in a home without liquor or tobacco. Later he made casual biblical references in courtrooms, and he always conducted himself with a high sense of moral obligation. As a New York lawyer, though, he smoked heavily, liked to drink and dance, and when visiting his parents would keep a flask in his suitcase. His clients included breweries for which he prepared briefs opposing the Eighteenth Amendment.

When he became U.S. attorney Buckner stopped drinking, made his staff follow suit, and did his utmost to enforce a law of which he disapproved. He hired bright young assistants such as

John Marshall Harlan, later a Supreme Court justice, and William E. Stevenson, a Rhodes Scholar and later president of Oberlin College. Accompanied by some of his men, Buckner spent $1,500 of his own money on a tour of New York speakeasies; then he got injunctions to close fourteen of them. "The policy of my administration will be Prohibition by padlock so far as the open selling of liquor is concerned," he explained. "My padlock policy will pinch the pocketbook of the men higher up, who for the most part at present escape. A padlocking court operates without a jury." It was mainly a symbolic act. New York had some thirty-two thousand speakeasies and nightclubs, far beyond the available supply of padlocks.

Buckner then went directly after the kingpins. He raided Waxey Gordon's headquarters at the Knickerbocker Hotel, arrested twenty-seven people, but the case went nowhere. He did better with a major indictment against Big Bill Dwyer. In his summation to the jury, Buckner admitted his wet sympathies, assumed the jurors felt the same way, but told them the law was the law. Dwyer was convicted and given a $10,000 fine—small change for him—and two years in Atlanta, of which he served one. Another big trial, of Frank Costello and his associates, was buttressed by mounds of evidence but ultimately foundered on a hung jury. "There was one very seedy man on the jury," recalled William Stevenson, who conducted the prosecution, "whom we were suspicious of from the start of the trial. After the case was over, I visited and interviewed several jurors who told me that the jury had been eleven to one for the conviction of some of the defendants and that the seedy character was the one." After only two years Buckner gave up and returned to private practice; New York's bootleggers collectively exhaled. Soon Buckner was urging the repeal of Prohibition, "this monstrous and crime-breeding thing foisted upon us by our national government."

Willebrandt stuck it out for eight years. A controversial figure in the 1928 presidential campaign, she wavered not at all in the face of ridicule, but it wore her down. "Very nervous," George Read Nutter decided after meeting her. "She seemed neurotic." At last she resigned in the spring of 1929 and wrote an apologia, *The Inside of Prohibition*. "Federal enforcement does not need more men, more money and more ammunition," she declared. "All difficulties and just criticisms come back to the human flaws in enforcement." She had little toleration for "human flaws." Yet shortly she was counsel to California Fruit Industries, maker of a grape concentrate that was easily and widely turned into serviceable wine.

❧ ❧

Organized crime in America was permanently transformed by thirteen years of Prohibition. The old, clear line between underworld and upperworld became vague and easily crossed. With so many everyday Americans casually defying the law, gangsters took on an oblique legitimacy. "Prior to Prohibition," Sol Gelb, a New York criminal attorney in the 1920s, said later, "a hoodlum was a hoodlum. A fellow who committed crimes never mixed with respectable people. . . . Came Prohibition and these people began to cater to the great part of America with their speakeasies and nightclubs. Soon they began to look and act the same as respectable people. They began to know respectable people, associate with them." Who was more guilty, the bootlegger or his customer? Did it matter?

During Prohibition the gangs moved for good beyond their own neighborhoods and cities. The informal cooperation among bootleggers in different states was increasingly systematized. By the late 1920s the major bootleggers of the Northeast had organized themselves into a "Big Seven" or "Seven Group." It included Johnny Torrio (now back in New York), Lucky Luciano and Frank Costello, Charlie Solomon, Waxey Gordon, Longy Zwillman, the Reinfeld Syndicate, and Meyer Lansky and Bugsy Siegel, among others. Most of these men in May 1929 attended the first national convention of organized crime in Atlantic City, along with Al Capone and others from the Midwest. Such an extraordinary summit would have been impossible, indeed unnecessary, before 1920. Crime was nationalized by Prohibition, as most of the men who would dominate organized crime for the next three or four decades got their start as bootleggers.

Finally, the history of Prohibition and the mobs it created cannot be understood without careful attention to ethnic aspects. "Blood ties" mattered, both among the gangsters and between them and their legal adversaries. The ethnic patterns of Prohibition endured for at least forty years afterward. The gangsters remained mostly Irish, Jewish, and Italian. The would-be gangbusters remained mostly WASPs with Protestant consciences.

TWO

THE FORK IN THE ROAD

The end of Prohibition in 1933 was a crucial fork in the road for big-time bootleggers. Some, the Irish rumrunners in particular, had not been criminals before 1920. As for the rest, typically they had been quite young men in 1920, engaged in small ways in minor crimes. They could not then have imagined the easy money and power that Prohibition would drop in their laps. Now they were richer and stronger than they had expected, and perhaps more deeply into the underworld than they had planned. Could they now return to the upperworld if they wanted to? Did they want to?

Given the occupational hazards of the trade, many bootleggers never had to decide. Dion O'Banion was killed in November 1924 by his business rivals the Gennas. Arnold Rothstein was killed in December 1928 by unknown parties, perhaps Irish, for unknown reasons. Frank Wallace and a Gustin gang colleague, Dodo Walsh, were killed in December 1931 by Italian business rivals. Larry Fay was killed in January 1933 by a drunk and disgruntled employee. Charlie Solomon was killed, also in January 1933, by Irish gunmen, shortly after his federal indictment in a major bootleg-ging ring. Max Greenberg and Max Hassel were killed in April 1933, probably by Italian business rivals, in an ambush that their partner Waxey Gordon either treacherously planned or miracu-lously escaped.

The surviving bootleggers now had to think hard, an endeavor for which many of them were not well equipped. During Prohibition it had been easy to cross the line downward into the underworld. After Prohibition it might be less simple to climb back up. Bootlegging had become a running bad joke, a "crime" that people winked at and laughed over. Rumrunners could plausibly regard themselves as entrepreneurs offering a tolerated public service. But other crimes were different, still *crimes*, committed by *criminals*, not by useful bootleggers. Between rumrunning and other "rackets"—a newly popular term—lay a murky no-man's-land, as yet unpenetrated and uncharted. Bootleggers were left wondering what to do.

Three years into the Depression, with the economic system collapsing and one worker in four unemployed, the presidential campaign of 1932 was still punctuated by arguments about Prohibition. Franklin Roosevelt, urging repeal of the Eighteenth Amendment, was elected in November. With that push, Congress voted for repeal in February and sent the Twenty-first Amendment to the states, which finished ratifying it in December 1933. So for thirteen months everybody knew Prohibition would end, and the bootleggers had time to ponder their futures.

Many decided to stay in the liquor business. Sam Bronfman moved himself and Seagram's main office down to New York. In 1935 the Internal Revenue Service dunned Seagram and three other Canadian liquor companies for unpaid taxes on their Prohibition shipments; Seagram agreed to pay $1.5 million, a fraction of its true indebtedness. Once past that embarrassment, Sam Bronfman applied all his rough, explosive shrewdness to the goal of turning Seagram into "the silken gown," as he liked to say, of the American booze industry. At times he indulged the amiable fiction that Joseph E. Seagram was actually some distant Canadian ancestor of his, probably Jewish. In the Bronfman home no one was henceforth allowed to use the words "bootlegger," "rumrunner," or "Prohibition."

Bronfman's main competition in the newly legal American market came from an old bootlegging confederate, Lewis S. Rosenstiel, and his Schenley Distillers Company. So alike in personality and ambition, these two men cooperated briefly, had a rancorous falling-out, and then became the feuding giants of booze, forever throwing plots and invective at each other. Rosenstiel had grown up in Cincinnati—his father was a commercial broker—and as a teenager went to work at an uncle's distillery in Kentucky. During Prohibition he bought and sold "medicinal" whiskey. Expecting Prohibition to be temporary ("I thought repeal was just around the corner the day Prohibition took effect"), Rosenstiel packed his warehouses and acquired the Schenley distillery in Pennsylvania. On his many trips to Montreal he purchased liquor from the Bronfmans and shipped it back to Cincinnati by way of St. Pierre and Bermuda. He was indicted once for bootlegging, in 1929, but the case was dismissed.

Just before repeal, Rosenstiel went to Europe and picked up the American rights to Dubonnet, Noilly Prat, and other popular brands. He did not, however, acquire any of the "Big Five" Scotch whiskies that dominated their market. When Prohibition ended, Schenley trailed far behind National Distillers, an old American firm, in capital resources and stored products. Yet only two years later, Schenley had displaced National Distillers as the industry leader and was described by *Fortune* as "the craziest, the damnedest, the quickest, and the shrewdest outfit in American whiskey." Still without one of the Big Five Scotches, Rosenstiel achieved this miracle in part by cultivating and dealing with old bootleggers like Frank Costello, Meyer Lansky, Joe Linsey, Moe Dalitz, and Sam Tucker. Sam Bronfman maintained similar ties to similar effect. So far as the general public knew, meantime, Bronfman and Rosenstiel were just legitimate businessmen, good citizens, and deep-pocketed philanthropists.

The dominant forces in a richly ruthless business, Seagram and Schenley prospered with the help of aggressive distributors selling their brands in local markets. As important as advertising or the product itself, a distributor could establish a new label by relentlessly pushing it into retail stores, bars, and restaurants. Many of the big distributors were, like Bronfman and Rosenstiel, former bootleggers who knew something about pushing booze, and who retained all the right contacts as the old speakeasies were upgraded to "cocktail lounges." These distributing and importing firms seldom bore the names of their founding bootleggers. The corporate officers were often relatives and stooges fronting for the real bosses. But the money and power behind the fronts came from bootlegging, and some of the methods as well.

Thus the Reinfeld bootlegging syndicate became Browne Vintners. With Prohibition about to end, Joe Reinfeld and other members of his syndicate spent six weeks in Europe, arranging to become the American agents for Remy Martin, Piper-Heidsieck, Cointreau, and—the real prize—White Horse, one of the Big Five Scotches. There remained the problem of how to mask the syndicate's interest in the new firm. "Everybody was more or less panicky," Nig Rutkin said of his associates, "that they would lose their license for being bootleggers or being in trouble at some time or other." So they named it Browne Vintners after a compliant wholesale druggist in New York, and laundered their initial investment of $250,000 through a Seagram employee in Montreal. The Newark gangsters Longy Zwillman and Doc Stacher owned a big piece of the firm, perhaps as much as 50 percent. Well financed and better camouflaged, boasting Zwillman's fearsome authority as an unmentioned asset, Browne became a major distributor, with offices in Rockefeller Center and with White Horse as the largest-selling Scotch in America. Seagram bought Browne Vintners in 1940 for $7.5 million. Joe Reinfeld then moved a vowel and stayed in the liquor business as Renfield Importers, Ltd.

Joe Kennedy, never convicted or even arrested for his bootlegging, did not need such subterfuges. As repeal approached, Kennedy—like Lew Rosenstiel and the Reinfeld group—went to Europe seeking liquor franchises. He got three of the best: Gordon's gin and *two* of the Big Five Scotches, Dewar's and Haig & Haig. "Everywhere I went," a competitor on a similar mission lamented, "Joe Kennedy had been two weeks ahead of me. So I came back without anything." Kennedy set up his distributing firm, Somerset Importers, with an initial investment of $100,000. Its New York office was under Ted O'Leary, formerly in charge of Kennedy's bootlegging. Somerset then brought Kennedy an average profit of a quarter-million dollars a year.

For Johnny Torrio, the end of Prohibition meant shifting his attention from the Seven Group of bootleggers to his Prendergast-Davies firm, the biggest wholesale liquor dealer in New York City. He provided the founding money but kept his name hidden behind a brother-in-law and other old retainers from his rumrunning days. The brains of the operation, just as he had been with Capone in Chicago, Torrio was known as J. T. McCarthy at the

Prendergast-Davies office. He ran the place, called board meetings, and oversaw successive manipulations of the firm's stock. After rival liquor dealers reported the situation to the feds, Torrio sold his interest at a 150 percent profit.

Frank Costello owned Alliance Distributors with Irving Haim, formerly of Boo-Boo Hoff's gang, and other old bootleggers. Alliance obtained the franchises for two more British Scotches, House of Lords and King's Ransom, from their parent company, William Whiteley. The connection proved so rewarding that in 1938 Alliance bought Whiteley, with Costello appointed—at an annual stipend plus a percent of the sales—as a kind of supersalesman for the company's brands. That arrangement with Costello fell through, perhaps, and in 1940 he officially cut his ties with Alliance, perhaps. But he still did liquor deals with Irving Haim, and for years afterward Costello still referred to House of Lords and King's Ransom as "my whiskies."

In Boston, Joe Linsey spent the first years after repeal stepping nimbly from one liquor purveyor to another. At first he was president of the F. H. Jackman Company, a distributor of Browne Vintners' imports. Next he became general manager of Eastern Wine and Spirits, the Boston affiliate of McKesson and Robbins. Finally he settled as president of his own Whitehall Distributors, Ltd., a wholesaler for Schenley products, thereby cementing his friendship with Lew Rosenstiel. The common thread running through these corporate arrangements was Linsey's network of local contacts from his bootlegging days.

The Capone gang's legitimate booze operations were supervised by Joe Fusco, a veteran of Chicago's beer wars of the 1920s. Overtly a mere salesman for Gold Seal Liquors, the dominant wholesaler in Chicago, Fusco actually owned the company behind fronts. Competing firms accused him of intimidating them, in the manner of the old days. For the record, though, Fusco had a more innocent explanation of how he got business from Schenley, Seagram, Somerset, Renfield, Alliance, and others: "I knew my way around town and I thought I could do a job for them. . . . I had been in Chicago all my life, born and raised here. I knew a lot of saloonkeepers. . . . I had made a lot of friends all my life. I never made any enemies." (No enemies that worried him, at least.) Other associates of the Capones owned the Canadian Ace Brewery and a chain of liquor stores in Chicago, and Fusco held interests in four other liquor distributors across northern Illinois.

In any city, the Seagram and Schenley agencies were the two main prizes, usually held by separate and very competitive distributors. Joe Fusco started with Seagram, switched to Schenley, but retained a piece of Seagram—as Fusco explained it—because of his special relationship with Victor Fischel, a top executive at Seagram. But the arrangement was atypical, testifying to Fusco's exceptional clout. In Kansas City, the Di Giovanni brothers got around the problem by running two agencies: Joe's Midwest Distributing had Seagram, and Vincent's Superior Wine and Liquor had Schenley. This family of old bootleggers thus monopolized booze in Kansas City. After a rival gangster, Wolf Riman, picked off part of Schenley's business in Kansas City, he was killed in an unsolved murder.

These patterns of old bootleggers and gangsters involved with legal booze were visible elsewhere across the country—in Cleveland, Detroit, Minneapolis, Los Angeles, Tampa, New Orleans, Newark, Buffalo, Des Moines. In many other places, no doubt, similar conditions prevailed but not visibly. The largest distributing firm in New Jersey was owned by a former bootlegger who was never known as such to the public—though Longy Zwillman held stock in his company. Once established legitimately, the bootleggers held on, and on. Over forty years after the end of Prohibition, the head of the New York State Liquor Authority surveyed the major distributors he was supposed to regulate and concluded, "All those guys were in bootlegging. That's how they got into the wholesale liquor business."

❧ ❧

But most bootleggers left the liquor business after repeal. The question of what to do next was easiest for those with significant pre-Prohibition criminal histories. They just resumed their usual pursuits. Pete McDonough and his men still controlled the rackets in San Francisco. Gamblers, prostitutes, and other crooks paid the McDonoughs a million dollars a year for the privilege of plying their trades. Anyone unwilling to pay could not do business in the city. A special report by a former FBI agent in 1937 described the McDonough Brothers firm as "a fountainhead of corruption, willing to interest itself in almost any matter designed to defeat or circumvent the law." Briefly perturbed, a grand jury then forced the resignations of sixteen top cops and two of the city's three police commissioners. A new state law directed at Pete McDonough put him out of bail bonding, and a few years later even his saloon had to close. (Yet certain circumstances did not change: in 1946 Pierre Salinger made his name as a young reporter in San Francisco by exposing corruption in the bail bond system.)

Of the Jewish bootleggers, Meyer Lansky went on to the longest, most important criminal career after Prohibition. Perhaps "the main architect of the giant conglomerate that is organized crime in the United States," Lansky succeeded to Arnold Rothstein's central position in the underworld as the banker, the money launderer and financial manipulator, the one man whom everyone knew and almost everyone trusted. Like his mentor, Rothstein, he was based not in a gang but in gambling. He ran the biggest bookmaking operation in New York City and a national clearinghouse for gamblers as well; thus he had many partners and men in his debt, whose strings could be pulled as needed. Always thinking ahead, he pushed American gangsters into lucrative scams in Cuba, Las Vegas, and the Bahamas. Only five feet four inches tall, known as the Little Man, he adroitly squirmed out of serious trouble with the law and described himself as an unfairly hounded businessman. "So why am I considered the criminal today," he said in old age, "because I was also part of the bootlegging business? Why is Lansky a 'gangster' and not the Bronfman and Rosenstiel families? I was involved with all of them in the 1920s, although they do not like to talk about it and change the subject when my name is mentioned." Lansky's net worth, according to mob folklore, ultimately amounted to a billion dollars.

A handful of major bootleggers who were honest before the irresistible bonanza of Prohibition did make apparent gestures toward going straight after 1933. But few of them could fully purge themselves of their criminal ties. Joe Linsey kept Mickey the Wise Guy Rocco, a high-level Boston mobster, on the payroll of his Whitehall distributing firm. Over the years Linsey had other dealings, discreet but evidently legitimate, with major local organized criminals. "When Prohibition ended, Linsey became the front man for the New England mob," recalled Vinnie Teresa, a Boston gangster. "What he does is invest their money in things like race tracks, hotels, liquor companies, real estate. There's nothing really illegal in that, but Linsey's been with the mob for years no matter what he says. . . . Linsey is kind of the Meyer Lansky of New England. He takes care of the boys' money." At the same time, perhaps in compensation, he donated hundreds of thousands of dollars to Brandeis University and other good causes in Boston. Linsey was once given a testimonial dinner attended by Lew Rosenstiel, three college presidents, and the attorney general of Massachusetts. "We have a way of dry cleaning Joe Linsey's money," one of his beneficiaries explained.

In Cleveland, Moe Dalitz and his old bootlegging partners took a middle ground between the ongoing rackets of Lansky and the overt respectability of Linsey. Operating from a suite in the Hollenden House hotel, Dalitz and his associates were linked to a sensational murder in 1931, but nothing was proven against them. Along with Tommy McGinty, the top Irish gangster in town, they ran gambling joints in Cleveland, Youngstown, and Covington, Kentucky. They dealt with gangsters from Chicago and New York. They helped create Las Vegas. For covers and diversion, they invested in legitimate businesses. Dalitz had interests in a railroad, a land development firm, a real-estate office, a steel company, and (especially) laundries: "I have been in that business all my life, practically," he later told the Kefauver committee. His partners Sam Tucker, Lou Rothkopf, and Morris Kleinman all had upperworld businesses too. Their associations and actions were questioned, but only questioned; in general this durable "silent syndicate" covered its tracks and stayed out of jail and the newspapers.

Big Bill Dwyer eased into a post-Prohibition life of similar ambiguity. He had always, in typical gangster style, hung around boxers, horse players, and other sporting types. When Emory Buckner indicted him in 1926, Dwyer was described by the *New York Times* as a "sportsman and race track owner." Convicted and awaiting prison, Dwyer—according to undercover gossip—traded his liquor interests to colleagues in exchange for their track holdings. After his year in jail he was not again considered an important bootlegger. He brought professional ice hockey to New York and was the first owner of the Brooklyn football Dodgers. But he also owned and managed racetracks with mob connections. The feds tried to get him for income tax evasion in 1934, lost the case, but then won another indictment in 1939. Dwyer was found guilty of evading $3.7 million in taxes from 1922 to 1936; almost $2.2 million of this came from just the three years 1923 to 1925, his rumrunning prime. He might have quit bootlegging, but it finally came back and nailed him again, six years after the end of Prohibition.

Joe Kennedy was a unique case. No other bootlegger had so large a reputation in the upperworld or so much to lose. After moving in 1926 to the greener pastures of New York, he had spent most of his time piling up fortunes there in securities and in the movies in Hollywood. Zipping back and forth between the coasts, he enjoyed a long run of good luck before stumbling in the late 1920s. He tried to produce an expensive "artistic" movie starring his girlfriend Gloria Swanson, but *Queen Kelly* was so bizarre and incoherent it could not be released in the United States. "I've never had a failure in my life," he told Swanson. Soon their affair ended and—after other reversals—Kennedy left the movie business, richer but frazzled and thirty pounds under his normal weight.

According to Doc Stacher, not a reliable source, Kennedy endured a concurrent disaster in bootlegging. As Stacher told the story, a Kennedy shipment of whiskey from Ireland was hijacked in southern New England by a gang taking orders from Lucky Luciano and Meyer Lansky. Kennedy's guards decided to fight the hijackers, and eleven men were killed. "It really wasn't our fault," one of the hijackers insisted. "Those Irish idiots hire amateurs as guards." Kennedy lost the shipment and then for months afterward was besieged by requests for money from the families of the dead men. No such hijacking involving eleven deaths—more than the seven killed in the St. Valentine's Day Massacre—was reported in newspapers at the time; but if it did take place, it might have made Kennedy rethink the implications of his bootlegging.

In any event, around 1930 Kennedy started behaving differently: less riveted on making money, more concerned over his family and his own public reputation. He established trust funds for his children. He bought homes in Bronxville, Hyannis Port, and Palm Beach, and spent more time with his family at them than he had previously. "This was a golden interval for me and for the children," Rose Fitzgerald Kennedy remembered later. On weekends he would take his children into New York from

Bronxville for lunch and movies at Radio City. Sunday afternoons he would spend in long walks with Rose, the children trailing behind. Throttling down from the frenzied pace of his varied enterprises, public and private, during the 1920s, Kennedy now puzzled over what really mattered to him. "The only thing I can leave them that will mean anything," he said of his children, "is my good name and reputation."

From this rumination he emerged with a newfound interest in politics. In 1932 he gave almost $100,000 to Roosevelt's campaign, and at the Democratic convention he delivered the crucial votes, newspapers, and money controlled by William Randolph Hearst ("I'm the one who got the Hearst check and gave it directly to Roosevelt"). For these services Kennedy in 1934 was made chairman of the new Securities and Exchange Commission. Before the appointment was announced, he met at the White House with Roosevelt, Raymond Moley, and Bernard Baruch. "Joe, I know darned well you want this job," said Moley. "But if anything in your career in business could injure the President, this is the time to spill it. Let's forget the general criticism that you've made money in Wall Street." Kennedy stonewalled them. "With a burst of profanity," Moley recalled, "he defied anyone to question his devotion to the public interest or to point to a single shady act in his whole life. The President did not need to worry about that, he said. What was more, he would give his critics—and here again the profanity flowed freely—an administration of the S.E.C. that would be a credit to the country, the President, himself, and his family—clear down to the ninth child."

In his new job, under new regulations, Kennedy then policed the very stock frauds and deceptions that had helped make him so rich a decade earlier. He performed well, and Roosevelt gave him two other important jobs later. "I prefer to have my activities referred to not as political," he with great dignity told his Harvard classmates, "but rather as an interest in public affairs." Yet his secret ties to gangsters continued (see Chapter Eight). In less obvious ways, he was no more successful than Joe Linsey or Big Bill Dwyer in shaking off his old associates.

All the major Italian bootleggers, whether involved in rackets before Prohibition or not, stayed in organized crime after 1933. They had started from farther down the ladder of social mobility than the Irish and Jewish rumrunners, so they had fewer options in going straight. More to the point, they also had a criminal advantage the Irish and Jewish gangsters did not: a secret criminal organization of compelling force and deadliness. Only Italians could join it. Irish and Jewish gangsters, no matter how powerful, could merely stand outside this organization, perform services and make requests, and await its decisions. The ultimate closed shop, it was—after Prohibition—the most consequential development in the history of American organized crime.

❦ ❦

They don't call it the Mafia. At different times and places, its members have named it the Outfit, the Clique, the Arm, the Syndicate, the Tradition, the Office, the Honored Society, the Combination, and La Cosa Nostra, "Our Thing." Sometimes no name at all is mentioned; a man is simply described as "connected," and the point is understood. Gangsters have used these terms to designate a national structure, or one of its local branches, or some other criminal group entirely, leading to confusion and arguments among observers over just how organized American organized crime has been. When the layers are peeled away, though, an essential core remains that may be called the Mafia.

It arose from medieval conditions in Sicily, and in America it succeeded precisely as a medieval anachronism in counterpoint to modern culture, each provoking and irritating the other. Modernity broke society down into atoms of mobile, free-floating, unaffiliated individuals with ultimate loyalties only to the state and its laws. The Mafia insisted on the enduring primacy of family, geography, ethnicity, and ultimate loyalties to persons and the Mafia itself—the group over the individual. Instead of contractual, legalistic, or economic ties, the Mafia bound its men with personalized relations of reciprocal obligations, often paid in services instead of money. While modernity presented endless choices and the option of periodically reinventing oneself, the Mafia required affective ties, birthrights that could not be chosen or altered. The essence of modernity was change, or "progress"; the Mafia offered a rock of stability, continuity, and protection from swirling modern tendencies. Other Americans might switch jobs, take new names, move to other states, join or leave families, slide up or down the class ladder. Mafiosi did too, but they still remained Mafiosi.

The Mafia in America was assuredly a predatory gang of crooks, vicious and merciless. But it was also a culture, a process, and an ideal that—however abused and manipulated—met basic emotional and psychological needs. It could hardly have prospered so well and long without these other, human aspects. "We didn't consider ourselves criminals," said Bonanno. "In fact, we considered our code of ethics stricter and fairer than any we encountered in America."

The American Mafia staved off modernity by stubbornly hewing to its Sicilian origins. For over two thousand years, successive waves of invaders from Europe and Africa had swept across Sicily, governing briefly and badly, then passing on. In the farms and villages of western Sicily, generations of peasants learned to regard state authority as distant and unfriendly. "The law works against people," a local saying had it. To fill the chasm between western Sicilians and their faraway governments, the feudal overlords formed private armies to enforce their authority. The armies evolved into secret societies with functions both protective and criminal: they were cops and robbers in turn.

These societies flourished during the century of political chaos between Napoleon and Mussolini. The old feudal system had collapsed under Napoleon's rule, and after his withdrawal the Mafia groups, as they were now called, stepped into the breach by mediating between peasants and aristocracy, and serving themselves as well. (Of the several versions of the word's origin, the most plausible is that it derived from a Sicilian adjective, *mafia*, implying "courage, strength, agility, quickness, endurance, and intelligence.") Dispersed across the island, the Mafia groups thrived on a weak state, strong kinship bonds, and an ethical code stressing masculine honor. The individual groups were called "families"—suggesting the importance of kinship—and they were headed by "fathers" or "men of respect." No single authority governed all the families, but a man especially respected by all the fathers would be deferred to as a *capo consigliere*, a "head counselor." The Mafia families controlled their own turfs and enterprises, exerted political influence, committed crimes, solved local problems with violence if necessary, and generally arranged matters between individuals and formal political powers.

Sicilian immigrants to America then brought along the Mafia as a culture, not as an organization. It arrived here in capricious fragments at scattered and unlikely places. Nobody in Sicily *sent* it. The blending of Sicilian traditions and American contexts spawned a particular hybrid, an American Mafia. Accustomed to unfriendly governments, Sicilian immigrants found the WASPs and Irishmen in American politics no more approachable than their old-country masters. The Mafia offered a familiar, nearby recourse and source of order in the local community. But it was also—mostly—a secret criminal enterprise threatening Italians, usually, with robbery, murder, kidnapping, and extortion letters. "It was a byword in every family," recalled Philip D'Andrea, a Capone mobster. "People were scared to death of having a little home for fear somebody would come over and blow it up, or for fear they would receive a letter." The American Mafia always presented this double edge: its constituents might at first need it, yet ultimately were harmed by it.

The Mafia first surfaced in America in New Orleans just after the Civil War, amid conditions of political disorder because of Reconstruction. Organized by Joseph Macheca, the son of Sicilian immigrants, this first American Mafia family flourished in the city's Second District and along the docks. For business purposes the New Orleans Mafia favored a weapon known as "the Mafia gun": a sawed-off shotgun with a hinged stock, folded and concealed under a coat. By the 1880s leadership had passed on to Charles Matranga and his brother Tony, a saloonkeeper. A feud between the Matrangas and the Provenzano family for control of the docks led in 1890 to the murder, apparently by Italians, of David Hennessey, chief of the New Orleans police. Afterward a lynch mob stormed the jail and hanged sixteen Italian prisoners, some of whom had not been charged with killing Hennessey. But the New Orleans Mafia went on, and Charles Matranga remained boss until 1922.

The coal mines of northeastern Pennsylvania brought a Sicilian colony to Pittston and other areas nearby. About a hundred families from one Sicilian town, Montedoro, lived in the Brandy Patch section of Pittston. There Stefano LaTorre and Santo Volpe, both immigrants, formed "the men of Montedoro," a second early Mafia family in America. Starting among the coal miners, their influence spread to the United Mine Workers and even the mine owners. Still based in the Brandy Patch, they eventually took over the UMW in their part of the state.

New York City's Sicilian immigrants lived mostly in Italian Harlem, while immigrants from Naples settled downtown on the Lower East Side. As early as 1888, according to a contemporary newspaper account, the American Mafia was centered in New Orleans and New York. The biggest Italian gang in New York around the turn of the century was led by Ignazio Lupo Saietta and Giuseppe Morello, two brothers-in-law from the same town in Sicily. "The city is confronted with an Italian problem," declared the *New York Tribune* in 1904, "with which at the present time it seems unable to cope." In 1910 Saietta and Morello were given long sentences for counterfeiting, one of their lesser crimes.

Los Angeles had no substantial Sicilian population, but it had gained a small Mafia colony by 1920. Jack Dragna was born in 1891 in Corleone, near Palermo, in Sicily. Brought to America as a boy, he returned to Sicily in 1908 ("I was here with my folks, and we all went back"), then emigrated on his own six years later, settling in California. A conviction for attempted extortion in 1915 landed him in San Quentin for a while. Then he bought a home in Los Angeles and grew rich bootlegging, becoming "the top man of my Tradition in the Los Angeles area," as Joe Bonanno described him.

The Mafia in Providence, Rhode Island, was founded by the five Morelli brothers of New York. Led by Joe and Butsey, they started a criminal gang in New York at the turn of the century. Later Joe bragged about having been a suspect in New York's famous Becker-Rosenthal murder of 1912. The Morellis moved on to Providence, with its large Italian community, and pillaged up into southeastern Massachusetts. They probably committed the holdup and murders for which Nicola Sacco and Bartolomeo Vanzetti were executed; a confession at the time implicated them, and Joe Morelli resembled Sacco. "These two suckers took it on the chin for us," Butsey Morelli later told Vinnie Teresa. "That shows you how much justice there really is."

Italian immigrants in Cleveland were clustered around Mayfield Road, from East 119th to East 125th Street. The local Mafia group, led by Big Al Polizzi, was known as the Mayfield Road Gang. A tall Mafioso at five feet ten inches—hence the nickname—Polizzi was born in Sicily in 1900, brought to America at age nine, and first arrested in 1920. Along with his Mayfield colleagues, John Angersola and the Milano brothers, Polizzi wiped out his

Sicilian rivals and then controlled the Italian rackets in Cleveland. The Mayfield gang coexisted with Moe Dalitz and his Jewish gang in the city.

Thus by the 1920s an American Mafia was operating on local levels, here and there. It appeared in major cities as well as almost anywhere Sicilians had congregated. The steel mills and smelting plants of Pueblo, Colorado, drew Sicilians, so it had a Mafia. The coal mines of central Illinois attracted Sicilians, so Springfield had a Mafia. Parochial by definition, unsophisticated and narrow-horizoned, these early Mafiosi cultivated their own local gardens without apparent larger ambitions.

Then an accident of history. Two unrelated events four thousand miles apart changed the American Mafia into something more. Mussolini assumed power in Italy in 1922. To consolidate his authority in Sicily he tried to subdue the Mafia, with methods running to torture and summary executions. Meantime Prohibition was making America a gangster heaven. Pushed by Mussolini and pulled by bootlegging, in the next few years a new group of Mafiosi arrived in America: Stefano Magaddino and his brother Antonio, Salvatore Maranzano, Joe Bonanno, Mike Coppola, Joe Profaci and his brother-in-law Giuseppe Magliocco, and others. The Magaddinos lived at first in New York City, then moved on to Buffalo and started a principal Mafia family there with lines into Canada. Most of the others settled in the New York City area.

This mix of new blood and easy pickings pushed the American Mafia—despite its discrete, localized origins—into a national structure. It seized on an existing framework, the Unione Siciliana, a mutual aid society founded in Chicago in 1895. Like its counterparts among other immigrant populations, the Unione provided life insurance, death expenses, and memories of the old country. Initially it also fought the Black Hand and other Italian lawbreakers. But in the 1920s Sicilian gangsters, operating behind its benign reputation, transformed it into a criminal front dominated by Mafiosi from New York and Chicago. During the decade six different presidents of the Unione in Chicago took office and were murdered in turn, suggesting both chaotic rivalries and the perceived importance of the job.

After one of these murders, that of Antonio Lombardo in September 1928, there occurred the first national meeting of the American Mafia (or at least the first to be discovered). Held at the

Hotel Statler in Cleveland in December 1928, it drew Mafiosi from the East, South, and Midwest. A hotel clerk alerted the police, who swept through several floors of the Statler, arresting twenty-seven men; others at a separate hotel, and probably on other floors of the Statler, escaped detection. Some of the bigger fish were Sam DiCarlo of Buffalo, Joe Vaglichio and Ignatzio Italiano of Tampa, and three New York kingpins: Vincent Mangano, Joe Profaci, and Giuseppe Magliocco. Italiano at seventy-two was the oldest; the rest were mainly in their thirties. They were booked, photographed, and released. Profaci, who ran a small olive-oil-importing company in Brooklyn, later explained that he was there "to expand my business . . . to open up the territory . . . because there was some friend of my father told me they had a friend over there, and he says they need me there in Cleveland." The actual purpose of the meeting remained a secret. Its real significance was simply that it was held at all.

The bloody showdowns among New York's five Italian gangs in 1930–31 nudged along the nationalization of the Mafia. The main conflict was between Salvatore Maranzano and Joe the Boss Masseria. Maranzano and most of his men came from the Castellammarese region of northwest Sicily; Masseria and many of his troops were from the town of Sciacca, forty miles to the south. Not confined to New York, this "Castellammarese War" drew support from allies in Buffalo, Cleveland, and Detroit, and the fighting stretched all the way to Chicago and the West Coast. Masseria, whose gang already included non-Sicilian Italians, accepted money and then gunmen from Al Capone, acts that implicitly extended the American Mafia beyond its Sicilian membership. "In exchange for Capone's more direct help, Masseria went ahead and accepted Capone, the Neapolitan, into our Sicilian orbit," noted Joe Bonanno. "Because of the melting-pot effect in America and the need for recruits during the Castellammarese War, we Sicilians found ourselves accepting into our confidence many non-Sicilians. Men joined our ranks who didn't fully understand our Tradition, or only understood it in a very rudimentary and superficial way."

When the killing stopped, the now-broadened Mafia was formalized by a new national Commission, an American invention without precedent in Sicily. Initially envisioned by Maranzano before he was murdered, then installed by his successor, Lucky

Luciano, the Commission met for the first time in the fall of 1931. At the outset it consisted of seven men, the five leaders of the New York families and one each from Chicago and Buffalo. The Commission wielded great power of a diffuse and shifting kind, depending on personalities and reputations instead of an organization chart. It reached decisions by consensus, not by formal vote. No one man dominated. Instead there was a conservative, Sicilian faction and a more liberal, Americanized one. Each Mafia family remained autonomous on its own turf. The Commission could not initiate actions, but it could sometimes veto them. Mafia families not directly represented on the Commission nonetheless accepted its authority; later it was expanded from seven to nine members. It met every five years in secret national conventions, unbothered by lawmen until a special out-of-sequence meeting at Apalachin, New York, in 1957. More a forum than a board of directors, the Commission gave the Mafia an expansive new scope, stability, and impact.

From the early 1930s on, the Mafia was the center, the main source of continuity and power, in the affairs of American organized crime. If the Mafia changed at all it was only by minor adjustments. Its essential internal procedures remained extraordinarily consistent. A prospective member had to be Italian on both sides of his family. Through some youthful display of criminal potential he would reach the attention of an established Mafioso, who would become his sponsor. The prospect would enter a long apprenticeship, often lasting for years, under the sponsor's eye. He would have to demonstrate the virtues of silence and obedience. At the bottom of the family's pecking order, the apprentice would undertake the most menial and dangerous jobs, usually including murders.

If he did well, and if the family needed new blood, the apprentice would become a "made" member in an initiation ceremony. Joe Valachi, a Neapolitan gunman inducted into Maranzano's family during the Castellammarese War, later gave the classic description of a Mafia initiation:

> After a time some guy, I forget who, comes to the door. He waves at me and says, "Joe, let's go." I follow him into this other room, which was very big. All the furniture was taken out of it except for a table running down the middle of it with chairs all around. The

table was about five feet wide and maybe thirty feet long. . . . I'd say about forty guys were sitting at the table, and everybody gets up when I come in. . . . Now Mr. Maranzano said to everybody around the table, "This is Joe Cago," which I must explain is what most of the guys knew me by. Then he tells me to sit down in an empty chair on his right. When I sit down, so does the whole table. Someone put a gun and a knife on the table in front of me. I remember the gun was a .38, and the knife was what you would call a dagger. After that, Maranzano motions us up again, and we all hold hands and he says some words in Italian. Then we sit down, and he turns to me, still in Italian, and talks about the gun and the knife. "This represents that you live by the gun and the knife," he says, "and you die by the gun and the knife." Next he asked me, "Which finger do you shoot with?" I said, "This one," and I hold up my right forefinger. I was still wondering what he meant by this when he told me to make a cup out of my hands. Then he put a piece of paper in them and lit it with a match and told me to say after him, as I was moving the paper back and forth, "This is the way I will burn if I betray the secret of this Cosa Nostra." . . . So Joe Bananas laughs too, and comes to me and says, "Give me that finger you shoot with." I hand him the finger, and he pricks the end of it with a pin and squeezes until the blood comes out. When that happens, Mr. Maranzano says, "This blood means that we are now one Family." In other words, we are all tied up. . . . Now the ceremony is over, and everybody is smiling.

The rituals of burning and bloodletting were not universal among Mafia families at the time, and later they passed out of fashion entirely. The key passage of initiation remained an elaborate dinner at which the initiate met family members previously unknown to him.

The Mafia's central idea, of the individual will subordinated to and for the group, did not change. "When you become a member they own you body and soul," Vinnie Teresa said later in explaining why he had not wished to be made. "God forbid, if they found out your kid was involved in some kind of a racket [and] they didn't like what he was doing, they would tell you to kill your own kid. . . . They come first above everything. That is the first rule of becoming a member of the organization." In America the "father" at the head of the family was typically called a boss or don. But the group itself was still called a family, and it retained salient aspects of kinship. Thus an incest taboo: a made member was strictly enjoined from sleeping with another member's wife. If he did, the cuckold had the right and expectation to kill the seducer. In the interest of family peace, no member could lay violent hands on another Mafioso, even from another family. This rule had special meaning in New York, where the five families constantly brushed against each other and were tempted to steal each other's rackets.

Later on, law enforcers trying to understand the Mafia drew schematic diagrams of an individual family's structure, with slots for the ruling council, the chiefs, the lieutenants or *caporegimes*, section leaders, and button men or soldiers at the bottom. These charts did capture one crucial reality: that the bosses were protected by layers from responsibility for the crimes committed on their orders. But otherwise the families were not organized so neatly. In an enterprise where nothing was ever written down, lines of authority might cross, be cut, or become entangled. Orders were conveyed by a hand gesture, a voice inflection, or a nod of the head. The words from a man's mouth might be rescinded by the simultaneous look in his eye. A simple handshake meant less than a handshake with the other hand on the shoulder, which meant less than a handshake with an embrace, which meant less than an embrace with kisses on both cheeks. A family's affairs turned on subtleties and shadings largely beyond an outsider's ability to comprehend or describe. Rules and traditions finally meant less than "a willingness in men," as Joe Bonanno observed, "to congregate around a greater man. In doing so, every man finds his place in relation to the greater man and thus friction is avoided. The result is harmony and a well-ordered society." Personal influence cannot be understood apart from the particular personalities at work.

Aside from that, controlling and expressing that, the Mafia was held together by the grim threat and fact of violence. At a certain point, all the rules and traditions become pallid rhetoric, just fine-sounding words and postures. The analogies to families and kinship patterns turn into euphemisms and evasions, like saying "hustle" to mean steal, or "hit" or "whack" or "clip" to mean kill. It comes down to murder: murder used as credential, admonition, proof of loyalty, payment, business tactic, sport, and final judgment. Among their underworld associates, the Italians had earned a reputation for killing. Their Mafia ultimately depended on the same specialty. Joe Valachi was once asked what he had done to ingratiate himself with his family. "Just kill for them," he said.

❧ ❧

"I know only one thing, Pete," Mike Scandifia of the Gambino family later told a colleague. "The Cosa Nostra is the Cosa Nostra. You just do what the fucking bosses tell you."

❧ ❧

With the Mafia as their vehicle, Italian gangsters began to dominate the underworld. Other criminals came to define themselves in relation to their Italian associates. Jews in particular fell into durable partnerships with Mafiosi, each group respecting the other's particular strengths. George Wolf, Frank Costello's Jewish lawyer, observed these ties for some thirty years, in New York and nationally as well. "The two groups have always worked in surprisingly good harmony," Wolf concluded, "the Italians respecting the Jews for their financial brains, and the Jews preferring to stay quietly behind the scenes and let the Italians use the 'muscle' needed."

Meyer Lansky's eminence derived initially from his special proximity to Lucky Luciano, the dominant figure among Italian gangsters of the 1930s. Luciano so depended on Lansky's advice that he asked permission to bring his associate to a crucial meeting of Italians in Chicago in 1931. (Lansky was allowed to make the trip but not to attend the meeting itself.) After Luciano went to jail, Lansky kept up similar ties with the later heads of the Luciano family, Frank Costello and Vito Genovese. "Anywhere where Meyer Lansky is, Vito Genovese is," Joe Valachi testified. "They do everything together." The most prominent Jewish gangster and the most prominent Mafia family fed off each other, succeeding together to degrees neither could have achieved alone. Greasy Thumb Guzik provided similar services for the Capone gang, as did Joe Linsey for the New England mob and Maishe Rockman for the Cleveland family. In the same way that Sicilians and Neapolitans had buried their ancient feuds to mutual advantage in the new Mafia, Jews and Italians—though retaining an acute sense of their partners' differentness—could now cooperate in criminal enterprises.

For such purposes Nig Rosen was transferred from New York to Philadelphia, just as a corporation would move a key employee. A Russian Jewish immigrant raised on New York's Lower East Side, Rosen was connected with Lansky and Bugsy Siegel, and through them with the Italian gangs of New York. The murder of Mickey Duffy in 1931 left open a key slot in Philadelphia gangdom, and Rosen moved down to fill it. (His own version was that he moved just to please his wife: "She was an entertainer and she worked around Philadelphia and she liked it.") At once, with remarkable speed, Rosen became the rackets boss of the city; the unspoken authority of the New York gangs may be inferred. Known as the Mahoff, with his Italian partners he ran gambling, narcotics, and labor racketeering. His power extended as far as Wilmington, Baltimore, and Atlantic City. Boo-Boo Hoff, the most notorious Jewish bootlegger in Philadelphia, was pushed aside. Hoff lost his money and wound up running a jukebox dance joint in West Philly. He died, an apparent suicide, at the age of forty-eight.

Longy Zwillman remained the boss in Newark because he had enough power to forge an honorable peace with the Italians. His bootlegging gang, though mainly Jewish, included Jerry Catena, a member of the Luciano family. Using Catena as the mediator, Zwillman worked out a settlement with Richie the Boot Boiardo, also a Luciano man and the leading Italian gangster in Newark. The Zwillman and Boiardo forces celebrated the peace over a fancy dinner party lasting two days. Zwillman of course was still barred from inner Mafia councils, but on his own turf the Italians granted him deference.

Other Jewish gangsters reached understandings with the Italians in their individual ways. For Mickey Cohen it meant becoming an Italian Jew. "Now I don't mean this degrading to the Irish," he said later, "but the Jews and the Italians also had a strong combine together—or as close as any Italian could be with any non-Italian." The son of Russian Jewish immigrants, Cohen grew up in the Boyle Heights section of Los Angeles and was first arrested, at age nine, for bootlegging. In his teens he ran away to be a boxer and gangster, winding up in Cleveland. There he fell in with Italian criminals, who called him "the Jew kid," and he started imitating them. "So naturally I'm going to pick up a lot of Italian ways. . . . The influence of the Italian loyalty and a respect for family, elders and women has remained a part of my way of life. But the violence about the Italians I associated with also rubbed off on me." He dressed in Italian gangster chic and was known more for muscle than brains. After a gunplay episode in which he killed two gangsters, he was anointed with Al Capone's approval, which inflated his reputation. Eventually he moved back to Los Angeles and hooked up with Bugsy Siegel, whom he respectfully called Benny (nobody dared address him as Bugsy). "So it was an organization, but it wasn't the Mafia. Being Jews, Benny and me and even Meyer couldn't be a real part and parcel of that."

Italian hoodlums dealt with less compliant Jewish rivals in characteristic fashion. In Detroit the Italians gradually reduced the Purple Gang to remnants, killing them one by one. Abe Bernstein, the head Purple, managed to hang on as a bookie—but he stopped contesting Detroit's Mafia for control of the city's underworld. Waxey Gordon in New York made a similar strategic retreat. A few days after the murders of his associates Max Greenberg and Max Hassel in April 1933, a Gordon enforcer named Murray Moll was also killed in the Bronx. By the time Gordon was jailed in a tax case later that year, his gang had been decimated. For days a vegetable truck loaded with machine gunners parked across the street from the jail, waiting for Gordon to emerge on bail. He chose to stay imprisoned and alive. After doing his time he returned to New York in 1941 and said he was reformed. He started dealing narcotics and in 1951, as a fourth-time offender, was sent away for twenty-five years to life. As a gangster he had peaked in the freewheeling Prohibition days before the Italian ascendancy.

Relatively few Irish gangsters became partners with Italians. If they chose to remain in rackets after Prohibition, Irishmen generally had the choice of being killed or retreating to a safe distance. In Boston the murders of Frank Wallace and Dodo Walsh in December 1931 ended years of squabbling between their Irish Gustin gang and the Italians of the North End. The Gustins, who had just hijacked a truck and still that belonged to the Italians, were invited to a peace conference in Joe Lombardo's office at 317 Hanover Street in the North End. They walked into an ambush. The following summer, Italian gangsters held a meeting at the Manger Hotel for the men who ran Boston's policy gambling. "We've knocked off men in the liquor racket," cops in the next room heard someone say, "so you had better take your medicine." The cops broke up that meeting, arresting Lombardo, Philip Buccola, and other ranking Italians, but could scarcely affect the growing Italian power in Boston. Dan Carroll, formerly Boston's major Irish bootlegger, lingered on as Buccola's associate, but he did as he was told.

Roger Touhy, the last major Irish bootlegger still alive in Chicago as Prohibition was ending, had been making concessions to the Capones for years. The Italians snatched Touhy's partner, Matt Kolb, and Touhy delivered the $50,000 ransom to Capone himself; then Capone shook down Touhy for another $25,000, and Touhy paid; finally Kolb was killed. In July 1933 the Capones helped stage the fake kidnapping of a noted swindler, Jake the Barber Factor, and set up Touhy to take the rap. Falsely convicted and imprisoned, Touhy was exonerated twenty years later. Shortly after his release from prison, as he sat on the front porch of his sister's home, he was murdered.

During Prohibition nobody in New York dared defy Owney Madden, the dominant Irish bootlegger in town. Yet "even Owney, with all his power, was a frightened man," according to his Broadway companion Walter Winchell. "He was always afraid of being betrayed or framed or killed." Madden attempted more legal ventures in boxing and laundries, but they tried his patience. "These legitimate rackets!" he complained. "There ain't no sense to 'em. You've got to wait for your money." In 1932 he went back to jail for a year after violating parole; the warden said he was glad to have him, that Madden would be a good influence on other prisoners. When he returned to New York in 1933 Madden decided not to fight the new Italian hegemony. He went south, all the way to the gangster resort of Hot Springs, Arkansas. There he married the WASP daughter of a Republican postmaster, lived quietly in a house next door to the police chief's, and controlled the rackets, such as they were, in Hot Springs. Every morning he would meet a train from New York to get the newspapers and greet anyone from home.

Perhaps Irish gangsters, who before 1920 had dominated the American underworld, were unwilling to accept the subordinated terms of the new arrangements. The partnership of Italians and Jews was symbiotic, but it was not equal. According to underworld convention, Jews might have the brains; Italians still had the muscle. When it came to a showdown, muscle always won. Even Lansky, privileged as he was, had to clear his projects through his Italian masters and cut them in. He could not act on his own. "Jews, outsiders, wind up on the short end in any sitdown chaired and run by the Mafia," a Jewish criminal named Michael Hellerman said later. "Somehow, we always wound up paying, even when we were right. . . . I was a Jew and a Jew doesn't win in sitdowns with the Italian mob over money."

As murder formed the base of the Mafia, it also established Italian authority in the affairs of organized crime. With time the Italians took control of the power of life and death in the underworld. Italians could kill Italians, and could kill others. But others could not kill Italians or even threaten them. Later, in New Jersey, a Jewish criminal named Jerry, an associate of the Mafioso Sam DeCavalcante, started planning his own big moves, even making threats against important people. "If you're not with us," DeCavalcante warned him elliptically, "don't bother anybody that has anything to do with us."

"All I want is a piece," Jerry replied, not seeming to grasp the point.

"But I want to tell you, Jerry," the Mafioso insisted, "if you ever come to me and say you're gonna do something to somebody outside of busting his head or leg—you're never gonna walk out of this office."

"I'm sorry I said that," Jerry apologized, in full retreat. "This would never happen! Believe me!" From the 1930s on, any Jew in organized crime had to know his place. The Italians surely knew theirs.

In time, organized crime gathered vast, unpublicized power in strictly criminal activities as well as in the allied fields of labor racketeering and urban machine politics. A blood thread of ethnicity ran through every underworld enterprise. Gangsters in illegal pursuits, ever suspicious of each other and with no recourse to police and state authority, needed any compensating source of mutual trust they could create. Lacking other bonds, they emphasized and insisted on ethnic ties. A man from the same "blood" was supposed to be more trustworthy; conversely, a hoodlum of a different ethnic background was to be watched skeptically. Ethnicity also established rough job specialties: Irish gangsters were more liable to handle politics and labor rackets, Jewish gangsters to deal in gambling and money matters, Italian gangsters to execute violence and run the whole show.

Over the course of the twentieth century, ethnicity functioned in conservative ways to help protect the stability of the underworld and stave off the ambitions of new gangsters from upstart ethnic groups. At the outset, in the 1920s, a combination of ethnic and economic factors brought Irish, Jewish, and Italian criminals into the underworld. The relatively low status of these groups at that historical moment made crime seem a reasonable, even inevitable way up and out. As time passed, ethnic forces became more compelling within organized crime than economic motives. Even while the honest majority of their ethnic cohorts ascended the class ladder by education and hard work, Irish, Jewish, and Italian gangsters kept running the underworld. Once established, the ethnic patterns were locked in, carried forward by their own internal uses and momentum, often regardless of changes in the external ethnic context of American life.

Yet to stress ethnicity may obscure the individual gangsters and the options available to them. This point cannot be overemphasized: only a tiny, slimy portion of these ethnic groups became gangsters. Most newly arrived Americans played the game straight, committed no crimes, and rose by their own legitimate efforts. Gangsters decided to kill and steal for their living not because they were Irish, Jewish, or Italian but because they were bad people. Organized crime finally derived less from social conditions or difficult childhoods or there-but-for-fortune bad luck than from a durable human condition: the dark, strong pull of selfish, greedy, impatient, unscrupulous ambition. The history of the underworld demands such moral judgments. Criminals—human beings—created organized crime. As human beings, they must be held accountable for the choices they made and the harm they wreaked.

THREE

THEIR OWN WORLD

angsters spent their time in occasional spates of killing and stealing, as well as in all the mundane activities of any conventional life. Somewhere between the killing and stealing and the conventional life, the gangsters made their own world: a middle-earth of smoky nightclubs, the flash of chorus girls in a spotlight, a sprinkling of trumpet and saxophone, and time stopped in a boozy moment of romance and glamor; of boxing arenas, the smell of sweat and liniment, the thud of leather into flesh, a spray of blood, and the rough ballet of the sweet science; of racetracks, the odor of horses and freshly turned earth, the dead reckoning of handicappers and rabbit's foot, the rhythm of sudden, thundering activity and lulls between post times.

In these milieus the men of the underworld met to loaf and plot. Here too the people of the upperworld came to stand back and gawk, to partake briefly of what they wanted only in small, safe doses. Because nightclubs, boxing, and racetracks had all been illegal—or at least improper—they offered a natural habitat for gangsters. The gangster presence made them all the more enticing to the upperworld, with a glistening edge of mystery and danger, and always the chance that something unusual might happen. In its way, the gangsters' own world extended a haven to anyone with the money and interest.

❧ ❧

During Prohibition the cabarets and jazz joints needed liquor. Bootleggers were the only reliable source, so they became involved in the nightlife business. They started in modest ways, bankrolling dives and small speakeasies with only a piano player and singer for entertainment. The gangster bosses paid off the relevant cops and other lawmen to avoid busts, and they installed reasonably clean managers to front the operations. As they prospered, and as public drinking in defiance of Prohibition became more tolerated, the bootleggers began to see themselves as showmen, as impresarios. The speaks became fancy nightclubs with plush interiors, full orchestras, and elaborate floor shows. "In the end," Nils Granlund, a theater publicist, recalled of the New York scene, "they virtually took over the industry, lock, stock, and whiskey barrel. It took plenty of money to set up a joint, with its garish fixtures, its illegal cellar, and its entertainment, and only the gangsters and professional gamblers had enough ready cash to invest in such swank places."

In strictly business terms, nightclubs were a riskier investment than just selling booze. The customers might come, or not; a particular band or entertainer might draw well, or not. Even if the local cops were bribed, federal Prohibition agents might still bestir themselves and close the place. Even the most popular spots would occasionally have to shut down and move to another address. What the nightclubs gave their gangster owners, though, was a modest dollop of respectability. Instead of skulking belowground in furtive ways, here the gangsters could come out in public, be recognized, say hello to famous people. "Hoods got in for the limelight, the name, the notoriety, and for the young girls," one old mobster said later. "They didn't care to make money. . . . They just wanted a place to hang out and ran clubs for this purpose alone." For men whose work was usually nocturnal and portable, the nightclubs amounted to an office and a kind of home.

So in most cities the celebrated night spots of the bootleg era were associated more or less openly with gangsters. In New York, Owney Madden and his partners owned some two dozen midtown clubs along Broadway and its side streets, between Forty-fourth and Fifty-eight streets. His Club Napoleon on Fifty-sixth was especially lush: an old mansion with three floors of velvet carpeting and mirrors, a revolving bar on the first floor, and a tennis court in back. Lucky Luciano was there often—"a quiet man," one musician remembered, "but those vibrations were deadly. When Lucky said go, you were gone." Luciano owned the House of Morgan, with its resident chanteuse, Helen Morgan, perched on her piano; Legs Diamond had the Hotsy Totsy, and Dutch Schultz the Embassy Club. Larry Fay ran a series of clubs including Fay's Follies, the El Fey, the Del Fey, and finally the Casa Blanca, where he was killed by an angry doorman whose pay he had just reduced.

Like Fay himself, most of these joints did not survive Prohibition. But a few did, to become fixtures of Manhattan life for decades afterward. The "21" Club, run by Two-Trigger Jack Kriendler and Charlie Berns, was first a speak known as Jack and Charlie's. It had a collapsible bar and a hidden cache for disposing of liquor during a raid. To avoid such difficulties, the owners would slip fifty-dollar bribes to police captains, a box of cigars to the cop on the beat, and free meals and drinks to others. After Prohibition the joint turned into a durably fashionable restaurant. John Perona's El Morocco managed a similar transformation when legal booze returned. An Italian immigrant with ties to the Unione Siciliana, Perona at first ran some West Side speakeasies. In 1931, probably with the help of unsavory silent partners, he opened the El Morocco on East Fifty-fourth Street, choosing a desert motif of tents and cushions because it meant less furniture to be replaced if the place was raided.

The Stork Club, the Morocco's only peer among New York's premier nightspots of the 1930s and 1940s, had a more complicated history. It was owned by Sherman Billingsley of the notorious Billingsley brothers, four remarkably well-traveled and resilient bootleggers. Originally from Tennessee, the boys—Logan, Fred, Ora, and Sherman—grew up in a small Oklahoma town. Since Oklahoma was a dry state even before national Prohibition, the brothers enterprisingly started running booze. Chased by lawmen, they headed west to Washington, also a dry state by 1916. In downtown Seattle they opened a drugstore and sold liquor "for medicinal purposes." After a police raid chopped up the store, the Billingsleys became major importers, bringing in one liquor shipment from San Francisco worth $250,000. A rivalry with the other big-time bootlegger in Seattle led to hijackings and murders, and finally to indictments. In pleading guilty, brother Logan said that in the course of doing business he had paid protection money to the city's mayor, sheriff, and police chief. After serving a few jail terms, the brothers—not easily discouraged—moved on to Detroit and resumed operations. Sherman was known as "the man with the black hearse" because he used a black truck to move his product. Caught once again, Sherman was sentenced to fifteen months in Leavenworth and a $5,000 fine; Ora got a lesser sentence, and both brothers did the time.

Already famous in three states, the Billingsleys came to New York in the early 1920s. Logan built apartment houses in the Bronx, served as president of the Bronx Chamber of Commerce, and constructed an ambitious subdivision in Westchester County. (At his death in 1963, the *New York Times* described him as "a real estate developer and an authority on American Indian affairs.") Sherman resumed bootlegging and again sold booze from a drugstore. In 1929 he opened the first Stork Club, on Fifty-eighth Street. "It was," he liked to say, "the first speakeasy that had a carpet on the floor and a canopy out front." Eddie Condon, one of the musicians who played there, remembered Billingsley's hanging around, "dressed like an Oklahoma horse trader," holding his chin in his right hand, squinting at everything, missing nothing. "You had only to be sober and rich to get into the Stork Club," according to Condon, "and you came out neither." After Prohibition agents applied axes to the bar, tables, glassware, and mirrors, Billingsley opened another Stork Club at Park Avenue and Fifty-first, and then finally settled into a permanent address two blocks away on Fifty-third Street. Working twelve-hour days and never taking a vacation, handing out gifts of champagne and perfume to the guests he liked, courting the gossip columnists and celebrities whose presence could help him, Billingsley made his joint the most famous nightclub in America. Neither he nor his friends much discussed his adventures before arriving in New York.

These clubs along and around Broadway were the best known, the only such places with national reputations, but any city with bootleggers and gangsters had its counterparts: Dan Carroll's Lambs Club and Charlie Solomon's Cocoanut Grove in Boston, Longy Zwillman's Blue Mirror and Casablanca clubs in Newark, and Tommy McGinty's Mounds Club in Cleveland, a fortress surrounded by a high iron gate, with old-rich chandeliers and leather furniture inside. Boo-Boo Hoff's Piccadilly Cafe in Philadelphia was managed by a former federal Prohibition administrator for the city. Only wealthy people and gangsters could afford the prices at these swanky establishments, blue-blooded cheeks nuzzling up against blue-tinted jowls. Mezz Mezzrow remembered playing in a hot band at Luigi's Cafe, an opulent club run by the Purple Gang in Detroit. "It struck me funny how the top and bottom crusts of society were always getting together during the Prohibition era," Mezzrow recalled. "That Purple Gang was a hard lot of guys, so tough they made Capone's playmates look like a kindergarten class, and Detroit's snooty set used to feel it was really living to talk to them hoodlums without getting their ounce-brains blown out."

In Chicago, Al Capone and an entourage of molls and shooters would appear at one of his clubs after midnight. With the doors locked, his men would have some hundred-dollar bills changed and pass the money around to the waiters and entertainers. "They sat in a corner, very gay and noisy but gunning the whole situation out of the corners of their eyes," a musician remembered. "Al's big round face had a broad grin plastered on it and he was always good-natured, which didn't annoy me at all." The guys in the band would get tips of five or ten dollars for playing Capone's favorite sentimental songs.

The Chicago underworld made its regular nighttime headquarters at Dennis Cooney's Rex Cafe in the First Ward. It opened an hour before midnight, never closing until eight or nine the next morning. In this ecumenical setting cops, politicians, and feuding gangsters drank and danced in brief affability, their guns checked at the door. "Arrests are never made at Cooney's," everyone was assured. Later a party might move on to the South Side, "and the South Side was running wide open in those days, I mean it was running wild," one Chicago gangster reminisced. "By that time, say it was about four o'clock, you get out to those joints to hit the peak of the shows, there was no stalling around in those days, you didn't want to waste no time, you wanted to get on to the next place. So maybe we'd shoot out to some of the northwest suburbs. There was wide-open gambling out there—big bank crap games, roulette, blackjack. We'd wind up staying for breakfast. It was all Outfit stuff. All your celebrities used to go there for gambling. One night I saw a movie star drop thirty-five thousand dollars in an hour and a half."

The entertainers playing the mob clubs fell generally into two categories: white, usually Jewish, singers and comedians; and black jazz musicians. Jimmy Durante, a stray Italian, was partnered with two Jews in the trio of Clayton, Jackson, and Durante. The son of immigrants from Salerno, Durante grew up on the Lower East Side and went to work playing ragtime piano in beer halls. "Maxine's was so tough," he said of one early employer, "that if you took off your hat you was a sissy." Durante then teamed with Lou Clayton and Eddie Jackson in a nightclub act of screwy, nearly indescribable comedy routines. They first surfaced in small clubs, "little more than hoodlum-backed dumps," in New York; at one of them Durante was busted for serving drinks to a cop. When Durante went solo Clayton became his manager, enforcer, and naysayer. "Lou Clayton was the most important person in Jimmy's life," according to Eddie Cantor. "A tough little guy with a sledge-hammer punch." Well acquainted in the underworld, once Clayton won and then lost $100,000 in three nights at one of Arnold Rothstein's floating crap games. At first through Clayton, then by himself, Durante did a lot of business with gangsters—especially Jewish gangsters—for the rest of his life. In 1933 Waxey Gordon invested $150,000 in a Broadway show, *Strike Me Pink*, because Durante was the star. Later on, when Bugsy Siegel opened his Flamingo casino in Las Vegas, Durante headlined the first show ("I always got along swell with Ben"); he paid a $20,000 fine to spring Mickey Cohen from jail; he was appearing at a mob casino in Newport, Kentucky, when it was closed down. "I don't go near the [gambling] tables," Durante explained.

Fanny Brice, up from a grim childhood when she had stolen to eat, was perhaps the most gifted woman comedian of her time, a star of Broadway and nightclubs. The arrant love of her life was a charming con man named Nicky Arnstein. "I never liked chiselers," she said of Arnstein. "I liked thieves if they were thieves, but not angle guys." Always dreaming she could reform him, after one of his arrests she borrowed the $75,000 bail from Arnold Rothstein. Then Rothstein sold her $13,000 worth of furniture for $50,000, collecting the difference of $37,000 as his interest on the loan. "Rothstein never said no when you asked a favor," Brice concluded, "but sooner or later you had to pay for it." Yet this episode was not typical for her. She was a *strong* woman, without fears or illusions. In her work and play she met many gangsters, and they seldom misused her. Once she sent a comedy writer, Billy Rose, to raise production money from a feared thug. When Rose's sketches flopped the thug wanted his money back. "I'm going to tell Fanny you're a welsher," said Rose, and the thug relented. "That's the kind of standing she had with the hoodlums in this town," Rose later observed. "In this town and all over the country."

Rose knew that because he became Brice's second husband and had his own brushes with the underworld. "Broadway during Prohibition was as glamorous as a thumb in the eye," he wrote from a safe distance, "and those of us who were mixed up in it are lucky to still be in one piece." In 1922 he had opened a speakeasy, the Backstage Club, over a Fifty-sixth Street garage. The omnipresent Rothstein, wanting to be cut in, had the cops raid the place twice, then sent his man Max Arronson with an offer: sell 25 percent of the joint in exchange for no more raids. Rose made the deal and Arronson became his liaison to the underworld. "Billy could talk these boys into doing things for him," as Arronson recounted it. "But the tough babies thought Billy was funny, cute, him and his songs and his showgals. He jumped around like a rabbit and he didn't drink. They figured he was an outfront business type who was making time in the rackets. They treated him like he was a connection." Just after the end of Prohibition, the Mafioso Tommy Lucchese and a gangster consortium asked Rose to stage the floor shows at a fancy theater restaurant, the Casino de Paree, on Fifty-fourth Street. Rose hired stars like Jimmy Durante and Benny Goodman, and the place did good business for about six months. But when Rose left town on vacation, the gangsters fired Goodman's band and beat up a union representative trying to organize the performers. Rose then quit the arrangement, losing his $16,000 investment but—he said—cutting his ties to the mob impresarios for good.

The break was probably not that final. The underworld ran on a system of mutual favors, of services given and taken, and gangsters had indelible memories of what was owed them. Yet the system worked both ways: if some notable from the upperworld was mistreated, gangdom might make elaborate amends. Joe E. Lewis, raised in a Jewish neighborhood on the Lower East Side, was singing at a mob cabaret in Chicago in 1928 when he was almost killed by Machine Gun Jack McGurn of the Capone gang. Lewis had wanted to leave McGurn's employ and sing elsewhere; McGurn disagreed and cut him up badly. The episode's real significance lay in what followed. "Why the hell didn't you come to me when you had your trouble?" Capone asked Lewis, giving him $10,000. "I'd have straightened things out." When Lewis was healthy enough to resume performing, Capone offered him $50,000 and partnership in a club. Instead Lewis went back to New York and worked for Dutch Schultz. Eventually he became the mob's favorite courier, peacemaker, and court jester, often seen in the company of underworld figures, often appearing at gangster nightclubs. In nearly being killed, Lewis had ironically earned a lifetime sinecure.

Milton Berle started his show business career as a nightclub entertainer toward the end of Prohibition. His first contacts with the underworld came from the implausible source of his mother, Sarah Berlinger, a fearsome stage mother. "Sometimes," he later acknowledged, "I wondered about Mama's friends and connections through the years"—about whether she had used her pull with mobsters for favors and good bookings, or to fix up problems. "I didn't want to know. I had even once been told that Mama had the clout to arrange for a hit. I refused to believe that, but I didn't want to check it out with Mama." For whatever reason, "I knew a lot of the mobsters around town." Berle played the Casino de Paree in New York after Tommy Lucchese ("sort of naive, a nice quiet gentleman") had taken it over from Billy Rose. Through Lucchese he met many other gangsters. "I never heard an angry word, never saw anything more than a suspicious bulge in a jacket. . . . I was so dumb back then and so sure of myself that I didn't know I was taking chances." Bugsy Siegel gave him a ring with an eight-carat diamond; Berle wore it occasionally but remained discreet about where he had gotten it. From 1938 on, Berle's manager was Lou Jackson, a mob associate from Chicago whom he had met at a boxing gym. "Lou was also mixed up in other things around Chicago, but you didn't ask questions about that." Like Durante and Lewis, Berle took regular turns on the underworld's nightclub circuit.

When black jazz musicians worked in gangster clubs it brought together two outlaw cultures. In peculiar ways they understood each other at a time when blacks and whites had little contact as peers. The gangsters and jazzmen shared an expansive common ground: nocturnal habits, flashy clothes, a code of silence, things to hide, disapproval by the straight world, the company of glamorous, pliant women, and an ethic of immediate pleasures instead of long-term planning. Jazzmen first played for money in whorehouses and gambling joints. "I came up," Willie the Lion Smith said proudly, "with all kinds of sharpies, pimps, pickpockets, snow birds, gamblers, con men, and ladies of the evening." "Back then everybody classified musicians as bums, which they were," Pops Foster recalled. "All the musicians back in New Orleans wanted to be pimps . . . and Jelly Roll Morton was one of them. He only played piano as a sideline because then you had to prove you were doing some kind of work or they'd put you in jail." The main centers of jazz—New Orleans, Chicago, New York, Kansas City—were all big mob towns, with protected sections where after-hours clubs and shady dives offered steady gigs to jazzmen, beyond the reach of moral guardians. Many white mobsters, not known for good taste in any other way, did like jazz. "It's got guts and it don't make you slobber," one of them remarked. Fats Waller played a command-performance birthday party for Al Capone that lasted for three days of champagne and hundred-dollar tips.

Gangsters inevitably ran the two most celebrated black nightclubs, the Grand Terrace in Chicago and the Cotton Club in New York. Capone's gang was behind the Grand Terrace, located at Oakwood Boulevard and South Parkway. After the last show a Capone man would linger at the cash register, checking the receipts for the night. "I knew a lot of the Capone mob that hung around the club and called them by their first names," Earl Hines said later. "Our relations were always cordial and sometimes it paid to know these fellows." Once Hines hired a singer for his band from Augusta, Georgia. The singer's white employer came all the way to Chicago looking for his handyman; when he appeared at the Grand Terrace and demanded the return of his employee, bouncers threw the white man out of the club, and he did not come back.

The Cotton Club in Harlem was nominally managed by Herman Stark, a cigar-chewing operator, for Owney Madden's gang. In 1928 the gang decided it wanted Duke Ellington's band, which had been playing for five years downtown at the Kentucky Club at Forty-ninth and Broadway. "That was one of the few times in my life that I wanted to leave the band," Ellington's drummer, Sonny Greer, recalled. "We were established and we were doing so well, but the pressure went on and we had to go up there." (Nobody turned down Owney Madden in those days.) A few years later Lena Horne, only sixteen years old, joined the chorus line at the Cotton Club. "My very youth protected me," as she recounted it. "I was jail bait and no one ever made a pass at me or suggested I go out with one of the customers, which happened all the time to the older girls."

By the 1930s the hottest jazz scene had shifted to Kansas City, running loud and flat out under the protection of Tom Pendergast and Johnny Lazia. Below them, the gambler Felix Payne and the jazzman Benny Moten controlled the clubs along Twelfth and Eighteenth streets, dictating who worked where, and with the pull if necessary to get errant musicians out of jail. "For twenty-five blocks, there used to be joints, sometimes three or four doors apart, sometimes every other block," Count Basie recalled. "There was an awful lot of good music, and it was like everything happened there. It was the first place I really heard the blues played and sung as they should be." The most fondly remembered club was the Reno on Twelfth Street between Cherry and Locust, managed by Papa Sol Epstein for the Pendergast machine. It was a long, narrow room with a divider down the middle separating black patrons from white patrons. Out in back loitered two-dollar whores and marijuana sellers looking for deals. On the bandstand, passing joints around, Basie's men played louder and faster as the night wore on, the air getting thicker, time slowing down. "That whole band didn't believe in going out with steady black people," Gene Ramey, a Basie musician, said later. "They'd head straight for the pimps and prostitutes and hang out with them. . . . Basie was down there, lying in the gutter, getting drunk with them. He'd have patches in his pants and everything. All of his band was like that."

For jazzmen as for anyone else, an arrangement with the underworld took on implacable Faustian aspects. With jazz being shunned by good and respectable people, gangsters gave it a place to romp—on a short leash. Ellington made his name at the Cotton Club, but when lucrative outside dates came his way he often had to decline them because his mob bosses would not let him go; when he did play elsewhere, he had to pay Cab Calloway's band to appear for him at the Cotton Club. Louis Armstrong was managed by a string of ruthless white guys with underworld connections. Joe Glaser, his bribing, cheating manager from 1935 on, also fronted for the Capones in boxing and other enterprises. "[Glaser] talked tough, acted rough," according to Armstrong's biographer James Lincoln Collier, "and was perennially threatening to have your 'leg broken' or have you 'taken care of' in some way." Armstrong left all the decisions about bookings, recordings, and investments to Glaser. "Speak to Papa Joe," he would say. Like Jimmy Durante, Armstrong could present his familiar image of simple amiability to the world because he had a thug of a manager to bluster and say no.

Again, though, the underworld depended on reciprocity, with mutual obligations extending in both directions. "In all the years I dealt with them," said Nils Granlund, "I never had a written contract with any of them. And I was never gypped or given a bad deal by a gangster owner." The musicians did as they were told—no arguments, no exceptions—and everyone knew the penalties. Lena Horne's stepfather once tried to extricate her from the Cotton Club; he was beaten up, his head shoved into a toilet bowl, and she stayed. But the entertainers were paid on time, even protected on occasion. "The underworld really ran the cabarets and they had a way of running them better than anyone else," the jazzman Dicky Wells reflected. "The clubs could be a front for other activities, but they had good producers and put on tight shows." "I keep hearing about how bad the gangsters were," Sonny Greer concluded later on. "All I can say is that I wish I was still working for them. Their word was all you needed."

❧ ❧

Al Capone's caddie learns about sex: aside from nightclubs, prizefights, and racetracks, for recreation Capone liked golf and young girls. At the Burnham golf course in 1925 he noticed Babe, the pretty sixteen-year-old big sister of young Tim Sullivan. "He asked me how would I like to be his regular caddie," Tim said years later. "What I didn't realize until I was a little older, he also wanted Babe to be his regular girl." Tim occasionally caddied for Killer Burke, one of Capone's gunmen. "He was usually in the company of a peroxide blonde. She didn't play. She just walked along beside him. One time, after they'd emptied his flask, they disappeared behind a bunker. They were gone about ten minutes and when they came back the blonde's dress had grass stains all over it. I was ten at the time and I couldn't figure out what they'd been up to.

"I learned the facts of life before I was too much older from Al and his boys. One afternoon on the links they kept talking about some kind of party they were going to throw at the clubhouse that night. An orgy, they called it. I'd never heard the word before and I was burning with curiosity. So after supper I went back to the clubhouse. . . . I was wearing tennis shoes that gave me enough traction to climb up to the second story where there was a little balcony and a window. I looked through and saw about twenty couples, most of them naked. Not Al, though. He just stood on the sidelines, watching and laughing. I found out then what an orgy was."

❦ ❦

Two men stand toe to toe and try to knock each other down. It is the most savage and elemental of sports; hence both its durable appeal and the periodic efforts by reformers to ban it. By its nature boxing is an especially corruptible sport. A man may absorb a punch by accident or on purpose, and he may be knocked out or just take a fall, and no outside observer can readily tell the difference. The referee, the third man in the ring, may exercise great independent control over the course of the fight, and unless there is a knockout the judges sitting at ringside will decide the outcome on whatever grounds they find sufficient, with no need to explain and no right of appeal. All these arbiters may be easily coerced by unseen parties. No single external authority has ever governed the sport: no big league, no national commissioner. Each state has its own boxing jurisdiction, subject to its own local political pressures. Even these local bodies may in practice yield to the power gathered around a particular champion, especially the heavyweight champion, and his appointed managers, promoters, and matchmakers. To an exceptional degree among major sports, boxing depends on shifting personal power and loyalties. The underworld, where power is nothing but personal, thrives on such conditions.

The fight game emerged from the backwoods of nineteenth-century America, out West or down South, anywhere groups of men were cut off from polite society and left to themselves for diversion. It lightened the dreary regimens of railroad gangs, lumber camps, mining towns, army posts. The contest itself gave men an excuse to bet, and this gambling aspect made a match's outcome more complicated than a simple matter of athletic superiority. Inevitably bloody, linked to gamblers and sporting men, spurned by respectable classes, fights took place on the fringes of urban America in secret, hurriedly announced rings, in barns and on barges in the middle of rivers between legal jurisdictions. In the late 1800s boxing pushed into urban immigrant districts and so became yet another concern of WASP reformers, tied in with saloons, gambling, and corrupt politics. At the time Irishmen dominated boxing and many of its allied activities as well. Big Tim Sullivan, the political boss of New York's Bowery and Lower East Side, controlled the illegal prizefights in the city. At his prodding the New York State Legislature legalized boxing in 1896, but after scandals and ring deaths the act was repealed four years later. "When money comes in at the gate," said Theodore Roosevelt, himself an avid boxer, "sport flies out at the window." Wellborn reformers typically deplored not the fight itself but the gambling and corruption that came with it.

At the turn of the century only four states formally allowed prizefights. Bouts in three widely scattered cities—Philadelphia, New Orleans, and San Francisco—kept the legal sport alive, aside from the inevitable illegal fights that laws could not reach. Driven underground, boxing became even more corrupt with fixes and phantom knockouts. "The fight game was a racket then," according to Nat Fleischer, the Boswell of boxing, "and truly could be referred to as the sport of rogues." The black heavyweight champion Jack Johnson irritated the situation by declining to conform to white America's notions of proper conduct. His easy thrashing of the white hope Jim Jeffries in 1910 led to racial friction and death knells for the sport. "It will probably be the last big fight in this country," former champ John L. Sullivan predicted. A few years later, at his trial on a Mann Act violation, Johnson crisply summed up the ethical level at which prizefights were being conducted. "They are all crooked," he said.

Jack Dempsey, a roughneck of dubious background, became the sport's unlikely savior. He fought his way east from mining camps and saloon brawls in Colorado and Utah. In 1916 he came to New York, where boxing was legal again, and acquired as manager John the Barber Reisler, a Broadway gambler and con man. "Many said he would have sold his mother's blood for money if the price was right," Dempsey recalled. "I had never come up against such a vicious person before"—quite a statement given the company Dempsey had kept. He soon quit John the Barber and went back West, where he took on another shifty manager, Jack Kearns. No more an innocent than the Barber, Kearns had served time for a morals conviction in Washington State and had been arrested for vagrancy and procuring in Vancouver. But Kearns did know boxing, and he efficiently maneuvered Dempsey into a bout with Jess Willard for the heavyweight title in 1919. Despite opposition in the Ohio legislature and from a group of Protestant ministers, the fight was held in Toledo, an open city known then as a haven for gangsters on the lam. Dempsey won easily; years later Kearns claimed that his man's gloves had been loaded with plaster of paris.

As Prohibition began, then, boxing already had a long, shadowy association with the underworld. Bootleggers did not have to force their way into the sport: it was an obvious, inevitable connection. "They were nice people," said Johnny Wilson, middleweight champ from 1920 to 1923, of his gangster managers. "It's like anything else. That was their business, what they had to do, just like you." Tommy McGinty in Cleveland, Boo-Boo Hoff and Nig Rosen in Philadelphia, Dan Carroll and Phil Buccola in Boston, the Capones in Chicago, and Owney Madden, Lucky Luciano, and Dutch Schultz in New York were all involved as managers, owners, or fight promoters. They owned fighters for the same reasons they owned nightclubs—not to make money, usually, but for the celebrity and precarious respectability of it. "The bootleggers did it not because of money," said Tommy Loughran, light heavyweight champion in the late 1920s. "They wanted to have a prize possession like a fellow wants a race horse or another fellow a baseball team. He wanted to have prime ownership of something. . . . Money meant nothing to them because they were making so much money from the liquor side of the thing." Mickey Cohen started his underworld career as a boxer during Prohibition, and he was always known for his boxing interests and fistic dexterity. "I got completely involved in the boxing world," he remembered of his youth, "and it and the racket world were almost one and the same. Most boxers were owned by racket people. And at one time, six of the boxing titles belonged to guys in the so-called racket world."

As unpopular champion, Dempsey did not fight for three years—from 1923 to 1926—because he was ducking a black challenger, Harry Wills, who outweighed him by thirty pounds. Eventually he agreed to a title bout with Gene Tunney, a white contender his own weight. Tunney was managed by Billy Gibson, a worldly veteran of the New York fight scene who also handled the lightweight champ Benny Leonard. Back when boxing was illegal in New York, Gibson had still run weekly bouts through his Fairmont Athletic Club, a rival of Big Tim Sullivan's National Athletic Club. Every week the cops would raid Gibson's fights at the Fairmont; Gibson would pay the fines and then hold more fights the next week. "It got so that I could run a monthly bill," he recalled, "send my check regularly at the first of the month for all four fines."

Now Gibson could avoid the cops and fines but not the gangsters. The New York Athletic Commission would not sanction the Dempsey-Tunney match because Dempsey had been avoiding Harry Wills. So the fight was held in Philadelphia, evidently with the cooperation of Boo-Boo Hoff. On the day of the bout, just a few hours before the bell, Gibson brought Hoff and his attorney to see Tunney. Gibson explained that he needed Tunney's signature on an agreement with Hoff. "I made a hurried inspection," as Tunney recounted it, "and, being assured it was as Billy claimed, witnessed it to get rid of them." Later Hoff sued Tunney and Gibson for $500,000, claiming they had accepted $20,000 from him in exchange for 20 percent of Tunney's share of the purse. (The suit inched along for more than three years, Gibson went insane from syphilis, and Hoff finally dropped the matter.)

Tunney won the fight and the title. They held the rematch a year later in Chicago, and this time it was Dempsey who had the local bootlegging king in his corner. Al Capone had been "one of my number one fans," said Dempsey, ever since they had met in 1920. "He was a rough customer who wanted to be accepted as a man, not a racketeer." When Capone visited Dempsey's training camps no cameras were allowed, and cooperative sportswriters neglected to note his presence. As the rematch with Tunney approached, rumors went around Chicago that Capone had bet $50,000 on his boy and was using money and muscle to ensure that Dempsey would win. As Dempsey told the story, he asked Capone to lay off in the interest of sportsmanship, and a day later his wife received a huge gift of flowers with a card saying, "To the Dempseys, in the name of sportsmanship." Still, as the fight was about to start, said Dempsey, "I was more afraid of who sat at ringside than of who was waiting for me inside the ring." He should have been afraid of all of them: Tunney won again—after the famous long count—and Capone lost his bet.

Perhaps Dempsey then believed, or was made to believe, that he owed Capone something. He retired from boxing and started promoting fights with Joe E. Lewis and others in the Capone organization. The arrangement was soon ended. "I quit because I was being used as a front, a promoter in name only," Dempsey later explained. "Capone's mob wound up telling me who was going to fight and how much I had to pay them. When they started giving orders who was going to win and who was going to lose—and naming the round—I got out." But his ties to the underworld were not so easily broken. In 1936 he formed a partnership with Nig Rutkin ("He was always around the fights, a sporting man"), Longy Zwillman, and Meyer Lansky to buy and run a hotel, which they called the Dempsey-Vanderbilt, in Miami Beach. With Dempsey again fronting for gangsters, they operated a gambling casino in the hotel. And Dempsey had other mob involvements later on.

All through the 1920s, while other gangsters flirted with Dempsey and Tunney, Owney Madden supervised his own stable of fighters, including title holders in the bantam and light heavyweight divisions. The biggest man in the biggest town, he still could not claim the heavyweight champion, the real prize in boxing. He got his chance after Tunney retired and vacated the title. From 1930 to 1937, Madden controlled four of the five heavyweight champs; only Max Baer escaped him. Not the manager of record for any of these men, Madden set up his friends and associates to run the operations. He held on to these boxers even after his voluntary exile to Hot Springs, Arkansas. Of his four heavyweight titleholders, the most outrageous fraud was Primo Carnera. A mountainous six feet six inches and 260 pounds, Carnera could neither give nor take a punch, and was so slow afoot he was called the Ambling Alp. Yet in one stretch of four months he knocked out sixteen straight opponents, in fights that everyone in boxing knew must have been fixed. One of his handlers, Good Time Walter Friedman, later conceded that many of these alleged fights were "mischievous." But, said Friedman, making his best case, "every once in a while Carnera could complete a perfect punch." (Not often enough for sixteen straight knockouts, though.)

Madden's men lost their hold on the heavyweight division with the advent of Joe Louis, the first black heavyweight champ since Jack Johnson. His personal habits were not so different from Johnson's, but he was at least discreet and deferential to whites and so was invariably described as "a credit to his race." Louis held the title for a dozen years, longer than anyone before or since. Because of that longevity, the black and white hoodlums behind him also controlled boxing for most of that time. The son of Alabama sharecroppers, raised in poverty in Detroit, he had won some amateur fights as a teenager and thus come to the attention of John Roxborough, a suave force in Detroit's black underworld. Behind the front of a real-estate office Roxborough ran the lucrative numbers gambling in the black neighborhoods of the city; his brother was a prominent lawyer, politician, and leader in the Urban League. For the shy, unsophisticated young Louis, Roxborough beckoned the way into a new and glossy world. "He didn't seem flashy, but stylish and rich-looking," Louis said later. "It was a kind of a charge to me to know a man like him was interested in me." Roxborough took him to a drugstore and told him to pick out all the boxing equipment he wanted. "First time I ever had so many clean bandages, rubbing alcohol, and such." Roxborough gave him pocket money and clothes and brought him home for dinner. "It was a beautiful house, and he had a good looking and gracious wife. I loved it. I never saw black people living this way, and I was envious and watched everything he did."

Early in 1934 Roxborough took his boxer, still an amateur, to Chicago for a Golden Gloves fight. Chicago gangsters with an interest in his opponent decided to intervene. Just before the bout, Chicago police detectives barged into his dressing room, arrested Louis on a concocted charge, took him to the police station, and held him long enough so that he missed his fight. This bizarre episode was actually a tribute to the young fighter's growing reputation. "After that Chicago incident was explained to me, I took on a greater sense of my own importance—I was a threat to other boxers." Now aware of his own possibilities, he started training harder. A few months later Roxborough told him it was time to turn professional.

Roxborough brought him back to Chicago, to Trafton's Gym on Randolph Street, a proving ground for boxers and their underworld owners. Roxborough had a friend in Chicago, Julian Black, a speakeasy owner and—like Roxborough—a big man in numbers gambling. "He was friendly enough to me, but I knew he was basically a tough guy." A few years earlier Black had loaned Roxborough money, and Roxborough was now returning the favor by giving him a piece of Joe Louis. At Trafton's they introduced him to Jack Blackburn, a trainer and former fighter who had served five years in prison for killing a man in a bar. Together these three black men would manage and train Louis for most of his career. To make their way upward in the heavyweight division, though, they had to connect with a powerful white ally.

They found their ally in Mike Jacobs of New York—"a true hustler," according to Louis, "but a damn good man." Louis needed Jacobs, Jacobs needed Louis, and in tandem they replaced Owney Madden's organization as the dominant force in boxing. The son of Polish Jewish immigrants, Jacobs was up from an Irish neighborhood on the Lower West Side. Mike had left school in the sixth grade to start scalping tickets near Madison Square Garden and the Metropolitan Opera. Standing around all day on the sidewalks of New York, cutting deals and watching for cops, he would go home at night with twenty dollars and bloody feet. During the 1920s he pushed his way into boxing by snapping up blocks of seats in advance, and through other services. In some mysterious fashion he helped arrange the Dempsey-Tunney fight in Chicago. "With Uncle Mike, the scratch was always up," one press agent remarked. "And his mouth was always shut." Through his Twentieth Century Sporting Club, Jacobs was feuding with the Madison Square Garden management for control of boxing in the city; a promising heavyweight like Joe Louis represented a potential trump card in this game. Jacobs inevitably dealt with the gangsters involved in boxing. "Mike's relations with the mob were usually cordial," as his biographer, Budd Schulberg, summarized the matter. "A pragmatist with no set code of ethics, Mike would neither encourage nor squeeze out the racketeers."

Joe Louis signed an exclusive contract with Jacobs and the Twentieth Century club in the spring of 1935. Jacobs then set up Louis's first big-time fight in New York, against Primo Carnera, whom Louis flattened in six rounds. With Jacobs making the matches, in less than two years Louis became the obvious contender for the heavyweight title held by Jim Braddock, the last in Owney Madden's string of champions. One day John Roxborough was plucked from a New York sidewalk by some white hoodlums who told him, "We're gonna take a ride." They drove him around the city for a while, explaining nothing, while Roxborough wondered if this would be his last ride. Eventually they stopped at the back of a nightclub and sat him down with Joe Gould, friend of Madden and manager of Braddock. Louis was sure to win the title, Gould explained, so he (and therefore Madden) wanted 50 percent of Roxborough's fighter; if no deal, then no fight with Braddock. Roxborough refused the offer. What about 25 percent? asked Gould. No. Or 20 percent? Still no. "And slow, easy, and cool," as Louis told the story, "Mr. Roxborough walked out of there, headed uptown, and had a double scotch on the rocks." Later Jacobs agreed to give Gould 10 percent of his share of the purse for as long as Louis might hold the title. With that the bout was arranged, between one fighter whom Gould managed and an opponent of whom he indirectly had a piece. Louis knocked out Braddock in eight rounds and claimed the title.

Riding his bond with Louis, Jacobs started to assume control of boxing through a near monopoly of promoting and matchmaking. His power came in layers, from the heavyweight division down, from New York out to the rest of the country. He had money available, more than anyone else in the game, and he readily advanced it to boxers and managers when they were broke, as they often were. Then he collected on his loans in loyalties and exclusive contracts. "He was a funny-looking old man," Sugar Ray Robinson said later, "bald and with false teeth that clacked, but Uncle Mike knew what was going on." During his years on the fringes of New York's underworld he had acquired an abrupt style, and he was often accused of arrogance and ruthlessness. If a conversation in his office took a direction he didn't like, Jacobs would end the discussion by making a phone call; his visitor would be left there, dangling, while Jacobs looked out the window and talked to somebody else. Robinson parted company with a manager because the manager wanted him to fight exclusively for Jacobs. Yet to break the contract Robinson had to borrow $10,000 from Jacobs, and so was bound to him anyway. "Maybe he had a monopoly and all that," one of his defenders allowed, "but he knew how to fill a house. And the more money he made for himself, the more he made for our fighters. . . . He stabilized this business."

The same could be said of most of the gangsters involved in boxing. They were real fight fans who loved the game, knew it at close quarters, and helped sustain it through fallow periods. They of all people were not likely to be offended by the violence in boxing. But they would also fix fights and manipulate the betting odds, and their belief in free, competitive enterprise was limited to their own enterprises. Their generally unmentioned presence hurt the game because they used it as a front and an excuse. When lawmen asked a gangster how he knew another hoodlum, he would explain that he had met the man at a fight. "He was always around the fights, a sporting man." When asked what he was doing in a distant city, a gangster would say that he was just there to see a fight. When asked the source of some mysterious income, he would say that he won it betting on a fighter he liked; just good luck, with no incriminating records to trace the money.

Yet this all had a certain plausibility. In their own world, they did meet each other at fights, they did make trips to see a major bout, and they did bet on their boys. The gangsters in boxing won and lost. The fight game won and lost because of their presence. Either way, it was all done in shadows. Sportswriters knew about the mobsters in boxing, but for various reasons—such as self-protection, libel laws, and a need to maintain sources—they usually kept the secret. For decades the sporting public had no sure idea of what was happening. Jack Dempsey and Gene Tunney were just clean young men in a rough sport, and Joe Louis was, as always, a credit to his race.

❦ ❦

Nicknames: to the upperworld and usually to each other they were known by their special nicknames. The newspapers loved these *noms de guerre* because they made dashing copy and fitted well into headlines. "Legs Diamond" and "Dutch Schultz" sounded more like gangsters' handles than the real names of John T. Nolan and Arthur Flegenheimer. In some embellished cases these nicknames existed mainly in the imaginations of newspaper reporters. After Vincent the Mick Coll accidentally killed a bystanding child he became Mad Dog Coll in the papers, and so he remained. Tommy Lucchese, missing a finger on one hand, was called Three-Finger Brown after a baseball pitcher who also lacked a digit. "The newspapers referred to me by that name,"

Lucchese insisted, "and I don't know anyone else that ever called me that." But Tommy Brown was actually one of his workaday criminal aliases.

In many instances the nicknames came from somewhere in their earlier lives and lasted into adulthood for nostalgic or descriptive reasons. Boo-Boo Hoff and Lepke Buchalter got their names as kids in the neighborhood, and the handles stuck as their boyhood pals stayed around to join their grownup gangs. Chick 99 Callace grew up on Ninety-ninth Street in New York. Longy Zwillman, always tall for his age, was called Der Langer—"the Tall One"—as an adolescent, and the name persisted, maybe because he preferred it to Abner. Paul Ricca, later a big man in the Capone gang, was called the Waiter because of an early restaurant job, and he disliked being reminded of this humble beginning. "I never worked as a waiter," he said between clenched teeth. "If you want to let it go for waiter, that is all right. I was manager at that time." As young boxers Vincenzo Demora, Girolamo Santuccio, Joseph Aiuppa, and Louis Fratto took the ring names of Jack McGurn, Bobby Doyle, Joey O'Brien, and Lew Farrell, and when they graduated from boxing to gangstering they kept the names.

As in the cases of these boxers, the sobriquets were often ethnic disguises. Jewish hoods might take Italian or Irish names, and Italian mobsters might take Irish or WASP names. No non-Jew ever assumed a Jewish name, though. "A lot of Jews in those days took Italian names," according to Mickey Cohen, "not really because of being in the underworld, but to get away from the stigma of being Jewish." Francesco Castiglia hit on the happy compromise of Frank Costello, an Irish name that at least sounded Italian. Tommy and Johnny Dioguardi cut their names down to Tommy and Johnny Dio. Paul (not the Waiter) Ricca's real name was Felice DeLucia. He changed it "just to make more easy to pronounce," he told a doubting congressional investigation. "Short name, that's all."

The mob nicknames most typically described certain physical or personal characteristics. The variety in these categories has been wonderful to behold. Physically descriptive: Big Bill Dwyer, Little Davy Betillo, Joe Adonis, Murray the Camel Humphreys, Tommy the Bull Pennochio, Nig Rosen ("I was dark and they called me Nig"), Black Bill Tocco, Black Tony Parmagini, Scarface Al Capone, Scarface Joe Bommarito, Cockeye Dunn, Jimmy Blue

Eyes Alo, Blinky Palermo, Vincent the Chin Gigante, Fat Tony Salerno, Skinny D'Amato, Pretty Amberg, Pretty Levine (in irony), Needle Nose Gioe, Big Nose LaGaipa. Personally descriptive: Charlie Lucky Luciano, Tough Tony Anastasia, Bugsy Siegel, Bugs Moran, Charlie the Bug Workman, Crazy Joey Gallo, Carmine the Cigar Galante, Greasy Thumb Guzik, Sleepy Barcelona, Cokie Dom Alongi, Waxey Gordon, Dodo Walsh, Dandy Phil Kastel, Loud Mouth Levin, Happy Maione, Yiddie Bloom, Shoes Caruso. Anthony, Benjamin, and Theodore DeMartino of the Luciano family apparently did not impress their colleagues; they were known as Tony the Bum, Benny the Bum, and Teddy the Bum.

More seriously, the nicknames might convey a man's underworld status or specialty. Nobody could mistake Joe the Boss Masseria's importance, or Killer Burke's trade, or Michael the Enforcer Rubino's job. Charlie Solomon was known as King Solomon in Boston, as Boston Charlie elsewhere. Abe Kid Twist Reles had a knack for strangling people. Trigger Mike Coppola was handy with a gun, as was Charlie the Blade Tourine with a knife. Sam Golf Bag Hunt liked to replace his golf clubs with a submachine gun. Owney the Killer Madden never lived down the name he assuredly earned as a young man running with the Gopher gang on the West Side.

Within any group of men turned tightly in on itself—within a college fraternity, athletic team, or combat regiment as well as a criminal gang—the men naturally give each other nicknames as symbols of camaraderie, trust, and exclusivity. For gangsters the names had special purposes as well, such as discreetly veiling a reference to a mob confederate. The underworld nicknames had their uses for the upperworld too. Outsiders liked to laugh at gangsters: from nervousness, and because they were sometimes buffoonishly amusing, and to avoid examining the situation more closely. These funny, colorful names encouraged the comforting fiction that gangsters were just Damon Runyon characters, affable louts too stupid to be really dangerous.

❦ ❦

The problem with moral reform movements was that they often made the situation worse. With their own emotions and pleasures carefully reined in, the moral reformers could not abide such frailties in other people—especially people of a different class, religion, and ethnicity. Believing in such abstract principles as ethical conduct and obedience to law, the reformers imagined they could excise any offending conduct by rendering it illegal. So they imposed Prohibition, which made bootleggers rich and established organized crime on a national level. They outlawed boxing and thus left it even more to the tender attentions of rogues. When legal booze and legal boxing came back, the gangsters in charge did not let go. The moralists might then deplore the underworld presence in these enterprises, but in so doing they had to flinch from conceding their own part in exacerbating the problem.

This ironic pattern was repeated when moral reformers decided to improve horse racing. The reformers came mostly from the sober middle class, menaced on one side by the sporting gentry— the Belmonts, Vanderbilts, Wideners, Whitneys—who generally owned the horses and tracks, and threatened on the other side by the raffish demimonde that trained and rode the horses and handled the bets. The horsey gentry gave racing its genteel aura as "the sport of kings," but by the 1890s the real power had already passed down to the ruffians in the stables and paddocks. One observer of New York's racetracks in 1893 found the sport governed on these two levels, by "amiable old gentlemen" who were losing touch and by urban political bosses from Brooklyn, New Jersey, and New York City: "This element has a very dense idea of turf morality, if it has any idea of morality at all, and insists on managing racing matters after the style most in favor with political machines." Gamblers and bookmakers were taking over, even starting to own horses and tracks. Horses were being painted and raced under false names, with electric prods slipped beneath their saddles. Sportswriters on turf beats were accepting payoffs and therefore speaking no evil.

Under such provocations, racetracks and betting were gradually outlawed by state legislatures as part of the Progressive impulse to cleanse public life. "Racing lowers the breed of men," said one reformer. "The chief loss is far more serious than the monetary one—the loss of character of men." New York tried a halfway measure: races and gentlemen's wagers among "friends" were allowed, but professional bookies were banned from the tracks. So the bookies stood just outside the tracks and plied their trade as before. "At the New York race tracks," someone noted in 1916, "there are about one hundred men who have large circles of friends." Across the country, though, almost one hundred tracks were shut down in fifteen years of moral reform. By 1920 only a half-dozen states, mostly in the South, still allowed racing.

Along with booze and boxing, the races went underground and became another favored habitat for bootleggers. "I run tracks when it wasn't legal," Tommy McGinty of Cleveland said later, without apology. Outside Kansas City the omnipotent Tom Pendergast's Riverside Park Jockey Club started running horses at a former dog track in 1928. Generally known as "Pendergast's Track," the operation was fronted by the boss's minions. Al Capone loved to bet on horses; once he won $750,000 in four days, then lost it and went $250,000 in the hole after three more days of betting, which at least suggested the races were not fixed. The Sportsman's Park track in Cicero was run for Capone by Edward J. O'Hare, an adroit lawyer whose deft touch brought him the nickname of Artful Eddie. A polite sophisticate of temperate habits, a rare orchid among the Capones, devoted to his only son, O'Hare imagined he could keep the rest of his life separate from his mob associates. But he could not. Later he managed dog tracks in Missouri, Florida, and Massachusetts for the Capones.

Legal racing came back after 1930 as moral fervor yielded to economic necessity in the Depression. A state could neither supervise nor tax outlaw tracks. But state-sanctioned racing might raise tax revenues, provide employment, and attract tourists. Accordingly Florida in 1931 legalized pari-mutuel betting, a system that in theory avoided the corruptions of individual bookies by letting the track management handle the bets, with odds adjusted to the cumulative drift of the wagering, and with a state tax on the proceeds. Formerly permitted only in Kentucky and Maryland, by 1934 pari-mutuel systems were clicking away in seventeen states. The gangsters who had been running underground tracks could now emerge into the light, blinking. A group of Canadian bootleggers organized by Big Bill Dwyer bought a dog track near Coral Gables, Florida, and converted it to the Tropical Park horse track, with Dwyer as the manager. Known as the Racket Track, in 1934 it was in turn acquired by a group that included Johnny Patton of the Capones, Meyer Lansky, and Frank Erickson, a bookie associated with Frank Costello. Dwyer, once a bottlegging partner of Costello's, stayed on as manager, steadily pushing the start of Tropical Park's season further back into the fall so it dovetailed with the end of racing for the year in New York and New England. Covering the calendar, Dwyer also ran the Rockingham Park track in New Hampshire with Edward Gallagher, a former Coast Guard commander whom he knew from his rumrunning days.

So it went, sometimes openly, sometimes behind fronts. In Massachusetts, Joe Linsey and other old bootleggers ran Suffolk Downs behind the respectable facade of John Macomber, a horsey gentleman who raised Thoroughbreds on his Raceland estate in Framingham and who wrote his horses and dogs into his will. Another group of Massachusetts bootleggers—Hyman Abrams, Lou Fox, and others—owned the Wonderland dog track in Revere. Joe Reinfeld had the Tanforan track in California. Longy Zwillman invested in tracks in New Jersey, Kentucky, and California. The Cleveland bootleggers ran tracks here and there. Joe Kennedy bought a piece of the Hialeah track in Florida. From his own box at the finish line, fitted with comfortable armchairs, Kennedy would amuse himself by making small bets of two or five dollars. "He was positive he could not beat the horses," a racetrack companion said later.

Gangsters by their natures would not play a game straight. Believing, or needing to believe, that the whole world was corrupt, they always sought an edge for themselves. The revival of horse racing attracted gangsters and, therefore, inevitable reports of horse doping. In 1934 federal agents working under-cover at tracks found over three hundred cases of horses injected with heroin, cocaine, and other drugs to make them run faster. Sometimes the drugged horses would heedlessly run themselves to death. "We found brutality, corruption and shame," said Harry Anslinger, head of the narcotics bureau. "No important stable was wholly exempt. Not a single great name in racing was excluded. Every track visited was involved in this slimy business." Newly imposed saliva tests somewhat controlled this abuse, but that still left many ways to fix a race. Jockeys could be bribed, ringers inserted in races at the last moment, horses overworked in training or loaded with water. Joe Fusco of the Capones was once asked how he managed to win, as he claimed, a steady $30,000 every year by betting on horses. "I don't know," said Fusco. "I follow a horse. I just took a crazy stab Saturday and bet one jockey. The jockey won four straight races." Remarkable.

Regardless of such abuses, racing and betting were back to stay. "Gambling is not a sport," scolded the *Christian Century*, a voice of mainstream Protestantism, in 1936. "It may be a business, a disease, a dissipation, or a form of insanity, but certainly it is not a sport." To which racing proponents could reasonably reply: We tried it your way, and see what happened. By 1939 some eighty tracks were running, in almost half the states of the union. Yet despite their impregnable innocence and busybodyism, the reformers did grasp the nub of the problem. Racetracks would not have prospered or even existed without the betting, and the presence of gamblers did corrupt the sport. The main point of fixing a race, after all, was to win a bet—or to make somebody else lose a bet. The moralists were right; the sport of kings was really a pretext for gambling.

On this cynical point was founded the vast horse-betting empire of Moses L. Annenberg. More than any other single force, Annenberg's tangled enterprises held together the sport and scam of betting on horses. Dozens of federal tax agents spent three years plodding through purposely muddled records before they managed a partial understanding of what Annenberg was doing. Essentially he was a publisher dealing in a particular kind of information. Bettors and bookies across the country required mounds of daily reports on the races that day. Annenberg provided this stuff through his *Daily Racing Form* (twenty-eight to forty pages long, published six days a week in seven editions in seven cities), his *Daily Racing Record* (six days a week in twelve editions), and his *New York Morning Telegraph* (daily) with its abridged version, the *Racing Guide* (also daily). These specialized publications offered a betting man more racing charts, tips, workout reports, handicappers' selections, odds, past records, track conditions, weights, and riders than any gambler could reasonably absorb, or reasonably skip.

None of these Annenberg sheets ever mentioned his other racing medium, the Nationwide News Service. Three of every four dollars bet on horses were handled not by the relegalized tracks but by illegal bookies operating from poolrooms, bars, horse parlors, and cigar stores. Bookies needed race results as they happened, quickly, in a form hard to trace. The Nationwide

News Service printed not one word. Its "news" came from binocculared observers at twenty-nine different tracks, calling races as horses left the gate, at various poles, and at the finish. These reports went by telephone and telegraph, instantly and invisibly, to 15,000 bookies in 223 cities and 39 states. Known in the underworld as The Trust, the phone company's fifth-largest customer, spread through fourteen corporations and thirty-six branches, Nationwide enjoyed a plush monopoly. It therefore charged customers whatever it chose, a total of at least $50 million a year.

His racing sheets and wire service made Moe Annenberg the most powerful non-Italian in organized crime. An unfortunate habit of grossly underreporting his income eventually put him in jail; but at his peak he was netting at least $6 million a year, the biggest individual income of any American. Looking around, he could see no eminence comparable to himself—except perhaps the British Empire. "Our position is similar to that of the English nation," he confided to one of his numerous sons-in-law. "We in the racing field own three-quarters of the globe and manage the balance. In other words, the few little nations that are left have to pay us tribute to continue. Now why isn't that the most beautiful and most satisfactory position to be in which ought to satisfy even me."

Along with many other gangsters, Annenberg owed his success in part to the flailings of moral reformers. At the turn of the century, the Western Union telegraph company had provided its own racing wire service; company employees collected results at tracks and sped them to any customer who rented a telegraph ticker. The immediacy of this service was important. The odds on a race changed right up to post time. Once the horses were off, the racing wire let a man in a distant poolroom or horse parlor call out the race in process, building a line of tension in the room, catching up the bettors and further loosening their wallets. The race over, a winner could at once put his new cash on the next race, while a loser might feel obliged to recoup his investment by digging deeper. A racing wire thus gave bookies an advantage that even daily racing publications could not match.

In 1905 reformers pushed Western Union out of its wire service business. Helen M. Gould, a prominent philanthropist and the eldest daughter of Jay Gould, led this effort. Her father had controlled Western Union, and she was a major stockholder; two other Goulds sat on the board of directors. Added pressure came from another group of patrician reformers at the City Club of New York. Badgered from within and without, embarrassed by the publicity, Western Union gave up its $2-million-a-year servicing of bookies. Then the irony: gangsters moved in and duplicated the service, but more roughly and with a tighter monopoly. Western Union at least had no interest in dominating bookmaking, but the mobsters who took over did. The wire service was so essential that it could be used to whip renegade bookies toward profitable cooperation. Western Union wires still might carry racing information, but the underworld collected it, received it, and gathered most of the profits. Reformers had once again outlawed something into the hands of gangsters.

After some preliminary squabbling, Mont Tennes and his General News Bureau emerged in control of the underworld wire service. Before that Tennes had been the gambling king of Chicago's North Side, the owner of saloons and racehorses. A city gambling war in 1907 with James O'Leary, his South Side rival, was punctuated by bombings and arson fires. Afterward Tennes was left supreme in Chicago, and from that base he got command of the national racing wire, with lines by 1911 into two dozen cities. A power in local politics, he could make and break police chiefs. Certain Chicago detectives were allowed to place bets in his rooms without putting up any money; if they won they collected, and if they lost they did not have to pay. Protected by his favored cops and politicians, Tennes acted like a good, very rich citizen, with an annual income estimated at a million dollars. "Why, I haven't been in the gambling game for years," he said in 1914. "I'm not a handbook maker. I'm a newspaper man." He bought a home in the fancy Edgewater district and was represented in court by Clarence Darrow.

Meanwhile Moe Annenberg was building his own career on a course headed toward the General News Bureau. Though not involved in horse racing until his forties, by then he was well experienced at both newspaper publishing and gangster methods. He was a German Jewish immigrant, born in a village in East Prussia near the Russian border. Brought to Chicago as a boy in 1885, he grew up on the South Side, in a second-floor apartment over a junk shop. His father was a peddler and grocer. Moe and his brother, Max, went to work selling newspapers and were caught up in the vicious circulation struggles among Chicago's dailies, pitting Hearst's *American* and *Examiner* against the conservative *Tribune*. All the contending parties hired gangs of sluggers and ex-boxers who used guns and blackjacks to persuade newsstands to feature one paper and slight a rival. Delivery trucks were waylaid, bundles of papers destroyed, and people killed. For young Moe, it amounted to an uncommonly brutal education in American business methods—an education he never escaped.

"I was a hungry wolf," he said later. "I had a large family. I had to hunt or starve. I learned how to hunt. And I kept it up." Hearst made Moe the circulation manager for the *Examiner* while brother Max took a similar job at the rival *Tribune*. The brothers quarreled, never to reconcile, and Chicago became too small for both of them. In 1907 Moe shifted to Milwaukee, where he handled circulation for several Hearst properties and bought up newspapers of his own. Hearst, recognizing a kindred personality, brought him to New York in 1920 to be circulation boss of the entire Hearst chain.

Annenberg was a tall, rangy man with a long-jawed, appropriately horsey face, his features "a mixture of jovial brutality and rapid perception." Some residue of the junk shop never left him: he affected an alpaca coat, like a pawnbroker's, and he spoke in South Side street patois. "I think you got somethin' on the ball," he would tell an employee who pleased him. In manner he was nervous, imperious, and abrupt. One day in the fall of 1921, he blew into the circulation office of the *San Francisco Call*, a Hearst paper fallen on hard times, and started giving orders. "Up to this time I had never heard of Mr. Annenberg, had never seen him, had never had any message from him of any kind or character," the astonished publisher of the *Call*, John Francis Neylan, reported to the Hearst office in New York. "To say that his attitude was offensive would be to put it mildly." Neylan reproached Annenberg for not paying his respects before issuing commands. "He then sneeringly apologized." Annenberg took some papers from an envelope and seemed about to discuss circulation rates, but then he changed his mind, stood up, and walked out. "He conducted himself," Neylan concluded, "in about as offensive, insulting, discourteous and nasty a manner as any person with whom I have come in contact in a good many years."

Annenberg obviously needed to run his own show. In 1922 he bought his first racing sheet, the *Daily Racing Form*, with two other

Hearst men. It did so well that Annenberg quit working for Hearst in 1926, bought into the *Form*'s main competition, the *Morning Telegraph,* and charged ahead, steadily buying out his partners and adding more bookie rags. "His world became more dangerous," according to his biographer, John Cooney, "and even death threats had to be taken seriously." Mont Tennes, under pressure in Chicago, sold half of the General News Bureau to Annenberg, then the other half to Jack Lynch, a Chicago gambler and saloon owner. For a few years Annenberg and Lynch ran the General News Bureau together in jittery tandem. Annenberg wanted all of it; Lynch resisted. So Annenberg started another bookie wire, the Nationwide News Service, to compete with himself. In two years of this odd arrangement, Nationwide took over nearly the whole wire service market. Lynch then accepted a settlement of $750,000, and Annenberg had the field all to himself.

By the late 1930s Annenberg could survey a wondrous domain: an intricate machinery for making money, all its parts gleaming and ticking. He lived in baronial homes in four states and fancy hotel suites in New York and Philadelphia. Aside from his own considerable family, he kept a mistress on the *Daily Racing Form*'s payroll as a clocker, at an annual salary of $16,300. He invested in hotels, office buildings, garages, movie theaters, an insurance company, a brokerage firm, liquor stores, bowling alleys, and a laundry. As a publisher he also owned pulp magazines and one very respectable newspaper, the *Philadelphia Inquirer,* the dignified organ of Main Line Philadelphia. Yet it was all built on horses and bettors, and illegal bookies.

One reporter investigating the Annenberg empire, following his leads to the source, made his way to a bookie joint near city hall in Chicago. It was a large room, crowded with over three hundred people. Clerks were kept busy chalking up racing entries, data, and results on the expansive blackboards covering the walls. Other clerks behind windows took bets and issued tickets. Every few minutes a voice over the loudspeaker called a race, from a half-dozen tracks around the country. "That was repeated forty or more times that afternoon," the reporter noted, "so the bettor got the benefit of risking his money and also a first-class bath of excitement. It was enormously more rousing and exciting than going to the track."

Like any major underworld figure, Annenberg was insulated from the real dirty work by layers of subordinates. But James M. Ragen, the man he picked to run his wire service, suggested a certain tone. The son of Irish immigrants, the product of a tough street gang, a veteran of Chicago's circulation wars, Ragen had shot and killed a man in 1906. Annenberg first made him circulation manager of a Hearst paper in Chicago, then promoted him to the wire service. Under Ragen the wire did business with Longy Zwillman, Meyer Lansky, and other big gangsters. Violent methods were reported in New York, Chicago, Philadelphia, and Houston. A wire service bookkeeper in Chicago was murdered after a dispute over missing money with Annenberg; "He is no better than Capone," said the widow. On the day Jack Lynch gave up the General News Bureau, Ragen delivered a mysterious $100,000 payoff to Frank Nitti of the Capones. Annenberg reputedly paid the Capones a million dollars a year for protection and enforcement services.

Annenberg was "a murderer and a thief," his tax attorneys were told by the Chicago district attorney. "I'll give you the names of three people he had killed in the city of Chicago in the last five years," said the DA. "He ought to be hung."

❧ ❧

During the twenty years from 1920 to 1940, organized crime penetrated American life in surprising and undetected corners. On some levels gangsters then had more power than ever before or since. The general public at the time was remarkably naïve, even willfully ignorant, of the situation. The upperworld met the underworld firsthand, if unknowingly, at nightclubs, prizefights, and racetracks. As popular as these amusements were, though, most Americans went to them infrequently, if at all. So most people, most of the time, had to glean impressions of the underworld secondhand from the mass media. In prebroadcasting days, that meant the print media of newspapers and magazines. There lay a key to understanding the public's underestimation of organized crime. Crucial editors, publishers, and writers were themselves involved with—identified with—the underworld.

Herbert Bayard Swope was, especially in his own mind, the most famous newspaper editor of the day. At the *New York World* he supervised a glittery staff that included Walter Lippmann, Heywood Broun, E. B. White, George S. Kaufman, Ring Lardner, Allan Nevins, Marc Connelly, and others of comparable gifts. Swope was not cowed by such headstrong personalities because of his serene bedrock conviction that he knew more facts, and more people, then anyone else in the universe. According to a running joke at the *World,* he would send a reporter to interview some big name and inevitably add, "Give him my regards." "If you wanted to meet God," David Sarnoff remarked, "he'd arrange it somehow." A tall, bustling man with a loud voice, Swope expected everyone, even his wife and children, to stand when he entered a room. He did not converse so much as hand down magisterial opinions. "If you started to give this guy an argument," someone noted, "he'd give you a push and say, 'Oh, go away.'" Larger than any job he held, even the executive editorship of the *World,* Swope was a primal force, unavoidable and unstoppable, with an influence cutting across social and political stratifications.

He came from a middle-class German Jewish family in St. Louis. As a small boy, only eight years old, he discovered horse racing at the St. Louis Fair Grounds; horses ran through the rest of his life, a beckoning line that pulled him toward dangerous waters. Already a rake and gambler in adolescence, he skipped college and went right into newspapering. He arrived in New York at age nineteen to write for the *Herald.* After the paper was put to bed, around three o'clock in the morning, Swope would move on to gamble and gambol in the tenderloin district. "It seemed one could always do pretty well at gambling," he remembered of those days. "If you won, you had lots of money, and if you lost, why, the problem was simple; all you had to do was go out and borrow some money and start over again." In 1917 his articles on Germany won the first Pulitzer Prize for reporting, and three years later he got the top job at the *World.*

What he brought to the position was contacts, in a stupefying profusion and variety. A consistent front-runner, he was closest to people when they were most prominent and useful to him. Thus when Joe Kennedy dabbled in high-level Democratic politics, he also became—for a while—Swope's best friend. They had a joint stock-market account and would talk on the phone every morning, sometimes for an hour. After Kennedy was appointed to the SEC, Swope lobbied newspapermen to treat him kindly, to "give him a good start in his new job." Young John F. Kennedy, applying to Harvard, listed Swope as one of three references, along with two other associates of his father's. Later on Swope and Joe Kennedy drifted apart as the war approached and Kennedy fell into public disfavor. For Swope it was a typical episode. "My whole capital," he reflected, "is my knowledge of things and my acquaintance with people."

Swope's complicated friendship with Arnold Rothstein must be understood in this context. Regardless of any other changes in his life, Swope never stopped betting on horses or playing high-stakes poker. In the early years of his marriage he would occasionally pawn his wife's engagement ring to get staked again. "I liked Herbert as a gambling fellow," Pearl Swope said later. "It was exciting not to know whether we had ten cents or a million dollars." Among high rollers on both coasts, Swope was known as someone who could arrange stratospheric wagers and games. Harpo Marx remembered a poker game on a private railroad car from New York to Florida that involved Swope, Harry Sinclair, Florenz Ziegfeld, and others. "Those guys' stakes made me feel I was a kid back on 93rd Street, hustling for pennies," said Marx. "Before I got dizzy from counting, I saw a million dollars change hands."

Such pastimes naturally put Swope in contact with Rothstein, the gambling boss of New York. For his part, Rothstein craved the implicit cachet of hanging out with famous people from the upperworld. When Rothstein got married, Swope was the best man. When Rothstein bought his own racing stable, Swope named the first six yearlings. "The feature about him that most impressed me," Rothstein's wife said of Swope, "was that he succeeded in making you think that you of all the persons in the world were the one he most wished to be with at that particular moment. He had an astonishing gift for making valuable friendships, and of having his own way with his friends." And when Swope owed Rothstein money, as he frequently did, the gangster was lenient about being paid.

Swope was of course entitled to his own private habits and friendships. His gambling and ties to Rothstein gained public significance because they affected how the *World* covered the news. "While he is a sporting man, he comes of a decent, respectable Jewish family," Swope defended Rothstein on one occasion, "and I am inclined to think that once his word is given he will offer no further cause for complaint." Again: "I have no paean of praise to sing for him but, on the other hand, I can see that injustices have been done in having every crime on the calendar charged to his account." These were private expressions, but Swope's friendship took more public, direct forms too. After Rothstein won $5,000 shooting pool at John McGraw's poolroom, Swope blared the news in the *World*. After Rothstein was accused of complicity in some gunplay, Swope helped quash the case. When the New York Athletic Commission would not allow the first Dempsey-Tunney fight in New York—a potential windfall for Rothstein—Swope warned a balking commissioner that the *World* would "get after" him. More generally, Swope would slant his paper toward an underworld viewpoint. He posted a notice in the *World*'s city room: "Members of the staff are doubly cautioned not to take the oftentimes irresponsible utterances of the police as final or authoritative."

A similar bias was visible among the employees of and publications belonging to William Randolph Hearst. The Hearst empire embraced two dozen newspapers, eight magazines (*Cosmopolitan, Harper's Bazaar, Good Housekeeping*), a news service, and widely syndicated columnists. The Hearst newspapers alone had a combined circulation twice that of the nearest competition, the Scripps-Howard chain. Well into his sixties and seventies, Hearst remained an attentive, nudging boss, and all his people reflected in some measure the old man's barnacled cynicism. He was a buccaneer among newspaper publishers: intent only on money and power, indifferent as to means and ethics, utterly flexible as to political principles. After a clamorous lifetime of talking one way and acting another, he probably no longer sensed his own contradictions. He prated about competition and free enterprise, and wanted nothing more than a monopoly in his field. He sang hymns to true democracy and was himself a political boss. (It was quite in character that someone like Joe Kennedy would deliver Hearst's California delegation at the 1932 Democratic convention.) Hearst's editorialists dilated on hearth and motherhood even while the old man lived openly with Marion Davies.

This inveterate hypocrisy extended to Hearst's treatment of organized crime. On occasion the Hearst papers mustered crusades, long on rhetoric and short on commitment, against the underworld. Meantime, day in and day out, Hearst and his people had close if unrecorded ties to gangsters. "The master," Mickey Cohen called Hearst, "who I looked upon with awe and great admiration. He was a benefactor for me throughout my career and when I needed him. There was nothing the Hearst people could call on me for that I would refuse or not attempt to do." Amster Spiro, city editor of the *New York Journal,* and Nate Gross, a columnist for the *Chicago American,* both maintained durable friendships with hoodlums. Hearst's papers would deplore fixed horse races on the editorial pages even while the sports pages promoted them. Working in this racy atmosphere, many Hearst employees not surprisingly liked to play the ponies. This particular enthusiasm reached a point that tried even Hearst's toleration. In 1935 he sent a memo to his publishers: "Many of our employees are spending entirely too much time perusing race-track form charts, making bets and watching results of races during business hours. I have also noticed that a number of employees leave the building during business hours to go to adjacent bookmaker establishments. . . . I do not wish to do anything drastic in this matter, but if the condition is not materially improved, it will be necessary to take decided steps." The problem ran too deep to be excised. One Hearst editor, Emile Gauvreau of the *New York Daily Mirror,* later commented that "if the 'decided steps' had been taken on Hearst's papers in New York alone, perhaps a corporal's guard might have been left on each publication to carry on their work."

Arthur Brisbane, Hearst's ace editorial writer, held forth to 30 million readers a day through his syndicated columns. Considered "the highest-paid editor in America," he produced torrents of estimable words about idealism, genteel culture, fair play, and religion. Yet when asked to state the significance of his work, he said Hearstily, "I don't know of any tribute to my writing that would be worth printing except possibly the exact facts as to the weekly tribute that I receive from the cashier of the Hearst organization." In his editorials Brisbane said he hated boxing, but he knew the sport well and he covered all the big bouts. Brisbane persuaded Moe Annenberg to come work for Hearst in 1920, and for a time the two men mingled their investments. At the Hearst office in New York, Brisbane, Annenberg, and other executives would play a ruthless dice game at lunchtime, with a minimum stake of five dollars a roll.

Brisbane's underworld contacts at least brought him occasional scoops. After the Lindbergh baby was kidnapped in 1932, Brisbane obtained an exclusive interview with the imprisoned Al Capone. Given a big play in the Hearst papers, the interview treated Capone deferentially, including his offer to find the kidnapper if he was only let out of jail. "I have given work to the unemployed," Brisbane had Capone saying. "At least three hundred young men, thanks to me, are getting from one hundred fifty to two hundred dollars a week, and are making it in a harmless beer racket, which is better than their jobs before." Just a selfless measure to relieve the Depression. "If I am a bootlegger, so are they all." (As Prohibition was winding down, Brisbane sent a colleague a magnum of champagne, warning that "those infernal things sometimes explode and I hope that particular sample won't be kept in too hot a locality, such as next to the engine in an automobile.")

Walter Winchell, based in the *New York Daily Mirror,* was Hearst's imitated but sui generis gossip columnist. His daily column of show business news and romantic developments ran in over one hundred papers, with a total circulation of 7.25 million; for this he was paid $1,000 a week plus half the gross syndication fees. His Sunday night radio show ("Good evening, Mr. and Mrs. America," telegraph key peenting in the background, "and all the ships at sea") brought him another $3,000 a week and a devoted audience. Winchell was the first and most important dispenser of his own kind of news, which included his version of the underworld. The son of Jewish immigrants from eastern Europe, raised in a railroad flat on the Upper East Side of New York, he grew up stagestruck. For a while he tried a vaudeville act—a little hoofing and patter—but found his true calling when he switched to writing for *The Vaudeville News.* Later he moved over to the *Daily Mirror,* bringing along his Broadway idiom of brisk, slangy worldliness.

In the Hearst fashion, Winchell made a ritual obeisance toward clucking over gangsters. "Prohibition has made the underworld reckless," he said in 1929. "The ruthless code is to bait the sucker and take him, and the racketeers are ready for all comers. That's why I call Broadway 'The Sappian Way.' " Yet he enjoyed the fruitful confidence of big mobsters. At the Stork Club, his favorite joint, Sherman Billingsley introduced him to various gang luminaries. Owney Madden, knowing that favorable notices in Winchell's column would bring business to his nightclubs, escorted him around town and fed him underworld gossip. Once the two men barged into the office of the *Herald Tribune* and chided an editor over the paper's references to Madden's murderous youth. Winchell, like Brisbane, was also granted exclusive interviews with Al Capone. "Everything in those papers is all lies," he quoted Capone as saying. Another time, he caught the mobster feeling blue ("I have no friends"). How had he made all that money? Winchell asked. "Presents," said Capone. "My friends and cousins gave me it all."

Later on, after Madden left town and Capone went to jail, Winchell's best underworld source became Frank Costello. They lived in the same apartment building at 115 Central Park West, exchanging pleasantries in the lobby. Winchell admired him, in a way, and called him Francesco. Introducing Costello to somebody else one day, Winchell said, "Meet Mr. Costello, the gambler," using a favorite euphemism for a more baleful designation. "The people who come to my places are gamblers, Walter," Costello nonetheless corrected him. "I'm a business man."

By respecting such niceties Winchell ensured a flow of information from the underworld—and more practical services too. His gamier gossip items might dangerously anger people, and at various times Madden, Capone, and Lucky Luciano all provided bodyguards for him. Yet Winchell was not himself a crook. He was driven, as Henry F. Pringle observed, by "a passionate, almost adolescent, interest in policemen, detectives, and crime." His only hobby was to cruise around New York late at night, ears tuned to the police radio in his car. When he heard a juicy report of a crime, he would turn on his police siren and chase it, tearing through the streets like a cop. He palled around with Owney Madden, and with J. Edgar Hoover as well. In Winchell's world they were both just names in his column, players in a diverting game.

Damon Runyon was Hearst's chief feature writer, a privileged columnist with the freedom and popularity to cover anything that caught his attention. His chosen place to play, and the source of his most durable writing, was the gangster world of nightclubs, prizefights, and racetracks. Runyon's column for Hearst gave him a name and platform. From there he wrote his famous short stories about Broadway life. Published in mass magazines, collected in books that sold millions of copies, made into popular plays and movies, Runyon's tales about the guys and dolls along Broadway etched an amiable image of these characters in the public mind. The premier social historian of the underworld, Runyon fixed a notion of the gangsters' milieu as a place of moral relativism, implacable social forces instead of personal choices, and comedy instead of tragedy.

Runyon at least did his research, and not in books. From the thousands of hours he spent hanging around hoodlums he knew his setting viscerally, experientially. Yet he remained an outsider in background, personality, and job, and that softened his approach to the subject. He had been born in Kansas and grown up in Colorado, working on newspapers there and in California until the age of thirty. He came to New York in 1910 to cover sports for Hearst's *American*. Despite the tough, knowing tone he later achieved in his Broadway stories, he was always rather a tourist in the big city, dazzled by the bright lights and sights, intimating a convert's zeal by his enthusiasm. In contrast with the unbridled Irishmen, Jews, and Italians of whom he wrote, Runyon was a tightly buttoned WASP, "a man as emotionally guarded as any who ever lived." He married a Broadway doll and dressed like a gangster with class, but in general he did not behave like them. Mobsters were pure act, without much thinking before or after. Runyon had a classic writer's personality: he stood off, watched and listened, kept his nose pressed to the windowpane, and wrote it down later, but he did not *do* it. "Of course it is none of my business," said the narrator in one of his stories, "so I take no part in the conversation."

This tension between looking and doing thrummed all through Runyon's life and work. Before he bumbled into the underworld in the early 1920s, he had been getting bored with his life, his first marriage, and with writing straight short stories. Prohibition moved gangsters up a bit, Runyon moved down a bit, and they connected. At Saratoga in the summer of 1922 he encountered horse racing, was at once fascinated, and began to enjoy life again.

He prowled the midtown speaks and met bootleggers. He knew Arnold Rothstein, in fact had a long talk with him just hours before he was shot. Big Bill Dwyer, trying to market ice hockey in America, took Runyon and two other sportswriters to Montreal to see a game. ("It was just a large hall," said Runyon, not impressed, "with the temperature down to nothing and a crowd of excited Canadians.") Where he felt most comfortable was in poking around his Broadway, from Forty-second Street fifteen blocks to the north, and between Sixth and Eighth avenues from east to west. Runyon settled into this land of the Friars Club, Lindy's Restaurant, Madison Square Garden, and Billy LaHiff's Tavern. After he left his family Runyon even lived there for a while, in an apartment over LaHiff's.

Sticking a toe into the fight game, he owned some boxers, none of them any good, with Billy LaHiff. Runyon was particularly close to Jack Dempsey, giving him the nickname the Manassa Mauler and celebrating him in many columns. "Damon would sit and talk with me for hours," Dempsey recalled. "He was the most patient man I knew." Runyon was the only newspaperman invited along on Dempsey's trip to Europe in 1922; competing writers resented his special ties to Dempsey and rushed to publicize the more accessible Gene Tunney. After Dempsey lost the title, Runyon trifled with other fighters. He helped foist Primo Carnera on the sport, and later helped arrange a bout between Joe Louis and Max Baer.

Still, this was all just play, not quite real life. Other men around and about Broadway lived and died by what they did there. As a writer Runyon was merely watching the show. Finally in 1929, forty-nine years old, he was ready to start writing his Broadway tales. The omniscient, after-the-fact narrator never had a name in the stories, but the voice was unmistakably Runyon's: cool, ironic, and uninvolved. From his distant perspective, Runyon caught the ornamental idiom of Broadway vernacular, everything expressed in the present tense and acted in present time. Some of the characters were transparently based on real people. Armand Rosenthal was Arnold Rothstein, Waldo Winchester was Walter Winchell, and Black Mike was Al Capone. ("This Black Mike is a Guinea, and not a bad-looking Guinea, at that, except for a big scar on one cheek which I suppose is done by somebody trying to give him a laughing mouth. Some Guins, especially Sicilians, can swing a shiv so as to give a guy a slash that leaves him looking as if he is always laughing out of his mouth, although generally this is only for dolls who are not on the level with their ever-loving guys.") Johnny Brannigan was a ferocious New York plainclothes cop named John Broderick, and "Ike Jacobs, the ticket spec," was Mike Jacobs.

These more or less genuine denizens of the underworld lent the stories an edge of historical truth. Runyon knew it all depended on Prohibition, and he did not neglect that experiment's absurdities. "I am a bootie for a long time," one rumrunner explained, "and supply very fine merchandise to my trade, as everybody knows, and it is a respectable business, because one and all in this country are in favor of it, except the prohibitionists." Runyon's characters bet on horses and usually lost, just as Runyon himself did. Careful distinctions in social status at the track hinged on where one's horses had been finishing. "A tout is a guy who goes around a race track giving out tips on the races, if he can find anybody who will listen to his tips, especially suckers, and a tout is nearly always broke. If he is not broke, he is by no means a tout, but a handicapper, and is respected by one and all, including the Pinkertons, for knowing so much about the races."

Yet despite the measured sociological clarity and the ironic laughter audible in the distance, the moral perspective was faithfully internal: a gangster's peculiar sense of right and wrong. In these stories cops were abusive, troublesome, and worse than useless. "Coppers always blame everything no matter where it happens on the most prominent guy they can think of," said the narrator. "The way I figure it there are a great many coppers in this world, and a few less may be a good thing for one and all concerned." On the other hand, the narrator had only whimsical objections to various underworld specialties. Breaking and entering was OK, although "I am greatly opposed to house-breaking, or sneak jobs, as I do not consider them dignified. Furthermore, they take too much time." What about kidnapping? "While snatching is by no means a high-class business, and is even considered somewhat illegal, it is something to tide over the hard times." Mugging? "Personally, I do not consider this occupation at all essential or even strictly ethical, but I always say every guy to his own taste."

This was not just the amorality of a fictional underworld character. This was Damon Runyon's own voice, speaking directly to millions of American readers. In soaking up the Broadway scene, he had displaced his own moral sense and picked up another. Toward the end of his life, in the 1940s, he thought over his sportswriting days. "I had softened up too much long before I quit it," he concluded. "I had become too relenting and too friendly and had too many personal contacts. . . . I found myself too often playing the part of the counsel for the defense. . . . There is nothing more engaging than an engaging rogue and there are many engaging rogues in professional sports. I fear I knew most of them and that is not good for a sports writer." For "rogues," read gangsters; for "professional sports," read the underworld. But the romanticized, soft-focus image of mobsters he created would survive permanently in his stories and movies.

To sum up the matter: the most celebrated newspaper editor in America, the biggest chain of newspapers and magazines, the most widely read editoralist, the most popular gossipmonger, and the main literary chronicler of the underworld. It was no wonder that organized crime enjoyed an uninquiring press. "The 'mob' ruled the town," Emile Gauvreau said of New York. "If it did not rule some of its newspapers it had little to fear from them."

❦ ❦

Certain rules, never written down but generally understood, governed contacts between the underworld and the upperworld. The underworld dealt in money and murder, and these volatile commodities had to be handled in predictable, rational ways—especially murder, since transactions in that coin could not be recalled.

The simplest exchange was murder for murder. If a friend was killed, only one kind of vengeance could truly balance the offense. This might take ludicrous forms. After Nails Morton, a top gangster in Chicago, was killed in a horse-riding accident, his friends went out and shot the horse. But this was atypical. A normal underworld slaying took place for some adequate reason, though authorities might not discover the cause, leaving the newspapers to creative speculations. "I've done a lot of things in my day," said Mickey Cohen, "but I never killed for just killing." Anyone who killed too easily, capriciously, was considered a true loose cannon, not to be trusted. "He was always unpopular," they said of Legs Diamond. "He would kill a friend."

Gangsters were especially careful about killing anyone from the upperworld. Cops, prosecutors, judges, and federal agents in general have had nothing to fear, no matter how irritating or zealous their pursuit of organized crime. "There is a twisted logic in the underworld code," Harry Anslinger reflected after thirty years at the Bureau of Narcotics as the dread nemesis of dope dealers and the Mafia. "Where an informer would be shot or stabbed to death, the Bureau agent, who makes his case and brings the violators into court, is in no danger of reprisal; the hoods accept him as a part of the routine business risk. . . . It is their delicate differentiation between one of us and one of their own." The crucial distinction between an informer or witness, and a cop or narcotics agent, was occupational. It was not an informer's or a witness's job to help catch criminals. But it *was* the work of cops and agents, and professional criminals respected the function of their professional adversaries. "One of the strictest rules we had toward outsiders was the injunction against killing a policeman," said Joe Bonanno. "My Tradition recognized that a cop was merely the servant of the government and thus was not to be held fully responsible for his actions. He merely had a job to do. We understood that, and very often ways could be found so that he would not interfere with us and we wouldn't interfere with him."

This occupational distinction was extended to reporters as well—again, people just doing a job. A reporter could accuse a gangster in print of murder one day, meet him the next day, and neither would mention the subject. Reporters knew they could write almost anything about a hoodlum without being taken for a ride. In fact they had more latitude with an underworld figure than with an average good citizen who might sue the paper for libel, a legal recourse that would not occur to a gangster. Reporters were safe more for practical reasons than due to any principle of honoring a free press. "If there is any 'code of the Underworld,' " said Willie Sutton, "it is that you do not knock off any ordinary citizens or newspapermen. To knock off a citizen is the surest way to bring the heat down on everybody."

If an honest newspaperman was molested, it was considered a breach of the code, and amends were made. Robert St. John, a crusading editor in Cicero, Illinois, who had been fighting the Capone gang's hold on his town, was beaten up by four Capones on a busy street while two cops watched and did nothing. Al himself came to see St. John at the police station to apologize. "Never should have happened. Sure the boys were sore at you. But they ain't smart," said Capone. "They made a mistake and now I gotta straighten it out. Always I gotta fix up their mistakes." Capone paid his hospital bill and offered him hundreds of dollars more, which St. John declined.

And a good thing that he did. If cops or journalists took money or favors from the mob, they thereby lost their immunity. Gangsters would expect services in return. At the very least, they would expect not to be bothered by the bribed parties. Two famous murders in 1930 made this point clear. Jake Lingle, a *Chicago Tribune* reporter, and Jerry Buckley, a political commentator for a Detroit radio station, were executed in gangland style. Both men, it developed, had been doing racket business. Despite an income of only $65 a week, Lingle had managed to spend at least $60,000 in the year before his death. He ran with the Capones and wore a diamond belt buckle they had given him. "You guys ain't giving me the runaround, are you?" a federal wiretap heard him warning the Capones three months before his murder. "Just remember, I wouldn't do that if I was you." As for Buckley, he had recently extorted money from three gamblers and had been accused of using his radio show for blackmail. A few years earlier, according to another theory, he had promised to help two ranking Italian gangsters get out of jail, but he had not come through. In any case, whoever committed these unsolved murders apparently had sufficient grounds.

Journalists on underworld beats therefore had to be careful to pay their own way. Walter Winchell ate and drank for free in mob nightclubs, but he drew the line against more direct contributions. Once, after his column had puffed one of Owney Madden's joints, Madden offered him a thousand-dollar bill. "I can't be under obligations to a man like you," Winchell demurred. "I'm a newspaperman.... I couldn't do you any favors." Madden bristled at the absurdity of the prospect. "What the fuck," he asked Winchell, "could *you* do for *me?*" In those days supplicants approached Madden for favors—never the other way around.

Gambling was the common thread stitching together many overtly good citizens who dabbled on the fringes of the underworld. A love for cards or dice or betting had first pulled them toward gangsters, and once in hock to the underworld they could not escape, could only do favors and services to buy time. Joe E. Lewis, Lou Clayton, and George Raft were all addicted and losing gamblers. It was not coincidental that they jumped when gangsters snapped their fingers. Milton Berle estimated that he'd blown at least $3 million betting on horses. "I was as hooked on the ponies as any junkie with his brand of drugs," he said later. "It wasn't long before I was betting not to win more money, but to cut down my losses. Through the bookmakers I met the shylocks, and when my debts got too high and the threats started coming, I turned to them for quick money, which put me in even worse trouble than I was in before." Damon Runyon would bet on races, boxing matches, ball games, card games, roller-skating contests in Miami, ratting contests in waterfront dives that pitted several rats against a single dog. Once Runyon had to hide from an angry bookie named Gloomy Gus for three days until a friend sent the scratch. Such obligations may have sweetened Runyon's treatment of the underworld in his Broadway tales.

Herbert Swope's gambling finally caught up with him, though not in a way made public at the time. When New York legalized betting at horse tracks in 1934, Swope was appointed chairman of a state racing commission intended to watch over the sport. After all, who knew more about betting on horses—legal or otherwise—than Swope? He liked to stroll around the tracks, responding to greetings of "How are you, Commissioner?" Meantime he continued as always to place his own wagers. His betting became a public issue when his appointment was about to expire in 1941, but he was reappointed anyway. A few years later, a wiretap on the telephone of the bookie Frank Erickson revealed that Swope owed him some $700,000—an obvious compromise of Swope's impartiality in regulating horse betting. So he was forced to resign from the racing commission, under the disguise of a voluntary departure. Swope at least was not killed; in his position he had been worth more to the underworld alive than dead.

General relations between the underworld and upperworld, then, have turned on these two essential principles. Ordinary citizens, cops, prosecutors, and journalists have normally been safe. But if they took favors from the underworld, and then did not cooperate, they needed to worry.

BOOTLEGGERS, LATER BIG-TIME GANGSTERS

Charlie Lucky Luciano, main architect of the national Mafia and its Commission; mug shots taken in 1936 after Thomas E. Dewey's office had brought him back from Hot Springs, Arkansas, to face charges of compulsory prostitution
COLLECTIONS OF THE MUNICIPAL ARCHIVES OF THE CITY OF NEW YORK

Meyer Lansky, lifelong friend of Lucky Luciano and, because of that connection, the most powerful and respected Jewish gangster in American history
COLLECTIONS OF THE MUNICIPAL ARCHIVES OF THE CITY OF NEW YORK

Frank Costello, successor to Charlie Lucky as boss of the Luciano family; the most prominent gangster in America during the 1940s and 1950s

Bugsy Siegel, leader with Meyer Lansky of the Bug and Meyer gang; the founder of Las Vegas as a mecca for gamblers

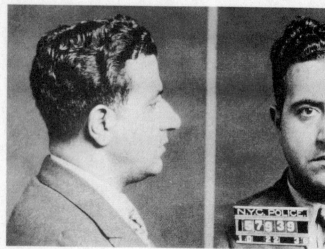

Albert Anastasia, boss of Murder, Incorporated, and one of the five New York families until his close shave in 1957

POLICE DEPARTMENT, BOSTON, MASS.

WANTED FOR MURDER

JOSEPH LOMBARDO, alias LOMBARDO

Above, Joe Lombardo, bootlegger and then a boss of the Boston Mafia for four decades

Left, Vito Genovese, successor to Frank Costello as boss of the Luciano family; the most vicious and feared Mafioso of his time

CLEVELAND MEETING

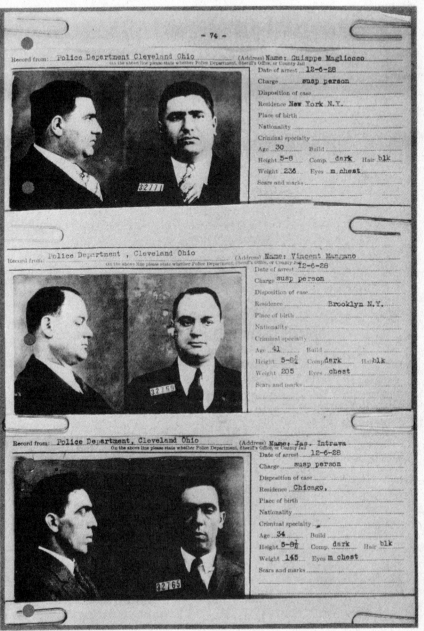

Record from: **Police Department Cleveland Ohio**
On the above line please state whether Police Department, Sheriff's Office, or County Jail

(Address) Name: Guispppe Magliocco
Date of arrest 12-6-28
Charge susp person
Disposition of case
Residence New York N.Y.
Place of birth
Nationality
Criminal specialty
Age 30   Build
Height 5-8   Comp. dark   Hair blk
Weight 236   Eyes m chest
Scars and marks

32771

Record from: **Police Department , Cleveland Ohio**
On the above line please state whether Police Department, Sheriff's Office, or County Jail

(Address) Name: Vincent Mangano
Date of arrest 12-6-28
Charge susp person
Disposition of case
Residence Brooklyn N.Y.
Place of birth
Nationality
Criminal specialty
Age 41   Build
Height 5-8½   Comp dark   Hair blk
Weight 205   Eyes chest
Scars and marks

32759

Record from: **Police Department, Cleveland Ohio**
On the above line please state whether Police Department, Sheriff's Office, or County Jail

(Address) Name: Jas. Intrava
Date of arrest 12-6-28
Charge susp person
Disposition of case
Residence Chicago,
Place of birth
Nationality
Criminal specialty
Age 34   Build
Height 5-8½   Comp. dark   Hair blk
Weight 145   Eyes m chest
Scars and marks

32765

Six mug shots from the meeting at the Hotel Statler in Cleveland in December 1928, the first national conference of the Mafia to be discovered by lawmen; Joseph Profaci and Vincent Mangano were later bosses of two of the five New York families.

Record from: **Police Department, Cleveland Ohio**

(Address) Name: Ignatzio Italiano

Date of arrest 12-6-28

Charge susp person

Disposition of case

Residence Tampa Fla

Place of birth

Nationality

Criminal specialty

Age 72   Build

Height 5-7   Comp. florid   Hair blk grey

Weight 190   Eyes lt chest

Scars and marks

Record from: **Police Department, Cleveland, Ohio**

(Address) Name: Jos. Profaci

Date of arrest 12-6-28

Charge susp person

Disposition of case

Residence New York City

Place of birth

Nationality

Criminal specialty

Age 30   Build

Height 5-6   Comp. dark   Hair blk

Weight 178   Eyes dk chest

Scars and marks

Record from: **Police Department, Cleveland Ohio**

(Address) Name: Mike Russo

Date of arrest 12-6-28

Charge susp person

Disposition of case

Residence

Place of birth

Nationality

Criminal specialty

Age 35   Build

Height 5-9½   Comp. dark   Hair blk

Weight 175   Eyes chest

Scars and marks

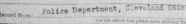

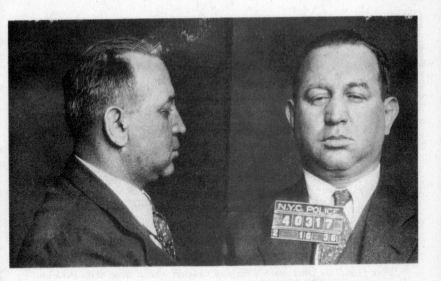

Above, Gurrah Shapiro, a leading labor rack-
eteer in New York during the 1930s
COLLECTIONS OF THE MUNICIPAL ARCHIVES OF THE CITY
OF NEW YORK

Right, Willie Bioff ran the Stagehands union
for the Hollywood producers and large payoffs.
BOSTON PUBLIC LIBRARY, PRINT DEPARTMENT

Johnny Dio of the Luccheses; as a top labor racketeer, a major target of the McClellan committee from 1957 to 1959
COLLECTIONS OF THE MUNICIPAL ARCHIVES OF THE CITY OF NEW YORK

Above left, Sidney Hillman, New Dealer and labor racketeer; as president of the Amalgamated Clothing Workers, he paid the gangster Lepke Buchalter $350 a week (and larger sums on special occasions) for muscle work and favors. Above right, Dan Tobin, Teamster president from 1907 to 1952, under whose regime the underworld took control of his union

LIBRARY OF CONGRESS; BOSTON PUBLIC LIBRARY, PRINT DEPARTMENT

THEIR WORLD

Above, Walter Winchell, underworld chronicler and amateur crimestopper

Right, Frank Hague, photographed with his wife in 1925, eight years into his thirty-year reign as the corrupt lord of Jersey City and the Democratic boss of New Jersey

Frankie Carbo, gunman for the Lucchese family; the omnipresent "Mr. Gray" of boxing during the 1940s and 1950s

Below, three heavyweight boxing champions. *Left to right:* Jack Sharkey (1932–33) dealt with Owney Madden; Rocky Marciano (1952–56) dealt with Al Weill and Frankie Carbo; Gene Tunney (1926–28) dealt with Billy Gibson and Boo-Boo Hoff

FOUR

THE WASP RESPONSE

How to counter the romping, stomping gangsters? The essence of organized crime was a triangular collusion among politicians, lawmen, and the underworld. Wherever the representatives of governmental power were safely bought off, nobody (or nobody strong enough) remained to chase the hoodlums. Newspapers and magazines could run worried articles. Clergymen could declaim from their pulpits. It all amounted to just words, though, as long as duly constituted authority turned its back—with a hand extended, palm upward, toward the gangsters. An average good citizen felt helpless.

Good citizens admittedly had helped create the situation by their feckless moral reform movements, especially Prohibition. Now they responded to the recent extension of organized crime with yet more gestures of reform. These latest WASP reformers worked both within and outside formal legal machinery. Either way, their efforts suggested the importance of the individual personality in history: spurred on by their own private consciences, they drove public opinion instead of responding to it, spontaneously creating or enlarging a role for themselves, acting admirably from mostly admirable motives. All this was clear. Whether they actually managed to diminish the powers of organized crime remained a murkier question.

Frank J. Loesch of the Chicago Crime Commission was the first of this new wave of WASP reformers. Born in Buffalo in 1852, Loesch was the son of a German immigrant from Baden who became a building contractor in America. At fourteen Frank went to work, delivering messages and then keeping books for Western Union. In 1870 the company transferred him to Chicago, where he attended Northwestern Law School. Eventually he started his own firm and prospered at corporate law, acting as general counsel for the Union Station and for the Pennsylvania Railroad lines west of Pittsburgh. At the same time he immersed himself in the civic and cultural affairs of his adopted city, serving on the board of education, presiding over the bar association, joining other groups and clubs around town. As a special state's attorney for Cook County, he prosecuted voting frauds committed during Chicago's first direct primary election in 1908; the experience made him an inveterate crusader against any conspiracy of politicians and criminals.

From this civic-minded background Loesch was appalled at what happened to Chicago after 1920. He helped start the Chicago Crime Commission, a private watchdog group organized through a local business association. For a few years the commission made vigorous noises about the crimes that were going unprosecuted in the city. But the gang wars continued, the Capones consolidated their power, and the commission began to wilt in defeat. On primary election day in April 1928, the voting was corrupted by frauds, felonies, bombings, kidnappings, and the murder of a black candidate in the notoriously bloody Twentieth Ward. For Loesch it called up memories of the primary in 1908; he took over as president of the crime commission, intending to revive the group and thereby "to lift Chicago out of the mire," as he put it. As a private citizen pursuing gangsters on his own, without the immunity the underworld allowed to cops and newspapermen, he received various threats on his life. He decided against hiring guards on the theory they could not stop a serious mob gunman anyway. "Those men know what an avalanche they will bring down upon themselves if they attack me," he declared. "And they are cowards at heart."

In that spirit he decided to visit Al Capone himself, "to

remonstrate with him about his conduct," he explained, to tell him that "a man of his ability ought to be a better American citizen." Loesch had concluded that Capone ran the city, with lines into every department of the county and municipal governments. Capone put him off for a while but then, perhaps amused, invited Loesch to his headquarters at the Lexington Hotel one day in the summer of 1928. It was a peculiar scene: the reformer, tall and thin, seventy-six years old but still quick and alert, bearding the gangster, fat and complacent, twenty-nine years old, in his lair. "There were 25 or 30 men around his place," Loesch noted, "evidently all dark-skinned fellows, probably none who could talk English." In his office Capone sat at a desk beneath portraits of Washington, Lincoln, and Big Bill Thompson, the unabashedly corrupt incumbent mayor of Chicago. A half-dozen guards loitered around the room, hands on their weapons.

Loesch asked Capone how long he could escape both the law and the gun. Capone replied that he would always beat the law, though he expected rival gangsters to shoot him eventually—"but they'll only get me when I'm not looking." Loesch then came to the point. "I am here to ask you to help in one thing," he said. "I want you to keep your damned Italian hoodlums out of the election this coming fall." Apparently intrigued by the novel idea of himself as a good-government man, Capone promised to do his bit. He said he could control the North Side "because they are all Dagoes up there," but would need reinforcements from his police stooges to subdue the Irish gangs on the West Side. So on election day some seventy police squad cars were dispatched to keep gangsters off the streets, and the city enjoyed "the only honest election that we had had in 30 years," as Loesch told the story later.

In other efforts, undertaken without Capone's support, Loesch fared worse. Certain judges of Cook County's criminal courts were working short hours and granting suspiciously large numbers of continuances, *nolle prosequis,* and felony waivers to mobsters. Over a three-month period, three judges in particular had waived some 450 felony cases. Loesch sent a statement of the situation to every judge in the area; "as expected," he noted, "no attention was paid to it whatever." After further agitation, the three most offending judges were not reappointed to the bench.

The Illinois attorney general made Loesch a special prosecutor to investigate the crimes committed on primary day in 1928. When the county board of commissioners tried to frustrate the investigation by denying him the money to hire a staff, Loesch raised the necessary $150,000 privately and then brought in sixty-three indictments. But the ensuing trials led mainly to acquittals and light sentences. "In the whole of my investigation experience," said Loesch, disgusted, "I saw that none of those leading criminals were ever gotten. It was just impossible"—because, Loesch surmised, enough lawmen had been bribed or threatened.

For the most part he had to rely on publicity. In 1930 Loesch coined a phrase, "public enemies," and released a list of the twenty-eight most egregious offenders in Chicago, with Capone and his brother Ralph at the top. Sent to newspapers and lawmen, the list included no surprises. Its novel aspect was simply to put names on the record, despite the risk of libel and retribution. "These men were walking the streets of Chicago," Loesch said later. "As a result of focusing public attention, the law officers got busy, and we got some of them." By 1933, four of the twenty-eight named public enemies—including both Capones and their main strategist, Greasy Thumb Guzik—were in jail for tax evasion; five others were dead, three were awaiting trial for vagrancy, and eight were fugitives from various charges.

Loesch headed the crime commission for ten years, until he was eighty-six, fueled by a combination of civic righteousness and nativist outrage. He was a high Presbyterian church man, twice a commissioner to his denomination's national general assembly. Quotations of Old Testament scripture came naturally to him. "It is the hand of Esau," he said of the alliance between gangsters and politicians, "but the voice of Jacob." As a WASP reformer confronting the gangs of Chicago, he could not miss the obvious ethnic aspects. Trying to account for the rise of organized crime, he came up with nine root causes—the first being the introduction of what he called "largely unassimilable foreign immigrants from Eastern and Southeastern Europe." At a crime conference in Princeton, New Jersey, in 1930, he said the perpetrators of Chicago's recent political frauds were all Irish, Polish, or Italian. "The American people are not a lawless people," he declared. "It's the foreigners and the first generation of Americans who are loaded on us." When the audience stirred in protest, Loesch asserted that he was himself first generation, and he conversely allowed that Chicago's crooked Mayor Thompson was an old-stock American. But he did not retract his basic point. "The real Americans are not gangsters," he said a few months later. "Recent immigrants and the first generation of Jews and Italians are the chief offenders, with the Jews furnishing the brains and the Italians the brawn." He didn't give a damn; he named names and did not mind offending anyone.

After Al Capone's removal to federal prison, and then the end of Prohibition, the worst of Chicago's gang wars ended. An illusory truce settled over the city. Actually Thompson's successors as mayor, Anton Cermak and Edward J. Kelly, were at least as corrupt as Thompson. And the Capone gang, under new leadership, held Chicago as tightly as ever, if more discreetly. But Frank Loesch could at last survey conditions with a measure of satisfaction. "We live in a pretty lawful town now," he said in 1938. "All you need to do is to put command of the law into the hands of the right officials."

❧ ❧

Samuel Seabury of New York came from a long, dignified line of lawyers and preachers. One of his ancestors, a prominent Tory during the American Revolution, had become the first Episcopal bishop in North America; another had helped found the New York bar. Both Seabury's father and grandfather were Episcopal rectors and seminary professors in New York City. For himself Seabury chose a career in law and reform politics, urging the ideals of Henry George and the municipal ownership of public utilities. Elected a judge of the city court at the age of twenty-eight, he went on to two other judicial posts before resigning in 1916 to run (and lose) as the Democratic nominee for governor. He then settled into private practice, but he always looked like a judge, with a definite courtly demeanor, a ruddy face, and white hair parted down the middle, tall and broad-shouldered, speaking with precise diction in a powerful baritone voice.

Childless himself, Seabury was motivated by a strong paternal concern for the public welfare. In his library he sat surrounded by portraits of ancestors, bewigged and bewhiskered, caparisoned in the robes of bench and pulpit. They looked down on him, stern and admonishing, and he sensed their living presence. On his annual vacation trips to England he would research the family genealogy in county and church records. He felt his family history as a moral imperative to do good, to be serious. "He was a little hard to kid," a cousin remarked. "It was that judicial mien he acquired so early." Seabury saw himself as a kind of twentieth-century Cincinnatus, always ready to leave the plow and serve his community. "We have labored under the delusion that the public business should be left to the professional politicians," he said. "Each and every one owes it to his country to take part in some measure in its public affairs."

Seabury got his call after an implausible chain of events originally set in motion by the murder of Arnold Rothstein in November 1928. For some months the New York underworld had been passing around rumors that Rothstein would be killed for not paying gambling debts. But he had a hand in so many scams, was so disliked—and so vulnerable because he had no protecting gang of his own—that any number of hoodlums might have, could have shot him. Investigators looking through his effects found many interesting documents with many interesting names. Under pressure, Mayor Jimmy Walker ordered his police commissioner, Joseph A. Warren, to solve the murder quickly. Warren hurriedly brought two of Rothstein's cronies to trial, but the evidence was so thin that the judge ordered an acquittal. Needing a scapegoat, Walker then fired Warren as police commissioner and replaced him with a department store manager.

The lid on the city's politics had been raised, and it could not be pushed back down. The dead Rothstein became an issue again in the fall of 1929 when Mayor Walker ran for reelection against a Republican congressman, Fiorello La Guardia. The challenger asserted that Walker and his police knew who had killed Rothstein, but would bring no indictment because of the political scandals it would stir up. To illustrate the point, La Guardia produced one of those incriminating documents from Rothstein's files: a letter showing that Rothstein had loaned $20,000 to city magistrate Albert H. Vitale, who had been coordinating Walker's campaign in the Italian neighborhoods of the Bronx. The mayor nonetheless buried La Guardia by almost five hundred thousand votes. Elected with him as district attorney was an old Tammany horse, Thomas C. T. Crain, who in campaigning had promised to solve the Rothstein case within fifteen days of taking office. Once installed as DA, Crain did nothing about the Rothstein murder, or about anything else.

The cynical tolerance of even the New York electorate was being strained. One evening in the summer of 1930, Justice

Joseph F. Crater of the state supreme court—the famous disappearing judge—got into a taxicab and drove off into the night, never to be seen again. Earlier that day he had taken several thick piles of documents from his official chambers and had cashed checks worth over $5,000. He was known to like nightclubs and the company of showgirls, and he kept a mistress in a midtown apartment. The previous spring, just after his appointment to the bench, Crater had withdrawn a total of $23,279 from securities and a savings account—a little more than a prospective supreme court justice supposedly had to pay Tammany to be appointed. Crater had also been implicated in shady financial manipulations relating to the sale of a hotel on the Lower East Side. As these details emerged, it became obvious that Crater had many possible reasons to vanish, or to be made to vanish.

The odor wafted north all the way to Albany. Governor Franklin D. Roosevelt needed the friendship of New York City's Democrats, and he would rather have ignored the whole situation. Jimmy Walker was not about to probe his own failings, though, so Roosevelt had to step in. Two weeks after Justice Crater was vaporized, the governor asked the appellate division of the state court to investigate the magistrates' courts of Manhattan and the Bronx, Albert Vitale's playpen. Needing someone of undoubted integrity, the appellate division after consulting with Roosevelt named Samuel Seabury to conduct an inquiry. He soon had two other appointments: one by Roosevelt, to investigate charges filed against DA Thomas Crain, and one by the state legislature, to serve as counsel for a general inquiry into New York City's government. Thus for twenty months, from the fall of 1930 to the summer of 1932, Seabury went looking for municipal corruption and found it.

The magistrates, fifty in all, presided over the lowest courts in the city judicial system. They were appointed by the Tammany organization at the recommendation of local district leaders, for services to the organization and a $10,000 bribe. "That is the way we make Democrats," explained James W. Brown, district leader of the Bronx. Once in office, the magistrates were expected to return favors to the Democratic leadership. If a gangster was arrested and wanted his case fixed, he would call on his district leader (with whom he had already probably done business). The leader would pull the string to his magistrate, and the case would be dropped, no explanation given. The criminal records of major gangsters were thereby littered with minor arrests never prose-cuted. During 1929, for example, of 4,328 bookmaking cases brought into the magistrates' courts, only about 3.8 percent were held for trial.

In the early stages, before hard evidence was turned up, Seabury's first investigation was sustained by Chief Magistrate Joseph E. Corrigan, a Walker appointee but inexplicably honest. He had started his own probing of the magistrates, and he gave Seabury his findings and other material from his files. Seabury's best evidence later came from blanket subpoenas served on two thousand banks and brokerage houses. Many crooked cops and court officers had made the mistake of depositing and investing their stolen money. One police lieutenant could not explain the source of $184,000 saved over five years. Five cops on the vice squad had accumulated a total of $550,000 above their salaries. When asked about this they gave creative answers.

The most elaborate and vicious enterprise uncovered was a ring of cops, bondsmen, lawyers, and magistrates operating in the women's night court, which dealt mainly with prostitution. Inno-cent women would be arrested and accused of whoring. They could then either accept an automatic conviction or pay a bribe of up to $1,180 to exonerate themselves. One assistant district attorney admitted to a total of $20,000 derived from his share of six hundred cases. Some of the women arrested were actually working prosti-tutes who then paid to have legitimate sentences reduced or dis-missed. One woman visited Seabury and told a story of being framed. She was asked to come back with evidence she had left at home. Before she could return she was found murdered.

Aside from the minor players that Seabury caught, three magistrates were forced to resign, two others were removed by formal proceedings, and a sixth fled the state. The public then was ready to believe the worst when Seabury turned his attention to DA Crain. But he found only incompetence and negligence, not overt corruption and criminality. Crain had staged his own perfunctory investigation of the magistrates' courts, turning up nothing to prosecute. Crain had looked into charges of racketeer-ing in various industries—millinery, cloth shrinking, and the Fulton Fish Market—but again could find no crimes. Seabury examined those same industries and easily found patterns of extortion and bribery. Yet Crain's failings had been omissions, not commissions, so Seabury could not recommend his removal. The net result of the Crain inquiry was criminal proceedings against seven bondsmen; of these, three were convicted, leading to one fine and two suspended sentences.

Seabury found more scoundrels when he directed the legislature's probe of the city government. In public and private hearings he made 2,435 squirming witnesses sit down and talk, producing some 52,000 pages of testimony. He emphasized the issue of political graft, the easiest crime to prove from the evidence turned up by his subpoenas to banks and brokers. A buffoonish parade of Irish politicians, grown sleekly fat at the public trough, could not explain the source of their wealth. William J. Flynn, commissioner of public works in the Bronx, had mysteriously piled up a net worth of over a million dollars in thirteen years of serving the public. The clearest links to organized crime that Seabury found were the "political clubs" run by Tammany district leaders. Supposedly just social and political headquarters of the local organizations, the clubs were actually fortified, protected gambling dens for which the district leaders received heavy payoffs from the underworld. James A. McQuade, the sheriff of Brooklyn, had managed to bank over $510,000 despite his modest salary. It was "money that I borrowed," he said, because through a series of family misfortunes he had become the sole support of thirty-three other McQuades. But he could not remember the name of anyone who had loaned him money for all those McQuades, nor did he have any records of the transactions. Why, he was asked, were professional gamblers found in a raid on his clubhouse? They were, he explained, "only reading books in the library I put in for the boys."

Thomas M. Farley, the sheriff of Manhattan, leader of the Fourteenth Assembly District, had accumulated over $360,000 in seven years while his annual salary varied from $6,500 to $15,000. All this came, said Farley, from "moneys that I saved" in a tin box at his home. "Kind of a magic box?" Seabury inquired, throwing him a straight line. "It was a wonderful box," Farley conceded. The sheriff was asked what a group of gamblers were doing at his clubhouse when it was raided at two o'clock one morning. "The members that was there," he insisted, "was busy packing baseball bats, skipping ropes and rubber balls, because our May Day outing took place on May 29th." Unable to come up with any less ludicrous answers, Farley was removed as sheriff.

And finally to the biggest fish, Hizzoner Jimmy Walker. As he sat before Seabury, the natty little mayor cracked jokes and played to his adoring gallery, contriving a good show of not being worried. Seabury stood off to the side, not making eye contact with Walker, inexorably painting him into a corner. As mayor, Walker was ultimately responsible for all the shenanigans of his subordinates and appointees; of these he claimed ignorance. But he had demonstrably taken huge bribes from companies hoping to establish transportation monopolies in the city. The key evidence again came from bank records. An accountant, Russell T. Sherwood, had maintained joint accounts for Walker into which flowed dividends, stock certificates, bonds, coupons, debentures, checks, and cash reaching a grand total of almost a million dollars. Under subpoena, accountant Sherwood left New York, turning up in Atlantic City, Chicago, and Mexico City, and he never came back. Walker tried to stick it out, never admitting anything, but Governor Roosevelt—prodded by Seabury, and in the midst of running for President— forced him to resign in September 1932.

Seabury's investigations gave him such a formidable reputation in New York that he became a political kingmaker. For the mayoral election in 1933, Seabury put together a Fusion ticket (since no Republican could be elected mayor of the city) and persuaded Fiorello La Guardia to head it. The Tammany forces were vanquished in the election, and La Guardia gave New York a relatively honest administration for the next dozen years. Seabury faded back into private life. Toward the end of La Guardia's third term a reporter went to interview Seabury at his law office on Nassau Street. "I just work along here from day to day, trying to be obscurely good," said Seabury. "The city is in fine shape now, but if anything should happen to it, if I should ever be called on, I'd be ready and willing to do what I could. Everybody knows where I am."

Harry J. Anslinger of the federal Bureau of Narcotics was the first important lawman to see the Mafia clearly. He was a Pennsylvania Dutchman, born and raised in Altoona. His father had emigrated from Switzerland in 1881, eleven years before Harry's birth. "I was brought up by a saintly mother," he said of his Protestant youth, "who gathered all the family together after dinner to read a verse from the Bible and to kneel in prayer." Two childhood experiences foreshadowed his later career. Visiting a nearby farm one day, he heard a woman screaming upstairs; the man of the house sent young Anslinger racing into town to buy morphine for her. He ran the errand, and the woman—addicted to morphine, then available over the counter—was quieted. "I never forgot those screams," Anslinger wrote many years afterward. "Nor did I forget that the morphine she had required was sold to a twelve-year-old boy, no questions asked."

At about that same time, or a few years later (Anslinger told different versions of the story), he first became aware of the Mafia. Big Mouth Sam, the local boss of Italian crime in Altoona, had demanded that a Sicilian railroad laborer hand over part of his wages every week. The laborer balked and Big Mouth Sam shot him, but he survived. When the matter came into court, a curious Anslinger watched the proceedings, astonished. As the gangster yelled out threats, the wounded laborer became too frightened to testify. "Such was my first direct encounter," wrote Anslinger, "with this transplanted brotherhood of plunder, extortion, thievery and murder."

From the age of fourteen Anslinger worked on construction gangs for the Pennsylvania Railroad, taking time out to graduate from high school and attend Penn State for two years. During the First World War he served in the Ordnance Division in Washington, then went into the State Department for eight years, posted to consulates in the Netherlands, Germany, Venezuela, and the Bahamas. Restive at trying to ascend the clogged ranks of the foreign service—"I was frozen"—Anslinger in his Bahamian assignment endured the particular absurdities of trying to enforce Prohibition in a British colony reaping fortunes from bootlegging to America. "I firmly believe that the colonial authorities here lack the courage to prosecute any persons connected with the liquor traffic," he concluded in 1926. "One of the most powerful politicians here, who is a liquor dealer, has boasted repeatedly that he put the controlling majority in the House of Assembly and that when he wanted anything he asked for it and got it. . . . The prosperity of the Colony today is attributed entirely to the revenue derived from liquor smuggled into the United States." Later that year he was glad to transfer into the Treasury Department's division of foreign control, trying from Washington to stem the flow of foreign booze. When Treasury created the Bureau of Narcotics in 1930, Anslinger was made its commissioner, a job he held for the next thirty-two years.

Boss of his own new domain, freed of the bogs he had contended with in the State Department, Anslinger fashioned the Bureau of Narcotics in his own image. He was a tough, unsmiling man, an inch under six feet and 190 pounds, with a large, bald head that reminded people of Mussolini. "The world belongs to the strong," he believed. "It always has—it always will." As an investigator accustomed to sizing people up quickly, he had a chilling habit of looking up and down a new acquaintance, noting and filing. One man meeting Anslinger for the first time felt himself being catalogued as the commissioner took in his features, build, and clothes; "it gives you a funny feeling," the man reflected uncomfortably.

In the rough business of pursuing international dope dealers, Anslinger emphasized the controversial use of paid informers and undercover agents. The informers, criminals themselves willing to tell secrets at the risk of being killed, were paid in cash, immunity from prosecution, or lightened sentences. "Getting an informer at the top echelons of a mob," said Anslinger, "is not so difficult as the public—or the racketeers—may believe. There is always someone willing to sell out. We have special employees in places where the hoodlums could not believe an informer would dare go." Still, any informer was skirting the most fundamental mob code—death to stool pigeons—which made it dangerous work. "This morning one of our informers was killed by a machine gun," a bureau agent matter-of-factly reported to Anslinger from Kansas City in 1931. Later on, Joe Valachi in New York was given the contract on a Bureau of Narcotics informer named Eugene Giannini. "There goes my couple of thousand that he owes me," Valachi mused, before having him killed.

From the early 1930s on, Anslinger's bureau at any given time had at least four of its own agents working undercover, posing as gangsters. Close to their quarry, resembling them in ways, sharing illicit activities in order to be trusted, these undercover men earned the bureau a raffish reputation. Some agents were said to ignore legal niceties when they broke down doors and beat people up. Anslinger was not moved by his occasional critics. (He referred to one unfriendly journalist, Florabel Muir, as "the old douche bag.") "Your bureau's work is pretty unusual," someone told him, picking the last word carefully. "Our enemies' work is unusual," he replied.

George H. White, one of the bureau's most effective undercover agents, had started out as a crime reporter in San Francisco. Pudgy and bald, with a cherubic face and heavily lidded eyes, he looked like a harmless Buddha. He had a fortunate knack for adding or taking off weight easily, which helped his disguises. When he first joined the Bureau of Narcotics, Anslinger almost fired him for not working hard enough. He never did take orders well. "George was a loner. He didn't like to carry the other men around on his back," according to Anslinger. "White could almost smell a crook, and he had an obsessive hatred especially for trusted officials who abused public responsibility." To understate the matter, he also did not mind using violence. As an OSS operative during World War II, he killed a Japanese spy in Calcutta. He then kept a picture on his wall of the bloody corpse lying in a gutter. "George would just as soon kill a man," said a wartime acquaintance, "as have a steak for breakfast."

Such men and such methods, however excessive, at least gave Anslinger and his men the information they needed to figure out the Mafia. This recognition did not come quickly. As Anslinger began his work, in the early 1930s, dope traffic in the United States was dispersed among many individual gangs. On the West Coast, the Chinese tongs—especially the On Leong and Hip Song—monopolized the opium trade. (In 1937 George White broke up a Hip Sing operation in Seattle.) In Chicago an Irish woman, Kitty Gilhooley, was considered "the undisputed narcotics boss of the Windy City" until one of Anslinger's agents busted her. The most active group consisted of Jewish gangsters in New York: Waxey Gordon, Lepke Buchalter, Saul Gelb, Mendy Weiss, Abe Stein, and others. They brought in Japanese heroin by way of Tientsin in China, and from New York it was distributed across the country to such dealers as Louis Oppleman in Baltimore and Nathan Biegler in Chicago. The narcotics bureau convicted many of these men. George White had the pleasure of arresting Mendy Weiss on the lam in Kansas City. "At that occasion," White recalled fondly, "the terrible and ferocious Mendy had a childish accident in his trousers when faced by two not so awfully tough narcotic agents."

The American Mafia had been trading in narcotics for years, at least since 1909, but Jewish gangsters dominated the business until the mid-1930s. At that point, as part of the general Italian ascendancy in organized crime, the Mafia began taking over narcotics, mainly through the Lucchese family in New York and the Mafia organization in Kansas City. Hounded by Anslinger on one side and Italian gangs on the other, Jewish dope dealers had to yield. The arrests made by the narcotics. bureau started bringing in more Italians, fewer Jews; the significance of this shift was not at once obvious. In the late 1930s, a Sicilian informer came to see Anslinger and an associate. The Mafia had shot a relative of the man, who then sought revenge by giving Anslinger valuable information about Mafia dope operations. When the interrogation ended, the informer stood up, took Anslinger's hand, and kissed it. What did that mean? "We knew that there were very powerful Italian gangs, of course," Anslinger recalled of those days. "They seemed to have an extraordinary cohesion. But none of us were aware that they were predominantly Sicilian or what that meant. It took us a while to find that out."

Bearing down on the Mafia, the bureau hired Italian-Americans to work undercover among Italian gangsters. Charles Siragusa had grown up in the Bronx, watching Ciro Terranova's gang and hating Italian hoodlums. One of his grandfathers, back in Sicily, had been killed by local Mafiosi after refusing to pay extortion money. As a boy Siragusa heard his father, who had come to America at sixteen, discussing the Black Hand in frightened whispers. Going to school in the Bronx, he found the sons of Mafiosi charging weaker kids fifteen to fifty cents a week for protection from beatings; periodically he would be stopped and searched for loose change. "I made a vow," Siragusa recalled, "to fight the Mafia when I was a grown man." He got his chance after joining the Bureau of Narcotics in 1939. George White put him in undercover work, costumed in a pinstriped suit and fancy shoes. Siragusa averaged two hundred arrests a year ("I have a lot of Sicilian in me. I feel things and I can talk to people"), sticking it to the Mafia and incidentally hoping to redeem the reputation of all honest Sicilian-Americans. "I would like it made clearly known that I am of Sicilian parentage . . . and extremely proud of my ancestry," he said later. "There are so many other Sicilians who have worked hard and raised decent families. Then there is this small group of Mafiosi who make us all look like jerks. I just wish that more Sicilian-Americans would do more about getting rid of them instead of attacking the people who are trying to."

By around 1940 Anslinger and his men could recognize the Mafia as something more than just another criminal gang. A major investigation of the Kansas City Mafia's dope dealing kept getting bigger, like a pebble thrown into water, sending out wider and wider rings, until finally the bureau could glimpse the Mafia's extent and some of its internal procedures. Acting on information from an informer who worked at gambling tables for the Kansas City syndicate, Anslinger's men arrested the local Mafia narcotics bosses, Joe DeLuca and Nicolo Impostato, with some of their confederates. One of these underlings, Carl Carramusa, decided to sing. With his secret testimony the bureau then arrested Mafia conspirators from other cities: Paul and Joe Antinori of Tampa, Florida, and Tom Buffa (Joe DeLuca's cousin) and Tony Lopiparo of St. Louis. All these men were involved in the Kansas City dope ring.

There the investigation stood in January 1943 when Joe Antinori and Tony Lopiparo, free on bail, traveled to Kansas City for a mob conference about the situation. The two men met for a long, rambling talk in room 1823 of the Phillips Hotel. Somehow the feds knew in advance. A microphone secretly placed in room 1823 fed the conversation to a suite on the twentieth floor, where narcotics agents listened and a stenographer wrote it all down. Tony Lopiparo had recently been added to the indictments. "Somebody must have put the finger on me," he said, "and I have a hunch who it was." He wondered if Joe Antinori or his brother, Paul, had squealed.

Tony: "Some of the guys said that you talked, but I would not believe it, and I told them that I would bet both my eyes that Paul wouldn't talk."

Joe: "Hell, no, I ain't said nothing, and I know damn well Paul hasn't talked. He wouldn't even tell me anything about this business. . . . You know you don't have to worry about me. Whatever I know I am going to keep to myself. It don't do you any good to talk and have to face three or four tough blank blank blank on the outside when you come out. . . . I admit that Paul is not so good, but you know a man is not going against his own brother, good or bad."

Tony: "He has his faults, but I think he can be trusted."

Joe: "He won't even tell me his troubles so you know he won't say anything to anybody else."

Tony: "I don't trust anyone."

Joe: "That is the best way."

They discussed how to deal with the narcotics indictments. Tony: "When something like this happens, you don't need a lawyer. You need a fixer to get you out of it."

Joe: "I think I will take my chances with the judge. I don't want no jury. I am looking to save time this way. Anyway, I haven't got any money for a lawyer."

Tony: "I haven't got any, either, but I am telling you if you ever get any, keep it in a safe deposit box. Then they can't find it, when they check up on you. . . . When those guys ask you questions, just put ice on your head and think twice before you answer."

Joe: "I don't know what to do. Maybe the best thing is to cop a plea."

Tony: "When the time comes to cop a plea, let me know and I will see that you get a good fix. Joe DeLuca knows how to do it."

In passing, Tony asked Joe about gambling conditions in his hometown of Tampa. "Hell, the Dagoes couldn't do any good gambling in Tampa," Joe replied. "The city charges, the sheriff charges, and the mayor charges. They just won't let you make any money. They used to be pretty strong out here in Kansas City, but they sort of lost out. They even asked me about the Mafia"—a loud laugh—"as if I would say anything about that."

The conversation kept drifting back to the indictments, as the two men wondered how much help they could expect from leaders further up the Mafia chain of command. Tony: "That damn DeLuca spent plenty of dough to get out. . . . About $50,000. Ten for the lawyers alone."

Joe: "The odds are all against us. I am smart enough to know that the big guys are out to save themselves, and we are going to get the worst of it."

Tony: "Yeah, that is the way it is."

Joe: "If these blank blank ever come to Florida and ask me what to do and ask me to do them a favor, I won't do it for a million dollars. . . . What are the big guys going to do for us?"

Tony: "Buffa said DeLuca was going to see his lawyer as soon as he got out. . . . He is going to try and put in a fix for you and Paul. . . . Tom said that Joe had his fix in already. . . . You just wait until the time comes and we will come out O.K. You know these government charges are pretty tough, but there is ways of getting around them, too. Money talks. . . . Those big shots have to take care of us and they know it. Unless you are scared to death like Paul, and then they won't do a damned thing for you. Don't think that the big boys are not out to save their own necks, and they will talk too, but they do it in a different way."

Joe: "If anything is ever said about what we talked about in this room and it comes from me, I hope that God strikes me dead."

Joe and Paul Antinori each wound up with five-year sentences. DeLuca and Impostato, the big guys with the power to fix things, got off with three and two years each. Lopiparo's indictment was dismissed for lack of evidence. Carl Carramusa, the crucial informer, was given four years, later reduced and probated. Once out of jail, Carramusa changed his name and moved his family to Chicago, where he tried to make a new life in a woodworking business. One day in June 1945 he was changing a tire in front of his home, while his teenage daughter sat on the porch watching. Another car drove up quickly; a shotgun blast tore off his head. No witnesses came forward, not even the daughter.

After such intelligence breakthroughs as the Kansas City case, Anslinger and his men had a general grasp of the Mafia's nature. The concept was so preposterous, so neatly conspiratorial, that for years most other law enforcement agencies dismissed the Mafia as a myth: a peculiar fantasy maintained at the Bureau of Narcotics, perhaps under the influence of its own contraband. Some salient details, such as the role of the Mafia's national Commission and its regular meetings, would not become clear until much later. But Anslinger and his men understood the basics, and they warned anyone who would listen. "For many years," a bureau memo summed up, "there has been in existence in this country a criminal organization, well-defined at some times and places, and at other periods rather loosely set up. This is composed of persons of Sicilian birth or extraction, often related by blood and marriage, who are engaged in the types of criminal specialties in which a code of terror and reprisal is valuable. These people are sometimes referred to as the MAFIA."

❧ ❧

Senator Royal S. Copeland of New York initiated the first congressional hearings on organized crime. He had been born in

1868 of old WASP stock on a farm outside Detroit. His earliest American ancestor on his father's side had come to Plymouth, Massachusetts, in 1650. As a young man Copeland taught at a country school before taking a medical degree at the University of Michigan. Settled in Ann Arbor, then a town of fifteen thousand people, he taught medicine and engaged in small-town politics, serving two years as a Republican mayor. His first exposure to a wider, national world came through his church. A devout Methodist, he was a delegate to the Methodist Episcopal general conference and became national treasurer of the Epworth League, the Methodist young people's organization. For the rest of his life, when he gave a speech he would address the audience as "brothers and sisters," in the style of his church.

Copeland's life changed markedly when he was forty years old. He moved to New York City to become dean of the New York Homeopathic Medical College and director of Flower Hospital. Yet he retained some aspect of the small-town, civic-minded busybody. During the First World War he went to see Mayor John F. Hylan, concerned about wartime health conditions in the city. Hylan, a Tammany regular and a creation of William Randolph Hearst, responded by making Copeland the city health commissioner. In this post he became quite visible, lecturing the public about preventive medicine and the value of pure food and drugs. He switched to the Democrats and started writing a daily column of health tips for the Hearst newspaper chain, which brought his name to a wider audience.

A political impasse in 1922 landed him in the Senate. The state Democratic party nominated Al Smith for governor and William Randolph Hearst for senator. But Smith refused to run on a ticket with Hearst. In the ensuing confusion, Copeland was thrown in to take Hearst's place as a harmless compromise candidate. Popular upstate and with women voters who read his Hearst column, Copeland—to general amazement—won the election. As a senator, still carrying on with his Hearst column, "the general practitioner of politics" filed many bills for constituents and made many speeches in Congress, usually emptying the hall when he rose to speak. "At Washington everybody likes him," a friendly observer concluded toward the end of Copeland's second term, "but he has made no deep or definite impression on Capitol Hill. He is still the practitioner, running errands for the voters and special groups." He was hard to place in the political landscape: a big-city

Democrat, but conservative; a country doctor, always friendly and helpful in his personal contacts, but tied to Hearst and the Tammany machine.

In his efforts against organized crime, Copeland danced to a tune called by Hearst. For his own muddled reasons, Hearst ordered his newspapers to stage a campaign against racketeering in the spring of 1933. Damon Runyon wrote a series of sixteen unrevealing articles, blared in the Hearst press, on crime conditions around the country. Hearst editorialists urged their readers to join an "Order of the Crusaders," a national group to fight gangsters. And in the Senate, Royal Copeland set up hearings through the Commerce Committee "to destroy this growing evil."

That summer, while his staff made the arrangements, Copeland gave newspaper interviews about his intentions. It was startling, he said, to learn how deeply involved racketeers had become in business, labor, the production of food and clothing and other necessities. "Alien criminals brought methods of violence from abroad," he explained, "and with them, making use of methods particularly our own, a system efficiently organized, thoroughly financed and broadly protected has been developed. That system must be destroyed." (Like Frank Loesch, Copeland was both a gangbuster and a xenophobic bigot. His motives for fighting the underworld were profoundly ambiguous. To harmful, incalculable degrees, the crimes of a few Irish, Jewish, and Italian gangsters reinforced existing prejudices among some WASPs against the honest majority of Irish, Jewish, and Italian Americans.)

In the spring of 1933, Copeland's Tammany friends were reeling from Samuel Seabury's probings, and they were about to lose the mayoralty to Fiorello La Guardia. They surely wanted no added problems from their man Copeland. "It is inconceivable to me," Copeland loyally announced, "that politics should be involved in any sort of racket in this state." The Senate hearings could have no jurisdiction over local rackets, he said, and would deal only with interstate violations such as kidnapping and concealed weapons.

In the fall of 1933, then, Copeland's committee held eight days of hearings in New York, Detroit, and Chicago. "There is a growing conviction in our country that the administration of justice has fallen down," Copeland said in his opening statement. "Everything we buy, every purchased pleasure, every service we employ—the payment for these is made harder because of the added tribute imposed by the underworld. . . . The rats of the underworld have found ways to crawl through the meshes of the law and to carry on their slimy business." Then he gave way to a range of witnesses: prosecutors, cops, criminologists, teachers, social workers, Methodist and Presbyterian ministers, the head of the Boy Scouts, the head of the Girl Scouts, the president of New York's Metropolitan Museum of Art, and police chiefs who described how they kept their communities so remarkably clean. "Organized crime has not been allowed to come into San Francisco," said the police chief of that city, which must have amused Pete McDonough. "It is a well-known fact," said a New York State cop, "that a large percentage of racketeers coming under our observation are aliens." "If we are going to exterminate our foreign army of racketeers, estimated at 400,000," agreed a criminologist from Detroit, "then we need some definite and drastic policy."

Two criminal attorneys from New York, grown rich in the cynical business of defending gangsters, raised the touchy issue of political corruption. "I dare say, Senator Copeland," Samuel Leibowitz testified, "that there is not a detective in the city of New York who cannot, within five hours' time—and that is exaggerated—put his finger on every racketeer from high, if he wanted to, and if he were permitted to." Local law enforcement, he added, was a joke. Big gangsters feared only the intervention of federal authorities. George Z. Medalie explained why: an all but universal alliance between gangsters and urban politicians. "In almost every large city," said Medalie, "your racketeer and your gangster are a part of the machinery for municipal control, and not until politics is divorced from municipal operation will you ever get rid of it." If he dared, Medalie added, he could name four New York politicians controlled by the underworld.

The most startling testimony, because it came from a universally respected authority, was by Lewis Lawes, warden of Sing Sing prison. A year earlier, Lawes had published a best-selling autobiography, *20,000 Years in Sing Sing*. He was known for humane, progressive views on penal reform and the treatment of prisoners. But he showed no comparable restraint in describing crime conditions. Policemen, he said, were as efficient as crooked politicians allowed them to be. He agreed with Samuel Leibowitz: "Everybody in this city in the police department knows who the racketeers are. They know where they are living, what kind of car they have, and what rackets they are in." Crime had become national in scope, and could be met only by declaring national war on it. All major crimes should therefore be made federal offenses. "In the battle with crime, state lines must be utterly abolished," Lawes insisted. If all the relevant authorities would cooperate, gangsters could be wiped out in sixty days, he concluded. "If I were Mussolini I could do it in thirty days. . . . If I cannot have the Constitution changed, I would declare martial law against them— and I am a liberal and realize what that means."

Meantime the Roosevelt administration was conducting its own well-publicized war on crime, and it did not welcome competition from an enemy of the New Deal like Copeland. Roosevelt's aide Raymond Moley showed up at the Copeland hearings to describe the initiatives underway at the White House. "I am here to listen to the suggestions offered and to think them over," Moley testified. "That is about all I have." After his hearings concluded, Copeland submitted a cluster of about thirty crime bills to Roosevelt—mostly minor revisions or cancellations of existing laws. FDR as usual had his own plans. The following spring, the administration pushed its crime package through Congress, extending the Lindbergh kidnapping law, making extortion through interstate mail or by telephone a federal offense, and giving the FBI the power to use guns and make arrests. The publicity churned up by Copeland's hearings presumably helped pass these laws. As for Copeland, he went back to his real passion, a stubborn crusade for a pure food and drug bill.

❦ ❦

Earl Warren, whom Raymond Moley called "the most intelligent and politically independent district attorney in the United States," was the son of Scandinavian immigrants, a Norwegian father— the surname had been Varran—and a Swedish mother. He grew up in Bakersfield, California, where his father worked for the Southern Pacific Railroad as a repairman and shop foreman. "He was devoted to both industry and thrift," Warren said of his father. "He lived a Spartan life, which meant a more or less Spartan life for my mother also. I always thought too Spartan for both of them." Both parents abstained from liquor and tobacco, "not as prohibitionists, but merely as a matter of personal forbearance." The family spent its extra money only on education, on books, music lessons, and lectures. From the age of nine Earl had jobs in summer and before and after school. The first person from Bakersfield's "railroad section" to attend college, he took his undergraduate and law degrees at Berkeley. Following a classic American scenario, he rose by education and hard work from a working-class immigrant childhood to a professional career and (eventually) great influence. He moved up by his own efforts, playing it straight, so he had little patience with anyone who bent rules. "He has a strong sense of moral right," a political associate said later, "and if what you propose doesn't square with that, heaven help you!"

A large, ambling man, persistent rather than brilliant, Warren backed into political life. In 1920 he took a $150-a-month post as an assistant district attorney for Alameda County. The third most populous county in the state, Alameda included Oakland, Berkeley, and—tucked between them—the tawdry little gamblers' town of Emeryville. After five years Warren was appointed acting district attorney and then, in his first election, won the office on his own in 1926. As DA, Warren aimed to set a good example in public and private. When he got married his wife, a Swedish immigrant, received a gift of Chinese jade jewelry from Lim Ben, the main Chinese lottery operator in the county; Warren sent it back and demanded a written receipt. Before Prohibition he had liked to drink. But as district attorney, believing "that I could not honorably prosecute liquor violators in the daytime and then go to parties where hard drinks were served in the evening," Warren and his wife became "almost hermits" until the end of Prohibition. To fill his staff of twenty-five lawyers and ten inspectors, Warren hired mainly young people willing to work long hours at low pay for the legal experience. They were inevitably called Boy Scouts, "and we did have the fervency of the Scout movement," Warren admitted.

Across the street from his office in Oakland was Caddy Wells' Parlor House, a notorious brothel. An entire block of such enterprises throve within three blocks of the county courthouse. Unable to abide the provocation, Warren started closing them, padlocking the houses for a year under an obscure state law, the "Red Light Abatement Act." The loudest objections came not from the madams or the grafting cops who had let the houses run, but from local bankers, furniture retailers, and real-estate men.

The whorehouses, it turned out, paid unusually high rents that supported large mortgages, and they bought expensive furniture at inflated prices. With Oakland's houses shut down, hundreds of men went across the bay to San Francisco at night, hurting Oakland's nightlife and real-estate values. Warren asked the worried businessmen to repeat their complaints to a grand jury; they said they couldn't do that. Warren asked them just to write letters to him stating their positions and offering remedies; a few said they would. But none did. For a long time Warren would run into one of these men and—ever persistent—remind him of the promised letter. Warren would get a mumbled assurance of good intentions and nothing more. For the young DA, this ironic experience showed how deeply and secretly rackets could penetrate into overtly respectable sectors. That insight stuck with him. More than forty years later, as Chief Justice of the United States, he recounted the episode in a major speech on organized crime.

This example of the good citizens in favor of prostitution was only symptomatic: much of the county was a mess. In the city of Alameda, bordering Oakland to the south, the mayor, city manager, and all but one of the councilmen were stealing public funds and forcing merchants to pay protection money. Mike Kelly, the political boss of Oakland, controlled a tight organization undisturbed by crusading lawmen or journalists. John F. Mullins, a county supervisor and part of the Kelly machine, ran the area's railroad and waterfront section, ornamented by the gangster lair of Emeryville. This town of three thousand inhabitants had actually been invented by gamblers. The owners of the Oakland Trotting Park, the local horse track, had incorporated Emeryville in 1896 as a haven for their own pursuits. Since then it had specialized in no-limit draw poker, prostitution, Chinese lotteries, and bootlegging. Emeryville had no police department, and the harmless city council was paid off.

In 1926 a local police chief, Burton F. Becker, was elected sheriff of Alameda County by promising to restore law and order to an alarming situation. But even before he took office, Becker made agreeable financial arrangements with major underworld figures. Warren heard about it and had Becker come to his office. Advised of the malodorous rumors, Becker shrugged them off. Warren warned him two more times. "You take care of your business," Becker replied, "and I will take care of mine." Which

Warren did, by indicting Becker for bribery. The sheriff responded by taking to his bottle and muttering threats. Deep in an alcoholic haze, he would place his gun on the table and describe how he would take care of that Warren. Even Becker's wife told her friends how the DA had better watch out for his children. Warren's wife received a threatening phone call one afternoon; Warren rushed home to comfort her. "A barking dog rarely bites," he said later.

One of Becker's henchmen was found hiding in Los Angeles. Given the choice of testifying against Becker or being indicted for grand larceny, the man agreed to testify—because he feared being killed if handed over to Becker's jail. Until the trial the witness was stashed in a summer home on the Russian River, sixty miles north of Oakland. At the trial, after further hesitation, this man and other criminals told about the payoffs they had made to Becker or his bagmen. The sheriff was convicted and sent to San Quentin prison. "I disliked very much to assume this job of policing the county," Warren recalled, "but it was either that or permit the county to become a sink of organized vice and crime. If the county's authorities did not have integrity, its police departments would deteriorate comparably. There was no other choice than to do it."

Yet Warren's cleanup had distinct limits. Mike Kelly had agreed not to obstruct the Becker investigation, and Warren did not interfere with Kelly's political control of Oakland. If not an explicit arrangement, it was at least a stalemate between adversaries unwilling to risk a direct confrontation. "As a result of the Sheriff's Office convictions," Warren later claimed, "the iniquitous little city of Emeryville became as quiet as a churchyard, and during my later years as district attorney presented no major problems." Again, it was the muted truce of a standoff. Gambling still flourished in Emeryville, and down to the present day it remains one of the last strongholds of old-fashioned, no-limit draw poker.

During his fourteen years as district attorney, no case tried by Warren was ever reversed by a higher court. Trial work still left him anxious, though. "I never heard a jury bring in a verdict of guilty," he said, "but that I felt sick at the pit of my stomach." Each morning at 8:30, six days a week, Warren would meet for an hour with a different group of deputies, each in charge of a specific aspect of the DA's office. He thus kept in touch with all the cases under way but left most of the detail work to his associates. "I could give some time to other things with a broader base, and I did," he said later. "I was particularly interested in coordinating the law enforcement agencies of the entire state to prevent the Prohibition era rackets that had spung up in many of the eastern communities from spreading to California."

From his base in Alameda County, Warren took charge of a statewide board of investigation and of a lawmen's association, pushing the extant crazy-quilt pattern of law enforcement toward professionalization, uniformity, and shared intelligence. After Stanford, Berkeley, and USC turned the idea down, Warren set up a police training school at San Jose State, taught every summer by a faculty of cops, prosecutors, and lab technicians. (Warren still believed in education.) The training school in turn led to a legislative clearinghouse, run through Warren's office, which tracked every bill in the legislature affecting law enforcement. During the legislative session Warren kept an assistant on hand in Sacramento, and the DA often went there to testify about a proposed bill. In 1934 he drew up a constitutional amendment extending the powers of the state attorney general, giving that office the right to step into any local prosecution by replacing a wayward sheriff or district attorney. When the amendment was ratified, Warren decided to run for attorney general himself. In 1938 he filed in all three major party primaries. Nominated by all three, he won the office with no opposition—the only Republican elected to a major state job in California that year.

Taking over from an aged incumbent who had been attorney general for thirty-six years, and with the expanded powers recently conferred by his own amendment, Warren had to reconstruct the office. He found no central filing system, no calendar control of litigation, no system of fiscal accountability, and little supervision of the deputies. To demonstrate the new statewide power of the attorney general, Warren decided to make an example of dog tracks. Dog racing was illegal by state law, but a half-dozen tracks ran on a staggered schedule all year at various places around the state, tolerated or ignored by the local cops. When Warren took office the only dog track running at the time was Black Jack Jerome's in El Cerrito, just across the county line from Alameda County. The ferocious Jerome, formerly a hired strikebreaker, was told to come see Warren, who gave him the bad news. Jerome asked if he might stay open just through Saturday night. Warren said he could not formally authorize any such lawbreaking, but since it was then Wednesday he doubted he would be ready to move before Saturday. Jerome's track then closed for good on Saturday. Jerome took his money, invested in parking garages in San Francisco, and died a rich man. Later on, when other dog tracks gave signs of doing business, Warren would send someone to ask the operators, "Do you think you are tougher than Black Jack Jerome?" Apparently none did, and no dogs ran.

Despite his thunderous reputation, Jerome was small time, without dangerous ties to the underworld beyond El Cerrito. What most concerned Warren was that major criminal gangs from the East, especially Chicago and New York, were moving into California. "The main thrust of my activities as attorney general," he said later, "was against any intrusion of organized crime." For years many eastern gangsters had been spending winter vacations in southern California. "When the snow flies," the saying went, "the hoodlums fly with the snow." During the winter months crime decreased in eastern cities while it increased in Los Angeles. Some of these winter visitors took up permanent places in the sun. The resident associates of Jack Dragna, the Mafia boss of southern California, included Frank Bompensiero of Milwaukee, Johnny Roselli of Chicago, and Joe Sica of New Jersey. Dragna was briefly arrested in 1931 and charged with having ties to the Capone gang. As part of the national Italian ascendancy in organized crime, Dragna began to assert himself in the mid-1930s. He and Roselli informed the leading bookies in Los Angeles they had new partners. "Who in the hell is Dragna?" one of the bookies wondered. After knocking over a few bookie joints around town, the Italians were cut in.

However, Jack Dragna was a parochial, old-country Sicilian who had come to America for good at the late age of twenty-three. He was also limited by the absence of a real city government in Los Angeles. With no political machine in place, he had few politicians to corrupt. He was protected by close ties to the Lucchese Mafia family in New York, but the stronger Luciano family decided he needed help. Around 1935 Bugsy Siegel moved from New York to Los Angeles for that purpose. "Jack wasn't pulling the counties or the political picture together," according to Mickey Cohen, who himself arrived from Chicago a few years later. "There wasn't even a casino open. There was no combination; everyone was acting

independently. The organization had to pour money on to help
Dragna at all times. So Benny come out here to get things moving
good." For Dragna it was embarrassing to be displaced, and by a
New York Jew at that. "Dragna was really from the old moustache
days," Cohen elaborated. "The worst thing you can do to an old-
time Italian mahoff is to harm his prestige in any way, and that's
what took place when Benny came out here."

Siegel rented a home on McCarthy Drive in Beverly Hills,
joined the snooty Hillcrest Country Club, and enrolled his two
daughters in a private school and riding academy. He made
friends easily at Hollywood studios and was often seen with his pal
George Raft, mingling at the new Clover Club casino on Sunset
Boulevard. He told people he wanted to become an actor. "The
most fascinating young man," as the screenwriter Anita Loos
remembered him: "tall, dark, and rather Italian in appearance."
(His Italian bosses may have picked him for the assignment
because as a Jew he might move more easily among the Jewish
moguls of Hollywood.) Later Siegel built a $200,000 mansion in
the Holmby Hills area above Los Angeles, thirty-five rooms in
size, with the master bathroom done in maroon marble. He was
said to have an interest in every gambling enterprise in the Los
Angeles area, including the Clover Club, and he performed other
tasks as requested. On Thanksgiving Day in 1939, he drove the
getaway car as Frankie Carbo, a Mafia gunman from the Lucchese
family, killed a gangster named Big Greeney Greenberg outside
his Hollywood home.

With eastern money behind him, the ever resourceful Tony
Cornero—the most notorious California bootlegger of the
1920s—emerged again and caught Earl Warren's attention. After
getting out of jail in 1931, Cornero had caused no trouble for a
while, tending quietly to his oil interests in Corpus Christi, Texas.
The IRS tried to collect $5,907 worth of taxes owed on the
bootlegging case that had put him in jail. "I dont owe you
anything or never did owe you anything," he wrote the feds.
"Your volumeous records were probably made up by some
super-diligent investigator seeking to agrandize his own position
in the eyes of his superior. . . . I cannot argue with the United
States government, because it has nothing to do but argue and I
am busy trying to make a living. Further, I have been paying my
Income Taxes in recent years religiously, and if you insist up on

putting a plaster on me you cause me to lose interest in trying to make money because of the said unjust plaster hanging over my head waiting to swoope down on any little earnings that I might have. So therefore you would stop me by your said actions to cease being a prolific tax payer, and therefor a direct loss as a tax payer to the government. Hopeing the above will cause you to with draw your claim and let me live." Arguing that he had already paid a $5,000 fine in the case, Cornero offered to settle for $100.

Since the 1920s, gangsters had been operating gambling ships anchored off the southern California coast. Beyond the three-mile limit, high rollers could play games that might get them arrested ashore. Lucrative and apparently unbustable, the gambling ships drew outside investors. One night in 1930, at two o'clock in the morning, Los Angeles cops arrested Jack Dragna, Johnny Roselli, and Charles Fischetti of the Capone gang in a car with a night's receipts from one of these gambling ships. By 1938 there were four such floating casinos: the *Tango* and *Showboat* off Long Beach and the *Texas* and *Rex* off Santa Monica. Of the four, Tony Cornero's *Rex* was the most elaborate. Financed in part by Bugsy Siegel and the Capones, the *Rex* boasted an array of slot machines, roulette wheels, and dice and blackjack tables. It was anchored by cables at the four points of the compass, so the boat could be maneuvered not to take waves broadside; naval men came to study the arrangement. The *Rex* had a telephone line to the Santa Monica pier, three miles away, to bring race results and allow bookmaking on board. All the gambling ships advertised in full-page newspaper ads, on billboards and over the radio, even by skywriting, proclaiming their wares and advising patrons where to catch the water taxis. "With things like this going on," Attorney General Warren told the head of his criminal division, Warren Olney III, "nobody can take us seriously when we're talking about dog tracks and gambling houses on the shore." Olney spent days in a law library, coming up with the necessary legal arguments, and the four ships were raided simultaneously on an afternoon in August 1939.

Three of them were boarded easily, but Cornero decided to stand and fight. A heavy steel door and an iron mesh gate blocked the gangway. Three fire hoses played on the lawmen, pushing them back. Tossing bottles of imported brandy to the press boats circling the fray, Cornero yelled his defiance through a megaphone. The lawmen could not get aboard, but they could prevent Cornero from leaving the *Rex*. Both sides settled into a blockade. "I won't give up the ship!" Cornero announced after two days. "We've got plenty of provisions and we're having a good time. I'm not worrying none." Finally after ten days, out of food and patience, Cornero surrendered. He settled the case by forfeiting the *Rex* and its gambling equipment, paying about $26,000 in expenses, taxes, and penalties, and by promising not to operate gambling ships in the future.

The *Rex* episode made national headlines and entertained the public for months. But Warren could not substantially affect the more general problem of inroads into California by eastern gangsters. An elaborate case against Moe Annenberg's wire service operations in the state, labored over for two years by Warren and his staff, was thrown out by the state supreme court, no explanation given. After four years as attorney general, Warren was elected governor of California. With his nemesis safely occupied in Sacramento, Tony Cornero launched another gambling ship.

❧ ❧

Thomas E. Dewey, the most celebrated racketbuster of the 1930s, came from Owosso, Michigan, twenty-five miles west of Flint. His father edited the newspaper in this small town of eight thousand people, its wide streets lined with maple trees, its political life uncomplicated by diversity. "It was assumed that all good people were Republicans," Dewey recalled, only half kidding. (He didn't kid around much.) The first Thomas Dewey in America had settled in Dorchester, Massachusetts, in 1634. The Deweys lived in New England for over two centuries until Tom's grandfather, a crusading abolitionist and prohibitionist, moved to Michigan just before the Civil War. He bought the *Owosso Times* and used it to inveigh against everything that looked evil—a tendency passed on to his grandson.

Tom was a good boy, never late or absent in twelve years of school, congenitally serious and striving. One summer he read most of the works of Shakespeare. "Life was always very full and busy. There wasn't any opportunity for juvenile delinquency. There was too much to do, both by way of fun and working," Dewey said later. "Our home was always comfortable and it was a lovely atmosphere. I could not remember ever hearing my mother and father have an argument." His mother was a strong Episcopalian. They went to church every Sunday—"it was one of those things we took for granted"—and Tom was confirmed in his early teens. (Later on he was a vestryman and always said grace before dinner.) After graduating from the University of Michigan he went on to Columbia Law School and then stayed in New York to work for a Wall Street firm.

As a midwestern Republican WASP in Jimmy Walker's New York of the 1920s, Dewey was drawn into reform politics. "I'd heard from my father and others that Tammany Hall was the epitome of all evil," he later recalled, "and I found it to be true." With other members of a Young Republican Club he served as a poll watcher on election day in 1928. At a school on 110th Street he saw gangsters bring in unregistered voters while the cops avoided noticing. "The Dutch Schultz mob had people there for the Democrats," Dewey said thirty years later, "and there were gangsters with guns that you could see sticking through their clothes at each of the polling places in the school. When some obviously unfit voter would come in, they'd raise such a hullabaloo that everybody was intimidated, and the public did nothing, nor did the police.... Some of my friends got beaten up in that election." Nothing like this ever happened in Owosso. The episode remained with Dewey for a long time. For several years after the election, Dewey's group of Young Republicans met every few weeks to discuss reform strategies—a quixotic mission until the advent of Samuel Seabury. Some of these Young Republican associates would stay with Dewey for the rest of his career.

"We were seeing massive, organized, orchestrated crime for the first time in America, and the public was fed to the teeth," said Dewey of his early racketbusting days. "In the 1930s and in the years that followed, it seemed to me that organized crime, linked with corruption in government, was the greatest single threat to our freedom in America." The solution, as he saw it, was to reverse the course of history: to return to an older, simpler, uncorrupted vision of America, to make New York more like Owosso. "We would return to the way of common honesty," he vowed, back to "a revival of our traditional concepts of justice" and "the restoration of a sense of public morality and the redefinition of an example to be set to our children."

A contact through his law firm brought him into the United States attorney's office for New York as the chief assistant. In March 1931, nine days short of his twenty-ninth birthday, he took charge of a staff of sixty lawyers, most of them older than their new boss. Of average height and build, Dewey always looked smaller and younger than he really was. His guileless, boyish face gained definition only from the trademark mustache. Among themselves, newspaper reporters at the criminal courts took to calling him the Boy, short for the Boy Scout. Perhaps in compensation, needing to demonstrate his seriousness, he projected a chilling, humorless sobriety. "He never was a great relaxer," an associate remarked. "He did not luxuriate around the office, chinning or passing the time of day." He did have serious business at hand.

In the most elaborate effort of this first phase of his gangbusting, Dewey stalked the bootlegger Waxey Gordon, known as Public Enemy Number One in New York. A special IRS unit, assigned to the Al Capone case in Chicago, was transferred to New York and the Gordon case following Capone's conviction in the fall of 1931. Preening themselves after nailing Capone, supposing they knew a little about how to catch gangster tax delinquents, the IRS men collided with the "glacial perfection" of young Dewey. "Dewey was the perfectionist to end all perfectionists," said Elmer Irey, head of the IRS unit. "His thoroughness is beyond description, although some of my boys made some handsome efforts to describe it in exquisite flights of profanity." An IRS agent, after what he thought was a careful, finished investigation, would sit down with Dewey to present the evidence. Dewey "would look off into space for a couple of minutes," according to Irey, "then turn his attention back to the agent. He would then bestow a smile—a medium smile, at that—on the agent and methodically tear the perfectly good evidence to shreds with about a million questions, give or take ten. Wearily the agent would leave, determined to get more evidence. He got more, of course, and that is what Dewey wanted."

The Gordon investigation lasted almost three years. For the final six months, six government lawyers and a dozen IRS agents worked full-time on it; they really wanted Gordon. Two hundred bank accounts and the toll slips of over one hundred thousand telephone calls were sifted. At some New Jersey banks, government agents would request records and be told to wait; while they sat there, Gordon's men would suddenly, mysteriously arrive to withdraw the accounts in question and remove all the evidence. In Hoboken, local cops arrested the feds and held them on contrived charges of forged credentials until the records they sought were made to disappear. Despite such examples of how far Gordon's power reached, the agents closed in on him. He had endorsed checks with his own and other names, and handwriting experts showed that all the signatures were in Gordon's hand. Like the politicians writhing before Samuel Seabury, Waxey Gordon in his apparent impregnability had made the mistake of using banks.

The case came to trial in November 1933, with Dewey representing the government. "His courtroom technique was superb," noted Elmer Irey, who had seen many trials. "I don't think Dewey ever forgot anything in his life. He generally kept his fine voice very low but he could do all sorts of tricks with it. And he never lost his temper unless he thought it good tactics to do so." For the year 1930 Gordon had reported an income of $8,000, on which he had paid a tax of $10.76. The prosecution estimated his beer income alone for that year at $1,338,000, and at $1,026,000 for 1931. With penalties and interest, he owed a million dollars. Gordon took the stand, admitted his bootlegging, but said the nature of the business prevented recordkeeping. "There's something you don't understand, Mr. Dewey," said Gordon. "We never ask questions in the beer business." The jury deliberated for only fifty-one minutes, found Gordon guilty on all counts, and gave him ten years in prison. Afterward the judge described the prosecution's conduct as "astounding"—"The spectacle of four or five young men under such a young leader presenting this complicated case in a manner that could not be surpassed by the most experienced or the most famous trial lawyer, has left with the court a sense of admiration."

A few weeks after the Gordon trial, a Democrat appointed by FDR took over the U.S. attorney's office, and Dewey returned to private practice with an enhanced reputation. Eighteen months later he was called back to racketbusting. A grand jury had been (once again) probing New York's underworld. "We were just an average bunch of citizens," explained the jury foreman, a businessman named Lee Thompson Smith, "whose names were drawn from the grand jury wheel—a wholesale butcher, a manufacturer, a real estate man, a coal dealer—twenty-three men of about the same caliber as you'll find on most grand juries. The city was full of talk of rackets, open or secretive, and we began nosing into it as part of our job. And were we surprised! We discovered almost every line of business in the city was getting threats from racketeers, or already paying them off." The Manhattan district attorney would not cooperate, so the jury bolted; it excluded the DA's men from the proceedings and demanded that a special prosecutor be appointed. The jury wanted Dewey for the job, but the DA said no. The grand jury took its case to New York's Governor Herbert H. Lehman. He suggested the prosecutor be chosen from a list of four senior, distinguished New York lawyers; all four declined and urged the selection of Dewey. So Dewey became the special prosecutor.

Instead of taking on a staff hired by someone else, he could now pick his own. Given his reputation, and all the unemployed talent around New York during the Depression, he was besieged with applicants: three thousand for twenty slots as lawyers, seven hundred for ten as accountants, five hundred for twenty as secretaries. Dewey chose carefully. Fourteen of the twenty lawyers he hired came out of Columbia or Harvard Law School. ("You know," he told a man from the Brooklyn School of Law, "you're the only one I'm interviewing from a lousy law school.") The oldest attorney on the staff was only forty, seven years senior to Dewey. "We were all young enough to be very ardent crusaders," one of his men said later. "We were battling the whole, organized underworld in New York City, and we were the forces of decent living." As young enthusiasts, contemptuous of the occluded legal structures that had failed to enforce the law, Dewey's people were said to be arrogant and impatient. Simply being hired from so competitive a field could swell a lawyer's pride. "There was an air of cockiness in the office," one man later conceded. "There was a truculence, a swaggering toughness about them. . . . It was an interesting job and you had the world by the tail. It couldn't have been easy to live with guys like that."

Half of Dewey's lawyers were Jews, including three of his top four assistants, the main trial strategist, and the most respected legal scholar in the office. Again Dewey took advantage of the historical moment. At the time even the brightest Jewish lawyers might be shut out of New York's old-line law firms; so they were hired by Dewey to chase racketeers, many of whom were Jewish.

"It was a fact of life that there were Jewish criminals," recalled Jacob Grumet, one of Dewey's Jews; "no one liked to see them but there they were." Stanley H. Fuld—"our real law man and brain," according to Dewey—found legal precedents, went over points of law, and drew up almost every indictment that Dewey filed. Sol Gelb, the trial strategist, would quickly digest the salient facts of a case and plan the right approach with dazzling, impossible speed. "Sometimes this quality used to drive Dewey with his passion for thoroughness almost nuts," a staff member said later, "but Gelb seldom if ever erred." At one point, worried for political reasons that his staff was too Jewish, Dewey told his investigators to go out and hire some Irish Catholics. They came back with Ed Walsh, Jim O'Malley, and Herman McCarthy, who turned out to be Methodist, Presbyterian, and Jewish.

Surrounded by headstrong stallions straining at their traces, Dewey held the reins tightly. Nobody thought he was smarter or worked harder than the boss. "He could quell any uprising with one look," someone recalled, "and he was tough enough himself so that nobody fooled around with him." Anyone who spoke up at a staff meeting just to brag or to curry favor would have his head bitten off. "You are all lazy," Dewey told one meeting. "In heaven's name, learn how to write English and to write it so that it makes sense." He cautioned his people not to leave themselves vulnerable to blackmail or indiscretions by going where gangsters went. If you want to have fun, it was said, better leave Manhattan and head over into New Jersey. "I would like to prohibit night clubs," Dewey admonished, "and I think the race track is probably not a very good place to be, but if you have an overwhelming yen for the races I suppose it is all right. About prize fights . . . I don't think that is bad, and if anybody wants to go to a conspicuous fight, it is all right. But I warn you to watch where you go and with whom."

Dewey began his work as special prosecutor with general targets—industrial rackets, policy gambling, prostitution—and the small fish who operated them. But the man who had put Waxey Gordon in jail most wanted to catch the big guys. Dutch Schultz, for example, controlled the vast empire of policy gambling in Harlem and the lower Bronx. Back when he was in the U.S. attorney's office, Dewey had tried to convict Schultz of tax evasion. Schultz had fled the indictment, surrendering only after Dewey had left office. His first trial on the charge then foundered on a hung jury, his second in an acquittal. "Gentlemen," the judge addressed the jury afterward, "a verdict such as you have just rendered shakes the confidence of law-abiding people. You have reached a verdict based not upon the evidence, but on some other motives." This escape from justice only enhanced the Dutchman's jittery sense of his own invulnerability.

By 1935 Schultz was the last major non-Italian hoodlum still functioning on his own in New York; everyone else was dead, jailed, exiled, or allied with Italians. Schultz and his gang were alone, with the creeping megalomania of a Napoleon complex. The Dutchman's lawyer, Dixie Davis, gave him a biography of Napoleon to read, not imagining how it would affect his personality. "For months thereafter he would sit brooding about Napoleon and Schultz," Davis recalled. "Henceforth the Dutchman refused to realize what changes were taking place in the underworld . . . thinking of himself as a scheming, powerful, Napoleonic figure." Two great leaders, the Dutchman mused, both hounded by lesser men . . .

Always noisily erratic and unpredictable, Schultz acted crazier and crazier. One day he was arguing with one of his men, Jules Martin, about money. As Davis watched, Schultz suddenly ended the argument by pulling his gun, sticking it into Martin's mouth, and shooting him dead. Davis was a lawyer, a member of the bar, and by mob convention he was not supposed to witness such crimes. "It is wrong in the underworld to kill a fellow for no reason at all," Davis said later. "You have got to have a reason. . . . The Dutchman did that murder just as casually as if he were picking his teeth."

Isolated within the underworld, loonier all the time, Schultz now felt Dewey bearing down on him again. Striking out, he conceived the ultimate lunacy: kill Dewey. It would have breached the underworld rule of not harming honest lawmen. Yet Dewey had the gangsters so worried that the idea had even been discussed at a meeting of the five Mafia family bosses in New York. Albert Anastasia, second-in-command of the Mangano family, had argued for killing Dewey. "The audacity of his suggestion made the Fathers pause in disbelief," recalled Joe Bonanno, who was there. "The rest of us turned to Luciano to see how he reacted. Lucky hesitated to give his view. Since Albert and Lucky were such close friends it could have been the case that

Lucky had let Albert make his suggestion to see how the rest of us felt about it. In any case, both Albert and Lucky seemed at least willing to entertain such a stupid notion, whereas the rest of us were totally against it. Seeing us recoil at the suggestion of killing a law-enforcement agent, Luciano deferred the matter to the other Fathers present, all of whom rejected it outright." So when the Italians learned that Schultz was planning to hit Dewey, they decided to kill Schultz first—thereby both avoiding a messy complication and removing their last big underworld rival in New York. The contract went to Jewish gunmen in Lepke Buchalter's gang. They shot the Dutchman on October 23, 1935, as he was taking a piss at the Palace Chop House in Newark.

A while later Lucky Luciano summoned Dixie Davis to a tenement on the East Side. Davis was scared but knew he could not refuse the Mafioso. "My knees trembled as we climbed the dark, evil-smelling stairs. I was led into a shabby kitchen, and there sat a swarthy, hard-eyed man with six guns before him on a table. He was cleaning them." In the front room, "surrounded by all the leaders of the Italian mob," sat Charlie Lucky. He spoke pleasantly, sympathetically, though Davis thought he saw a hard glint in his eye. "All I want you to do," he said, "is tell me about the Dutchman's affairs." Davis quickly recited what he knew about Schultz's enterprises. "His investments," said Luciano. "You would know about those." Davis replied that he knew of no investments, hoping Luciano would belive him. Apparently he did, because he let Davis go. "The boss himself had given me permission to quit," Davis concluded. "The Italians had moved in, and so far as I was concerned they were welcome to everything they found."

With Schultz fortuitously removed for them, Dewey's staff picked up an inquiry into prostitution. After twists and surprises the trail led to Luciano, the biggest fish of all. It started when Eunice Hunton Carter of Dewey's staff heard stories that the whores in Harlem were all bossed by a single organization. The only black and the only woman among Dewey's lawyers, Carter had been hired to work on policy gambling in Harlem; in that undertaking she learned of the prostitution ring. Dewey resisted the idea at first, but eventually Carter and others on the staff persuaded him to authorize a full investigation. What they turned up was another aspect of the Italian takeover. Prostitution in New York, formerly dominated by Jewish procurers, madams, and

whores, was yielding to Italian gangsters with their Jewish partners. A "combination" controlled the business, led by Tommy the
Bull Pennochio, Jimmy Frederico, Little Davie Betillo (whose
name was also spelled Petillo), and Abie the Jew Wahrman.

Indictments were brought—not including Luciano—and eighty
whorehouses were raided on a night in January 1936. About one
hundred women were arrested, along with various pimps and
procurers. "We just locked them up," Dewey said later, "held
them in high bail as material witnesses not knowing whether they
were going to testify or where they were going to fit in the jig
saw." Under pressure and threats (some of the women were
addicts suddenly removed from their dope sources), the prisoners
began to talk. Luciano's name came up—exactly what Dewey's
inquisitors wanted to hear. Meantime a New York cop assigned to
Dewey's office, Anthony E. Mancuso, developed his private
sources on the East Side. About two weeks after the raids,
Mancuso submitted his conclusions: "Petillo is of greater importance to the current investigation than assumed. He has been
classified as of lesser importance than Jimmy Frederico and Tom
Pennochio but is in reality the real leader of the syndicate, making
direct contact with Lucky Luciano." At one time a favored
member of Al Capone's gang, Betillo had returned to New York
after Capone's conviction and connected with the Luciano organization. "Petillo was taken under the wing of Luciano," Mancuso
reported, "and since this organization has a hand in most every
racket in the city, Petillo because of this direct connection with
Luciano was the most important man in the vice racket. Petillo's
youthful appearance tends to divert police suspicion from his
importance." If Betillo was the real boss of the prostitution
combination—so the thinking now ran—and if Betillo was so close
to Luciano, ergo Luciano was the real culprit.

"We were always interested in the boss," Dewey recalled, "and
in no one else. "Luciano was added to the prostitution indictments.
As afraid of Dewey as any other gangster, Luciano then acted
guilty by hiding out in Hot Springs, Arkansas. The local government in Hot Springs was so corruptible that extraditing Luciano
was not easy. Dewey pulled every imaginable string and sent two
of his detectives down to Arkansas. "As you know," he wrote to
one of these detectives, "but which I do not think you should
discuss or disclose, Luciano as the executive head of the racket did
not personally place any women in houses. I think that you should

play on the theme of his importance in his many rackets and on the fact that he is indicted as the chief of all organized vice in New York, but I do not think you can safely admit that he did not personally place the women or the courts will use that to hang their hats on. . . . This case will not be decided on law or the facts probably, but on the amount of fuss you can make, and you may have to issue statements to the Press and make a real first class row." After elaborate efforts and a crucial mistake by Luciano's lawyers, he was taken from the Hot Springs jail, locked into a railroad car stateroom, and rushed home. He was held under bail of $350,000, the highest to that point in New York State history.

Yet could they prove that Luciano was not merely Betillo's boss, but demonstrably in active charge of the prostitution ring? They never found the direct evidence, though they came close. In the fall of 1933, they learned, a group of Jewish procurers and bonders was ordered to a meeting with Betillo and other Italians at a café on Broome Street. When Luciano entered the room all the Italians stood up to greet him, "just as if he were a general." Betillo spoke to him in Italian, after which Luciano addressed the whole group: "Listen, you fellows are all through; from now on Little Davie is taking over the bonding." At other times, when trying to assert his own authority, Betillo would flourish Luciano's name. Later, in the fall of 1935, Luciano complained about the use of his name; prostitution was too much trouble, he said, not enough money in it—they shouldn't be involved. Betillo convinced him to give it more time. It was always Betillo's enterprise, though. Luciano lent his approval and the force of his underworld reputation, but—apparently—nothing more than that.

Dewey brought Luciano and the others to trial in May 1936. A few prostitutes and procurers testified that Luciano was the real boss, but they were too far down in the organization to know for sure. One important and willing underworld witness, Benny Spiller, was not called to testify because he had insisted he did not know Luciano. Charlie Lucky's attorneys again served him poorly by maintaining he had never even met the other defendants. Telephone records and witnesses at Luciano's hotel easily proved otherwise. Calling Luciano "the greatest gangster in America," Dewey brought up the narcotics case back in 1923, when Luciano had turned informer to avoid a heroin conviction.

Dewey: "What were you—a stool pigeon?"

Luciano: "I told him what I knew."

"Were you a stool pigeon?"

"I says, I told him what I knew."

"For a consideration?"

"I don't know what you mean by that."

Dewey addressed the jury in summation. "I could not break the entire underworld," he said. "I guess probably we have in this case more underworld testimony than has ever been produced in any twenty cases before in American history. More people have broken that unwritten rule, 'Thou shalt not squeal,' because they had to; because they had to, they were not voluntary." All the major defendants were found guilty. Luciano got thirty to fifty years, an extraordinary sentence for a mere prostitution case. Dewey and his racketbusters were so good at their jobs, and so well regarded by the jury, that they convicted Luciano of one of the few crimes he had *not* committed. "I have been in many rackets," he later admitted to a prison psychiatrist, "but not in that one."

(Nine months after the trial, three of the prostitutes who had implicated Luciano recanted their testimony. Even among his convict friends in prison, with whom he in underworld fashion might have bragged about his exploits, Luciano always insisted on his innocence. Years later, the gangster Joe Bendix confided to a Luciano biographer that Dewey had induced him to help frame Luciano. And Polly Adler, New York's most famous madam, delivered an emphatic vote for acquittal in her memoirs, published in 1953. "I was astonished to learn that he [Dewey] was seeking to link Charlie (Lucky) Luciano with the prostitution racket," Adler wrote. "It was inconceivable to me that any such connection could exist. For one thing, I used to supply the girls when Charlie Lucky entertained in his plushy hotel suites, and it hardly seems logical that if he had the alleged tie-ups, he would patronize a madam outside the combine. Of course it was no secret that Charlie Lucky was mixed up in all sorts of rackets . . . but not once was it ever even implied that he derived any part of his income from prostitution. I think Mr. Dewey never called me as a witness because the only testimony I could possible give was in favor of the defense. . . . Certainly I believe that in the many years I was associated with prostitution if there had been even a hint of a rumor of a tie-up between Charlie and the combination, I would have heard of it.")

Dewey went on to other prosecutions. In 1937 Samuel Seabury and the Fusion leadership persuaded him to run for district attorney. By then he was a national figure; whenever a movie newsreel showed his face, the theater audience would applaud. A syndicated pundit declared Dewey the most admired young man since Charles Lindbergh. Damon Runyon told a Dewey story in his column: a Broadway guy on the street was approached by a panhandler sporting a neat black mustache who said, "I'd like a word with you." "Guilty, Mr. Dewey," said the guy with a resigned tone. No, said the panhandler, he was only looking for a small touch. "The mustache fooled me," said the guy. "Here's a dollar for you."

Dewey was elected DA and went after New York's corrupt politicians. "Today," he said in April 1938, "there is not a racketeer of first importance left in New York." Later that year he narrowly missed being elected governor of New York. In 1940 he made his first run for the presidency.

Lucky Luciano was sent to Dannemora prison. (Frank Costello replaced him as boss of the strongest Mafia family in New York.) Isolated in the far reaches of northern New York, Dannemora was known as "Siberia" in the underworld. One prisoner cleaned Luciano's cell in return for gifts of cigarettes, candy, cakes, and salami. Another convict was paid to do Luciano's prison work in the laundry. Davie Betillo prepared his food. Dressed in a silk shirt and pants with a razor crease, Luciano spent his time playing gin rummy and hanging around the handball court, professing his innocence. "He practically ran the place," a prison guard marveled. "He used to stand there in the yard like he was the warden. Men waited in line to talk to him. Charlie Lucky would listen, say something and then wave his hand. The guy would actually *back* away. It was something to watch."

❧ ❧

History seldom arrays itself so neatly. In the decades after 1920, organized crime developed by a pattern of provocation and response. WASPs fretting over the drinking habits of non-WASPs had imposed Prohibition. That gave rise to a bootlegging trade run mainly by Irish, Jewish, and Italian Americans. WASPs like Mabel Willebrandt and Emory Buckner tried to enforce Prohibition. When the dry years ended, the non-WASP bootleggers created a national system of organized crime with an American Mafia at its core. Other WASP reformers then tried to subdue the flourishing underworld, winning many battles but few wars.

For WASPs, enforcing the law was the same as enforcing themselves, given their class and historical advantages. The American legal and political system was derived from British traditions of common law and representative government. Since the founding of the American republic, WASPs had been running the legal machinery. They were more inclined to play by the rules because the rules were their own. The immigrant gangsters came from different traditions. Italians in southern Italy and Sicily, Irish Catholics in Great Britain, and Jews in eastern and southern Europe all had bitter reasons to distrust the law as distant, unfriendly, and beyond reach. Instead of the American traditions of orderly, impersonal contractual relations and a respect for such abstractions as laws, the immigrant cultures depended on local, tangible, personal bonds, and ultimate loyalties to persons instead of to abstractions. Laws were made by other people, for other people.

Yet an analysis that emphasizes class status and privilege goes only so far. Frank Loesch, Harry Anslinger, and Earl Warren were all first-generation Americans, not born to wealth. In making their own way upward they took routes available to most other sons of immigrants, with the edge of being WASP men swimming in a WASP men's sea. The only common ground they shared with their fellow WASP racketbusters Samuel Seabury, Royal Copeland, and Thomas Dewey was that all were Protestants descended from immigrants from Great Britain and northern Europe. They all to some degree were prodded by a Protestant conscience, that unrelenting internal monitor. "The fact stands out like a sore thumb," said Royal Copeland at his rackets hearings in 1933, "that there has been a serious decline in churchgoing and a marked increase in crime. You must draw your own conclusions from these figures."

Protestants and Catholics in these unecumenical years lived in different ways, proud of the differences. The Catholic Church, part of childhood for most Irish and Italian gangsters, arranged a forgiving structure of mediators—sacraments, saints, miracles—between heaven and fallible mortals. The Protestants had dispensed with all that in favor of a demanding God up there and a worried individual human down here, with only Christ to help out. "It broke the continuity," Peter Berger has suggested, "cut the umbilical cord between heaven and earth, and thereby threw man back upon himself in a historically unprecedented manner." Protestants could not well escape their internal need to play the game straight; the Protestant God expected nothing less. Catholics were overtly handed more prescriptive rules by their church about how to behave—but they also were cushioned by a structure of confession and penance, of expiation and forgiveness. "Protestantism is not as oppressive in its *laws* as Catholicism is; it is oppressive in its *attitude* toward law," as Michael Novak has summarized the matter. "The Catholic spirit leaves judgment of the soul in God's hands alone, distinguishes sharply between the external forum and the internal forum, and expects its laws to cover outward conduct merely and internal conduct only insofar as the person so chooses." For the WASP gangbusters, then, chasing hoodlums was in part a religious mission.

This train of thought also has its limits, though. Neither class nor religious analysis can explain a basic mystery: why a small minority of Irish, Jewish, and Italian immigrants became gangsters while the huge majority of their peers, contending as immigrants with the same obstacles, still worked hard and lived honest lives. Lepke Buchalter had three brothers; one was a rabbi, one a pharmacist, one a dentist. Lepke went into the rackets. It came down to choices made. For reasons ultimately beyond explanation, buried in the mysteries of private, unconscious motivation, some individuals chose the underworld.

"Being an uneducated person," said Mickey Cohen, "what walk of life could I have gotten into that I could have become involved with such people? I'm not talking about racket people. I'm talking about celebrities, politicians, people in higher walks of life and education and different things like that." Instead of the dull job and meager income for which he was equipped, Cohen enjoyed bright lights, easy money, easy women. Gangsters loved their work and enjoyed reminiscing about it, sometimes to their misfortune. And always that focused, vitalized, existential moment of doing the crime, committing the murder. "Yeah, I would be lying if I said I didn't enjoy giving a guy a deal," Cohen admitted. "The chances that you took was just part and parcel—they made it more invigorating, they added to the challenge of it." "It wasn't that I craved for anything," said a Chicago gangster in looking back. "It was more the excitement than anything else. It was more fun getting the apple than it was eating it."

Organized crime was hard to wipe out, always being replenished by new recruits, because it took so little aptitude to become a gangster. A man needed only willingness and a limited coolness under pressure. With a few exceptions, gangsters were remarkably stupid and ignorant, dim of bulb and narrow of horizon. Robert Sylvester of the *New York Daily News* covered Broadway and nightclubs for decades, encountering many gangsters as a reporter. "I never met a professional hoodlum," he concluded, "who was a wit, a good conversationalist, showed a likeable personality or gave any evidence of having brains enough to do anything worthwhile."

Even gangsters, though, felt human emotions. They loved their sons and spun the usual hopes for them. As time passed, the sons of Irish and Jewish hoodlums typically climbed into the upperworld. The sons of Italian gangsters were more liable to remain in crime. During these years, in general, Italians had neither the Irish access to the structures of church and politics nor the Jewish knack for business and higher education. What the Italians did have was durable family ties, strong fathers bound to their sons, fathers whom the sons wanted to emulate. "Pop always said," one Italian hoodlum in New York recalled of his hoodlum father, "that he trusted Italians more than Americans, Sicilians more than Italians, his *paesani* more than other Sicilians, but most of all he trusted his family." Even Mafiosi who were habitually unfaithful to their wives remained attentive, loving fathers and—in their way—good husbands. Lines between generations were unbroken by the diseases of alcoholism, neurotic family patterns, or too much education. Italians were more liable to stay within their ethnic cultures and neighborhoods, less likely to move up and out, more likely to preserve the bond from grandfather to father to son, unless disrupted by schooling and modern progress. So the sons of Mafiosi often became Mafiosi in turn.

To leave the underworld was not simple, for either a gangster or his son. Artful Eddie O'Hare of the Capone gang was devoted to his only son, peppering his conversation with the latest exploits of "my son, Butch." He hoped Butch might attend the naval academy at Annapolis, but he knew such an appointment would be jeopardized by his own criminal history. To break with Capone, then, and—as he explained it—to get Butch into Annapolis, O'Hare became an informer, feeding the government crucial tips about Capone's tax case. According to an IRS agent working on the case, O'Hare's assistance was "the most important single factor resulting in the conviction of Al Capone." But Capone apparently learned of O'Hare's treachery. From jail in 1937 he threatened to kill O'Hare. Two years later, just before Capone was released, O'Hare was murdered in gangster style. Butch O'Hare did go to Annapolis. In World War II he was a navy pilot, shooting down seven Japanese planes in one dogfight, receiving the Congressional Medal of Honor, before he was killed in action. The airport in Chicago was named for him.

Moe Annenberg had seven daughters and one son, Walter. When the boy came of age, Moe gave him a harmless job in the family business. "Though he engaged some of his sons-in-law in the more sinister sides of the operations," according to the Annenberg biographer, John Cooney, "Walter was excluded. He was always reserved for the wholesomeness that Moses wanted to achieve." But when Moe was indicted for massive tax evasions, Walter was dragged into the proceedings, charged with aiding and abetting the scams. Moe pleaded guilty to one count; as part of the deal the charges against Walter were dropped. Like Eddie O'Hare, Annenberg wanted something better for his boy. Moe was sentenced to three years in jail and $8 million in taxes, penalties, and interest, the largest such assessment to that point in American history.

After Moe died in 1942 Walter took over the Annenberg empire. He built it up, adding *Seventeen* magazine and *TV Guide,* the most popular magazine in America. As if to atone for his father's crimes, Walter Annenberg gave away hundreds of millions of dollars to schools, hospitals, and the Republican party. In 1969 Nixon appointed him ambassador to Great Britain. At the confirmation hearing, someone asked about Moe's tax case. "That episode is a tragedy in the life in the family," Annenberg replied, "and for the past thirty-some years I have attempted to operate and I have actually found the tragedy a great source of inspiration for constructive endeavor." Of all his homes, Annenberg's favorite was the Palm Springs estate called Sunnylands, with its 209 acres of rolling hills, nine-hole golf course, twelve artificial lakes, and $50 million art collection. Here Moe Annenberg's only son entertained an American elite. In 1986 Ronald and Nancy Reagan attended their twentieth New Year's Eve party as guests of the Annenbergs at Sunnylands.

FIVE

PRIVATE SECTOR: GANGSTERS, UNIONS, EMPLOYERS

Think for a moment of organized crime as just another form of private enterprise. Reserve moral judgments, overlook the blood and muscle, and imagine the market situation. Over here, a variety of goods and services, some dangerous, all considered illegal or immoral. Over there, an inchoate throng of willing consumers, mostly good citizens but with some illicit tastes and plans. Between the products and consumers, the gangsters offer themselves as necessary entrepreneurs, with the skills and expertise to protect the illegal commerce flowing from underworld to upperworld. Recognizing these opportunities, underprivileged ethnic groups step in and profit by making the trade their own domain. What could be more American? Or more reflective of the fluid prospects extended by American life?

Consider the hoodlum as entrepreneur, then; and not merely in his own peculiar trades, but as a forceful presence in legitimate business as well. Before 1920 organized crime dealt in formal terms mainly with the public sector—with lawmen and politicians, whether bribed or honest. Employers and labor unions occasionally hired gangsters as goons and strikebreakers, but otherwise the underworld and real private enterprise had only glancing, trivial contacts. From the 1920s on, and especially after the end of Prohibition, organized crime sprawled into the private sector too. In labor-management disputes, each side accused the other of initiating violence as each side raised the ante by welcoming more gangsters to perform their specialties. So the situation spiraled, and the gangsters often went from hirelings to cohorts to dictators.

These involvements eventually reached the highest levels, all the way to the leaders of the Ford Motor Company, to the major Hollywood movie studios, and to the New Deal's favorite labor statesman. Quickly, invisibly, coercively, gangsters entered hiring halls and boardrooms. Once inside they preferred to remain, with their own plans.

❧ ❧

At first the private-sector rackets were discrete. The line between underworld and upperworld still meant something. A union or employers' association might engage gangsters temporarily, as muscular consultants providing special services. Or a particular union local or group of businessmen might be corruptly governed, through kickbacks and extortion, by free-lance crooks without formal ties to organized crime. But the underworld, strictly defined, did not control the situation—except when beckoned forward, at intervals, and within understood limits.

Dopey Benny Fein, raised on the Lower East Side, the son of Jewish immigrants, was New York's most notorious labor racketeer before Prohibition. His gang included such future luminaries as Waxey Gordon, Lepke Buchalter, and Gurrah Shapiro. Initially they worked for the United Hebrew Trades, the focus of union organizing in the Jewish-dominated garment industry. Dopey Benny and his men knocked heads and protected picket lines; a violent strike on the East Side in 1914 introduced, according to an assistant district attorney, "a use of gangsters and thugs in labor troubles, unparalleled in the history of this country." The gangsters were just hired guns doing a job. A few years later, during the First World War, a group of employers engaged the Fein gang to break strikes called by the same union that used to pay them. As consultants they worked for anybody.

It was always pointless to ask labor racketeers which side they were on. They recognized no sides, had no labor ideologies. When they saw money and power they became interested. Socks Lanza, so named because of his heavy hitting in sandlot baseball games, went to work at the Fulton Fish Market when he was eighteen years old. Perched at the southern tip of Manhattan, from Peck Slip to Beekman Street, the Fulton market unloaded fish from oceangoing boats and freshwater catches from as far away as the Great Lakes. Once an Irish domain—Al Smith had gotten started there thirty years earlier—by Lanza's time the fish handlers were mostly Italian. Moving easily among them, husky and not shy, Lanza organized a local of the Seafood Workers union in 1922. From that power base he turned the market into his own fiefdom, controlling every aspect of the trade, essentially by himself. (This was some years before the Italian gangs consolidated their power in New York.)

Under Lanza's regime the fishing boat crews were not allowed to unload their own catches. They sat by while Lanza's men took off the fish, for a fee. Lanza also charged each boat another ten dollars "for the union's benevolent fund." If a skipper balked at the surcharge, a five-hundred-pound bucket of fish might be accidentally dumped into the harbor. And Lanza did not restrict himself to the union side. He ruled and made money from the open-air market at Peck Slip where pushcart merchants bought fish in small lots. He ran a watchmen's service to protect the automobiles of retail merchants who came to the market at midweek. Fish-processing plants each paid Lanza $2,500 a year to keep their shops nonunion; Lanza even owned part of a cannery, an evident conflict of interest that did not perturb him. Shaking down anyone in sight, Lanza and his main men pulled in perhaps a half-million dollars a year in the 1920s. New Yorkers paid more for their fish.

So did Chicagoans, but there a racketeer had taken over not the union but the Fish Dealers Association, a retailers' group originally set up to ensure fair prices from the big wholesalers. A Russian Jewish immigrant, Maxie Eisen, formerly keeper of a saloon at Division and Potomac streets, barged into the Fish Dealers Association in the early 1920s. He was arrested at various times for throwing stink bombs, pouring kerosene on fish, carrying concealed weapons, assault with intent to kill, and larceny, but he was acquitted in each case except the last. By these methods Eisen intimidated Chicago's fish dealers, most of whom were also Jewish. "The Business Agent of the Fish Dealers Association he come by the store and tell my husband he must have $25 that they were going to put into a Cadillac car for a present by Maxie Eisen," the wife of one dealer said later. The agent also wanted six dollars every month, or no fish. "The next day they come around again and my husband say he no got the money and they tell him unless they get it the next day after that they going to stop him getting fish from the wholesale house." Her husband refused to pay, "and we had to go out of business, and it worried my husband sick, and now we're all living on $12 a week from the United Jewish charities. *Vai iss mere!* [Woe is me!] There was more freedom in Russia under the Czar."

"When I tried to keep them from making our Association a racket," another dealer testified, "they broke all the windows in my store and then warned the wholesalers to sell me no fish—and then I could buy no more fish from any of the fish firms in Chicago, so I had to go out of business. I am an old man—I only know the fish business—so I live with my daughter now." In a third case, a dealer could not afford to pay ("Max's business agent wanted $500 from me to join—but I got only a wagon, and no store, so I couldn't pay that much"). When the man then tried to buy seventy-five pounds of whitefish and suckers from Booth Fisheries, one of Eisen's men intervened: "He grabbed me and choked me and hit me in the face, and knocked the fish out of my hand. And then he kicked the fish all around in the sawdust on the floor and walked out. And the Booth Fisheries gave me my money back. And now what am I going to do?"

Business rackets, union rackets: it was hard to tell them apart. Sometimes a businessman was squeezed from both sides at once. For years Morris Becker ran cleaning and dyeing shops in Chicago and its suburbs, maintaining union pay and conditions. One morning all his employees went on strike; the union told Becker to see Walter Crowley, manager of the Master Cleaners Association. Crowley explained that Becker had the choice of losing his business or paying a bribe of $5,000 and raising his retail prices. "We had to go to Walter Crowley," Becker lamented afterward, "and stand on the carpet and receive our punishment for being born in America and thinking we had some rights as American citizens in a free country."

At the same time Becker was leaned on by another group of cleaners and dyers run by Bugs Moran's gang. Becker's shops and main plant at 2506 South Parkway were bombed, windows broken, and acid thrown on cleaned garments hanging in delivery trucks. Feeling besieged and helpless, without legal recourse, Becker called on a neighbor, Al Capone, Moran's mortal enemy. "Our shops had been bombed 40 times," he said later, "the union had bled us for $3,000 to call off a strike. The police, the state's attorney, and the United States attorney would or could do nothing. So we called in a man that could protect us—Al Capone. He did it well." Too well, in fact—Becker soon gave up and sold his business. "The Frankenstein set up by businessmen and labor leaders," said a man from an employers' association, "this alliance between them and the gangs—the use of hoodlums by all against one another—now threatens to take over the entire [cleaning] industry."

It was indeed a Frankenstein monster, misbegotten by the triple parentage of business, labor, and underworld, none willing to admit paternity but all fighting over custody of the little darling. In this strife a firm's merchandise and physical plant meant as much as the people involved, so the favored weapon was not a machine gun but a bomb tossed through a window. During a sixteen-month period in the late 1920s, 157 Chicago businesses were bombed. The Capone gang did most of the damage, working through its non-Italian associates Murray the Camel Humphreys, Red Barker, and Three-Fingered Jack White. Barker and White, from an Irish bootlegging gang on the West Side, made their peace with the Capones by fronting for them in union affairs, starting with the Teamsters and quickly diversifying. By 1932 Barker was running fifteen hundred public garages and at least fourteen—perhaps as many as thirty-three—different unions in Chicago.

Once again, the racketeers were mostly working-class Irish, Jews, and Italians while the most visibly, audibly concerned outsiders were WASPs from the middle and upper classes, not members of unions. When WASP reformers deplored conditions in the labor movement, union leaders could reasonably doubt the purity of their motives: did they really disapprove of labor rackets or of unions in general? The Chicago Crime Commission tried to expose labor racketeering; Victor Olander, a local union leader, thereupon described the commission as "antagonistic to the Chicago Federation of Labor and its purposes." Not quite, but then the commission admittedly had no union men on its board of directors and no perceptible union constituency. In March 1932 Frank Loesch, eighty years old and still president of the commission, asserted that two thirds of Chicago's unions were controlled by the Capones. "Maliciously untrue," Olander replied, adding that Loesch was an enemy of labor. Yet only five months later Olander appended a statement on "The Gangster Menace" to the Illinois Federation of Labor's annual report, "in order to sustain the standing and reputation of the Federation to face this issue by a public declaration." The statement described the muscling of locals, the kidnap of one leader, the murder of another, and the mute acquiescence of employers. Labor leaders could make such remarks without being accused of anti-union prejudice.

The general situation, already bad enough, became worse for two reasons in the early 1930s. The Depression made both workers and bosses desperate, willing to prostrate themselves and pay extortionate prices for the privilege of getting a job or staying in business. Then—a second blow—the end of Prohibition left bootlegging gangs in need of a new scam and looking greedily at industrial rackets. So the Depression decade brought more gangsters into more rackets—a geometric explosion of the problem.

At the Copeland hearings in the fall of 1933, most of the substantive testimony involved business and labor rackets. The United States attorney for Chicago testified that ten industries in his city were "subjected to the racketeer": cleaning and dyeing, laundries, carbonated beverages, building, trucking, paving, garbage collection, food markets, amusements, and coal delivery. A lawyer from New York, Adolph Dzik, recalled the fatuous investigation he had conducted for the American Federation of Labor in 1931. "Most of the unions in New York," Dzik concluded, "particularly the building trade unions, were saturated with rackets right within the unions. We had a lot to contend with in officials. . . . The membership at large did not have any voice."

The Copeland committee heard firsthand from a few labor leaders brave or foolish enough to come forward. Steve Sumner, eighty-four years old, had been secretary-treasurer of the Chicago Milk Drivers union for thirty years. "I did not come with any prepared talk," Sumner told the committee. "The racketeering started here in Chicago several years ago. It was first brought in by big business. The men to whom we generally look as being above the average were the very men that were the lowest. They brought them in." With Prohibition waning, a gang of bootleggers had visited his office. "They told us plainly that the milk business looked to them like a good business for their boys to engage in after Prohibition, whiskey, and beer and all that stuff had gone down. Of course, we argued with them. . . . So in time they offered $100,000 for us to step out and for them to step in. To that we told them nothing doing." Sumner fortified his home and office with armor plate in the walls and steel window screens. "The people have got in the frame of mind that they are afraid of those fellows. Whenever you say anything about Murray Humphreys, or Three-Fingered Jack White, or Al Capone, the majority of people begin to shiver. They said, 'Why, you can't cope with those fellows. There is no good of saying anything against them. If you do, your life is in danger.'

"I might be murdered, for instance—and that is liable to happen to me at any time," said Sumner. "It is my opinion from what I have found with these racketeers—and believe me, we have met up with a lot of them in the last 18 months—it is my belief that they are the lousiest, most cowardly skunks on the face of the earth."

❧ ❧

Once a matter of random thugs and extortions here and there, labor racketeering became a formal part of organized crime when it meshed with the major underworld gangs. The mob-afflicted unions and the criminal gangs went national together, carrying each other. Gangsters picked on small-scale, relatively competitive industries with casual, semiskilled labor markets fed by unions with unusually autonomous locals and corruptible or somnolent national leaders. Thus the mobs could seldom penetrate the big railroad, steel, and automobile unions, but they found easier pickings in the building-trade, laundry, garment, trucking, longshore, and restaurant unions. Because these latter industries generally ran on modest scales and investments, new business competitors could easily enter and disrupt them. Their unions therefore might serve crucial regulatory functions, rationalizing and stabilizing situations prone to disruption, in ways pleasing to employers. The corrupt union leadership and the corrupted (or corrupting) bosses might act in collusion—by agreeable sweetheart contracts or by disagreeable extortions. Either way, it was the labor force itself that suffered. The most broadly harmful aspect of union racketeering was that mobbed-up unions neglected their responsibility of standing for the worker against the boss.

Two building-trade unions, the Laborers and the Operating Engineers, were among the first labor organizations to be manipulated at a national level by gangsters. The Laborers union, which represented the least skilled, lowest-paid construction workers, was dominated by its Italian members: thousands of honest workingmen wretchedly served by their leaders. Founded in 1903, the Laborers union elected its first Italian president, Dominick D'Allesandro, five years later. An Italian immigrant who had settled in Boston, he moved the union's headquarters to Massachusetts and served as president until his death in 1926.

At that point a group in Chicago with ties to the Capones took control of the Laborers. The new president—elected by the executive board, not the general membership—was Joseph Moreschi, thrust upward from his old job as third vice president. Born in Italy, brought to Chicago at age eight, he had been active in the city's Local 1 since 1912. As president, Moreschi saw no evil and took orders well. He was abetted by Michael Carozzo, the acknowledged boss of Chicago's Laborer locals. Also an Italian immigrant, Carozzo had come to Chicago in 1909 to serve as bodyguard to Jim Colosimo, the major Italian gangster in Chicago before the Capone era. Carozzo went into union work around 1919; a year later he was indicted for murder, but the case was dropped.

Until the 1920s the building trades in Chicago and New York were controlled by Irish labor leaders. Even the Laborers, the most Italian of the construction unions, had to contend with remnants of an Irish faction. Patrick McNicholas, a former president of New York's Laborer locals, showed up at the Copeland hearings in 1933 to complain about the Italians who were running his union. Joe Moreschi ("the gunman from Chicago") had been fined for income tax evasion, said McNicholas, "and he is supporting certain men who appeared in the public press and who, I believe one of them, was in jail for murder and was the head of the Black Hand gang and sentenced to 15 years in jail for counterfeiting. These are the kind of men that the district attorneys of this state or the city wish us to pay tribute to, and they have the cheek to tell the people that the citizens have not the courage to fight against these Black Hand scoundrels. I say to you that I presented the facts to the officials and I told them everything." Presiding over the hearings, Royal Copeland brushed this testimony aside. "You are giving us history which is very valuable," he told McNicholas, "but it is a long time ago." Copeland listened for a while longer and then changed the subject.

Moreschi and his cohorts operated a secure oligarchy beyond democratic control. For thirty years, from 1911 to 1941, the

Laborers held no national conventions or general elections. Moreschi sat in the president's chair for forty-two years, until he was eighty-four, pliantly leaving the decisions to others. Individual locals were allowed to run their own affairs as they chose. At one New York construction site in the early 1930s, the plasterer's helpers made union scale of $8.50 a day; from this they had to kick back $2.50 a day to the foremen who had hired them. When they complained to their union—Local 30 of the Laborers—they got no help, in fact were fined for working below union scale. One man who pressed his case was blinded with acid. Moreschi and the national leadership were not moved to intervene.

When they did timorously intervene, as in the case of Nick Stirone and Local 1058 in Pittsburgh, it was only after years of crimes, accusations, and bad publicity for the Laborers. Moreschi had sent Stirone, his trusted crony, to Pittsburgh in 1936 to organize the traditionally open-shop heavy construction industry in western Pennsylvania. With big projects at hand—the Pennsylvania Turnpike and, later, defense jobs for the war—Stirone lined up major contracts from the construction companies. He also extorted bribes from them and let employers pay his men less than union wages. Stirone lived well beyond his purported salary, driving a Cadillac around town, residing in a luxurious suite at the William Penn Hotel and at a 742-acre farm out in the mountains of Bedford County. Along with John S. LaRocca, a Sicilian immigrant high in the Pittsburgh Mafia, Stirone owned a linen supply business that undercut the competition until it was sold.

His domestic life was not tranquil. One day in 1939, his blond girlfriend was mysteriously shot in the shoulder at his suite in the William Penn. She explained that a revolver had accidentally discharged when she was examining it, and there the matter ended. A few years later, Stirone's wife and daughter appeared from New Jersey to swear out warrants for desertion and nonsupport. Stirone left town for a few days and his family went back to New Jersey.

He rode out those troubles, but not a series of accusations by colleagues in the Laborers:

- One man, John Paull, charged that Stirone had threatened "to cave my head in" over some disagreement. Nine months later Paull's home was bombed. The police blamed it on "labor trouble."

- Albert L. Russell of Johnstown said that Stirone had ordered him to blow up the equipment of contractors who would not recognize the union, to extort money from contractors, and to kill a contractor and two union organizers. "Stirone wanted every contractor in Pennsylvania," Russell claimed, "to shiver in his shoes when he heard the name of Nick Stirone."

- Ross Adams, a former aide to Stirone, filed an equity suit alleging that he "has set up a tyranny in the field of labor under his control in this area and has by gangster tactics, vicious assaults, threats and intimidation, domineered both workers and employers"; has "extorted large sums of money from businessmen and contractors in the wrecking industries, the linen supply industry, the scrap iron industry, the construction industry and in many public improvement contracts in the Pittsburgh area"; has "converted to his own use funds belonging to the local union"; and "has always carried firearms and has surrounded himself with gunmen who were put on the payroll of the local union."

This was too much even for the national leadership of the Laborers union. Stirone's Local 1058 was dissolved, its charter withdrawn. FINIS WRITTEN ON LONG CAREER OF IRON-HANDED BOSS STIRONE, a newspaper headline announced. It was all "a joke," Stirone shrugged, and in fact he remained the boss of a restored Local 1058 and of Pittsburgh's Laborers. Eventually he was convicted of extortion and given ten years in jail.

Brazen as he was, Stirone was a petty hood compared with Joseph S. Fay and William E. Maloney of the Operating Engineers union. A notch up the building-trade pecking order from the Laborers, the Operating Engineers ran the steam shovels, cranes, earth movers, and other heavy equipment at a construction site. Joe Fay started working as a teenager at his father's gravel pit in Port Washington, Long Island. Drifting around the construction business, by 1918 he had settled in Newark as the business agent for Local 825 of the Operating Engineers. Local 825 remained his base for the rest of his life, though his power reached far beyond it. From the 1920s on he accumulated an impressive arrest record, which he excused as an inevitable aspect of union work at the time. "There were fights," he told the McClellan hearings thirty years later, "and I want you to know . . . that I lived through the years that the busting of unions and breaking of heads was more or less the tool of our opponents." The gangster Longy Zwillman, a fellow resident of Newark, did some of Fay's strong-arm work.

Fay also was tightly bound to Frank Hague, the lord of Jersey City, just across Newark Bay. Once, when Fay was returning from Europe, Hague sent a boat and a police band to serenade Fay as he sailed up New York Harbor.

A turbulent, overstated Irishman, Joe Fay enjoyed an evident gift for friendship and good times. An acting governor of New Jersey described him in 1933 as "one of the real forces in American life," which was surely true. Fay owned a fancy house in the Forest Hills section of Newark, drove a new Cadillac every year, and gave lavish parties all through the Depression. Often seen at the casinos in Atlantic City, he dropped as much as $50,000 in a single night of gambling. In the tradition of labor racketeers, he did not mind conflicts of interest; for a time he owned an excavating company with two other officials of Local 825. "Fay was not an Italian," Max Block of the Butchers union said later, "but he was a mob man, strictly rackets."

Fay's direct influence in the Operating Engineers sprawled across three states. He controlled all of New Jersey, the New York City locals through his appointment as receiver for Local 125, five upstate New York counties to the west of the Hudson River, and Local 542 in Philadelphia. "When he came over to the local union," a member of 542 later testified, "a gang of men, hoods as we characterized them, . . . would stand on the side of the meeting hall or patrol up and down the aisles, and anybody who asked a question about finances, or anything else affecting the membership of the local union, would be told to sit down and shut up. These men would glare at him and make gestures, and threatening gestures toward them." Fay and his men stole millions of dollars from Local 542. Anybody who protested was beaten up.

William E. Maloney of Chicago was Fay's sometime ally, sometime rival at the top level of Operating Engineer leadership. As Fay was tied to Longy Zwillman, Maloney had connections with the Capones through Michael Carozzo of the Laborers and Three-Fingered Jack White and Charles Fischetti of the Teamsters. Appointed to an office in Operating Engineer Local 569, from that position Maloney plotted to dominate all his union's locals in Chicago. His main obstacle was Dennis Bruce Zeigler, 569's secretary and an honest man.

Zeigler was a hoisting engineer, the father of eleven children, descended from German and Welsh families settled in America for two centuries. He placed the steel girders in the Palmer House and Bismark Hotel and the stone columns in front of the Field Museum. To house his considerable family he bought a six-room cottage. While the family lived in it he added to the back; they then moved to the back while he added to the front. "No pioneer ever worked any harder at making a home for his family," his daughter Pauline said later.

When Zeigler resisted Maloney's designs on Local 569, Maloney pointed a gun at him and warned him to get out or be killed. Others threatened to kidnap Zeigler's children and bomb his home. The police stationed guards at his home and office. One day Maloney chased him down a street and into a taxi. "You son of a bitch," Maloney shouted, "I will get you yet." To raise money for the struggle, Zeigler mortgaged his home, which until then had had a clear title.

He took his case against Maloney to the union's national office but got nowhere. Since 1928 the Operating Engineers had held no conventions, hence no general elections. So in January 1933 Zeigler asked William Green, president of the American Federation of Labor, for a new charter to start a rump local. "The rank and file of our organization has completely lost confidence in the integrity and ability of the officers of the international," Zeigler told Green. "Many of the officers have so muscled their way into many of the local unions that the members feel it is impossible ever again to have the international union again function as it should in the interest of the members and in accordance with the principles of the AFL. The membership of the organization is sick and tired and disgusted with being classified as being dominated and controlled by the worst form of racketeers, hoodlums, and murderers in America. We want and demand freedom from this stigma. . . . Among our men are to be found the very best mechanics, and oldtime members are in the vast majority. We have a keen sense of responsibility."

"I would strongly advise against the action which you are planning to take," Green replied. "It will serve no good purpose."

Zeigler was running out of options. "We are not permitted to assemble in convention," he wrote back to Green. "Whole local unions are voted by supervisors appointed by the president of the international. Other local unions are bodily disenfranchised. The votes of other local unions are flagrantly miscounted so that we may be denied the privilege of assembling in convention and correcting the ills from which the organization suffers. In the absence of a convention the only remaining tribunal is the officers themselves whom we charge with misconduct. Are they to be permitted to pass upon the propriety of their own acts? Are they to be the judges of their own stewardship?"

In February 1933, Zeigler's police protection was withdrawn after eighteen months and no overt attempts on his life. Three weeks later, as Zeigler approached his home one evening, a car sped up. Five shots were fired into the back of his head, blowing half his face away. His son David, twenty years old, came out to the street and cradled his father as he died. No one was arrested for the murder. David, who had a bad heart, suffered a series of strokes and died nine months later, on Thanksgiving morning. The fatherless family could not meet its mortgage payments. "What hurt the most," Pauline Zeigler recalled, "we had to give up our precious house that Pop built and Mom's heart was broken." As for William Maloney, in 1940 he became international president of the union.

Another honest labor leader, Norman Redwood of New York, was caught between crooked factions of the Laborers and Operating Engineers. Joe Fay, always reaching for more power, absorbed four New York Laborers locals into his own union—with the collusion, oddly enough, of James Bove of the Laborers. Norman Redwood, business agent of Laborers Local 102, refused to accept the arrangement. He made Fay even angrier in February 1937 by calling a strike on a sewer project under construction by Fay's associate Samuel Rosoff. "If this strike is called, I will have you killed," Rosoff warned Redwood. "You will be a dead man. You can tell that to the police." Two weeks later, after more arguments with Fay, and after Redwood had gone to see Special Prosecutor Thomas E. Dewey, he was murdered outside his home in Teaneck, New Jersey. The county prosecutor immediately blamed Fay and Rosoff, but no indictments were brought.

In 1943, though, Fay and James Bove were indicted for extorting the contractors on a massive water supply project in those five upstate counties that Fay controlled. The two men were convicted of receiving $368,000; the DA placed the actual total at over a million dollars. Fay held on to his office and power during the four years of trials and appeals. Finally he went off to prison for eight years. A parade of big labor and political names came to visit him, seeking his advice and favor. When he got out of jail a union pension was waiting for him.

The AFL had its gangsters and the CIO had its Communists. "This local has been captured by radicals and Communists," said Joe Ryan about the San Francisco longshoremen led by Harry Bridges. But what of "the way they sweat and graft on the East Coast longshoremen," said Bridges, referring to Ryan's locals. "You see men working there ten times worse than we ever worked here, and five per cent of their pay paid to racketeers alone."

The labor factions came down to gangsters and Communists, bristling enemies, forever squabbling over turf and deploring each other in public. Yet the gangsters and Communists shared more than they could acknowledge. Both were secretive conspiracies, veiling their purposes, speaking in cryptic argots behind contrived facades. Both drew their troops from immigrant and ethnic populations. Both believed in monopolies—their own—instead of free markets and democratic choices. Both were contemptuous of cops as mercenary lackeys serving evil, bloated masters. Both pursued larger goals, beyond the labor movement, with an absolute unconcern as to means and ethics. But gangsters and Communists split on one final, distinguishing point. If they had to choose, gangsters would line up with employers, Communists with workers. The criminals ultimately wanted money. The Communists—for their own peculiar reasons—wanted to build a labor movement. In the labor wars of the 1930s, the Communists were the surest allies of working people.

President Green of the American Federation of Labor functioned merely as a clerk and mouthpiece for the strongest unions in his organization. When stories about racketeering in AFL unions came his way, Green would boldly say a few well-intentioned words, maybe. "If there is brought to my attention the racketeer moving under the garb of trade unionism," he declared at an AFL meeting in 1930, "and I can place my hands on him with convincing evidence, I will drive him from the movement, if I can." Two "if's" in one sentence: typical of Green's mild, accommodating style.

A renegade member of the Operating Engineers, George B. McGovern, told the Copeland hearings about his frustrated attempts to clean up his union. "Recourse to the labor movement is futile," said McGovern. "It is absolutely useless. The American Federation of Labor and its executive council have robed themselves in charity. I am personally acquainted with the majority of so-called 'leaders' in the labor movement. They are not leaders; they are misleaders." He had appealed to William Green, "personally told him what was being done to the workingman, depriving them of their rights, and he told me that everybody is doing it." So now New York's unions were being dominated by bullets and bullies. "If we cannot run our own affairs," McGovern wound up, "we are a menace to the community. If we are a group of bandits, who are holding up men for wages, labor unions should be dissolved and should be caused to go out of existence."

In part because of these conditions, in 1935 John L. Lewis of the United Mine Workers led a group of unions out of the AFL to form a new labor movement, the Congress of Industrial Organizations. The AFL had always practiced craft unionism, that is, organizing workers by the skills or tools they used instead of the product they made or the plant in which they toiled. The effect of this approach was to restrict the AFL to the more skilled workers and to dissipate the impact of a strike on a given industry. The CIO's industrial unionism, on the other hand, urged the more militant theory of binding all a particular industry's workers into one big union, with more power to worry employers. Left-wing unionists naturally flocked to the CIO; by one estimate, 40 percent of the CIO unions were partly or wholly controlled by Communists. "Industry should not complain if we allow Communism in our organization," Lewis asserted as head of the CIO. After all, he pointed out, "who gets the bird, the dog or the hunter?" The departure of left-wingers from the AFL, meantime, left it even more to the manipulations of its mobbed-up unions.

Within an afflicted union, the gangsters and Communists feuded in predictable patterns, each group to a degree hating the other just because they so resembled each other. One conspiracy understood all the devices used by the other conspiracy. In the Hotel and Restaurant Employees union, the battle was sharpened by the organization's ancient ties with saloons and booze. At the turn of the century the HRE was known as "the Irish bartenders' union."

Its president, Edward Flore of Buffalo, a Roman Catholic of French and Alsatian descent, had started washing beer glasses in his father's saloon when he was nine years old. As president from 1911 to 1945, Flore was an agreeable figurehead, distant and innocuous. During Prohibition the union lost half its members. Many locals were transformed into speakeasies and centers for gambling and bootlegging. When legal booze brought the old members back, gangsters already had lines into the union's affairs.

Dutch Schultz's gang, in its last big coup before the Dutchman was killed, set up the Metropolitan Restaurant and Cafeteria Association to shake down employers as well as Locals 16 and 302 of the HRE union. Paul Coulcher, Schultz's stooge in Local 16, hired a Schultz lawyer as the union attorney and expelled members for selling Communist literature and complaining about his rackets. Coulcher called and settled strikes without consulting the members, replaced duly elected shop chairmen with hoodlum flunkies, and conspired with employers to subvert union standards. The restaurant owners paid fees of $250 to $25,000 a year to ensure Coulcher's favor. "I'll do for your union the same as Local 16," a Schultz gangster told another HRE local in New York. "Coulcher is the boss of his union, and if anybody wants to see him they have to knock on his door. If you have 25 or 50 members who are squawkers, give me the names of the squawkers. I wouldn't kill them, but I have ways of cooling them off." The whole operation brought the gang about $2 million a year.

But only for a while. Schultz was ventilated, Dewey busted up the Metropolitan racket, and Communists moved into the vacuum. At the HRE's 1936 convention in Rochester, New York, three delegates were gunned down on a sidewalk; one of them, a thug connected to Local 16, soon died. In the ensuing commotion, President Flore needed a fresh crew of leaders in New York untainted by organized crime. A few years earlier, Communists had organized the Food Workers Industrial Union to compete with the bemobbed HRE locals. Employers preferred the less demanding contracts they could sign with gangster unions. But after Flore embraced the FWIU left-wingers, and Dewey put the HRE's racket leaders in jail, the union's New York locals were delivered from gangsters to Communists.

The HRE locals in Chicago were promotional devices for the underworld's more or less legitimate liquor enterprises. The

Capones owned bars, nightclubs, breweries, and liquor distributorships; they wanted to own the staffs working at their night spots as well. Claude Maddox—a Capone gunman since the early 1920s, suspected in the St. Valentine's Day Massacre—ran HRE Local 450 in the Capone stronghold of Cicero. To control Chicago's bartenders, though, the gang needed Local 278, with its forty-five hundred members and its assertive boss, George B. McLane, the local business agent since 1913. Later, after falling out with the Capones, McLane described his seduction to a grand jury—and then withdrew his testimony. His version of events may be doubted, especially in its chronology and in McLane's professed resistance to the gangsters. But as to what the Capones did, their statements, and their motives, McLane probably conveyed the essential if self-serving truth.

In 1935, or perhaps a year or two earlier, McLane was called to a series of meetings with Frank the Enforcer Nitti and other top Capones. They wanted him to take one of their boys, Louis Romano, into a leadership role in Local 278. (They claimed Romano was clean, with no criminal record; actually he had been arrested in the 1920s for shooting four men.) McLane said he could not accept Romano without his executive board's approval, and furthermore Romano was not a union member. "Give us the names of anyone who opposes," said Nitti, "and we will take care of them. We want no more playing around. If you don't do what we say, you will get shot in the head. How would your wife look in black?" So Romano came into Local 278 as president.

Later McLane met with Nitti, Joe Fusco, and other men in charge of the Capones' liquor interests. They instructed him to have his bartenders push such Capone products as Gold Seal liquors and Canadian Ace beer. "I said I was afraid the union would get in trouble with the Fair Trade Practices Act," McLane testified. "Nitti said: 'See that your men do this, and let us worry about fair trade.'" Under these pressures, the harassed McLane took to his bottle. That brought another directive from the Enforcer. "Nitti said for me to quit drinking and get on the wagon or I would get shot in my head. Nitti said it was an unwritten law with the outfit that they did not allow anybody to drink that belonged to them."

Within the national leadership of his union, though, McLane was a rising star, the subject of adoring articles in the HRE's official journal, elected to an international vice presidency in charge of the Midwest district. In 1938, as McLane told the story, Nitti made him run against Edward Flore for the presidency of the whole HRE union. Nitti cited the Capones' previous experience in such matters: how they had made Michael Carozzo the boss of Chicago's Laborers, and how they now ran the whole union. When McLane still hesitated, Nitti pulled out his revolver and ended the discussion in his usual way. "Either I would run," McLane recalled, "or I would be found in an alley."

He ran. The 1938 HRE convention was held in San Francisco. Membership was up to two hundred thousand, making it the fifth-largest union in the AFL. Charges went back and forth. McLane accused Flore of being allied with "New York Communists" (true); Flore said he was fighting gangsters (also true). One Flore supporter from New York was beaten up by McLane's goons. Another Flore man was kidnapped. But Flore won the election easily, 1,095 votes to 612. McLane was also defeated for reelection to his vice presidency.

Thwarted on a national level, the Capones dumped McLane from his job in Local 278 and installed another stooge. On a local level their hegemony remained nearly absolute. Edward Flore sensibly did not try to disturb it. As manufacturers, distributors, retailers, and union bosses, the Capones made money almost every time a glass was raised in Chicago.

❧ ❧

Organized crime damaged American labor most by taking over two crucial transportation unions, the Longshoremen and Teamsters. Both were led, or unled, by indifferent executives in the mold of William Green of the AFL, Joe Moreschi of the Laborers, and Edward Flore of the HRE. Joseph Patrick Ryan presided over the Longshoremen from 1927 to 1953; Daniel Tobin lasted even longer at the Teamsters, from 1907 to 1952. During their entrenched, less than vigorous reigns, gangsters moved into most of the important locals of both unions. Meantime Ryan and Tobin were all noise and bluster, puffing up and down the captain's deck, overtly ignorant of conditions down in steerage.

The Longshoremen had only fifty thousand members in 1936—but the union controlled the port of New York, which gave it leverage beyond its size. The Teamsters had both size and leverage. "No other union has the power that we have," Tobin liked to say. "We touch every trade and industry." With some five hundred thousand members in 1940, the Teamsters made up the biggest union in the AFL, second only to the CIO's United Mine Workers among all American labor organizations. This combination of union power and degree of mob influence made the Longshoremen and the Teamsters the two most significant cases of labor racketeering.

The port of New York—the finest natural harbor in North America, the geographic factor that had made New York the greatest American city—provided the setting for the Longshoremen's gangsters. Anchored on the East and West sides of Manhattan, the port extended east and south to Brooklyn, west and south into New Jersey and Staten Island. It took in over seven hundred miles of wharves and shoreline, two hundred deepwater piers, nineteen hundred piers in all. The waterfront ran on its own rules and time clock. When a ship came in, the work was there, to be done quickly; a ship resting in port made no money. Longshoremen often toiled at night, in the fog and damp, under murky light and nasty conditions. The work was hard, heavy, and dangerous. If a man was murdered it could easily be explained as an accident on the job.

The work force was casual and unpredictable, filled with ex-convicts and transients of unsteady habits. They were hired not by seniority or rotation but by a shape-up: a hiring boss stood in front of a group of longshoremen and picked the men he wanted for a work gang. The job required few skills beyond a strong back, and too many men always showed up for the task at hand. In such conditions of surplus, unskilled labor, the hiring boss's whim depended on kickbacks, up to 20 percent of a day's wages. (In Hoboken and Jersey City, a longshoreman willing to kick back displayed his intention by putting a toothpick behind his ear, thus alerting the boss.)

Beyond the docks, the streets were narrow and congested, lined with trucks waiting to pick up or deliver at the floor of the pier. That led to the abuse called public loading: gangs of men charged extortionate fees for moving goods between trucks and piers, even when other men did the work. The boss loaders, members of the Longshoremen's union, were employers as well, hiring their own loading gangs and collecting their fees through coercion and intimidation. Truckers might also pay "hurry-up fees" to advance their place in line—all in the interest of speed, to get back on the road, in the same way the ships wanted to get back to sea.

These two essential aspects of waterfront life, the shape-up and public loading, caused most of the crime along the docks. As lucrative rackets they drew the attention of criminal gangs anxious to control them. Because dock jobs were so scarce and capriciously given, longshoremen often went into debt to the loan sharks hovering nearby. The shark then might strike a deal with a hiring boss to employ the men who owed him money. While workers waited in waterfront saloons for job calls that might not come, they drank and gambled and bet with bookies. If they lost heavily they could be leaned on to set up cargo thefts and narcotics smuggling, with forged documents and diverted shipments. On a given dock the gang boss was king. The men only wanted to work, and nobody else was watching them.

The Longshoremen's union, organized on the Great Lakes in 1892, was controlled by its New York locals by the 1910s. In Manhattan and Brooklyn they were mostly Irish at first. Joe Ryan, the son of Irish immigrants, joined Local 791 on the West Side in 1912. He made thirty cents an hour, working shifts up to forty-five hours long, with each man expected to lift three thousand pounds an hour, all day long, into the night. "The work was hard and we had no security," Ryan said later. "I went up through the various jobs. I had a shape every hour of the day." After a load of lead ingots fell on him, breaking his arm and shoulder, Ryan became Local 791's financial secretary, then a vice-president of the union. Though he liked to call up grim recollections of the bad old days, for Joe Ryan a working stiff's perspective was just a memory. He took his cues from elsewhere.

Across the East River, longshoremen lived in the Irishtown section of Brooklyn, between the Fulton Ferry and the Brooklyn Navy Yard, clustered around the bridges to Manhattan. The bankrobber Willie Sutton grew up in Irishtown, learning about crime by laboring on the docks. "Since it was all muscle," he recalled, "the gang members were generally in their late teens or early twenties and therefore very easy for a kid to identify with. The dock boss—the leader—would usually be a little older, all the way up into his mid-twenties, maybe. They gained control by killing their predecessors, and they in turn were killed by their successors. Two years was a long time for a dock boss to stay alive; the turnover was very rapid. They were beaten to a pulp on a dark street; they were shot or stabbed and dumped into the water." Sutton idolized Wild Bill Lovett, a dock boss so tough he was supposed to have run Al Capone out of town, a gifted leader "with a sure sense of command and a vibrant personality. Or, at any rate, he was before he had his head bashed in along the docks one night." Another man, Dinny Meehan, "was the only dock boss I can remember who died in bed. By which I mean that somebody slipped in through his bedroom window while he was asleep and put a bullet in his brain."

From 1920 to 1930 at least eighteen dock bosses or pretenders were murdered in Irishtown. "No one was ever convicted," Sutton noted. "A code of silence was observed in Irishtown more faithfully then *omertà* is observed by the Mafia." Eddie McGuire enjoyed the briefest waterfront reign. With the leadership open in 1928, the pier leaders rolled dice for the job and McGuire won, sort of. Five minutes later the others left the pier and McGuire stayed behind with five bullets in his corpse.

During and just after World War I, new piers were built near Italian neighborhoods of South Brooklyn, Hoboken, and Staten Island. Italians and Italian gangsters thereby began to influence the Longshoremen's affairs. In Hoboken Anthony Strollo of the Luciano Mafia family was often seen around the docks. The East River piers on the Manhattan side were run through Local 856 by Mike Clemente of the Lucianos. For two decades Emil Camarda and his relatives held six Italian locals in the Red Hook section of Brooklyn. They in turn deferred to Mafiosi: Joe Adonis of the Lucianos and Albert Anastasia and his brother Tough Tony of the Manganos.

The Anastasias came from a family of five brothers who had immigrated to America. One brother became a priest and went back to Italy; the other four became gangsters. Tough Tony loved ships and cargoes, the dead reckoning of loading a ship just right, and he actually worked on the docks. He dismissed the suspicion that "all longshoremen are hoodlums and gamblers" as an unaccountable rumor. "It's about time they stopped persecuting us," he insisted. "We won't stand for this. We are Americans." But he was a capo in the Mangano family, a career criminal with a dozen arrests on his record.

The six Camarda locals were run from a single office on

President Street in Brooklyn. They had been amalgamated without a rank-and-file election, and the Camardas never bothered to call any union meetings. Records were destroyed and forged and the treasury looted of $600,000 a year. In protest, an ardent young longshoreman named Peter Panto started demanding free elections and an end to shape-ups and hiring kickbacks. When he called a protest meeting, some twelve hundred angry longshoremen showed up to urge him on. That caught the attention of the forces behind the Camardas. "I wish you'd stop doing what you're doing," Emil Camarda warned Panto. "The boys don't like it."

Two weeks later Albert Anastasia and two henchmen took Panto for a ride, strangled him, and buried the body in a lime pit in New Jersey. "Panto wasn't a longshoreman at all," a union leader insisted. "He was just a 'red,' trying to stir up trouble." Soon Emil Camarda offended his masters and was also killed. Joe Ryan named a brother-in-law of Vincent Mangano's to replace him.

Meantime Irish gangs held on to the piers on the West Side of Manhattan. Mickey Bowers and his men ran the midtown area above Forty-second Street, including the choice terminals where passenger liners docked. Tim O'Mara's gang had the Chelsea district to the south down to around Twentieth Street. Two newcomers, Cockeye Dunn and Eddie McGrath, took over the Greenwich Village piers below O'Mara's turf. Dunn and McGrath were just garden-variety hoodlums, with no prior experience on the docks or in unions, when in 1936 they got a charter for Local 1730 of the Longshoremen. An ex-con named Buster Smith later described their organizing technique: "In 1936 me and George Keeler and Tom Porter had the loading at Pier 59 at 18th Street. Dunn's gang was trying to get bigger control, and they just moved in on us. Dunn and his boys opened up on us one day with pistols and shotguns. I was wounded. A few weeks later, Dunn, Matty Kane, and some others killed Tom Porter and his girl in Long Island City. Tom and his girl were sitting in an automobile. They killed her because they didn't want no witnesses, I guess. A month later Dunn and two of his gunmen knocked off George Keeler at his home in Brooklyn. They shot George as he was asleep in his bed. With me wounded and Keeler and Porter dead, Dunn's boys took over our loading at Pier 59."

With Dunn and McGrath providing some of the muscle, and ties to the Lucianos, the West Side loading bosses established a central collection agency under the bland name of Varick Enterprises, Inc. It rationalized the public loading racket by gathering information on every shipment of goods arriving in New York by rail or water. Every morning the boss loaders would check the various terminals for the names of consigned truckers and the weights of their loads. They would compute their fees—a minimum of three cents per hundred pounds at first, and more later—and issue loading tickets. Then Varick's goon squads would make the collections. With over a thousand accounts, Varick wielded a serene monopoly. Many cops were later found on its payroll.

Waterfront conditions were more easily described than proven or reformed. Newspapers ran exposés, lawmen conducted investigations, government bodies held hearings. None of this much affected the situation or provoked Joe Ryan's curiosity. When asked about all the bad reports, Ryan would pound his desk and deny everything. Crime on the waterfront? "We got a Police Department, haven't we? The police wouldn't stand for a situation like that. Our men wouldn't stand for it." Kickbacks? "I defy anybody to prove there's any kickback in our organization. I don't care who says so, and they have been saying it for years." Shape-ups? "The men have never asked for a change. They could change it if they wanted to." The loading racket? "Loading is hard work. The men themselves split the fees. It's all divided up. Gangsters do not pocket that money. That's simply not true. Why, the men wouldn't stand for it!" Ex-cons in the union? "Because a man's done wrong once, it don't show he's a criminal. Why, a man can't get paroled unless somebody'll give him a job, and those are the very men who stop other men from stealing." He blamed the parole system, not his union. "They dump them on us all the time—the parole boards. There are some criminals on the waterfront, but they are in the minority and don't run in packs."

As chairman for ten years of the AFL Central Labor Council of New York City, Ryan was one of the most powerful union leaders in the AFL. Within his own union, though, he took orders from his corrupt locals and, beyond them, from the steamship and stevedore companies. Between 1919 and 1945 no major strikes hit the New York waterfront. "Nobody wants strikes," said Ryan. "Remember that we are a vital part of the steamship industry." A typical labor racketeer, Ryan favored the employers over the workers. "We call Ryan in once a year or so," a stevedore company official explained, "and say, 'Joe, how much of a raise do you need to keep the boys in line?' " At contract negotiations, when terms were on the table and Ryan had to reach a decision, he would make a phone call to receive instructions.

The biggest man on the waterfront was not Ryan but his dear friend William J. McCormack, the main force in the New York Shipping Association. Up from a West Side childhood and grammar school education, a former teamster and owner of a trucking company, McCormack ran two stevedore firms that served ten piers, making him a dominant operator. Every year McCormack, properly grateful for favors extended, staged a fancy dinner dance in honor of Joe Ryan, attended by an interesting mix of top gangsters and top politicians. (Ryan denied the stories that McCormack did his thinking; they were just good personal friends, he said, for McCormack had "a capacity for true friendship which . . . is a rare gift, becoming even rarer in these troubled times.")

While McCormack was the big boss, other employers had the same friendly attitude toward gangsters on the docks. "This may sound terrible to you," one of them allowed, "but I don't care whether they are criminals or not, just so long as they don't hurt me. In fact, to be perfectly frank, if I had a choice of hiring a tough ex-convict or a man without a criminal record I am more inclined to take the ex-con. Know why? Because if he is in a boss job he'll keep the men in line and get the maximum work out of them. They'll be afraid of him." It was good business; end of discussion. The businessmen had to pay bribes and kickbacks, hidden by inventive and potentially embarrassing bookkeeping. In return they got labor peace and stable, predictable conditions in an unstable industry. "I liked to do business with him because he got results," an employer said of a hoodlum murdered in Hoboken. "That's what I pay for—results. I am not concerned with how anybody gets them. You see, I'm no reformer. That's the church's business, not mine."

If the New York Longshoremen were led by gangsters, the San Francisco Longshoremen were led by left-wingers under Harry Bridges. "We as workers have nothing in common with the employers," Bridges insisted. "We are in a class struggle." An Australian immigrant, cynical and unrelenting, Bridges never admitted to being a Communist party member. But he seldom diverged from the Soviet catechism in foreign policy, and he welcomed Communists into his union. "I found them good union men," he explained. "They have generally fought for progressive and democratic trade unionism. I have very few complaints against the Communist Party as a whole." (Ryan by contrast collected secret funds from employers "to fight Communism on the waterfront." He kept the money in his private bank account and dispensed it for mysterious purposes.)

No two labor leaders could have had less in common than Joe Ryan and Harry Bridges. When the San Francisco locals under Bridges went on strike in 1934, Ryan flew out to California, met with the employers, and announced a settlement that left the shape-up and other bad hiring practices intact. At a mass meeting in San Francisco, Ryan ordered the men back to work; they refused, and Ryan barely escaped the hall without a beating. He received ominous phone calls day and night. "Clear out of California," he was warned, "before you go back in a box." Ryan returned to New York. After two longshoremen were killed in a street fight with cops, the crisis escalated into the first general strike in America since 1919. Eventually the Longshoremen settled on better terms, including the abolition of the shape-up on the West Coast.

A few years later Bridges took his men out of the AFL into a new CIO union of longshoremen. At their first convention they held a mock funeral for Joe Ryan. "Here lies Joseph P. Ryan," they hooted, "who was both phoney and finky, knowing that he believed in the eternal principle of the shipowners. He valued the almighty dollar, never spoke the truth, and was unjust in his dealing with all union men."

❧ ❧

"The crookedest, stinkingest goddamn union I ever heard of," said a member of the Teamsters. "I don't know anything about these situations," Dan Tobin offered. "If dishonesty and racketeering exists, they keep it covered up."

❧ ❧

As the Depression began to lift, and prodded by New Deal measures, unions swelled in size and militancy. The factions of gangsters and Communists competed in organizing new groups of workers. Total union membership tripled from 3 million in 1933 to 9 million seven years later. The Teamsters grew the most, from eighty-two thousand in 1932 to a half-million members in a thousand locals by 1940. Because almost every industry used trucks, the Teamsters included workers in poultry, produce, flour and groceries, construction, laundries, breweries, cleaning and dyeing, taxicabs, garages, parking lots, gas stations, warehouses, freight terminals, racetracks, jukeboxes. Like longshore work, trucking was a fluid commodity that could not be stored up—as coal or wheat or steel could be—against the possibility of a strike. The trucks had to roll every day; many deliveries would spoil if delayed; strikes could wipe out the small-scale industries involved. That gave the Teamsters enormous, threatening power.

The union was organized from the bottom up. Locals were literally that, organized by local people, and Dan Tobin's office was not particular about who got charters. Money flowed to the general treasury but not from it. With over $6 million on hand in 1940, it still paid out no sickness, unemployment, or disability benefits. Tobin sat at his old-fashioned rolltop desk at Teamster headquarters in Indianapolis, safe behind a locked iron gate, bellowing defiance to his critics. "Uncle Dan fundamentally doesn't care who runs the locals," said an anonymous member of the union, "so long as they take orders and fork over to the International treasury."

Tobin's flaring pugnacity merely expressed his union's general temperament. Founded at the turn of the century, the Teamsters accumulated a consistent history of fistfights and violent strikes. In the early days, it took a rough, strong man to muscle cargo on and off his wagon, to handle a team of heavy dray horses, to sit on an exposed driver's seat all day long the year round. Even if employed by someone else, a teamster might work by himself in his own way—not like a factory hand punching a time clock, or a work gang with an impatient foreman nearby. Teamster work often suggested a lingering echo of an earlier time, when men worked humbly but for themselves, answering to nobody; a spirit of bellicose, fuck-you independence. "They are not college graduates," explained an attorney for the lawless Teamster Local 202 of New York. "They have grown up on the streets of New York, and the vast majority of them are second-generation Americans, American citizens, and they are law-abiding, but very often we do find a dereliction." Even if Dan Tobin had wanted to supervise his locals, he could not have managed it.

He lasted forty-five years as president because he left his locals alone. An Irish immigrant, he had come to Boston in 1890 as a fifteen-year-old. He drove a three-horse coal wagon twelve hours a day for eleven dollars a week. Teamsters, he said later, "were kicked around as the lowest sort of creatures." After the incumbent Teamster president was charged with extortion, Tobin was elected in 1907 as a reformist, cleanup candidate. Thereafter he lived well in two homes bought by the union, employed two sons in his office, and took long winter vacations in Miami. But he was never charged with any crimes of his own.

A bulky, ruddy-faced man, Tobin had a loud, unmodulated voice that evidently lacked a volume control. It served him well in making speeches—a Teamster crowd would sing "Danny Boy" as he approached the rostrum—and in dominating meetings. He loved whiskey, dice, and horse races ("My losses are known only to God and me," he would shout confidentially). Gifted with the constitution of a dray horse, he could retire dead drunk at four o'clock in the morning and then trumpet forth, in utter control of the situation, only four hours later. "Dan Tobin drank too much," Jimmy Hoffa concluded, "and lived too long."

Given the vacuum at the top, Tobin's eventual successors as president were already, in the 1930s, climbing the union structure in the usual Teamster style. Dave Beck of Seattle, the chief West Coast organizer, had the president's ear; Tobin usually consulted him before any important decision. "While Tobin was not a good organizer (he couldn't have organized his mother)," Beck said later, "he was the slickest politician I have ever known in the labor movement." As head of the labor division for all four of Franklin Roosevelt's presidential campaigns, Tobin spent long blocks of time in Washington, drinking and shouting with public servants. Beck meanwhile organized Teamster locals in the hostile territory of southern California, fielding many threats on his life, registering under different names in four or five hotels at once to avoid his enemies. "It got pretty rough," Beck recalled. "My safety wasn't worth a plugged nickel."

Young Jimmy Hoffa was organizing Detroit locals under similar Teamster-like conditions. His brother was shot. A Teamster business agent was killed by a strikebreaker. "Our cars were bombed out," Hoffa remembered. "Three different times, someone broke into the office and destroyed our furniture. Cars would crowd us off the streets. Then it got worse. They hired thugs who were out to get us, and brother, your life was in your hands every day. There was only one way to survive—fight back. And we used to slug it out on the streets. They found out we didn't scare. The police were no help. The police would beat your brains in for even talking union. The cops harassed us every day. If you went on strike, you had your head broken." Once Hoffa was arrested eighteen times within twenty-four hours for marching on a picket line; arrested, released, back to the line, arrested . . . Police also brought him in sixteen other times in ten years for extortion, assault and battery, conspiracy, and so on.

In these violent times for the labor movement, the Teamsters had more fights and more arrests than most other unions. Gangsters fought against the Teamsters, with them, and on both sides at once. The Mafioso Jimmy Fratianno, starting out in Cleveland, did muscle work for Teamster organizers. To persuade parking lot attendants to join the union, they would pour acid on car bodies, slash tires, and break windows. Babe Triscaro of the Cleveland Mafia was first a strikebreaker for a Black and Decker plant in Kent, Ohio. "I went down there to protect the plant," he later explained. Why had he stayed in the plant during the strike? "I would have gotten my head blowed off, so I couldn't get out. I had to stay there." For his efforts he was arrested and convicted of shooting to kill. Out of jail, he crossed the line and became president of Teamster Local 436 in Cleveland.

Given their ancient affinities for guns and violence, the Teamsters made easy accommodations with the underworld. If the gangsters played dirty, so did the cops and employers; better to have the thugs on your side. "Mob guys had muscle," Hoffa pointed out, "and where in hell do you think employers got the tough guys when they wanted to break a strike?" In 1935 "they" sent remnants of the old Purple Gang to fight the Teamsters in Detroit. "It was a real bloody business of bombings and beatings. So we made it our business to get to know them," as Hoffa told the story. "We made our point. They could let us alone and we'd let them alone. We didn't join forces with them and we didn't take any mobsters into our ranks." It was merely "an arrangement under which they'd stay out of our business and we'd stay out of theirs." (Twenty years later, Hoffa tried to arrange a retrial for one of the Purples convicted of killing a politician. Neither Hoffa nor his underworld partners forgot their friends.)

All over the country, Teamsters and gangsters worked out

similar arrangements. In New York Dewey sent eight officers of three Teamster locals to jail. "I am surprised at this tirade against labor," said the Longshoremen's Joe Ryan in defense of one of these crooks. "There are certain persons who think high wages constitute racketeering." Tony Sasso of Local 863 in Newark got three to five years for shaking down produce merchants. In Minneapolis a baking company paid hoodlums $16,500 to settle a dispute with Local 289. In Chicago, Joey Glimco (Local 777) and Joseph Aiuppa (Local 450) of the Capones were big men among the Teamsters. In Philadelphia, Turk Daniels and Shorty Feldman of Local 929 controlled the Dock Street Market, the main produce outlet for the city. "I'm putting you out of business because I don't like you, and there's not a thing you can do about it," Daniels told one offending merchant. "The hell with you and the hell with the farmers. You're closed. Let the produce rot." Teamsters had their ways.

On the record, Tobin denounced any stray gangsters that might have unaccountably wandered into the union—"one or two so-called cheap racketeers in New York, Chicago, Cleveland, Detroit, or some other large city"—and he had a Teamster convention resolve that any convicted criminal would be expelled. But more revealing was a curious, secret episode in 1933. Paddy Berrell, head of the Chicago Teamsters, had been murdered. Leslie Goudie, who took his place, got a phone call in June 1933 from somebody who said he was a lawyer. "He said he represented certain men who were interested in the International Brotherhood of Teamsters, and that they wanted to see me. I said I would see them and suggested they come to my office or that I'd meet them in any office or hotel they'd name." No, they—Capones, presumably—wanted to see Goudie on the street. He agreed to meet them the next day at the corner of California and Peterson avenues.

At the appointed time three cars drove up. Goudie was called to the middle car, in which sat three men armed with revolvers and a machine gun. "You've taken Paddy Berrell's place. We want $300,000," he was told. "Go get the money from Dan Tobin. We came to you because you took Berrell's place. Go tell Tobin we want it." So Goudie went to Indianapolis and advised Tobin and his national secretary, Tom Hughes, of the shakedown. "Tobin and Hughes listened, then went into another room to talk it over. When they came back into the room, they asked me what I thought should be done." The money was not paid, at least according to Goudie, and Tobin later appointed him international organizer for Chicago. The most suggestive aspect of the story, though, was that Tobin considered the matter at all—and then handed it back to Goudie for his opinion.

In the fashion of Joe Ryan, Tobin worried more about Communists than gangsters in his union. The tradition of local autonomy allowed Communists to penetrate some Teamster locals. In Minneapolis, Farrell Dobbs and the Dunne brothers—all of them members of the Trotskyite wing of the Communist party—got control of Local 544 and led an epochal strike in 1934. After four months, four deaths, scores of injuries, and the calling of the National Guard, the Teamsters won a good settlement. Dobbs then started organizing "over-the-road" drivers, intercity and interstate truckers scorned by Tobin. Eventually these over-the-road members became the dominant faction within the Teamsters and the main source of Jimmy Hoffa's power. But Tobin expelled Local 544 for Communist activities. The Dunnes then took their local to the CIO. Organized crime settled down into the Teamsters. No mobbed-up union had to fret about Communist infiltration; the two conspiracies could not coexist.

❦ ❦

The collusion of gangsters and employers went farthest and lasted longest at the Ford Motor Company. Organized crime had never before come so close to a major American corporation. In true underworld style, this came about through the singular personality and personal influence of one man, Harry Bennett, an anomalous WASP gangster. He knew nothing about cars or the car business. His job title—director of Ford's Service Department—by itself carried no authority. He worked from an inconspicuous office, with a private, unmarked entrance, in the basement of the administration building in Dearborn. He never gave speeches and seldom appeared in public. Curious journalists found him inaccessible. The company's publicists did not mention him or celebrate his works. Yet for two decades Harry Bennett reigned as the second most important man in the Ford Motor Company.

It was essentially a family matter, driven by the tangled relations among three men: old Henry Ford himself; his only son and heir apparent, Edsel Ford; and Bennett, a year older than Edsel.

Henry Ford turned seventy in 1933. Still the absolute boss—when he chose to be—of the company he had founded, Ford was getting old, his attention sporadic, his judgment capricious. He whipsawed his son by badgering him to be strong, to take charge, yet not extending the authority he needed to do it. The company president in name only, Edsel Ford was a gentle, civilized man with interests that ranged into territories unknown to his ignorant father. He had married a society woman from old-money Detroit. They lived in Grosse Pointe, moving in social circles scorned by Henry Ford as effete and self-indulgent. The father wondered if his son was too weak, too sickly, too far from the shop floor to run his company the right way.

Then there was Harry Bennett. Out of school after the eighth grade, a former Episcopal choirboy, he had spent six years in the Navy, boxing and roaming the world. Tattoos covered his arms. Known at Ford as "the little guy downstairs," he was small and wiry, tightly muscled, quick and jaunty in his movements. Even when relaxed he seemed alert, his eyes on high beam; nothing escaped him. "He was wound up tight like a watch spring," an associate observed. "He looked like a man who found life interesting and fun." He kept lions and tigers as pets, sometimes bringing them to work. Fond of guns and hunting, he would punctuate meetings in his office by firing an air gun shaped like a Luger toward a target at the other end of the room. His more peculiar habits were perhaps a conscious act, to keep people off balance and wondering what he might do next. To an exceptional degree he had the habit of command. Expecting to dominate any situation, he made decisions easily and barked orders in a clipped, clear voice not to be questioned.

In Bennett the old man found the son he wanted Edsel to be. They were introduced during the First World War by Arthur Brisbane of the Hearst syndicate. Ford soon made him boss of the Service Department, the euphemistically named security force that policed every Ford operation. By the late 1920s Bennett was spending more time with Ford than anyone except Ford's wife. Every morning at 7:30 Ford would telephone; often they rode to work together. For most of the day Bennett went wherever Ford went. Every night, no matter where Bennett was, Ford would call him at 9:30 for a final exchange. They discussed every aspect of company business, and Bennett did not withhold his opinions. This extraordinary access to the throne, regardless of job descriptions or organization charts, gave Bennett his power. "What I like about Harry," said Ford, "is that if I want something done he will do it; I don't have to tell him twice." On his own Bennett could hire or fire almost any employee, arrange transfers, and manipulate expense accounts. Edsel Ford, detesting Bennett, must have felt displaced and jealous—but he was helpless to resist his own subordination by the little guy downstairs. "I supervised anything that was wrong," Bennett later claimed. "That is, if there was a department wrong, I was sent in to straighten it up, any department."

Bennett ran his Service Department like an underworld gang. He kept no records, wrote no reports, answered only to Henry Ford; certain conversations in his office were secretly recorded by a Dictograph. "Don't try to catch me on dates," he later told the Kefauver committee. "I never made a note in my life." To staff his gang he hired hoodlums, ex-cons, football players, army veterans, boxers, and wrestlers. "They're a lot of tough bastards," Bennett said proudly, "but every goddam one of them's a gentleman." (An arguable point; "they never looked or acted like Ford men," according to the general manager Charles Sorensen, "and Edsel and I were continually apologizing for their bad manners.")

Aside from the Ford offices in Dearborn, the Service men roamed the Highland Park and River Rouge plants nearby. River Rouge was the largest industrial complex in the world, spread across 1,100 acres, taking in coke and iron ore at one end and disgorging cars at the other, with an assembly line 950 feet long. In this self-enclosed empire, Bennett's men looked for tiny job derelictions—talking or whistling on company time—as well as the larger crimes of Communist and union agitation. Feared and hated by everyone else in the company, they skulked around at the bottom of the Ford pecking order. "The army of 'servicemen' give the impression of a last dilution of the lusterless middle-class power which dominates the workers at Ford's," Edmund Wilson concluded after a visit. "Openly jeered at by these, upon whom they are set to spy, not particularly beloved by the lower white-collars, whom they are supposed to have an eye on, too, they must keep to the right side of the middle-class line, and they prowl in the plant and the offices like sallow and hollow trolls, dreaming no doubt of executive desks."

The Service Department functioned merely as Bennett's launching platform. From it he forged ties to the world outside by an inexhaustible flow of favors and inside information—the reciprocal services, asked and rendered, of any underworld king. When River Rouge was running flat out, it employed over one hundred thousand workers; in Dearborn, Ford property amounted to 62 percent of the city's tax base. As Ford went, so went the local economy. Nearby governments and police forces therefore deferred to Bennett's whims, knowing that he spoke for the old man. Carl Brooks, the Dearborn police chief, a former employee of Bennett's, gave special attention to any crimes reported at Ford. "I don't know why," a Dearborn cop remarked, "but he seemed to be more interested in those cases." But then—the reciprocity—Brooks could always get a man hired at Ford. "You can have a job as long as you want on the police department," he told one of his cops; "if not, then you can have a job over at the Ford Motor."

Bennett's power rippled outward across the state. He sat on the Michigan Prison Commission and on the board of trustees of the University of Michigan. (He gave the school football players easy summer jobs and let them practice on company time.) He paid the bills and traveling expenses for Republican state conventions. Grateful politicians courted his favor. Supplicant officeholders, businessmen, journalists, celebrities, and movie stars found their way to the inconspicuous basement office. Sitting there, tilted back with one leg on the desk and the other folded under him, natty in his colorful silk shirts and bow ties, Bennett loved the attention, the diversity of the show. "I talked to governors and racketeers and judges," he said, "and everybody in my office all at one time."

Racketeers in particular. The effectiveness of the Service Department—the fear and respect it extracted—depended finally on Bennett's gangster contacts. Even his congeniality with his companion Henry Ford hung, to some extent, on these ties; Ford evidently enjoyed the vicarious titillation of hearing about Bennett's underworld colleagues. (Edsel Ford had nothing to do with such people.) To perform his muscle work Bennett hired many gangsters. He kept up friendships with cops and robbers all over the country, and he liked to show off these connections. The head of the Michigan state police would bring famous criminals to meet Bennett. On a selective basis, Bennett fed helpful tips to the FBI and other law enforcement agencies. "On numerous occasions when serious crimes occurred in Detroit and elsewhere in the state," the FBI's Detroit office reported to Washington in 1939, "he has personally entered activities of the investigation and been of considerable assistance."

It was a dangerous tightrope act, moving back and forth between crooks and lawmen, making both believe he was their useful friend. Many stories were told about Bennett and his obsession with crime. He solved one murder by taking the suspect to his home, beating him up, and forcing a confession. On the other hand, he protected a witness to the Purple Gang's Collingwood Massacre by stashing the man on a Ford freighter bound across the Atlantic. Once he was shot by a gangster whom he had interfered with in a kidnapping case. As he was recovering, Bennett received a photograph of the gangster's bullet-perforated corpse and a message: "He won't bother you any more, Harry." Thereafter he was more careful. His elaborate home near Ann Arbor had secret rooms and passages and a tunnel, hidden behind a bookcase, to other buildings on the property. He was driven to and from work at high speeds, sometimes with an escort car of bodyguards, and he kept a .45 revolver at hand while en route.

For his most powerful and dangerous gangster friends, the Mafiosi of Detroit, Bennett arranged legitimate business deals with the company—evidence of his power outside the Service Department. According to Bennett, it started when Henry Ford, acting on one of his unpredictable humanitarian impulses, decided to mediate the bloody feuds among the local Italian gangs. "Mr. Ford heard about it and the papers wrote it up," Bennett recalled, "and he said, 'By God, we will straighten this out.'" Bennett contacted Chet La Mare, boss of the West Side faction. "I am the king," La Mare told him. "You deal with me, and nobody gets killed." To grease the arrangement, La Mare was given a Ford dealership (Crescent Motor Sales) and the fruit concession for the food wagons at River Rouge. But La Mare "didn't know a banana from an orange," Bennett said later, and he was soon murdered anyway. La Mare was not the king he claimed to be, and Bennett omitted unbecoming motives in his recounting.

Two other deals with Mafiosi lasted longer. Around 1931 Anthony D'Anna asked Walter Hancock, the River Rouge police chief, to arrange an appointment at Dearborn because he wanted a Ford agency in Wyandotte, a few miles downriver from River Rouge. In one of the strange-bedfellows encounters so typical of Bennett's reign, the police chief took the Mafioso to meet the little guy downstairs. D'Anna got not only the agency—Pardo Auto Sales—

but an exclusive contract as well to haul new cars from Highland Park and River Rouge. D'Anna's company, E. & L. Auto Transport, kept this lucrative privilege for at least twenty years. What D'Anna did in gratitude was not on the record. By the nature of such exchanges, he must have done Bennett substantial favors.

In 1932 Bennett lined up another Mafia haulaway contract, this one for Joe Adonis of the Luciano family of New York. The Automotive Conveying Company of New Jersey, controlled by Adonis, hauled cars from the Ford plant in Edgewater, across the Hudson River from Manhattan, to various points in the Northeast. It was good business for Adonis—$8 million worth up to 1940—and a lucky connection for Bennett, as it happened, after he squabbled with Pete Licavoli of Detroit. Bennett had hired Licavoli's thugs into the Service Department. When Licavoli demanded a raise from six to fifteen dollars a day for each man, Bennett fired the whole crew. Striking back, Licavoli's gang ran Bennett's car off the road one day in 1937 and nearly killed him. The contending parties then called in someone from the New York Mafia—where Bennett was, through Adonis, already well met—to settle it peacefully.

Aside from indulging Bennett's boy-detective tendencies, the main point of hiring gangsters was to fight unions. Henry Ford and Harry Bennett disliked all labor organizations, the United Auto Workers in particular. Affiliated with the CIO, the UAW was led by two left-wing factions, one Communist, the other socialist under Walter Reuther and his brothers. In March 1932 they staged a "Hunger March" on River Rouge; Bennett drove through the plant gate, stepped from his car, was hit on the head by a brick, and went down. With that the cops and Ford men started shooting from inside the gate. Four strikers were killed. They all received Red funerals: Communist eulogies, coffins draped in red, mourners with red armbands, interments to the strains of the "International."

Once again it was gangsters against Communists and left-wingers. General Motors settled with the UAW in February 1937. Chrysler followed two months later. Only Ford held out. To do battle the Service Department, nominally a force of four hundred, grew to some three thousand troops: the biggest private army in the world. UAW organizers were routinely beaten by gangs of Service thugs at Ford plants. "They got a small sample of what they will get," Bennett warned, "if they ever come out again."

On the evening of April 9, 1938, Walter Reuther's family and friends celebrated a birthday at his home. They called out for Chinese food. An hour later someone knocked on the door. "There stood two toughs with drawn revolvers," Victor Reuther later recalled. "They pushed their way into the room, shouting, 'Okay, back against the wall!' At first it was as unreal as a clip from an old silent movie. The shorter gunman wore a dark hat with the brim turned down to conceal his eyes; he was obviously the trigger man. The other gangster spotted Walter immediately, put his gun in its holster, and drew out of his rear pocket an enormous blackjack with a leather strap, which he twined around his wrist. 'Okay, Red, you're coming with us,' he said. Only gradually did we realize this was no joke."

The birthday party saved Reuther; the presence of so many people confused the situation. While the short man kept the others covered, the thug with the blackjack went after Walter Reuther. They parried blows briefly. "Kill the son of a bitch," the tall man shouted to his partner. During the commotion one of the party-goers jumped out a kitchen window to a concrete alley two flights down and yelled for help. The neighborhood awoke as people gathered in the street. Afraid of being caught, the two thugs fled.

Two days later Reuther paid an informer for the names of the intruders: Eddie Percelli, a former bootlegger in Detroit, and Bud Holt, a former employee of Harry Bennett's. Reuther was told it was a conspiracy among Bennett and Detroit's city hall and police department to kill Reuther and dump his body in the Detroit River. Each of the people at the birthday party, brought in to view separate lineups, identified Percelli and Holt as the men who had broken in. At the trial the defense emphasized the radical politics of the Reuthers and dismissed the incident as a ruse concocted by the UAW. The jury bought it, and the two men were acquitted.

Outside Detroit, though, Bennett could not control the legal and political machinery. A series of rulings by the Supreme Court and the National Labor Relations Board revealed the lawless workings of the Service Department and forced Ford to deal with the UAW. In May 1941, 70 percent of the Ford workers voted to join the CIO union; "a great victory for the Communist Party," Bennett announced. As part of the settlement, the Service Department was disbanded and plant security employees were required to wear uniforms and badges.

A few years later, after Edsel Ford's death at forty-nine, his son

Henry Ford II took over the company. The day he assumed power, Harry Bennett was gone. But a gangster influence lingered. Tony D'Anna and Joe Adonis kept their haulaway contracts. In 1948 a Mafia hitman, Raymond Patriarca of the New England Mafia family, fired a shotgun at Walter Reuther as he stood in his kitchen. A refrigerator door absorbed most of the blast, and Reuther escaped again.

🌿 🌿

The case of Willie Bioff and the Hollywood moguls suggested the Ford episode turned inside out. Again employers and gangsters conspired together, with the flexing national muscle of an emergent Mafia as the enforcement power. In Hollywood, though, the gangsters worked from within the union—the International Alliance of Theatrical Stage Employees and Motion Picture Operators, better known as the Stagehands union—subverting it to the employers' purposes, to the mutual benefit of all but the union members. The case became notorious because the conspiring employers included the biggest names in the business: Joseph M. Schenck of Twentieth Century–Fox, Louis B. Mayer of MGM, Harry Cohn of Columbia, and Harry and Albert Warner of Warner Brothers.

Joe Schenck, one of the founders of Hollywood, president of the Association of Motion Picture Producers, was the key figure among the moguls. He and his brother, Nick, were Russian Jewish immigrants from a village on the Volga River. After a childhood of selling newspapers on the Lower East Side, they had operated nickelodeons and concessions in an amusement park, then migrated with the movie business to southern California in the 1920s. Rising on the success of Buster Keaton, Fatty Arbuckle, Mutt and Jeff cartoons, and Norma Talmadge (Joe Schenck's wife), by 1927 the brothers were said to be worth $20 million, with an annual income of a million dollars. Not a hands-on producer like Mayer, or an imperious tyrant like Cohn, Joe Schenck excelled as a diplomat and lobbyist for the movies.

He showed some of Harry Bennett's knack for keeping an unlikely collection of allies happy. Schenck handed out many dollars and favors to crucial politicians, and they remembered him. "Whatever Joe Schenck wanted," recalled Arthur Samish, the boss of the California Legislature, "I got for him." As one of the most generous donors to Franklin Roosevelt's campaigns, he could always get the attention of Jim Farley, dispenser of New Deal patronage. Well connected in Sacramento and Washington, Schenck did not neglect William Randolph Hearst either. "I am quite sure that everything will turn out to your entire satisfaction in Southern California," he wrote Hearst's attorney. "You can depend on me for all assistance that I can possibly give you." Sliding further down the scale of respectability, Schenck had old friends in organized crime as well. (All his life he bet heavily on horse races.) According to Anita Loos, his screenwriter and loyal advocate, "He came to know every element of the gangster world, from its lowest ranks on up to the top echelons." When Norma Talmadge fell in love with the actor Gilbert Roland, some of Schenck's hoodlum pals offered to murder Roland. Schenck— ever the conciliator—said no thanks and arranged for his wife's divorce and remarriage.

Joe Schenck and Willie Bioff came from similar backgrounds. Also a Russian Jew, Bioff was brought to America at age five, grew up on the Southwest side of Chicago, and made it through the third grade. Thereafter, as he told the story, he was on his own. As a young man he joined the labor movement, in a way, by doing muscle work for Mike Galvin, boss of the Eighteenth Ward and a leading Teamster. Bioff was short and brawny, fast-tempered and often arrested, well educated in the streetways of Chicago. In 1922 he was convicted of running a whorehouse on South Halstead Street. "I was a youngster at the time," he said later. "I never had no bringin' up. I never knew no better." Sentenced to six months, he did eight days in jail.

Affiliated with the Capones as a labor specialist, Bioff was trying to organize the city's kosher butchers in 1932 when he connected with George E. Browne, business agent for Local 2 of the Stage-hands. The union—which included movie projectionists, electricians, carpenters, painters, and other theater workers—was already gangster ridden. Locals in New York, Newark, Cincinnati, St. Louis, Chicago, and southern California were using violence and extorting protection money from theater owners. "We are being unmercifully persecuted by a notorious method of racke-teering by a gang of inhuman scoundrels," protested an owner in Alhambra, California. "Our theatres are being stench bombed, tear gas bombed. Three have been burned. They are broken into at night and motion picture equipment machines, seats, carpets, draperies are destroyed." Tommy Maloy, who ran a projectionists' local in Chicago for the Capones, had been suspected in nine murders. One resisting theater owner was even killed in Maloy's office. His local was a closed shop, with no new members admitted since 1916; Maloy stole at least half a million dollars from the treasury.

So Willie Bioff was on familiar territory when he joined George Browne in Local 2 of the Stagehands. Never actually a member of the union, Bioff did the thinking for Browne, a pickled oaf supposedly capable of drinking a hundred bottles of beer every day. When beered up, Browne liked to wander from saloon to saloon, sticking his face and pistol through the door, shouting, "Anybody here think he's tougher than I am?" The Capones did and were. In the spring of 1934 they told Browne he had a new partner: the Capone gang would thereafter take half the earnings of Local 2. The percentage increased later.

In return for services, of course. At a meeting in suburban Riverside, the top Capone bosses—Frank Nitti, Paul the Waiter Ricca, Louis Campagna, and others—ordered Browne to run for the presidency of the whole Stagehands union at the national convention in Louisville that summer. Browne worried about his tepid support in certain locals out of state. No problem, said the Capones; they would make arrangements with their associates Lucky Luciano and Lepke Buchalter in New York, Longy Zwillman in Newark, Big Al Polizzi in Cleveland, and Johnny Dougherty in St. Louis. At Louisville, in an atmosphere of bribes and intimidation, Browne was duly elected president. A few months later Bioff and Browne were summoned to a Mafia dinner party at Tommy Lucchese's Casino de Paree in Manhattan. Among the luminaries on hand were Jack Dragna from Los Angeles, Paul Ricca from Chicago, Luciano and Frank Costello from New York, "and many other heads from the different cities that I don't know," as Bioff put it later. Ricca told Bioff "to be free to call on Charlie Lucky or on Frank Costello if we find any difficulties here in our work, and if we need anything to call on them and be free to call on them, because that is their people."

The Mafiosi were aiming at Hollywood. Instead of just shaking down random theater owners, the Capones and their associates wanted the plush movie studios. When Bioff came out to Hollywood in 1935, he found other gangsters already on hand, moving around the studios and talent agencies. Johnny Roselli of the Capones and Bugsy Siegel of the Lucianos were there. Mickey Cohen would soon arrive. Roselli did labor conciliation work (strikebreaking) for the producers, and Siegel had clout in the union of movie extras. Jimmy Durante and George Raft maintained durable underworld friendships. Frank Costello was close to Harry Cohn of Columbia and George Wood of the William Morris Agency. "The guy's all right," Costello said of Cohn, "and he's done some favors for us back here." At Warner Brothers, Bryan Foy produced B movies, including numerous gangster epics, and he later employed Roselli in his own production company. Mark Hellinger, once a Broadway scribe in New York, worked for Foy in Hollywood. Hellinger helped his old Broadway pals stay out of trouble while he placed bets "on anything," according to his biographer, "from the spin of a wheel to the color of the next license plate coming down a road."

Bioff did not have to "corrupt" Hollywood any more than he had needed to corrupt the Stagehands union. In both instances he folded smoothly into the environment. As a union organizer in Hollywood he achieved wonders—because, it later turned out, he had the help (at first dragooned and then more or less willing) of the producers. A failed strike in 1933 had decimated Stagehands Local 37 in Hollywood. Before Bioff appeared it had shrunk to thirty-three paid-up members, no longer held meetings, and was not part of the "basic agreement" between unions and studios. Bioff went right to the producers and demanded $2 million. After howls and threats the costs came down to an annual $50,000 from the major studios, $25,000 from the lesser ones. (Joe Schenck could work anything out.) Suddenly the Stagehands were again made part of the basic agreement. Studio bulletin boards announced that employees must join the union; membership zoomed overnight to twelve thousand.

The producers thought Bioff's fees excessive, running to a total of $1.1 million from 1936 to 1940. But their money bought privileges and stable labor relations. They no longer had to deal with volatile memberships or union elections, just with Bioff and Browne, who could be bribed to call off strikes and cut wage scales. The Stagehands helped the producers break a strike by a rival CIO union, and they forced a favorable settlement with the Screen

Actors Guild. (Employers always preferred gangsters to Communists.) Under Bioff the Stagehands also jacked up wages and costs for live theater, which helped the competing movie theaters.

As Harry Warner acknowledged, it was "good business" to stay on friendly terms with Bioff. Joe Schenck gave Bioff and his wife an ocean cruise to Rio de Janeiro and Europe, with a send-off party and orchids from Harry Warner. "We have had less interruption of employment," said Sidney Kent of Twentieth Century–Fox at the 1938 Stagehands convention, "less hard feeling, less recrimination, and have built more good will than any industry I know of in the country."

Bioff had put an opulent distance between himself and the whorehouse on South Halstead Street. He bought an eighty-acre farm in the San Fernando Valley and started raising alfalfa. "My wife is nuts about flowers, and so am I," he purred. "We grow all our own fruit and vegetables. I'm building a playhouse, so I can have a place to entertain my pals." He had the grounds landscaped with cedars, palms, and $600 olive trees. The dining room was furnished in mahogany, the living room in Louis Quinze, all of it executed in typically overstated gangster chic. Did this all suggest great wealth? "It's the union that's rich, not Willie Bioff," he laughed. "We got four and a half million dollars in our war chest and we're ready for anything." ("We had about 20 percent of Hollywood when we got in trouble," he said later, more candidly. "If we hadn't got loused up we'd of had 50 percent. I had Hollywood dancin' to my tune.")

The pimp's empire started to unravel when an abused group of dissidents within Local 37 asked Carey McWilliams, a radical labor attorney in Los Angeles, to help them. He found enough evidence to force investigations by the state legislature and the district attorney of Sacramento County. They turned up a smoking gun: a check for $100,000 to Bioff from Joe Schenck's nephew. Neither Bioff nor Schenck had plausible explanations. Federal agencies became interested. The columnist Westbrook Pegler got on the case, winning a Pulitzer Price for his exposures. Bioff and Browne were convicted of labor racketeering, Schenck of evading over $400,000 in taxes, and they all went to jail.

After three years of prison life, Bioff decided to testify against the Capones lurking behind the whole enterprise. On the day the indictments came down, Frank Nitti shot himself, a rare Mafia suicide. The other Capones involved were convicted on Bioff's relished, reckless testimony. Once out of jail, Bioff changed his name and moved to Phoenix, Arizona. But he foolishly surfaced a few years later, and the Mafia never forgot. A car bomb blew him apart.

❦ ❦

Sidney Hillman was the exception to the rule: a CIO leader with deep, criminal ties to the underworld. As president of the Amalgamated Clothing Workers, Hillman hired the regular services of Lepke Buchalter, successor to Dopey Benny Fein as the main labor racketeer in New York. That was Hillman's secret life. In public he was known as Franklin Roosevelt's most influential labor adviser. A frequent guest at the White House, he became a key administrator of the National Recovery Act and later of the wartime Office of Production Management, and from time to time was mentioned as a replacement for Secretary of Labor Frances Perkins. Straddling his two milieus, Hillman bestrode a jagged knife edge, a secret schizophrenic between underworld and upperworld.

No wonder that Hillman was nervous, rushed, and prone to collapsing from stress and overwork. The double life exacted its toll. Born in Lithuania, educated in rabbinical studies, briefly imprisoned in Russia after the Revolution of 1905, he had come to America on his own at age twenty, without contacts or knowledge of English. After a short period of cutting fabric in a clothing factory, he went into union work. Hillman had qualities of imagination and shy ambition that attracted useful patrons such as Jane Addams and Louis Brandeis. In 1914, only seven years after arriving in America, he became the founding president of the Amalgamated Clothing Workers. Leaving behind his youthful socialism, he fought Communists in his union and was known as a unionist with whom employers could bargain, to avoid strikes and keep everybody working. "One is more likely to get concessions while one is on speaking and bargaining terms," he pointed out. "In Russia I discovered how universal is the fear of chaos. Only a few can nourish their lives on the promises alone of things to come. Most of us need to make a living now, mate now, enjoy now a reasonable degree of social stability." A pact with organized crime helped stabilize the chaos.

Louis Buchalter, the gangster commonly known as Lepke, came

from a more favored background than Hillman's. As one acquaintance noted, Lepke "should have turned out better." Ten years younger than Hillman, he had been born on the Lower East Side of Russian Jewish immigrants. The father ran a hardware shop on Henry Street, and Lepke's siblings entered honest professions. Lepke managed to stay clean through elementary school. Then he went into the streets and started stealing. He looked inoffensive: of average height, with nondescript features, soft eyes, and an apologetic manner. Never a bootlegger, he played golf and read good books. Associates called him the Judge or Judge Louie. Lawmen held him responsible for over eighty murders. "His eyes were so expressive," noted a fellow prisoner at Leavenworth; "he could think of a million things and they'd be in his eyes. That head held so many secrets. . . . I'll never forget that guy's eyes."

Lepke was boss of the Jewish-Italian gang in Brooklyn that newspapers liked to call Murder, Incorporated. Most of the boys had grown up in the Brownsville section, hanging around a pool hall and candy store under the Elevated tracks at the corner of Livonia and Saratoga avenues. Pittsburgh Phil Strauss, one of the leaders, was tall, handsome, athletic, and a prolific killer. "He was a pleasant enough guy to meet," a Brownsville friend remembered, "and one of the sharpest dressers I ever saw. But he was an impatient punk who would poke a fork in a waiter's eye if the restaurant service wasn't fast enough, and with a gun in his hands he had the itchiest fingers in Brownsville." After these Jewish hoods combined with Italians from the adjacent Ocean Hill neighborhood, the gang came under the hegemony of Albert Anastasia and the Mangano Mafia family, lords of that part of Brooklyn. "We thought Lepke ran his own mob," recalled Harry Anslinger of the Bureau of Narcotics, "but it later turned out that he was an important cog in the Mafia and subject to the orders of the big boys of that organization."

Caught in this corner of the Mafia's national ascendancy, Lepke's gang surrendered its autonomy in return for the privileges of association. "Everybody knew that Albert was the boss of the different mobs in Brooklyn," one gang member, Seymour Magoon, later confessed. "His power lay in the fact that he was part of the national combination; in other words, if he were crossed, the one incurring his displeasure verily incurred the displeasure of the national underworld. Albert A., in turn, put Louis Capone in the Brownsville mob as his front man there.

Albert always seemed to side with the Brownsville mob in their entanglements or trouble with members of other mobs. For instance, if they were very wrong, it was only then that they were reprimanded, but always with a secretive 'Go ahead.' " As part of the arrangement, Lepke's gang killed Dutch Schultz, the last big Jewish hoodlum who had refused to accommodate the Italians. "We had to go down and get their permission," agreed Abe Reles, another Brownsville gangster. "Albert goes down and puts the pressure on for us. Even if you're wrong he can make it right. Small things here and there, they wouldn't be in on, but where large sums were involved, they would get a share."

Lepke meantime kept his own labor rackets, dealing usually with Jewish victims. Deploying a crew of up to 250 enforcers and collectors, pillaging flour and baking companies, garment workers, projectionists, leather workers, milliners, handbag makers, shoemakers, taxis, cleaning and dyeing, poultry markets, and restaurants, Lepke's men hauled in $5 million, perhaps $10 million a year from both unions and employers. "They were all through the garment district," one businessman said later. "Everybody around the garment district knew them. You had to know them."

Inevitably Lepke collided with Hillman's Amalgamated locals. On the record Hillman struck bold postures against "the curse of underworldism," as he put it in 1931. "Racketeers have established themselves in parts of the industry and labor has been made to pay the price," he said. "We must rid ourselves and the industry of the hold-up men." In a noted episode that year, Hillman flushed hoodlums from his Cutter Local 4, announcing a clear victory afterward.

It was just smoke and verbiage, a fine-sounding diversion. A few years later, when Dewey started pursuing labor rackets, he had Hillman and David Dubinsky of the Ladies' Garment Workers union come to his home for dinner. "They both dealt with these gangsters and knew all about them," Dewey recalled years later, "but they wouldn't give me the slightest bit of help of any kind, and they never did. . . . We had to make our own, tough way."

Hillman's dealings with Lepke proceeded through stages, from resistance to détente to criminal cooperation. At first Hillman decided to have Lepke and his top assistant, Gurrah Shapiro, killed. The contract went to an Italian, one Bruno from New Jersey, who passed it on to Salvatore Maranzano's Mafia family. The job was botched; shots were fired but missed.

Hillman liked to settle things. For five years, from 1932 to 1937, Hillman paid Lepke a regular $350 each week; of this, the Luciano family took a weekly $50 in tribute. Usually Hillman gave the money to Murray Weinstein, his trusted associate in the Amalgamated since 1914. Weinstein would pass it along to Danny Fields, a labor goon and former boxer, who delivered it to Lepke. Sometimes, if the occasion warranted, Hillman and Lepke would bypass their intermediaries and meet face to face in a suite at the Governor Clinton Hotel in Manhattan. Hillman would set up the meeting through Weinstein or Fields.

For these payoffs Lepke performed various kinds of muscle work. According to the subsequent secret testimony of Albert Tannenbaum, a Lepke gangster, "Tannenbaum did 'slugging' work on occasion for Hillman." When Hillman "experienced trouble in connection with the Amalgamated," he would tell Fields or (more often) Weinstein, "and they would transmit the matter to Lepke. If the nature of the trouble was such as in Lepke's opinion called for 'slugging,' he would get Harry (Greenie) Greenberg, who had charge of such work for Lepke, and 'Greenie' would pick perhaps Tannenbaum and others in the gang who could do the work and the troublesome people were 'slugged.' Generally two men would be picked for a 'slugging' and would be paid a hundred dollars. This money would be paid by 'Greenie,' who would receive the money from Lepke."

Special occasions cost more. The Amalgamated paid Lepke a $25,000 bonus for his help in winning a strike, and other fees for other extra services in labor disputes. Once Hillman gave $20,000 to Lepke's emissary to fix a murder charge involving the garment industry. Lucky Luciano—Lepke's ultimate boss as the top Mafioso in New York—also had influence in the union. At around this time, Luciano offered Joe Bonanno "a piece of the action in the garment district" as a gesture of friendship from one Mafia family head to another. "As I understood it, Luciano and his men received regular payoffs from the Amalgamated," Bonanno said later. "Luciano had extensive interests in the clothing industry, especially in the Amalgamated." Bonanno declined the offer in order—he said—to keep his independence from the stronger Luciano family.

Of course stories about Hillman's gangster dealings were passed around the garment district. In 1935 Max Rubin of the Amalgamated's Local 240 took some delivery business away from Morris Blustein, a garment trucker, and gave it to another trucker tied to

Lepke. Trying to fight back, Blustein got nowhere with Rubin, so he went to see Hillman, who brushed him off. Losing his temper, Blustein grabbed Hillman hard. "Listen, Mr. Hillman," he said, "I know that your hands are full of blood. You've killed plenty of people. I'll be damned if you're going to kill me." "I've got nothing to do with it," Hillman replied. "Go and see Max Rubin." A day or so later, Danny Fields met Blustein on Fifth Avenue and warned him not to bother Hillman again. "Then I figured the best way out of it was to keep quiet," Blustein decided, "because I knew who Danny Fields was." (A Lepke enforcer, that is.)

Lepke's weekly stipend from Hillman ended in 1937 only because he then went underground, chased by the feds on a narcotics charge and by Dewey for murder. Even while on the lam, Lepke still received a helpful $1,400 from the Amalgamated. While Lepke hid in an apartment on Foster Avenue in Brooklyn, Dewey and federal agents searched the country for him. Every Sunday, Walter Winchell used his radio show to urge Lepke to turn himself in. With the pressure being jacked up, notch by notch, and spilling over onto other New York gangsters, Lepke's Italian masters ordered him to surrender to the lesser federal narcotics charge. Albert Anastasia drove him from the Foster Avenue hideout to Madison Square Park in Manhattan, where Lepke presented himself to Walter Winchell—glorying in the crimestopping role he loved to play—and his friend J. Edgar Hoover of the FBI.

The scheme worked at first. Convicted in the dope case, Lepke was safely sent to Leavenworth for a fourteen-year stay. But the feds then handed him over to the New York authorities. Convicted of murder, he was condemned to the electric chair; not what he had in mind. Hoping to save his life, Lepke started singing about his dealings with Sidney Hillman. Two Lepke henchmen under other indictments, Albert Tannenbaum and Paul Berger, supported Lepke's revelations. Lepke added another story: that Hillman had been himself involved in the 1931 murder of Guido Ferreri, a clothing manufacturer who had been fighting the Amalgamated's organizing efforts.

Lepke's stories about Hillman circulated among the FBI, the Bureau of Narcotics, and the Manhattan DA's office, along with the separate confessions of Tannenbaum and Berger. "The facts fitted together too precisely for error," Harry Anslinger recalled. "Lepke was willing to talk, so far as we could gather, in an all-out attempt to save his neck. While I do not believe any deals should have been made with this mass murderer, I believe his testimony and that of his associates who wanted to corroborate his story should have been taken, the evidence presented to a grand jury, and an indictment obtained." But under New York law, the mere testimony of accomplices was not enough, and the necessary outside corroboration did not turn up. It may be assumed as well that Hillman's political connections and prominence helped save him. "He is a big shot," Max Rubin loyally pointed out. "He knows President Roosevelt—he wouldn't know any of this stuff."

Lepke went to the chair in March 1944—the only big-time American gangster ever to be legally executed. Hillman, after a period in limbo while Lepke told his tales, resumed his place in New Deal circles. "Clear it with Sidney," Roosevelt is supposed to have said before the 1944 Democratic convention. The phrase became a jeering Republican slogan in the campaign that fall, as Dewey lost his first presidential election. Hillman died in 1946, only fifty-nine but already worn out, and was canonized as a great American labor statesman.

❧ ❧

In the aftermath of World War II, the two labor conspiracies from the Depression decade fared quite differently. The Red scare of McCarthyism drove the Communists from the labor movement. This retreat left their natural enemies, the gangsters, in yet stronger positions. The underworld presence in American unions has proved to be quite durable and consistent. For a half century after the 1930s, the Laborers, Hotel and Restaurant Employees, Longshoremen, and Teamsters remained the four most bemobbed labor organizations. Public perceptions of these circumstances came and went, but the hoodlums stayed on.

During these five decades the analogy of organized crime as just another form of private enterprise could be tested at different times and places. In the end the analogy made little sense. Gangsters most depended on muscle, not on market forces. American capitalists, for all their failings, did not habitually extort bribes, beat people up, and kill their business rivals. Organized crime was not productive but parasitic in function. It generally did not produce goods and services or develop new products and markets. It merely leeched on those who did.

SIX

PUBLIC SECTOR: GANGSTERS AND POLITICS

Without crooked politicians, the triangular collusion of gangsters/cops/public servants would have lost a leg, tottered, and collapsed. The gangsters delivered money and services to the pols, who controlled the cops, who as ordered would jail the gangsters or not: a self-enclosed, self-generating machine, menaced only by the yammerings of reformers. The final power of autonomous decision usually rested with the politicians—except for certain times and places, from the 1930s on, in which the underworld turned it around and gave orders to the public sector. Yet while politicians held the ultimate authority, they were also the most vulnerable part of the triangular collusion.

Americans expected their elected officials to behave better than cops, gangsters, or even upperworld business people. In the private sector, executives might accept extra financial inducements, fill payrolls with worthless relatives, and lead unbuttoned personal lives—all without having their fitness as captains of industry questioned. If a politician was caught in such practices, by contrast, newspapers would run alarmed editorials about bribe taking, nepotism, and threats to the sanctity of the home, and urge that the offender be retired to the (implicitly) lower standards of private life.

Political corruption thus gave reformers their best opening. Unlike cops and gangsters, politicians at intervals had to offer themselves to voters. Safe in private life, the voters measured their public servants by hypocritically lofty standards. No wonder elections made so many officeholders sweat, especially those with friends in the underworld.

The varieties of underworld political corruption took many forms: from the incongruity of a small resort town deep in the Protestant heart of Arkansas, to the overt—indeed, self-advertised—wheelings of "the secret boss of California," to the familiar urban political machines of the Northeast and Midwest. Amid this variety, two general themes predominated. Most corrupt regimes depended finally on illicit money and muscle, those underworld specialties. And if the rascals ever got thrown out, it was probably an accident. A corrupt boss might gamble too much or not pay his taxes and so leave himself at risk. A jilted woman might kill herself after sending lethal evidence to the newspapers. In the absence of such unfortunate caprices, though, the crooked politicians were usually safe from reformers.

❧ ❧

Fifty miles southwest of Little Rock, Arkansas, in a valley ringed by the gentle hills of the Ouachita Mountains, the forty-six hot springs bubble up from somewhere deep below, heavy with minerals, at a steady 143 degrees Fahrenheit. Long before the advent of white people, the local Indians took the waters for various ailments, internal and external. In 1832 President Andrew Jackson signed an act of Congress that made Hot Springs a federal preserve, safe from any commercial monopoly of its waters. After the railroad arrived in 1874, the town grew up as a place apart from the rest of Arkansas, becoming one of the first national health and recreation centers in the country. Ultimately this apartness made it a favorite underworld playground, "the wickedest city in the United States," governed by a tightly corrupt political machine.

The corruption was based on cards, dice, and horses. The healing waters brought rich vacationers who in turn attracted gamblers, then casinos. From the 1870s on, Hot Springs was known as an open town, a haven for confidence men and criminals on the run from other places. Just before the turn of the century, horse-racing tracks were built to give people something else to bet on. Reformers closed the tracks twice, until the Arkansas legislature in 1934 legalized pari-mutuel betting for

Hot Springs. But the gambling never stopped. Down one side of Central Avenue, the main drag, a row of bathhouses offered healing waters; across the street, diverse gambling joints did their own roaring business.

Local political affairs were scarred by noisy voting scandals and killings until the mostly serene administration of Mayor Leo P. McLaughlin, the Irish Catholic boss of a Baptist town. Born and raised in Hot Springs, the son of Irish immigrants, a good student and athlete in high school, he came from a substantial family. His father ran a hardware store and owned property around town. For most of his adult life Mayor McLaughlin lived in a big house with his mother and two unmarried sisters. "His love for his mother beat anything I ever saw," a political associate recalled. "Half of what he did, as I knew him, was predicated on advice from his mother." He was married, briefly, but his family did not approve and he soon went back to his mother and sisters.

Aside from his family and his stable of horses, McLaughlin devoted himself to machine politics. He won every election by manipulating the poll tax—which a voter had to pay before casting a ballot—and corruptible conditions in the black Second Ward of Hot Springs. He was first elected mayor in 1926, beating a candidate favored by "the good people." According to one man's recollection many years later, "All the good people came out and voted, the prominent people, the high class people; everything was going beautifully until about two o'clock in the afternoon. They backed two trains into the Missouri Pacific Railroad Station and unloaded about 1500 to 2000 people from down at Prescott, Hope, Malvern. Each of them had a poll tax receipt in his hand and they asked where to go to vote for McLaughlin. They all went and voted in the Second Ward," and McLaughlin was the new mayor.

For twenty years he was impregnable. To staff his administration he pulled in many trusted old high-school friends. One high-school classmate, Vern Ledgerwood—a WASP and a Methodist—became a city judge, with the power to run the police department. Ledgerwood made his wife's brother the police chief; the man gratefully did whatever he was told. "We had an airtight machine," Ledgerwood said later. "We didn't have to do anything crooked." Anything discoverably crooked, that is. At election time, Ledgerwood would tell municipal employees to pay poll taxes for all their relatives and get them to the polls. "I don't know how they got the money to pay for it; cost a dollar, but nevertheless, I said, 'You show up with them anyway.' I'd keep the books. I credited the Captain of Police with 45. He had 45 relatives. He was a country boy. So I copied 'em and election day I had the stenographer give him the list. I said by 11:30 you have those 45 to the polls, so they vote just one way. Meant his job, you know." ("If you don't want to vote like they say, you are going to lose your job," agreed a Hot Springs minister, a solitary critic of McLaughlin brave enough to raise his head. "The people are afraid to talk; they are afraid to make a move that is not in harmony with the administration.")

The machine's gambling boss was William S. Jacobs, brought in from Memphis, unflappable and mysterious. "He is a large, dark, taciturn man," according to one observer, "who, legend has it, hasn't exhibited an emotion since the moment of his birth." Jacobs ran the two biggest Hot Springs casinos: the Southern Club, across Central Avenue from the very dignified Arlington Hotel, and the Belvedere, a few miles outside town on the road to Little Rock. As many as three thousand people a night came to the Belvedere for roulette, twenty-one, craps, and bingo. Other, lesser casinos paid monthly "fines" to City Hall. Jacobs gave jobs at his two joints to many relatives of the McLaughlin machine and so was granted the privilege of paying no fines. "We, on our side of the street, accept Mr. Jacobs," purred the owner of a Central Avenue bathhouse, "and were very glad when Mr. Jacobs made it clear that he accepted us."

In simple terms, the casinos and the bathhouses needed each other. The town's permanent population of sixteen thousand at times was outnumbered two to one by visitors. Most Hot Springs citizens—good and otherwise—agreed that local prosperity depended on giving outsiders what they wanted. A half-dozen bookie joints were ready to accept bets on sports events elsewhere; they also paid monthly "fines" to stay in business. Some one hundred slot machines were scattered around town; a regular 60 percent of their take went to city hall. At the end of each month, employees of the five white and two black whorehouses would appear in court. Each madam paid twenty dollars, each working girl five dollars. The whorehouses stayed open and their contributions paid the wages of the police department. In Hot Springs, it was said, "you can do practically anything you can pay for."

Thus perfect conditions for a gangster resort. The most celebrated underworld names from around the country came to Hot Springs twice a year, after the World Series in October and again during the racing season in February and March. Some actually came for the waters: before penicillin, the mineral springs were thought to relieve venereal diseases, those occupational hazards of underworld social life. (Waxey Gordon explained at his tax trial that he made annual trips to Hot Springs for "a chronic ailment.") Other hoodlums came to escape cold weather, or to watch boxers like Jack Dempsey and Joe Louis work out, or to play at golf, gambling, and whoring. Al Capone liked to stroll down Central Avenue, convoyed by a retinue of bodyguards. The gangster reunions had more serious purposes as well. As organized crime was nationalized from the late 1920s on, these semiannual mob meetings—reliably unmolested by the McLaughlin machine—gave the underworld a safe, neutral place to meet and plot. The occasions provided their own cover. If later asked about such meetings, a gangster could plausibly say he'd just been there for the healing waters and happened to run into his dear friend from Cleveland.

On its surface Hot Springs was amiable, tolerant, hedonistic, and well organized. An admiring article in *Collier's* magazine in 1931 praised "the remarkable civic health of Hot Springs, its uncommon serenity, its freedom from run-of-the-mill crime." This was only the surface. Dutch Akers, the chief of detectives, sold bootleg guns and diamonds on the side. Sometimes his cops would arrest outsiders on pretexts, jail them, and split their fines with the lawyers hanging around the courthouse. In 1936 John Dickson, a local farmer suspected in the burglaries of two gambling clubs, was beaten to death in the Hot Springs jail.

More notorious, significant criminals, chased from out-of-state jurisdictions, could expect a protected haven in Hot Springs, presumably for a price. Pretty Boy Floyd, Creepy Karpis, and dozens of others hid out in McLaughlin's underworld. When Lucky Luciano was running from Dewey's indictment in 1936, he predictably turned up in Hot Springs. "The whole crowd are a complete ring, the Chief of Police, the Chief of Detectives, the Mayor and the City Attorney," Dewey confided to the man he sent to bring Luciano home. "The Mayor owns the gambling houses and the detectives sleep all day and dress up in Tuxedos all night to guard the gamblers." Luciano hired the city attorney as one of his lawyers. Held in the Hot Springs jail, confidently expecting to be sprung, he slept on plush sheets and blankets from the Arlington Hotel and ate special food brought to him by Dutch Akers. After the Arkansas attorney general intervened for Dewey, Luciano finally was returned to New York.

When dealing with visiting dignitaries as important as Luciano, McLaughlin sometimes became a mere figurehead. He *looked* like a mayor in his tailored suits and trademark red carnation. He loved parades, speeches, his box at the racetrack, and being seen around town. Possessed of a glossy surface, he faithfully represented the burnished exterior of his town. "We put him out in front," Vern Ledgerwood said later. "He wanted the credit for everything."

Owney Madden, not McLaughlin, actually controlled the rackets in Hot Springs. Madden's redoubtable presence after 1933 gave the national underworld a reliable, universally accepted agent on the scene. "Owney was really a guy to respect and admire," Mickey Cohen noted. "If Owney felt that you were an all right person, there wasn't nothing that he wouldn't do for you." Officially he was paroled from New York to Hot Springs for his health; in fact it was probably a strategic retreat by the strongest Irish gangster in New York as the Italians and their Jewish associates came to run organized crime. In Hot Springs he could still do favors for hoodlums from around the country, and in return he was granted a kind of pension. One of Meyer Lansky's men brought him regular packets of cash. No one knew just what Madden did with the money. Lawmen passed around rumors that outside investors owned pieces of the Hot Springs casinos.

Only rumors, though. As far as anybody could tell on the record, Madden was retired, devoted to golf and good works, and living quietly with his second wife, the daughter of a former postmaster in town. One of his golf partners, Frank Costello, claimed that Madden's wife had "tamed" him to the point of restricting his golf bets to two bits a hole. Childless himself, Madden liked to buy ice cream cones for neighborhood kids and pay college expenses for poor students. "He was a pretty nice fellow, really. He did his dirty work in New York," one Hot Springs resident said later. "He lived in Hot Springs without causing a ripple."

Once settled in, Madden hardly ever left his new home. In 1940 he was arrested at a prizefight in New York; he gave his occupation as mineral water salesman. Again, seven years later, he returned to Manhattan for his mother's funeral. But in general he stayed down south, apparently content to be the biggest man in Hot Springs. On occasion, as needed, the old qualities for which he was called "the Killer" might flare up. He could not abide nosy writers. Once a journalist specializing in organized crime took a cab to Madden's home at 506 West Grand. The cabbie, a former deputy sheriff, thought he could arrange an interview. The cabbie went in a back door and quickly came out again, looking scared. "Mr. Madden said," he explained, "if I ever brought anybody to his house again he hadn't sent for first, he'd cut my heart out." Madden could live quietly, arranging deals for his old friends, because everyone still knew who he was.

❧ ❧

Artie Samish never ran for office and was never appointed to a political job. For a quarter century he nonetheless dominated political life in California. No other Californian has ever held so much political power for so long and in a manner so insulated from shifting gubernatorial administrations and the electoral will. Mere officeholders came and went, fools to be manipulated. Samish was the king of the lobbyists. Anchored in "Samish Alley"—his suite on the fourth floor of the Senator Hotel in Sacramento, within beckoning distance of the legislature—Samish handed out bribes and favors for his shady clients and his gangster friends. "I'm the governor of the legislature," he proclaimed, sure of getting no arguments. "To hell with the governor of the state."

Risen from poverty, self-invented and self-confident beyond arrogance, Samish looked and acted the way a political boss was supposed to look and act. He had been born in 1897 in the Boyle Heights section of Los Angeles. (Mickey Cohen came from the same neighborhood.) Samish's father, an Austrian immigrant, deserted the family before his son was in grade school. Thereafter the household consisted of the boy; his mother, Henrietta; and her mother. Living in San Francisco, he took the name of Arthur Henrietta Samish and attended school until the seventh grade. By his own account, his teachers were glad to see him go forth to work. When he was about twenty-one he took a job as a minute clerk in the state legislature. Watching how politics was conducted on the inside, he recognized his true calling.

In his prime, Samish resembled a W. C. Fields balloon inflated to a point near bursting: three hundred pounds of lobbyist draped on a six-two frame, a rosy face heavy around the nose, mouth, and jowls, a bald pink pate with a desperate fringe of gray-white hair barely holding on. After a self-indulgent young manhood he neither drank nor smoked; his only obvious vice was food. During the day, meeting callers in his hotel suite, he dressed in a loose robe. Belts and buttons cut into his bulk. Out for the evening, to dinner or an informal reception, he wore meticulously careless sports clothes. In any face-to-face meeting, power cascaded from his overwhelming presence and personality. Loud and large, he filled any room. Anybody standing next to him felt smaller.

Samish used money and muscle when needed, but ordinarily he dealt in information. He kept a black book—useful during election campaigns and when bills came to a floor vote—on every California legislator. "My staff and I found out everything there was to know about the lawmakers," he recalled, "and I mean everything." His employees attended all the important meetings around the capitol, taking notes on friends and enemies. Samish had free-lance informants as well, clerks and secretaries lodged in various corners of the state government. "Such people could be very helpful in picking up bits of information about senators who were planning to change their votes or assemblymen who needed convincing. Naturally I rewarded these informants in my usual beneficent manner."

At Samish Alley four adjoining rooms held waiting visitors who were intentionally shielded from each other's identities and purposes. "I didn't like my own agents to know each other; I knew their reports would be franker if they preserved their anonymity." While biding their time, the boss's wondrously assorted visitors might enjoy a sumptuous bar and buffet of lobster, shrimp, and caviar. Taking their ease and pleasure, the parade of clients and lawmakers, of gangsters and spies and journalists, all came to Samish and made him the best-informed, best-connected man in Sacramento. "I've got the damndest Gestapo you ever saw," he bragged to an impressed writer.

"On matters that affect his clients," Governor Earl Warren conceded, "Artie unquestionably has more power than the governor." When described schematically, his lobbying had no inherently sinister aspects; it remained a matter of style and execution. A business interest had a legitimate right to be directly heard by the legislature. Samish stood between the two, cutting deals and trolling bait, keeping each side ignorant of just what the other side knew. The involved parties saw only what Samish chose to reveal. He dealt in cash, kept no records that could ever be found, and suffered an oddly vague memory when asked about the details of what he was doing. "I've always been known in my line as the highest-priced in the business," he liked to say. "The results, I'll leave to you." Clients cared most about results.

His two main clients were racetracks and liquor interests: that is, enterprises that had been driven down to the underworld when outlawed, and then had retained gangster influences when re-legalized. Ties to these raffish clients brought the Samish operation an implicit, sometimes explicit association with organized crime—but they also formed the base of his power. Racing and liquor clients led in turn to deals with gamblers, pinball kings, and slot machine entrepreneurs.

Though personally immune to booze, Samish did like to bet on horses. "I'm always looking for a tip," he allowed. "I always kept a wad of bills in my pocket, just in case I had a hunch." In 1933, just starting to rise as a lobbyist, he co-authored the bill that legalized horse racing in the state. Thereafter he represented the Santa Anita track (receiving $55,000 in fees, officially, from 1935 to 1938, and then an annual $50,000 retainer) and Hollywood Park in southern California and the Bay Meadows track up north. A state legislator, William Hornblower, who also was an attorney for Bay Meadows, received a monthly $100 from Samish. (Later they claimed the money was for legal work Hornblower had done for another Samish client.) Samish did admit to other services that pleased his racetrack clients: restricting the state tax on pari-mutuel betting and keeping competitive tracks out of the state.

Just before national Prohibition came down, Samish had worked for a liquor trade association hoping to stave off the drys in California. After Prohibition ended in 1933 he renewed this business connection. The California State Brewers each year gave him $30,000 for himself and $150,000 for an "educational fund," as it was called, "and I put that money to good use." So good that brewers in California were taxed only two cents per gallon of beer produced, the lowest rate in the country. For twenty years, as long as Samish held power, this modest tax was never raised.

Such results brought Samish the fat Schenley account and the friendship of its president, Lewis Rosenstiel. These two men—kindred buccaneer spirits, rough and cynical—liked to call each other "Pops." Samish would stage elaborate birthday parties for Rosenstiel, who sent Samish the key to his home and said it was always open to him. Rosenstiel had hard, practical reasons to be amiable. At one point he was fretting over competition from Hiram Walker's 10 High Whiskey, a brand aged for three years. So Samish passed a law, over the governor's veto, that whiskey sold in California had to be at least four years old. "I didn't hear until later," Samish insisted, "that Schenley owned the great bulk of four-year-old whiskey in the United States." For such deliveries Rosenstiel paid Samish at least $36,000 a year, and another $18,000 for the Schenley-owned California Vineyards.

Grounded in Schenley and the brewers, Samish's power through the liquor business reached into wholesalers, retail outlets, advertising, nightclubs, bars, delivery trucks: a half-million workers behind "the damndest political machine you ever saw," Samish said fondly. "Every branch of the alcohol industry consults me. I'm the daddy of the whole thing. Men on my staff represent various branches, including labor. But it's a one-man show, and don't forget it. I control the purse strings, and sweetheart, there's a lot of dough in that purse." If newspapers printed unfavorable reports, Samish would cut off their liquor ads. If legislators voted disagreeably on booze bills, Samish would deploy his forces to defeat them at the next election. He controlled over four thousand billboards around the state. Friendly candidates got cheap space while unfriendlies got no space. "People are suckers for a picture and a slogan," as Samish explained his advertising technique. "Trying to educate them is a waste of time and money."

Most of what Samish did, though not described in civics textbooks, was still technically legal. Because of cross-filing and other reforms installed to cleanse the old bossed political machines, California's party organizations lurched from election to election, weak and unstable, respected by nobody. In this power vacuum, business clients went right to the lobbyists, bypassing the impotent parties and pols. Samish's stooges in the legislature shared no politics as such, merely self-interest and fealty to Artie. His bloc could usually elect the Speaker and name the chairmen of key committees. The Committee on Public Morals—in charge of liquor, racetracks, and gambling—drew Samish's particular attention. From his lifetime of watching the democratic process in Sacramento, he knew all the rules and customs, the whole arcane system of how bills could be stopped or passed. "Procedure is the secret of success around here," he pointed out. "There isn't a short cut around the place I don't know."

As to his certain if unproven illegal operations, he covered his tracks well. If he gave money to a politician, he called it a campaign contribution, not a bribe. If he did business with gangsters, he could explain it, or veil it through third parties. In San Bernardino County the local slot machine king, Edward Seeman, owned lucrative liquor distributorships with a woman friend of Samish's. In San Francisco, Samish shared an office suite with Otis P. Murphy, a bookie and casino owner from Chicago. Murphy owned a major slot-machine-distributing firm along with Samish's secretary. In Los Angeles, Samish was often seen with his home boy Mickey Cohen; they talked on the phone once a week. "See," Cohen said later, "if I had any problems with legislators in Sacramento on things like slot machines on premises, he nipped it in the bud. I was his right hand, and he was my godfather, my senior statesman." (Cohen did not specify just what he did as Artie's "right hand.") Frank Costello of New York was asked if he considered himself a "fairly good friend" of Samish. "Yes, I would say so," Costello replied.

Merely social contacts, Samish insisted. He acknowledged his regular visits to Hot Springs, Arkansas, "just for the baths and to take off a little weight," he said. "You are down there in a hotel, and it is more or less of an assembly place where you meet everybody." He had seen Joe Adonis of the Luciano family there and in New York, but "I don't know anything about him. I never had any business with him." What about the contacts with Mickey Cohen? "Some of these guys like Cohen call me up and give me tips on races and things. That's all there is to it."

In 1938 a political enemy induced the state senate to investigate Samish and his fellow lobbyists. The resulting report showed that Samish since 1935 had received at least a half-million dollars for political purposes, with no records or reasons to explain how he had spent it; liquor interests had contributed a little over half this total. Samish had become, the report concluded, "a powerful—if secretive and unofficial—'fourth branch' of state government . . . responsible not to the public but only to individuals or interests able to pay high fees." The report was filed and then in effect expunged from the official record. Nothing came of it. Soon copies of the report itself became mysteriously scarce.

The report turned up thirteen years later, though, at the Kefauver hearings on organized crime. Samish appeared before the Kefauver committee to dismiss the report's findings as ancient history. "I have been a strong advocate of strict enforcement of the law," he said.

"You have a lot of lawyers on your payroll," Kefauver noted. "What do you use them for?"

"I really don't know what I use them for, Senator," Samish replied. "I am kind of fond of some of them personally."

Kefauver, persisting, asked about his services for Lew Rosenstiel and Schenley: "You must do a lot of work for them for $36,000."

"Well," said Samish, "I do at times, Senator. I do. But not always. I mean I'm callable when they want me." They couldn't touch him. He knew his business.

"A national reputation," a *Fortune* profile concluded, "as the most arrogant political corruptionist operating on any state legislature."

❦ ❦

The most embarrassing political scandal in Detroit's history began to be exposed when Janet McDonald decided to kill herself. She was an Irish immigrant, thirty-three years old, raising a young daughter by herself. She worked as a clerk in a numbers gambling joint, the Great Lakes, at 9116 Oakland Avenue in Detroit. There she met and fell in love with William McBride, a minor gambling figure. In the fashion of gangsters bragging to their girlfriends, he told her how important he was, how he carried bribes from the Great Lakes house to the cops. The house did in fact seem well connected. After it was raided in the spring of 1939, the owner went to the police station, sprang all his people from jail, and resumed business the next day.

But he could not control Janet McDonald's passion. Billy McBride was not true to her; he spurned her and consorted with other women. McDonald could not accept it and could not face life alone. Things closed in around her, and she decided on her revenge. On August 5, 1939, a lonely Saturday night, she sent letters to the

Detroit newspapers: "On this night a girl has ended her life because of the mental cruelty caused by Racketeer William McBride, ex–Great Lakes Numbers House operator. McBride is the go-between man for Lieut. John McCarthy. He arranges the fix between our dutiful Lieut. and the Racketeers. Should you care to learn more of this story get in touch with McBride. . . . He glories in telling lies, so don't believe everything he tells you, as I did."

She also sent a note, defeated and triumphant, to McBride: "Billy, you remember how I always told you the only way you could have another mama would be over my dead body. You didn't think I really meant it, but I did. I can't and won't think of living without you. . . . In spirit I'll return and curse any woman that you make a friend of until the day you die." Then McDonald killed her daughter and herself.

Sex, tragedy, corruption. The Detroit papers blared it and demanded redress. Mayor Richard W. Reading, Police Superintendent Frederick Frahm, and county prosecutor Duncan McCrea all issued conventional statements of concern. But they took no substantial action. Five days after the suicide, McCrea said his office would not spend any more time on the matter. "We have only three investigators of our own," he explained. Given this puzzling failure by public lawmen, the Detroit Citizens League, a private good-government organization left over from the Progressive era, stepped forward. On August 19 it petitioned a local circuit judge, Homer Ferguson, to start grand jury proceedings. Under Michigan law he could form a one-man grand jury on his own authority. As his first witness Ferguson called John McCarthy, the crooked cop named by Janet McDonald. When Ferguson caught him lying he sent McCarthy to jail for five days; this judge meant it.

For the next year Ferguson heard witnesses and drew indictments that pulled in everyone from small numbers runners to the biggest political names in Detroit. He became one of the most effective WASP racketbusters of his time. A Presbyterian Republican who never smoked or drank, a church elder who prayed every night before bed, Ferguson had grown up in a small mining town outside Pittsburgh. "In the 1880s when I was born," he said later, "I was fortunate to have parents who believed they had a duty and privilege to teach their children moral and religious principles. Working on a farm and walking five miles a day to and from high school gave me a strong body and mind. I was fortunate to love work—hard physical work, or the work necessary to get an education." He mined coal and taught country school before taking his law degree at the University of Michigan. After a legal practice in Detroit he was appointed to the bench in 1929. He looked stolid and solid, a little under six feet and two hundred pounds, with a blandly handsome face marked off by wire-rimmed glasses and spiky gray hair. In manner he was understated and tenacious. "My old Dad used to say," he joshed, " 'Even a blind hog will find an occasional acorn if he just keeps his nose down.' "

The grand jury demanded all the tenacity he could bring to it. He hired a small staff of attorneys and investigators, as well as six volunteer lawyers who worked for a dollar a year. His chief attorney, Chester P. O'Hara, became invaluable, but Ferguson held it all together and made the hard decisions. At his secret office on the nineteenth floor of a bank building, reached through an inconspicuous garage entrance, Ferguson kept a printed sign on his desk bearing a couplet from Walter Scott: OH, WHAT A TANGLED WEB WE WEAVE, / WHEN FIRST WE PRACTICE TO DECEIVE! Witnesses seated before the desk, squirming and avoiding Ferguson's eyes, would gaze instead at the sign, and it seemed to prod their memories. At times witnesses were brought to two other secret meeting places, and were also interrogated in private homes, hotel rooms, taxicabs. Once Ferguson sat up all night interviewing a man on a train to Chicago. Tongue-tied witnesses often loosened up after dark, fueled by caffeine and nicotine, so the grand jury worked many late nights.

Occasionally Ferguson worried about threats on his life and his family. He hired a former FBI agent from Chicago as an investigator; the man turned out to be employed by numbers gamblers and was fired. Ferguson received many ominous messages and phone calls. In theory he was safe because the underworld did not harm honest lawmen, but a theory offered little real comfort. Policemen guarded his home around the clock. One of these guards was later indicted for corruption, as the Fergusons with a chill wondered how sincere his guarding had been. On Sundays, to blow off tension and perhaps to make a point, Ferguson would fire guns at a shooting range. One Sunday at the range he ran into a gangster about to be indicted. The encounter left him shaken and fretful. (The fears lingered a long time. Years later, after a stroke in old age, Ferguson suffered terrible, recurrent nightmares about being chased and killed by gangsters.)

It was a murky, dangerous business for the stammering witnesses. Shadows flickered on a wall, teased and danced away. As the inquiry reached the mayor's office, the police department, and the county prosecutor, the line between good guys and bad guys faded to nothing. Whom to trust? Whom to fear? In preliminary interrogations Ferguson and his staff had to break witnesses, to persuade them to give formal testimony first to the confidential grand jury and then, after indictments, in open court. Those witnesses with the most to tell also had the most to lose, and the keenest sense of the inevitable underworld penalty for squealing.

Dictographs recorded some of the early interviews by the grand jury staff. A box of these recordings was discovered at the home of Ferguson's widow in 1985. Never made public at the time of the investigation, they show how two crucial witnesses—Sam Block and Buddy Boettcher—were induced to sing. Both were major bagmen, the people who actually delivered cash from underworld consortiums to public officials. Without their cooperation, Ferguson could not land the biggest fish. (At the outset Ferguson had consulted Tom Dewey, who was visiting his mother in Owosso, Michigan. You'll never get the big shots, Dewey had warned him.)

Sam Block ran a bookie joint in the suburb of Hamtramck. "You come from a good family," Ferguson told him, invoking a sense of class responsibility. "Don't you have a moral obligation?" Nothing doing. Chet O'Hara tried another family angle: "What does your wife think about all this?"

"Oh, God, she's beyond that stage."

"Well, she doesn't want to see you go to jail. . . . That's the trouble with these things. . . ."

"Yeah, it don't hurt the fellow that's really supposed to get hurt, it hurts them poor innocent people [like himself] that aren't really entitled to be hurt."

O'Hara told Block they weren't really after him anyway. "We're not reformers," he said. They did not expect to stop bookmaking or wipe out the gambling instinct. "We do want to get the men who were sworn to enforce the law and didn't." Some of his associates had already broken, Block was informed. "Every place we look we see Sam Block." They had mounds of evidence pointing right at him. "They're playing you for a sucker." After long hours of cajoling, coffee drinking, and discussions of potential tax problems and how hard it was to make a living as a bookie because his employees cheated on him, Block began to waver. "Understand I haven't made any promises," he said. "I want to give it serious consideration, and if I decide I'm going to try to do what I consider the best thing for myself."

Block was teased with pieces of information about his crimes. He wondered how the lawmen had found out: "I still would like to know what you did to those people that did talk to make them talk. I'm not saying that they're right, understand, but what the hell you did to make them talk I still can't understand. I don't know whether you put a pistol up against them or what. . . ."

"No," O'Hara assured him, "we never used any force on anybody."

"Sure you didn't hang them out the window?"

"Well, I've been so tired I'm afraid I might've dropped 'em!"

Finally Block caved in. Starting in 1935, he said, Harry Colburn—the county prosecutor's chief investigator—had demanded bribes from Block and his bookie associates. In less than four years they had given Colburn over $100,000. Under pressure, Colburn then flipped and implicated his boss, Duncan McCrea, the county prosecutor. One big fish was caught.

Buddy Boettcher, the son of a retired cop, was a police lieutenant, on the force for eighteen years. He was implicated along with other cops in the first wave of newspaper stories after the McDonald suicide. Mayor Reading and Police Superintendent Frahm defended the other cops under fire but said nothing for Boettcher, leaving him dangling and feeling deserted. "Looks like I've been made the goddamn goat out of the whole thing," he complained at one of his first sessions with Ferguson's staff. "You don't *have* to be the goat, Buddy," offered John Kelly, one of the staff investigators.

"I've been suspended, and I'm the only one suspended, and I've gotten smeared in the newspapers . . . for a lot of things that I never done."

"And they'd all stand up tomorrow and smear you again, every one of 'em, to save themselves. . . . Freddy Frahm is not gonna do a damn thing for you."

Angry at being betrayed, and with his father in the room, Boettcher at first claimed he had started taking graft only after Reading became mayor in January 1938. The money had come, said Boettcher, from Monk Watson, the black numbers boss: a monthly $2,000 for Reading and $2,000 more for Frahm. His inquisitors were not satisfied. Well, Boettcher allowed, he'd also taken $1,000 a month from a bookie, Ed Hall, in 1938 and 1939. What else? he was asked. They knew of money he had received from a whorehouse years earlier. "So think *hard*," Kelly warned him.

Bearing down, Kelly talked to Boettcher alone, without his father present. Boettcher admitted he "might have" taken bribes before the Reading administration came in. "I'm scared," he said. "I don't know the hell which way to turn." Kelly agreed that he had made the best possible presentation in front of his father; but now better tell the full truth. "I'm not innocent by any means," Boettcher admitted.

Finally to the main gangster in the story: Elmer Buff Ryan, head of the Consolidated News Bureau, the local outlet for Moe Annenberg's bookie wire. Through the Consolidated, Buff Ryan wielded power over all the bookmakers in Detroit. A friend to Boettcher since childhood, Ryan had courted the cop, palled around town with him, and started his payoffs to Boettcher in 1936, over a year before Reading took office. "Ryan was the class of the gambling operators in Detroit," Boettcher said later. "He was a gentleman. He had no bad habits. . . . I met a lot of fine people through Ryan. A lot of classy people liked him and did business with him."

And now Boettcher was turning on him. "Now you know this is a terrible thing," he told Kelly, flinching from what he had to do. "Elmer Ryan's been a friend of mine for 30 years. . . . After all, friendship is a big thing, you know that."

"Quite true," Kelly agreed, "but you'd be surprised how many friendships have been shattered already, by people that don't give a damn."

All right, said Boettcher: "This thing all started between Buff Ryan and I." He then gave an honest account of all the bribes he knew about.

Kelly at once went to a phone and called Ferguson. "I want you to come out," he said, "because this thing is taking a slight different turn, and much more illuminating and very valuable." In a little less than three years, Boettcher had collected and delivered over $300,000. Along with the monthly $2,000 for

Reading from Monk Watson, he gave the mayor and his son $4,000 from the bookies, making the deliveries every month at—appropriately enough—the Book-Cadillac Hotel. He gave the rest of the money to various cops and city officials. His own cut was $500 a month for fifteen minutes' work. Over the course of a year, in a total of three hours he made double his police salary.

Reading, defeated for reelection, had left office by the time of his trial. He was sentenced to four to five years in jail, of which he served three. Also imprisoned were McCrea, Frahm, dozens of top cops, and scores of gangsters and gamblers, including Buff Ryan and Monk Watson. John Roxborough, a manager of Joe Louis, was convicted with Watson for numbers payoffs and given the same two-and-a-half-to-five-year sentence. Roxborough had run his gambling from an office at the corner of Beacon and St. Antoine, the same office he used to manage Joe Louis's affairs. The jailed hoodlums were mostly Irish, Jewish, and black. Few of the Purples and Italians who ran Detroit's underworld, and who annually split $125,000 in gambling protection money, were caught. Ferguson did miss the biggest gangster fish.

Like Earl Warren and Tom Dewey, Homer Ferguson found that racketbusting pointed the way upward. In 1942 he defeated a popular Democratic incumbent for his seat in the United States Senate. He left Detroit with a reform mayor, Edward Jeffries, in city hall, but without illusions as to the lasting effect of his prosecutions. The Detroit underworld continued to make book and take numbers bets. Cops and public servants had been paid off before the Reading administration, and doubtless would be after it too. "People say it's no use trying to clean up a city," Ferguson concluded, "because graft is bound to spring up again. Sure it is. That's why you have to keep after it all the time. You might as well say that it's no use to clean your house because it will get dirty again. This is a democracy and we have got to make it work."

❧ ❧

"I decide," said Mayor Frank Hague. "I do. Me. Right here. And if the people of Jersey City don't like the way I run the town, they can get another mayor."

❧ ❧

Leo McLaughlin stayed within his own small pond in Hot Springs. Artie Samish was sui generis. Richard Reading was a minor political hack, a Detroit city employee since 1921, who was elected mayor in 1937 mainly because his CIO-backed opponent scared too many voters. All three of these crooked political figures were aberrations. The most typical, durable, powerful alliances of gangsters and politicians flourished in the entrenched political machines of older American cities, where the major underworld gangs were based. The machines and the gangs needed each other, fed into each other, reaching their apex of authority together during the years between the world wars. Their mutual influence stretched beyond their own cities into their states and—during the presidency of Franklin Roosevelt—all the way to Washington. The leaders of these machines included some of the most capable, corrupted politicians in American history.

Of the urban bosses, Frank Hague enjoyed the longest, most totalitarian reign. As mayor of Jersey City for thirty years he ran an American version of a fascist state. Not for him the higher ethical postures of public life; instead he treated government as a form of private enterprise to be judged by its products, stability, and profits. "Politics is a business," he would cry in his authoritative voice, jabbing an emphatic forefinger like a dagger toward his listener. "That's what the reformers don't get. They think it's a sort of revival meeting, with nothing to do but nominate some bird who's never seen a polling place, make a lot of speeches about clean government, and then sit back and wait for voters to hit the sawdust trail. It's a laugh. You got to have *organization*." After an electoral victory in Jersey City, patronage jobs naturally went to loyal campaign workers. Reformers called it the spoils system. Hague called it fair promotion for work well done. "Of course workers get the jobs," he admitted. "And why not? What would you think of an executive who hired fellows that knocked the company or didn't take any interest in it? We deliver for those that deliver for us. And as the district leaders and ward men make good, we move 'em up. Follow me? The merit system just like in business!"

Hague in full bellow loved to point out the hypocrisies and contradictions of his hapless adversaries. As a purported businessman in politics he represented the beau ideal of the Progressive reformers that had spawned him. See what you have wrought, he implied. Some observers were taken in by "his free tongue and amazing frankness," as George Creel, the old Wilsonian, put it in 1936: "He bars no subject from discussion, even checking over the list of crimes charged against him in order to make sure that none has been overlooked." Yet his unchallenged rule depended on decades of frauds, thefts, and secret alliances with the underworld. He was essentially a gangster, not an efficient captain of industry. Far from building up his enterprise, he left it pillaged and near ruin.

Intellectually and ethically, Hague never left the Horseshoe, the rough Irish section of Jersey City from which he sprang. "I was what folks call a bad boy," he said later. The Horseshoe lay near the Hudson River docks, across from the southern tip of Manhattan. Men there worked for the railroads, packinghouses, and factories that gave the ward its sooty ambience, and they drank in the forty saloons that let them end the day with a buzz or more. Frank Hague, the fourth of eight children born to Irish immigrants, found no model in his father, who toiled as a blacksmith, then a bank guard. Instead he admired his older brothers, stalwarts of the Red Tigers street gang. "You didn't do anything worse than I did," he later told an audience of reformatory kids. "I grew up in a tough part of Jersey City, and most of my friends swiped things out of freight cars, and by the time I was twelve I had played hooky so often I was kicked out of school." Into the streets full-time, he served an underworld apprenticeship as a protégé of Denny McLaughlin, a saloon and racetrack owner and the political boss of Ward 2. At times Hague managed a prizefighter. (Years later he helped stage the Dempsey-Carpentier heavyweight bout in Jersey City.)

The once and future hoodlum rose through the police department and good-government reforms. Political connections brought him appointments as a constable, then a deputy sheriff. Despite perjuring himself at the trial of a burglar buddy in Boston, Hague rode upward on his reputation as an expert on police matters. In 1913 Progressive reformers installed the commission form of city government, a favorite remedy for corrupt bossed machines. Hague was appointed the public safety commissioner, or top cop. He then noisily, ruthlessly "cleaned up" the police department by breaking the police union, hiring his friends and firing his enemies, and creating a special hundred-man squad to watch cops and citizens alike. In subduing the police he created his own springboard to power. After four years he was elected to the city commission; the new members of the board, pulled along in his wake, appreciatively elected him mayor.

Once enthroned, Hague continued to present himself as a moralist in politics. Tall and erect, with the hooded looks of a suspicious basset hound, he dressed in austere suits and dignified high collars. He was easily perturbed. Thin of skin and devoid of humor, he accelerated quickly from arguments to sputtering rages to possible fisticuffs. According to a *New Yorker* profile, "Probably nobody in the country, with the possible exception of Donald Duck, is as persistently indignant as Hague." In his constant state of high dudgeon, he insisted that Jersey City could have no red-light district, no burlesque shows or taxi dances, no women or entertainment in the saloons, no poolrooms open after midnight, no bucket shops selling fraudulent securities, no payroll or bank robberies or street crime. Some of these enterprises did operate in Hague's broader turf of the surrounding Hudson County. But "Jersey City," said Hague in the argot of the Horseshoe, "is the most moralest city in America."

Up to a point. Hague neither smoked nor drank. (Every year he took the city hall staff over to Manhattan for a banquet at Dinty Moore's; nobody had a drop until the boss left.) But Hague loved to gamble, and therefore so did his city. Visibly fond of horses, he was often seen in prominent boxes at Saratoga in New York, Churchill Downs in Kentucky, and Hialeah in Florida. In his own state of New Jersey he led political movements to legalize horse racing and to repeal a state antigambling amendment. He also bet on boxing and his beloved New York Giants.

"No vice, no crime, no racketeering" was his favorite campaign slogan. By which he meant: none that the mayor did not control. His gambling bosses—Charles Goode of Ward 2 and Newsboy Moriarity—watched over an orderly system of graft. Each ward was allowed a given number of card games, numbers wheels, and bookies. Every month they paid off the ward leader, who brought the money, more or less intact, to city hall. "You pay only *one* guy in Jersey City," explained a resident bookie. The town was known as "the Horse Bourse" among gamblers around the country. Bookmakers in downtown tenements took off-track bets by phone and telegraph. After the collapse of Moe Annenberg's national gambling wire service, the system was reorganized with Jersey City as its eastern headquarters.

Bristling and reddening, Hague of course denied his underworld payoffs. "I've cleaned up vice and gambling and racketeering," he insisted. "It's all a goddam lie. I'd be crazy to take that kind of money." From gamblers alone, as local folklore had it, he pulled in $2 million a year. He made comforting arrangements with other gangsters as well. During Prohibition his cops maintained friendly ties with bootleggers. Many liquor shipments came ashore in Hague's Hudson County, especially in Bayonne and Weehawken. One prominent beer baron, Frank Dunn, was tipped off by Hague men two days before business rivals killed him. For decades Hague was allied with Longy Zwillman, the gangster king of Newark. Every Christmas Zwillman sent the mayor a box of fine cigars.

None of this was public knowledge at the time. On the record Hague spoke admirable words against "the gangsters and labor racketeers" while his men cut backstairs deals. "I found that four gangsters was the head of that union," he said of a Teamster local. "I drove them out of the city and disorganized the union." Other mobbed-up unions encountered no such difficulties. Hague was especially close to Joe Fay of the Operating Engineers. The Second Ward organization in Jersey City worked amicably with the Longshoremen's Local 1247 and its gangster leaders, Charlie Yanowsky and Edward Florio. Through 1247 and other locals in Hoboken, Jersey City's neighbor to the north, Yanowsky and Florio ran all the Jersey docks. At one point some of Harry Bridges's CIO Longshoremen tried to take over these underworld locals. Jersey City cops stopped the pickets, harassed the organizers, and pushed them out of town.

Thus the base of Hague's money and power: secret arrangements with gamblers, bootleggers, gangsters, and labor racketeers. His loud Irish Calvinism was merely a cover. As his political power grew beyond Jersey City and Hudson County, he hid behind other plausible fronts. He could not manipulate the state legislature, which remained stubbornly Republican and largely WASP. The governor of New Jersey, however, was usually his boy—especially A. Harry Moore, governor for three terms of three years each. Elected with Hague to the Jersey City commission, Moore owed his political life to the mayor. He was a Scotch-Irish Protestant who taught the men's Bible class at a Reformed church. (Hague knew that would play well downstate.) Governor Moore kept Hague's loyalty because he knew his place. "I do not have the power to appoint to these Federal positions," he told a patronage seeker. "They are made upon the recommendation of the local organizations to Mayor Hague, who, in turn, sends them in [to Washington]."

Hague's stooge in Congress was Mary Teresa Norton, the first woman elected to Congress from an eastern state and the first woman from anywhere to chair a congressional committee. If Harry Moore's WASPiness made him electable outside Hudson County, Hague wanted somebody more like himself to represent Jersey City in Congress. Mary Norton was the daughter of Irish immigrants. After the death in infancy of her only child, she started a nursery for children of working women. Hoping for municipal support, she went to see Hague. He helped her get the money and then pushed her into politics, moving her through local jobs and finally to Congress in 1924.

During her twenty-six years in Washington she never questioned the ethics or discipline of the Hague machine—though she fit no stereotype of a machine politician. "An ample figure with flashing dark eyes," according to one observer, "wholesome as a windy day, she has the directed energy of a steel riveting machine." On occasion she obviously danced to Hague's tune. In 1928 she introduced the first bill in Congress to repeal Prohibition. As chair of the District of Columbia Committee, she legalized booze and boxing in Washington. For the record, though, "I never have had any interference from Mayor Hague with the way I voted," she said. "He has never asked any of us to do anything our conscience would not approve our doing." Her main services were unflinching loyalty and the steering of federal money and patronage toward Jersey City.

Within Jersey City, the glue binding the Hague machine to voters was ethnic and religious ties. The city population was 75 percent Roman Catholic, mostly Irish and Italian. Almost all the major police and political figures were Catholics. Hague kept up an outward display of religious piety. A regular at confession, whenever he was in town he made the 10:30 mass at St. Aedan's each Sunday. He gave his parish a fancy main altar that cost $50,000, and he served as honorary chairman of the Mount Carmel Guild, the charity drive for Jersey City's twenty-eight Catholic churches. (Conversely, his few persistent enemies were mostly Protestant clergy: a Methodist minister in Jersey City, an Episcopal rector in Bayonne.)

Hague's appeals to ethnic and religious loyalties were classically fascist. Played against the international developments of the 1930s, they echoed Mussolini's cries of redeeming ancient glories and Hitler's hymns to the fatherland. "The Republican party is not a party of your people," Hague told a group of Italians in 1931. "It is high hat, without interest in your welfare." Hague's favored Italian, Mike Scatuorchio of the Fifth Ward, was given the city's garbage and ash contract—but only on a measured, year-to-year basis. Though Italians were displacing Irish as the largest ethnic group in town, most of Hague's plums still went to Irishmen; he practiced his own discriminations. But once again he said all the right words. "The Democratic party welcomes the foreigner," he promised another immigrant group, "and offers him a chance to make good, but the Republican party ignores the strangers on our shores."

Toward real or imagined enemies Hague behaved like a dictator, or like a gangster. Every night a police lieutenant sat in the Western Union office in Jersey City, looking over the day's volume of telegrams in and out, checking for plots and traitors. Hague had other spies in the banks and post office. At one city election, several hundred well-intentioned college boys came over from Princeton to serve as poll watchers against voting frauds. They were cuffed and beaten, five of them sent to the hospital. "Animal spirits, that's all," Hague explained. "I told my boys to lay off, but it was a pretty dull election, and they couldn't resist the temptation to have a little fun." In 1937 Hague won his sixth term by a vote of 110,473 to 6,798; no wonder.

As a fascist state, Jersey City under Hague allowed no freedom of press, speech, or assembly. "Whenever I hear a discussion of civil rights," he said, "and the rights of free speech and the rights of the Constitution, always remember you will find him with a Russian flag under his coat; you never miss." After the *New York Post* ran a damaging series on Hague in 1938, two hundred Jersey City newsdealers were ordered not to carry the paper. *Life* magazine published unflattering photographs of the boss (his looks were not easily flattered) and was also banned. A few years earlier a brazen local newspaper, the *Jersey Journal,* had dared criticize the "slimy" Hague record. Hague decreed that any city or county employee seen reading the paper would be fired. Cops and firemen went door to door, distributing leaflets about the *Journal's* perfidies and soliciting subscriptions to a rival paper of approved loyalties. Theater owners were forced to withdraw their advertising; one resisting owner was harassed by building, health, and fire inspectors until he capitulated. The city council even changed the name of Journal Square to Veterans Square. Under these assaults, the *Journal* caved in and began to celebrate Hague's works. The name of Journal Square was restored. One of the paper's publishers was tossed a judicial appointment. Hague's absolute control of the police meant that no suspicious meeting or speech could be held. Cops would break it up, no explanation given or necessary, and dump the offenders into jail or out of town.

And finally, Hague acted the fascist dictator by living in opulence while his city fell into debt and ruin. Aside from his underworld bribes, Hague extracted a regular kickback of 3 percent from the wages of all public employees. "Sure, he had the 3 percent thing going," one Jersey City cop said later, "but those of us who paid it looked on it as union dues." Other extortions and patronage brought Hague more barrels of money, with regular deliveries to Manhattan banks and brokers. An investigation by the New Jersey Senate in 1929 found that Hague, on a city salary of no more than $8,000, had somehow managed to accumulate almost $400,000 worth of stocks and property in a dozen years—and that was merely the portion the investigators could find. Hague kept homes in Jersey City, on the Jersey shore in Deal, in Manhattan hotel suites, and on Biscayne Bay, Florida. Often hard to find in Jersey City, he governed by telephone from these homes or from his many vacations in Europe. Late in life, he privately acknowledged a fortune of $8 million. By other estimates his worth amounted to perhaps ten times that much.

At great and permanent cost to his city. Corrupt regimes like Hague's, it was said, at least provided humane and accessible city services. Hague did lavish money on his beloved police and an elaborate medical center. Because of these extravagances, and the inevitable price of stealing public money and handing out non-jobs, Jersey City had the highest per capita payroll of any American city with a population over one hundred thousand. In twenty years under Hague the tax rate tripled, property assessments doubled, the budget went up 450 percent, the public debt up 500 percent. Despite all this spending the city streets remained unswept and sputteringly brightened by ancient gaslights. Children played in the streets because they found few parks or playgrounds. Hague built his medical center but hardly any schoolhouses or libraries. At some schools the students still had to use outdoor toilets. Factories and businesses were leaving town for freer, cleaner environments. Jersey City slid toward a long, slow decline. "Nobody can beat me as long as I give the people service," Hague promised. "And I give them service."

❧ ❧

"I'm not bragging when I say I run the show in Kansas City," said Tom Pendergast. "I am boss. If I was a Republican they would call me 'leader.' "

❧ ❧

The boss's day began at five o'clock in the morning. He awoke in an upstairs bedroom of the French Regency mansion at 5650 Ward Parkway in Kansas City, Missouri. Built at a cost of $175,000 in 1928, the Pendergast home was nouveau plush, "all immaculate," a visitor recalled, "in a set order, and very delicate looking." The furnishings of each upstairs room and attached bathroom—drapes, bedclothes, rugs—were all done in a given color, varied from room to room. The three marble hearths and mantles on the first floor were in the respective styles of Louis XIV, XV, and XVI. The basement recreation room was nautical, with a bar down one side of the room and chrome-and-leather stools. The closets bulged with fur coats belonging to Pendergast's wife and daughters. ("We're very close—all of us," the boss said of his family circle. For the first five years of his marriage, he never spent a night away from home—and then did so only because business took him to St. Louis. After his daughter Marcelline was married, she still came home every evening to kiss her parents good night.)

At six o'clock, after a plain breakfast, T. J. Pendergast arrived for work at the headquarters of the Jackson Democratic Club at 1908 Main Street, in a shabby downtown business district, two blocks from a railroad yard. In contrast with the elaborate home he had just left, Pendergast ran his political machine from an ostentatiously dingy office. It consisted of three rooms on the second floor of a two-story brick building engulfed by taller structures on both sides. One room held the organization's larger meetings; an anteroom filled quickly with men who chatted, read newspapers, and smoked cigars as they waited to see the boss; the third room, his inner sanctum, boasted only an old rolltop desk on a worn green rug, a brass cuspidor, and a few chairs. Pendergast sat there in a comfortable swivel chair, a gray flannel hat on his head. "All right," he barked. "Who's next?"

A visitor felt the immediate presence of a primal force, barely contained, ever on the verge of bursting forth. Of average height, Pendergast nonetheless seemed huge, weighing around 230 pounds, with a thick neck and an oversized skull strong in the mouth, jaw, and nose. Perched forward on the edge of his chair, punctuating his terse conversation with forceful gestures, he was all business. "He seems to be about to spring," one caller noted. "His strength beamed out of him," said another. "He looked as if he could reach out and with a bare hand crush the inkwell on his desk." Pendergast had no Irish blarney, no backslapping hand, no jokes or stories to tell. Instead he watched and listened. People noticed his unwavering eyes: "They were large, cold, cat-like and inscrutable. They nailed you with an almost hypnotic gaze." Through the morning, the boss pinioned a stream of callers with those eyes. He heard their requests, said yes or no, and shouted for the next supplicant.

After lunch Pendergast moved on to the nearby office of his Ready-Mixed Concrete Company. NO POLITICS DISCUSSED HERE, warned a sign on the wall, and the boss meant it. In the afternoon he ran the affairs of his concrete company, his wholesale liquor company, his asphalt, paving, construction, and other businesses. Many of these enterprises prospered on municipal contracts. "My concrete is good, nobody denies that," Pendergast pointed out. "Why haven't I got as much right to do business with the city as anybody else?" By six o'clock he was home for supper with his family. He seldom went out in the evening, even to a movie or political meeting. At nine o'clock he went to bed, just as the fabled Kansas City night life of jazz clubs, gambling dens, and whorehouses began to stir.

Not a public-office holder himself, the boss ran his machine through an administrative triumvirate of Henry McElroy, Harry Truman, and Johnny Lazia. Like Frank Hague in Jersey City, Pendergast had ridden to power on the manipulation of Progressive political reforms. The son of Irish immigrants, he had grown up in St. Joseph, Missouri. In 1890, eighteen years old, he followed his big brother Jim down to Kansas City. The brothers ran a saloon in the Irish West Bottoms section, the "Bloody First" Ward with its railroads, slaughterhouses, and meat-packers. After Jim's death in 1911, Tom took over the ward political organization, serving a few years on the city council, but losing control of the city to a Republican regime in 1920. Five years later reformers passed a new city charter providing for a weak mayor, a strong city manager, and nine councillors—all designed to clean up city politics for good.

Pendergast endorsed the reforms, got his own slate of councillors elected, and thereby appointed his man Henry McElroy city manager. Known as Old Turkey Neck, McElroy was a Presbyterian country merchant from Dunlap, Iowa. Disliked for his testy irascibility and curtness toward impertinent reporters, he took orders only from Pendergast. "Tom and I are partners," McElroy explained. "He takes care of politics and I take care of the [municipal] business. Every Sunday morning, at Tom's house or mine, we meet and talk over what's best for the city."

For ten years Harry Truman, an army buddy of Pendergast's nephew, served as a county judge for the machine. The position in Missouri was really more executive than judicial; Truman had the power to set budgets, hire employees, let contracts, assess taxes, deposit monies, and control patronage. According to the pleasant mythology Truman later created about those years, he was the solitary rose in the manure pile, an honest public servant unaware of the crimes around him. But—as he recorded in private notes at the time—he did know about the machine's corruptions and wondered about his part in them. In one instance, Truman acceded to Pendergast's request that he give road contracts to crooked contractors. "I had to compromise with him," Truman reflected. "I had to let a former saloon keeper and murderer, a friend of the Big Boss, steal about $10,000 . . . from the general revenues of the County to satisfy my ideal associate and keep the crooks from getting a million or more out of the bond issue. Was I right or did I compound a felony? I don't know."

In later episodes the total boodle stolen under Truman's eyes ran to a million dollars. "I was able to expend $7,000,000.00 for the taxpayers' benefit," he wrote. "At the same time I gave away about a million in general revenue to satisfy the politicians. But if

I hadn't done that the crooks would have had half the seven million. . . . I wonder if I did right to put a lot of no account sons of bitches on the payroll and pay other sons of bitches more money for supplies than they were worth in order to satisfy the political powers and save $3,500,000.00. I believe I did do right."

As Truman trimmed his conscience in other ways—such as making two justice-of-the-peace appointments that he knew were illegal, in the absence of the other two county judges—he fell into mordant ruminations about basic human integrity. He had believed most men to be honest. " 'The Boss' says that instead most of them are not when they are put into a position where they can get away with crookedness. I guess I've been wrong in my premise that 92% are not thieves." Truman even wondered if he had done right not to steal money himself. "I could have had $1,500,000.00. I haven't $150.00. Am I a fool or an ethical giant? I don't know." But it was more than graft and dirty contracts. The machine that Truman then served and later defended also took part in beatings, kidnappings, bombings, and even murders. "I think maybe that machines are not so good for the country," he concluded timorously, probably understating his own moral confusion. "I have been doing some deep and conscientious thinking. Is a service to the public or one's country worth one's life if it becomes necessary to give it, to accomplish the end sought?"

In 1934 Pendergast sent Truman on to the United States Senate. Thereafter, according to Truman's later recollection, Pendergast spoke to him only once about a Senate issue. If literally true, the statement was essentially false. Truman may have received orders only once from the boss's mouth, but other instructions came to him by mail or through intermediaries. In Washington, Truman remained unblinkingly loyal to the machine that gave him political life. As Richard Lawrence Miller, the most careful student of Truman's rise to power, has summed up the matter: "The fanatic, unthinking, and eternal devotion Truman demanded from anyone ever associated with the Pendergast machine has no justification in normal American political practice or in the history of Kansas City politics. Clearly he protested too much, perhaps to ease his own guilty conscience about his role as an honest front protecting the power of thieves and murderers."

The murderers and other overt hoodlums came under Johnny Lazia's aegis. The leader of Kansas City's Italian mob, based in the

North Side, Lazia in 1928 organized the North Side Democratic Club to work for Pendergast. Among other services, Lazia's gangsters got the vote out at election time. "I used to go to talk to the old people and ask them," the Mafioso James Balestrere said later. "With the old people, practically every one used to say, 'All right, we vote for Mr. Pendergast.' I had just to mention Pendergast and it would have been all right." Less officially, the Lazia gang took charge of gambling joints, bootlegging, prostitution, narcotics, slot machines, numbers gambling, and speakeasies all over the city. The taverns and dives on Twelfth Street and the whorehouses on Fourteenth all had to pay tribute. Lazia dealt with laggards in his own underworld fashion. Pendergast did not have to issue specific enforcement orders.

Under Pendergast by way of Lazia, Kansas City became an open town, a bigger and brassier version of Hot Springs. "This town was fast," a thief named Red Rudensky said fondly, "had good booze joints, plenty of targets and some of the laziest cops in the country." (Indeed, about seventy-five Kansas City cops were ex-cons appointed through Lazia.) Gambling casinos operated all day within a few blocks of a snooty shopping district; the employees emerged for lunch blinking, still wearing their green aprons and eyeshades.

Businessmen would come to Kansas City, sell their wheat or livestock, then go on the town with money to spend. The bars and joints beckoned, twenty or thirty blocks at a stretch. The Chesterfield Club offered strippers and nude waitresses. The bands at the Reno played state-of-the-art jazz. "Most of the night spots were run by politicians and hoodlums," the jazz pianist Mary Lou Williams recalled, "and the town was wide open for drinking, gambling, and pretty much every form of vice. Naturally, work was plentiful for musicians, though some of the employers were tough people." Count Basie had a misunderstanding with one big gangster and had to play for two weeks without pay.

Unmolested by local lawmen, Lazia was convicted early in 1933 of evading almost $50,000 in federal income taxes. The IRS had found unreported income from a dog track and a nightclub. So Pendergast wrote a "Dear Jim" letter to Postmaster General James A. Farley, the New Deal's political fixer: "Now, Jim, Lazia is one of my chief lieutenants and I am more sincerely interested in his welfare than anything you might be able to do for me now or in the future. He has been in trouble with the Income Tax Department for some time. I know it was simply a case of being jobbed because of his Democratic activities. . . . I wish you would use your utmost endeavor to bring about a settlement of this matter. I cannot make it any stronger, except to say that my interest in him is greater than anything that might come up in the future." Farley could not help, and Lazia was sentenced to prison. Later on, after a St. Louis newspaper obtained and published this letter, Pendergast was asked about it. "Yes; I wrote it. I stand by it, too," he said. "Whenever I get to the stage when I accept the help of an organization—no matter if it is composed of Jews or Italians, anybody—and then won't go to bat for it in an honorable way, I ought to have my head cut off."

In July 1934, freed while his tax case was being appealed, Lazia was shot outside his apartment at the Park Central Hotel. DEMOCRATIC LEADER SLAIN IN KANSAS CITY, read the headline in the *New York Times*. Before he died, Lazia told his friends—but not the law—who had done it: Jack Gregory, a killer Lazia had imported from St. Louis to work in labor rackets. After Gregory then tried to muscle into Lazia's operation on his own, he had been ordered out of town. Not cooperating, he had killed Lazia instead. Lazia's men found Gregory and took him for a ride. Knowing what was coming, Gregory asked for a last cigarette. Defiant to the finish, he ground the lighted end into the eye of a man sitting next to him. Lazia's men, showing their own inventiveness, beat Gregory and stuffed him, still alive, into the blazing furnace of an apartment building on Independence Avenue. Pendergast attended the Lazia funeral and sent a floral offering in the shape of a wheel attached to an axle, with the second wheel missing, implying the dead man's importance. Arrangements were made with Lazia's gang successor, Charles Carollo, and the Pendergast machine rolled along.

It worked so smoothly, with so few disruptions, that the actual extent of its reach was not easily appreciated. The good citizens of Kansas City may have winced at their town's reputation. But they liked the low taxes, the absence of petty crime and labor violence, and the civic improvements. Pendergast—unlike Frank Hague—did not bleed his town white. "We have turned Kansas City from a hick town into a metropolitan city," Pendergast bragged. "Look at our streets and our parks and public buildings and everything!"

Favored businessmen got illegal tax breaks, and troublesome local ordinances were changed or ignored. Business groups—the Better Business Bureau, chamber of commerce, real-estate board, and merchants' association—made no public objections to the Pendergast regime.

The full power at the boss's fingertips became clear when a local reformer dared squeak his defiance. Rabbi Samuel S. Mayerberg of Temple B'Nai Jehudah, a prominent Kansas City congregation, was one of the few non-WASP would-be racketbusters of the 1930s. Himself the son of a rabbi, Mayerberg had arrived in Kansas City in 1928. Intensely concerned with civic affairs (he had done graduate work in political science before his rabbinical studies), Mayerberg was appalled by how the machine intruded into the most private aspects of life. "People were actually told what physicians they might use," he said later, "what lawyers might practice, what merchants might do business. Personnel men in our factories came under the domination of the machine; and for years they would refuse to employ men unless they had passes from the boss. All city insurance and all surety bonds for contractors working for the city or county had to be negotiated through one insurance broker, a very good man, a close personal friend of the boss. Respectable business men soon found it a matter of safety to have Pendergast or McElroy identified with them in their concerns; in some instances they received blocks of stock; in others they were paid for serving on executive boards."

Starting with one of the governing triumvirate, Mayerberg gathered evidence on Henry McElroy's crimes as city manager and presented it to a women's government study club in May 1932. The *Kansas City Star* gave it two columns on the front page and editorial approval. For a while, some Pendergast critics emerged from hiding, poked their heads out windows, and looked around. A few days after Mayerberg's speech, the Ministerial Alliance, 125 ministers strong, passed an endorsement; but of these 125 preachers, only 4 stayed with the crusade to the end. Mayerberg started the Charter League to recall the corrupted city council. For this temerity his phones were tapped, his office files ransacked. One night his car was forced to the curb, and a shot was fired that missed. For months Mayerberg slept with a loaded pistol on the floor by his bed.

Prodded and annoyed, the machine gathered itself. The city

clerk declared the Charter League's petitions fraudulent and destroyed them. Mayerberg could not persuade any prominent citizens to run as recall candidates. "One of my hardest jobs was not fighting the underworld," he said later, "but in using my energy and time to convince thoroughly nice people, honorable men . . . that, as respectable citizens, they ought to be in it [the fight] also." Many members of his congregation resigned under threats from the machine. After a year the Charter League expired, unfulfilled and $3,600 in debt. The city election in 1934—marred by four killings, a dozen serious injuries, and sluggings of reformers—finally scared the movement into silence. Mayerberg remained an implacable enemy of the machine, but he crusaded more quietly.

Immune to reformers, Pendergast was undone by himself. This man of such granitic self-possession, so shrewd and disciplined, so ascetic and understated in every other way, was a horse-betting fool. All his instincts for thrills and pleasures were gathered and channeled into one roaring, consuming vice. Pendergast's none-too-expert racing tout, Roy Offutt, lingered around the office at 1908 Main Street. After the morning's business was done, Pendergast would sit back and shout, "Where the hell is Offutt?" The two men would pore over racing papers and dope sheets and then phone in the boss's bets. As the races were run at tracks around the country, Pendergast sat with a telephone to his ear, hanging on the accounts that came over Annenberg's racing wire, living and dying with each race.

Horses became his only interest outside his work and family. At times the horses overwhelmed everything. In 1928 Pendergast brought horse racing back to Kansas City after reformers had managed to keep it out for two decades. The Riverside Park Jockey Club, usually called "Pendergast's Track," ran five miles north of the city, out in Platte County. In season Pendergast was there every afternoon. He kept his own stable of a dozen horses; they seldom won, but he liked to watch them work out. When the boss traveled he brought along his obsession. He made annual trips to Saratoga and Churchill Downs. At Belmont Park in New York he was often seen in the company of Lucky Luciano and Frank Costello. Once Senator Harry Truman and his aide Victor Messall called on the boss in his suite at the Waldorf in Manhattan. "T. J.'s penthouse looked just like a stockbroker's office," Messall noted. "It was a madhouse with ticker-tape machines bringing him racetrack news and results, and the place was filled with jockeys and bookies. He told us that some jockeys had doublecrossed him with wrong tips and he almost killed a few of them."

Occasionally he put his money on a winner. In 1934 a bet of $10,000 on a long shot brought him a payoff of $250,000. He won just often enough to be pulled in deeper and deeper. He bet up to $50,000 a day, sometimes $2 million over a year. From 1933 on, according to friends, his average net loss was a million dollars a year. Frantic to keep up, Pendergast raised his take from the Kansas City underworld, had McElroy steal more public money, roused his associates in the middle of the night to bring him $10,000, or $100,000. He never had enough money to fill the ravenous maw of his addiction.

Bearing his load, he arranged for a bribe of $750,000 from a group of fire insurance companies seeking friendly legislation in Missouri. The boss had received $440,000 of it before one of the conspirators died, killing the deal. A routine IRS audit of a lawyer's estate in Chicago turned up traces of the arrangement. Pendergast was indicted for tax evasion. "I never desert a sinking ship," said Harry Truman. "He was my friend when I needed him, and I will be his."

With the boss at bay, his whole machine suddenly came apart. The structure, so sleek and stable in appearance, could not stand without the leader. Henry McElroy resigned under fire. Pendergast pled guilty to two counts, paid $330,000 in taxes and penalties, and was sent to Leavenworth penitentiary for fifteen months. The *Kansas City Star* printed his convict mug shot, in prison garb, on the front page. The prison director received a phone call from Senator Truman: "I want you to know that he's a friend of mine. . . . I'm not asking any favors for him, do you understand, but I want him treated no differently from anybody else." Charles Carollo, Police Chief Otto Higgins, and other municipal luminaries soon joined the boss in jail.

Reformers took over at the Kansas City elections in 1940. They installed a new mayor and a new city manager. The jazz joints and gambling dens gradually closed down, and the city became safely dull. Truman ambled toward the White House. "The terrible things done by the high ups in K.C.," he confided to his wife, "will be a lead weight to me from now on."

❦ ❦

"To be a real mayor you've got to have control of the party," said Mayor Edward J. Kelly of Chicago. "You've got to be a potent political factor. You've gotta be a boss!"

❦ ❦

In Chicago the names changed and the corruption went on forever. "The visitor to Chicago is not there very long," one writer observed in 1940, "before he becomes aware of a mysterious, shadowy power that everyone speaks about, seems to know about, but actually is unable to describe save in the foggiest terms. It is that invisible, sinister organism known as the Syndicate." By which was meant the old Capone gang. More diverse ethnically than most Italian gangs, it included non-Italians—Greasy Thumb Guzik, Murray the Camel Humphreys, Gussie Alex—at its highest levels. Most of the troops, though, and the ultimate power of decision, the authority to kill, remained Italian. Al Capone's successors at the top, Frank Nitti and Tony Accardo, were quieter, shrewder, less flamboyant than the big guy. They imposed a "Pax Caponeum" on the city's underworld that made it seem—even to Frank Loesch of the Chicago Crime Commission— that conditions had improved.

The mayor's office passed from Big Bill Thompson to Anton Cermak to Ed Kelly, all corrupt and comfortably aligned with the underworld. Of the three, Kelly was the slickest and most durable, holding the mayoralty for fourteen years. Senator Paul Douglas of Illinois, initiated into politics by dealing with Kelly on the Chicago City Council, and who as a professor at the University of Chicago had been surrounded by impressive minds, recognized a "great native intelligence" in Kelly. During his reign as mayor Kelly indulged in various self-improvement measures, driven in part by the early death of his only son. He stopped drinking and all-night poker games, and watched his diet and health to the point of hypochondria. Wishing to refine his diction, he critiqued his speech on a home recorder. In conversation he would drop knowing references to legitimate theater and current literature. He got himself admitted to a choosy club. He dressed well and lived well in homes on Lake Shore Drive and at the Ambassador East Hotel.

The Chicago underworld, said Kelly, no longer even existed. "We have purged the city of gangsters, hoodlums and racketeers," he declared. "The underworld, realizing that we mean business, has moved to other places." Yet Frank Nitti and Tony Accardo remained prosperously ensconced in Chicago. Behind a canny front, Kelly was still the tough kid, brawling and crooked, from Back of the Yards on the Southwest Side of town. His father, an Irish immigrant, had worked as a cop and fireman. The oldest of nine children, Ed Kelly left school when he was twelve and took up the diversions of street life. At eighteen, he liked to recall, he threw rocks at the federal troops during the great Pullman strike of 1894.

That same year he started working for the Chicago Sanitary District, an association that lasted almost forty years. On his own he learned enough about the engineering of sewers and water-works, and about the politics of city contracts, to ascend through the hierarchy of the Sanitary domain. From 1919 to 1929, he later admitted, his total income ran about $66,000 a year despite an average city salary of under $14,000. Some of these unreported bonuses presumably came through his friend Patrick A. Nash, the Twenty-eighth Ward committeeman, whose family ran sewer contracting businesses. After Kelly became chief engineer in 1920, in position to control who got the jobs, Nash's family was awarded $13 million worth of contracts in three years. Thus greased, the two men formed a complementary team in city politics: Kelly the public contact man, tall, robust, and gregarious; Nash the diplomat in the background, "the great harmonizer" who got along with everybody but seldom appeared in public.

Kelly was taking his ease at a Havana racetrack in 1933 when he heard that Mayor Cermak had been shot. After Cermak died, Patrick Nash—as chairman of the Cook County Democratic organization—had Kelly appointed mayor. In the tradition of Frank Hague and Tom Pendergast, Kelly took power as a reformer. "When I first came here," he said later, "this place looked like a junk shop. Some boys kept their heads glued to a racing form, playing the horses right in the mayor's office. I cut that stuff out." In his early years as mayor he performed fiscal miracles: at a time of grim depression and declining municipal revenues, Kelly somehow brought in balanced budgets and trea-sury surpluses. According to the *New York Times*, "He turned one of the worst-governed cities into one of the best-governed." In 1935 he won his first full term by a vote of 799,060 to 167,106. (No more than half his margin came from stolen votes.)

Cynics did wonder, though, how much of the city's financial health depended on illicit money. The Kelly-Nash machine took in a huge tribute, estimated at $12 million to $20 million annually, from protected gambling outfits. Thus it did not have to loot the public treasury, to the improvement of Chicago's fiscal soundness. Kelly himself listed $50,000 in "gambling" income on his federal tax returns; this probably represented only part of his share of the boodle. "It was commonly known," said Paul Douglas, "that City Hall, the ward organizations, and the police all shared in the payoffs. I never learned the ratios but I knew each captain had a man who picked up the tribute." The administration had internal sources of graft as well. Jobs and promotions in the police, fire, and other city departments were given in exchange for bribes. According to a man from the Thirteenth Ward, "Everybody knows how promotions are made in the police department. Most captains are appointed by the mayor on recommendation of the ward committeeman. Every ward committeeman knows that civil service examinations for promotion are mostly a sham—it's all handled through the mayor."

The serious money came from gambling. Near city hall, within the Loop, over one hundred bookie joints and gambling houses prospered under Kelly's protection. Perhaps eight hundred more ran elsewhere in the city. Kelly thought it should all be legalized, "like the race tracks." As he explained his position: "Gambling isn't a violation of divine law, and you'll find it wherever there are human beings, beginning with kids who play marbles for keeps. All you can do is keep the strong-arm boys, the muscle, from moving in." The muscle, of course, did not have to move in because it was already there. During the 1937 primary campaign, Kelly's opponent accused the mayor of—gasp!—underworld ties. "The mayor is part and parcel of the syndicate which controls gambling," it was said. "The fix is in at the top." Kelly still won easily. A few years later, worried about a renegade grand-jury investigation, Kelly had the joints shut down for a few weeks. The reformers then relaxed and business soon resumed.

While the Capones controlled most of Chicago's underworld, the Kelly machine had one other, independent source of income:

the numbers or "policy" gambling on the black South Side. In other cities, the white underworld by the 1930s had taken charge of the numbers game. In Chicago the black numbers men had enough money and clout to remain on their own a while longer. The Depression had made them even more important to the black community. As legitimate businesses suffered in hard times, policy rackets still offered stability and employment to five thousand people every week. About five hundred "policy stations" were sprinkled across the South Side. The Jones brothers, sons of a Baptist preacher from Vicksburg, Mississippi, had the biggest franchise. Their headquarters at 4724 South Michigan was staffed by up to 250 workers. The Joneses also owned hotels, apartment buildings, and a large department store on Forty-seventh Street. "They may come under the head of racketeers," said one black restaurant owner of the brothers, "but as long as they have done something that no other one of our group has done, they should be given a lot of credit and are entitled to the support of our people." Part of the Kelly organization, the Jones brothers served as precinct captains in Ward 2.

Before the Kelly regime consolidated the process, local policy bosses had to pay the cops in their districts. By the late 1930s the money went directly to city hall, as described by a black attorney who worked in the South Side office building where the transactions took place: "A string of white and colored come into this building to make their weekly payments. Later in the day a man from downtown comes to take the money. Sometimes he has a bodyguard and sometimes a squad car comes with him." Police captains would then be told which operations in their precincts to lay off and which to bust.

In 1939 Kelly appointed William L. Dawson, a black attorney, to be the new Ward 2 committeeman. As a criminal lawyer Dawson had specialized in defending black gamblers and gangsters. Elected to Congress in 1942, Dawson eventually became the most powerful black politician in America: the boss of six wards in Chicago, the chairman for eighteen years of a major House committee, and a vice chairman of the Democratic National Committee. His political organization, ruthlessly efficient, depended on contributions from black policy men—as Dawson himself acknowledged. The money came every month to his Chicago office at 180 West Washington Street. "Betting is a human frailty, but it isn't evil in itself," Dawson explained. "There's bingo played in the churches, and not too much racket is made about it." To Dawson it made sense that black gambling money should stay within the South Side. "Negroes don't create money. They usually go outside their area to work for it and bring it back into their community," said the congressman. "If anybody is to profit out of gambling in the Negro community, it should be the Negro. It is purely an economic question."

Dawson's underworld connections and obligations, however, extended beyond the South Side. A few years after Dawson went to Congress, the Capones finally had taken over Chicago's black policy syndicates. After one of the Joneses was kidnapped and ransomed, the brothers took their money and removed to Mexico. Representative Dawson, by contrast, got on fine with the Capones. Greasy Thumb Guzik collected the policy protection money at Dawson's office each month. As Dawson assumed more power during his twenty-eight years in Congress, he did occasional favors for organized crime, such as defending crooked Teamsters under attack by investigating committees. No criminal charges were ever proven against him. As a practicing politician, he said, he dealt in favors, not in money. After all, how could he as a congressman protect the underworld? "I have never been in a position to give gamblers protection," he pointed out. "That is the province of the mayor and the police commissioner." The powers at city hall probably wished he hadn't said that.

❧ ❧

Organized crime dealt in surprises and deceptions, so underworld politics produced unlikely alliances and startling combinations. It was admirable, for example, that women and blacks achieved a measure of power in national politics. It was ironic, though, that Mary Norton (the first substantial woman in Congress) and William Dawson (the first substantial black in Congress) were both creations of corrupt urban machines. Norton could not survive the end of Hague's power, but Dawson constructed his own base and picked his own successor before retiring at the age of eighty-four.

In the same fashion, organized crime and corrupt urban machines formed the dark underside of the New Deal. Bemobbed union leaders like Sidney Hillman and Dan Tobin were always prominent in Roosevelt's presidency. When FDR first ran for the White House, none of the major city bosses had supported him. The New Deal of the first two terms—the New Deal of progressive social legislation, the New Deal beloved by liberals, intellectuals, and social workers—owed little to the city machines. But as federal patronage and WPA jobs came to such good Democrats as Frank Hague, Tom Pendergast, and Ed Kelly, the machines and the New Dealers settled their differences. Toward the end of the second term, Postmaster General Farley warned Roosevelt that Hague's men were reading the mail of their enemies in Jersey City. Tell them to stop, the President told Farley, "but keep this quiet. We need Hague's support if we want New Jersey."

Without the city bosses, especially Ed Kelly, Roosevelt would not have won a third term. The Democratic convention of 1940 was held in Chicago for good reasons. "I am not overlooking the fact," Roosevelt confided to Harold Ickes, "that Kelly could pack the galleries for us." Kelly led the movement, subtly encouraged by the White House, to draft FDR for a third term. At the convention, Frank Hague served as a floor manager for Roosevelt. After the reading of an oblique statement by the President—not saying yes to another term, not saying no—Kelly's men engineered an arranged demonstration. A loud, disembodied, mysterious voice came over the PA system, calling for Roosevelt. (It was Kelly's superintendent of sewers, down in the basement, pressing his lips to the mike.) Other Kelly minions led a "spontaneous" demonstration that lasted an hour and stampeded the convention. The next day Roosevelt was nominated.

As the 1944 convention approached, Kelly suggested that Harry Truman's friend Bob Hannegan, a machine pol from St. Louis, be made chairman of the Democratic National Committee. After some consideration FDR, busy with the war and losing his grip on domestic affairs, gave his approval. The 1944 convention—dominated by Hannegan, Hillman, and the city bosses—added Truman to the ticket. Roosevelt died three months after his fourth inauguration, and Tom Pendergast's boy became President.

SEVEN

THE WASPS PERSIST

For most Americans, World War II meant emergency austerities, sacrifices, and the submission of individual ambitions to a greater good. For gangsters, the war meant flush times, easy money, and fewer lawmen. In wartime, as in most times, life from an underworld perspective implied a world turned upside down and inside out. The war economy—factories roaring straight through three shifts, full employment, households with two or more incomes—left Americans with extra money on their hands for the first time since the 1920s. But the usual recreations and consumer goods became scarce. Filling these voids, gambling and betting and horse racing grew and throve. With federal agents switched to pursuing domestic spies and saboteurs, and with local police forces depleted by reduced budgets and drafted manpower, gangsters enjoyed both fewer adversaries and blooming opportunities.

Organized crime, expert in such matters, helped run the flourishing underground consumer economy—the black market of tires, gasoline, liquor, meat, silk stockings, and other rarities hard to buy legally. Waxey Gordon, out of jail and back in New York, was caught diverting five tons of sugar to an illegal still. Other gangsters dealt in precious federal ration stamps and coupons, obtained usually from crooked government officials. Carlo Gambino of New York made over a million dollars on one such deal alone. Joe Valachi, a mere soldier in the Luciano family, cleared $150,000 in a year of handling genuine stamps ("There were so many legitimate stamps around," he said later, "I didn't think it was wise to go around with counterfeit stamps"). Total war was good business for war profiteers and gangsters too.

The war mood itself loosened restraint: the upheavals of families dislocated, individuals moved about, normal ways in suspension, daily casualties overseas, and a general sense of live this day because tomorrow is a crapshoot. One Chicago hoodlum loitered through the war as a guard at a booming gambling joint run by the local outfit. Nobody at the club seemed to suffer from wartime shortages of ration coupons or anything else. "The members of this gambling club were very good about giving me extra coupons," the guard remembered. "They had pockets full of every kind of ration coupon there was. If they didn't have it, all they had to do was call someone."

Even in wartime, then, the WASP racketbusters still had culprits to stalk. Though engulfed at the time by overwhelming news of the war, crusading WASPs in Boston, Minneapolis, and Chicago did their utmost to catch bad guys. After 1945, both hounds and hares settled into an endless chase: the hounds running for the principle and the hares running for their lives and fortunes. No wonder the hares usually won.

❦ ❦

Robert T. Bushnell, attorney general of Massachusetts during World War II, mounted a most ambitious crusade against organized crime at a most difficult time. All his life he plunged forward despite any odds; gifted in ways, he lacked discretion and a sense of proportion, flaws that finally pulled him down. Born in New York in 1896, he had grown up as a child of reduced circumstances. His father, a manufacturer, died when he was eight. His mother then baked loaves of Boston brown bread, which the boy delivered to food shops around town. Later he peddled newspapers and raised chickens to help the family get by. Scholarships took him to prep school and Harvard. He worked his way through college by waiting tables, pulling weeds, and doing other odd jobs.

With time out for army service in World War I, Bushnell graduated from Harvard in 1919. At his commencement he flashed the singleminded zeal (or unawareness of context) that so dominated his personality: after reciting the traditional class ode he stepped forward, declared that he could not contain himself, and announced his disapproval of Bolshevism, anarchism, socialism, and pacifism. The audience, startled but caught in the spirit of the day, clapped loudly. Three years later, fresh out of Harvard Law School, he spurned the customary small job in a big firm and started his own practice, making a quick reputation as a trial lawyer. He went, as usual, his own way.

In 1926 Bushnell was elected district attorney of Middlesex County, bordering Boston to the north and west. Thirty years old, he was the youngest man ever to hold the job. His corrupt predecessor had run budget deficits; in three years Bushnell actually returned $144,000 from his appropriations to the county treasury, despite a greater volume of litigation. Even Bushnell could not enforce Prohibition, however. Once a dry, by 1930 he had given up on the noble experiment because it had sent "a vast subterranean flow of wealth into the hands of the worst and lowest element of society," as he put it.

Returning to private life in 1931, for a decade Bushnell practiced law and Republican politics before coming back to public office as attorney general. Once again he had to confront "the worst and lowest element," which Prohibition had made so rich: old bootleggers still ran the Boston underworld. Since the early 1930s, Italian gangsters from the North End and East Boston had extracted fealty and tribute from the Irish and Jewish hoodlums operating elsewhere around Boston. According to a confidential memorandum prepared in 1936 by John C. Bresnahan of the Boston police, "All rackets are controlled and supervised by the following men: Daniel J. Carroll, Philip Buccola, and Joseph Lombardi [Lombardo]. Carroll, formerly associated in business with the notorious Charles Solomon, now deceased, is the 'front man' and 'fingerman' for this organization. Although in the legitimate enterprizes of trucking and prize-fight manager, his main source of revenue is derived from 'Part of cut' of all types of rackets being carried on in this City. Buccola, formerly of Brooklyn, N.Y. is the 'boss' or 'king' of the above organization. . . . Lombardi, formerly of Brooklyn, N.Y., nefarious dealer in drugs and alcohol; also during Prohibition a notorious bootlegger and the direct cause of the shooting of Frankie Wallace and Dodo Walsh in his office on Hanover Street a few years ago." Lombardo's sumptuous Pinetree racing stable, out in the suburb of Framingham, was the protected site of occasional national Mafia conferences with luminaries from New York, Buffalo, Chicago, and New Orleans.

Below the ruling Italians and the amenable Carroll, two Jews and an Irishman supervised the betting parlors, numbers pools, and gambling joints around town. Joseph Hotze, based in the working-class enclave of Somerville, specialized in the numbers racket, known locally as nigger pool because it had originated in black districts. In the South End, the veteran Paddy Coleman ran a bookie empire extending into the Back Bay, Roxbury, and South Boston. A bookie since 1913, Coleman was proud of never having been convicted or losing his telephone service. One of his associates in South Boston, Knocko McCormack, was the brother of Representative John W. McCormack. Knocko's Wave Cottage restaurant boasted a gambling den on the second floor. His congressman brother, once a lawyer for the late Gustin gang of the Wallace brothers, kept himself apart from Knocko's underworld life.

Harry Sagansky, the most wily and durable gambling boss in town, operated from an office building on the main square of Charlestown, across the street from a police station. Born and raised in Boston's West End, he had graduated from Tufts Dental School in 1919 and practiced dentistry for a few years. He seemed so respectable, so mildly well mannered and ungangsterlike; it provided superb cover. "This defendant is a prominent dentist in the City of Boston who has no previous record," said an assistant DA in explaining why he was dismissing one of Sagansky's first gaming arrests. "There is a grave question of identity and in view of the defendant's record and standing there is a doubt as to whether he violated the law." Sagansky went on to accumulate two dozen arrests over the years, but nothing stuck. With his gambling scams delivering a personal income of over a million dollars a year, he owned parts of three racetracks, three Boston nightclubs, and a finance company. He kept his wife and four children in Brookline and his girlfriend in a Back Bay apartment. The girlfriend, known as the Duchess, worked as hostess at one of his nightclubs, the Mayfair, which he had thoughtfully bought for her.

Beneath the ruling triumvirate of Buccola-Lombardo-Carroll,

and the second tier of Sagansky-Coleman-Hotze, toiled thousands of small-time crooks: numbers runners, telephone men, clerks, and gofers. The whole system prospered without police interference, most of the time, because the pertinent cops were paid off. Within a given police precinct, the captain ran his own barony as he chose. Bribes might net him $100,000 or more each year. Among the plusher precincts were Division 2, downtown, with nightclubs nearby; and Division 16 in the Back Bay, near Gangster's Row at the corner of Boylston Street and Massachusetts Avenue. The precinct captains in turn had to pay higher-ups at headquarters to get and keep their jobs.

The top cop, the commissioner of police, was appointed by the governor of Massachusetts. In 1885 the WASP Republican legislature, dismayed by police conditions in Irish Democratic Boston, had given the governor the power to name the city's police commissioner. This system worked only as long as the governor was himself honest. Whenever reformers grew especially upset about police corruption in Boston, the commissioner became the fall guy. From 1930 to 1936, five different commissioners served the public, each yielding in turn to embarrassing but brief scandals. Governor James Michael Curley, the most egregiously crooked Boston pol of his time, made two of these appointments. The first, an advertising man with no police background, lasted nineteen months. The second, Joseph F. Timilty, got the job in November 1936 and held on for seven tumultuous years.

Like his dubious predecessor, Joe Timilty knew nothing about police work. He was, however, charming, widely acquainted, and adroit: nobody else could have retained the simultaneous good wishes of both Curley and the Kennedy family, ancient enemies in the politics of Boston. Timilty was one of Joe Kennedy's tightest buddies. They played golf, took trips, and did business deals together. When Kennedy was away, Timilty—a lifelong bachelor noted for his flashy clothes—might escort Rose Kennedy to parties or the theater. In the late 1930s, Joe Kennedy, Jr., then a Harvard student, often accompanied Timilty to racetracks and on the commissioner's nocturnal inspection tours around town. Both Timilty and young Joe loved to gamble.

Yet these ties to Kennedys somehow survived Timilty's even closer connections to Curley. "If it wasn't for Curley I wouldn't have anything today," said Timilty. "He gave me my start."

Timilty's father, Diamond Jim, the son of Irish immigrants to Boston, had started the family construction business. In the 1920s, Curley during one of his terms as mayor of Boston had given the Timiltys some $3 million worth of construction contracts. As usual with Curley, these arrangements did not lack shenanigans. In 1926 the Timiltys were indicted for conspiring to monopolize road-paving materials. The case was impeded long enough for a new and friendlier district attorney to take office, at which point the indictments went into limbo, neither dropped nor pursued. "I sought to do exactly what the NRA tried to do years later," Timilty subsequently explained, "to fix prices and eliminate unfair competition." After Curley went up to the statehouse in 1935, Timilty became his military aide—resplendent in uniforms with brightly lined capes and gold braid and epaulets—and his closest adviser and confidant. Curley then made him police commissioner because he could expect absolute personal loyalty, the mother's milk of Boston politics.

Following the pattern of his briefly tenured predecessors, at the outset Timilty promised to end police corruption in Boston. "I'm going to clean up this city," he announced, banging his fist on the desk. In a week his men arrested fifty-six minor bookies and gamblers (but no big shots). Timilty even then fretted about the social effect of bearing down on gamblers. "Such men are used to soft living and easy money," he pointed out. "So we've got to be alert and ready for whatever they might turn their hands to." After a year Timilty claimed to have closed 150 bookie rooms and arrested 1,000 numbers men. Yet nobody, he insisted, could entirely wipe out gambling in Boston. "We can never really hope to rid the city of the so-called little racketeer," he said, "so long as the citizens of the city themselves want to make illegal bets." But it was just small fry: "There is no real organization in Boston. I mean that. There may have been. There isn't now."

The Watch & Ward Society was characteristically not satisfied. Founded in 1884 as the New England Society for the Suppression of Vice, sustained over the years by Protestant ministers, the Watch & Ward was a private group of WASP reformers worried about gambling, prostitution, and smutty books and plays. The group's Protestant-conscienced zeal—especially to ban certain books—made it controversial even among reform-minded WASPs. "Quack doctors of public morals," Robert Bushnell said of the Watch & Ward in 1930. "Many of them have been high-minded clergymen, possessed of knowledge of criminal investigation as naive as that of a child of four." Police forces were not perfect, Bushnell admitted, but "the worst of them function better than a motley crew of private investigators under the leadership of narrow-minded seekers of evil."

Surveying crime conditions in Massachusetts during the 1930s, the Watch & Ward perceived a "wave of gambling" sweeping over the commonwealth. Pari-mutuel betting and beano games were legalized. Legal lotteries were staged for charities. Slot machines and numbers pools, though still illegal, were more visibly tolerated. "We have come to a day," the Watch & Ward declared in 1936, "when members of the legislature, sitting in a public committee hearing, may be heard to boast about the number of lottery tickets they buy in violation of the law. We have come to a day when candidates for the highest offices in the commonwealth accept large sums of money from the gambling element to help in their campaigns for election."

The Watch & Ward carefully tracked Joe Timilty's announced reforms in Boston, at first with relief, later with misgivings. When advised of some gambling operation like Paddy Coleman's, Timilty would thank the group for its vigilance and promise action. As time passed, Timilty acted less the reformer. After a private talk with him in March 1941, the Watch & Ward's secretary, the Reverend Charles Bodwell, concluded that Timilty had abandoned his promises. "The commissioner advanced any number of reasons," Bodwell noted, "as to why it was better to leave the small bookies alone. Among them being the following: 'Gambling keeps them from committing hold-ups.' The commissioner went on to say that he had raided Coleman's off and on and 'bawled him out.' This is a sad commentary on law enforcement."

In the summer of 1942, after years of private warnings, the Watch & Ward went public with its criticisms of Timilty. "Morality has gone haywire in Boston since the outbreak of the war," said Bodwell's successor, Louis Croteau, in an interview with the *Boston Post*. "Vice has become smart. That's an actual fact. Young girls who never before strayed from the path of decency now regard it as smart to have easy morals." Bookies, numbers, and floating dice games were all thriving. And why? "Starting with the crooked politicians," said Croteau, "you get some politically appointed police officials, who know on which side their bread is buttered and obey only the wishes of their politician-backers. You will also find police officials who are inefficient and scared of their jobs. They condone gambling and other forms of crime in their district because they haven't got the moral courage to stamp it out." Timilty, the implicit though unnamed culprit, demanded a retraction but did not get it.

Meantime Robert Bushnell had taken office as attorney general. He started slowly, feeling his way, not wishing to seem a Watch & Ward zealot. "I'm not a crusader for or against anything," he said. "I dislike the term and the practice." In 1941, after receiving various complaints about gambling in Boston, Bushnell sent Timilty a letter, in private, just a warning shot off the bow: "It is not my disposition to conduct any sensational or headline investigation of any police department. On the other hand, I find the number of complaints relative to number pools and horse-racing rackets sufficient to give me some concern. Before taking any other step, I prefer to call the complaints, of which these are fair specimens, to your attention."

Poked and prodded, worried into action, Timilty started a *pro forma* investigation. A police underworld specialist, James V. Crowley, reported that a certain "big shot" racketeer alluded to in Bushnell's letter was probably Harry Sagansky. "I do not believe that Sagansky now has the police under his control," Crowley noted, denying an allegation in Bushnell's letter. "It has not been the policy of this office to take notice of number pool backers and their agents for several years and thus it is impossible in this short space of time to accumulate the entire activities of Sagansky." One section of Crowley's internal report, describing Sagansky's headquarters near the police station in Charlestown, was secretly deleted at the behest of Timilty or his superintendent of police, Edward W. Fallon, or both.

That was revealed later. At the time, Bushnell only knew he kept getting complaints that left Timilty oddly unconcerned. In December 1941 the attorney general received a long, detailed memo from the publisher and editor of the *Boston Herald*, a newspaper that catered to Yankee Republicans. The memo described a vast numbers syndicate, headed by Sagansky, employing three thousand people, taking in up to $300,000 a day, six days a week. "There isn't an office building in the entire city—City Hall, the State House and Police Headquarters NOT excluded—where one has any difficulty in placing a number," according to the memo. The most damning accusations hit the police: "A part of every dollar collected by pool writers in Boston, is set aside for police protection.... As far as the police are concerned those behind the syndicate have been known to be behind the transfer of officers and men, have dictated promotions and shifts and have operated practically unmolested."

Bushnell's patience, not his long suit, was being stretched. Sending such reports on to Timilty, he found, was like punching a pillow. The reports were absorbed, Timilty made gestures, and nothing changed. Skeptical of the Boston police, Bushnell finally assigned six Massachusetts state policemen to make their own investigations. For five months they tailed, watched, and took movies of the busy gambling venues around town. They were almost ready to make arrests when a terrible fire engulfed the Cocoanut Grove nightclub in the South End. In its complex aftermath, everything in Boston stopped for a while.

Like other big-time Boston nightclubs, the Cocoanut Grove was an underworld enterprise. Its original owner was Charlie Solomon, the city rackets boss in the 1920s. After Solomon was murdered in 1933, the Cocoanut Grove passed on to his lawyer, Barney Welansky. The nightclub retained its underworld associations under Welansky's management. As a gangster joint, the Cocoanut Grove enjoyed special privileges from the police and city inspectors. Its operating license was renewed each year with no formal review or hearing. "In all the time I was there," the maître d' said later, "I never saw any fire or building inspectors in the place. I didn't know anything about fire exits, and no one ever told me. The police would come in occasionally, ask me how things were going, pass the time of day, and then go out." Welansky bragged of his friendship with Mayor Maurice Tobin; in the summer of 1942 Tobin appointed him to the city war rationing board. (Later over four thousand cases of outlaw booze, without federal tax stamps, were found in the nightclub's ruins.) A workman at the club in the fall of 1942 told Welansky he needed a building permit. "You won't have to get a permit," Welansky replied, "because Tobin and I fit. They owe me plenty down there."

On the Saturday night of November 28, 1942, the Cocoanut

Grove was jammed with some 1,000 patrons. The club's legal occupancy limit was 460. At one of its bars that evening sat the local night police captain, oblivious to the overcrowding. A fire started in a downstairs lounge. The furnishings, supposed to be fireproof, were not. An emergency exit, required by law, had been welded shut to foil check dodgers. In only twelve minutes the fire exploded through the place, sucking up oxygen, choking and killing with its smoke. Bodies piled up at the available exits, trapping others inside. The final toll came to 491 deaths. It remains the second-deadliest building fire in American history, surpassed only by a Chicago theater fire in 1903 that killed 602.

While Bushnell's office tried to assign blame for the fire, his delayed offensive against gambling in Boston finally pounced. As Bushnell and his men pondered their leads and evidence, they decided to go after Sagansky. On January 12, 1943, a force of fifty-two state troopers in plainclothes descended on twelve sites simultaneously, taking betting equipment and making twenty-three arrests. Sagansky himself, who had moved from his Charlestown headquarters after the Cocoanut Grove fire, was arrested at his girlfriend's apartment at 12 Commonwealth Avenue. Among the papers taken from his home in Brookline was an insurance policy on the life of James Michael Curley that named Sagansky as beneficiary. (Curley said it was security on a loan from Sagansky.) The evidence of corrupt connections pointed more generally at the Boston police and Joe Timilty. The state police had taken movies of Boston cops moving in and around Sagansky's betting premises, talking and loafing, parking their cars, but making no arrests.

Bushnell was broadening his net to catch cops as well as robbers, and Timilty was squirming. In the weeks after the Sagansky raids, the police commissioner behaved like a guilty man. He went to a bank safe-deposit box—a box to which he alone had access—removed $37,370 in cash, and took it home. A while later, on February 8, he was called before a grand jury to answer questions from Bushnell about that money and his conduct as commmmissioner. Timilty said he had removed the $37,370 "because if that money was discovered I figured a misrepresentation would be placed on it. They could figure I got the money since I was police commissioner, and that is positively not so." He had put the money in a safe at home; or maybe his cousin or brother had placed it there, he wasn't sure. Two days later, called back to the grand jury, Timilty made a different guess as to just when he had taken the money, and added that he had left it in his room at home, not in a safe. When giving his previous, contradictory testimony, he explained, he had been "all in a fog-like."

Not a reassuring performance. In March the grand jury indicted Timilty, Superintendent Fallon, and five of their police subordinates for conspiring to allow gambling in Boston. On the day the indictment came down, Timilty again performed a suspicious errand: he removed four drawers of his personal files from his office to his home. All seven police defendants pleaded not guilty and were suspended by Governor Leverett Saltonstall. In effect, Bushnell had taken over the Boston Police Department.

It was too much for him. Along with all his routine business as attorney general, hampered by war shortages of men and resources, he was conducting four major investigations at once: the Cocoanut Grove fire, the Sagansky raids, the police cases, and a related inquiry into the Timilty family's financial dealings. In all these he needed the cooperation of Governor Saltonstall, a fellow Yankee Republican of undoubted integrity. Unfortunately Bushnell had, as one of his admiring assistants later acknowledged, an "absolute knack for antagonizing people who weren't really his objectives." In criticizing one of Saltonstall's judicial appointments, he called a press conference and hinted of an alliance between the governor and the underworld. Bushnell started feuding with the press, even with the Republican *Herald*, which had helped push him into racketbusting. "I have never had a particle of help from any newspaper in Boston," he said, twisting the facts, "nothing but a deliberate tearing down."

Flailing around, bristling easily, Bushnell alienated the very political forces that should have been on his side. In presenting one of his police cases to an Irish Catholic judge, Bushnell filed a motion to sequester the jury. When the motion was denied, Bushnell picked up his bag of lawbooks, dropped it loudly on the table, said he expected such a decision from such a judge, and stalked from the room, leaving a young assistant to pick up the pieces. In early June, after another Irish Catholic judge quashed the police indictments with no explanation, Bushnell disappeared from Boston.

For three months he was absent from the courts and his office.

If his staff knew his whereabouts, it would not discuss the matter. The *Herald* sarcastically announced that Bushnell was "wanted for questioning" and provided a description of the fugitive: "Bushnell is short and stocky and wears a moustache on his upper lip, of all places. He also smokes cigars and pipes and usually carries a brief case well-lined with indictments." Late in August he surfaced in Boston, looking thinner and deeply tanned. "I have tried press conferences in the past," he told the press. "My remarks have been betrayed or distorted. I do not intend to have any more."

Timilty and the other police officials were re-indicted. A judge again dismissed the indictment against Timilty, on the questionable grounds that the commissioner was only supposed to administer the department, not enforce the laws or make arrests. As the other police cases moved forward, Timilty's term as police commissioner expired in November 1943. Bushnell urged Saltonstall not to reappoint him. Timilty, twice indicted but never brought to trial, wanted to keep the job—if only to outlast his nemesis, Bushnell. On his side, Bushnell had already lost the good wishes of Saltonstall and the press. For his part, Timilty offered a supporting petition with 120,000 signatures and endorsements from the Boston City Council and nearly 200 labor unions and other groups. While Saltonstall pondered a decision, Timilty spent his weekends with Joe Kennedy in Hyannis Port, concocting strategies and calling in debts.

Saltonstall resisted these pressures, swallowed his animosity toward Bushnell, and properly replaced Timilty as police commissioner. "The hypocrisy and arrogance of the attorney general have gained him a temporary victory," Timilty announced. "It's obvious I am going to be a candidate for public office." A few years later Timilty ran for mayor and lost badly.

Bushnell's crusades wound to varied conclusions. The other indicted cops were exonerated except for John Dorsey, the captain at the station house across the street from Sagansky's headquarters; found guilty of neglect of duty by a police review board, Dorsey was reduced to the rank of lieutenant. Barney Welansky, convicted of manslaughter in the Cocoanut Grove case, served three years and seven months in jail and was released early just before he died of cancer. Harry Sagansky pleaded guilty to one count and did thirty months in prison. Out of jail, he married his girlfriend and resumed bookmaking. He was arrested at intervals for the next four decades, was punished lightly, and lived to a prosperous old age.

Robert Bushnell retired from politics in 1945, moved to New York, and died of a heart attack—alone in a hotel room—at the age of fifty-three.

❧ ❧

Hubert Humphrey began his political career as the racketbusting mayor of Minneapolis. During his brief term in the mayor's office he moved quickly from a callow idealism to the real-life compromises of an ambitious politician. Only thirty-four years old when elected in 1945, he looked even younger, with bright eyes and headlong vitality; friends called him Pinky. He had grown up in Doland, South Dakota, a prairie village of white Protestants with one Jewish family and no blacks at all. From his WASP father, Humphrey acquired a talkative interest in politics; from his mother, the daughter of Norwegian immigrants, he absorbed a tireless, ecumenical Protestant piety. Baptized a Lutheran, he spent his early years in a Methodist church: Sunday school, youth groups, Wednesday prayer meetings, singing in the choir at Sunday services. After he moved to Minneapolis for college and graduate work in political science, he switched to a liberal Congregational church, where he taught the adult Sunday school class. Still a young man, revering his mother's example of faith and good works, he was guided by what he called "the plain and unambiguous Christian teachings upon which our society is based."

This deeply felt Protestantism nudged him toward political life. "It is not enough just to be a prayerful and religious person," he said. "The very essence of the Christian religion is a philosophy of action and positive deeds." Well acquainted around Minneapolis through university circles and his jobs as a federal administrator, and deferred from military service for medical reasons, late in 1942 he started to think about trying for the mayoralty. "If I run for mayor," he asked a supporter, "do you think I'll get shot?"

It was a reasonable question. For years the Minneapolis underworld had been serenely protected by corrupt mayors and police chiefs. Accustomed to its entrenched privileges, the underworld would not welcome a mayor of Humphrey's announced intentions. Two old bootleggers—one Irish, the other Jewish—

controlled organized crime in the city. Tommy Banks owned the Casablanca nightclub, gambling joints, bars, liquor stores, and other businesses around town. (From 1941 to 1945, according to a later federal tax indictment, his unreported income amounted to over $291,000.) His sometime partner, occasional rival was Isadore Blumenfeld, the gangster known as Kid Cann. A Romanian immigrant, Cann during Prohibition had run the La Pompadour bootlegging ring with Meyer Schuldberg and other Jews in Minneapolis. After repeal, La Pompadour—following the national pattern—had turned into Chesapeake Brands, a legitimate liquor distributor. Along with Banks, Cann also owned bars and liquor stores. Both men, despite their acknowledged reputations and power, had somehow escaped the attention of the city police.

Beyond this general situation of police neglect, Humphrey had more pointed reasons to wonder about his safety as a gangbusting candidate. A few years earlier two newspapermen, crusaders against the underworld, had been murdered in Minneapolis; neither case was ever solved. Howard Guilford, shot in September 1934, had been attacking gambling and vice operations through his small weekly tabloid. Walter W. Liggett, killed fifteen months later, had been using *his* weekly newspaper to accuse Minnesota's Governor Floyd B. Olson of corruption and gangster connections. Liggett's widow and another witness to his murder identified Kid Cann as the shooter. "Sure I've done a lot of funny things in my life," Cann told reporters. "But for the past two years I've been in a legitimate liquor business. And I'm innocent of this and I can prove it."

What made these murders remarkable, even inexplicable, was that they seemed to violate the traditional underworld rule against harming adversaries who just did their jobs and played it straight. "Criminals, racketeers, mobsters have their own code," Governor Olson pointed out, partly to defend himself from an allegation by Liggett's widow that he was involved in the murder. "They respect, or at least tolerate, an honest policeman, prosecutor, or newspaper man. The underworld never assassinates an honest man on the other side of the line. But once they cross the line, let them look out." As it happened, both Guilford and Liggett had pursued erratic journalistic careers. Guilford had been tried and acquitted of extortion. Cann and his partner Schuldberg both claimed that Liggett had demanded $1,500 or

$2,000 from them to be left alone by his newspaper. Perhaps Guilford and Liggett had indeed crossed the line, or perhaps they were killed by rogue gangsters not abiding by the usual rules, or perhaps the murderers were not gangsters at all, but others aggrieved by the dead men's uninhibited scandal sheets. (Cann produced an alibi witness and was acquitted of Liggett's murder.) In any case, these mysterious killings must have weighed on Humphrey's mind as he pondered whether to run for mayor.

He did have potential allies. The Good Government League, a counterpart to Boston's Watch & Ward, was the organizational expression of a one-man vice crusade. The Reverend Henry J. Soltau, a Methodist minister, prowled the city, spying on saloons, whorehouses, and gambling joints, and peppering unshocked lawmen with reports of what he saw. The Good Government League, for which Soltau claimed a membership of three thousand, had risen from the shards of his earlier vehicle, the Anti-Saloon League. Soltau once scolded Humphrey for taking an occasional drink; you must, he urged, "be honest with yourself and God, and not be trapped by the great deceiver."

Humphrey found a more solid and reasonable—but no less persistent—ally against the underworld in Bradshaw Mintener. While Soltau sniffed around the lower reaches of Minneapolis, Mintener was securely lodged in the city's corporate and social elite: an alumnus of Yale, Oxford, and the University of Minnesota Law School, a deep-dyed Methodist and Republican, a trustee of Macalester College, general counsel and vice-president of Pillsbury Mills—and deeply perturbed by his city's roistering underworld. "I was dedicated," he said later, "to obtaining law enforcement for Minneapolis." For years he had been trying to install an honest mayor. Repeatedly disappointed, he kept hoping anyway.

As a power in city affairs, Mintener had helped elect Marvin Kline, the incumbent mayor in 1943, and had watched over his administration. One city policeman later remembered "this white-haired guy [Mintener] hanging around the Court House, in and out of Kline's office all the time. . . . He spent more time in the Court House than he did in the Pillsbury Building." Eventually Kline fell back into the sleazy ways of previous mayors. "I'm disgusted with this Kline," Mintener decided. "He promised to clean up this town and this town is still wide open."

So one day early in 1943, Mintener received young Humphrey

at his office in the Pillsbury Building. Gangsters were out to take over Minneapolis, said Humphrey, and he aimed to stop them. Mintener, ever hopeful, promised to help. "What a tragedy it is," said Humphrey in one of his first campaign speeches, "that in our city campaign every two years the chief issue seems to be whether the city has more gangsters, more gambling joints, more vice dens, more sneak drinking places than it had two years before." The challenger and the incumbent accused each other of being allied with racketeers. Kline won the election of 1943, but it was close.

Two years later Humphrey tried again. The underworld expected to control the police department by simple political leverage: it would select an agreeable candidate for mayor, push him to victory, and thereby gain the power to name a cooperative police chief. Humphrey had to break that arrangement. "I am no blue-nose," he explained to the publisher of the *Minneapolis Tribune*, "and I am no crusading reformer that seems to see vice and corruption in every nook and cranny of our city. I for one happen to believe that too much emphasis has been placed upon the filth and rackets of Minneapolis. . . . However, I do not propose to be placed in the position of having some outside influence, some invisible government, select the Chief of Police. . . . I intend to do something about the police department."

The challenger's prospects brightened in January 1945 with yet another unsolved murder of a newspaperman. Like Howard Guilford and Walter Liggett, Arthur Kasherman had published a superheated weekly tabloid and had a complicated personal history. Convicted of extortion in 1937, Kasherman had served thirty months of a five-year prison term. Just before his death he had threatened to expose Mayor Kline's offenses in office; popular suspicions therefore implicated Kline in the murder. "He was a shakedown artist," Kline said later, "and I was blamed for it. And I didn't even know the joker." But Kasherman's murder, along with a recent grand-jury report that had blamed Kline for the "open flaunting of gambling and liquor laws," pushed Humphrey to an easy victory. He took office on July 2, announcing he would enforce all the laws. Within thirty minutes, some operators started removing their gambling devices.

To be the new police chief Humphrey picked Ed Ryan, his near neighbor in southeast Minneapolis, a police detective and twenty-year veteran of the force. An honest cop—a bit of a maverick—and a graduate of the FBI's special training course for local police, Ryan had grown cynical watching a parade of Minneapolis politicians over the years, all promising reforms and delivering nothing. When Humphrey first ran in 1943, Ryan later recalled, he thought, "Well, here's another one of these clowns with the same yack that I had been listening to for 18, 19 years." Eventually Ryan, Humphrey's senior by fifteen years, began to believe the boy politician. Humphrey made him chief and told him to close the city to major underworld rackets. And "God damn it," the mayor added, "I want it kept closed." ("He could swear beautifully," Ryan noted. "One of the reasons I liked him.")

To monitor the cleanup Humphrey appointed an ex-officio law enforcement committee. For political reasons it included three union men, but its most active members were Humphrey, Ryan, and its chairman, Bradshaw Mintener. Under Mintener's steely direction, the committee construed laws quite strictly. At one meeting, three men from the Retail Beer Dealers Association asked about the "14" game, a slight game of chance played in bars around town. One of the union men on the committee saw no danger to it. They should concern themselves with major organized rackets, he said, not with independent penny-ante stuff. No, Mintener insisted; all the laws must be obeyed, and "14" was illegal.

For a time, Minneapolis contracted a racketbusting fever. The city council even outlawed bingo games. The newspapers were generally enthusiastic about the cleanup ("This is quite a surprise," Humphrey remarked). Chief Ryan promised to close down any joints open after hours. "When you see a lot of cars, drunks, and hear jive music at 4 a.m.," he observed, "you know it isn't a revival meeting." During his first year in office Humphrey liked to visit police stations around midnight, to listen in on phone calls, talk to cops, ride around in their squad cars, watching and noting. "I understand that the jail is full and that the vast majority of police officers are really out doing a job," he wrote Ryan in the fall of 1945. "Crack down on a few of these fellows who apparently are unwilling to play the game squarely," he urged. "A few more complaint orders must be issued and action must be taken."

The Reverend Soltau, ever alert, watched a whorehouse on Thirteenth Avenue South for four hours one night and counted twelve customers. He reported it to the police; "We hope this shameful spot has been dealt with according to law," he warned Ryan. The place was raided two weeks later. In the first eight months of the new regime, convictions for gambling and prostitution more than doubled over the same period a year earlier. "For the first time in my memory, organized crime no longer exists in our fair city," Mintener declared in the spring of 1946. "Business can now be done without being shaken down—almost."

Almost. The racketbusting fever burned at full intensity for about a year, but a fever by definition could not be sustained. Ed Ryan quit as police chief after ten months to run for sheriff of the surrounding Hennepin County. His successor as chief, Glenn MacLean, was—like Ryan—an honest and experienced Minneapolis police officer. But he was more of a "regular" than Ryan, and less zealous and effective as chief.

Two police episodes in January 1947 suggested a change in tone. Jack Lally, a veteran cop, was granted a license to open a liquor store in a building owned by an associate of Tommy Banks. According to rumors, Banks himself might even have bankrolled Lally's store; thus the peculiar situation of a liquor store fronted by a policeman for a gangster king. Chief MacLean nonetheless defended his brother officer in the matter. At about the same time, Kid Cann got into a fistfight at the Nicollet Hotel; afterward the police treated him deferentially and arrested only his pugilistic opponent. "It was just a Saturday night brawl," Humphrey declared during the uproar that followed. "Because one of the participants is reported to have been a man of considerable reputation in the underworld is no reason for persecuting him." Humphrey absolved MacLean and the department, assured the chief of his unbroken loyalty and trust, and added only that the mayor should be spared any blame in such cases in the future.

In general, Humphrey's crackdowns had landed just smaller fish. Tommy Banks and Kid Cann went their usual ways, defying the law by holding multiple liquor licenses under false names. Later on Humphrey claimed that Banks and Cann had never much concerned him, that he mainly had wanted to end police corruption. "I never tried to have—or wage any particular war with them," he said of Banks and Cann, "except that I insisted they abide by the law and that they quit tampering with the police department." After his first year, Humphrey stopped his midnight forays into police work and paid less attention to the law enforcement committee. He thought about adding new people to the committee to strengthen it, but "I am going to leave this in your hands," he told one of his assistants.

As to the minor rackets around town, in the long run they were hardly affected by Mayor Humphrey. "How do you get rid of prostitution?" Ed Ryan was asked later. "You don't," he replied. Bingo, merely driven underground by the city council's ban, was formally relegalized in the fall of 1947. Pinball and slot machines were played more openly. The Reverend Soltau's persistent alarms were no longer heeded at city hall. After he bought illegal football jackpot tickets and indignantly displayed them to the press, Humphrey scolded him for "meddling with petty things." The police department, Chief MacLean added, "needs no help from professional reformers."

By then Humphrey's attention had turned to other city issues, to state politics, and to the campaign that would send him on to the United States Senate in 1948. These larger ambitions demanded accommodations that dimmed the brightly burning moral reformer's flame of his first year as mayor. He had won in 1945 over the rough opposition of a corrupt Teamster local, 544, and its crooked leader, Sid Brennan. "I never got along with Sidney Brennan," Humphrey later claimed; "he threatened me many times." But in fact the two men had struck certain mutually helpful bargains. Humphrey thanked Brennan "for all that you are doing for me" in the summer of 1947. "I know that we can work together," he went on, "and I know that this relationship will be of great benefit to all of us. It is a real relief to me to know that at last we are beginning to understand each other and to recognize the importance of cooperation. By the way, thanks for the tent. The kids are surely enjoying it."

Humphrey's tightening friendship with Fred Gates epitomized this veering away from reformist purity. Gates, the son of Lebanese immigrants, ran a penny arcade on Hennepin Avenue in downtown Minneapolis. On the side he was involved in various rackets ("all of them," according to Bradshaw Mintener). From 1945 on Gates hitched himself to Humphrey's ascending star with an adoring, uncritical loyalty. At first Humphrey used him mainly as a source of intelligence on the underworld. "He knew everything that was going on in Minneapolis," Humphrey recalled. "He had to live by his wits and that meant that he had to know what was going on." Gates got his information from an underworld character named Billy Cohen. Humphrey kept the source confidential, trusting it more than any reports from the police department.

With time Gates—the former small-time racketeer—became Humphrey's closest political associate, his expediter and campaign finance manager. For years they talked on the phone at least once a day. To raise campaign money they worked the telephones together, sitting side by side, with Gates dialing and arranging and Humphrey making the pitches. Occasionally Humphrey was urged to get rid of him, but he would not. When Humphrey was sworn in as Vice President of the United States in 1965, Fred Gates held the Bible. It was an odd, revealing tableau for a man who had started out as a gangbuster.

❧ ❧

Virgil W. Peterson was operating director of the Chicago Crime Commission for twenty-eight years, from 1942 to 1970. For most of that period he was considered the preeminent expert on organized crime in America. From Chicago he tracked the varied and ever-expanding operations of the Capone gang; its interests extended as far as Florida, Texas, Nevada, and California. At a time when the FBI barely acknowledged a national underworld, and when local police forces did not readily share raw intelligence, Peterson alone had the perspective, contacts, and information to recognize fully the interstate aspects of the problem. Tireless and tenacious, a meticulous keeper of files and cross-references, Peterson gave out material to lawmen and journalists, as well as through his own books, articles, speeches, and testimony before congressional committees. Nobody did more to create an informed public understanding of organized crime.

After the fashion of most other WASP gangbusters, Peterson was shaped by a background quite different from those of his gangster quarries. He came from the farming town of Olds, Iowa, population 250, in the southeastern part of the state. All four grandparents were Swedish immigrants; his parents had grown up on farms. The family attended the Lutheran church in Swedesburg, two miles away. Peterson's father ran a dry goods store in Olds. Virgil, an only child, worked there after school. "I had a lot of self-discipline," he later recalled. When not waiting on customers he kept busy, washing windows or stocking shelves. At play he showed other hints of his adult personality. He was the catcher on the school baseball team, the quarterback on the football team. He liked to take charge and control his own situation.

After undergraduate study at nearby Parsons College, he went on to Northwestern's law school in Chicago. During his final year there he saw a letter from J. Edgar Hoover on a bulletin board, inviting lawyers to apply for work with the FBI. Joining the bureau as an agent with his law degree, in a dozen years he served at nine different field offices around the country. In Chicago Peterson was chief assistant to the celebrated G-man Melvin Purvis, writing his reports for him and managing the office. Peterson helped catch John Dillinger, Baby Face Nelson, and other famous hoodlums of the 1930s. He was ascending the FBI's stringent career ladder, but not contentedly. "When I was there," he said later of his FBI days, "well, then, everything was just autocratic." The old catcher and quarterback wanted to run his own show.

In 1942 the Chicago Crime Commission, having lost both Frank Loesch and its longtime operating director, and in need of revitalization, invited Peterson to take over. He quit the FBI and settled into the commission, now his own boss. His budget, privately funded by concerned citizens, gave him an office in the Loop and a staff of about a dozen people. He hired former FBI agents to work as investigators, sometimes undercover. "From the very beginning . . . my primary concentration of effort was on organized crime," he recalled. "I frequently publicized misconduct or ineffectiveness of local officials, including the police and other agencies of the administration of justice. . . . Our task was to observe and report to the public on the effectiveness or integrity of the duly constituted officials."

Peterson could not trust the brazenly corrupt Chicago police, with the notable exception of a detective named Joe Morris—"the most honorable individual in the department," according to Peterson. He also had one vital contact within the Capone gang: a snitch who would telephone Peterson's office, identify himself as "a friend," and speak only to the director. Peterson never met him in person, never learned his name. For years the man, evidently a disaffected member of the Capones, provided accurate, invaluable tips on the gang's meetings and internal affairs. "The most remarkable informant anyone could possibly have," as Peterson remembered him. Eventually he stopped calling; Peterson assumed the snitch had been discovered and killed.

This particular situation, with its edge of mystery and danger, was not typical of how Peterson operated. He could hardly have less resembled his old bosses at the FBI, the flamboyant and publicity-chasing Purvis and Hoover. Living peacefully in the suburb of Riverside with his wife and two sons, he was a voting member of the local Lutheran church. "Those who belong to churches help raise the mores and morals of the community," he said. "When religion makes an impact on individuals, it also makes an impact on the institutions of the community." Contained and well ordered, mild in voice and appearance, passionate only about his favorite Chicago baseball and football teams, Peterson did his work quietly, just another job. He received no major threats on his life and lost no sleep to nightmares about being chased by gangsters. He knew the underworld code and hewed to it. "I always assumed," he said later, "that they would never attack you, as long as you were not trying to play both ends toward the middle."

Peterson started his work at the commission just as American gangsters, pumped up by their easy wartime bonanzas, zoomed into a national postwar expansion. Trailing after them, taking notes and filling his files, Peterson was pulled into prominence by the very success of his adversaries. During the first peacetime years, gangs based in the North and East opened fancy gambling casinos in Louisiana, Florida, and Nevada. Frank Costello and his man Dandy Phil Kastel, both of New York, launched their Beverly Club in Jefferson Parish outside New Orleans. (Costello stayed at the Roosevelt Hotel in New Orleans for over three months in 1945.) "I have had no complaint about it from the neighborhood around there," the sheriff of Jefferson Parish explained later. The comedian Joey Bishop played the Beverly Club one Christmas season. Invited to a Christmas party at Kastel's home, he went and found dozens of Mafiosi on hand for the occasion. "What should I have done?" he wondered.

In Miami Beach, Costello and another group of partners—including Meyer Lansky, Bugsy Siegel, and Joe Adonis—opened an even plusher gambling joint, the Colonial Inn. Worried that Walter Winchell would blare the Colonial's gangster ties, the partners made a preemptive strike by donating $5,000 to the columnist's favorite Damon Runyon Cancer Fund, ensuring his mute cooperation. Joe Kennedy and Ed Sullivan, the Broadway columnist turned TV host, were among the nonpaying guests of the management soon after the club opened. Sullivan lost $36,000, mainly at roulette, but the debt was forgiven because the house knew it might come back in other forms.

The Capones, the only peer of the New York gangs in the national underworld, took over other gambling operations in the Miami Beach area: horse tracks, dog tracks, and several hundred bookie joints. Agents of the Capones moved in and bought homes, bars, hotels, restaurants, oceanfront property, a radio station, and other businesses. A local group of businessmen, displaced and concerned, hired Daniel P. Sullivan (another former FBI agent) to investigate. "We wrote the Chicago Crime Commission," Sullivan later recounted, "—they have a lot of records—and they sent us a lot of names on a lot of people. And through informers we found more, and by checking occupational records and tax records, liquor permits, and then checking the corporate records in the State Capitol and finding their officers and directors and which property was held, we found more. And we came up with an astounding story." The Capones could not be removed, but the investigation did lead to the founding of the Miami Crime Commission, on the model of Chicago's, with Sullivan its director.

All these enterprises, however audacious, were ultimately dwarfed by the underworld's invention of Las Vegas. Gambling had been legalized in Nevada as a Depression-fighting measure in 1931. Tony Cornero and his brothers opened an elaborate nightclub outside Las Vegas in 1932, but it went broke. The town only started to hum after the war. Earl Warren's scuttling of the gambling ships off southern California had left local high rollers without a game. At the same time, the extension of regularly scheduled airline flights after 1945 made Las Vegas accessible to gamblers from back East as well. Airplanes brought the suckers; the national underworld brought the bankrolls, muscle, and expertise.

Jewish gangsters, sometimes with Italian partners, got there earliest. The first big-time Las Vegas casinos were the Flamingo (Bugsy Siegel, Meyer Lansky, and others), the Desert Inn (Moe Dalitz and the Cleveland syndicate), the Thunderbird (Lansky again), and the Sands (Longy Zwillman, Doc Stacher, and others from New Jersey), all by 1952. Then a wave of Italian casinos: the Riviera (the Capones), the Stardust (Tony Cornero, then the Capones), the Dunes (Raymond Patriarca and the New England Mafia), and the Tropicana (Costello and Dandy Phil Kastel). Tony Cornero died a gambler's death at a Desert Inn dice table just before his own Stardust was about to open in 1955. He had lost about $10,000 and was still there the next morning, trying to win it back. After a loud argument over paying a $25 tab, he suffered a heart attack, collapsed onto the table and expired, utterly in his element.

Given the testy presence of all these competing mobs from around the country, Las Vegas was declared an open town, controlled by nobody. At first the casinos were notoriously crooked. "The people who ran the casinos cheated *everybody*, including each other," recalled Jimmy the Greek Snyder, who worked there at the time. This led to bloodshed and inefficiencies. So the major owners picked Meyer Lansky to act as referee and banker. "They had to have somebody that everybody had implicit trust in," one informed gangster said later. "That guy became Meyer. Absolute unequivocal law when it came to cutting up the pot okay. . . . The top guy would say: Meyer's word is law. We will hear from Meyer. He will give us an explanation and that's it. . . . He had control over hundreds of millions of dollars. But he never fucked anyone."

Regardless of Lansky's crucial role, the Italians kept their traditional power of life and death. Even Lansky, the strongest Jew in the underworld, still took his orders and authority from the Mafia. Around 1950, Jimmy the Weasel Fratianno felt obliged to beat up Doc Stacher, who did not resist. "He knows I'm a made guy," Fratianno noted. "He'd get clipped in a minute and he knows it. The Jews don't fuck with the Italians. They learned that lesson a long time ago."

In the aftermath of World War II, then, the national underworld became even more nationalized, obliterating lines between states and regions, making issues of turf and territory more bristlingly complex. Virgil Peterson in Chicago saw these developments with special clarity because the Capones, the local boys, were especially restless and inventive. Tony Accardo had taken over the gang leadership after Frank Nitti's suicide in 1943. Far more intelligent and sophisticated than Nitti or Al Capone himself, Accardo was perhaps "the most capable leader in the history of the Chicago group," as one FBI agent later described him. He pushed the gang beyond its parochial local scams.

The Capones imposed a kind of diplomatic sphere of influence down through the Midwest. In Des Moines, Iowa, Luigi Fratto (a.k.a. Lew Farrell) watched over the Capones' local brewery and other interests in the state. Clark Mollenhoff, a young police reporter in Des Moines during the war, was astonished by how Farrell—despite his underworld ties—was warmly embraced by cops, judges, and respectable people because of his conspicuous charities. In downstate Illinois, in East St. Louis, the Capones offered a partnership to the local Shelton brothers, veteran bootleggers. The Sheltons were not agreeable. Three Shelton brothers were murdered, and the Capones came in anyway. The Capone influence reached behind prison walls as well. At the federal penitentiary in Leavenworth, Kansas, "the clique from Chicago always had the best of everything," one convict recalled. "I mean in outside connections, inside connections, whatever the best in the institution was, they had it."

Most remarkably of all, in 1946 the Capones went all the way down to Dallas, Texas, intending to take over the rackets there. That fall a new sheriff, Steve Guthrie, was elected in Dallas, promising a cleanup after a scandal. The Capones saw an opening. A delegation of them—notably Pat Manno, Jack Nappi, and Paul Jones—went to Dallas and worked on Guthrie. They promised him an income of $150,000 a year if he cooperated. They would bring in slot machines and their own dice experts to run a huge floating crap game. They would not deal in narcotics, they said, because that would bring down the FBI, "and that's one guy you don't want to fool around with." They had connections all over the country, they bragged, even into Harry Truman's White House through the postmaster general, Robert Hannegan.

Guthrie played along, pretending to be interested. He invited the Capones to a meeting at his home in Dallas on November 7, 1946. While they all conspired together, a microphone fed the proceedings to a recorder elsewhere in the home. "We have told

Steve that he's going to have a clean administration," Jones explained to the group, "and that we're going to guide him and not embarrass him in any way, shape, or form. The program is just this, horse booking, slot machines, dice, numbers, everything. We're going to keep it clean. We're going to take over quietly. . . . We'll pick a local man who will be the front man for that. So far as everybody knows, he's the man who's putting these machines in, the local man. We put the money up and train him and advise him and show him how to set up."

Manno promised that with the Capones on hand, no small free-lancers would ply their trades. "They should be run out of town anyway," he said. "If they are undesirable characters, they have no business in the city. . . . You should go right on through and prosecute, because they are a menace to society. When you get in office, you should go out and bring them in. After all, you got a law here. You don't have to take things like that from those petty hoodlums. For what? They only embarrass you again while you're in office . . . going out in the street and shooting up Main Street, whatever your main street is here." The Capones, on the other hand, offered law and order.

A month after this meeting, the conspiring Capones were arrested for attempted bribery. Some were jailed, others run out of town. But a Chicago presence did linger in the city. One Chicago hoodlum who moved to Dallas in the late 1940s, and stayed there, was Jacob Rubenstein, a small-time thug who called himself Jack Ruby. The Capones might have been snared by Sheriff Guthrie, but they still kept their man Ruby on the scene.

The episode was symptomatic. Even when the Capones were apparently beaten, still they crawled out of some distant corner, ever relentless. They gave Virgil Peterson plenty of work to do.

Warren Olney III, counsel and leader of the California Commission on Organized Crime in the late 1940s, came from a family deeply rooted in Congregational theology and independent Republican politics. One observer perceived "an almost puritanical, hair-shirt sort of dedication to duty" in Olney; and in fact the first of the family line in America, Thomas Olney, had been among the contrary-minded founders of Rhode Island in the seventeenth century. His descendants took their civic obligations seriously.

The first Warren Olney moved out to California in the mid-1800s and was serving as mayor of San Francisco when his grandson, Warren III, was born in 1904. The boy grew up in a home shaped by politics, the law, and a Protestant conscience. His father and father's father were both lawyers; his mother's father was a Congregational minister across the bay in Oakland. In college Warren III, fascinated all his life by history and archaeology, thought about becoming a history professor. Finally he yielded to the tradition of his namesakes and went to law school at Boalt Hall in San Francisco.

Determined "to housebreak myself of a congenital shyness," as he later put it, he joined a local district attorney's office to force himself to think and speak on his feet in a courtroom. (Do the hardest thing, his upbringing had taught him.) There he came to the attention of Earl Warren, then the DA of Alameda County. Warren brought him over to his own staff: the start of a vital connection that lasted the rest of their lives. Olney became Warren's closest friend and associate outside his own family, the recipient over the years of five different law-enforcement appointments through his political mentor. The son of Scandinavian immigrants and the scion of an old WASP line were virtual alter egos, down to their shared names. Thirteen years Olney's senior, Warren evidently saw some of his own muted intensity in his protégé. "He is as much of a crusader, in his quiet way, as anyone I ever knew," Warren said of Olney. "He must have some real cause to serve."

As the head of Warren's criminal division when he was attorney general of California in the late 1930s, Olney was assigned to investigate horse betting and Moe Annenberg's wire service in the state. "We found it very difficult to get an understanding of what the bookmaking racket was," Olney recalled, "what it was that made it go, why there was so much money in it and where the money went and who the people were behind it. Not even the bookmakers seemed to have any clear idea." So he spent three days at a legal bookie joint in Reno, the Bank Club, watching the play and no doubt trying to appear inconspicuous. He could not have folded easily into the environment at the Bank Club. "He was exactly the opposite of a flamboyant personality. He was almost self-effacing," according to his law partner, Scott Elder. "He certainly had little to say unless he had something important to say." "When he made up his mind to do something, he did it but he didn't do it loudly," agreed his wife, Elizabeth. "Sometimes almost without your realizing it he'd accomplish something." For recreation Olney normally went outdoors, not inside to a gambling joint; he loved fishing, swimming, horseback riding, and mountaineering trips to the Sierras with his family. (His grandfather Olney had helped organize the Sierra Club in 1892.) In the noisy, rococo atmosphere of the Bank Club, redolent of tobacco smoke and indoor pleasures, he must have felt and looked like a man out of place.

"We kept hearing that wire service was important, but it was difficult for us to see why," he said later. "We couldn't see why a man couldn't make book by what you could get on the radio or in the newspapers." It came down to a bookmaker's need for immediate results, delivered right after each race. "We saw the need for rapid play to make money," Olney noted. "The big money in it comes from the $2 bets in the horse parlors, and people won't make a $2 bet unless they know how they came out on the previous race, and you have to have fast results and fast information to keep a rapid turnover in a place like that." The sport of kings amounted to pure gambling, built on the return from the last money down, connected but slightly to tout sheets, hot tips, and a handicapper tugging at one's elbow. "Bookmaking has nothing to do with horse races," Olney concluded. "It's a strict lottery, nothing more than that."

Cut the bookie wire, then, and bookmaking would be crippled. Olney filed an injunction against some one hundred bookie defendants, many of whom kept operating anyway while the cases inched forward. Brought in for contempt, the culprits applied to the state supreme court for writs of habeas corpus. In granting the writs the court knocked out the legal basis of the attorney general's case, ruining the entire prosecution. But "we felt that we had at least learned as a practical matter that the wire service was the key to the bookmaking racket," Olney said later. That insight stayed with him.

When the war came, Olney—thirty-eight years old, married, with children—enlisted in the Marines and served in the South Pacific. (Do the hardest thing.) While he was away, Earl Warren moved up to the governor's office. Artie Samish, boss of the legislature, thus could make his man Fred Howser the new attorney general. "I got him elected," Samish admitted later, ever ingenuous. "I didn't know he had all the funny money behind him." Howser's résumé was not promising: as a criminal attorney he had defended gamblers and other gangsters; as district attorney of Los Angeles he had impeded Attorney General Warren's prosecution of the gambling ships anchored offshore; in running for attorney general he did not conceal his ties to the notorious Samish and his liquor clients.

Howser was a crook. As attorney general he conducted his office predictably. Gambling in the state expanded and slot machines proliferated amid rumors of new payoffs to lawmen. "The word was out through the underworld that the state was to be opened up to gambling and other illegal activities," Warren recalled. "I told Howser several times that I understood what was going on. He protested that he knew nothing about it, and would take whatever action was called for. But he never did." Governor Warren therefore went around him, to the legislature, and got authorization to appoint five special crime-study commissions. By then Olney was back home, just starting up a two-man legal practice in San Francisco. "I induced him to become chief counsel and executive officer of the Commission on Organized Crime on a part-time basis," Warren noted later. "True to his nature, however, it was not long until he was working around the clock."

Olney and Howser were already acquainted. They had brushed against each other during the gambling ship episode, and both men now expected a showdown. At the outset of the crime commission, Howser on some pretext held up $7,500 that the legislature had designated for Olney's work. Olney went ahead anyway, neglecting his own law clients. For a few months the family had to live on stocks owned by Elizabeth Olney; she also took a part-time job in a doctor's office. Eventually the $7,500 came through. (Later on, Olney suspected a tap had been placed on his home telephone in Berkeley. At the time Olney's two teenaged daughters were monopolizing the family telephone. "He said anybody who bugged his phone deserved it," one of the daughters recalled.)

As a gangbusting mechanism the crime commission was severely limited. Though fronted by a board of five prominent Californians, all its work was done by Olney and a small staff that at its fullest included only an assistant counsel, Arthur Sherry, and four investigators. They had no legal power to make arrests, to search and seize, or to issue subpoenas. "The problem was that we were not official," Sherry noted. "We were not policemen. We were just private citizens. We obtained nothing by way of evidence except by persuasion or people volunteering information to us." Under Olney's direction, though, the commission—with Governor Warren's approval and to Attorney General Howser's dismay—went beyond its modest mandate. "It became an investigative agency," Olney said later.

For his first major target, Olney picked on his old nemesis, the bookie wire. After Moe Annenberg's conviction and jail term for huge tax evasions, the wire service had passed on to two competing underworld groups. Bugsy Siegel, murdered in Beverly Hills in June 1947, was the most notorious casualty of this struggle. "Naturally I missed Benny [Siegel]," Mickey Cohen later reflected, not quite in sorrow. "We were real close and he taught me many things. But to be honest with you, his getting knocked in was not a bad break for me. Pretty soon I was running everything out here." Eventually the Capones—whom Cohen vaguely represented in California—won control of the wire, renamed the Continental Press.

To Olney it meant another intrusion into his state by the national underworld. "From evidence furnished our commission by the Chicago Crime Commission, and other sources," he wrote in one of his public reports, "it is plain that the 'wire service' and the national bookmaking racket is now in the hands of the notorious Capone Syndicate of Chicago and other middle western cities. . . . It is a fact, which should never be overlooked or forgotten, that no matter what organization or persons may front for the racing news service, in dealing with the 'wire service' in California today we are in reality dealing with the Capone Syndicate and its agents."

When Howser would not help Olney go after the Continental Press outlets in California, Olney persuaded the state public-utilities commission to hold hearings on the matter. A month after the hearings, on April 6, 1948, the utilities commission ordered all telephone and telegraph companies in the state to refuse service to bookmakers. With that order, Olney reported, the wire service was gone: "The organization of bookmakers in this State has become far more difficult than formerly. The monopolistic aspect of the bookmaking racket has almost disappeared in this State."

In the meantime Olney kept hearing peculiar reports about Howser and his staff at the attorney general's office. During a gang war in Los Angeles, Howser even assigned a bodyguard to protect Mickey Cohen. The guard was seriously wounded when somebody shot at Cohen outside a restaurant. In another episode, the Los Angeles police raided an office of the Mafioso Jack Dragna and found several checks from Dragna's wire service outlet made out to George Rochester, a special assistant to Howser. Olney gave photostats of the checks to the press, which drew the obvious conclusions that Olney had prudently not made explicit.

These incidents were mere shenanigans when measured against a larger scheme hatched by the attorney general. Howser's investigators moved around the state, county by county, explaining to concerned parties that they were going to organize all the gambling in the vicinity. In return for up to half the total proceeds, Howser's men would guarantee protection to the local purveyors of bookmaking, slot machines, punchboards, cards, and dice. "They said they were representing the attorney general of the State of California, Fred Howser," the former police chief of Bakersfield later testified. "They named him directly. They didn't pull no punches. They talked right out in the open. They also told me this, the people in on the deal would be ex–deputy sheriffs, retired police officers and so forth." It was an amazing, audacious plan—conceived by the top lawman in the state.

Olney and the crime commission got on the case. Three of Howser's men were convicted in one of these schemes in Mendocino County. Olney gave out reports of similar Howser designs on fourteen other counties in the state. Caught and embarrassed, Howser dismissed the crime commission as "a tumorous growth on the body politic, conceived in Warren's political ambitions." It was merely the bleating of a stuck pig. A federal narcotics investigation in Los Angeles came close to indicting Howser for obstruction of justice in a dope case; the attorney general's venality cut across all jurisdictions. Voters started recall efforts in Los Angeles and San Francisco. Admitting nothing, Howser ran for reelection in 1950 but was denied the nomination of his own party.

Aside from snipping the wire service and retiring Howser to private life, Olney published detailed reports on slot machines and the Los Angeles gang wars. The legislature passed a tighter ban on slots, including their component parts. More generally, the commission fed tips to local lawmen and prosecutors—and to the media. "The thing that made us most effective," Arthur Sherry said later, "was the fact that we kept the spotlight on the mobsters all the time. They can't operate with that kind of thing happening."

One more shoe had to drop. Artie Samish, the power behind the departed Howser, remained king of the lobbyists in Sacramento. In one of his crime commission reports, Olney had devoted three pages to Samish's ties to Mickey Cohen and other gangsters. But for the most part, perhaps in deference to his power and cleverness, the commission had avoided Samish. "Our policy was never to be seen with him or talking to him," Sherry recalled. "We stayed strictly away from Samish. . . . He could see that people like Howser were fools and these other things were dangerous. There was no point in it. He was getting along well with his breweries, trucks, bus lines, and other interests—why bother?"

Olney did not let go. In 1953 he went to Washington to take charge of the criminal division in the new administration's Justice Department. When he arrived he found a tax case already underway against Samish. Olney sped it along. Convicted on eight counts in November 1953, Samish was ordered to pay $70,000 in taxes and $40,000 in fines, and to serve three years in jail. The secret boss of California had finally been caught. "Has Artie Samish a chance to beat his case?" his old friend and fellow horseplayer Herbert Bayard Swope asked John Francis Neylan, a Samish attorney in San Francisco. "I hope so, because I hate to see a man go to jail."

Nothing doing; Samish paid up and did twenty-six months in prison. "He started away back from scratch," his attorney Neylan concluded, "overcame a thousand difficulties, and collected a crew who did not dare tell him he was not a genius. He got weary of hearing me tell him to get out of the lobbying racket. . . . He thought he knew human beings, and yet was bewildered when he saw his quondam friends scurry to cover when he got in trouble."

❧ ❧

Senator Estes Kefauver of Tennessee opened his hearings on organized crime in Miami in May 1950 and concluded them in New York, ten months and thirteen cities later. The fullest, most public investigation of the underworld up to that time, the hearings were breakthroughs on three unrelated levels. Well covered by all media, the proceedings made millions of Americans aware of the national underworld—and especially of the Mafia—for the first time. The televised New York hearings, starring Frank Costello as a witness both writhing and willing, gave an early demonstration of TV's latent, overwhelming impact. ("It is the best thing we have had since television came in," said a viewer in Brooklyn.) And for Kefauver himself, a senator only since 1949, the hearings manufactured an instantly credible presidential candidacy. Voters always liked a gangbuster.

Only a dozen years earlier, the junior senator from Tennessee had been a Chattanooga lawyer who had never run for office. He came from Madisonville, a small country town in Monroe County, near the North Carolina border. His father was a dairy farmer and hardware merchant. The Kefauvers were conventionally religious for the time and place—just good, churchgoing Baptists. Every Sunday young Estes endured his preacher grandfather's two-hour sermons at First Baptist in Madisonville. Following college in Knoxville and law school at Yale, he came back home and started a practice in Chattanooga. Tall and courtly in a Dixie way, apparently unambitious, with a gravely impassive bearing later called Lincolnesque, he seemed to be settled down for the rest of his life.

A local reform movement drew him into active politics. Sent to Congress by a special election in 1939, he joined the small group of southern progressives in Washington: supporting the New Deal and TVA, introducing bills to outlaw lynching and the poll tax. After five terms in the House he ran for the Senate, taking on the state political machine run by Boss Ed Crump of Memphis. Crump called him a pet coon; Kefauver therefore campaigned in a coonskin hat, his trademark ever after, and won again as a reformer. The label stayed with him in the Senate. He took independent stands and filed legislation that usually did not pass. Too much of a maverick to be admitted to the Senate's inner club, impatient with its hoary rules and customs, Kefauver remained his own man with his own agenda.

Reports published by the crime commissions of Chicago and California persuaded Kefauver that organized crime's interstate aspects brought it within the purview of Congress. He introduced bills in the fall of 1949 to ban the interstate shipment of slot machines and gambling news. "We are not naive enough to believe that any group or anybody can stop gambling," he explained later. "What we hope to help do is to throw blocks in the way of the interstate ramifications and the operation of it across state lines so that it might be reduced to a local problem." In January 1950 he started badgering the Senate leadership to authorize a full investigation by a special committee. After complex maneuvers the committee was picked: two Republicans and three Democrats, including Kefauver as chairman.

Of his four colleagues on the committee, Senator Charles W. Tobey, a Republican from New Hampshire, turned out to be the most persistent and controversial scourge of witnesses. A Bible-quoting Yankee, seventy years old in 1950, Tobey had grown up in a strict Baptist household that Kefauver would have recognized. As a child Tobey was not allowed to play cards, attend the theater, or read a Sunday paper. As an adult he remained a lifelong teetotaler and prohibitionist, with a weakness only for strawberry ice cream. "There is no place in our world today for the expression of uncontrolled emotions," he believed. "For many years an unbelievable number in America have been trying to live without God." Instead, he was sure, Americans should turn back to "the solid rocks of the nation's foundation, thrift, self-reliance, courage, energy, high aspiration, and all the ideals of the Pilgrim fathers of long ago," to those "ideals of Christian living, so essential to the tradition of our forefathers."

Kefauver, understated by nature and mindful of his political future, spoke carefully when facing witnesses. Tobey had no such restraints. On the Kefauver committee he represented a Protestant conscience to its purest, most unrelenting degree. Lecturing witnesses that displeased him in formal, stentorian tones, Tobey invoked nothing less than divine wrath and eternal damnation. Thus at an executive session in Kansas City, with no reporters present, Tobey in colloquy with a local Democratic politician, Henry McKissick:

"Do you feel a hatred toward all this chicanery, toward the numbers racket, toward prostitution, toward anything that is evil and anti-Christ?"

"No, I don't."

"Why do you not?"

"Because I don't."

"Why do you not feel that way? What is your church? Are you a Catholic or Protestant?"

"I don't go to church."

"Why do you not? You know what decency is and righteousness is, do you not?"

"Yes, I do."

"Then knowing that in your heart, do you not feel hatred of anything that spoils this country? It is a fair country and decent men let it be so. You are only going to live 60 like the rest of us. Some day you and I are going to meet our God."

McKissick was not worried. "I never took any dirty money," he said.

As the committee moved from city to city, most of its investigative leads came from private, unofficial sources. Newspaper reporters on local crime beats gave invaluable tips. "Some of our good gentlemen of the press," Kefauver noted in San Francisco, "know more about this nationwide crime picture than anyone else that I know of." Because congressional testimony was legally privileged, the committee and its witnesses could freely name names without being sued for libel. Local experts could take satisfaction in putting sensitive facts on the record that could not safely be published in any other forum.

The committee also substantially relied on the directors of three local crime commissions: Virgil Peterson in Chicago, Warren Olney III in California, and Daniel P. Sullivan in Miami. Peterson in particular assumed enormous authority within the investigation. When the committee touched down in Chicago in July 1950, Peterson testified for two days, engulfing the hearings with details about the underworld in Chicago and a dozen other cities. The transcript of his presentation filled eighty-nine closely printed pages. He described a national underworld dominated by old bootlegging gangs from New York and Chicago: "For convenience, we might refer to the New York mob as the Frank Costello gang and the Chicago gang as the Capone syndicate. Naturally, this constitutes an oversimplification of the problem, but it really is surprising when there is a full realization of the tremendous influence these two organized groups still wield throughout the nation today." It was an interstate problem, he stressed, demanding federal remedies. "We get letters from all over the country asking for help from duly constituted officials," he said. "The criminal population today is very mobile, moving from one area to the other, with connections all over the country."

The Kefauver committee gained remarkably little help from the main federal law-enforcement agency, the FBI. Ever since the 1920s, J. Edgar Hoover had steadily refused to admit the reality of organized interstate crime. "They're just a bunch of hoodlums," he would say, as though that settled the matter. Some of his critics, looking for an explanation of this gaping blind spot, found patterns in his social contacts that would have seemed suspicious in anyone else. He kept up close ties with people on the edge of the underworld such as Walter Winchell, Joe Kennedy, Sherman Billingsley of the Stork Club, and Lew Rosenstiel of Schenley. Hoover played the horses at the tracks around Washington almost once a week; he would let himself be photographed at the two-dollar windows while FBI agents placed other bets for him at the hundred-dollar windows. Hoover got betting tips from Winchell, who in turn received them from a major New York bookie. So the top G-man placed wagers using underworld information: a potential scandal if it had been reported, and compromising at best.

Still, Hoover had more plausible, less sinister reasons to ignore big-time gangsters. His essential conservatism was both political and temperamental; he characteristically played it safe, too safe. He took the easy, politically marketable path of chasing unprotected minor hoodlums and bank robbers—John Dillinger and Baby Face Nelson—and harmless leftists on the political fringe. To confront the national underworld, by contrast, would have meant expending major resources with no certain outcome. The FBI was always supposed to get its man. Hoover construed his legal authority narrowly, kept his bureau small and controllable, and guarded his entrenched autonomy, ever reluctant to share information and manpower with other agencies.

For whatever causes, the Kefauver committee got nowhere with the FBI. In the fall of 1950, after two promising witnesses for the committee were murdered before they could testify, Kefauver asked Hoover to protect his subpoenaed witnesses. "I regret to advise," Hoover shot back, "the Federal Bureau of Investigation is not empowered to perform guard duties." Appearing before the committee the following spring, Hoover dismissed organized crime as a purely local problem, not within the FBI's jurisdiction: "The federal government can never be a satisfactory substitute for local self-government in the enforcement field." The bureau, he added, did not need more money and agents. "I think it is too big today," he said.

Hoover's ancient rival among federal lawmen, Harry Anslinger of the Bureau of Narcotics, gave Kefauver vastly more help. (That by itself may have discouraged Hoover's participation.) Anslinger's top agent, George White, was even assigned to the committee staff for a while. At an early point, in June 1950, Anslinger came before the committee and was asked whether a national crime organization existed. "I would say that all the members of this combine are very well acquainted with everybody else throughout the country," he replied. "It is interlaced, and intertwined . . . but I wouldn't say that one section of the country controls another section." To prove his point, Anslinger showed the committee his guarded master list of eight hundred top gangsters from around the country. Unlike Hoover, he said he could use more agents. Understaffed and less celebrated than the FBI, the narcotics bureau still knew more about the national underworld. "They are far more conversant with the people we are interested in than any other agency in the United States," an organized crime specialist from the Los Angeles Police Department told the committee. "For example, here in Los Angeles the federal narcotics have only three men, but they have more information for three men than anyone I have ever known of. I can't see how they assemble the information that they do. . . . The FBI so far has not been interested in this type of individual that we are talking about."

Following Anslinger's lead, Kefauver and his staff became intrigued by the idea of a Mafia organization at the core of the national underworld. Since around 1940, the Bureau of Narcotics had accepted the Mafia as a fact, however evanescent and hard to prove. Most other lawmen, at least on the record, would not yet buy the concept. Those who did sometimes confused the Mafia with the Black Hand (not an organization at all) or the Unione Siciliana (overlapping in places, yet still distinct from the Mafia). Virgil Peterson, who knew more about organized crime than anyone else, remained a skeptic. Warren Olney in his four California crime commission reports made only one brief, non-committal reference to "the little-known and secretive Mafia."

Rudolph Halley, Kefauver's chief counsel, at first dismissed the Mafia as "almost fictional." Eventually evidence from narcotics agents and other witnesses made him a believer. Edward J. Allen, the police chief of Youngstown, Ohio, gave the committee reasonable guesses about the Mafia's internal procedures. "They have no elections. There are no members elected or appointed as such," Allen testified. "There are certain district leaders in various parts of the country, but they gain their leadership through the sheer force of their own character, much as an attorney becomes known nationally because of his ability, only theirs also runs to ruthlessness, and the whole fabric of which is based upon murder." As to fighting the Mafia, Allen concluded, "Only a tyrant could eradicate it. Mussolini made great strides in that direction, but no constitutional government can succeed very well."

At the hearings in San Francisco, a local police chief mentioned the Mafia. "What is the Mafia?" Kefauver asked. "Sort of a loose-knit national syndicate," the chief replied, "dealing in narcotics, extortion, control of legitimate enterprise, and operating throughout the Italian element, not encroaching necessarily upon the other types of nationalities; primarily interested in the Italian field and only able to operate within that field; at least, that is true from our investigation." Did anyone ever admit to membership? "No; they claim it doesn't exist, but it does exist." Rudolph Halley listened to various Mafia tales on this occasion and finally said, "It seems to me that this is the point at which we should agree to try to work out a campaign to prove this thing rather than simply get a story. There must be some way to either seize these men, find their records, or find some actual evidence on which we can prove the existence of the Mafia, or get some testimony."

Not easily done, at least from the men who knew the Mafia on the inside. In New York, Halley asked Sal Moretti of the Luciano family, "Do you know what the Mafia is?"

"What?"

"The Mafia, M-a-f-i-a."

"I am sorry, I don't know what you are talking about."

"Have you ever heard of the Mafia?"

"No, I never have."

Later on, Halley asked Joe Profaci why he had been arrested at the national Mafia gathering in Cleveland in 1928. Just there for business, Profaci explained. "You don't expect anybody here to believe," said Halley, exasperated, "that when you had a little business in Brooklyn, you suddenly went to Cleveland in 1928 to try to sell a little olive oil?"

The hearings climaxed in March 1951 with the testimony of Frank Costello, at the time the most famous and best-connected Mafioso in America. For ten months his name had wound through the testimony, the mystery man in the background, seemingly always about to spring forth. Harry Anslinger had been trying to nail him for years—to Anslinger's utter frustration. As boss of the strong Luciano family, Costello started from a substantial base. His power rippled far beyond that because of his universally acknowledged reputation for wise and just counsel. "A complete gentleman and a guy that done business correctly—who never misused anybody and who would only try to make everything even up and square with everybody," as Mickey Cohen remembered him. "There was nobody in the world—I don't give a goddamn about your presidents, your kings, or whatever—nobody compared with Frank Costello. He was a dignified man; class just leaked out of him." From the other side of the line, a New York newspaperman acquainted with the underworld spoke in similar terms: "Believe me when I tell you he was a force for good in this town. If he hadn't been around there would have been a lot more killing and rough stuff. He kept the animals in line. He had so much power and prestige that he could settle a tense situation with a phone call."

On the Mafia's national Commission he was deferred to as the first among equals, but he was not the big boss. The other fathers on the Commission recognized no such ultimate authority. Costello urged the others not to deal drugs, arguing that dope would bring down the feared Bureau of Narcotics. Some bosses—such as Tony Accardo of Chicago—cooperated with Costello on this point while others—Tommy Lucchese of New York and Stefano Magaddino of Buffalo—did not. The local families kept their independence, to Costello's annoyed impatience. "Throughout my long relationship with Frank," his attorney George Wolf said later, "I felt he viewed the Mafia leadership as a burden he had to bear, and would have loved to disavow."

In some ways Costello was already legitimate. He had major investments in nightclubs, liquor companies, real estate, oil wells, and other businesses. But the capital in these ventures was dirty, derived originally from gambling, slot machines, bootlegging, and murder. This blood money also bought Costello's legendary clout in New York City politics. Through his Tammany connections, Costello had lines into ten of the city's sixteen electoral districts— partly because of underworld muscle, but more because of his diplomatic finesse and carefully placed money. "How can you analyze it?" Senator Tobey asked former mayor William O'Dwyer at the New York hearings. "You look him over, you wouldn't mark him except pretty near minus zero. But what is there? What is the attraction?" "It doesn't matter," O'Dwyer replied, "whether it is a banker, a businessman, or a gangster, his pocketbook is always attractive."

A few years earlier, New York newspaper editor Emile Gauvreau had visited Costello at his opulent penthouse apartment on Central Park West. Costello greeted him dressed in lush Japanese silk pajamas. At the art deco bar, backed by a huge mirror of blue glass, two gangsters in blue serge suits handed out refreshments. A couple of city magistrates were on hand, friskily drunk. Costello's wife sat at a gold-plated piano, picking out "The Farmer in the Dell" slowly, with one finger. Each corner of the room had a slot machine. "Try your luck," Costello urged. Gauvreau played a quarter and won four dollars, played another quarter and again won four dollars. When he tried to give the money back, Costello flared: "What the hell do you think I am, a punk? Nobody loses in my house!" Gauvreau and the tipsy magistrates all departed with their winnings and gift bottles of booze.

By a lovely irony, Costello's political connections—not his lifetime of crime per se—finally made him notorious. For six months in 1943, the Manhattan district attorney placed a legal tap on Costello's home telephone. The tap picked up conversations about the approaching local elections. "I am tied up on account of the election although I'd like to be away," Costello told his man Dandy Phil Kastel on July 29. "All these guys bothering me. I don't know one third of them who are running. . . . Who wants to know these bums. They see you talking to one and right away they think you are behind him." A few days later a grateful nominee for the state supreme court, Thomas Aurelio, phoned to pay his respects:

"Good morning, Francesco, how are you, and thanks for everything."

"Congratulations. It went over perfect. When I tell you something is in the bag, you can rest assured."

". . . Right now I want to assure you of my loyalty for all you have done. It's undying."

The DA released this exchange to the press. From that point on, Costello was thrust into an unwanted, embarrassing celebrity. "He is the real big shot of the underworld," a long profile in *Collier's* asserted, "where he is known and referred to as the 'Prime Minister.' He has been boss of half a dozen rackets and dominates gambling throughout the country." In the single month of November 1949, Costello made the covers of *Time* and *Newsweek* and was examined in a five-part series syndicated by the *Washington Post*. "Fast becoming a figure of U.S. legend," according to *Time*. "Millions of newspaper readers considered him a kind of master criminal, shadowy as a ghost and cunning as Satan, who ruled a vast, mysterious, and malevolent underworld and laughed lazily at the law."

The master criminal innocently gave a benefit party for the Salvation Army at his Copacabana nightclub in New York. A reporter for the *New York Journal-American,* Igor Cassini, posed as a waiter at the affair, took note of the eight judges, the congressman, the borough president, and the other politicos on hand, and splashed it onto the front page. "It was a mistake," Costello said afterward. "I knew it was, but what the hell. I got the Salvation Army $15,000." (As for the intrepid reporter, Cassini wondered if the mob might strike back at him. The underworld code protected him. "We talked about you," Joe Adonis later told him, "but we don't like to mess with you guys in the press. And you were a Wop!")

As suggested by this effort for the Salvation Army, Costello craved respectability in ways both comic and poignant. He read widely, especially for a gangster, and threw ostentatiously big words into his conversation ("tangible," "recoup," "authentic"), though he stumbled occasionally ("importancy"). At a dinner party in his home he would pick some topical issue, go around the table soliciting opinions, and then deliver his own measured conclusion. Conscious of his street accent and lack of education, he soaked up ideas and mannerisms from people of more polish. "All I know I stole," he told a reporter. "If I saw you hold a cigarette in a certain way, and I liked it, I would steal it from you."

For two years Costello maintained a deep, platonic friendship with the Indian writer Santha Rama Rau. Impressed by his courtesy and gentleness, she introduced him to artists and writers around New York. "What I saw," she said later, "was an amused kind of tolerant man with a great many regrets about his life, but not the sort of ones you'd expect. He didn't give the impression he regretted anything he had done. I think he regretted the things he missed in his life." For a time Costello even consulted a Park Avenue psychiatrist. "To me he is a fascinating and picturesque character," said the shrink. "I never took a nickel from him. Oh, I might have accepted an occasional case of Scotch."

This yearning for a good name, despite everything, led Costello to cooperate—up to a point—with the Kefauver committee. Virgil Peterson's testimony had described Costello as "the most influential underworld leader in America," possessed of "tremendous political power, public relations and publicity men, a personal attorney and enormous wealth." Costello hoped to prove otherwise by answering questions in seeming candor; most gangsters brought before the committee had taken the Fifth Amendment and said nothing. Costello wanted exoneration in this most public forum. The New York hearings, the last stop on Kefauver's ten-month tour, were broadcast live over national radio and TV. Bashful about showing his face, Costello instead allowed the television camera to focus on his hands. So TV viewers—estimated at 20 to 30 million, twice the audience for the 1950 World Series—saw the gangster's hands kneading nervously, playing with a water glass, twiddling his glasses, picking at a cuticle, while he fenced with his interrogators in a high, strained voice.

For two days he sweated and parried. "I am not expecting you to believe anything," he said. "I knew you weren't going to believe anything when I first come here. I have been prejudged." At the start of the third day he stalked from the room: "When I testify, I want to testify truthfully, and my mind don't function." Threatened with contempt of Congress, he came back a few days later and resumed his punishment, still declining in most instances to take the Fifth. Charles Tobey was relentless, as usual:

"Bearing in mind all that you have gained and received in wealth, what have you ever done for your country as a good citizen?"

"Well, I don't know what you mean by that."

"You are looking back over the years, now, to that time when you became a citizen. Now, spending 20-odd years after that, you must have in your mind some things you have done that you can speak of to your credit as an American citizen. If so, what are they?"

"Paid my tax." (Laughter in the room.)

". . . Isn't he [Frankie Mario] actually, in the last analysis, your contact man to collect money from bookies, and so forth?"

"Why, that's ridiculous, Senator."

"You needn't say it is ridiculous. Is it true; yes or no?"

"I am sorry; no."

"Save that voice of yours; we are not through with you yet. . . . You don't vote? Is that a test of good citizenship to refrain from voting?"

"Well, there are millions who don't vote."

"That isn't the question, sir. Guilt is personal in this country."

So it went, to a testy stalemate. "I am not ashamed of nothing, but I want to be correct," Costello said toward the end, still trying. "I know there's a lot of technicalities here, Mr. Halley. . . . I am not in a friendly place. I know that." When it was over, Costello had not cleared his name and the committee had not pulled any important revelations from him. "Ladies and gentlemen," Kefauver announced, "Mr. Costello has been a rather mysterious figure to you of the television audience because he was not photographed, but at this time Mr. Costello is willing to face the camera and let you have a good look at him. Mr. Costello, as the photographer says to the little boy, will you smile a little bit?" Still doing his best in public, Costello weakly obliged.

After some 600 witnesses and over 11,500 pages of testimony, the Kefauver committee finished its work. By some criteria the tangible results did not justify all that effort. Forty-five contempt citations were issued to uncooperative witnesses, leading to only three convictions; the courts generally accepted the Fifth Amendment's protections. The committee proposed nineteen bills to improve law enforcement; only one passed Congress, the Wagering Stamp Act, which proved unenforceable. Joe Adonis was pressured to sell his Ford haulaway business by the committee's publicity, but he sold it to another Mafioso, Charles Chiri. The Immigration and Naturalization Service was ordered to review the deportability of 559 alien gangsters ("Very bad, you know," Kefauver had said, "that people come here from other countries to be American citizens and they have such little respect for the United States Senate as to perjure themselves before a Senate committee"). Of the 559, only 24 were deported, mostly small fry except for Joe Adonis and Doc Stacher.

On the other hand: the Continental Press had to shut down for good in March 1952. Though it was replaced by a loose confederation of local wire services, the national bookie underground had lost its lifeline. The IRS set up a special rackets squad that convicted 874 gangster tax delinquents in the next six years, with Artie Samish prominent among them. Costello was convicted of both contempt and tax evasion and spent almost half of the next decade in jail. The Kefauver committee never came up with absolute proof of the Mafia. "If there had been two years' time instead of just 11 months," Halley said afterward, "and if there'd been a staff of 200 investigators instead of just a dozen, we might have learned the truth about the Mafia." But just by submitting whatever evidence came to hand, and discussing it in public, the committee moved along a process of discovery. "It's a criminal way of life which is just in another world," Kefauver concluded. "They never call on the police, they report nothing to the police, they give no information, they enforce their own orders, they cut one another in on investments, and they all know one another all over the country."

A few secret ironies remained. Organized crime had so penetrated the American upperworld by 1951 that the committee could not reveal all it knew. Mayor deLesseps Morrison of New Orleans was allowed to testify about how he had purged his city of Costello and other out-of-state gangsters. "In this city we believe we have run them out of the city limits," Morrison told the committee, "but they still hover around our borders, ever watchful for the opportunity to return to the lush pickings of the past." Meantime the committee had affidavits and other evidence in its files of how Morrison had taken large payoffs from *local* gamblers and vice operators, both as a candidate and as mayor. None of this incriminating material was revealed at the time.

Kefauver himself had his own complications, again most unpublicized. He liked to gamble and bet on horses, tastes he had perhaps acquired during a year in Hot Springs, Arkansas, between college and law school. He attended the races at the Laurel and Pimlico tracks near Washington, making bets and expecting free passes and courtesy badges from the managements. Meyer Lansky later remembered a private meeting with Kefauver during the hearings. "What's so bad about gambling?" Lansky asked him. "You like it yourself, I know you've gambled a lot." "That's right," Kefauver replied. "But I don't want you people to control it." Harry Bennett also suspected Kefauver of hypocrisy. With the committee after him in Detroit, Bennett sent out inquiries to his underworld friends. "He never knew how much I had on him," Bennett recalled, "but it would have embarrassed him."

Perhaps because of his gambling, Kefauver was constantly, vulnerably broke. When he bought a home in Washington, he had to give weekend lectures to pay the mortgage. The furniture came secondhand from an apartment auction. Kefauver's checking account at a Chattanooga bank was often overdrawn by as much as $1,700. Yet on January 3, 1951, with his rackets investigation about two-thirds complete, he deposited $25,000 in the account. The source of this large sum remains a mystery; the hearings brought him a book contract, but not until some months later. Normally he deposited no more than $1,500 at a time. Kefauver at once wrote a check for $10,500 to pay off the second mortgage on his home in Washington. By that fall the account was again overdrawn by more than $1,600.

Flora and Herbert Brody, a married couple in Knoxville, Tennessee, were among Kefauver's political and financial supporters back home. Flora was a schoolmate of Kefauver's; Herbert was a numbers boss in Knoxville. Herbert Brody was arrested for gambling in March 1951 after a police raid seized incriminating records and checks. A rumor passed around town that Brody had given $5,000 to Kefauver's Senate campaign in 1948, though Kefauver had reported only a $100 donation from him. Three weeks after Brody's arrest, Kefauver suddenly and unexpectedly resigned as chairman of his committee. "I can't go on," he said. "I have got to get some time to get home."

"Jeez, everything is a racket today," Willie Moretti had told the committee in New York. "Everybody has a racket of their own."

EIGHT

KENNEDYS

November 22, 1963. All the main strands of organized crime converged on Dallas: the ethnic trinity of Irish, Jewish, and Italian; the decades of collusion among unions and the mob, nightclubs and show business and the mob, Democratic political machines and the mob. On a personal level, the tragedy of an old Irish gangster with Faustian ambitions for his sons, but who still wanted to keep them clean. Binding it all, the unrecorded but well-established criminal code that governed relations between underworld and upperworld. And enveloping it all, the usual miasmic underworld cloud of swirling mysteries and mirrors, of dark shadows and smoke.

The motorcade turned left onto Elm Street and drove slowly past the Texas School Book Depository. Up on the sixth floor, Lee Harvey Oswald drew a bead. In front of the motorcade and to the right, behind a fence above the Grassy Knoll, a second gunman raised his weapon. A car bearing Secret Service men and two White House aides, Ken O'Donnell and Dave Powers, followed less than ten feet behind the presidential limousine. O'Donnell and Powers heard two gunshots close together. Powers saw the President slump to his left, toward Jacqueline, and Powers told O'Donnell, who crossed himself. Both men were staring at the wounded President when another shot blew off the top of his head. "We saw pieces of bone and brain tissue and bits of his reddish hair flying through the air," O'Donnell remembered later. "The impact lifted him and shook him limply, as if he was a rag doll, and then he dropped out of our sight, sprawled across the back seat of the car. I said to Dave, 'He's dead.' "

(Based on what they heard, O'Donnell, Powers, and dozens of other witnesses were sure that some of the gunfire came from the Grassy Knoll. At least ten witnesses also saw smoke hanging in the air by the fence on the knoll. In 1979 newly discovered acoustical evidence, as analyzed by the House Assassinations Committee, placed—with 95 percent certainty—a gunman behind the fence. The lethal head shot may have come from the front or the back. Muddled evidence on this point would never allow a final conclusion. It does not matter. The presence of two gunmen meant a conspiracy.)

Two days after the assassination, Jack Ruby—the smoking gun, the Rosetta stone, the trout in the milk—lunged into history. For thirty years he had been scrabbling through lower reaches of the underworld in Chicago, San Francisco, Dallas, Las Vegas, and Cuba. Since 1947 he had run strip joints and mob business in Dallas. On Sunday, moving easily among his friends at the police station, Ruby shot Oswald and at last became somebody. "You all know me!" he shouted. "I'm Jack Ruby!"

As attorney general, Robert Kennedy had devoted more time and resources to the pursuit of organized crime than all his predecessors put together. And now Jack Ruby, a man with long and deep ties to the underworld, had silenced John Kennedy's accused killer. Simple logic therefore said: the mob murdered Jack to stifle Bobby's crusade. Kill the head and the body dies.

This line of reasoning ignored the underworld code. Gangsters did not normally harm honest lawmen. For such an extraordinary murder—*to kill a President*—they must have been extraordinarily provoked. In their terms, it could only have involved a double cross. The Kennedys must have dealt with the underworld in compromising ways. When the Kennedys then turned around and nonetheless went after organized crime, they breached the code and put a contract on the President.

❧ ❧

Shakespeare knew: "The sins of the father are to be laid upon the children."

❦ ❦

The tragedy in Dallas began with the father. Joe Kennedy was the shrewdest, most complicated, most mysterious of all the Kennedys. He roared around the country, piling up money, operating face to face or over the telephone, leaving scant, discreet records on paper. Awed by nobody, he knew people from many fields better than they knew him. "Time after time, while growing up," his son Robert said later, "I remember listening to him talk with an important figure in business, the theater, or politics, and always observing that he was the dominant figure— that he knew more; that he expressed it better." Sitting by the pool one day at his Palm Beach home, he called up—and reached—Mayor Richard Daley of Chicago, James Reston of the *New York Times,* Chet Huntley of NBC News, Frank Sinatra, Janet Leigh and Jack Warner of Hollywood, and his sons, the President and attorney general of the United States. "Now," he said, "who else can we call?"

Beyond the intimate circle of his family and closest friends, he was widely, cordially hated. Looking back later, Franklin D. Roosevelt, Jr., dismissed him as "one of the most evil, disgusting men I have ever known." "Dishonorable," said Walter Annenberg; "the most ruthless operator I ever saw in my life." "A tough customer . . . quite touchy," agreed Joe Schenck, who knew many underworld and upperworld toughs. "As big a crook as we've got anywhere in this country," said Harry Truman.

All these statements, though, were by enemies personally distant from Kennedy who knew him through business and politics, endeavors that he conducted as guerrilla warfare. His oldest, tightest friends—men like Morton Downey, Joe E. Lewis, Joe Timilty, and Carroll Rosenbloom—came to him through the more relaxed milieus of show business, sports, and the Ould Sod of Irish Boston. They saw a different man from the one his business and political acquaintances did, and they stayed fiercely loyal to him. Downey, Lewis, Timilty, and Rosenbloom were among the very few associates who visited Kennedy after his disabling stroke in 1961, and who at the end were invited to his small, private funeral in 1969. ("I was surprised," Kennedy's chauffeur noted, "that a man who had been so powerful and was so rich did not have more close friends.") Yet these devoted retainers, by their own lives, merely added to the sinister gangster atmosphere that always clung to Kennedy. In his choice of best friends, Kennedy was actually the same upperworld hoodlum so detested by his enemies.

Morton Downey, an Irish tenor from Connecticut, trilled "When Irish Eyes Are Smiling" in public more than ten thousand times. His friendship with Joe Kennedy started in 1923, when he was singing with one of Paul Whiteman's bands. A few years later Kennedy gave him a role in his film *Syncopation,* an early movie musical. For the most part, though, their relations were unclouded by business arrangements. They were often seen at the Stork Club, drinking together and telling ribald stories, and they both owned summer homes in Hyannis Port. "I saw more than Joe's usual casual facade," Downey said later. "He loved to walk and discuss absolutely everything in the world, for he had a strange, almost turbulent interest in more seemingly unrelated topics and things than any man I ever knew." In their four decades of friendship, Kennedy at times showed Downey a surprisingly introspective quality, an unexpected deft grasp of human psychology, a genius for reading people and spotting phonies—as well as the impervious shell he normally presented to the world. "He was always fearless," Downey observed. "No one could shake or worry him. I think I admire that quality as much as all his others, because it governed all his others. When people went a trifle too far with him, I could see the wall go up."

Downey was not a crook. His worst tangle with the law brought him only a suspended sentence in 1931 for punching a process server in a quarrel over a twenty-dollar laundry bill. But making his way upward in show business when he did, the way he did, he could hardly avoid underworld contacts. He sang at gangster nightclubs: the Mayfair in Boston, the Mounds Club in Cleveland, a Mafia joint in New Orleans, and the Casanova, the Silver Slipper, Texas Guinan's Playground, and his own Delmonico Club in New York. He owned a perfume company with the Stork Club's Sherman Billingsley, an old bootlegger. In the 1940s Downey served a term as president of the American Guild of Variety Artists, the mob-infested nightclub union. Along with Frank Costello, Carlos Marcello, Dandy Phil Kastel, and Jimmy Durante, he owned part of the Tropicana casino in Las Vegas. At Tony Cornero's lavish mob funeral in 1955, Downey stood up and sang his composition

"Wabash Moon," the late gangster's favorite song. None of these associations amounted to indictable offenses. Downey merely did business with gangsters, at times making his living from them, at other times mingling his money with theirs in joint ventures.

Joe E. Lewis, the cabaret singer who became a comedian after Machine Gun Jack McGurn sliced him up in 1928, met Kennedy while he was appearing at a Palm Beach nightclub in the mid-1930s. Lewis was a stock character from an endless Damon Runyon story. Homely and profane, a vagabond who lived out of trunks and hotel rooms, Lewis drank, joked, whored, and gambled his way through a playground of low comedy and earthy pleasures. He appealed to the raffish aspects of Joe Kennedy's personality. They liked to gamble together at casinos in Nevada and racetracks in Florida. "He's a real smart bettor," Lewis said of his friend, "but he never bets a lot of dough. He used to bawl me out about my big bets and used to tell me to make smaller bets on the sure ones, like him." Once, in an atypical fit of propriety, Lewis got briefly married; Kennedy sent over three cases of his Haig & Haig whiskey, which may have outlasted the marriage.

Like Downey, but to a greater degree, Lewis owed his living to his gangster friends. During the 1930s he ran mob nightclubs in New York, Los Angeles, and Chicago, none of them successfully. His own performing career began to soar after he played thirty-three weeks in 1940 at Frank Costello's Copacabana nightclub in New York. For the next twenty-five years he did annual turns at the Copa, usually opening the club's season in September. At other times he made stops on the underworld nightclub circuit, performing and gambling at joints in Las Vegas, Miami, New Orleans, Cleveland, Chicago, and New York, always well publicized by the gangster-chroniclers Walter Winchell and Ed Sullivan. Especially close to Johnny Torrio and Sam Giancana, Lewis quietly carried messages and did favors for his criminal cronies, making them laugh and relieving tensions. When he opened his final season at the Copa in the fall of 1965, a crippled Joe Kennedy was brought down to see him.

Joe Timilty, the corrupt (if untried) Boston police commissioner from 1936 to 1943, was to Joe Kennedy as Lem Billings was to Jack Kennedy. Timilty and Billings were both jovial, predictable companions, lifelong bachelors unencumbered by families or demanding careers, always ready to come and be cheerful when beckoned forward by a Kennedy. Timilty and Joe Kennedy first knew each other as fellow rogues from Irish Boston; their real friendship began after Governor James Michael Curley made Timilty the top cop in Boston. During his crisis in the fall of 1943, as he tried and failed to get himself reappointed commissioner, Timilty spent weekends with Kennedy in Hyannis Port. Thereafter the Kennedys still obligingly called him Commish.

For his part, Timilty was there during hard times for the Kennedys. When Joe's favorite daughter, Kathleen, died in a plane crash in 1948, a reporter telephoned the news to Kennedy and Timilty at their hotel suite in Paris. Timilty answered the phone, woke Joe up, and told him. After Joe identified the body, Timilty accompanied him on the slow, sad ocean voyage home to New York. "He hasn't talked to anybody—won't talk to anybody," Timilty explained. "He hasn't left his stateroom much." Fifteen years later, following the assassination in Dallas, Timilty again helped shepherd the family through its grief.

Carroll Rosenbloom, owner of the Baltimore Colts during their glory years of Johnny Unitas and three championships, first encountered Joe Kennedy in Palm Beach in the late 1930s. "I was not his employee," Rosenbloom said later, "nor his subordinate in any official or business relationship, yet he had such effective powers of leadership that I instinctively and happily called him 'Chief.' " Rosenbloom met his second wife, a Las Vegas chorus girl, at a Kennedy party in Palm Beach in 1957. Every Sunday afternoon during the fall, Rosenbloom would call Joe with the Colts score; he gave Bobby the game ball, signed by all the Colts, from the epochal 1958 title game against the New York Giants. As an intimate member of the family circle, Rosenbloom saw Kennedy's gentler traits and heard about his unpublicized philanthropies. "Maybe because he has such inner security he does not need public acclaim to fulfill himself," Rosenbloom suggested. "Maybe also he rather enjoys being thought of as 'tough' rather than 'soft.' . . . In his personal relationships he has always been the 'softest touch' I have ever known."

Rosenbloom himself was an elusive, mysterious man, known to hang out with gamblers and lowlifes. The son of a Polish Jewish immigrant who had become a Baltimore clothing manufacturer, Rosenbloom by obscure means parlayed a small stake from his father into a major fortune. Evidently he made a pile by leasing tote machines to racetracks; an underworld air of horses and bets stayed with him. Tied to Lou Chesler, a Toronto gambler, and to Max Orovitz, an associate of Meyer Lansky's, Rosenbloom in 1958 invested $240,000 in a Havana mob casino. Expansively and repeatedly flouting NFL rules, he bet hundreds of thousands of dollars on Colt games—sometimes against his own team. On occasion he illegally scalped tickets for Colts games as well. Rosenbloom lived, dressed, and carried himself like a hoodlum, and he may have died the same way. Officially he drowned while swimming in the surf off Golden Beach, Florida; but a witness on the beach saw a skindiver pulling him under.

People who are themselves enigmatic may still be defined by the closest company they keep. Downey, Lewis, Timilty, and Rosenbloom all maintained legitimate reputations and sources of income. All four also operated on the fringe of the underworld. It made sense that they should be Joe Kennedy's best friends because he dallied in that same fringe.

Outside this inner foursome, Kennedy kept up less personal ties of mutual favors to others in the murky zone between underworld and upperworld: Herbert Bayard Swope, William Randolph Hearst, Walter Winchell, Harry Bennett, and many others. "I want you to know Kennedy," Swope once wrote Eugene Meyer of the *Washington Post*. "He is worth knowing. He has courage, capacity, clarity, cordiality, and character. I could exhaust the other letters as I have the Cs in finding adjectives to suit him." "He is very able," Hearst said of Kennedy to his doubting attorney Neylan, "very interested, very friendly, and very influential." (Hearst and Kennedy shared another bond: they both loved Marion Davies. After Hearst's death, Kennedy kept a picture of Davies on the night table of his bedroom in Hyannis Port—the only photograph in the room. "She was a woman who understood men," said Kennedy. "She understood men who wanted great things. She understood me.")

Farther down, closer to the real underworld, Frank Sinatra entered the Kennedy circle through his friendship with Joe and their common grounds of nightclubs, Hollywood, and Las Vegas. Sinatra's own gangster ties went back to his childhood in Hoboken and merely deepened over the years. The son of Italian immigrants, he had grown up among uncles involved in loan sharking, numbers gambling, and possibly murder, and a mother who was the neighborhood bootlegger and abortionist. Once he started singing in saloons and nightclubs, Sinatra routinely exchanged favors with gangsters. "Some of them were kind to me when I started out," he privately conceded in 1951, understating the matter, "and I have sort of casually seen them or spoken to them at different places, in nightclubs where I worked or out in Vegas or California." A few years later he acquired a 9 percent share in the Sands casino in Las Vegas, run by Doc Stacher and Longy Zwillman with other mobsters; for the next dozen years Sinatra was the joint's resident headliner and sucker-magnet. Always agreeably sycophantic when summoned by the mob, Sinatra acted starstruck around his gangster buddies, falling over himself to serve them. "I'd rather be a don of the Mafia," he told Eddie Fisher, "than President of the United States."

Through his friend Joe Kennedy, Sinatra could at least cultivate a President. From the late 1950s on, as it became clear that Jack would run for the office, Sinatra drew closer to the Kennedys, often visiting at their homes. Once Sinatra brought a dubious companion and two women of commercial virtue to see Joe in Hyannis Port. (Sinatra knew how to please the old man.) Late that night someone on the household staff encountered Kennedy and one of the women in a hallway; he had her backed against a wall and was fondling her breasts. The staffer, flustered, explained that he had shined up Kennedy's riding boots. "My riding boots!" Kennedy laughed. "Just in time!"

And finally, descending from Kennedy's mob-connected friends and associates, down all the way to his own dealings with real gangsters. As an old bootlegger he never forsook the under-world; as a man of feral, imperious will, used to making his own rules and getting his way, he probably never wanted to forsake it. Like many other former bootleggers, after Prohibition he owned a legitimate liquor-distributing company (Somerset Importers) and part of a racetrack (Hialeah). These ventures kept him in contact with mobsters, as did his passion for gambling. He revealed himself in his amusements. He played a carefully re-strained golf game, settling for a three-quarter swing and short, straight drives—but he bet up to $10,000 a match. Away from the links, he placed so many other bets on other games that he called his own private bookmaker once a day or more. Given his vast wealth, no matter how much he lost the underworld could never

have "owned" him as it owned, for example, his friends Joe E.
Lewis and Herbert Bayard Swope. But his gambling did maintain
a pattern of potentially compromising situations over decades.

In 1947 Kennedy's quondam bootlegging partner Frank Costello and other top New York hoods opened their plush Colonial
Inn casino in Miami Beach. "I got a friend coming in tomorrow,"
Costello told the casino's PR man, Harold Conrad, one night,
"and I want that you should keep an eye on him and see that he's
taken care of. Big man, name's Joe Kennedy, use' to be ambassador to England." Costello had someone else look after Kennedy
because he knew a public display of their connection might
embarrass his upperworld friend. The next night, Conrad introduced himself and watched over the famous visitor from
Costello's past. "Kennedy is getting a big kick out of the show,"
Conrad noted, "especially when the girls are on. For some reason
he looks to me like a priest on the cheat. He asks me if the girls
come out into the club after the show. I tell him yes, but I don't
take the hint. I notice that not once does Costello approach him
during the whole evening." Apparently pleased with the Colonial
action, of varied kinds, Kennedy returned often. "Everybody
used to come to my Colonial Inn," Meyer Lansky said later:
"judges, senators, respectable businessmen. Joe Kennedy used to
come four or five times a week."

For reasons of business or pleasure, or his own private impulse
to defy propriety, Kennedy liked gangster hangouts. In New
York he favored the Waldorf-Astoria barbershop, where Costello
appeared every day, and the Black Angus restaurant, run by Max
Block of the Amalgamated Meat Cutters union. Many leading
hoods came to the Black Angus for steaks and privacy. "Some
mob business was undoubtedly conducted in the Black Angus,"
Block later allowed, not without pride. ("A no-good bum," Block
said of Joe Kennedy. "Now John was supposed to be the gentleman, but everyone forgot how the old man made his money.")

When he gambled in Nevada, Joe usually stayed at the Cal-
Neva Lodge, a mob haven on Lake Tahoe that straddled the
California-Nevada state line. Built by the California gambler Bill
Graham in the 1930s, the Cal-Neva was the first successful casino
at Tahoe. The state border bisected the main lodge, with a dining
room on one side and gambling on the other; a guest could violate
the Mann Act, it was said, just by walking across the lobby. Twenty

comfortable cottages allowed discretion to visitors with something to hide. Over the years, various mob accomplices fronted and managed the place. Sinatra once tried to kill himself there after a fight with Ava Gardner.

Joe Kennedy came so often that at Christmas the Cal-Neva management in appreciation would send him two 10-foot Tahoe Christmas trees. Kennedy stayed there with Joe Timilty, and with his children and grandchildren. "He may be old," Walter Winchell later said of Kennedy's recreations at the Cal-Neva, "but he's still in there pinching." He also met there with various hoodlums for mysterious reasons. According to a confidential Justice Department report, Kennedy was "visited by many gangsters with gambling interests"; no details available. The FBI ultimately compiled 343 separate case files on Kennedy.

The old man covered his tracks well. As his boys warmed to their own careers, Kennedy withdrew from public life, sold his interests in Somerset Importers and the Hialeah track, and kept his money in more respectable enterprises. At some point he dropped his old partner Costello. Always craving the respectability of knowing famous people, Costello resented the break. "The way he talked about him," one of Costello's friends said later, "you had the sense that they were close during Prohibition and then something happened. Frank said that he helped Kennedy become wealthy. What happened between them I don't know. But the way Frank talked you had the feeling that in later years he had tried to reach Joe Kennedy for something and that he was completely ignored. Frank didn't mind if someone said no to him. He could understand that. But nothing made him angrier than to be just ignored, as if he didn't exist."

No damaging reports of Kennedy's gambling and underworld ties appeared in print during his lifetime. In October 1950, though, his name was mentioned—briefly and innocuously—at the Chicago hearings of the Kefauver committee. Joe Fusco, who managed the Capones' legal liquor interests, was explaining his dealings with Tom Cassara, a gangster who had run a mob hotel in Miami Beach. "Cassara when he first came to Chicago I think was in 1944," Fusco testified, "he was working for Kennedy, the Somerset Import Co. He was their representative here. He used to call on the trade as a missionary man." With Cassara as the contact, Fusco added Somerset's lines to his own distributing company. Three months after

Cassara was shot in front of a Chicago restaurant, Kennedy sold his liquor business to Joe Reinfeld, another old bootlegger. "When they bought Somerset, Kennedy's company, we were distributor for Kennedy," said Fusco. "Automatically they left us on as a distributor for Reinfeld."

Intriguing information: that Joe Kennedy had employed a murdered gangster, had done business with the Capones, and had sold his company to the notorious Reinfeld. Yet no one on the Kefauver committee or its staff seemed curious. They did not even ask Fusco just which Kennedy he was discussing. The matter was left dangling—not coincidentally, perhaps. Kennedy had many allies in high, strategic places.

Mobsters recognized him as one of their own. The underworld ties that started during Prohibition lasted all his life. If the general public remained unaware of these associations, gangsters knew them firsthand and might eventually find some use for the old man's secrets. Sam Giancana of Chicago told his girlfriend Judy Campbell "that Joe Kennedy was one of the biggest crooks that ever lived," she later recalled. "He often intimated that he knew a great deal of derogatory information about Joe Kennedy's background."

So far as anyone can tell, Kennedy's family actually knew little about that background. As the children grew up, they surely became aware of his gambling and the Runyonesque tone to his friends. But he carefully kept the family ignorant of how he made money and what he did all day. "Business, even his own operations, were so seldom discussed at home," Bobby said later. "Despite his rather extensive holdings, none of us was encouraged to go into business, even for the purpose of carrying them on after his retirement." He groomed two of his sons-in-law—not his own boys—to take over the family's business interests. Not wanting Jack, Bobby, or Teddy to become "just another businessman," as he put it, he shoved them toward political careers. The Kennedy brothers therefore remained chastely innocent about business affairs in general and their father's in particular. "When they talked about business they really were just naive," Jack's friend Charles Spalding recalled. "Listening to them talk about money was like listening to nuns talk about sex. It was awkward."

At the Palm Beach home where the family spent winters, Joe's office was a solarium by the pool, ten feet square, with cushioned benches and wicker chairs. Known as the bullpen, this box gave him protection from the wind and privacy from his kids and their friends. Dressed in a towel and a big hat, sweat streaming down his body, he spent mornings in there alone with a telephone and a notebook "while we sat around outside," said his daughter Eunice, "getting tan and wondering what he was doing." "Although you could not hear what he was saying," noted Jack's Navy buddy Red Fay, "you could feel the power in that voice as he directed one of the great American business empires from his post there beside the pool."

He built a literal wall between his family life and his outside life. "He could be tough in a business deal," an associate noted, "but when it came to his children, he melted." "He was careful to make sure we understood," Bobby added, "that his enemies were not to become our enemies." The psychological aspects here are irresistible: a man so rough and unprincipled in the outside world, but so correspondingly insistent and meticulous in creating a safe haven inside for his children; the latter a compensation for, even an unconscious admission of, the former. Many other gangsters, especially Irish and Jewish gangsters, displayed the same pattern. Meyer Lansky sent his son to West Point.

In the Kennedy household, the old man ruled everyone, mother and sons and daughters alike. "His personality was so strong," Bobby remembered, "his ideas so definite, his views and outlook so determined, that he dominated our home and our lives." Rose Kennedy was not even allowed to hire and train servants. When nurses and governesses had questions about the children, they went to Joe. If he was away on business, as often happened, they had orders to reach him by phone. One visitor to family dinners in the 1930s recalled the noisy babble of talk and laughter and an overwhelmed Rose attempting to cut through the cacophony: "Mrs. Kennedy would be heard trying to say something at the end of the table. She hardly ever got it out though, didn't have a chance." Once the children were of school age, their mother was seldom heeded.

Kennedy might hope to protect his children from the world he knew, but—with Rose only a muffled spectator—he could not protect his children from himself. They perforce absorbed his amoral ways. "Winning is what counts," he said, over and over, in many forms. All summer long, the children competed at organized swimming and sailing races, at golf and tennis and other games. "We did well," Eunice recalled, "—but I hesitate to think about the consequences if we had lost them all!" At Kennedy's twenty-fifth Harvard reunion week in 1937, Kathleen was paired at tennis against the wife of a classmate. With no linesman on hand, Kathleen cheated repeatedly on line calls, lost anyway, and then burst into tears.

Winning mattered, not doing your best or playing the game straight. "You must remember," he taught, "it's not what you are that counts, but what people think you are." Over two hundred letters from Kennedy to his children have survived; they prate endlessly of looking right and beating everyone, never of doing right and acting fairly. Kennedy taught his children about winning and appearances, at which he was adept, but not about ethics and values, of which he knew nothing. "One rule always to remember," he once told Harry Bridges, "is don't get caught."

Even when the Kennedy children moved away, to schools and jobs, emotionally they remained in their father's house. They matured and settled down slowly and married late—three in their thirties. "I used to think of him as a tiger mother," Jacqueline said later, "swatting his cubs when they were out of line, and drawing them in with his paw when they were troubled. When you married into his family, you became one of those cubs: as loved, as protected, as chastised, as much an object of pride as one of his own. I have never seen that anywhere else."

As grown-ups, with families of their own, Kennedy children in effect stayed on an allowance. The Kennedy office in New York handled—and therefore examined—all their living expenses, bank accounts, taxes, hotel and travel reservations. Such privileges also gave their father one more line of control. Once, when Jack was in Congress, Joe Kennedy had the office ask him about a check he had written for $3,000. Jack, thirty-one years old at the time, a bad boy making an implausible excuse, said it was to pay off an election bet—though he had written the check before the election took place.

At every stage of John Kennedy's political career, the old man was there with mounds of money, assertive advice, and secret connections—facts consistently minimized and denied by the family. (Don't get caught.) "Joe Kennedy was the mastermind of all Jack's campaigns," Joe Timilty concluded. "He was completely

KENNEDYS   319

in charge of everything, every detail." Just out of the Navy in 1945, Jack was ordered to run for Congress. "I can feel Pappy's eyes on the back of my neck," he told Red Fay. "Dad is ready right now and can't understand why Johnny boy isn't 'all engines ahead full.'" During the campaign Joe made only one public appearance on behalf of his son. But for some reason the *Boston American,* owned by Joe's friend Hearst and widely read in the district, never in the final two months mentioned Jack's main primary opponent. "The essential campaign manager through all of these things was probably Mr. Kennedy," recalled Mark Dalton, the putative campaign manager. "He was deeply interested in every campaign, at least those that I had anything to do with. . . . And I think for history, that that should be clear."

In 1952 Joe pushed Jack into challenging Henry Cabot Lodge for his Senate seat. The old man came up to Boston for the campaign, settled into an apartment at 81 Beacon Street with a bank of telephones, and deployed his forces. "The father was the distinct boss in every way," an insider remembered. "He dominated everything, even told everyone where to sit. They are just children in that house." Only once did he drop by the formal campaign head-quarters. "And boy!" a worker said later. "You know, everybody was jumping to attention, and I was trying to look inconspicuous because I was really a little frightened at meeting him because he had such a formidable reputation." At a crucial point, Joe bought the support of the *Boston Post* with a $500,000 loan to the publisher. "We had to buy that fucking paper," Jack later admitted in private, "or I'd have been licked." Lodge was defeated by what one of his supporters called "the First Kennedy Bank."

Joe Kennedy never let up and never let go. In 1953 Bobby, recently out of law school, pondered joining the staff of the Senate Permanent Subcommittee on Investigations. Joe favored it, Jack opposed it, Bobby did it. Late in 1956, Joe urged Lyndon Johnson, the Senate majority leader, to appoint Jack to the coveted Foreign Relations Committee. Estes Kefauver also wanted that plum; Kefauver had seniority over Kennedy and was Johnson's first choice. "But I kept picturing old Joe Kennedy sitting there," Johnson said later, "with all that power and wealth feeling indebted to me for the rest of his life, and I sure liked that picture." Jack was anointed and in appreciation, for three years in a row, nominated Johnson's man Bobby Baker to be one of the Jaycees' Ten Outstanding Young Men of the Year.

The sons of course resented any suggestion that they owed their success to Daddy. Occasionally they took public issue with their father on small political matters. "They are entitled to their own identities and positions," Joe said for publication. "Except to try to be a good father to both, I have never tried to influence their careers nor their thinking." The boys did, with time, think for themselves. But their careers could not have bloomed so soon, if at all, without the unbalancing effect of their father's manipulations and bottomless checkbook.

In terms of the eventual assassination in Dallas, then, these aspects of Kennedy family history stand out: the children probably did not appreciate the extent of Joe Kennedy's ties to organized crime. Despite this innocence, they did absorb his devotion to winning and ethical anarchy. As adults they remained extraordinarily dependent on their father's money and authority. Without quite realizing it, they therefore had their own implicit underworld associations. If neither they nor the general public understood that situation, gangsters did. "The problem is that you can't separate one Kennedy from another," Sam Giancana later told Judy Campbell. "Maybe Jack would be okay if you could get rid of that damn family."

And one more Kennedy quality, an aspect of classic tragedy: the family hubris. "You watched these people go through their lives and just had a feeling that they existed outside the usual laws of nature," Charles Spalding reflected. "The Kennedys had a feeling of being heightened." They seemed richer, prettier, bolder, more alive than ordinary mortals; they laughed more, lived more, got laid more, won more, suffered more. "Men who wanted great things," as Joe described himself. One of his grandsons, trying to define the Kennedy spirit, finally said, "It means that we're exactly the same as everybody else, except better."

Such people could disregard the usual rules and restraints. They could do anything, at any time, to anybody. They could defy all the available gods and chortle about it. They could take wing and fly toward the sun. They could play with the underworld and fight it as well.

❧ ❧

At Christmastime in 1956, Bobby came home to Hyannis Port and told the family he was going racketbusting. As chief counsel to the Senate Select Committee on Improper Activities in the Labor or Management Field, chaired by Senator John L. McClellan of Arkansas, Bobby planned a full-blown inquiry into lawbreaking by labor unions, including their underworld connections. His father's advice, fast and definite, was not to do it. Bobby argued back, Joe persisted, and they steamed into a furious confrontation, the worst the family had ever seen between the two. For Bobby— always a sweet child and pliant son, thirty-one years old, married and already with five children of his own—it marked the first real defiance of his father's will.

The planned investigation would produce no significant reforms, Joe insisted, and might alienate labor support from the Kennedy presidential campaign he was already planning for 1960. The father, of all people, also knew how the underworld might flare back if provoked. "The old man saw this as dangerous," recalled Lem Billings, who was there, "not the sort of thing or the sort of people to mess around with. He felt Bobby was being awfully naive." His private, unspoken fears of where such an investigation might lead, what it might dredge up about his own past, may be inferred. Only Joe Kennedy could fully gauge the ironies—the possibly tragic ironies—if one of his sons went after the mob.

Bobby, stepping out on his own, was not dissuaded. For the next 30 months, he took executive charge of what became the most thorough exposure of organized crime that Congress had yet undertaken: a staff of over 100 lawyers, accountants, and investigators; more than 1,500 witnesses in over 500 open hearings, and some 14 million words of testimony filling 20,432 printed pages. Holding together this deluge of assorted details, teasing leads, and loose ends, Kennedy came to assert unusual discretion over where the trails led next. For some Republicans on the select committee, the brash young man was grabbing too much unsupervised power. "I simply do not believe the Committee should be run by the Chief Counsel," Karl Mundt of South Dakota urged McClellan. "Frankly," agreed Barry Goldwater of Arizona, "I am getting a little tired about reading that the Chief Counsel has made up his mind as to what direction the investigation will take." "He is tops," McClellan replied to Kennedy's critics. "I trust him; I know he has superb judgment; he is conscientious and doing an excellent job."

At the time, and especially later on, Kennedy's prominence obscured his chairman's part in the whole undertaking. John McClellan, like Estes Kefauver before him, was a Democrat, a southerner, and a WASP racketbuster in the Senate. As southern Democrats, unobligated to the mob-connected Democratic machines of the North, they had a political option to probe the underworld. Otherwise these two scourges of organized crime shared little. Kefauver was a progressive maverick, only one year into his first term when he launched his crimebusting crusade, and ambitious beyond the Senate. McClellan was a conservative, states' rights segregationist, two years into his third term in 1957, content within the Senate and a powerful member of its inner club. In contrast with Kefauver, McClellan could pull the wires and levers to sustain an investigation that lasted twice as long as Kefauver's and reached further.

McClellan came from Malvern, Arkansas, population 9,243, a county seat twenty miles southeast of Hot Springs. (In pursuing bad guys, McClellan retained a protective, states' rights soft spot for the nearby gamblers in Hot Springs.) He had been born on a farm in 1896, descended from humble generations of Baptist tenant farmers. When he was eleven his daddy passed the bar and became a country lawyer. John followed him, reading lawbooks in his office, and was admitted to practice at the callow age of seventeen. The younger McClellan made his local reputation as a prosecuting attorney, independent and righteous. Sometimes father and son met in a courtroom on opposite sides of the same case.

McClellan went to Congress in 1934, to the Senate eight years later. Aside from the usual voting patterns of a conservative Dixiecrat, he acted out a Protestant conscience and was known as a ferocious enemy of waste and corruption in government. "McClellan has the astringent, disapproving demeanor of a stern man of the cloth," one journalist observed in 1957, "his outlook on the world rooted in the Baptist church." He needed that religious faith. His personal life brought a melancholy, almost unbelievable series of sorrows: the breakup of his first marriage, the death from spinal meningitis of his second wife, and the successive deaths of one son in the war, of another son in a car crash, and of the remaining son in a plane crash. "There are two places where all men stand equal," he confided to a friend after the last of these blows. "They are at the foot of the Cross and at the grave. So, may I say that it is my prayer that God may find it well in His wisdom and mercy to spare you and your loved ones and all others from the burden now laid upon my soul, and which, through faith in Him and, by His grace and dispensation of strength, I shall be able to bear."

So this southern WASP, of deep and necessary Protestant belief, confronted the alien, non-WASP underworld. As he watched the parade of Irish, Jewish, and Italian gangsters, many of them immigrants, brought before his committee and taking refuge in the Fifth Amendment, McClellan on occasion lashed out in nativist outrage. "We should rid the country of characters who come here from other lands," he said one day, "and take advantage of the great freedom and opportunity our country affords, who come here to exploit these advantages with criminal activities. They do not belong to our land, and they ought to be sent somewhere else. In my book, they are human parasites on society, and they violate every law of decency and humanity." "Mr. Chairman," Karl Mundt, a fellow WASP, added from the other side of the aisle, "I would like to associate myself emphatically with that fine statement."

But then the chief counsel, the first important non-WASP racketbuster, was the Irish Catholic son of an upperworld gangster. Confronting witnesses, seated elbow to elbow in close quarters, McClellan and Kennedy made a peculiar team. The older man, twenty-nine years Kennedy's senior, resembled a large mastiff, slow and deliberate, measured and dignified. In rough going he often took over the interrogation. A scowl line between his eyes deepened, his face darkened into an expression of incredulous exasperation, as he leaned forward and tapped the table in cadence with his deep, rumbling drawl. Beside him, the younger and smaller Kennedy, sarcastic and needling, an excitable terrier occasionally brought to heel by his boss, yapped at the witnesses in his flat, nasal Boston Irish voice. As the investigations unfolded it became essentially a joint undertaking of these two oddly matched allies.

The McClellan committee escalated through three distinct phases. It first examined the theft of union funds by Dave Beck, president of the Teamsters, and other Teamster officials in the Pacific Northwest. These matters, though criminal, did not involve the formal underworld. Next the hearings went into specifically mob-related violations by unions with long organized-crime histories: the Operating Engineers, Longshoremen, Hotel and Restaurant Employees, and (especially) the Teamsters again and

Jimmy Hoffa, Dave Beck's successor as Teamster president. Finally the committee moved to a direct look at organized crime and the Mafia at its core. Thus the hearings raised the ante, from crooked unions to mobbed-up unions to the mob.

On all three levels, Hoffa and the Teamsters became the prime villains. Repeatedly the testimony returned to them, showing a pattern of squandered and stolen union funds, sweetheart contracts, conflicts of interest among employers and union leaders, phony "paper locals" and denial of democratic process to members, collusions and coercions and violence always about to break out. These patterns were demonstrated at Teamster locals in New York and Chicago, in particular, but also in Detroit, Cleveland, St. Louis, Minneapolis, and Pittsburgh. Of 141 Teamsters brought before the committee, half took the Fifth and refused to testify. "This has become a sordid story," McClellan scolded Hoffa. "Lord Almighty, you are the man at the head of it. You have the responsibility. But apparently instead of taking any action you are undertaking to do everything you can to perpetuate this situation."

Hoffa was not the real problem. Here the committee, lacking historical memory, underestimated the situation. At one point, Senator Irving Ives of New York asked Kennedy how long labor rackets had been afflicting his state. "I think many of the racketeers and hoodlums came into the union movement starting back in 1950, Senator Ives," Kennedy replied, "but I think there has been racketeering in the labor movement up in New York for many, many years." How many years, Ives asked. "Certainly through the 1930s," Kennedy guessed. First he said 1950, then pushed it back further.

This exchange was not typical. The committee was overwhelmingly present-minded, leaving a general impression that current leaders—not the bemobbed, entrenched locals—had corrupted the Teamsters from the top down in the recent past. "The source of the cancer in the International Brotherhood of Teamsters today," McClellan concluded late in the proceedings, "obviously stems from the leadership and influence of James R. Hoffa." No; Hoffa just inherited the mess and went along with given procedures. He could have reformed the Teamsters only at the cost of his power.

Hoffa took cues—not orders—from gangsters. The hearings showed his dealings, inside and outside the union, with Angelo

Meli, William Bufalino, and Pete Licavoli of Detroit, Babe Triscaro of Cleveland, Paul Ricca and Joey Glimco of Chicago, and Johnny Dio, Tony Ducks Corallo, and Vincent Squillante of New York. Most of these hoods were both Mafia members and Teamster officials. Thus a phone call, legally tapped on March 10, 1953, by the Manhattan district attorney, between Hoffa and Dio, who controlled Local 227:

Hoffa: "He [a troublesome Teamster] promised me that he would straighten that situation out; there would be no more interference at where you're having elections or anything else if you'll just let him know where, where you're working and he'll keep the hell out of there. . . ."

Dio: "I'll get in touch with him tomorrow and give him a rundown just in case so there'll be no mistakes about it."

And another tapped call, on May 26, 1953, between Dio and Anthony Doria, who had introduced Hoffa to Dio at the 1952 Teamster convention:

Doria: "There is a misunderstanding as far as Jimmy is concerned."

Dio: "What is the misunderstanding?"

"Jimmy is still under the impression that everything is the way we left it with Beck, with the exception of the financing of the organizational drive. . . ."

"Now, the answer is this: That Jimmy was supposed to let me know."

"You haven't been able to get ahold of him?"

"I haven't tried."

"Well, you ought to try."

"Well, do you remember, he said he would like to be left alone."

"Don't worry about it because he is under a misapprehension on the whole thing."

The tone suggested the dynamics of the arrangement. The Mafiosi needed Hoffa's cooperation; he was the union boss even before he formally took over Beck's office. Hoffa on his part needed the authority and muscle of the gangsters. In labor rackets, as in the underworld generally, the Mafia retained the ultimate power of life and death—and the chilling respect that generated.

As the Kefauver committee had learned, and as the general public had then forgotten, the trail finally led to the Mafia. On November 13, 1957, with the McClellan committee winding up the second phase of its work, it heard testimony by Joseph Amato, a Mafia specialist from the Bureau of Narcotics. In passing, Amato mentioned that Vincent Squillante of New York's Teamster Local 813 belonged to the Mafia. Kennedy picked up the point: "Is there any organization such as the Mafia, or is that just the name given to the hierarchy in the Italian underworld?" "That is a big question to answer," Amato allowed. "But we believe that there does exist today in the United States a society, loosely organized, for the specific purpose of smuggling narcotics and committing other crimes. . . . It has its core in Italy and it is nationwide. In fact, international."

On the very next day, coincidentally, came the most compelling proof yet of the nationwide Mafia. The New York State Police raided a meeting at the rural home of Joseph Barbara in the small western New York town of Apalachin. The cops arrested fifty-eight gangsters, half of them immigrants, all Italian, mostly from the Northeast and Midwest, with others from points as distant as Florida, Texas, Colorado, California, and Cuba. Among the luminaries were four current and two future heads of New York City's five Mafia families. Perhaps fifty other Mafiosi escaped into the woods and back roads around the home. Among those who fled, but later were placed at or near the Apalachin meeting, were the boss of San Francisco (James Lanza), the missing fifth head of a New York family (Tommy Lucchese), and three other members of the national Mafia Commission (Sam Giancana of Chicago, Stefano Magaddino of Buffalo, and Joe Zerilli of Detroit). These five pushed the total to sixty-three embarrassed gangsters.

"Well, I hope you're satisfied," Giancana congratulated Magaddino afterward on a bugged telephone. "Sixty-three of our top guys made by the cops."

"I gotta admit you were right, Sam," Magaddino said. "It never would have happened in your place."

"You're fucking right it wouldn't," said the boss of Chicago. "This is the safest territory in the world for a big meet. We could have scattered you guys in my motels. We could've given you guys different cars from my auto agencies, and then we could have had the meet in one of my big restaurants. The cops don't bother us here."

Apalachin (pronounced "Apple-*ay*kin" by the local residents) was an intelligence breakthrough so massive and unprecedented that lawmen took years to absorb it and draw conclusions. Since 1931 the Mafia Commission had met every five years, in secret, with no such problems. The most recent meeting in 1956, also at Barbara's home in Apalachin, had passed calmly. There Joe Zerilli and Angelo Bruno of Philadelphia were added to the Commission, bringing it to nine members.

During the year since the 1956 meeting, though, the Mafia world had fallen into crisis: squabbles over making new soldiers, over conservative and liberal factions on the Commission, and over the imperial ambitions of Vito Genovese, who had replaced Frank Costello as boss of the Luciano family in 1955. Always suspicious of Costello's authority, perhaps jealous of his upper-world contacts, Genovese had him shot in May 1957. ("It was just uncalled for," Mickey Cohen said later. "See, nobody believed that they could shoot at the god.") Costello recovered and later invited his failed assassin to a conciliatory dinner at his home. Then in October, a scant three weeks before Apalachin, Albert Anastasia—who had taken over the Mangano family in 1951—was murdered and replaced by Carlo Gambino. The five New York families, so stable for twenty years, suddenly had new bosses and problems. Therefore Apalachin, a special Commission gathering within the usual five-year interval.

The next summer, the McClellan committee convened hearings just on Apalachin and the Mafia. It heard from Mafiologists eager to testify and Mafiosi not so eager. "I am a dress contractor," Tommy Lucchese explained before taking refuge in the Fifth. Kennedy submitted evidence of Genovese's wealth from his ex-wife's testimony at a separation hearing in 1952: his bulging safe-deposit boxes scattered around New York, New Jersey, and Europe; his interests in racetracks, gambling, greyhounds, water-front piers, nightclubs, union kickbacks, and the Italian lottery. Genovese, who had reported an income of only $6,881.72 in 1952, was understandably not a happy witness. "He was the only one that really frightened me," recalled Ruth Young Watt of the committee staff. "He had the coldest eyes. He would look right through you and just make chills."

The least plausible witness was John C. Montana of Buffalo, one of the Apalachin 58. A handsome, white-haired man, he looked rich, intelligent, and distinguished. He had no police record and was a prominent, respected citizen of Buffalo. He

owned the largest taxicab fleet in western New York, with a virtual
monopoly at the airport, train station, and better hotels. A former
member of the Buffalo City Council, a delegate to the state
constitutional convention in 1937, he had been named Man of the
Year by a local civic group in 1956. "I don't understand how you
got into this gang," Irving Ives, who also came from western New
York, told him at the hearings. "I have known nothing but good
of you until now."

His cover was blown. For decades he had been a high-ranking
member of the Magaddino Mafia family, at times second only to
Don Stefano himself. Born in Montedoro, Sicily—hometown of
many American Mafiosi—he had come to America in 1907 at the
age of fourteen. By the 1920s he was running with the Magaddinos; later, in the usual pattern of old bootleggers, he owned a
liquor-distributing firm with them. In 1931 he seconded Magaddino at a national Mafia meeting in Chicago. On the record,
though, Montana had managed to hide his underworld life.
Squirming before the McClellan committee, he explained his
presence at Barbara's home: he had been driving to a business
meeting in Philadelphia, had car trouble, and so had gone to see
his friend Barbara, who he knew employed good mechanics.
Montana was not believed. To compound this humiliation, the
Magaddinos then demoted him to a plain soldier in the family.
(When he died in 1964, the *New York Times* obit called him a Mafia
leader.)

Of the Apalachin 58, the committee was told, twenty-two were
involved in unions or labor-management relations, seventeen in
taverns, restaurants, or hotels, sixteen in the garment industry,
twelve in real estate, eleven in import-export businesses, eleven in
olive oil and cheese, ten in groceries, nine in vending machines
and in construction. "The testimony we have heard can leave no
doubt that there has been a concerted effort by members of the
American criminal syndicate to achieve legitimacy through association and control of labor unions and business firms," McClellan
concluded. "The criminal syndicate which we have identified here
as the Mafia has revealed an arrogant challenge to the government
and to the decent people of this country."

The hearings stretched on until the summer of 1959, mopping
up and filling in gaps. Over the next five years, ninety-six criminal
witnesses before the committee were convicted of various offenses.

Because of the hearings, Dave Beck was driven from the Teamsters, William E. Maloney from the Operating Engineers, Max Block from the Butchers, and James Cross from the Bakers union. Longy Zwillman, facing a committee subpoena, killed himself. Illegal gambling centers in Newport and Covington, Kentucky, run by the Cleveland syndicate, were shut down. Congress passed the Landrum-Griffin Act of 1959, which set standards for union elections and required unions to send regular financial reports to the Labor Department.

For Bobby Kennedy, the hearings established a fateful personal agenda. Jimmy Hoffa remained boss of the Teamsters, out of jail and brazen as ever. The Apalachin meeting, however awkward for the snared gangsters, hardly affected the Mafia's power and upperworld penetration. If not lethal to organized crime, the hearings did give Kennedy his first national fame. He impressed almost everyone, and that would not harm the presidential campaign he was about to direct. "We learned that he was fearless," noted Harry Anslinger of the narcotics bureau, "and we supplied him with all of the information he asked for concerning the big criminals. He used it wisely and the underworld had reason to hate and fear him when he became attorney general."

As for Joe Kennedy, at some point fatherly pride had overridden his objections, spoken and silent, to his son's racketbusting. Always conscious of public relations, he suggested that Bobby have a reporter ask Bobby Jr., then three years old, what his father was doing, and that the little boy should say his daddy, like a cowboy, was chasing bad guys. Another time, after finding Bobby still at ease in Hyannis Port on a Monday morning, Joe ordered him back to Washington. Occasionally the old man attended the hearings in person. "You knew when he was there," Ruth Young Watt observed. "Bob was a little keyed up, a little tense and so on. There was a strong paternal influence over all the Kennedys. He really was a strong, strong person."

Joe Kennedy's name unremarkably never came up at the hearings, but his influence probably did. Probing Teamster affairs in New York City, Bobby delved into a conspiracy among Hoffa, Johnny Dio, and Tony Ducks Corallo to install a stooge, Johnny O'Rourke, as the head of Teamster Joint Council 16. A veteran Teamster, connected in mysterious ways with Mickey Cohen and Frank Erickson, O'Rourke also knew Joe Kennedy. On August

15, 1957, when O'Rourke came before the committee, Bobby had been interrogating the previous witnesses, but then stepped aside. "He looks like a nice, pleasant Irishman," McClellan said of O'Rourke. "I believe he is going to tell us something directly." McClellan turned to Kennedy, who said nothing; after a pause, the assistant counsel picked up the questioning. O'Rourke pleaded the Fifth eighty-nine times. When he left, Kennedy came back and resumed his questions to the next witness. Afterward a rumor passed around town that William J. McCormack, the big boss of the New York waterfront, had called Joe Kennedy and asked him to have Bobby go easy on Johnny O'Rourke.

Maybe so. Given the range of the committee's curiosity and the range of Joe Kennedy's underworld friends, they logically would have intersected somewhere. The committee staff learned the old man owned a building on Fourteenth Street in New York that included the offices of several unions under investigation. The building superintendent, subpoenaed by the committee, replied, "I take my orders from the father, not the boys." Like anyone in the Kennedy circle, he knew where the power lay.

"I don't apologize," Jimmy Hoffa told a journalist at the time. "You take any industry and look at the problems they ran into while they were building up—how they did it, who they associated with, how they cut corners. The best example is Kennedy's old man." And later: "To hear Kennedy when he was grandstanding in front of the McClellan committee, you might have thought I was making as much out of the pension fund as the Kennedys made out of selling whiskey."

❧ ❧

"Senator Kennedy is a charming young man," said Eleanor Roosevelt late in 1958. "His father has been spending oodles of money all over the country and probably has a representative in every state by now. I realize that if you have done it for yourself, it is a perfectly permissible thing to do, but [only] if you really had organized it yourself."

❧ ❧

Lifting his son into the White House was the ultimate score by a lifelong gambler, the climax of his long haul up from East Boston. Joe Kennedy started working on it right after the 1956 election. Jack began with heavy burdens: his youth (the youngest President ever elected), his religion (the first Roman Catholic President), and his father's reputation (political and otherwise). "I'm not against the Pope," said Harry Truman in explaining his resistance to Kennedys. "I'm against the Pop." Yet the old man helped far more than he hurt. Calling in all his chips, Joe deployed the whole stupefying range of his personal contacts, spent uncounted millions of dollars, and led the cheers. "Jack," he told his boy in December 1959, "I'm willing to bet one million dollars today with the gamblers in Las Vegas that you'll win the nomination and election."

The candidate's Catholicism offended some parts of the electorate, but—a neglected point—it attracted others, notably the archaic Irish Catholic political bosses such as John M. Bailey of Connecticut, Richard Daley of Illinois, William J. Green and (eventually) David L. Lawrence of Pennsylvania, and Charles A. Buckley, Eugene Keogh, and Peter J. Crotty of New York. "He knew instinctively who the important people were," Keogh later said of Joe's efforts, "who the bosses behind the scenes were. From 1958 on he was in contact with them constantly by phone, presenting Jack's case, explaining and interpreting his son, working these bosses."

For the younger men around the candidate, the bosses called up unpleasant tintype images of graft and boodle, cigars and underworld connections. But the bosses still held key blocs of convention delegates, and Joe was best equipped by old ties and old ways to make deals with them. "He firmly believed that Jack's political affairs should have been handled by the same type of old Democratic pols who worked for Jim Farley and Ed Flynn on the Roosevelt campaign of 1932," according to Ken O'Donnell. "If Jack had known about some of the telephone calls his father made on his behalf to Tammany-type bosses during the 1960 campaign, Jack's hair would have turned white."

In New York State, the liberal Democrats had Eleanor Roosevelt and Herbert Lehman while the bosses had the power. Charles Buckley, who had succeeded Ed Flynn as boss of the Bronx in 1953, was a short, jowly, popeyed, old-fashioned dictator. A Bronx-bound member of Congress, he went down to Washington only to cast important votes. Joe Kennedy had known him for years. In April 1960, Peter Crotty of Buffalo became the first

Democratic county chairman in New York to endorse Kennedy. Arthur Schlesinger, Jr., the candidate's liberal conscience, fretted about such courting of what he called "the Buckley-Crotty crowd." No problem; at the Democratic convention, the bosses delivered 104½ of New York's 114 votes to Kennedy.

Billy Green, the Democratic boss of Philadelphia, son of a saloonkeeper, was acquitted in 1959 of fraud in a federal construction project. "I tried to get Billy Green with me," Jack Kennedy teased Schlesinger, "as I feel that if I had his support it would be an effective answer to your statement, 'The trouble with Kennedy is that he has no politicians with him.'" While Green came along readily, David Lawrence—the first Catholic governor of Pennsylvania—kept his cards hidden. (During the 1930s, Lawrence had twice been acquitted of contract and campaign fund violations.) In the winter of 1960, Joe Kennedy invited Lawrence down to Palm Beach. Lawrence declined, pleading legislative business, so Kennedy ingratiatingly came up to Harrisburg for a secret meeting at the Penn Harris Hotel. "Nobody was there," Lawrence recalled. "The papers never discovered it. I went down there and had lunch with him instead of at the mansion because the mansion would have been covered by newspapermen if they'd ever found out. Of course he couldn't understand why I wasn't for his boy, Jack. We had a very interesting lunch. He was very vigorous . . . very friendly, but very vigorous!" Lawrence came through later; at the convention Kennedy got sixty-four of Pennsylvania's eighty-one delegates.

In Chicago, Mayor Richard Daley owed Joe Kennedy a favor. Ever since buying Chicago's enormous Merchandise Mart in 1945, Kennedy had maintained an office and political connections in the city. Sargent Shriver, the Mart's manager, married Eunice Kennedy in 1953. One year later, Daley—then a county clerk—came to see Joe, hat in hand, at the Mart. He wanted to run for mayor. Kennedy asked a few questions about money and the likely opposition, then gave his imperial blessing. Daley left quickly, his heels beating a fast staccato as he hurried down the corridor. As 1960 approached, Jack Kennedy paid Mayor Daley brief, ceremonial visits while "the long, tough talks were between the mayor and Joe Kennedy," according to Sargent Shriver. Hizzoner came across with 59½ of his state's 69 votes at the convention.

While Joe worked the Irish Catholic bosses, the underworld approached the Kennedys through the old man's friend Frank Sinatra. In January 1960, Jack came to Sinatra's Sands casino in Las Vegas for a Rat Pack show by the cast of the movie *Ocean's Eleven*, then being shot on location. After the show, the group partied and discussed what they could do for Jack. "We got caught up completely in the Kennedy optimism," Sammy Davis, Jr., said later, "and it was an exciting time for all of us, especially Frank. It was very much Sinatra's baby, and he played it to the hilt." Sinatra recorded a campaign song—a variation of his hit "High Hopes"—and pulled strings in New Jersey, where his mother had lines to the Jersey City machine. Prodded by Joe, Sinatra arranged a secret meeting between the old man and Harold J. Gibbons, a Teamster vice president. The Teamsters need not fear the Kennedys, Joe told him: "I hardly hear the name Hoffa in our house any more."

On his own, or perhaps at someone's direction, Sinatra set up a dangerous tie between the presidential candidate and the Mafia boss of Chicago. On February 7, 1960, while sitting at Sinatra's private table at the Sands, Jack was introduced to Judy Campbell, a pretty young woman who ran in fast Hollywood and Las Vegas circles. As she told the story, they started having sex together one month later. Two or three weeks after that, Sinatra introduced her to Sam Giancana at the Fontainebleau hotel in Miami. Giancana courted her with elaborate gifts and favors, always generous and available, and did not press her for sex. Given her intimate connection to the candidate and (later) President, Giancana wanted her friendship more than her body. "When I think of it now," Campbell reflected years later, "I realize it was all too ideal, all too studied and planned." At the candidate's request, she set up meetings between Kennedy and Giancana in New York and Florida during the campaign.

For the crucial West Virginia primary in May, Sinatra provided equally private but more political services. Along with Giancana, he had bought a majority interest in the Cal-Neva Lodge, the underworld joint at Lake Tahoe so heavily patronized by Joe Kennedy. To manage it Sinatra brought out his crony Skinny D'Amato, who for years had been running the 500 Club, a mob-connected nightspot back in Atlantic City. The Kennedys needed a decisive victory in West Virginia to prove a Catholic could win a Protestant state; so the old man went low down. According to D'Amato, Joe Kennedy asked him to help out; D'Amato agreed, if the Kennedys would later allow the deported Mafioso Joe Adonis back in the country; Joe said sure. Moving around West Virginia, D'Amato spent an acknowledged $50,000—and probably more—from underworld sources. A New Jersey attorney, Angelo Melandra, dispensed other mob funds from Sinatra and his friends. The first meeting between Giancana and John Kennedy, on April 12, perhaps involved this issue. "I don't think elections should be bought," said Hubert Humphrey, the swamped opponent. "I can't afford to run through this state with a little black bag and a checkbook." Kennedy won thumpingly, 61 to 39 percent, and Humphrey dropped from the race.

The Democratic convention was held in Los Angeles in July. Kennedy had won all seven primaries he'd entered. Those delegates, with the three bossed states of New York, Illinois, and Pennsylvania that Joe Kennedy had pulled in, gave Jack over half the votes he needed for the nomination. On the way to California, Joe stopped in Nevada and put enough money on his son to swing the quoted betting odds in his favor.

The Kennedy forces settled into the Beverly Hills mansion of Joe's old friend Marion Davies. At one point Jack answered the phone and told Bobby that George Meany of the AFL-CIO wanted to come by. "You mean to see Dad?" Bobby asked. "No, to see me," said Jack, surprised that the most powerful labor leader was not dealing with his father. Sinatra wandered through the house, handing out drinks. Kennedy won on the first ballot and then appalled his camp by adding Lyndon Johnson to the ticket. Amid general gloom, the old man stood in the doorway of the Davies home, dressed in slippers and a smoking jacket, and said, "Don't worry, Jack, in two weeks they'll be saying it's the smartest thing you ever did."

And so to November. At the Cal-Neva, Ted Kennedy bet $25,000 on his brother. Four days before the election, Jack was scheduled to exhort a big crowd at the Chicago Stadium. "Get me a network," Mayor Daley told his press secretary, who went to see the old man at the Merchandise Mart. Kennedy wrote a check for $125,000, and the speech went nationwide.

It was the closest presidential election since 1916. The city machines of New York, Philadelphia, and Chicago came through.

In Philadelphia, Billy Green's turf, Kennedy's margin of 331,000 gave him the state by 116,000 votes. Sam Giancana's political organization in Cook County delivered by methods best not examined too closely. The mob wards (1, 25, 28, 29) and William Dawson's affiliated and equally corrupt black wards (2, 3, 4, 6, 20, 21, 24) gave Kennedy 80 percent of their votes and a margin of 165,667. The rest of Chicago went 60 percent for Kennedy, who won Illinois by fewer than 9,000 votes. Giancana could plausibly conclude that he—not Daley—had given the state to Kennedy.

Joe Kennedy's part in all this was, as always, well concealed. Through the campaign, father and son made no public appearances, were never even photographed together. "He's really had less to do with my campaign," said the candidate, "than any of the other members of my family." After the convention, Joe went to Europe for two months. Back home in September, he was asked if he was staying in touch with the campaign. "I read the papers," he admitted. He spent most of the fall in Hyannis Port, living alone except for the servants, trying to stay invisible.

In so close an election, many supporters could claim to have provided the crucial margin of victory. Because of Joe Kennedy, organized crime had helped elect a president: indirectly through the urban bossed machines, more directly through Sinatra, the West Virginia primary, and the syndicate wards of Chicago. Gangsters might self-servingly inflate their contribution. Their perception here, not the carefully analyzed reality, was what mattered. "Listen, honey," Giancana told Judy Campbell, "if it wasn't for me your boyfriend wouldn't even be in the White House." "Frank won Kennedy the election," Skinny D'Amato later said of his buddy Sinatra. "All the guys knew it." As they understood such exchanges, they had bought some consideration.

❦ ❦

Instead of favored treatment, they got Bobby Kennedy as attorney general. He had not sought the job. "I thought nepotism was a problem," he said later. "Secondly, I had been chasing bad men for three years and I didn't want to spend the rest of my life doing that." And furthermore, "I had been working with my brother for a long time and I thought maybe I'd like to go off by myself." Joe Kennedy whisked all these objections aside: he wanted Bobby in the cabinet, close to Jack and utterly loyal to his interests. "My father was very strongly in favor of me going as attorney general. He wouldn't hear of anything else," Bobby recalled. "I would never have been attorney general if it hadn't been for him ... nor my older brother wouldn't have been President." Jack went along with his father, and together they wore Bobby down. The old man had forced the next step on the road to Dallas.

The racketbuster from the McClellan committee went in with clear priorities. During the first year he steered five bills through Congress aimed at gambling and interstate flight by gangsters on the lam. He expanded the Justice Department's organized crime section from seventeen to sixty lawyers, and added field units in Chicago, New York, Los Angeles, and Miami. In the final year of the Eisenhower administration, Justice had indicted 49 gangsters; that increased year by year to 121, then 350, then 615 in 1963. Convictions went from 45 in 1960 to 73, then 138, and 288 in 1963. Most of these were tax cases, as Kennedy persuaded the IRS to shift major resources to underworld prosecutions. Because of his fraternal bond with the White House, he had the interdepartmental clout to badger law enforcement agencies from mutually suspicious cabinet departments into cooperating. "There was no question that I could do it because of my relationship [to the President]," Kennedy acknowledged. "They wouldn't have paid any attention to me otherwise."

For Harry Anslinger at the Bureau of Narcotics, the new administration vindicated his three decades as the federal government's resident—and often unheeded—Mafiologist. Over the years, Anslinger had assembled a thick black book with the names of eight hundred gangsters, in the United States and abroad, linked to the Mafia. "Many law enforcement officers have testified before congressional committees and have babbled to the press that no such thing existed," Anslinger noted. "In the meantime the Mafia thrived and the agents of the Bureau continued to bring in members who were engaged in narcotic trafficking, but we were at a standstill in our attempts to convince lawmen of the syndicate."

A few weeks after Kennedy took over the Justice Department, Anslinger brought him the Mafia book. Kennedy scanned it intensely, called in the chief of his organized crime section, gave him the book, and told him to get moving. For the next three years, Anslinger watched Kennedy follow through: reviewing cases, calling special meetings, moving around the country, remembering details, and pushing, always pushing. "The attorney general wasn't afraid to admit that there was an association of highly organized gangsters in the country, and he wasn't afraid to term this organization the Mafia," Anslinger concluded. "It was a revelation to me to see what a strong, courageous, and intelligent attorney general could do."

Presumably Anslinger allowed himself an uncharacteristic smile at the conversion of his old rivals, J. Edgar Hoover and the FBI. Until then, nothing—not the Kefauver committee, the McClellan committee, or Apalachin—had shaken Hoover's see-no-evil disbelief in the Mafia or a national underworld. In the early 1950s, two FBI agents had induced a Mafioso to talk; he told Mafia stories, the agents filed their reports, and nothing came of it. A few years later, Hoover formed a small group within the FBI specifically instructed "to determine and document the nonexistence of organized crime." After Apalachin, Kennedy as the McClellan counsel asked the FBI for files on the nabbed Mafiosi. The FBI had nothing on most of them while the Bureau of Narcotics knew them all. "The FBI didn't know anything, really, about these people who were the major gangsters in the United States," Kennedy said later. "And that was rather a shock to me." Hoover did let a subordinate assign nine agents to the subject. They produced a two-volume study that accepted the Mafia as real. Hoover buried it within the bureau by refusing to send copies to Anslinger or the Justice Department.

With Bobby now his boss, Hoover came around, grudgingly at first, then with all the zeal of a convert. "They started to get informants," Kennedy said of the FBI. "I asked them to go into it like they went into the Communist Party." The FBI made a list of thirty gangsters to receive special attention, among them Sam Giancana, Tommy Lucchese, and Joe Profaci. A secret, illegal campaign of electronic surveillance, begun after Apalachin, was vastly expanded. Wiretaps and bugs were planted at gangster homes and hangouts all around the country, with seventy-five to one hundred devices active at a given time. In Las Vegas alone, the FBI monitored twenty-five telephone lines to various mob casinos. Gangsters heard of these devices, to their general paranoia. "I need to get hold of a guy in Las Vegas," one New Jersey

Mafioso told another on a tapped line, "and how the hell am I going to get hold of him? They don't even want you to make a call there." "You can't call the state of Nevada," his friend insisted. "That's the orders."

Perhaps through these bugs and taps, the Kennedys learned more about the mob ties of their avid campaigner Frank Sinatra. As part of cracking down on organized crime, they then dumped Sinatra. In the summer of 1961, Joe Kennedy invited Sinatra and the Rat Pack to his summer home at Antibes on the French Riviera. After Bobby flew to Nice for a talk with his father, the old man announced that he had no room for Sinatra and his friends after all. For the record, Bobby had the Justice Department compile a nineteen-page confidential report documenting Sinatra's bonds with ten ranking hoodlums. Thereafter he was no longer welcome at the White House. Sinatra took it badly; aside from the simple ingratitude of the Kennedys after all his efforts, he had told his underworld cronies he could reach the administration for them. Multiply embarrassed, he applied a sledgehammer to the concrete landing pad, specially built for the presidential helicopter, at his Palm Springs home.

Before the election, before Sam Giancana helped carry Cook County so heavily, Bobby Kennedy had brought him to face the McClellan committee. For over a year the Mafioso had dodged a subpoena. He finally appeared in June 1959 and took the Fifth, leading to this testy exchange:

Kennedy: "Would you tell us anything about any of your operations or will you just giggle every time I ask you a question?"

"I decline to answer. . . ."

"I thought only little girls giggled, Mr. Giancana."

The election over, Kennedy resumed his pursuit. Giancana was bugged, tapped, and followed everywhere, even across a golf course. With the FBI listening in, Giancana discussed his problems with Johnny Roselli.

Roselli: "Between you and I, Frank saw Joe Kennedy three different times—Joe Kennedy, the father. He called him three times. . . ."

Giancana: "After all, if I'm taking somebody's money, I'm gonna make sure that this money is gonna do something, like, do you want it or don't you want it. If the money is accepted, maybe one of these days the guy will do me a favor. . . . The last time I talked to him [Sinatra] was at the hotel in Florida a month before he left, and he said, 'Don't worry about it. If I can't talk to the old man I'm gonna talk to the man.'. . ."

"He's got big ideas, Frank does, about being ambassador, or something. . . . They don't want him. They treat him like they treat a whore. You fuck them, you pay them, and they're through. . . . He's got it in his head that they're going to be faithful to him."

"In other words, then, the donation that was made. . . ."

"That's what I was talking about."

"In other words, if I ever get a speeding ticket, none of these fuckers would know me."

"You told that right, buddy."

The word passed through the underworld: double cross. "They used him [Sinatra] to help them raise money," Vinnie Teresa of Boston later said of the Kennedys. "Then they turn around and say they're great fighters against corruption. They criticize other people for being with mob guys. They're hypocrites." "Sam did a lot to help Kennedy get elected President with all that Teamster money," said a friend of Sinatra's. "He bought Cook County for Jack, and Frank could never understand why Jack Kennedy wouldn't accept Giancana as a friend. Frank thought if politicians can take the money they need to get elected, why can't they consent to take the friendship that goes along with the money." Skinny D'Amato reminded Joe Kennedy of his promise to help arrange the return of Joe Adonis from Italy. Joe reported that Jack was agreeable but Bobby was not, so no deal—and another offense to the underworld code.

Of all the hounded gangsters, Carlos Marcello of New Orleans had particular reasons to avenge himself on the Kennedys. Though relatively small (with only about fifty made members), New Orleans was the oldest and one of the richest, most stable Mafia families in the country, serenely bossed by only three men since the 1880s. Marcello, born in Tunis, North Africa, of Sicilian parents in 1910, had been brought to New Orleans as a baby. At nineteen he began to establish a criminal record, charged with robbery along with his father and one of his six criminal brothers. Later he served five years for armed robbery and ten months for selling twenty-three pounds of marijuana. After 1939 he stayed out of jail. By 1948, according to an IRS investigation, Marcello had interests in forty assorted businesses scattered around southern Louisiana. His shrimp boats brought in narcotics from Mexico and Central America. Local politicians and lawmen owed him favors. Based in Jefferson Parish, across the Mississippi from New Orleans, his power reached as far as Dallas. Joseph Civello, Marcello's underboss there, represented him at Apalachin.

"He is the head of the underworld in the southeastern part of the United States," Bobby Kennedy said of Marcello at the McClellan hearings in 1959. A year later, according to a Marcello associate, Bobby sent someone to ask Marcello's help with the Louisiana delegation at the convention. Marcello was committed to Lyndon Johnson. "Bobby was pissed off at Carlos," the associate said later, "and promised he'd get even."

Maybe; as attorney general, Kennedy did very quickly expedite a deportation order that had hung over Marcello since the Kefauver hearings. Not a U.S citizen, Marcello held only a dubious Guatemalan passport issued on a forged birth record. On April 4, 1961, Marcello came to the immigration office in New Orleans for his regular quarterly appointment. As he reached across a desk to sign a form, he was handcuffed and arrested. At once, with no lawyers or hearings, he was zipped to the airport, placed on a waiting Border Patrol airplane, and flown to Guatemala.

"They dumped me off in Guatemala," Marcello testified seventeen years later, still amazed and furious. "They just snatched me, and that is it, actually kidnapped me!" The local authorities were even less friendly. After a political explosion over the Mafioso's unwelcome presence, the Guatemalans deposited him in a village in the jungle of El Salvador. Salvadorian soldiers held and questioned him for five days, then shunted him across the border to Honduras, leaving him stranded on a mountain. Out of shape, not dressed or shod for the occasion, he walked seventeen miles to a village, falling three times, breaking two ribs. Finally the most feared man in Louisiana reached a coastal town and flew illegally back to New Orleans. He found an IRS tax lien for $835,396 awaiting him. The feds soon indicted him for illegal entry and for faking his Guatemalan birth record. Reeling from these assaults, his pride hurting more than his ribs, Marcello asked Sam Giancana to try to reach the administration through Sinatra and Joe Kennedy. Once again, it didn't help.

After his stroke in December 1961, Joe Kennedy was useless anyway. The stroke left him able to see, hear, and comprehend—but paralyzed on his right side and unable to speak or write. He could only say "no, no, no," occasionally an extended "NNNnnnooo!" Beyond that, he could not express himself. "Sometimes he could squeak a yes," according to his chauffeur, Frank Saunders, "and sometimes he'd use his good left hand and arm to make gestures and motion us. He tried to write with his left hand, to give us instructions and tell us what he wanted, but it frustrated him. I would see this look of fear creep into his eyes, and at times there would be something more fleeting in his eyes too—the look you can get from a wild caged animal. He was trapped, and he knew it." This man—so self-created, always so sure and commanding—spent the last eight years of his life without the simple power to make himself understood, as though in a dream, trying to cry out but mute. "He's the one who made all this possible," said Jack, "and look at him now." He could not warn his sons of dangers, could not—had he wanted to—intervene for the underworld. And organized crime no longer had to worry about his vengeance.

Even with Bobby hounding hoodlums, the Kennedys still took favors from the Mafia. (Kennedys made their own rules.) They continued an arrangement, begun in 1960, whereby the CIA hired Sam Giancana and Johnny Roselli to kill Fidel Castro for $150,000. During 1961, Judy Campbell carried mysterious, unmarked envelopes back and forth between her lover, the President, and Giancana and Roselli. "Don't worry," the President assured her. "Sam works for us." Although various plans failed or were delayed—the Mafiosi may have strung it out to exploit the contract—the Kennedys did not cancel the arrangement. At one point, in May 1962, the CIA even asked Bobby to let up on its hired guns. His mob prosecutions still went forward. While one hand tried to jail them, the other hand paid them to kill. "Here I am, helping the government," Roselli told an associate at the time, "helping my country, and that little son of a bitch is breaking my balls."

Double crosses on double crosses, and always the Kennedy Justice Department bearing down, the FBI listening in. *"Livarsi na petra di la scarpa!"* Carlos Marcello exploded (Take the stone from my shoe!). "Don't worry about that little Bobby son of a bitch," said Marcello. "He's going to be taken care of!" "Mark my word, this man Kennedy is in trouble, and he will get what is coming to him," said Santos Trafficante, boss of the Tampa Mafia. "Kennedy's not going to make it to the election. He is going to be hit." The FBI bugs and taps picked up other threats. "See what Kennedy done," said an associate of Angelo Bruno's in Philadelphia. "With Kennedy, a guy should take a knife, like one of them other guys, and stab and kill the fucker. . . . Somebody's got to get rid of this fucker." "Bob Kennedy won't stop today until he puts us all in jail all over the country," warned Mike Clemente of the Genovese family. "Until the Commission meets and puts its foot down, things will be at a standstill." "They know everything under the sun," said Stefano Magaddino of Buffalo. "They know who's back of it, they know Amici, they know Capodecina, they know there is a Commission." "They should kill the whole family," Peter Magaddino told his father Stefano, "the mother and father too!"

All this before the final provocation. Joe Valachi, the son of Neapolitan immigrants, was a Mafia soldier in New York for thirty years. Involved in at least thirty-three murders, he also stole, ran dope, owned racehorses, and traded in the black market during World War II. Vito Genovese was best man at his wedding. In June 1962, doing fifteen years at the Atlanta penitentiary on a narcotics rap, he became convinced he was marked for death as a suspected informer. Lashing out in fear, he killed another prisoner—his appointed murderer, he thought—but got the wrong man. To buy protection from the prison system, he started talking: the first Mafioso ever to sing at length, on the record, and finally in public.

The Bureau of Narcotics, which had put him in jail, had him first. "Before you knew it," recalled the narcotics agent Charles Siragusa, "Bobby Kennedy, because of his hatred of the mob, had completely taken possession of Valachi. Frankly, we were pretty upset about it, because Valachi was helping to make a number of our cases." Within the limits of his lowly perspective and his New York myopia, Valachi told what he knew: old unsolved murders and who had done them, the Commission, Apalachin, and the structure, evolution, folkways, and members of the five New York families. Some of it corroborated what the FBI already knew. Valachi's testimony, unlike evidence from the illegal bugs and taps, could be used in court, and he added many details, placing 289 individuals on the rosters of the five families. Valachi was blowing away *omertà*, the traditional code of silence that had generally protected the Mafia's inner workings. (Later on, Valachi told a jailmate "that Bobby Kennedy had promised he [Valachi] would get out of jail, but it was all a snow job.")

In the fall of 1963, Valachi was the star of televised hearings before McClellan's investigations subcommittee. (Just before the hearings, McClellan visited Valachi in jail and asked him not to mention Hot Springs.) The Valachi hearings began on September 25. One day later, the White House announced the itinerary of the President's trip to Dallas in November.

❧ ❧

Classic tragedy: the hero brought down by family, hubris, and the ramifications of his own success. Without Bobby Kennedy's unwearied pursuit of organized crime, and without Joe Kennedy's lifetime of underworld connections, Jack Kennedy would not have been hit. In that sense, brother killed brother, and father killed son.

❧ ❧

Jack Ruby, born of Polish Jewish immigrants in Chicago in 1911, had bumbled his way through a conventional underworld résumé: running errands for Al Capone as a teenager, then a racetrack and gambling in California, back to Chicago in 1937 for union racketeering and nightclub work. In 1947 the Capones sent him to Dallas to help their designs on dominating the rackets there. "Jack Ruby at that time was a 'small time peanut' with this group," as Sheriff Steve Guthrie remembered it. "Ruby's name came up on numerous occasions ... as being the person who would take over a very fabulous restaurant ... the upper floor would be used for gambling."

Ruby's big plans never turned out right. The Capones did not assume control, and Ruby was left not with a fancy gold mine of a restaurant-gambling den but with a string of tawdry strip joints. Not what he had in mind, but evidently he was given no choice. "Jack Ruby would sit at the table where I was seated," an acquaintance recalled, "and discuss how he was sent down here by 'them'—he always referred to 'them'—meaning the syndicate in Chicago. He always complained that if he had to be exiled, why couldn't he have been exiled to California or to Florida? Why to this hellhole Dallas?" Gangsters came to Ruby's clubs for meetings and to watch the strippers. "Whenever I wanted to find anyone from the syndicate," said Sheriff Guthrie, "I went to Ruby's Silver Spur." For the proprietor it was a small, dreary world of neon lights and G-strings, fistfights and minor arrests, and constant worries about money.

During the fall of 1963, though, he was working on something big. He met with Frank Caracci, an associate of Carlos Marcello's, in New Orleans, and with Johnny Roselli in Miami. Usually he made only twenty-five to thirty-five long-distance phone calls a month: but he placed seventy-five such calls in October, and ninety-six more in the first three and a half weeks of November. Some of these calls were with underworld figures linked to the Teamsters and the Capones. A few months earlier, he had been broke and owed $60,000 in taxes. Suddenly and mysteriously he came into money. He bought a safe, told his tax attorney he had a good connection, and was carrying $7,000 in cash on November 22.

At various times that autumn, Lee Harvey Oswald was seen with Ruby at his Carousel Club. He was a young man, only twenty-four, a ninth-grade dropout, of febrile and inchoate left-wing politics. Oswald had spent part of his fatherless childhood in New Orleans, where his uncle and substitute father Charles Murret worked for a gambling syndicate under the Marcello organization. In April 1963, Oswald returned to New Orleans and lived with Murret for a time. He went back to Dallas in October and took a job at the Texas School Book Depository. (Marcello had told an associate the best way to kill the President. Set up some unconnected "nut," he said, who could be manipulated to take the fall.)

On November 22: in Washington, Bobby Kennedy held a morning meeting on the department's efforts against organized crime in Chicago; that afternoon they were going to discuss specific actions aimed at Sam Giancana. In New Orleans, Carlos Marcello was acquitted by a jury of defrauding the government over his forged Guatemalan birth record. In Dallas, Jack Ruby went to place his regular nightclub ads at the advertising office of the *Dallas Morning News*. After the noon deadline, he hung around the office, sitting by a window on the second floor at the front of the building from which he could see out into Dealey Plaza, a few blocks away. At 12:30 he watched the motorcade drive toward the Texas School Book Depository and the Grassy Knoll.

❧ ❧

A best guess as to how they got away with it: Oswald, the patsy, was supposed to be killed as he was captured. A description of him, derived quickly and mysteriously from unknown sources, went over the police radio only fourteen minutes after the assassination. Oswald then might have died during his encounter with Patrolman J. D. Tippit, whom Oswald shot instead, or in gunplay when he was caught at the movie theater. But Oswald survived both occasions, and that left it up to Jack Ruby. Facing possible mob vengeance for botching this most significant, most potentially damaging murder contract, Ruby had no choice but to stalk Oswald. Attending the midnight press conference on November 22, Ruby stood at the back of the room. When the DA said Oswald belonged to the anti-Castro Free Cuba Committee, Ruby pointedly, revealingly corrected him: it was rather the pro-Castro, left-wing Fair Play for Cuba Committee. Then on Sunday, preferring to face legal justice over mob justice, expecting leniency for his patriotic act, Ruby finally silenced the patsy.

From that point, it became not a single underworld conspiracy but layers of upperworld conspiracies, overlapping and self-reinforcing, all needing to believe Oswald had acted alone. Key parties had something to hide: the CIA (its Mafia plots to kill Castro), the FBI (its sloppy investigation of Oswald, before and after the assassination), and Bobby Kennedy (his family's ties and debts to organized crime). The needs of national security and reassuring the public slammed a curtain down.

Hence the Warren Commission's laughably self-willed focus on Oswald as the lone assassin. In preliminary interviews for the commission, Ken O'Donnell told the FBI about hearing two shots from the fence above the Grassy Knoll. The FBI insisted that was impossible. "So I testified the way they wanted me to," O'Donnell later said in private. "I just didn't want to stir up any more pain and trouble for the family. . . . The family—everybody wanted this thing behind them."

The family. The cruel, teasing question is whether Bobby ever knew why his brother had been killed. If he did know, that would explain the family's remarkable silence ever after. Bobby wanted no investigation of the assassination, interfered with the Warren Commission, then endorsed its report without reading it, and later refused to speculate on Dallas theories with his own staff. Bobby, if anyone, should have pursued every lead to find and punish his brother's killers. Under a cover of dark, disabling grief, he did nothing, and so the family followed his example. "Even those of us close to the Kennedy household never witnessed a discussion regarding it," noted Joe Kennedy's nurse. "There was no open speculation either among the domestic staff, the professional personnel, or any members of the family. There was, however, an apparent dread in everyone, a jumpy nervousness."

Meantime the underworld, by contrast, relaxed in the wake of Dallas. During the nine months afterward that he lingered on as attorney general, Bobby never again met with the organized crime unit he had convened on November 22. He no longer pushed his furious crusade against the underworld, even seemed reluctant to think or talk about it. On April 13, 1964, he was interviewed for an oral history memoir to be deposited in the Kennedy Presidential Library. He mentioned "the day of the President's—on November 22nd" in passing. "Would you make a note," he said, "of we are to talk about the—I suppose we will anyway—November 22nd."

The interviewer, leaping across an awkward moment, moving unaware from the murder to its cause, suddenly switched subjects and asked about the Justice Department's efforts against organized crime. "Well, I don't know," said Kennedy, flinching. "Do you think there's anything really of—I made speeches about it and talked about it. I don't know whether there's any great—anything that I could really add on this." But he warmed to the topic, describing the new racketeering laws, the emphasis on underworld prosecutions, the increases in gangster indictments and convictions. "And so," he concluded, "it's made a helluva impact around the country." The zeal still flickered, but his brother was dead, and the Kennedy gangbusting campaign died with him. The mob had won.

NINE

AFTER DALLAS: PROSPERITY AND MAFIA CHIC

They murdered a president of the United States—the crime of the century—and they were not caught. As the final act in the Kennedy war on organized crime, Dallas was all too symptomatic.

Granted that the mob had absorbed casualties and lost skirmishes along the way. The FBI's bugs and taps did let lawmen inside private meetings and phone calls. Not realizing the extent of this electronic snooping, seeking explanations for spilled secrets, gangsters worried about traitors and stoolies among themselves. "We got to retrench ourselves," Mike Scandifia of the Gambino family told a colleague while lawmen listened in. "We had a meeting one time—who did you bring there? Who was he? Where was he born? How was he born? What is he doing right now? Every fucking friend should be screened. . . . I don't want to be bloodthirsty. Leave a couple of fucking heads hanging on a fucking pole. The stool pigeons that are flaunting it in our face, they'll think twice. They'll think fucking twice before going over to the law." The bugs and taps broke down the implicit trust cementing the underworld.

Nor did the federal effort against organized crime collapse after Robert Kennedy resigned as attorney general in the summer of 1964. During 1963, its most active year under Kennedy, the Justice Department tallied up 615 indictments and 288 convictions of mobsters. Over the next five years, Justice did even better, averaging an annual 929 indictments and 479 convictions—even though Kennedy's successors in the department did not make chasing gangsters a priority, as Kennedy had done.

But these prosecutions had no apparent impact on overall underworld operations. Serenely undiminished, gangsters kept killing and stealing, forever developing new scams, usually without interference by lawmen. "Almost nobody ever got caught," recalled Henry Hill, an associate of the Lucchese family during the 1960s. "That's what people from the outside don't understand. When you're doing different schemes, and everyone you know is doing these things, and nobody is getting caught, except by accident, you begin to get the message that maybe it's not so dangerous. And there were a million different schemes. You didn't have to sell swag or stick up anybody." Arrests were rare, convictions rarer, hard time rarer still. "None of them should ever happen," Hill added. "They are always more because of your own stupidity than any cop's smarts."

Lawmen did not have the statutory tools they needed. President Lyndon Johnson pulled out the FBI's underworld bugs and taps in 1965; they were illegal, after all, and inadmissible as court evidence. The feds still pressed all those mobster prosecutions, but they caught mostly small fish, random individuals, and could not affect the gangs as criminal enterprises. "Our principal problem is insulation," Bobby Kennedy had told the Valachi hearings. "The kingpins of the rackets—our main targets—are often far removed from their illegal activities. In fact, when we see that one of our subjects has become operational, we know he is no longer a kingpin." Kennedy hoped Valachi's testimony would shock Congress into passing new laws to allow legal wiretapping and immunity to witnesses in rackets cases.

Such legislation was not enacted until 1968 and 1970. Meanwhile the underworld was annoyed but not hindered, and the murderers of John Kennedy remained at large.

❧ ❧

It was now three decades since the end of Prohibition had sent bootleggers into other criminal lines. Gangsters never rested long enough to be examined and measured, and they filed no credible financial reports. All estimates of their total incomes were merely loose guesses. In general, though, since the 1930s their surest, richest moneymaker had been gambling: a blandly simple term taking in vast and complex empires of numbers games, card and dice games, sports betting and bookmaking, and the allied industry of loan sharking.

The numbers game—and its variant form, policy gambling—had begun in nineteenth-century black neighborhoods as a poor man's way of betting. (In Boston it was called nigger pool.) A bettor put down a nickel, dime, or quarter on a random three-digit number, the winner picked each day by lot or (more typically) from stock exchange reports in the newspaper. The bettor faced odds of 999 to 1 while the numbers banker paid off at odds between 450 to 1 and 650 to 1. The difference gave the bankers their profits. Black migrations from the South during the 1920s spread the game to most big northern cities. "The Negroes owned and controlled things to start," recalled the black jazzman Willie the Lion Smith, "but they cheated each other, and outsiders moved in to take over."

White outsiders, that is. The numbers and policy games were so popular—hitting a nickel bet meant a payoff of thirty dollars or so—that they moved beyond black ghettos. New York in the early 1930s had a hundred policy bankers in Harlem, but fifty more in lower Manhattan, a hundred in Brooklyn, and sixty in the Bronx, with an aggregate gross of $300,000 a day. In Chicago, around 350,000 bets each day yielded a monthly income to the bankers of a million dollars. With Prohibition ending, bootleggers barged into numbers through their usual persuasions of muscle and murder. Dutch Schultz controlled the games in New York until his demise in 1935, after which Trigger Mike Coppola and Fat Tony Salerno of the Luciano family took over. In Detroit, Philadelphia, Cleveland, and Boston the local Mafiosi had generally seized control of numbers gambling by 1940. The black bankers in Chicago held on longer, yielding to the Capone gang around 1950. In the usual underworld pattern, the Italian hoods took charge of enforcement and profits while Jewish associates, like Nig Rosen in Philadelphia, ran the business and counted the money. Blacks still often did the footwork, roaming a given territory each day to make collections and (rarely) payoffs.

The numbers runners and bankers were so numerous and visible that they could prosper only behind regular payoffs to lawmen. In Philadelphia during the 1950s, a patrolman in the twelve lucrative numbers districts could expect a hundred dollars a week; a police captain made a thousand. Busts were not encouraged. "If you do happen to bother these numbers men," according to one Philadelphia cop, "you are put on a beat where there ain't none. You are growled at right and left about it." The Italian bosses did their own policing. A black numbers boss in Detroit, Johnny White, ran a bank at the Gotham Hotel that took in $21 million a year. After complaints in 1962 that White would change the winning number if too many people hit it, his Mafia overlords, Pete Licavoli and Tony Giacalone, made him stop cheating the winners.

If the Mafiosi themselves wanted to cheat, though, that was different. Gangsters ran notoriously crooked high-stakes card and dice games in cities all around the country. The hoodlums in charge protected the games from interference by lawmen or free-lance thieves; and they raked in the profits, held the money, and approved the devices by which unaffiliated sheep were fleeced. The cards might be marked with white ink, or bleached, or scraped with a knife to vary the designs on the backs and identify their value. A bevel mark at a certain point on the edge would do the same, as would fine lines, spots, or curlicues. Luminous marked cards could be read only through tinted glasses. Stripper cards with trimmed edges were narrower or shorter in meaningful ways. A card mechanic with gifted hands could make the deck dance. A clip under the table would hold cards secretly removed from the deck. A cold deck previously arranged by the dealer might be deftly substituted for the deck in play. A holdout man could palm valuable cards, hold them, and bring them back into play at the right time. With low-belly strippers, a deck in which the edges of high cards were concave rather than straight, a cheat would cut a low card at will. A small mirror hidden in a ring, pipe, or matchbox might reflect card faces as they were dealt.

In dice games, the man in charge had similar advantages. Dice could be altered in many ways: rounded edges, bricks that were not true cubes, tops and busters with the wrong spots, peculiar angles on the edges, gaffed dice, dice loaded with weights, dice loaded with steel slugs played on a table with a concealed electromagnet. The man throwing the dice might use a soft surface, like a blanket, or "cackle" the dice by making them seem to rattle in the hand while they were actually held in a concealed finger grip. If a cup shook the dice, a polished inner surface could fix the roll. A whip shot could spin the dice from the hand onto the table with a flat motion that left the right numbers on top.

Racetrack bets depended on odds and quick information that could easily be fixed. Bookies might take comeback money from bettors and wager it themselves to change odds. If a bettor, on the other hand, learned a race's outcome sooner than a bookie, he might past-post a bet on known results. From a vantage point outside the track, someone with binoculars could watch the tote board for fast results to beat a bettor, or a bookie. In other situations, a "pitcher" inside the track might wigwag hand signals to a "catcher" on the outside. A crooked owner could hold back a good horse in several races, raising the odds against him, then let the hot horse win at the right time with long odds. Horses might be drugged to run faster or slower, and jockeys bribed or coerced. "Hell, you know, the races are fixed," explained Virginia Hill, Bugsy Siegel's last love.

The point of all these gambling frauds was to give the underworld an edge. Gangsters hated to play any game straight; it insulted their honor as thieves. The thrill of getting away with something added to the pleasure they took in their work. If the wrong people, such as made members of the Mafia, were cheated, that could mean dead scammers. But if average suckers were swindled at games that were already illegal, they had no recourse. They could not complain to the local police, who were probably bribed anyway, and the gangsters with muscle usually protected only their friends. So the legions of good, anonymous citizens who dallied with the underworld because they liked to gamble were routinely cheated.

To sharpen its edge in sports betting, organized crime poked into the management and ownership of horses, dogs, boxers, and big-time pro sports. The extent of these underworld intrusions was grossly underreported at the time. Gangsters always covered their bets: in New York in the late 1940s, Irving Cohen and other managers behind the boxer Rocky Graziano made regular cash payments to the city's sportswriters working fight beats. Again, a few years later, it was revealed that racetracks in Massachusetts paid off the local turf press, especially writers on the Hearst-owned *Boston Record* and *American*. Such arrangements helped deflect public curiosity about the steady underworld presence in boxing and racing.

That presence went back decades, back to when "sportsmen" and "sporting life" were euphemisms for gangsters and the underworld. When the major baseball, football, and basketball leagues were formed, "sportsmen" were there in every capacity. Among owners in the National Football League, Tim Mara of the New York Giants, Mickey McBride of the Cleveland Browns, Charlie Bidwill of the Chicago Cardinals, and Carroll Rosenbloom of the Baltimore Colts all had tight connections to bookmaking and criminal syndicates. Some of the best football players—Sammy Baugh in the 1940s, Bobby Layne in the 1950s, Paul Hornung in the 1960s—were known to bet on games and consort with hoodlums. With such ties, the underworld at least had inside betting information about crucial injuries and at best could arrange for shaving points and throwing games.

Owners and players came and went, though, and could not always deliver. The underworld's oldest, most reliable pipeline to big-time sports ran through Louie Jacobs and his sports concession companies, Sportservice and Emprise. From a humble base in popcorn and hot dogs, his veiled deals with gangsters made Jacobs the main man in the risky middle ground between legitimate sports and the underworld—and thus a key to sports betting. Louie Jacobs had been born on New York's Lower East Side, the son of a Polish Jewish immigrant who worked as a tailor. At the turn of the century the family moved to Buffalo, where little Louie sold peanuts at a ball park and popcorn at a burlesque house. During the 1920s he started dealing with both his worlds: he got his first big-league concession contract, for the Detroit Tigers, while he bankrolled rumrunning boats moving booze from Canada across Lake Erie into Buffalo.

Sportservice's concession business grew on an endless flow of favors by Jacobs. If a team owner needed money quickly, Jacobs delivered. He once saved Connie Mack of the Philadelphia Athletics with an interest-free loan of $250,000. "Jacobs money meant the difference between staying afloat and sinking for many a club," declared *Sporting News*, the bible of baseball. The loans came with implicit strings. At his height Jacobs sold the refreshments for two dozen major-league teams, as well as over fifty racetracks, various jai alai frontons, horse shows, golf tournaments, and the 1960 Olympics in Rome. It was a *large* business, with over seventy thousand employees in thirty-nine states and many subsidiaries and associated enterprises. The boss lived simply, never took a vacation, and never kept a personal bank account.

As a man swimming in two worlds, Jacobs attracted other amphibians. Bill Veeck, whose father had owned the Chicago Cubs, met Jacobs around 1940. The connection helped Veeck acquire control of three big-league baseball teams over the years. Veeck bought his first team, the Cleveland Indians, with a loan—arranged by Jacobs—of $150,000 from Sammy Haas, the main mob attorney in Cleveland. The money was laundered through several banks so it could not be traced to Haas. "I associated with a lot of hoodlums in Cleveland myself before I was through," Veeck said later. "I've always found the so-called hoodlums to be colorful people. And good customers of a ball club." Gamblers came to Veeck's ball park and passed wagering money around; Veeck asked them to keep the money out of plain sight. Happy Chandler, the commissioner of baseball, asked Veeck about his gangster friends. "You can tell me who to hire on my ball club," Veeck replied, "but you can't tell me who to sell tickets to." Veeck nonetheless kept his reputation as one of the most admired, inventive men in sports. On occasion he testified to the fine character of his friend Louie Jacobs.

Across the line and farther down, Jacobs cut deals and performed services for celebrated underworld names and associates as well: Raymond Patriarca at the Berkshire Downs track in Massachusetts, Joe Zerilli and Bill Tocco at the Hazel Park track outside Detroit, Anthony Zerilli at a Las Vegas casino, Tony Ducks Corallo in a slot machine deal, and, in other arrangements, the Capones in Chicago, Jerry Catena in New Jersey, Russell Bufalino in Pittsburgh, the Gambino family in New York, and Sam Tucker and Moe Dalitz in Cleveland. With utter impartiality, Jacobs would loan millions of dollars to ball club owners and to Mafiosi; it was all the same to him. "Anytime you want more than $3 million, give us 24 hours' notice," he told a potential partner. "Any less than that sum, we'll get you immediately." Raymond Patriarca, annoyed at losing $215,000 in Berkshire Downs, had an associate "tell Sportservice to OK an additional mortgage for $215,000" so Patriarca could get his money back. (Sportservice already held a large mortgage on the track and would surely protect its investment.)

Through Jacobs and his easily summoned favors, the underworld took on protective coloration, with lines into the highest levels of sports management. It may be assumed that these connections affected bookies and sports betting around the country. Jacobs was discreet, and he kept no incriminating records. Most of his underworld dealings went unnoticed. Few curious lawmen asked Jacobs about them. Devoted to work and to making money, he died at his desk at ten o'clock one evening in 1968. *Sporting News* said he belonged in the Baseball Hall of Fame. Bill Veeck served as a pallbearer.

Of all Louie Jacobs's underworld partners, Frankie Carbo—whose boxers Jacobs helped underwrite during the 1950s—had the most clout in a particular sport. As an expert gunman for the Lucchese family, Carbo was suspected in five crucial murders that notched the Italian ascendancy in organized crime: those of Mickey Duffy in 1931, Max Hassel and Max Greenberg in 1933, Big Greeney Greenberg in 1939, and Bugsy Siegel in 1947. In between hits, and a dozen arrests on other charges, Carbo followed boxing. "He did know a great deal about fighters," according to Bernie Glickman, a promoter in Chicago. "He knew a great deal about styles. He knew a great deal about, within a thousand dollars, of what a bout would draw in California or anywhere else. He was a student of boxing." Carbo's reputation as a killer eased his way into gyms. "Everybody was scared of him," said Nat Fleischer of *Ring* magazine, and no wonder.

Carbo and his fight-game sidekick, Blinky Palermo of Philadelphia, were both gambling men. While they may genuinely have loved the sweet science, they hung around boxing mainly to manipulate odds and outcomes. Palermo served sixty days on a numbers conviction in 1934. Once back on the street, he continued as a numbers boss in Philadelphia. Carbo also ran bookmaking and numbers operations and bet heavily on many sports. "I seen him watching the baseball game where he is crazy," said his associate Hymie the Mink Wallman. "I know he gambled on horses and everything."

Carbo and Palermo ensured the underworld its demanded edge in betting on the fights. The middleweight Jake LaMotta dumped a fight in 1947 after Carbo and Palermo called on him. Two years later, he was awarded a title fight and won it. The word went around: Frankie and Blinky might help a boxer's route upward. Ike Williams, a skilled lightweight without a manager, could not get bouts, couldn't even find sparring partners. So in 1947 he signed with Palermo ("I didn't know anything about the man's reputation"). He won his title seven months later. Over the next four years, as Williams told the story, Palermo four times passed along bribe offers of up to $100,000 to throw fights. Williams refused the offers and won all the bouts but the last. The boxer and the Mafioso parted company after Williams lost the title in 1951. "He robbed me of quite a bit of money," Williams said later.

"As far as bribes in fighting are concerned, 'payola' offers for throwing a bout come your way all the time," the middleweight Rocky Graziano admitted in 1955. "If you reported each and every one, not only would the cops laugh you outa the station house, but you wouldn't have no time to train." Sugar Ray Robinson, the most gifted boxer of his era, had no formal ties to Carbo. But just before his title bout with LaMotta in 1951, Robinson got a phone call from Frankie. ("When the man known as Mr. Carbo wanted to see somebody," said Robinson, "it was a command performance.") Claiming to represent LaMotta, Carbo offered a three-fight deal: Robinson to win the first, LaMotta the second, with the third on the level. Robinson declined and won the championship belt.

A year later, just before a fight in Chicago with Graziano for which Robinson was a three-to-one favorite, Robinson was summoned by the top Chicago Mafia boss (unidentified by Robinson). The Mafioso proposed a similar scam: a million dollars for the favored Robinson to lose the first fight, giving the underworld a betting bonanza, with Graziano to lose the rematch, setting up a third, legitimate fight. No, said Robinson. "No hard feelings," said the Mafioso. Years later, in retirement, Robinson did acknowledge "carrying" overmatched opponents, intentionally not knocking them out so the fights would last longer than most bettors expected. "I never considered it morally wrong," Robinson insisted. "I'm sure some guys in the know made some money betting on an opponent going the distance with me, but ... my responsibility wasn't to the bettors, it was to the spectators." By this punch-drunk logic, Robinson squared his conscience while the underworld honed its edge.

From 1953 on, Carbo lurked behind the respectable front of the International Boxing Club and its respectable president, James D. Norris. For decades Norris and his father had owned sports teams and arenas, notably Madison Square Garden in New York. Aside from running racehorses, and a peculiar friendship with Golf Bag Hunt of the Capones, the younger Norris had no underworld history. To keep Madison Square Garden profitable, though, he needed prizefights. "My father . . . was very much against my going into boxing," Norris later claimed, "but he did understand that we had a big investment in Madison Square Garden, and someone ought to protect it." After his father died in 1952, the son meandered toward Carbo, a lamb to the slaughter.

Norris struck deals with NBC and CBS to telecast weekly Wednesday and Friday night fights from the Garden. To fill his cards he needed many boxers, more than he could find: "I was floundering and afraid I was going to blow my contracts. I was having a great deal of trouble with the managers, with the lack of talent coming up, and I was grasping at straws." So he talked to Frankie Carbo. "Mr. Carbo had been there many years before I," Norris pointed out. "I didn't bring him in the business. . . . He knew everybody, and I think everybody sort of looked upon him as knowing a great deal about boxing. He had done them favors and he had a great acquaintanceship."

Once Norris added Carbo's girlfriend to his payroll, his problems vanished. The key promoters, managers, and matchmakers around the country—all tied to Carbo—sent boxers to New York for the IBC's televised fights. With that leverage, Norris and "Mr. Gray," as Carbo was known, monopolized boxing as completely as Mike Jacobs had during the hegemony of Joe Louis. "Carbo and Norris had a vice-like grip around the neck of boxing and were strangling it to death," recalled Angelo Dundee, a manager outside the monopoly. "So if you were in boxing, somewhere along the line you had to do business with them."

Anyone who defied the monopoly courted underworld revenge. Ray Arcel, a trainer who had worked for champions, arranged yet a third TV deal, for Saturday night fights—but without going through Carbo, an act of reckless independence. His belief in free enterprise nearly got Arcel killed. One night, after a renegade match at the Boston Garden, Arcel was beaten over the head with a lead pipe in the presence of many eyewitnesses. "They used a couple kids from Boston to do it," a Carbo associate later explained. The local police made no arrests and quickly dropped the case. Arcel's TV deal soon collapsed.

As always, the rich heavyweight division was the boxing prize most coveted by the underworld. Between 1951 and 1964, mobsters controlled three of the five heavyweight champions. Jersey Joe Walcott was managed by Felix Bocchicchio, an ex-con with deep bonds to organized crime in Philadelphia and Camden, New Jersey. In 1952 Rocky Marciano knocked Walcott out for the title. Marciano was managed by Al Weill, a matchmaker at Madison Square Garden. "I was lucky enough to have a manager who protected me from all outside influences," Marciano later said on the record. "Al Weill was the boss as far as I was concerned, and I sort of took orders from him." In turn, Weill—"a boxing politician who held hands with the mob," according to his rival Teddy Brenner—took orders from the omnipresent Carbo. "He's very close with Gray [Carbo]," said a Carbo associate, Honest Bill Daly, in a bugged conversation. "Weill is. Very close. . . . He pays off like a [bleeping] slot machine. . . . If he has a fighter, he gets a crack at the title right away." Later on, after he retired undefeated in 1956, Marciano confided that he had been forced to give half his earnings to the underworld.

For six years, while Floyd Patterson and Ingemar Johansson held the title, the mob grip on the heavyweights loosened—though not completely. Al Weill promoted one of Patterson's fights in 1958. And in June 1959, when the promoter of the first Patterson-Johansson bout needed money, Patterson's management arranged for the publicity costs to be borne by Fat Tony Salerno of the Genovese family. In return, Salerno got one third of the proceeds.

Carbo retrieved the heavyweight title in September 1962 when Sonny Liston unexpectedly flattened Patterson in one round. A glowering block of muscle, testy and explosive, Liston had graduated from a reformatory and a penitentiary. As a fighter he was owned by Carbo, Palermo, and John Vitale, a gangster from Liston's hometown of St. Louis. When Liston again disposed of Patterson in one round in the rematch, it appeared he would hold the title for years. In February 1964 he was matched against Cassius Clay, as he was then known, a lightly regarded loudmouth. Oddsmakers established Liston as a prohibitive seven-to-one favorite.

The odds invited a fix. Just before the fight, Patsy Lepera—a scam man in the mob town of Reading, Pennsylvania—heard from Felix Bocchicchio's nephew that everything was arranged.

Lepera put $25,000 on Clay and watched the fight on TV. At the start of the seventh round, an apparently undamaged Liston refused to leave his stool. "This guy didn't just take a dive—he did a one and a half off the high board," Lepera recalled. "It was so bad I figured we blew everything. But no, everybody got paid off. We had to give up 40 percent for the information. I come out with $75,000." No doubt Frankie Carbo and many of his friends also made killings that night.

❦ ❦

"Gambling is the standby and the foundation," said Vinnie Teresa in 1971 after forsaking the Boston underworld. "From it comes the corrupt politicians and policemen, the bribes and the payoffs, and sometimes murder. If you could crush gambling, you would put the mob out of business."

❦ ❦

Most of the suckers who gambled with the underworld wound up losing. They could not consistently beat the gangster edge. In losing they would then compound their problems by turning to loan sharks: the vultures, parasites, and enforcers of underworld gambling. "You find most loan sharks hanging around crap games, gambling parlors, the private clubs that usually house the poker games and other games," said a client of a Mafia loan shark ring in New York. "They make it known that they have money to loan at high interest rates. What usually happens is that a person who wants to borrow money has to give his marker, and his marker states that when he borrows the money he will pay it back in a certain amount of time. . . . Most loan sharks only accept one or two markers. If the money isn't paid by that time, the whole operation is then handed over to the enforcement part of the organization and they begin to take action."

It was a rough yet elegant operation, meshed and self-reinforcing. The gambling bosses, with huge cash profits that could not be legitimately invested, put the money back on the street by loaning it to sharks at, say, 2 percent a week. Losing gamblers would then borrow from the sharks at 5 percent or more a week. Desperate for money, the suckers would gamble more, lose more, borrow more, in a tightening spiral that could squeeze a man beyond his endurance. Under such pressures, honest suckers might then disclose useful inside information that led to other crimes by their underworld owners. In short order, an upperworld citizen who just liked poker or craps could become an accomplice in major crimes, if he cooperated, or dead if he did not.

By some criteria, loan sharks had the best jobs in organized crime. They needed no office or extensive, incriminating records, no regular employees or overhead, no special equipment or skills. A shark ran his affairs out of his wallet and memory. He met his pigeons in gambling dens, bars, nightclubs, restaurants, union halls, racetracks, boxing arenas—the usual underworld places of business. Unlike other gangsters, he left behind no special tools or evidence beyond the unmarked cash in which he dealt. Seldom bothered by lawmen, he had no need to bribe them. "I have never heard of there being any kind of payoff of any nature to anyone in the criminal justice system in order to run a loan shark operation," said Ralph Salerno, an organized crime expert with the New York police, in 1968. "Arrests, convictions, and jails almost never happen in the area of loan sharks. . . . It may not equal gambling in dollar volume, but on the bottom line, net profit as to risk, loan sharking is a much better business than is gambling."

Repeating the familiar pattern, reformers had outlawed usurious loans and so—like boxing, racing, booze, and the bookie wire—had driven the enterprise down to the underworld. Early in the twentieth century, "salary lending" by shady businesses had forced employees to accept high interest rates or risk losing their jobs. A reform movement under the Russell Sage Foundation abolished salary lending, state by state, through limiting interest rates and licensing small lenders. So the underworld in the 1920s began to lend money.

Evidently "shark" as a term for the practice was a vernacular corruption of "Shylock," Shakespeare's Jewish moneylender in *The Merchant of Venice;* "shark" then became "loan shark," precisely descriptive. For centuries, some Jews had practiced usury on the fringes of the Gentile world. Italian gangsters in the United States at first scorned the practice as unworthy, beneath them, but then began to take it over as part of the Italian ascendancy in organized crime. Early in 1937, Thomas E. Dewey's office arrested nearly one hundred sharks in New York; they were mostly eastern European Jews and (already) Italians.

The "juice racket" in Chicago, as it was known there, was not well organized until after World War II. Before then, according to Charles Siragusa, "only disreputable thugs, petty pickpockets, and those at the very bottom of the underworld ladder would even stoop to becoming Shylocks." Money overrode ethics. Of obvious potential as an earner, sharking was upgraded in Chicago, just as in New York and elsewhere. Sam DeStefano, raised in Sam Giancana's 42 Gang on the near West Side, consolidated the local sharks for the Capones. DeStefano earned so much money for his Mafia bosses that—despite his base in a once-deplored "Jewish" business—he achieved the rare social status of playing regular gin rummy games on Sunday mornings at Tony Accardo's suburban home.

Some West Side bookies started switching to loan sharking as a richer, more predictable way to earn a living. The penalty for misconduct, though, remained conventionally harsh. One juice collector in Chicago, Action Jackson, failed to meet his weekly payments and withheld his collections. Jackson, a large man, was impaled through the rectum on a meathook in the basement of a restaurant. While he hung there, writhing, a piece of his buttocks was sliced off. After being stabbed many times with ice picks and burned with an acetylene torch, Jackson mercifully died from shock. The juice business in Chicago perhaps ran more smoothly for a while.

In 1964, according to one study by lawmen, the five Mafia families in New York included at least 121 loan sharks. The Genovese family (fifty-one sharks) and Gambino family (thirty-seven sharks) were most heavily involved. Nick Forlano, a Profaci capo, and his partner Ruby Stein ran the single most ambitious loan operation in the city, with up to $5 million on the street at a given time. (Stein was the real brains behind Forlano, said Joe Valachi, "although he [Forlano] does not let them [his Mafia associates] know.") If any free-lance shark tried to practice without Mafia protection and enforcement, he risked—at best—not collecting on his loans. Henry Hill, tied to Paul Vario's crew in the Lucchese family, took over the debts of a horse-playing restaurateur in exchange for the sucker's restaurant. "I knew some of the guys he owed, and they weren't very strong," Hill recalled. "They didn't have the weight. So I knew I wouldn't have to pay. I just strong-armed them out of the money—and who could they go to? If you were with Paulie and our crew, you could tell most of the city's half-assed wiseguys to get lost. I made them eat the debts."

Like any underworld enterprise, loan sharking depended finally on who had the muscle. "The only thing a Shylock has is his reputation," said Gary Bowdach, a shark in Miami who later testified for the law. "If you show weakness, nobody is going to pay you. You have got to make it understood by the other people." That understanding could only come from demonstrations and object lessons like Action Jackson. "There is one thing a loan shark has to have if he's going to be a success," agreed Vinnie Teresa, reflecting on his career in the field. "He's got to have big culonies [balls]. You have to show you are afraid of no one, even if you are. . . . It don't take just guts. You got to be scared—afraid that if you don't do it you're out of business. No one will take advantage of you then. They won't say: 'He's got no balls. Fuck him.' So it's fear and courage that make you go in and do what you have to do."

From its mother lode in gambling, loan sharking spread toward the upperworld. Any good citizen, if desperate enough for money and spurned by legal lenders, might turn to the sharks. A corrupted loan officer at a bank could pass along referrals of rejected applicants. Gary Bowdach dealt mainly with car salesmen and their eager customers, willing to pay interest at 7 percent a week for the cars they craved. Jack, a businessman in New York, first borrowed $3,500 from a shark to meet his small company's bills. When the business failed, and Jack got in deeper to another shark, the matter went to Dom, a Mafia enforcer. Jack in desperation told the police and let them bug his room before Dom came to collect. With lawmen next door listening in, Dom looked for evidence of a bug.

Jack: "You won't find one. You won't find one. That's all I got to say. . . . Look, I can't take any more of this. . . ."

Dom: "What you fucking around with the guy for? Grab eighteen hundred? You ain't even a fucking man, do you know that? You ain't even a man. . . ."

"I'm not giving no money any more, Dominic. I'm not going to give any money. I can't. I'm going away. I'm taking off. I'm leaving. . . ."

"Am I shaking you down in other words you're telling me? Am I shaking you down?"

"Well, aren't you? Aren't you?"

"You say I'm shaking you down? I'm shaking you down? I'll bust your fucking mouth. I'm shaking you down. You prick. I'm shaking you down?"

"Look, Dom, cut it out now."

"Cut it out? What you mean, cut it out? You made a fucking patsy out of me, you cunt. . . ."

"I'm leaving town one way or another. [Sounds of Dom assaulting Jack] I've just had it, Dominic. That's all. I've just had it. I can't pay any more. . . . You're not going to accomplish nothing by beating me up. You know that. . . ."

(Pause while Dom telephones for instructions; after a while the phone rings, Dom talks on it briefly, then hangs up.)

"I say you owe me three fucking hundred. Now I want my fucking money. [Sounds of Dom assaulting Jack] Or I'll put you down the fucking hill. Give it to me. Give it to me."

"I don't have it. [Sounds of Dom assaulting Jack] Owwwwww. . . . I'm not going to—I'm not going to take this any more [Sounds of Dom assaulting Jack]." At last, and none too soon as far as Jack was concerned, the cops broke down the door and put Dom against the wall.

By the late 1960s, some lawmen were guessing that loan sharking had become the underworld's second most productive scam, yielding income levels surpassed only by gambling and betting. No longer scorned, it had become a functionally integrated part of organized crime in most cities.

❦ ❦

Coming up fast, lethally enticing, narcotics would eventually blow apart given arrangements in organized crime. Big-time junk pushers never bothered much with marijuana deals, bulky and low-profit. They preferred the compact, high-profit killers: opium, heroin, morphine, cocaine. Different from any other gangster enterprise, these drugs were the wildest of wild cards, deranging for everyone involved, with peculiar, unpredictable powers of their own. From the 1960s on, as consumer demand in the United States for harder drugs kept building, the underworld got in ever deeper, both dealing and using. It was a fateful bargain, offering big money in the short run at the ultimate price of cohesion, security, and organization. No less than any street addict, gangsters in the end paid dearly for their high.

None of this was obvious in the 1960s. At that time, outsiders and lawmen saw drugs as just another mob scam, based in a classic pattern of underworld ethnic succession. In the beginning, back in Prohibition, Jewish gangsters had dominated narcotics: Arnold Rothstein and Waxey Gordon in New York, Charlie Solomon in Boston, the Purple Gang in Detroit, and others. As these dealers were jailed or killed by business rivals, other Jews—Lepke Buchalter, Saul Gelb, and Mendy Weiss of New York, Nig Rosen of Philadelphia, Happy Meltzer of Los Angeles, Wady David of Boston—took their places, to be jailed or killed in turn. By 1950, Mafia families around the country generally controlled the importing and distribution of hard drugs to American addicts.

From his exile in Naples, Charlie Lucky Luciano directed this dangerous embrace of narcotics by the American Mafia. In 1936 Thomas E. Dewey had sent Luciano to jail on concocted charges of compulsory prostitution; almost ten years later, still on the case, Dewey as governor of New York commuted the sentence on condition that Luciano be deported to the country of his birth. As Dewey told the story, he let Luciano out because the Mafioso—from prison—had assisted wartime security and union cooperation in the war effort along the New York waterfront. ("You go up and mention my name," Luciano had instructed an associate, Socks Lanza, "and in the meantime I will have word out and you won't have no difficulties. . . . Go and see Frank [Costello] and let Frank help along, this is a good cause.") For his part, Luciano later told his friends conflicting versions of why Dewey had released him: a guilty conscience on Dewey's part over what he knew was a false conviction; or because Luciano's friends in New York had blackmailed Dewey with mysterious, incriminating information about Dewey or someone close to him; or because Dewey had simply been bribed with $500,000 delivered to one of his associates. For whatever reason—probably for several of these reasons—Luciano was exiled to Naples, where he operated a restaurant, the San Francisco Bar and Grill, that catered to American tourists. Apparently unemployed, Luciano sat in his bar, signing autographs and greeting visitors from home, yearning to return to America.

According to Harry Anslinger and his federal Bureau of Narcotics, many of those American visitors came to Luciano on narcotics missions. Luciano had a long drug history, starting with his first arrest, at eighteen, for heroin possession. As a young thug he also smoked opium, sold heroin, and went to Europe in 1930 to arrange a narcotics shipment from Paris. Once settled into his Neapolitan exile after the war, Luciano mediated among corrupt Italian officials and those American Mafia families—especially the Lucchese and Genovese gangs in New York—most involved in drugs, arranging shipments from sources in France and the Near East. "Luciano is uncannily shrewd in avoiding entangling evidence," Anslinger allowed in begrudged admiration. "He talks to his relatives and intimates on the beach, away from casual listeners, and he avoids any open statements. He leaves no trace because there is no trace. And still we know he is the man."

Anslinger could not nail him, but neither could Luciano escape the narcotics bureau's relentless attention. When Luciano surfaced in Havana in 1947 to gamble at the mob casinos and meet with American gangsters, Anslinger smoked him out and got him expelled by Cuban authorities. "That son of a bitch Ass-slinger," Luciano complained in the presence of an American undercover agent, Salvatore Vizzini, "you cannot tell where any of his men are going to pop up. When Russia lands a man on the moon one of Ass-slinger's narcotic boys will be there to search him when he gets off his ship." Luciano's companions laughed at this remark; Charlie Lucky did not.

Early in 1953, Luciano sent a beseeching letter, laboriously handwritten, to his old friend Dewey, still governor of New York. "I hope you dont mind the way this letter is written," Luciano apologized, "and also that I am writing to you, it is the best I can do, and also my only hopes for some relief. . . . They dont want to let up, the agents that Anslinger has here are stooping to everything to get me. I wish you would take some interest in this matter, because I never gave it a thought in going into the dope busines, direct or indirect, and if it wasn't so I wouldn't be writing to you. If you dont believe me I make a sujestion, and that is to have the Attorney General appoint one investigator to investigate the Narcotic Division there and all the European Interpol, including me. I have another sujestion if you want to. I could send direct to you my side of the story, of what I know, which I would like it much better. Governor, since I left the U. S. A. I haven't had a day in peace, and there isn't any let up in sight. If you dont want to do it for me, please do it for yourself, that you didn't let out of jail an international dope smugler. That great power that the Narcotic Division has, is in the wrong hands." Evidently Anslinger's agents were coming close enough to worry Luciano. Nothing came of the letter to Dewey, and Luciano lived out his days in exile. "Just six months, that's all I want," he told Sal Vizzini, "three months in New York and three months in Miami, then they could bury me, I would be satisfied."

Slowly and inexorably, amid internal debates, the Mafia got hooked on its own drug problem. Even while Luciano was arranging dope deals from Italy, the head of Charlie Lucky's own family in America, Frank Costello, had ordered his men not to handle narcotics. Drugs were still exotic, outside the familiar nexus of gambling–betting–loan sharking, and more difficult for the public to dismiss as just another harmless, unfairly outlawed amusement. Drugs also brought special heat from the law, especially from the dread Anslinger and his undercover agents. For these practical reasons, not from any pathetic wisps of moral outrage, Costello tried to stop the Mafia drug traffic. Not even Costello, with his peerless underworld name, could do it.

Officially, on the record, the Mafia Commission went along with Costello. "You are in serious trouble if you were arrested for narcotics," Joe Valachi testified. "After Anastasia died in 1957, all families were notified—no narcotics." Some families cooperated. The Chicago gang even paid troublesome soldiers $200 a week not to deal drugs; Paul Ricca, whose son was an addict, had personal reasons to fear dope. As admonishing examples, a few Capone members were killed for defying the ban in Chicago.

But the Mafia, no less than the American upperworld, could not resist drugs. Valachi and his boss, Vito Genovese, died in prison after narcotics convictions. The families in Tampa and Kansas City had traded in dope for decades, and the Commission could not now stop them. (Individual families always guarded their local autonomy from the Commission.) John Priziola of the Detroit family dominated heroin trafficking in his city. In New York, the Gambino family split on the issue, as a faction under Aniello Dellacroce brushed aside the aging Don Carlo's resistance to the drug trade. For many families, again as in the upperworld, it became a generational issue. Older men had their traditional sources of income; younger men, looking for easy scores, saw dope dealing as a quick way upward. "It was too profitable," a crooked mob attorney named Martin Light said later. "There was too much money involved."

It was dirty money, the dirtiest kind of money. By contrast, the traditional underworld businesses of gambling, stealing, extortion, union rackets, and political corruption seldom killed outsiders directly and inevitably. Drugs were more dangerous. Some big-time gangsters got hooked on drugs themselves. When Waxey Gordon, a heroin addict, was arrested for the last time in 1951, he fell to his hands and knees and begged the narcotics agent to shoot him right there, preferring death to facing withdrawal in jail.

Even criminals who did not sell or use drugs had to put up with harmful incidental consequences spilling over into their own businesses. "I wouldn't put out any money even at 15% now because operating costs are so high," said one Mafia loan shark in Brooklyn around 1969. "Half the guys who borrow are on dope and no matter what you do, they aren't going to pay you back because they end up on Rikers Island or getting shot by the cops." Twenty years later, such problems would seem mild indeed. The beast had escaped and the underworld was going to suffer too: a rough kind of justice.

❧ ❧

For the time being, organized crime boomed along, spreading and prospering, menaced mainly by the specter of Joe Valachi. At least a year before his public testimony, the underworld knew Valachi was singing in private to the feds. "I hear he's talking like a bastard," Angelo De Carlo of Newark told an associate. "He must have known something about this thing?" As Valachi was moved around for his safety, the mob traced him to New York, then to Washington. The day before he finished testifying to the McClellan committee, the FBI received an anonymous phone call: an illegal Italian alien, posing as a photographer, was going to place a bomb in the hearing room, set to explode sixty seconds later. The FBI tightened its security that day, and no bomb appeared. "Vito [Genovese] should have killed Valachi," growled Stefano Magaddino of Buffalo. "He talks too much. He's gonna get himself killed for that." The underworld put an open contract on Valachi, offering $100,000—later $250,000—to anyone who could hit him.

At the hearings, John McClellan asked Valachi why he was talking. "To destroy them," he replied. "They have been very bad to the soldiers and they have been thinking for themselves, all through the years." Ever the gangster, keeping his cards hidden, Valachi had less noble motives as well. If he had not cooperated fully, the feds would not have kept him in protective custody—and somebody could have collected on his contract. Valachi also nursed the lifelong resentments of a humble soldier ("They never gave me nothing") not allowed to rise in the Genovese family structure. "Lieutenants automatically make money," he explained. "They have a hundred percent edge over the soldier. The soldier has to do it, himself, whereas the lieutenant, they bring it to him." At the end of his small-time career, Valachi finally struck back at the bosses who had overlooked him.

From whatever motives, this otherwise insignificant button man did get his revenge. As Sam Giancana observed at the time, even if Valachi's testimony sent no one to jail, its worst damage was simple publicity. By talking so openly about the Mafia—or the Cosa Nostra, as he called it—by naming names and telling stories, Valachi raised the subject to an unprecedented level of public attention. That would eventually prod the curiosity of politicians and lawmen. The Mafia throve in darkness and silence, and Valachi put that at risk. During the ten years before the Valachi hearings, the *New York Times* had mentioned the Mafia only about once every three months. In the ten years after Valachi, the *Times* on average brought up the Mafia every other day. Gangsters squirmed.

For decades Americans had shown an intermittent fascination with organized crime. The main change in public perception during the 1960s was a narrowed focus on the Italian crime families at the heart of the underworld. (Harry Anslinger, retired in 1962, might have nodded grimly.) A presidential commission in 1967, following Valachi's lead, described twenty-four Mafia families around the country with formal memberships ranging from twenty to eight hundred men, reinforced by thousands of unmade associates outside the organization itself. Above them, a council of nine members—one each from Chicago, Detroit, Buffalo, Philadelphia, and the five New York families—held the whole Mafia structure together. "Organized crime in its totality thus consists of these twenty-four groups," the presidential commission concluded, "allied with other racket enterprises to form a loose confederation operating in large and small cities. In the core groups, because of their permanency of form, strength of organization, and ability to control other racket operations, resides the power that organized crime has in America today." Two consultants to the commission, Ralph Salerno of the New York police and Donald R. Cressey, a sociologist, then published well-received books bristling with secretly recorded Mafia conversations and inside information. "There is no longer any doubt," *Time* magazine explained in a cover story on organized crime in the summer of 1969, "that its most important part, its very nucleus, is La Cosa Nostra."

Two other books, both thumping bestsellers in 1969, popularized this new (and overdue) orthodoxy: *The Valachi Papers* by Peter Maas and *The Godfather* by Mario Puzo. To fill his blank, endless prison days, in necessary but lonesome isolation from other convicts, Valachi had scrawled out a handwritten, book-length manuscript of memoirs. Peter Maas, a magazine writer, agreed in the fall of 1965 to shape it into a publishable book. But word got out, and an angry group of Italian-American judges, politicians, and others pressured the Johnson administration to stop the book.

Nothing was more ethnic than organized crime in America. The subject could hardly be touched without offending those ethnic groups historically most involved in the underworld. Just before the Valachi hearings, Representative John J. Rooney— chairman of the crucial House Appropriations Committee, whose Brooklyn district included many Italian voters—had responded to constituent protests by criticizing the Justice Department for wasting too much money on the Valachi case. Duly sensitized, the hearings then walked on ethnic eggshells. "I'm not talking about Italians," Valachi insisted. "I'm talking about criminals." At the hearings, New York's Senator Jacob Javits, who was Jewish, objected to the phrase "Jewish ties" on a chart of the Buffalo Mafia family. "I would like to point out," said Javits, "that the staff here has gone to great pains to eliminate a national or ethnic reference to the whole organization, and I think that is a splendid thing." The phrase was deleted from the chart, along with the names and photographs of three Jewish associates of the Magaddino family.

With that background, the planned collaboration of Valachi and Maas was bound to meet ethnic resistance. Caving in, the Johnson

White House sent Justice Department lawyers into federal court seeking a permanent summary injunction against the book. "The pretext was that Valachi was still a federal prisoner under Justice Department control," Maas said later, "and any use of the manuscript he had written about his career in the Cosa Nostra, or anything he had said in subsequent interviews, would be, of all things, 'injurious' to law enforcement." The judge didn't buy the government's case, so the lawyers from Justice offered a deal: Maas could write a book drawn from his own interviews with Valachi, but not from the handwritten manuscript itself. Assisted by a sympathetic Justice official, Maas then had Valachi orally repeat the material he wanted, and the book was done.

Twenty-two publishers—perhaps scared off by the ethnic squabbling, certainly underestimating the commercial potential of the Mafia—rejected the book before Putnam finally took it. *The Valachi Papers* reached bookstores just after New Year's Day, supposedly a flat time to sell books; Putnam had tried to sell the paperback rights before publication but been spurned. Despite these problems, the book wound up selling 2 million copies in all editions and was translated into fourteen languages. Again a celebrity, but still unable to savor it in freedom, Valachi lingered in federal prison. Always hoping to be released for his cooperation, he died of natural causes in 1971.

The Godfather, a novel with the right real-life touches, meant an ironic homecoming for its author. Mario Puzo, forty-nine years old in 1969, had grown up as the son of illiterate Neapolitan immigrants in Hell's Kitchen, around Tenth Avenue and Thirtieth Street in Manhattan, overlooking the New York Central's noisome railroad yards. When Mario was twelve, his father—a trackman laborer—deserted his wife and seven children. The boy grew up in profound alienation from the Italians around him: "coarse, vulgar, and insulting," as he remembered them, "always shouting, always angry, quicker to quarrel than embrace," they "wore lumpy work clothes and handlebar mustaches, they blew their noses on their fingers . . . and the furthest limit of their horizon was their daily bread." Escaping to a neighborhood settlement house and the public library, Puzo early on decided to become a writer, the occupation most removed from his surroundings that he could imagine. "My mother looked on all this reading with a fishy Latin eye. She saw no profit in it."

For a long time his mother was right. Puzo scraped out a bare living as a writer, publishing two novels that nobody bought. Without understanding him, his relatives yet tolerated him as the family "chooch," the donkey, always broke and borrowing money from them. In 1965, $20,000 in debt and with his proposal for a third novel rejected by his publisher, Puzo decided to bend artistic integrity and write an intentionally commercial Mafia novel. In part he drew on childhood memories: "Stories about crime were part of the culture," he said later. "A couple of things I saw when I was a kid ended up in *The Godfather*. A guy once passed guns to my mother across the air shaft from another apartment. My brother had a dog and the landlord wanted to throw us out. My mother went to some guy and he straightened everything out for us."

Beyond that, and the gambling world that Puzo knew well firsthand, he wrote the saga of the Corleone family from research, never meeting a real gangster in person. The book's paperback rights brought $410,000, then a record in the book business, and in two years the novel sold a million hardcover and 8 million paperback copies. "I felt very unnatural being out of debt," Puzo reflected. "The book got much better reviews than I expected. I wished like hell I'd written it better."

The several *Godfather*s, the book as well as the two Oscar-winning movies that followed it, were so universally popular that they created what social scientists call a Hawthorne effect, by which people under observation change their behavior because of being observed. In one Brooklyn Mafia family, a younger member started referring to the patriarch as "the Godfather." An outlaw motorcycle gang, a chapter of the Hell's Angels, used the book to model itself after a traditional organized-crime pattern. Mobsters would ask each other if they had seen the *Godfather* films; a young gangster claimed to have seen one of them ten times. At dinner in a New Jersey restaurant, the hoodlum son of Joe Adonis had the waiter play the musical theme from the movies on the jukebox, over and over, all through the meal. After Philip Testa, a Philadelphia Mafioso, was murdered, a videotape of one of the *Godfather* films was found in his home. "I think it was a good book," Raymond Patriarca, boss of the New England Mafia, told a congressional committee in 1972. "To me it was nothing but a lot of fiction, good seller. People like to read that after all the publicity you people give it about organized crime and all this kind of stuff. People die to go out and buy it. You can come out tomorrow with the 'Patriarca Papers' and make a million dollars."

If Patriarca didn't mind the book, what did that imply about its treatment of the Mafia? *The Godfather* did not in any general way glorify organized crime. Gangsters for the most part were accurately depicted as selfish, vicious killers concerned only for money and themselves. But as the story's crucial twist of plot—when Michael, the straight, college-educated son, decides to join the Corleone criminal enterprises—Puzo offered an innocent notion of underworld motivation. Michael turns crook not because he sees organized crime as an easy way to a plush living, but because of an admirable love for and loyalty to his father after the father is almost killed. The effect is to turn the moral implications of Michael's decision upside down: he becomes a gangster because he is a good son. Nobody could object to that.

Gay Talese repeated that motivation in his bestselling book on the Bonanno family, *Honor Thy Father*, published in 1971. Talese wrote his book from long interviews with Joe Bonanno's gangster son Bill, whom the old don wished to appoint his successor as boss of one of the five New York families. Bill Bonanno fed Talese a self-flattering line; Talese believed him and essentially adopted the Mafioso's perspective. ("In plain English," Vinnie Teresa remarked, "he was conned.") Thus in the book Talese implied the Bonannos had gone legitimate, were no longer much involved in crime. That was not true. Again, Bill Bonanno said he had committed himself to his father's ways out of filial love and devotion. So, wrote Talese, given "the responsibilities he felt toward his father's world," Bill "could not turn against his father, nor did he really want to." Granted that Bill did love his father; that still did not adequately explain his drift toward the underworld. Bill had dropped out of college, had no other means to earn a comparably fat income, and had never shown any aptitude for a life of hard, honest work. He still had choices, but his own self-interest pointed the way downward.

At some point the newly enormous public interest in organized crime slid over into romanticization and Mafia chic. Nicholas Pileggi, a crime reporter in New York (and Gay Talese's cousin), published a remarkable hymn to the Mafia in the *Saturday Evening Post*, an oracle of mainstream American opinion. "Without question, the success of the Mafia in America today depends upon the excellence of its services," Pileggi declared. "The Mafia has been dependable, ubiquitous and a friend to those in need." In need, that is, of various harmless products and pastimes that the American upperworld had foolishly rendered illegal by its "unrealistic, unenforceable and unpopular laws." Stepping into this breach, the Mafia went about its business, dealing fairly and benignly. Since America was itself "a land of moral expediency," it followed that Mafiosi were just regular guys, no different from you and me, "far more a symbol of contemporary American society than an aberration."

To illustrate the point, for a few months in 1972 New York's café society embraced Crazy Joey Gallo, a loony renegade member of the Profaci family. "It was the thing to do," said one fashionable hostess. "If you hadn't met him, you weren't in." Crazy Joe started it: he had befriended Jerry Orbach, an actor who played a Gallo-like character in the movie version of Jimmy Breslin's comic Mafia novel, *The Gang That Couldn't Shoot Straight*. On Sundays Orbach and his wife, Marta Curro, would invite selected friends over to meet the Mafioso and eat spaghetti. Gallo had done a little reading in prison, and he liked to strike intellectualish postures. "He was the brightest person I've ever known," said the actress Joan Hackett. "He'd sit around my kitchen with those sad, sad eyes," said Curro. "When he asked me whether I preferred Camus or Sartre, I almost fell into a plate of spaghetti."

But what about Crazy Joey's underworld past and present? "I know there was another side to Joey," Curro conceded. "But I can't comprehend it. He told us he was going straight." ("They'd rather you thought they all dealt with honor and respect," a Gallo associate, Peter Diapoulos, said later, "all that crap, and that they all were right out of *The Godfather*.") Appearing to straighten up, Gallo got married at the home of Orbach and Curro. Bob Dylan wrote a song about him. This all ended when Gallo, not as free of his past as he pretended, was killed late one night at a restaurant in Little Italy. His society friends were not on hand to be splattered. All but inevitably, Curro started writing a book about this strange friendship.

Even Frank Costello considered doing a book. Out of jail for the last time, no longer boss of his family, he lived quietly in New York in semiretirement. "I never see Sherman Billingsley," he wrote an old friend in 1966. "The Stork Club is demolished. And for Shor's bar, I don't get there too often. New York isn't the same anymore." Toward the end of his life, he evidently wished to retrieve something from the old days of power and prominence, to erase the croaking impression he had left at the Kefauver committee. Costello started preliminary talks with a willing co-author, Peter Maas. Over two months they met once a week for two or three hours of conversation.

"My most difficult problem was drawing him out on the Mafia," Maas said later. "He considered himself a man of stature. His attitudes, even his manner, said that he felt he had maintained a life on a level far above the conventional rackets. He was much more interested in talking about himself in relation to Joe Kennedy, Huey Long and Fiorello La Guardia." Costello died only ten days after finally deciding to go ahead with the project, and Maas never wrote the book. It doubtless would also have been a bestseller; no other gangster could have approached the stories that Costello might have told.

❧ ❧

According to a Harris Poll in 1971, 78 percent of Americans agreed that "there is a secret organization engaged in organized crime in this country which is called the *Mafia*."

❧ ❧

All this attention to the Mafia was annoying Joe Colombo. While other ethnic groups were demanding their civil rights, Italian-Americans were not getting theirs—and were smeared as gangsters to boot. "We say there is a conspiracy against *every* Italian-American," said Colombo. "Show me what Italian is in what caliber of position in the police, the fire department, the board of education, in every field and every endeavor. How do we figure that no President in the history of the country had enough confidence to appoint an Italian to the Supreme Court?"

A reasonable question, and Joe Colombo presented himself as a reasonable man, just an average good citizen concerned over the treatment of his people. Born and raised in the Bath Beach section of Brooklyn, he still lived there with his wife and children in a prosaic split-level home. A good athlete, he liked to play handball and golfed in the respectable mid-eighties. Outwardly he behaved like anyone in the aspiring American middle class.

Colombo made his living, he said, selling real estate. "He's got the most sincerest group of clients," said his boss at the office. "They never try to cheat him out of his commissions."

Actually Joe Colombo was head of the Profaci crime family, and deeply rooted in the underworld. His mobster father had been murdered when Joe was fifteen, found garroted in the backseat of a car with his girlfriend. "They say I was brought up in a life of crime," Joe said later, very offended. "Would you believe any father would bring up his son to do anything bad?" With his father's example showing the way, Joe climbed upward through the Brooklyn docks, dice and gambling, and contract murder. In 1963, only forty years old, he took over the Profaci family after titanic, bloody struggles within the gang. Lawmen knew him well: a Valachi chart in 1963 and a list published in *The Congressional Record* in 1969 identified him as a top Mafioso, Ralph Salerno's book of 1969 mentioned him, and federal wiretaps had picked up traces of his underworld dealings. But Colombo had ducked any serious convictions, so news media had to refer to him as a "reputed," "alleged" gangster.

In April 1970, the FBI arrested one of Colombo's sons for conspiring to melt down $300,000 worth of silver coins into more valuable ingots. Convinced that the feds were persecuting his family because they could not reach him, Colombo and his associates started picketing the FBI office on Third Avenue in Manhattan. Taking cues from the civil rights movement of the time, Colombo then organized an Italian-American Unity Day at Columbus Circle. With about one hundred thousand enthusiasts on hand, New York's Deputy Mayor Richard Aurelio conveyed the regards of city hall. That led, in August 1970, to the Italian-American Civil Rights League, founded and dominated by Colombo. Frank Sinatra sang at a benefit in Madison Square Garden that raised $450,000 for the league.

Big money, big names; Colombo did not lack chutzpah, or a sense of irony. "Is it *possible* in New York that only *Italians* have committed crimes?" he asked. "I wasn't born free of sin but I sure couldn't be all the things that people have said—I got torture chambers in my cellar, I'm a murderer, I'm the head of every shylock ring, of every bookmakin' ring, I press buttons and I have enterprises in London, at the airports I get seven, eight million dollars a year revenue out of there. Who are they kiddin' and how far will they go to kid the public?" Colombo knew all about kidding the public.

Still, he had a point. The great success of *The Godfather* had reinforced a popular association of Italians with organized crime. The book used the words "Mafia" and "Mafioso" some sixty-eight times, and Colombo did not approve. With production on the first *Godfather* movie about to start, he sent a protest to Paramount Pictures: "The book, *The Godfather*, although fiction, is a spurious and slanderous account of the Italian-American. . . . You should do everything in your power to delete the words 'Mafia' and 'Cosa Nostra' and the characterization of Italians being 'gangsters' from this movie."

Scores of politicians, notified by Colombo's league, also leaned on Paramount. The movie's producer, Albert Ruddy, met with league representatives and agreed to change "Mafia" and "Cosa Nostra" to "family" or "syndicate" in the script. "One thing you've got to say about the Mafia is that it at least conducts crime in a reliable way, like a business," Ruddy later explained. "I'm a moviemaker and I just want to make movies; I wanted to create the circumstances under which I could make *this* movie." ("I never wrote this book as a putdown of Italians," Mario Puzo insisted. "I'm sort of proud they're so clever in crime," he went on, not helping his case. "In fact I even believe they have a natural gift for it—the southern Italians and the Sicilians.")

As a civil rights leader, Colombo might have gone on to other coups. But at the second annual Unity Day celebration, in June 1971, a black street criminal—presumably hired by someone else— shot him down. The shooter was immediately killed by Colombo's bodyguards, leaving the mystery of who had sent him on a suicidal hit. Colombo lay in a vegetative state for seven years before dying. Three of his sons later pleaded guilty to racketeering charges—the third generation of Colombos in the underworld.

As a Mafia boss denying that Italians were much involved in organized crime, Joe Colombo was an obvious fraud. His life and death denied the fine-sounding words he spoke; his crimes reinforced the stereotypes he wished to refute. Yet he was right for the wrong reasons. Gangsters did comprise a tiny proportion of all Italian-Americans, and the Mafia taint did make the honest lives of most Italian-Americans more difficult. Even after his murder and exposure, then, Colombo remained a hero to many admirers. "Without courageous Joseph Colombo at the helm, the Italian-American Civil Rights League and its Unity Day were eventually shattered beyond repair," mourned John Scarne, a cardsharp and gambling consultant. "The millions of Italian-Americans without a Joe Colombo to lead them are again politically and economically impotent."

Scarne worked on the edge of the underworld and was perhaps too close to the subject. For an academic perspective, consider the judgment of Luciano J. Iorizzo and Salvatore Mondello, both Ph.D. historians: "For one brief moment in their history, it seemed that Italian-Americans would be united to eradicate the long-standing plague of criminality. . . . Many respectable individuals have since entered the fight against the Mafia, but *none* has exhibited the kind of charisma and leadership which enabled Colombo to light a fire under his countrymen." Italians in America had many other leaders equally aggrieved at the slights they endured. Yet no one before this Mafia boss had taken such positions with such impact. Neither American society nor Americans of Italian descent could escape that terrible irony.

❦ ❦

Colombo aside, there were more serious challenges to the new orthodoxy about the Mafia. In some hands, the orthodoxy had been stretched to fit a simplified version of organized crime in America, too neat and conspiratorial. Thus the underworld was sometimes seen as an alien intrusion, imposed by criminal immigrants on an America theretofore free of any organized crime. Italian gangsters were described not merely as the dominant underworld group, but as having the entire underworld to themselves. Strong connections were drawn between the Mafia in Sicily and the American Mafia, as though the Sicilian organization had craftily sent emissaries to the United States who still took directions from home. The American Mafia's internal procedures were described as quite rationalized and orderly, to be reproduced on an organization chart with clear hierarchies and lines of control. The national Mafia Commission was said to dictate local policies to all the families around the country, and therefore to all organized crime in America.

Responding to such simplified notions, and to the Mafia's overdue notoriety, a group of Mafia-as-myth writers doubted the new orthodoxy. Some, like Murray Kempton, were political liberals suspicious of the Justice Department's use of Mafia stories to justify wiretapping and other intrusions on the right to privacy. Others, like William J. Chambliss, were Marxists for whom organized crime merely confirmed the failings of private ownership and a free economy; the underworld was no more corrupt than the social system in which it was embedded. ("The logic of capitalism," said Chambliss, "is a logic within which the emergence of crime networks is inevitable.") Still others, like Giovanni Schiavo and John Scarne, were loyal Italian-Americans defending their ethnic group from what they saw as simple bigotry. "There is no Mafia in America," Schiavo declared, only a name "which some thugs appropriate to give themselves importance and awe the ignorant people, with the unwitting complicity of reporters and politicians who toss the word around with utter recklessness." "These officials and writers hate Italians," Scarne agreed, "and use the Mafia label as cover-up for crimes committed by their own people."

The most substantial exponents of Mafia-as-myth were social scientists, especially sociologists and anthropologists. The Mafia orthodoxy did not fit comfortably within a conventional social-science construct, which, at the complex intersection of self and society, emphasized general social forces instead of individual choices and personalities. Most traditions in social science regarded people as more shaped than shaping; therefore social disorganization caused crime, not the other way around, and the underworld was more symptom than sickness. Since people usually did what they must, not what they chose, and because social science aimed to be neutrally "scientific," questions of morality—right and wrong—were irrelevant. Organized crime was rather part of a functional social system, meeting rational needs and providing necessary services, neither right nor wrong but logical. The (alleged) Mafia had become merely a convenient scapegoat, finite and identifiable, for inchoate social forces. The underworld could not be effectively attacked without first making fundamental changes in society; and perhaps, given that the underworld had its legitimate causes and uses, it should not be attacked at all.

The first powerful statement along these lines came from the sociologist Daniel Bell in two articles, one written after the Kefauver hearings, the second after Valachi's testimony. Bell dismissed the existence of the Mafia as a fictional, self-serving concoction by the Bureau of Narcotics. As to organized crime in general, it had functioned as "a queer ladder of social mobility" for successive waves of immigrants. Frustrated by unfair social conditions, said Bell, the Irish, then Jews, then Italians had seized on crime as a way out and up. Once well established in American life, each group would forsake crime for honest livings. By 1963, Bell concluded, most of the old rackets had become legitimate, to be replaced by the upperworld's preferred forms of white-collar crime. "The real domain of organized crime in the U.S., then," said Bell, "is no longer the old one of outright illegality, but the more shadowy one of dealing and corner-cutting." *The Public Interest,* a journal co-edited by Bell, later published other articles in the same spirit by Gordon Hawkins, Peter Reuter, Jonathan Rubinstein, and others.

Joseph L. Albini, a sociologist who favored "a structural-functional method of analysis," extended the argument in his book *The American Mafia: Genesis of a Legend* (1971). Albini wished to explode "the widely held misconception that the innocent, unguarded American public is a victim of foreign evildoers who secretly rob it of its moral virginity." Organized crime predated the major Italian immigrations to America, Albini pointed out, citing the nineteenth-century Irish syndicates of Mike McDonald in Chicago and John Morrissey in New York, among others. Later immigrant groups then folded into criminal arrangements already in place. Even so, organized crime was a method, not an organization but a system of shifting power struggles and informal patron-client relationships that could not be tracked on an organization chart. Valachi's testimony, at times vague and contradictory, proved nothing to Albini; if Valachi's version of a tightly ordered Mafia were true, then Frank Costello's edict against dope would have been obeyed. The Mafia Commission ("if it does exist") had no formal structure because it lacked consistent form and membership procedures.

On other points, the logic of Albini's position forced him into intellectual contortions not easy to follow: "We wonder how segments of the public and writers can continue to speak of a secret society when daily the names of the so-called bosses, lieutenants, and others are published openly in newspapers across the country. What then is the secret?" The Mafia certainly *intended* secrecy. Needing to deny Italian domination of the underworld, Albini mentioned the murder of Dutch Schultz, the decline of the Purples in Detroit, and the eclipse of the Shelton gang in southern Illinois—without noting that Italian gangsters had caused them all. As for the Apalachin conference, "we cannot even find agreement about how many were present at the meeting" (because an unknown number escaped into the woods). Again, Albini neglected to admit that only Italians had attended Apalachin. What about bugged recordings of Italian gangsters making respectful mention of the Cosa Nostra? "The mere use of the word," said Albini, "does not constitute proof of the existence of such an organization."

Francis A. J. Ianni and Elizabeth Reuss-Ianni took in less territory and—at first—argued their case more tightly in their book *A Family Business: Kinship and Social Control in Organized Crime* (1972). As anthropologists, the Iannis saw family and kinship where other observers saw criminal structure. Francis Ianni, the son of immigrants from the Abruzzi region near Rome, had grown up in an Italian neighborhood of Wilmington, Delaware. With the advantage of that background, he was allowed extraordinary access to what he called the "Lupollo" crime family of Brooklyn. During two years in the late 1960s, he mingled with the Lupollos at weddings and funerals, in their homes and restaurants, watching and listening. Presumably the Lupollos were careful about what they showed him. If only sketchily aware of their crimes, Ianni did acquire a uniquely full and inside sense of how they ran affairs among themselves. This crime family, it seemed, conducted itself like a literal family, organized by inherited cultural values, dependent on function instead of bureaucratic structure, with authority conveyed by seniority and blood ties. "We believe," the Iannis suggested, echoing Mario Puzo and Gay Talese, "that members of the Lupollo family are sustained in action by the force of kinship rather than driven by fear or motivated by crime."

From there, and without the necessary intermediary evidence, the Iannis vaulted to an ambitious conclusion that other Italian gangs around the country were equally based on kinship, not on blood and power, and that had created the Mafia myth. "We believe that it is the universality of this clan organization and the strength of its shared behavior system which makes Italian-American crim-

inal syndicates seem so similar. And we believe that it is this simi-
larity which has inclined observers to maintain that the different
crime families constitute some sort of highly national or even
international crime conspiracy." Almost half the men at Apalachin,
after all, were related by blood or marriage. As to the existence of
a national syndicate, the Iannis at first were agnostic, finding no
evidence from the Lupollos either for or against such a structure.
But in an article a few years later, the Iannis again jumped a few
necessary steps to a more definite statement: "We hoped that our
work would dispel the myth of a nationwide Italian-American
crime syndicate." It did not because the Iannis, drawing only on a
partial view of one family in Brooklyn, had submitted no new
evidence on the larger question of a national structure.

In his book *The Mafia Mystique* (1975), Dwight C. Smith, Jr.,
offered the most persuasive statement of Mafia-as-myth by keeping his argument within careful limits. Organized crime was real,
he acknowledged, but misidentified as a Mafia plot. Ever since the
murder of David Hennessey in New Orleans in 1890, American
perceptions of the underworld had depended less on verifiable
facts than on external anxieties such as nativism, xenophobic fears
of immigration, political hysterias, the upheavals of Prohibition,
and the Bureau of Narcotics' need to excuse its failure to stop
drug trafficking by constructing a Mafia monolith. The national
underworld conventions of the late 1920s and early 1930s reflected ongoing competition and instability, said Smith, not an
ascendant Mafia. After decades in eclipse, the Mafia specter was
revived by the Kefauver committee. All the varied speculation by
lawmen and journalists about the Apalachin meeting ("if it was
that") could not with certainty tie it to the Mafia. Joe Valachi,
whose underworld knowledge did not reach beyond his own
family, merely fed the McClellan committee what it wanted. "The
absence of bona fide corroboration for Valachi's tale does not
imply that it was necessarily wrong," Smith allowed. "It does
suggest that the subcommittee could have been more objective
and cautious in its analysis."

Like others in the Mafia-as-myth school, Smith blamed organized
crime on American society, not on the criminals. "The plain fact,"
he concluded, "is that organized crime is the product of forces that
threaten values, not the cause of them"—that is, the general level
of violence, greed, selfishness, and law defiance in American life.

Instead of blood, theft, and extortion, the underworld generally dealt in amicable corruption and collusion with willing legitimate segments of the American economy. According to this "theory of illicit enterprise," loan sharks were bankers, fences were retailers, drug smugglers were importers—all of them cooperating with overtly good citizens. Not a predatory criminal at all, a typical gangster was just another American businessman.

The Mafia-as-myth depended on two essential propositions: organized crime as routine American enterprise, and an "ethnic succession" whereby criminal ethnic groups, once well established in America, yielded the underworld to newer immigrants farther down the social ladder. Later events made both propositions less tenable. From the early 1970s on, a flood of new information on organized crime became available. Memoirs appeared by Joe Bonanno (of particular value), Mickey Cohen, Vinnie Teresa, Jimmy the Weasel Fratianno, Vincent Siciliano, Patsy Lepera, Willie Sutton, a killer named "Joey," Michael Hellerman, Peter Diapoulos, Henry Hill, and others. High-level Mafiosi, including acting bosses of the Los Angeles and Cleveland families, flipped and testified about mob life. A new wave of FBI bugs and taps recorded gangsters convicting themselves in their own words. An FBI agent, Joseph D. Pistone, infiltrated two Mafia families in New York, was almost made a member, and survived to write a book about it.

Given all this new evidence, nobody could still reasonably deny that the Mafia existed, included a national Commission, and exerted more power over the underworld than any other single group. Few major new statements of Mafia-as-myth appeared after 1975. It gradually became clear that gangsters did not just provide illicit goods demanded by the public. They often created their own demand; gambling and loan sharking fed into each other, one building the market for the other. Neither could have prospered so well without the mirror half of the scam. The public, far from "needing" gambling and loan sharking, was squeezed between them. Gangsters intruded on labor unions because of muscle and ambition, not market forces. Underworld business resembled no other form of enterprise: conducted without ethical norms, routinely crooked and cheating, dependent always on the threat of violence, casually arrogant monopolies of broken legs and murder.

Moreover, the predicted ethnic succession did not happen. New immigrant groups did enter the underworld, but none ever approached the ongoing reach and stability of the Mafia. Long after most Italian-Americans were comfortably assimilated into the American dream, some young Italians still aspired to be Mafiosi. Underworld families might stretch over two generations (the Bonannos, Barbaras, Boiardos, Zerillis, Patriarcas, Sicilianos, Profacis, and many others), three generations (the Colombos and Joe Adonis, his father, and his son), even four generations (Vinnie Teresa, his grandfather, his uncle, and his sons). In these hoodlum clans, the younger men grew up in nouveau opulence and could have entered any legitimate field they wished. Instead they *chose* the underworld, not from societal anger or frustration but from peer reinforcement, unprincipled greed, and an aversion to honest toil. "These people did not want to work," said Harvey Bonadonna, the son of a Kansas City mobster, about his friends and relatives in the rackets. "They would see how members flourished, had flashy cars, not doing anything, and they would try to find where they could make a score. . . . They weren't interested in legitimate jobs. They wanted to go out and prey upon the community, to steal." Far from expressing normal American values, they flouted a traditional American faith in work and education as the way upward.

Seventeen years after his celebration of the Mafia in the *Saturday Evening Post,* Nicholas Pileggi helped write the memoirs of Henry Hill, a convicted associate of the Lucchese family. Having once described the Mafia as "dependable, ubiquitous, and a friend to those in need," Pileggi now saw a different underworld. "The romantic notion of that world is *so* far from the truth," he explained. Instead of honor and loyalty, the underworld ran on treachery and betrayal. Gangsters loved their work, the easy money and thrill of stealing, and liked to tell fondly remembered war stories about past coups and murders. "It's a career filled with pain, much of it inflicted on others," said Pileggi. "They're not Sonny Corleone. They're not those characters in movies. There's nothing noble about them. They're quite loathsome." From this distance, Mafia chic and the apotheosis of Crazy Joey Gallo looked ridiculous, a temporary fashion well outgrown.

Above, Harry J. Anslinger, director of the federal Bureau of Narcotics, 1930–62; the first major lawman to see the Mafia clearly
HARRY J. ANSLINGER PAPERS

Right, Homer Ferguson, the one-man grand jury who investigated Detroit's political and criminal underworld during 1939 and 1940
JOHN HENDERSON STUDIOS

Robert T. Bushnell, attorney general of Massachusetts, just after returning from his mysterious absence in the summer of 1943

Hubert Humphrey, a few years after his term as the racketbusting mayor of Minneapolis, 1945–49

Virgil W. Peterson, FBI agent, then from 1942 to 1970 operating director of the Chicago Crime Commission
COURTESY OF VIRGIL PETERSON

Warren Olney III, counsel to the California Commission on Organized Crime, 1947–50
COURTESY OF ELIZABETH OLNEY

KENNEDYS

Joe Kennedy, five of his children, and three of
their spouses in Palm Beach, May 1957
LOOK COLLECTION, JOHN F. KENNEDY LIBRARY

John L. McClellan, Robert F. Kennedy, and
John F. Kennedy at a hearing before the
McClellan committee, May 1957
LOOK COLLECTION, JOHN F. KENNEDY LIBRARY

Congressman William L. Dawson of Chicago and the candidate, during the 1960 campaign

The widow and the brother, with other members of the family, November 25, 1963

GANGBUSTERS II

Above, Senator Estes Kefauver (*right*) with
Rudolph Halley (*left*), chief counsel of the
1950–51 Kefauver committee, the first important governmental investigation of organized
crime
WIDE WORLD PHOTOS

Right, Aaron M. Kohn, managing director of
the Metropolitan Crime Commission of New
Orleans, 1954–78.
COURTESY OF AARON M. KOHN

G. Robert Blakey, author of the RICO law
KEITH JEWELL

Rudolph Giuliani, head of the federal Justice Department's criminal division and then United States attorney for New York City; the most prominent Italian-American racketbuster of the 1980s
U.S. DEPARTMENT OF JUSTICE

TEN

GETTING SERIOUS

It began in the 1920s with Prohibition. Now, in the 1970s and 1980s, the big-time national underworld again dealt in illicit substances that millions of good American citizens wished to consume, laws be damned. Once again, new criminal gangs stepped forward to deliver the goods and prosper by the deals. Once again, law enforcers huffed and puffed but stopped only a trickle of the swelling flood. It all seemed so familiar: a huge underworld traffic, dominating an era in organized crime, revealing public fictions and hypocrisies. Many observers saw a new Prohibition, just as feckless and wasteful as the old Prohibition.

This analogy, at first so apparent, dissolved when examined more closely. For all its dangers, alcohol caused less health damage in a typical user than hard drugs. Americans before 1920 had long and mostly benign histories with booze. Prohibition then interfered with drinking habits deeply rooted in culture and tradition. Most Americans, by contrast, had no contact with illicit drugs before the 1970s. During Prohibition, public opinion gradually turned against the noble experiment, and the government gave up on trying to enforce it. During the 1970s and 1980s, public attitudes against drugs stiffened—instead of growing more tolerant—as their effects became clear, and law enforcers steadily poured more resources and new laws into fighting them. In the old Prohibition, the bootleggers consolidated their operations into regional and national networks, more rationalized and orderly all the time; in the new Prohibition, the drug gangs were ever wilder and more competitive, less organized and predictable, mean and wired on their own goods. On both sides of the law, conditions were getting serious.

❧ ❧

In this endless game of hounds and hares, the ethnic character of the chase was transformed. The gangsters, once mainly Irish, Jewish, and Italian, now prominently included newer immigrant groups, especially Latins and Asians. The gangbusters, once mostly WASPs, now were reinforced by many Irish, Jewish and Italian cops, crusaders, and prosecutors, along with assorted WASP holdovers. The simple pattern that had prevailed for a half century, of WASPs and non-WASPs fencing across the line, no longer existed.

Over the decades since Prohibition, the "acids of modernity" (in Walter Lippmann's suggestive phrase) had smoothed out the old-time differences among America's major white ethnic groups. Education, intermarriage, mass culture, and economic mobility made them all resemble each other, to be distinguished merely by a person's name or religious practice. Even religious differences among Protestants, Catholics, and Jews no longer showed the old sharp edges; given ecumenical tendencies and the general decline of religion as a force in American life, the Protestant conscience that had so animated the earlier gangbusters no longer separated WASPs as sharply from others. The plain bigotry that had kept non-WASPs from high offices in law enforcement had also diminished. The 1970s brought the first Jew (Edward Levi) and the first Italian (Benjamin Civiletti) to serve as attorney general of the United States. In the general population, most Irish, Jewish, and Italian citizens had moved from the old immigrant neighborhoods, of personalized relations and suspicions toward the law, to an American middle class of contractual relations and abstract belief in the law. Now firmly part of the social contract, governed by law instead of culture and tradition, these ethnic groups were more inclined to respect a legal structure that they finally helped run.

The new non-WASP gangbusters were typically modern personalities, perhaps with self-conscious affection for the old ethnic ties, but generically American in most other respects. This homogenization opened up the field of law enforcement. Even before Robert Kennedy's breakthrough prominence as a non-

WASP gangbuster, other ethnic lawmen had breached the Protestant hegemony. Since the 1930s, the federal Bureau of Narcotics had recruited Italians—Charles Siragusa, Joseph Amato, Salvatore Vizzini—to work undercover among Mafia drug dealers, and some of these agents rose to supervisory jobs in the bureau. Daniel P. Sullivan, an Irish Catholic retired FBI agent—and the father of fourteen children, of whom one became a priest and another a nun—helped found the Crime Commission of Greater Miami in 1948 and then served as its longtime operating director. Sullivan fed vital information to the Kefauver committee in 1950 and to later congressional investigations of organized crime as well. "I cannot too highly commend the Crime Commission of Greater Miami," said Florida's Representative Claude Pepper at hearings in 1969, "and that gallant gentleman [Sullivan] who has been Mr. Crime Fighter in Dade County for so long."

After 1960 such ethnic exceptions became typical. Ralph Salerno, a supervisor of detectives in the New York City Police Department's organized crime unit, helped prepare Joe Valachi for his public testimony, checking the Mafioso's memory against police records. ("His Italian was very poor," Salerno noted.) During his twenty years of police work, Salerno had hundreds of conversations with gangsters in police stations and courthouses, on the street and in their homes. When he retired from the department in 1966, the *New York Times* declared that Salerno probably knew more about the Mafia than any other lawman. He went on to a prominent career as a consultant and author on organized crime, an Italian gangbuster with special expertise about Italian hoodlums. "Unfortunately in the United States we give the greatest upward mobility to those immigrants who are willing to go into a life of crime as against what we offer immigrants who will be dutiful citizens and work hard,'" he said. "From time to time when the Mafia, the Cosa Nostra, has to be discussed, some Americans are angered by that fact. I would like the record to show that I am one of the Americans who is greatly angered when the necessity arises. I resent the fact that some criminals have formed an organization where they require that membership be limited to people of Italian background." Proud of his ethnic heritage, Salerno remained impatient with anyone who denied the reality of the Mafia.

Aaron M. Kohn of the Metropolitan Crime Commission of New Orleans was the Virgil Peterson of the 1960s and 1970s, the most visible example of a gangbuster operating from the peculiar advantages and vulnerabilities of the private sector. In his twenty-four years of fighting the New Orleans underworld, Kohn never carried a gun and was sued and threatened many times. (He never lost a lawsuit.) Once he opened his Sunday newspaper and found a dead rabbit, its throat slit. On three occasions he was jailed for guarding the identities of informants. Yet he felt safe, protected by the underworld code as long as he did not lie or exaggerate the facts. Picking his way through the endemic political corruption of southern Louisiana, ever suspicious of local politicians and lawmen, Kohn stayed carefully independent of the public sector. "The front line of private sector defense and offense against organized crime must be within the community," he urged. "Citizens can be most effective at that level through organizations and support of independent crime commissions, privately financed." Crime commissions, said Kohn, should never accept government funding: "They should be constantly free, and there is no surer way of removing freedom than by creating financial obligations."

Aaron Kohn's family history reflected a typical twentieth-century ethnic assimilation into the American mainstream. He was born in Philadelphia in 1910 of Lithuanian Jewish immigrants; his parents had met at the suspender factory where they both worked. Later his father ran a small dry-goods store in a neighborhood that was mostly Irish and German, with only a few Jews. The family lived over and behind the store, and his mother held forth as the neighborhood adviser. His father's best friend was a Protestant minister. Kohn was raised an Orthodox Jew, learning Hebrew, keeping kosher habits inside but not outside his parents' home. He married a Jewish woman and they brought up their daughters in ways Jewish but not Orthodox. (Years later, Kohn was married again, to a Gentile woman.)

Like Virgil Peterson and Daniel Sullivan, Kohn started his private-sector gangbusting after working for the FBI. Out of high school in 1928, disinclined to follow his older brother into medicine, he took a civil service exam that brought him an offer from the FBI. Stationed in Washington, he became a fingerprint expert and went to law school at night. He was promoted quickly and moved around the country to testify at trials and set up police training schools. His first wife could not abide these absences from home, so he quit the bureau in 1939. "My life has been much richer," he said later, "than it might have been if I'd stayed in a bureaucratic situation." After thirteen years in private business and two years spent investigating organized crime in Chicago, Kohn was hired by a group of New Orleans businessmen and civic leaders to look into police corruption in their city.

From that supposedly temporary assignment, the city's crime commission was launched in 1954 with Kohn as the managing director. The commission was always a shoestring operation, composed usually of just Kohn and his secretaries with occasional part-time undercover agents. The initial budget of $24,000 grew to an annual $50,000 by 1960 and $100,000 by the late 1970s—all of it squeezed from private donors and depending, said Kohn, "upon whose toes are stepped on." Backed by these modest resources and the quiet help of anonymous honest lawmen, Kohn contended with the corrupt mayor of New Orleans, deLesseps Morrison; a string of crooked sheriffs in Jefferson Parish; a U.S. attorney who was the son-in-law of an underworld political boss; and several corrupt district attorneys.

And behind them all, the Mafia don Carlos Marcello. "He is the most powerful, influential, and sinister racketeer boss in Louisiana," Kohn told the McClellan committee in 1961. "His wishes are considered orders by numerous persons in public office, obligated to him for their election or appointment to authority. He exerts a major influence upon elections and the selection of candidates. In some of his enterprises the record reveals his connection. But in most of them the open ownership identification is in the hands of trusted representatives, bound to him by obligation, loyalty, or fear." Despite the unbalanced odds, Kohn managed a few victories—a more professional police force in New Orleans, the election of a real sheriff in Jefferson Parish, the reduction of numbers gambling—and stayed on the job, persistently unscared.

On the national level, in 1970 G. Robert Blakey drafted the most important federal legislation against organized crime ever enacted. As a gangbuster, Blakey stood between the public and private sectors, shuttling back and forth from government jobs to teaching at law schools. Born and raised in the South, in the small Christian town of Burlington, North Carolina, Blakey had grown up thinking of ethnicity as a matter of white people and black people. His WASP father was president of the First National Bank of Burlington; his Irish Catholic mother raised him in the Catholic faith. "I guess—in the traditional sense—I am neither WASP nor Irish Catholic," Blakey said later. "Maybe just Amer-

ican." He went to college and law school at Notre Dame, a
Catholic institution. When he met his future wife, she—of French
Catholic background—asked about his ethnic ties. "I'm an Amer-
ican," Blakey replied, puzzled by the question.

Just out of law school in the summer of 1960, Blakey went to
work for the Justice Department's organized crime section in
Washington. He stayed on during the Kennedy administration,
exhilarated by Robert Kennedy's dogged expansion of federal
efforts against the underworld. Along with others in the organized
crime section, Blakey met with Bobby on the morning of November 22, 1963; they were supposed to meet again that afternoon,
but the news from Dallas intervened. Blakey left the Justice
Department in June 1964 with a nascent conviction that even the
most dedicated law enforcers could not then deal the underworld
a mortal blow. "We needed to start thinking about organized
crime as organized crime," he said later, "rather than as individuals committing individual offenses." The situation demanded
not only new people struggling within the limits of existing
statutes, but new measures.

Electronic snooping, for example. Blakey was a liberal Democrat, a member of the American Civil Liberties Union, philosoph-
ically tilted toward a citizen's right to privacy over the
government's right to meddle. While at Justice, he had not
known—and probably would not have approved—of the FBI's
illegal bugs and taps on underworld figures. In the spring of
1967, though, a Mafioso's tax case in Providence, Rhode Island,
released ten previously secret FBI reports on the bugging of an
office used by Raymond Patriarca, the local Mafia boss. Gathered
from 1962 to 1965, these reports documented crimes and conspiracies by the Mafia, its Commission, and families around the
country, showing the nuts and bolts of their domination of the
underworld. How then to balance the value of such intelligence
against its Orwellian source? "Nothing in the routine reports that
I read from any federal agency contained data of this quantity or
quality," Blakey told a Senate committee, recalling his tenure at
Justice. "The investigation reports I read were the product of the
use of normal investigative methods. There is just simply no
comparison in the two kinds of reports." If such surveillance were
legally authorized, under court orders, that might actually prevent
such abuses as the FBI's outlaw bugs and taps. "I support
court-ordered electronic surveillance because I think it is the only

way to secure privacy in this country," Blakey concluded. "It is because I love privacy more, not less, that I support a system of court-ordered electronic surveillance." In 1968, Title III of the Omnibus Crime Control and Safe Streets Act finally gave federal lawmen the power to install bugs and taps, with prior judicial approval, and to use the evidence gathered to prosecute cases.

In a political atmosphere defined by *The Godfather, The Valachi Papers,* and the new Mafia orthodoxy, Congress was ready to expand federal powers against the underworld. As chief counsel to a Senate subcommittee, Blakey drafted the crucial portions of the Organized Crime Control Act of 1970. The law mandated a federal witness protection program, expanded use of immunity for witnesses, more money and staffing, and special Justice Department task forces against organized crime. Most important, the Racketeer Influenced and Corrupt Organizations (RICO) section of the law allowed prosecutors to go after whole criminal enterprises, not just stray individuals or low-level fall guys. Under RICO, any two of several dozen defined crimes over a ten-year period could convict someone of taking part in an ongoing rackets enterprise; anyone planning or discussing a crime was as guilty as the actual perpetrator. Different crimes by different crooks could still point to a single underworld organization. Bosses were no longer insulated from subordinates acting on their orders. RICO also let lawmen seize any stolen loot through property forfeitures.

For John McClellan, the Organized Crime Control Act capped his career as the Senate's most effective gangbuster. Seventy-four years old in 1970, McClellan sat down with Blakey at various stages of the bill's evolution, tracking the revisions and tradeoffs. After shepherding it through the Senate, McClellan was the first witness at House hearings on the bill. "The public is demanding that we recognize that the right of society to be safe transcends the right of the criminal to be free," he said. "When the forces of right and peace clash against the forces of evil and violence, something has to give." This was not a McClellan bill, he added, denying the general impression around Congress. "I don't want the credit for it," he said. "There is enough glory in it for everybody if we can win." Despite opposition from civil libertarians, the bill passed the House essentially intact and was signed by President Nixon. The feds at last had the tools they needed to hit organized crime.

It took them about a decade to apply the new tools. Still focused on underworld gambling prosecutions, federal agencies shifted very slowly toward RICO cases. Beyond the usual inhibitions of bureaucratic inertia, the RICO law presented a brier patch of challenges. Instead of small, easy cases that led quickly to impressive numbers of indictments and convictions, RICO promised slow, complex investigations that might not succeed. Years of effort on a single case could lead nowhere. Not until 1981 did the Supreme Court, in the *Turkette* decision, make it clear that RICO could be applied to criminal enterprises. With some impatience, Blakey watched the nonuse of his brainchild. "A principal problem here is that the government lawyers haven't bothered to study the laws that you have already enacted," he told a Senate committee. "RICO is not a difficult statute," he added. "It's just that they won't do their homework and learn it."

Rudolph Giuliani did his homework. As head of the Justice Department's criminal division from 1981 to 1983, and then as an especially visible U.S. attorney in New York City, Giuliani became the most prominent Italian-American gangbuster of his time—and sharply representative of his time as well. An early admirer of Bobby Kennedy in New York, graduated from college and law school in the 1960s, then a McGovern Democrat in 1972, Giuliani moved rightward after his first prosecuting jobs in Republican administrations of the 1970s. He settled into a good prosecutor's certainty that criminals, not society, should be held responsible for their crimes. "During the Fifties and Sixties," he said later, "we socialized the responsibility for crime. We broke down the line between explanation and excuses, and explanations became excuses." Giuliani—a pale, intense man whose zealous looks reminded one observer of a medieval fresco of an obscure saint—accepted no excuses. "For purposes of ethics and of law, we elevate human beings by holding them responsible," he insisted. "Ultimately, you diminish human individuality and importance when you say, 'Oh, well, you're not really responsible for what you did. Your parents are responsible for it, or your neighborhood is responsible for it, or society is responsible for it.' In fact, if you harm another human being, you're responsible for that."

Philosophical issues came easily to Giuliani; until college he had expected to become a Roman Catholic priest. The grandson of Italian immigrants, he'd grown up hearing family stories about the Mafia and Black Hand, of how they had disgraced all good Italian-Americans. Giuliani was born in Brooklyn, where his father ran a pizza restaurant, and was raised an only child out on Long Island, in neighborhoods where most of his friends were Jewish. Living in generic suburbs, without siblings or other Italians his own age, attending parochial schools dominated by Irish Catholic priests and nuns, the younger Giuliani was a thoroughly assimilated, non-ethnic American. "There was one thing my father and I used to fight about all the time," he recalled. "He was an Italophile, and I couldn't see it. Without being able to speak Italian, he loved everything Italian. Even things you shouldn't love." Later on, though, Giuliani developed tastes for opera and Italian history that returned him to a willed affection for his roots.

That affection stopped where the underworld began. In private practice in the late 1970s, Giuliani would not represent mobsters. "Organized crime figures are illegitimate people who would go on being illegitimate people if I got them off," he explained. "I would not want to spend a lot of time with them . . . and become involved with people who are close to totally evil." Reading *The Valachi Papers* and Joe Bonanno's memoirs, *A Man of Honor* (1983), convinced Giuliani that the Mafia and its structure were real. Appointed by the Reagan administration to jobs with substantial clout, he pushed Justice prosecutors to use RICO and other new laws against the underworld. "It's like stuffing in a pipe," Robert Blakey reflected, seeing his handiwork at last applied. "You put it in at one end, and for a long time you don't see anything. And then finally it shows. Rudolph Giuliani is the guy lucky enough to be standing at the end of the pipe."

Working furiously, sleeping five hours a night, granting interviews to anyone with a microphone, Giuliani became the most celebrated racketbuster in New York since Thomas E. Dewey. "I don't think I can break the back of the Mafia *alone*," he made clear. "But I think we have a chance to break a lot of their power now, a chance we never had before." Giving the back of his hand to defense attorneys, civil libertarians, and liberal editorial writers, he pushed and pressed his cases with the born-again faith of a converted liberal. "My view is," he summed up: "The way you end corruption, you scare the daylights out of people." In cities around the country, away from the blare and glare of New York, other federal prosecutors—equally intent—together mounted the most sustained assault on organized crime in American history.

❧ ❧

A cold winter evening, January 19, 1981, in the North End of Boston. Around two o'clock on this quiet Sunday night, three FBI agents walked toward the headquarters of the Boston Mafia at 98 Prince Street. At the corner of Thatcher Street, the agents passed a van with FBI lookouts inside; all clear, the lookouts said over their radio, so the three agents briskly crossed the street and ducked into the entry at 98 Prince. Behind them, other FBI agents stalled their cars at the two intersections leading into this part of Prince Street, blocking any troublesome traffic for a while. At 98 Prince, one of the agents picked the outside door lock. Entering the first-floor hall of the old brick building, the three agents stood listening at the inside door of the Boston underworld's inner sanctum. They heard voices, a muted low burble, from behind the door. No one was supposed to be in there; the lookouts were sure.

Ten days earlier, the feds had obtained a thirty-day court order, under Title III of the 1968 act, to enter and wire this room. Three times in the past week, agents had tried to plant the bugs but pulled back because of suspicious pedestrians, then a faulty FBI radio, then those same voices behind the door that now froze the agents. Only twenty days remained on the court order, less than three weeks in which to collect evidence. Taking a chance, the agents guessed the oddly cadenced voices they were hearing came from a radio. They picked the lock and went in.

They found a small room, twelve feet wide and thirty feet long, the overheated air heavy with garlic and stale tobacco smoke. The only light came from—sighs of relief—a radio tuned to an all-talk station. Crouched in the darkness, the agents gradually took in the room's features. It was bare and tacky, with cheap wood paneling, a dropped ceiling, and flea market prints of Mediterranean scenes on the walls. Family photographs, a family crest, and two bicentennial American flags provided the other decorations. A long conference table and the boss's favorite chair dominated the front of the room. A bookcase held a few volumes, mainly lawbooks and the memoirs of Jimmy the Weasel Fratianno. In the rear, the kitchen boasted the room's one impressive aspect, bizarrely out of proportion: a full sized commercial stove with six burners and a double oven. The denizens of this modest one-room apartment evidently liked to eat well.

For ten minutes the FBI agents waited inside the room, wondering if they had tripped a silent burglar alarm. Nothing happened; the gangsters in their hubris had relied merely on the protection of the ever-playing radio and the xenophobic gossip network of this insular North End neighborhood. "The best crooking streets in the world," an old Boston hoodlum had said of the North End. "A stranger ain't got a chance around here, and neighbors ain't gonna help you much. A thief could hide in here five years and never get pinched."

With the room secure, however briefly, a second team of three FBI electronics specialists hurried in and set to work, shining flashlights under a black cloth. They planted two bugs in the ceiling's seams, fifteen feet apart. Above them, in the space offered by the dropped ceiling, they hid three power packs, each the size of a fireplace log. The work went in spurts, interrupted when the FBI lookouts warned of a car or pedestrian approaching on Prince Street. The bugs were tested; both worked, then one failed; while the electronics men tinkered and fussed, everyone else sweated; then both bugs again transmitted properly. All the agents cleared out, leaving the room carefully intact. It was now five o'clock under a brightening sky. After two slow years of planning and details, the FBI had penetrated "The Office" of the Boston underworld.

The object of all this effort was a Mafia gang led by Gennaro (Jerry) Angiulo and his four brothers. In a twisted sense, these hoodlum brothers never left home. The Angiulos had grown up across the way at 95 Prince Street. Their parents, Italian immigrants, ran a mom-and-pop grocery store. Giovannina Angiulo bore seven children in eleven years, kept the store going after her husband died, and became a neighborhood institution, extending advice and credit in hard times. "She was the hottest card player I ever knew," remembered Vinnie Teresa, who knew many professional cardsharps. "She'd clean me out. What a gin player that old lady was. . . . Jerry would get mad as hell when he'd see us playing cards. She'd call me Sonny and he'd explode. 'Don't call him Sonny, his name is Vinnie,' he'd shout. She'd tell him to shut his mouth and holler some cuss words in Sicilian."

Gennaro was the second-oldest son, the smartest and most ambitious. Graduating from Boston English High School in 1936, he said he hoped to become a criminal lawyer. His yearbook photograph caught a self-possessed young man, the eyes bright and intelligent, a complacent smirk (not a smile) playing around the mouth. He briefly drove a delivery truck—dabbling in honest work—but settled into the underworld. All his brothers went along with him. Running gambling joints without the protection of formal Mafia membership, the Angiulos were shaken down by local Mafiosi. So Gennaro went to see Raymond Patriarca down in Providence, Rhode Island. Boss of New England, Patriarca made Angiulo an initiated wiseguy in exchange for half his gambling income. Not previously known to Patriarca, Angiulo was made without having to prove his loyalty by the usual services, especially murder on demand. "Jerry Angiulo bought his strength like a buzzard," an underworld enemy said later. "They never did anything right," another Patriarca associate said of the Angiulos. "They did it upside down."

As the brothers prospered, all but Francesco bought homes out in the suburbs. The only bachelor among them, Francesco still lived in the old family home at 95 Prince, in a small apartment on the third floor. Every morning at nine o'clock, he crossed the street and opened The Office for business. Francesco remained in charge, collecting from bookies and loan sharks, until around four o'clock, when Gennaro came in from his million-dollar oceanfront home in Nahant. He was a testy martinet, abusing everyone on hand. Still the lawyer *manqué*, holding forth at windy length on fine points of the law, he fancied himself a legal genius. Nobody could even guess at his total wealth. In the early 1960s, according to street gossip, he had bought $10 million worth of real estate. Twenty years later, the feds knew of $45 million held by Angiulo in bank accounts—and that was only the portion the feds had managed to identify. In gathering this illegal fortune, Angiulo had served a total of sixty days in jail for trivial offenses. His larger, everyday crimes went unpunished.

The bugs at 98 Prince Street, however, might produce evidence that no gangster could scare or blow away. Two Boston Irishmen, alike in background, personality, and persistence, led the federal effort against the Angiulos. Jeremiah T. O'Sullivan, head of the Justice Department's New England Organized Crime Strike Force since 1979, was the chief prosecutor; Edward M. Quinn was the lead FBI agent on the investigation, the man at the scene who decided to enter The Office despite the voices behind the door. Both men were devout Roman Catholics, graduates of a Catholic high school and Catholic college (and, in O'Sullivan's case, a Catholic law school as well). Both had spent their whole careers in law enforcement. Both had quiet, contained personalities, with the grim patience to dig in and wait it out. "He is somewhat like a pit dog," an associate said of O'Sullivan. "Once he is onto something, once he gets his teeth into it, there is no way you are going to stop him unless you take a hatchet and chop his head off."

The feds needed all the patience they could muster. Every day, all day long, FBI agents in shifts listened to the secret transmissions from The Office. Sorting out the hoodlum voices from the background cacophony of a TV, radio, and police scanner that the wiseguys kept blaring to foil (they thought) any possible surveillance, agents taped only the conversations that seemed to veer into criminal topics. On the street outside The Office, a video camera hidden in the grill of a car parked at the corner of Prince and Thatcher caught everyone entering and leaving 98 Prince. These pictures would help identify the voices on the tapes. At three o'clock each morning, the camera car was deftly replaced by another with fresh batteries, thus holding the vital parking spot and camera angle. At one touchy moment, an Angiulo lookout peered into the car's grill but could not see the camera, which duly recorded his eyeball at close range.

In the twenty days remaining on the first court order, the bugs picked up enough gangster talk to justify extending the operation. On February 2, Gennaro Angiulo and Ilario Zannino, a capo and second to the boss, discussed the murder of Joe Barboza in 1976. An especially vicious enforcer for the New England mob, with twenty-six kills, Barboza had been hit in San Francisco because he had flipped and testified against his old employers, who then arranged his murder. "They got two chairs, Jerry," said Zannino, noting that a murder conviction in California could mean the gas chamber. "We can hold hands together."

"We'll go separate," the boss replied. "Sorry, Larry, you go first. Just your luck."

They wondered if their alleged hitman, J. R. Russo, was under suspicion. "Nobody in the world would ever indict J. R. for murder," said Angiulo.

"Wait a minute," Zannino warned. "They might have some witnesses."

Two days later, February 4, the conversation again wound toward murder. "We could use them," Angiulo said of the Winter Hill gang, his non-Mafia associates in Somerville. "I'll tell you right now if I called these guys right now they'd kill anyfuckinbody we tell 'em to." On reflection, though, the boss preferred his own hitmen: "I got Dominic, I got John Cincotti, I got Peter Limone Jr., I got Richie, I got my brother, Danny, I got you and I got four soldiers in East Boston that would kill anyfuckinbody." (In passing, the Mafioso wondered why anyone would be a policeman. "That's why all Irishmen are cops," he supposed. "They love it. Alone they're a piece of shit. When they put on the uniform and they get a little power, they start destroying everything"—exactly what Jeremiah O'Sullivan and Edward Quinn had in mind.)

The feds also heard continuous chatter about gambling and loan sharking, the everyday earners, and other routine underworld business. They went back to court and obtained secret writs for another thirty days of surveillance at The Office, and new bugs at a high-stakes poker game run by the Angiulos elsewhere in the North End. But the boss left town on vacation, and for a month the bugs yielded little of use. So on March 6 the strike force lawyers obtained another thirty-day extension.

The boss returned early from Fort Lauderdale on March 9 to deal with a related grand-jury probe of his empire. "They're saying Angiulo," he fretted. "It might be me, you, him, him, and him too. Nobody knows. Under RICO no matter who the fuck we are, if we're together, they'll get every fuckin one of us. . . . We've been sleepin. I've been jerkin off in Florida for three weeks." The grand jury summoned a strip-joint bartender who owed the family $2,000 in loan shark money. The boss learned the grand jury had granted the bartender immunity to compel his testimony. Where would that lead? The untrusted bartender was too dangerous alive. "Tell him to take a ride," Angiulo instructed one of his killers. "Bing! You hit him in the fuckin head and leave him right in the fuckin spot. . . . Just hit him in the fuckin head and stab him, okay. The jeopardy is just a little too much for me."

FBI agents monitoring the bugs heard the order to kill. At the risk of exposing the transmitters in the ceiling, they had to warn the intended victim. They told him their news came from "an informant." Less than grateful, the bartender still refused to cooperate with the government. Instead he told his designated murderer about being tipped off by the FBI. With that, the murder order was rescinded, the bartender mutely went to jail for refusing to testify, and the Mafiosi wondered about their security. Francesco Angiulo decided the feds must have tapped a nearby pay telephone favored by wiseguys. "I think that's where all this grand jury's coming from," he cautioned. "Stay the fuck away from it. . . . It has to be on that fucking telephone. Yep, has to be." A few weeks later, on a hunch he went looking for bugs in the ceiling at The Office. After a few pokes and thumps, he found nothing and gave up the search, still puzzled.

The gangsters never figured it out. After final thirty-day renewals on the bugs at The Office and the poker game, the FBI recorded Zannino describing the murders of Joe Barboza and three others; a worried Gennaro Angiulo ("we may not survive this thing") urging his son, Jason, an apprentice gangster, to disappear instead of facing the grand jury; and a reminiscent boss, recalling the time two decades earlier when the Angiulos had paid unwilling tribute—"we had to do it"—to the more powerful Genovese family in New York. And on April 27, an obliging inventory by the boss: "I wouldn't be in a legitimate business for all the fuckin money in the world," he said proudly. "We're a shylock . . . a fuckin bookmaker . . . selling marijuana . . . illegal here, illegal there, arsonists! We're every fuckin thing." The feds had heard enough. They pulled out the bugs and raided the premises on May 4 to gather physical evidence.

Almost five years later, after an eight-month trial that included twenty-nine hours of recorded conversations, Gennaro, two of his brothers, and one of their capos, Samuel Granito, were found guilty of RICO violations. It was a landmark case, the first conviction of the top leaders of a Mafia family for running a criminal enterprise, not just individual crimes. Gennaro, sixty-seven years old, was sent off to serve forty-five years. In later trials, Ilario Zannino, Jason Angiulo, and thirteen other Boston hoodlums were also convicted and given hard time. Younger, less experienced men took over the Boston family, and the chase went on. "They don't have the expertise of people who had been sitting in that seat for 20 years, the corrupt contacts in law enforcement, the insulation," said Jeremiah O'Sullivan, still in pursuit. "We ought to be investigating the hell out of them."

The Boston prosecutions had counterparts all over the country. During the 1980s, the leaders of some twenty-two Mafia families were indicted; most were convicted, usually by electronic surveillance and RICO. In New York, Fat Tony Salerno of the Genoveses, Tony Ducks Corallo of the Luccheses, and Carmine Persico of the Colombos were all found guilty, as family bosses, of operating the national Commission of the Cosa Nostra. The major families of Chicago, Cleveland, New York, Boston, Philadelphia, New Orleans, Kansas City, and Los Angeles were reeling from this federal assault. "This could be the beginning of the end for the Mafia," said

Robert Blakey, not given to facile hopes. "Families, they're no longer immune. It's taken us 20 years to do it."

※ ※

"The thing that frustrates people, I think legitimately so," said Sam Nunn, successor to John McClellan as the Senate's resident gangbuster, "is that no matter how many people you put in jail, the organizations seem to go on."

※ ※

By the 1980s the underworld had less clout in politics and most labor unions—but more because of general historical changes than because of any feats of reformers or federal prosecutors. The old bossed city machines of Frank Hague, Tom Pendergast, Ed Kelly, and their ilk, so tightly aligned with gangsters, were long and well gone. A few such regimes lingered on, slight imitations of the robust originals. Urban political corruption still festered, to the occasional titillation of voters, but it was no longer so systemic and entrenched. In the labor movement, the percentage of all American workers belonging to unions dipped year by year, down to about 18 percent by the late 1980s. Jobs for unskilled and semiskilled workers, the easiest pickings for labor racketeers, also declined in proportion to the whole work force. With fewer union members, especially of the kind favored by the underworld, organized crime's *aggregate* power in labor dribbled away.

However: once into a specific union or local, gangsters stayed there, immune to the best efforts of lawmen and crusaders. "Union corruption is at least as bad as it was during the period of the McClellan committee hearings," said a Labor Department official in 1983, "and, if anything, racketeers have become more deeply entrenched in the unions they have penetrated, and more sophisticated in their methods." The patterns of fifty and sixty years—especially in the four most bemobbed unions, the Teamsters, Longshoremen, Laborers, and Hotel and Restaurant Employees—remained astonishingly stable. Of 930 federal indictments against unions from 1980 to 1984, 45 percent involved just these four organizations. Individual labor leaders came and went, often to jail and back, and nothing changed. "We got our money from gambling," said Vincent Cafaro, an apostate member of the Genoveses, "but our real power, real strength came from the unions. With the unions behind us, we could shut down the city, the country for that matter, if we needed to, to get our way."

Robert Kennedy's Justice Department had convicted Jimmy Hoffa and 115 other Teamsters and their associates. It made no difference. Twenty years later, Mafia families still controlled the biggest, richest, strongest of all American unions, with its 1.7 million dues-payers and bulging pension funds. At least thirty-eight of the largest Teamster locals were mob-riddled. In New York City, ten of the twenty men on the Teamster Joint Council 16 were members, or sons of members, of the Mafia. As each Teamster general president in turn ran legally afoul of the feds, Mafiosi in Chicago, Kansas City, and New York picked his successor. "They was here a long time before any of us ever got here," President Roy Lee Williams told the government after his conviction for trying to bribe a United States senator, "and they have got pretty powerful. And you fellows haven't been able to do nothing with them either."

Mob power rippled through the Teamsters into legitimate industries, especially construction and garbage collection, notably around Detroit and the environs of New York City. In a bugged conversation, Sal Avellino, who ran the Lucchese garbage interests, explained his designs: "We're gonna knock everybody out, absorb everybody, eat them up, or whoever we, whoever stays in there is only who we allowing to stay in there." "You got big plans," said a garbage associate. "Well, isn't that the truth," Avellino allowed. The Lucchese boss, Tony Ducks Corallo, by himself made at least $200,000 a year in extorted cash offerings from the garbage industry on Long Island.

Directed by hoodlums, the Teamster pension funds made huge loans on favored terms to favored customers. Moe Dalitz and his fellow gangsters from Cleveland got $62 million to build the Rancho La Costa resort near San Diego. Morris Shenker, a mob attorney from St. Louis, was loaned $180.3 million to invest in California real estate. The Pritzker family from Chicago—which owned the Hyatt hotel chain. Braniff Airlines, *McCall's* magazine, and many other enterprises—received $54.4 million worth of Teamster loans from 1959 to 1975. Abe Pritzker, the founding father, and his associate Arthur Greene had ancient business ties to the Capones, Meyer Lansky, Longy Zwillman, and other thugs. Thereby vouched for, the Pritzkers and Teamsters naturally trusted each other. "You are making a legitimate borrowing at a legitimate rate of interest," said Jay Pritzker, "and you are going to pay it back. What difference does the lender's reputation really make, other than the risk of unfair accusations? Morally, I see nothing wrong with it."

On the New York–New Jersey waterfront, the Mafiosi in charge of the Longshoremen's union deflected successive waves of reformers and lawmen. After exposures and hearings, Joe Ryan's pliant twenty-six-year reign as titular head of the union had ended in 1953. A waterfront commission, appointed to clean up the port, abolished the hiring shape-up, a rich source of bribes and extortion money. Otherwise life on the docks went on as before. "I've lost," concluded John Corridan, the "waterfront priest" who had defied the gangsters for years. "The city and people of New York have lost. The mobsters won. They're still on the docks. The more unscrupulous elements within the shipping industry won. . . . We have a longer and harder fight here than the fight against Communism."

Mike Clemente of the Genoveses, boss of Manhattan's key Longshoremen's Local 856, was convicted of extortion in 1953 and banned from the union. So he installed a stooge, Fred Field, and kept running the piers through him. In 1963, unhappy with the incumbent union president, the gangsters replaced him with Teddy Gleason. A union veteran who had started out on the West Side docks at fifteen for ten cents an hour, Gleason was more amenable than his predecessor. "Teddy is number one," explained Thomas Buzzanca, a waterfront racketeer, in a secretly taped conversation. "First, he—he likes money. Second of all, he wants to be around and third of all he's Irish. If he could be Irish first and have the other two, fine, but if he can't, he's Irish third." In other words, he deferred without flinching to Italian gangsters.

Under Gleason's nodding supervision, the Gambino family ran the Brooklyn docks while the Genoveses held Manhattan, New Jersey, and a southern offshoot in Miami. Tino Fiumara, a young Genovese capo, watched over New Jersey with special panache. Moving among remorseless killers who did not frighten easily, Fiumara still scared everybody. He killed the godfather of his own child; he killed two brothers, Patsy and Nicky Colucci, then let their brother Vincent survive and preside over one of his locals. "Tino's good points is that everybody fears and respects him," Thomas Buzzanca pointed out. "That's a good thing. He has blind devotion. . . . I absolutely think that [if] this guy tempers himself, he'll be, ten years from now, he'll be awesome. . . . He'll have the best of two worlds. Good sense, good judgment plus, which we all live under, fear. Ya need to have that balance."

An ambitious federal investigation of the Longshoremen in the late 1970s used bugs and undercover agents to convict 110 gangsters, businessmen, and union officials. Clemente, Fiumara, and Buzzanca got ten to twenty-five years each for extortion. Once again, it hardly mattered. "It would be lovely to be idealistic and say we cleaned up the waterfront," a strike force attorney admitted. "I would be foolish to try and make that statement. The circumstances still remain." The Mafia families always had willing new men ready to take over the vacated union offices.

Among the Laborers, the same dreary pattern. Joe Moreschi finally retired as president in 1968 after forty-two years of inattentive, corrupted rule. The Capones picked his successors, Peter Fosco, then Fosco's son Angelo. As before, the real power rested with Mafia families around the country, especially in Chicago, Cleveland, St. Louis, Buffalo, Philadelphia, and northern New Jersey. In Manhattan, the Luccheses and Genoveses ran five Laborer locals. Because this underworld strength was so widely distributed and decentralized, no single prosecution could much affect its grip on the union. In concert with the Teamsters, the mobbed-up Laborer locals gave Mafiosi swaggering privileges at many construction sites, with a constant threat to shut down expensive projects if contractors did not provide kickbacks and no-show jobs.

By the 1980s, most of the six hundred thousand members of the Laborers were either black or Hispanic. They did the dirtiest, lowest-paid jobs in construction. Robert Powell, a black vice president of the union from Washington, D.C., was told by Arthur Coia, the secretary-treasurer, "that the Italians had organized the Laborers," according to Powell, "and that nobody black or anyone else was going to ever take control." Powell nonetheless thought about running for national president at the 1981 convention. "Powell, you're dead, you're dead," warned Angelo Fosco, who was then elected to another five-year term. A year later, a Hispanic protégé of Powell's, Ben Medina, ran for president of Local 332 in Philadelphia. Five men came to Medina's home at midnight, tied up his wife, and beat him to death. When Powell testified before a federal investigation in 1985, he was understandably cynical. "I remember when all of these other hearings was held," he said, recalling the Kefauver and McClellan committees, "but what happened? A watered down solution, just enough to pat somebody on the shoulder and go ahead on; business as usual. . . . As soon as you put one in jail, there is another one to step in his place. So let's not kid each other, sir."

From 1982 to 1984, Senator Sam Nunn's Permanent Subcommittee on Investigations held a series of five hearings on the affairs of the Hotel and Restaurant Employees union. Witnesses testified to illegal practices at HRE locals around the country: shakedowns of employers, membership dues deducted from paychecks with no apparent benefits to the employees, tight collusive arrangements with nearby Mafia families. For fifty years, the Capones had run the union from Chicago. Edward Hanley of Chicago's Local 450, elected international president in 1973, was a tool of Tony Accardo and Joey Aiuppa. Accardo and other Capones owned vacation homes in San Diego, where the local Mafia contact was Joe LiMandri, a convicted dope dealer from New York. Two HRE "organizers" were dispatched to San Diego in 1978 to add muscle to the local there. "I watched their organizing efforts in San Diego," reported an investigator from the district attorney's office. "It was an easy job. They would spend half the day playing golf at the Stardust [Hotel and Country Club], then attend the races at Del Mar and then confer with Joe LiMandri at the cardroom in the Stardust." They didn't need to bother with job sites and grubby union details.

After New Jersey voters in 1976 legalized casino gambling in Atlantic City, the town's HRE Local 54 became the springboard for designs by at least nine Mafia families on the expected windfalls from an East Coast version of Las Vegas. The authorized games and slot machines in Atlantic City were part of a national trend: repeatedly unable to beat gambling, authorities gave up and joined it. Most states now allowed some form of legal betting and odds defying, whether lotteries, off-track race betting, bingo and its variants, numbers games, or casinos. Atlantic City had long been a wide-open town, controlled by the Philadelphia underworld, with many bookies, numbers joints, and payoffs to cops and politicians. Despite these attractions, the old resort was crumbling, with thinner crowds and harder times on the boardwalk. Legal casinos were supposed to revive it and pump new tax revenues to the state.

Over the first six years after legalization, New Jersey made $436.4 million in casino taxes—but at the cost to Atlantic City of a fourfold increase in crime, the demise of 90 percent of the local businesses, a declining population and tax base, and boarded-up buildings in the shadow of the casinos, which kept roaring and fleecing all day while everything else withered. Local 54, serving the casinos, shared in this limited prosperity, with membership up from twenty-five hundred to fifteen thousand. Directed by his mob masters, President Frank Gerace of Local 54 passed along $125,000 from the Philadelphia family to a crooked Atlantic City politician. For this offense the New Jersey Casino Control Commission bestirred itself, removing Gerace from his union office. He was soon back as an HRE consultant, at $48,000 a year, and trustee of two union funds.

In every sense, Atlantic City was indeed another Las Vegas. "The days of James Cagney and George Raft is over," one interested Mafioso said to another, referring to the film gangsters always ready to shoot it out. "No one is going to fool around with your license in Atlantic City or anything like that. It will be done like any other corporate business is done. . . . And if a little pressure has to be applied it's applied where it hurts them. If they are getting gas deliveries, they don't get gas deliveries any more. The Teamsters just don't go there no more because the Teamsters are part of us. And whatever the reason is, they stall and stall and no one will go. That's the way it happens."

🌺 🌺

While the Mafia plied its familiar trades, the lush and verdant fields of dope dealing grew newer, younger groups of organized criminals. True to the patterns of Prohibition and its aftermath, many of the new gangsters were recent immigrants to the United States. They turned to crime not because American society was closed to them, but quite the opposite. Coming from countries in tight circumstances, under Draconian police methods, they found here fresh air and relative freedom, with lawmen diffused among city, county, state, and federal jurisdictions, and split further among a labyrinth of federal agencies. The sheer space and variety of America, the ease and speed of travel, and the anonymity of urban life made it simpler to commit the crime and melt away into protective ethnic enclaves.

Two of the new underworld groups, the bikers and black gangs, were homegrown. The outlaw motorcycle groups composed a category unto themselves: hoodlum clans with no definite ethnic or geographic base, more an expression of modern society than a retaliation against it. The Hell's Angels, the prototypes, were founded around 1950 in southern California, the least rooted part of the country. On their model came the Pagans (started in Prince Georges County, Maryland, in 1959), the Outlaws (in Chicago, also 1959), and the Bandidos (in Houston, in 1966). A typical member of these four major gangs was a white man of working-class background, alienated from work and family, fond of primitive amusements, and loyal only to his bike and gang. By common standards, the bikers barely existed on the fringes of decent society. But in a group of themselves, bellowing and billowing down a highway in formation, they had emphatic presence. Unlike other criminal groups, they proclaimed their identities. Their beards, regalia, and black leather jackets announced: We're Angels (or whoever). We're here. Watch out.

Always scary and dangerous, easily violent, the bikers for years committed mostly petty crimes. They stole and fenced motorcycles, did small-time drug deals, got drunk and busted up bars. Around 1970, a *Godfather* effect started changing them into more ambitious organized-crime groups. "I joined because of a brotherhood, and I thought it was a good idea," recalled one Angel who witnessed this transition. "We were all one family, one big brotherhood, we would all stay together. Our kids would be Hell's Angels. . . . And then people got into drugs really heavy and the dealing of drugs. They accumulated big money. They had different ideas. After the *Godfather* movie and everything, it kind of evolved all into just one big organization for profit. They got away from the brotherhood, the whole thing of it, and now it is nothing to kill anybody." Once a substitute family for rootless nomads, the biker gangs became just another bunch of thugs.

Their specialty was synthetic drugs—methamphetamines (speed), PCP, LSD—manufactured from available materials, therefore produced locally instead of imported across difficult borders. Explicitly taking cues from Mafia families, the bikers organized themselves with national officers and policy boards. A prospective member would enter a probation period during which he ran errands, fixed bikes, stood guard, and proved he could fight. As the final test he would have to kill someone—"roll his bones"—and then be awarded tattoos and gang colors for his jacket. (A fraudulently acquired tattoo, if discovered, might be cut from a man's arm, flesh and all.) If a prospect did not commit murder within six months, he would be killed for dereliction and knowing too much. This procedure shielded the gang from infiltration by undercover lawmen.

In the 1980s the four main motorcycle gangs had around three thousand members in about 130 chapters around the country. Perhaps another four thousand bikers belonged to smaller outlaw gangs, both affiliates and independents. Territories were shifted and individuals moved around, making them hard to trace. Often connected to Mafia families, the bikers performed murder, arson, assault, and loan-sharking chores for the Mafiosi. "Organized crime figures are wearing suits now," a Pagan explained. "The Pagans are out in the street doing the dirty work." The bikers were—remarkably—even more vicious than the Mafia. Not sweet-tempered to begin with, they ingested speed and cocaine all day long, growing ever twitchier and more paranoid. Glaring out at other people through their chemical tunnels, they recognized no traditional mob code for dealing with the upperworld. They would kill or beat up anyone, including cops and prosecutors, for any reason or no reason. The ultimate modern personalities, tied to nothing but the moment, bikers lived and died for that existential instant of violence. Their funeral rituals became quite practiced.

Organized gangs of American blacks came out of social upheavals of the 1960s. For decades, minor black hoodlums had worked black neighborhoods, dealing dope and running numbers as low-level employees of Mafia families. When formerly Italian inner-city neighborhoods turned blacker, and when the civil rights movement encouraged all blacks to consider their own possibilities, black gangsters moved up and took over their own turfs. In Buffalo, blacks seized control of numbers gambling from the Magaddinos, at first paying a token tribute of 10 percent of profits, then no tribute at all. In Newark, they snatched the numbers trade from Richie Boiardo, a Genovese capo, even to the point of robbing and shooting at Boiardo's men. "Everybody wants his turn at making it," said an Italian gangster pushed out of East Harlem. "We had ours and I guess it's their turn now. But if you watch the way they run the operation, it's not going to be the same. A lot of times they refuse to pay off. That leads to trouble and trouble always brings heat. In the 20 years I'm here in East Harlem, we never refused to pay off even when we were sure we were being taken. Now nobody knows what the hell is going to happen."

Along with most of organized crime, blacks moved on from

gambling to narcotics. "The blacks use more dope than anybody," said a white dealer active in New York, "but you don't see Italian pushers no more in Harlem or Bed-Stuy. Not healthy. The blacks run the streets now, and look after their own." In the late 1960s, Charles Green organized the first major black dope gang in New York, importing heroin and cocaine from South America and selling it through over one hundred distributors and couriers. After Green's arrest in 1970, Frank Matthews took over his operation. Connected for business purposes to the Gambino and Lucchese families, Matthews organized a meeting in Atlanta in October 1971 of about forty top black drug merchants—the first evidence of such national cooperation among black gangs.

Matthews in turn yielded New York to Nicky Barnes, who was especially slick. A heroin addict from the age of fourteen, Barnes had met Crazy Joey Gallo in prison during the 1960s and learned how to run a sophisticated gang. Back on the street after 1970, with contacts among the Bonannos and Luccheses, he organized a seven-man "Council" of Harlem drug lords. The Council controlled heroin trafficking through New York State into Canada and Pennsylvania for most of the 1970s. "We weren't subjected to any intimidation by any outside group," Barnes said later. "We competed by having the best powder because drug addicts don't buy names, they buy the quality." For his own habit, Barnes now preferred pure cocaine. He owned five homes, a fleet of expensive cars, and a boggling wardrobe. In 1978, after beating previous charges of murder, bribery, and drug and gun violations, Barnes was finally convicted of running his heroin empire and sentenced to life.

Up stepped Papa D's Family, another black group, run (according to sworn testimony) by Pop Washington from a brownstone headquarters at 119 West 130th Street in Harlem. The brownstone was protected by TV surveillance cameras and a twenty-four-hour armed guard. Women were crucial to the operation. They smuggled in dope, secreted in vaginas or rectums, or strapped under their breasts, from London, Florida, and the Bahamas. The drugs were distributed through New York and at least six other states. A woman lawyer, known only as Mother Superior, handled the gang's financial accounts and legal problems. "Every time that we were to pick up," one courier said later, "money would be tooken to her office, and a day or two later, we would be on the move again." The presence of women did not temper the Family's enforcement methods. Somebody who owed them money fled to California. They followed him there, killed him, and sent the body back to New York with synthetic heroin concealed in the coffin.

The criminals made even the law work in their favor. Children grew up quickly in black ghettos, skipping childhood and admiring the pimps and dealers in their rococo clothes and cars. Drug rings sometimes used children, legally immune, for the more public roles of making drops and collections. In Detroit, the Young Boys consortium employed up to 450 kids, most under eighteen, some as young as eleven. As recounted by former members of the gang, Butch Jones started the Young Boys in his Monterey-Dexter neighborhood in 1980. The members wore coded jogging suits: red suits for money runners, blue for heroin couriers. Drug envelopes were stamped with brand names and logos. Specialists provided fake driver's licenses, Social Security cards, and birth certificates. The conspiring adults, at least, were still vulnerable. Jones and other top dogs were convicted in 1983. Without them, remnants spun off a new organization, Pony Down, and conducted business along the same lines.

Back in the early 1970s, some observers had predicted a black succession in organized crime: the various black gangs would grow increasingly strong and stable, displacing the dominant Italians. By the late 1980s, this still had not happened. The black gangs held only black neighborhoods, dealing mainly in drugs and numbers. They never developed a national structure like the Mafia and its Commission. Among the Italian gangs, patrilineal kinship ties helped ensure the continuity and loyalty of the enterprise. In the black underclass that spawned the black gangs, family patterns were matrilineal and less orderly. Most of the young black hoodlums had no fathers on hand to emulate. The black gangs proved too short-lived and undisciplined to approach the ongoing might of the Mafia. "There was no loyalty," Nicky Barnes said of his experience with the Council. "We agreed to watch the back of one another if any of us had gotten into any trouble, and after I got arrested, and after I got sentenced, they forgot about me. So the Council was good as long as I was there, and I was able to contribute, but when I needed them to look out for me, they didn't do it." Barnes himself flipped after four years in jail and testified against his old friends, sending fifty of them to prison.

The new immigrant gangs were more loyal and durable, thus more dangerous. Two of these groups, the Cubans and Vietnamese, were legacies of failed American efforts to fight Communism overseas. Gangsters from the old country washed ashore in America and enjoyed all the benefits here of free, illicit enterprise. These recruits for the underworld owed their new prosperity to the authority of the American government, from the State Department to the police department. John Kennedy might have appreciated the ironies.

Before Castro's revolution, the Batista regime and American gangsters together ran lucrative casinos in Havana. Following the defeated Bay of Pigs invasion in 1961, Cuban hoodlums settled in America and renewed their friendships among domestic Mafiosi. Their leader was José Miguel Battle, known as El Padrino, "the Godfather." Thirty-two years old in 1961, a veteran of Batista's army and a former Havana vice cop, Battle survived the Bay of Pigs landing, came to south Florida, and was made a lieutenant in the United States Army by a special act of Congress. Assisted by the Trafficante family of Tampa, Battle and his associates ran dope and gambling in Cuban neighborhoods. In the late 1960s Battle switched his base to Union City, New Jersey, across the Hudson from Manhattan, again with the help of Mafia partners. They muscled into Hispanic criminal enterprises in and around New York City. During the 1970s Battle served thirty-one months in jail on gambling and murder-conspiracy charges. His partners kept his seat warm and welcomed him back.

By 1985 this Cuban gang, known as the Corporation, had some twenty-five hundred employees in New York City, branches in Miami and northern New Jersey, and boundless assets and cash flows. Grounded in drugs and gambling, they committed other crimes, arson and murder, as necessary. From 1980 to 1985 they were responsible for about thirty deaths in New York City. Gambling in New York alone earned the Corporation at least $45 million, perhaps up to $100 million, each year. The Corporation made additional millions by monopolizing tickets, mainly in Miami, Los Angeles, and New York, for the misnamed Puerto Rican lottery. Lawmen intercepted Corporation couriers in Miami and London with packages of $439,000 and $450,000 in cash— merely hinting at the extent of the profits. Each week the Cuban gangsters made grateful payoffs to sponsoring Mafia groups for the privilege of doing business in America.

The Colombian cocaine trade grew from a partnership with Cuban hoodlums. At first, in the 1960s, Colombian middlemen bought raw coca from Andean peasants and processed it into cocaine, which they sold to Cubans for distribution in the United States. As American consumer demand exploded, and as Colombian immigrants established colonies in Miami, New York, Los Angeles, and Chicago, Colombian gangsters stopped selling coke to Cubans and took over the distribution and profits for themselves. Most of this cocaine was smuggled in through south Florida. The Colombian gangs, about a dozen in all, dealt with anybody who had the cash. In so disorganized a trade, violence and ripoffs became routine. "I wish we were so fortunate, really, as to have the traditional organized Mafia-type families running the drug business," said Attorney General Jim Smith of Florida in 1981. "We might be able to keep up with that kind of activity, but our state law enforcement agencies have identified something like 1,000 major drug dealers in the Dade–Broward County areas." So much cocaine was available that the wholesale price dropped for a time from $60,000 to $14,000 a kilogram—still enough to generate huge revenues for the Colombian cartels.

The new Asian gangsters in America came—at first—from legal immigration and social organizations. After the nativist immigration quotas of the 1920s were liberalized in 1965, the Chinese population in the United States jumped 85 percent between 1970 and 1980, to a total of 806,000. During the single year of 1984, almost 50,000 Chinese settled in America, constituting the second-largest group of legal immigrants after Mexicans. These new citizens added members to various Chinese tongs, legitimate benevolent societies dating back centuries. These tongs, however, included criminal spinoffs and street gangs. Given the problems of multiple Chinese dialects and the inconsistent transliteration of Chinese names into English, American lawmen found these new gangs extraordinarily difficult to identify and track. With branches around the country, in most Chinatowns, the gangs dealt in gambling, prostitution, extortion, robbery, and drugs, usually within Chinese areas, exploiting latent tensions between FOB ("fresh off the boat") and ABC (American-born Chinese) groups. Fighting among themselves, the gangs heedlessly sprayed gunfire on innocent bystanders. During the 1970s, San Francisco police recorded about fifty Chinese gang-related murders, including five at a grisly massacre in a Chinese restaurant in September 1977.

The end of the Vietnam war in 1975 sent a new wave of Asian immigrants to America, with a small core of gangsters. Nguyen Cao Ky, a former leader of the Saigon regime, established an anti-Communist organization in exile with generals of the late South Vietnamese army. According to sworn testimony by a former member, this group of about a thousand members had an organized crime division, called the Dark Side or Black Side, with branches in San Francisco (the Black Eagles), Chicago (the Eagle Seven), Houston (the Fishermen), Los Angeles (the Frogmen), and other cities. Ky's men recruited recent Vietnamese immigrants and trained them to rob and kill. They sold drugs and preyed on Asian businesses and gambling dens. Victims were usually too frightened to testify; Vietnamese gangsters were rougher, more ruthless than the Chinese hoodlums with whom they competed. Back home, Chinese and Vietnamese had feuded for hundreds of years. Now they transferred their quarrels to America, frustrating lawmen who could neither comprehend nor stop them.

The Jamaican posse gangs also came to the United States after political turmoil at home. Named for the vigilante groups in spaghetti western movies, popular fare in Jamaican ghettos, the posses first surfaced during the bloody Jamaican election campaign of 1980, murdering hundreds of people from both political parties. The posses showed up in America shortly thereafter, most visibly in the drug centers of Miami and New York, dealing cocaine and killing anybody in their way. Their trademarks were Volvo automobiles and nine-millimeter handguns. By 1988 authorities knew of some thirty posses around the country with over three thousand members responsible for up to eight hundred murders. When in need of new blood, the posses returned home, to the slums of East Kingston. They flashed cars and money around and brought platoons of illegal immigrants back to the United States. A major federal investigation, Operation Rum Punch, arrested over one hundred posse members suspected of drug dealing, murders, robberies, and kidnappings.

With all this new competition, the American Mafia also went back home. From the late 1960s on, Sicilian immigrants—called zips—entered the United States, legally and otherwise, and joined Italian-American gangs. Cesare Bonventre, well connected through two uncles in the Bonanno family, came over in 1968 and rose quickly by killing up to twenty people. He was too ambitious, though, offending more-assimilated Mafiosi, and in 1984 was murdered, chopped in pieces, and stuffed into three oil drums. The zips did expedite dope deals such as an elaborate operation that smuggled in $1.65 billion worth of heroin over five years and distributed it through pizza joints around the country. But the Sicilians, because of their drugs and bumptious foreignness, further disrupted the diminishing level of trust within the beleaguered American Mafia. "You can't trust those bastard zips," Lefty Ruggiero of the Bonannos warned an associate. "Greaseballs are motherfuckers. When a zip kisses, forget about it. They hate the American people. . . . You cannot give them the power. They don't give a fuck. They don't care who's boss. They got no respect. There's no family."

As of the late 1980s, none of the new organized crime groups yet enjoyed the entrenched connections of the Mafia in America. The new gangsters had no power in labor racketeering, and few lines to crooked politicians or lawmen. Their turfs were smaller and more precarious. Taken together, though, they threw the underworld into chaos, a degree of disorganized confusion not seen since the early days of Prohibition. The new groups dealt mainly in drugs, and those volatile commodities wiped out all the old rules. "Anyone who deals in junk," said Gennaro Angiulo, "will tell the feds anything they want to hear." Coked-up gangsters would kill anyone, including cops and uninvolved women and children. That made lawmen even angrier and more intent on the chase.

Riven from within, besieged by the new criminal gangs, and pursued by waves and waves of federal prosecutions, Mafiosi faced difficult times, the worst they had known. The one-two punch of electronic surveillance and flipped wiseguys meant the effective end of *omertà*, the ancient code of silence toward the law. If authorized bugs and taps did not directly record the embarrassing evidence, someone high in the Mafia—Angelo Lonardo of Cleveland, Frank Bompensiero of San Diego, Vincent Cafaro of the Genoveses—would come forward to sing and inform, to buy mercy for himself and send away his old comrades instead. "People don't train their people no more," lamented Aniello Dellacroce of the Gambinos. "There's no more respect. There's no more nothing." The acids of modernity ate away at everyone, even the antimodern Mafia. The younger Mafiosi were bound together mainly by fear and self-interest, no longer by kinship, culture, and tradition. That was not enough. "My Tradition has died in America," said Joe Bonanno, himself the author of a revealing autobiography. "The way of life that I and my Sicilian ancestors pursued is dead. What Americans refer to as 'the Mafia' is a degenerate outgrowth of that life-style."

❦ ❦

Degenerate, maybe, but not dead. For years, hopeful observers had been announcing premature obituaries of the Mafia. According to theories of ethnic succession in organized crime, Italian gangsters should have disappeared by the 1980s. The general levels of education, income, and white-collar status of Italian-Americans were now at or beyond national norms. Italians could no longer be described as a marginal group, poor and ignorant, needing crime as a way out. Yet the Mafia remained the strongest group in the underworld, the only one with truly national scope and six decades of continuity and killing reputation behind it.

In fact, higher education and economic mobility did not necessarily turn younger Italians away from organized crime. Some of the Mafia's rising stars in the 1980s—Sal Testa of Philadelphia, Vincent Ferrara of Boston, Michael Franzese of the Colombos— were college educated, with the skills and discipline to make their way through the upperworld. Mafia fathers still hoped their sons would follow family tradition. Joseph Pistone, an FBI undercover agent, spent six years among the Bonannos and Colombos. "Their children were all involved in the Mafia," Pistone told the Nunn committee in 1988. "They were all well aware of what their fathers were doing, and they were all thieves in their own right. I did not find anyone that I dealt with that tried to steer their sons away from a life of crime."

It came down to this: underworld life was still too easy, plush, and thrilling for some people to resist. Greg Scarpa, a Colombo capo, dressed and spoke well, like any good citizen of brains and privilege. "He is very, very bright," said his former attorney in 1986. "He could have been a lawyer probably, or run any big business. But it would be no fun to him." *Fun:* the pleasures of deference and opulence, without the bother of working hard and earning them, kept organized crime attractive no matter how perilous the attention of racketbusters became. "As a wiseguy," Lefty Ruggiero exulted, "you can lie, you can cheat, you can steal, you can kill people—*legitimately.* You can do any goddamn thing you want, and nobody can say anything about it. Who wouldn't want to be a wiseguy?"

ACKNOWLEDGMENTS

I have drawn most of this book from manuscript collections, congressional hearings, and the vast—if unreliable—body of published material on the history of organized crime. In addition to these sources, I have conducted interviews with Elizabeth Olney Anderson, Amy Ferguson Beltz, G. Robert Blakey, Frank Devereaux, Morton Downey, Jr., Scott Elder, Myrtle Ferguson, Frank Havey, Maxine Temple Jones, Aaron M. Kohn, George Leary, Jacob Lewiton, Paul Fishman Maccabee, Matthew McGrath, Jr., Joseph Meldon, Bradshaw Mintener, Jimmy O'Keefe, Elizabeth Olney, Margaret Olney, Jeremiah O'Sullivan, Virgil W. Peterson, James Ring, Frank Saunders, Walter Seaver, Arthur H. Sherry, William Stevenson, David Strassel, Dwight S. Strong, and Charles E. Wyzanski, Jr. I have also corresponded with Joseph L. Albini, Stephen Birmingham, Joseph Boskin, Harold Conrad, Richard Dubow, John Robert Greene, Murray Kempton, Herman Kogan, Tommy Prior, Charles H. Trout, William F. Whyte, and Marda Woodbury. My grateful thanks to all.

Friends and colleagues of mine have helped shape this book. I am indebted to my associates in the Alliance of Independent Scholars, especially Lance Farrar, Eugenia Kaledin, Polly Kaufman, Joan Mark, Sherrin Marshall, Phil Nicholson, J. David Reno, Paul Wright, and Nancy Zumwalt. Katherine Poole, Robert J. Antonio, Norman Yetman, Justin Kaplan, Steven Spitzer, Vanda Sendzimir, Alice Van Deburg, and David Shiang gave me research tips and/or trenchant critiques. My editor, Harvey Ginsberg, and my agent, Robin Straus, have again been the absolute sine qua nons for a book project of mine, sending me an effective mixture of prodding and encouragement.

Alexandra Dundas Todd is a sociologist, my scholarly colleague, and my wife. Though she does not entirely approve of my remarks about some Mafia sociologists at the end of Chapter 9, she has sharpened my thinking there and elsewhere in the book. For that, and for many other reasons, this final, fullest expression of gratitude goes to her, the at-last love and light of my life.

MANUSCRIPT COLLECTIONS

Sidney A. Aisner Papers, Harvard Law School Library

Harry J. Anslinger Papers, Historical Collections and Labor Archives, Pattee Library, Pennsylvania State University

Newton D. Baker Papers, Manuscript Division, Library of Congress

Eleanor Margaret Baumgardner Papers, Bentley Historical Library, University of Michigan

Heber Blankenhorn Papers, Labor Archives, Wayne State University

Robert F. Bradford Papers, Massachusetts Historical Society

William Jeremiah Burke Papers, Joint Collection, University of Missouri Western Historical Manuscript Collection—Columbia and State Historical Society of Missouri Manuscripts

Royal S. Copeland Papers, Bentley Historical Library, University of Michigan

Thomas E. Dewey Papers, Department of Rare Books and Special Collections, Rush Rhees Library, University of Rochester

William O. Douglas Papers, Manuscript Division, Library of Congress

Herbert B. Ehrmann Papers, Harvard Law School Library

James A. Farley Papers, Manuscript Division, Library of Congress

Homer Ferguson Papers, Bentley Historical Library, University of Michigan

Josephine Fellows Gomon Papers, Bentley Historical Library, University of Michigan

Eugene Gressman Papers, Bentley Historical Library, University of Michigan

John Marshall Harlan Papers, Mudd Manuscript Library, Princeton University

Hubert H. Humphrey Papers, Minnesota Historical Society

Estes Kefauver Papers, Special Collections Library, University of Tennessee

John F. Kennedy Papers, John Fitzgerald Kennedy Library

Robert F. Kennedy Papers, John Fitzgerald Kennedy Library

Arthur Krock Papers, Mudd Manuscript Library, Princeton University

James M. Landis Papers, Manuscript Division, Library of Congress

Henry Cabot Lodge II Papers, Massachusetts Historical Society

Ralph Lowell Papers, Massachusetts Historical Society

John L. McClellan Papers, Ouachita Baptist University Library

James P. McGranery Papers, Manuscript Division, Library of Congress

James J. P. McShane Papers, John Fitzgerald Kennedy Library

Manhattan District Attorney Papers, New York Municipal Archives

Eugene Meyer Papers, Manuscript Division, Library of Congress

Maurice Milligan Collection, Joint Collection, University of Missouri Western Historical Manuscript Collection–Columbia and State Historical Society of Missouri Manuscripts

Raymond Moley Papers, Hoover Institution, Stanford University

Karl E. Mundt Papers, Dakota State College Library

Murder Incorporated Papers, Kings County District Attorney Papers, New York Municipal Archives

Frank Murphy Papers, Bentley Historical Library, University of Michigan

New England Watch & Ward Society Papers, Harvard Law School Library

John Francis Neylan Papers, Bancroft Library, University of California at Berkeley

George Read Nutter Papers, Massachusetts Historical Society

Victor Olander Papers, Chicago Historical Society

Westbrook Pegler Papers, Herbert Hoover Library

Roscoe Pound Papers, Harvard Law School Library

Joseph Pulitzer Papers, Manuscript Division, Library of Congress

John J. Raskob Papers, Hagley Museum and Library

George S. Robinson Papers, Harry S Truman Library

Arthur M. Schlesinger, Jr., Papers, John Fitzgerald Kennedy Library

Henry Lee Shattuck Papers, Massachusetts Historical Society

Carl Solberg Papers, Minnesota Historical Society

Theodore C. Sorensen Papers, John Fitzgerald Kennedy Library

Harlan Fiske Stone Papers, Manuscript Division, Library of Congress

Charles W. Tobey Papers, Special Collections, Dartmouth College Library

William Roy Vallance Papers, Department of Rare Books and Special Collections, Rush Rhees Library, University of Rochester

Harry H. Vaughan Papers, Harry S Truman Library

Mabel Walker Willebrandt Papers, Manuscript Division, Library of Congress

Alexander Woollcott Papers, Houghton Library, Harvard University

ABBREVIATIONS OF GOVERNMENT PUBLICATIONS

ACL   *Anticrime Legislation: Hearings Before the Committee on Interstate and Foreign Commerce, Senate, 82 Cong. 1 Sess., September 19–21, 1951*

AFH   *Arson-for-Hire: Hearings Before the Permanent Subcommittee on Investigations of the Committee on Government Operations, Senate, 95 Cong. 2 Sess., August 23–September 14, 1978*

AGV   *American Guild of Variety Artists: Hearings Before the Permanent Subcommittee on Investigations of the Committee on Government Operations, Senate, 87 Cong. 2 Sess., June 12–26, 1962*

ALE   *Adequacy of Law Enforcement Powers for Labor Department Criminal Investigations: Hearings Before the Committee on Labor and Human Resources, Senate, 98 Cong. 1 Sess., February 2–3, 1983*

CAO   *Crime in America—Aspects of Organized Crime, Court Delay, and Juvenile Justice: Hearings Before the Select Committee on Crime, House, 91 Cong. 1 Sess., December 1969*

CCT   *Controlling Crime Through More Effective Law Enforcement: Hearings Before the Subcommittee on Criminal Laws and Procedures of the Committee on the Judiciary, Senate, 90 Cong. 1 Sess., March 7–July 12, 1967*

CHI   *Organized Crime in Chicago: Hearing Before the Permanent Subcommittee on Investigations of the Committee on Governmental Affairs, Senate, 98 Cong. 1 Sess., March 4, 1983*

CLP   *Criminal Laws and Procedures: Hearings Before the Subcommittee on Criminal Laws and Procedures of the Judiciary Committee, Senate, 89 Cong. 2 Sess., March 22–May 11, 1966*

CSB   *Impact of Crime on Small Business: Hearings Before the Select*

Committee on Small Business, Senate, 90 Cong. 1 Sess., April 24, 1967–May 16, 1968

FEA *The Federal Effort Against Organized Crime: Hearings Before a Subcommittee of the Committee on Government Operations,* House, 90 Cong. 1 Sess., April 5, 1967–February 8, 1968

FEP *Federal Effort Against Organized Crime—Role of the Private Sector: Hearings Before a Subcommittee of the Committee on Government Operations,* House, 91 Cong. 2 Sess., August 13 and September 15, 1970

FID *Financial Investigation of Drug Trafficking: Hearing Before the Select Committee on Narcotics Abuse and Control,* House, 97 Cong. 1 Sess., October 9, 1981

GAC *Government's Ability to Combat Labor Management Racketeering: Hearings Before the Permanent Subcommittee on Investigations of the Committee on Governmental Affairs,* Senate, 97 Cong. 1 Sess., October 28–November 3, 1981

GLR *Profile of Organized Crime—Great Lakes Region: Hearings Before the Permanent Subcommittee on Investigations of the Committee on Governmental Affairs,* Senate, 98 Cong. 2 Sess., January 25–February 1, 1984

GOC *Gambling and Organized Crime: Hearings Before the Permanent Subcommittee on Investigations of the Committee on Government Operations,* Senate, 87 Cong. 1 Sess., August 22–September 8, 1961

HRE *Hotel Employees & Restaurant Employees International Union: Hearings Before the Permanent Subcommittee on Investigations,* Senate, 97 Cong. 2 Sess.–98 Cong. 2 Sess., June 22, 1982–June 21, 1984

IAI *Injunctions Against Illegitimate Labor Practices and Outlawing Racketeering: Hearings Before Subcommittee No. 3 of the Committee on the Judiciary,* House, 77 Cong. 2 Sess., April 2–May 1, 1942

IAP *Investigation of the Assassination of President John F. Kennedy: Hearings Before the Select Committee on Assassinations,* House, 95 Cong. 2 Sess., September 6–December 29, 1978

IIA *Investigation of Improper Activities in the Labor or Management Field: Hearings Before the Select Committee,* Senate, 85 Cong. 1 Sess.–86 Cong. 1 Sess., February 26, 1957–September 9, 1959

IMW *Investigation as to the Manner in Which the United States Board of Parole Is Operating . . . : Hearings Before a Subcommittee of the Committee on Expenditures in the Executive Departments,* House, 80 Cong. 2 Sess., September 25, 1947–March 11, 1948

IOC *Investigation of Organized Crime in Interstate Commerce: Hearings Before the Special Committee,* Senate, 81 Cong. 2 Sess.–82 Cong. 1 Sess., May 26, 1950–August 7, 1951

IRC   *Investigation of Racketeering in the Cleveland, Ohio, Area: Hearings Before a Special Anti-Racketeering Subcommittee of the Committee on Government Operations,* House, 83 Cong. 2 Sess., September 27–November 10, 1954

IRM   *Investigation of Racketeering in the Minneapolis, Minn., Area: Hearings Before a Subcommittee of the Committee on Government Operations,* House, 83 Cong. 2 Sess., April 9 and 10, 1954

IRP   *Investigation of Racketeering in the Pittsburgh, Pa., Area: Hearing Before a Subcommittee of the Committee on Government Operations,* House, 83 Cong. 2 Sess., May 21, 1954

ISR   *Investigation of So-Called "Rackets": Hearings Before a Subcommittee of the Committee on Commerce,* Senate, 73 Cong. 2 Sess., August 14–December 21, 1933

JRH   *James R. Hoffa and Continued Underworld Control of New York Teamster Local 239: Hearings Before the Permanent Subcommittee on Investigations,* Senate, 87 Cong. 1 Sess., January 10–25, 1961

LMR   *Labor Management Racketeering: Hearings Before the Permanent Subcommittee on Investigations of the Committee on Governmental Affairs,* Senate, 95 Cong. 2 Sess., April 24–25, 1978

MAR   *Profile of Organized Crime—Mid-Atlantic Region: Hearings Before the Permanent Subcommittee on Investigations of the Committee on Governmental Affairs,* Senate, 98 Cong. 1 Sess., February 15–24, 1983

MRO   *Measures Relating to Organized Crime: Hearings Before the Subcommittee on Criminal Laws and Procedures of the Committee on the Judiciary,* Senate, 91 Cong. 1 Sess., March 18–June 4, 1969

NJW   *Nomination of James H. Wilkerson: Hearings Before a Subcommittee of the Committee on the Judiciary,* Senate, 72 Cong. 1 Sess., January 21–March 29, 1932

OCA   *Organized Crime in America: Hearings Before the Committee on the Judiciary,* Senate, 98 Cong. 1 Sess., January 27–July 11, 1983

OCC   *Organized Crime Control: Hearings Before Subcommittee No. 5 of the Committee on the Judiciary,* House, 91 Cong. 2 Sess., May 20–August 5, 1970

OCN   *Organized Crime and Illicit Traffic in Narcotics: Hearings Before the Permanent Subcommittee on Investigations of the Committee on Government Operations,* Senate, 88 Cong. 1 Sess., September 25, 1963–August 5, 1964

OCS   *Organized Crime in Sports (Racing): Hearings Before the Select Committee on Crime,* House, 92 Cong. 2 Sess., May 9–July 27, 1972

OCV   *Organized Crime and Use of Violence: Hearings Before the Permanent Subcommittee on Investigations of the Committee on Governmental Affairs,* Senate, 96 Cong. 2 Sess., April 28–May 5, 1980

OSS   *Organized Crime—Stolen Securities: Hearings Before the Permanent Subcommittee on Investigations of the Committee on Government Operations,* Senate, 92 Cong. 1 Sess., June 8–August 4, 1971

PBX   *Professional Boxing: Hearings Before the Subcommittee on Antitrust and Monopoly of the Committee on the Judiciary,* Senate, 86 Cong. 2 Sess.–88 Cong. 2 Sess., June 14, 1960–March 31, 1964

PCD   President's Commission on Organized Crime, *Report to the President and the Attorney General: America's Habit—Drug Abuse, Drug Trafficking, and Organized Crime,* March 1986

PCE   President's Commission on Organized Crime, *Report to the President and the Attorney General: The Edge—Organized Crime, Business, and Labor Unions,* March 1986

PCEA   President's Commission on Organized Crime, *Report to the President and the Attorney General: The Edge—Organized Crime, Business, and Labor Unions,* Appendix, October 1985

PCH   President's Commission on Organized Crime: *Record of Hearings,* 1–7, November 29, 1983–June 26, 1985

PCI   President's Commission on Organized Crime, *Report to the President and the Attorney General: The Impact—Organized Crime Today,* April 1986

SDC   *The F.B.I. Transcripts: On Exhibit in U.S.A.* v. *De Cavalcante, Vastola, and Annunziata* (Lemma Publishing, 1970)

SFA   *Organized Criminal Activities—South Florida and U.S. Penitentiary, Atlanta, Ga.: Hearings Before the Permanent Subcommittee on Investigations,* Senate, 95 Cong. 2 Sess., August 2–October 25, 1978

UCL   *Use of Casinos to Launder Proceeds of Drug Trafficking and Organized Crime: Hearings Before the Subcommittee on Crime of the Committee on the Judiciary,* House, 98 Cong. 2 Sess., February 10 and June 21, 1984

WCC   *New Jersey–New York Waterfront Commission Compact: Hearing Before Subcommittee No. 3 of the Committee on the Judiciary,* House, 83 Cong. 1 Sess., July 22, 1953

WDI   *Organized Crime Links to the Waste Disposal Industry: Hearing Before the Subcommittee on Oversight and Investigations of the Committee on Energy and Commerce,* House, 97 Cong. 1 Sess., May 28, 1981

WFC   *Waterfront Corruption: Hearings Before the Permanent Subcommittee on Investigations of the Committee on Governmental Affairs,* Senate, 97 Cong. 1 Sess., February 17–27, 1981

WFI   *Waterfront Investigation: Hearings Before a Subcommittee of the Committee on Interstate and Foreign Commerce,* Senate, 83 Cong. 1 Sess., March 27–June 26, 1953

WPP   *Witness Protection Program: Hearings Before the Subcommittee on*

Administrative Practice and Procedure of the Committee on the Judiciary, Senate, 95 Cong. 2 Sess., March 20–April 14, 1978

WSP *Witness Security Program: Hearings Before the Permanent Subcommittee on Investigations of the Committee on Government Operations,* Senate, 96 Cong. 2 Sess., December 15–17, 1980

NOTES

CHAPTER ONE

12. "The minute regulations": John A. Ryan, *Questions of the Day* (1931), p. 24.

13. Prohibition in South: Lewis L. Gould, *Progressives and Prohibitionists: Texas Democrats in the Wilson Era* (1973), pp. 46–49; Jack S. Blocker, Jr., *Retreat from Reform: The Prohibition Movement in the United States, 1890–1913* (1976), p. 167; James Benson Sellers, *The Prohibition Movement in Alabama, 1702 to 1943* (1943), p. 101; Daniel Jay Whitener, *Prohibition in North Carolina, 1715–1945* (1945), pp. 69, 138, 142.

13. Prohibition leaders: Blocker, *Retreat*, p. 10.

13. Los Angeles and San Francisco: Gilman M. Ostrander, *The Prohibition Movement in California, 1848–1933* (1957).

13. "to preserve this nation": Joseph R. Gusfield, *Symbolic Crusade: Status Politics and the American Temperance Movement* (1963), p. 100.

14. "the kind of dirty": Virginius Dabney, *Dry Messiah: The Life of Bishop Cannon* (1949), p. 188; next quotation, ibid., p. 188.

14. "Is it not about": Peter H. Odegard, *Pressure Politics: The Story of the Anti-Saloon League* (1928), p. 27.

14. "Having banished": Jenna Weissman Joselit, *Our Gang: Jewish Crime and the New York Jewish Community, 1900–1940* (1983), p. 88.

14. "the Decennial Santa Claus": *Harvard College Class of 1912: Decennial Report* (1923), p. xviii.

14. "Joe was our chief": Richard J. Whalen, *The Founding Father: The Story of Joseph P. Kennedy* (1964), p. 58.

15. Irish stereotype: see Richard Stivers, *A Hair of the Dog: Irish Drinking and American Stereotype* (1976).

15. Tommy McGinty: Hank Messick, *The Silent Syndicate* (1967), p. 31.

15. "a gigantic wholesale": *New York Times,* October 24, 1924; and see *Cleveland Press,* October 25, November 3, 1924.

15. Tommy Banks: *Minneapolis Star,* June 19, 1959.

16. "Because I was in": *Minneapolis Star and Tribune,* September 12, 1985.

16. Pete Mc Donough: *Time,* August 18, 1941; J. W. Ehrlich, *A Life in My Hands* (1965), pp. 87–88.

16. "king of San Francisco's": *California Liberator,* March 1923.

17. McDonough case, 1923: Elizabeth Anne Brown, "The Enforcement of Prohibition in San Francisco, California" (M.A. thesis, University of California at Berkeley, 1948), pp. 32–34; Ostrander, *Prohibition,* p. 173.

17. "Billy was the best": interview with Frank Devereaux, January 17, 1984; and interview with Tommy Duris, December 29, 1983.

17. Gustin gang: clippings in Gustin file, *Boston Herald-American* library, at Boston University School of Public Communications: *Boston Herald,* July 26, 1928; Devereaux interview.

18. Gustins and McCormack: *Boston Herald,* July 16, 1923; cases 2926 (1921), 5770 (1922), and 2556 (1923), Superior Criminal Court, Boston.

18. "The Boston police strike": *Boston Herald,* January 5, 1929.

18. Carroll's bootlegging: Devereaux interview.

18. Gangster hangouts: Noel Behn, *Big Stick-up at Brink's!* (1977), p. 63; interview with Jimmy O'Keefe, February 8, 1984; interview with Matthew McGrath, Jr., January 13, 1984.

18. Carroll case, 1925: *Boston Globe,* March 19, 24, 1925; case 1986 (1925), Superior Criminal Court, Boston.

19. "All the trouble": *Boston Herald,* January 10, 1929; next quotation, ibid.

19. "The Kennedys were": interview with Wilton Vaughn, May 11, 1964, John F. Kennedy Presidential Library.

19. "My father": memo by Frank Murphy, July 14, 1941, box 1, Eugene Gressman Papers.

20. "My father taught": Joseph P. Kennedy to Arthur Krock, July 1, 1937, box 31, Arthur Krock Papers.

20. "Importer": Joseph P. Kennedy questionnaire, file 312.505, Records of Class of 1912, Harvard Archives, Pusey Library, Harvard University.

20. Currier and Stone: "The Reminiscences of Eddie Dowling" (Columbia Oral History Collection, 1964), p. 304; Bill Duncliffe, *The Life and Times of Joseph P. Kennedy* (1965), pp. 49, 65.

20. Kennedy bootlegging: Doris Kearns Goodwin, *The Fitzgeralds and the Kennedys* (1987), pp. 441–43, 534.

20. "Our present Mayor": Whalen, *Founding,* p. xv.

20. Fitzgeralds after 1920: Michael R. Beschloss, *Kennedy and Roosevelt: The Uneasy Alliance* (1980), pp. 102–3.

20.   Kennedy in Plymouth: interview with David Strassel, September 23, 1983.

20.   Kennedy at 53 State: interview with Joe Meldon, January 30, 1984.

20.   Kennedy on a dock: Doris Kearns Goodwin, speech at Boston Public Library, April 23, 1986.

20.   Ted O'Leary: Gloria Swanson, *Swanson on Swanson* (1980), p. 344.

20.   "ice cream": cf. James M. Landis to Joseph P. Kennedy, [1951], box 51, James M. Landis Papers.

21.   Dion O'Banion: Walter Noble Burns, *The One-Way Ride* (1931), pp. 80–83; Edward D. Sullivan, *Rattling the Cup on Chicago Crime* (1929), p. 6.

21.   "O'Banion was": Sullivan, *Rattling,* p. 12; next quotation, ibid., p. 28.

21.   "I set out": Roger Touhy with Ray Brennan, *The Stolen Years* (1959), p. 63; next two quotations, ibid., pp. 65, 67.

22.   Touhys later: Courtney Ryley Cooper, *Ten Thousand Public Enemies* (1935), p. 65.

22.   Fay bootlegging: Nils Thor Granlund, with Sid Feder and Ralph Hancock, *Blondes, Brunettes, and Bullets* (1957), pp. 100–101.

22.   "He always had": ibid., p. 119.

22.   "Now if you are": *A Treasury of Damon Runyon,* ed. Clark Kinnaird (1958), p. 114.

23.   Dwyer bootlegging: *New York Times,* July 17, 1926; John Kobler, *Ardent Spirits: The Rise and Fall of Prohibition* (1973), pp. 247–48.

23.   Owney Madden: Graham Nown, *The English Godfather* (1987).

23.   "Wildest bunch": Stanley Walker, *The Night Club Era* (1933), p. 117.

23.   Madden appearance: Denis Tilden Lynch, *Criminals and Politicians* (1932), p. 74; Walker, *Night Club,* p. 105.

23.   Madden bootlegging: Lynch, *Criminals,* pp. 59–60; Sean Dennis Cashman, *Prohibition: The Lie of the Land* (1981), p. 41.

24.   "Sure, I admired": Lewis Yablonsky, *George Raft* (1974), pp. 246–47.

24.   "You just had": St. Clair McKelway, *Gossip: The Life and Times of Walter Winchell* (1940), p. 107.

24.   "Now, to get": IOC 10:923.

24.   "Prohibition is": Joselit, *Our Gang,* p. 86.

25.   "If they were": Peter C. Newman, *King of the Castle: The Making of a Dynasty—Seagram's and the Bronfman Empire* (Atheneum edition, 1979), p. 63; next quotation, ibid., p. 80.

25.   "We loaded": Philip Siekman in *Fortune,* November 1966.

25.   "The attitude was": Newman, *King,* p. 54.

25. Jewish population, 1920s: *American Jewish Yearbook* (1925).

26. "The mobsters hated": Granlund, *Blondes,* p. 171.

26. "I didn't go": Donald Henderson Clarke, *In the Reign of Rothstein* (1929), p. 13.

26. Rothstein and 1919 Series: Craig Thompson and Allen Raymond, *Gang Rule in New York* (1940), p. 53; Eliot Asinof, *Eight Men Out* (1963), p. 286.

26. "My husband": Carolyn Rothstein, *Now I'll Tell* (1934), p. 164; next two quotations, ibid., pp. 139, 45.

27. "But pretty soon": William G. Shepherd in *Collier's,* March 13, 1926; next quotation, ibid.; and see statement by B. J. Samuels, [1926], in box 131.1, William Roy Vallance Papers.

27. Kessler's later troubles: *New York Times,* April 10, 1926, October 17–18, 1929, April 8, 1931.

28. "The heavy concentration": Joselit, *Our Gang,* p. 35.

28. Jewish arraignments: ibid., pp. 32–33.

28. "He was young": Dennis Eisenberg, Uri Dan, Eli Landau, *Meyer Lansky: Mogul of the Mob* (1979), p. 56; next two quotations, ibid., pp. 108, 103.

28. Bronfman and Lansky: Stephen Birmingham, *"The Rest of Us"* (1984), p. 153.

29. Schultz bootlegging: *Night Stick: The Autobiography of Lewis J. Valentine* (1947), pp. 53–54.

29. "Like anyone else": Willie Sutton with Edward Linn, *Where the Money Was* (1976), p. 100.

29. Schultz and Raft: Yablonsky, *Raft,* p. 42.

29. "He seemed to have": Polly Adler, *A House Is Not a Home* (1953), p. 238.

29. Waxey Gordon: Thompson and Raymond, *Gang Rule,* pp. 27–29.

30. Gordon bootlegging: Alan Block, *East Side—West Side: Organizing Crime in New York, 1930–1950* (Transaction edition, 1983), pp. 134–35; Justice Department case 23-53-230, Record Group 60, National Archives; FEA 2:208.

30. "He is an able": Joseph Driscoll in *New Outlook,* November 1933.

30. Longy Zwillman: Mark A. Stuart, *Gangster #2: Longy Zwillman, the Man Who Invented Organized Crime* (1985); IOC 18:773; Joselit, *Our Gang,* p. 97.

30. "I had the biggest": IOC 12:615.

31. Zwillman and Reinfeld: Hank Messick, *Secret File* (1969), p. 278; transcript of *U.S.* v. *James Rutkin,* Newark, October 10, 1950, et seq., p. 400, in box 1:28, Estes Kefauver Papers.

31. "I was stopped": *Rutkin* transcript, p. 1014; next quotation, ibid., p. 1007.

31. Reinfeld system: IOC 18:999.

31. "That was much": *Rutkin* transcript, p. 1028.

32. Charlie Solomon: *Boston Daily Globe*, January 28, 1933.

32. Solomon and Carroll: interviews with Matthew McGrath Jr., January 13, 1984, and with Jimmy O'Keefe, February 8, 1984.

32. Solomon case, 1922: Justice Department case 12-1751, Record Group 60, National Archives; next two quotations, ibid.

32. Joe Linsey: Hank Messick with Joseph L. Nellis, *The Private Lives of Public Enemies* (1973), pp. 154–55.

32. National Realty Company: statement by John A. Campbell, January 9, 1931, in box 133.1, Vallance Papers.

32. Linsey and Bronfmans: McGrath interview.

32. Linsey's later indictments: indictment 8561 (1928), Federal District Court records, Federal Archives and Record Center, Waltham, Massachusetts.

33. Cleveland syndicate: Messick, *Silent Syndicate*, pp. 4–5.

33. Shipments through Galveston: Justice Department case 23-74-90, Record Group 60, National Archives.

33. "I, frankly": IOC 10:907.

33. Jewish populations: *American Jewish Yearbook* (1925).

33. Purple Gang: ISR, p. 193; Larry Engelmann, *Intemperance: The Lost War Against Liquor* (1979), p. 143.

33. "He was small": *New York Times*, March 9, 1968.

33. "gamblers and big spenders": Milton "Mezz" Mezzrow, *Really the Blues* (1946), p. 96.

34. Purples and St. Louis gang: Lynch, *Criminals*, pp. 136–37.

34. Purples and Collingwood: Fred D. Pasley, *Muscling In* (1931), p. 203.

34. Boo-Boo Hoff: *New York Times*, April 28, 1941.

34. Hoff bootlegging: Mark Haller in *Pennsylvania Magazine of History and Biography*, April 1985; next quotation, ibid.

35. "I recognize": *New York Times*, March 29, 1929.

35. "Only the Capone gang": Sullivan, *Rattling*, p. 193.

35. Italians in old country: *The Crime Society*, eds. Francis A. J. Ianni and Elizabeth Reuss-Ianni (1976), pp. 47–8.

35. "The most vicious": Daniel Fuchs in *New Republic*, September 9, 1931.

35. "to restore": Arthur A. Carey in *Collier's*, February 15, 1930.

36. Italian felony arrests: Joselit, *Our Gang*, p. 33.

36. Black Hand: Thomas Monroe Pitkin, *The Black Hand: A Chapter in Ethnic Crime* (1977), pp. 135–36.

36. "Southern California": William R. Woods, Jr., to Prohibition

Commissioner, January 28, 1930, in Justice Department case 23-11-869, Record Group 60, National Archives.

37. "A very smart": Warren Olney III, "Law Enforcement and Judicial Administration in the Earl Warren Era" (Earl Warren Oral History Project, Bancroft Library, 1981), pp. 159, 166.

37. Cornero escape, 1926: Clinton H. Anderson, *Beverly Hills Is My Beat* (1960), p. 103.

37. Cornero in Germany: Justice Department case 23-100-629, Record Group 60, National Archives.

37. Black Hand in Kansas City: William M. Reddig, *Tom's Town: Kansas City and the Pendergast Legend* (1947), p. 250.

37. "My brother-in-law": IOC 4:347.

37. Johnny Lazia: Andrew Rolle, *The Italian Americans: Troubled Roots* (1980), p. 100; Reddig, *Tom's Town*, pp. 248–51.

38. "When I was": Behn, *Big Stick-up*, p. 60.

38. Philip Buccola: Andrew Tully, *Treasury Agent* (1958), p. 65; OCN 4:973.

38. Gustins and Italians: Behn, *Big Stick-up*, p. 61.

38. Buccola and Carroll: McGrath interview.

39. Joe Lombardo: Vinnie Teresa in *Saturday Review of Society*, February 1973.

39. "His cultural": report, January 23, 1932, in case 1476 (1932), Superior Criminal Court, Boston.

39. "Gentile is": IOC 9:305.

39. Italian bootleggers, Detroit: Engelmann, *Intemperance*, pp. 145–47.

39. Anthony D'Anna: IOC 9:10–11.

40. Zerilli and Tocco: OCN 2:410.

40. "Any time an Italian": *New York Times*, March 9, 1968.

40. "It was then": Charles Siragusa as told to Robert Wiedrich, *The Trail of the Poppy: Behind the Mask of the Mafia* (1966), p. 42.

41. "I thought": Joseph Bonanno with Sergio Lalli, *A Man of Honor* (1983), p. 65.

41. Five Italian gangs: ibid., pp. 84–85; chart facing OCN 1:162.

41. "I felt honored": Bonanno, *Man*, p. 70; next two quotations, ibid., pp. 76, 86.

42. "All of his": Leonard Katz, *Uncle Frank: The Biography of Frank Costello* (1973), p. 77.

42. "They were more": Eisenberg et al., *Lansky*, p. 143.

42. "Other kids": James A. Bell in *American Mercury*, August 1950.

42. Costello childhood: Giuseppe Selvaggi, *The Rise of the Mafia in New York* (1978), pp. 88, 107.

43. Costello and father: Katz, *Costello*, p. 39.

43. "If you're writing": George Wolf with Joseph DiMona, *Frank Costello: Prime Minister of the Underworld* (1974), p. 39.

43. Costello bootlegging: Katz, *Costello,* pp. 58–59, 63–64.

43. Costello and Kennedy: *New York Times,* February 27, 1973; Bonanno, *Man,* pp. 174, 308; John Scarne, *The Mafia Conspiracy* (1976), pp. 52, 203.

43. "You had the sense": Katz, *Costello,* pp. 68–69.

43. Madden and Kennedy: Nown, *Godfather,* p. 189.

43. "I used to hit": Tony Sciacca, *Luciano: The Man Who Modernized the American Mafia* (1975), pp. 30–31.

44. "An aggressive": report, 1946, by Dr. Harry L. Freedman in box 21, Herlands file, Thomas E. Dewey Papers.

44. Luciano case, 1923: Harry J. Anslinger and Will Oursler, *The Murderers: The Story of the Narcotic Gangs* (1961), p. 102.

44. Luciano and Rothstein: Sciacca, *Luciano,* pp. 8–9, 33.

45. "No one was close": IOC 5:51.

45. Capone and publicity: Kenneth Allsop, *The Bootleggers: The Story of Chicago's Prohibition Era* (1968 edition), p. 347.

45. "whose surname": Bonanno, *Man,* p. 86.

45. "He is remembered": Fuchs in *New Republic,* September 9, 1931.

45. Capone and Torrio: Humbert S. Nelli, *The Business of Crime: Italians and Syndicate Crime in the United States* (1976), p. 163; John Landesco, *Organized Crime in Chicago* (1929), pp. 94–95.

46. Capone and Guzik: John Kobler, *Capone* (1971), pp. 12, 120; NJW, p. 233.

46. Capone tax investigation: Frank J. Wilson and Beth Day, *Special Agent* (1965), p. 29.

46. Mabel Willebrandt: Dorothy M. Brown, *Mabel Walker Willebrandt: A Study of Power, Loyalty, and Law* (1984).

46. "in moderation": Mabel Walker Willebrandt, *The Inside of Prohibition* (1929), p. 10.

46. Woman suffrage and Prohibition: Eleanor Flexner, *Century of Struggle: The Woman's Rights Movement in the United States* (1959), pp. 181–85, 224–25, 296–98; Aileen S. Kraditor, *The Ideas of the Woman Suffrage Movement, 1890–1920* (1965); Ross E. Paulson, *Women's Suffrage and Prohibition* (1973). But see also David E. Kyvig in *American Quarterly,* fall 1976; Eileen L. McDonagh and H. Douglas Price in *American Political Science Review,* June 1985; paper by Eileen L. McDonagh delivered at Social Science History Association meeting, St. Louis, October 1986. The issue is best addressed by examining the motives of the advocates and opponents of suffrage, not by counting the final votes in Congress. The link between suffrage and

Prohibition was clearest outside the South, which was so strongly against the first and for the second.

46. "There is something": diary, December 13, 1922, Mabel Walker Willebrandt Papers.

46. "For all of my life": Willebrandt to parents, Christmas 1923, Willebrandt Papers.

47. "It was a *stag*": diary, March 20, 1923, Willebrandt Papers.

47. "manifestly utterly": Willebrandt to A. T. Mason, January 31, 1951, box 83, Harlan Fiske Stone Papers.

47. Willebrandt on Mellon: ibid.

47. Prohibition Bureau: Ira L. Reeves, *Ol' Rum River* (1931), p. 33.

47. "At first": Willebrandt to parents, October 13, 1926, Willebrandt Papers.

47. Drinking during Prohibition: David E. Kyvig, *Repealing National Prohibition* (1979), pp. 24–25.

48. "One can never": Stephen Graham, *New York Nights* (1927), p. 66.

48. "You used to have": Anonymous, *The Real Story of a Bootlegger* (1923), p. 118.

48. Al Smith and liquor: Edward T. Flynn, *You're the Boss* (1947), p. 66; "The Reminiscences of Mrs. John A. Warner" (Columbia Oral History Collection, 1967), p. 42.

48. Raskob's Christmas present: Raskob to Al Smith, December 29, 1930, file 2112, John J. Raskob Papers.

48. "I am having": Raskob to Walter Chrysler, September 27, 1928, file 396, Raskob Papers.

48. "As there was": diary, January 26, 1923, George Read Nutter Papers; next quotation, ibid., November 5, 1927.

49. New York State law: Kobler, *Ardent Spirits*, p. 223.

49. "drunkenness on duty": Willebrandt to Mason, January 31, 1951; next quotation, ibid.

49. "If I dethrone": Brown, *Willebrandt*, p. 74.

49. Emory Buckner: Martin Mayer, *Emory Buckner* (1968).

50. "The policy": *New York Herald Tribune*, March 6, 1925.

50. New York speakeasies: Willebrandt, *Prohibition*, p. 169.

50. "There was one": William Stevenson to author, September 27, 1983.

50. "this monstrous": Mayer, *Buckner*, p. 266.

50. "Very nervous": diary, October 24, 1929, Nutter Papers.

50. "Federal enforcement": Willebrandt, *Prohibition*, p. 196.

51. "Prior to Prohibition": Sol Gelb statement, September 11, 1958, in Harlan Phillips file, Dewey Papers.

51. Big Seven: Virgil W. Peterson, *The Mob: 200 Years of Organized Crime in New York* (1983), pp. 156–57.

51. Atlantic City conference: ibid., pp. 158–59; Nelli, *Business,* pp. 214–15.

CHAPTER TWO

age　52. Greenberg and Hassel murders: Justice Department case 23-53-230, Record Group 60, National Archives.

53. "the silken gown": Philip Siekman in *Fortune,* November 1966.

53. Bronfmans after Prohibition: Stephen Birmingham, *"The Rest of Us"* (1984), pp. 277–78.

54. "I thought": *Fortune,* May 1936.

54. Rosenstiel indictment: *New York Times,* March 12, 1971.

54. "the craziest": *Fortune,* May 1936.

54. Rosenstiel and old bootleggers: *New York Times,* January 29, 1971; Michael Dorman, *Payoff: The Role of Organized Crime in American Politics* (1972), pp. 228–29, 249–51.

55. "Everybody was": transcript of *U.S.* v. *James Rutkin,* Newark, October 10, 1950, et seq., p. 1036, in box 1:28, Estes Kefauver Papers.

55. $250,000 laundered: ibid., p. 131.

55. Zwillman and Stacher: IOC 7:547–48; 18:1000.

55. "Everywhere I went": "The Reminiscences of Eddie Dowling" (Columbia Oral History Collection, 1964), p. 491.

55. Somerset profits: Richard J. Whalen, *The Founding Father: The Story of Joseph P. Kennedy* (1964), p. 381.

55. Prendergast-Davies: Elmer R. Irey, as told to William J. Slocum, *The Tax Dodgers: The Inside Story of the T-men's War with America's Political and Underworld Hoodlums* (1948), pp. 160–63; *New York Times,* April 7, 1939; Jack McPhaul, *Johnny Torrio: First of the Gang Lords* (1970), p. 300.

56. Alliance: IOC 2:133, 7:985, 989–98, 10:183; Agnes S. Wolf, "Draft of Committee Report on Infiltration of Organized Crime into Legitimate Enterprises," March 22, 1951, p. 36, in box 1:25, Kefauver Papers.

56. "my whiskies": Wolf, "Draft," p. 36.

56. Linsey after Prohibition: *Boston Herald,* May 18, 1937; *Boston City Directory,* 1934–1940.

56. Joe Fusco: Wolf, "Draft," pp. 19, 23; IOC 5:609.

56. "I knew my way": IOC 5:594.

56. Other Capone interests: IMW, pp. 788–92, 804–11; IOC 5:558–59.

57. Di Giovannis: IOC 4:372–73.
57. "All those guys": Jonathan Kwitny, *Vicious Circles: The Mafia in the Marketplace* (1979), p. 242.
57. McDonoughs: *New York Times*, March 28, 1937.
57. "a fountainhead": *San Francisco Chronicle*, March 17, 1937.
58. Police resignations: *New York Times*, July 17, 18, 1937.
58. Salinger, 1946: Pierre Salinger, *With Kennedy* (Avon edition, 1967), pp. 32–33.
58. "the main architect": Nicholas Gage, *The Mafia Is Not an Equal Opportunity Employer* (1971), p. 50.
58. Lansky after Prohibition: Max Block with Ron Kenner, *Max the Butcher* (1982), p. 182; Joey with Dave Fisher, *Killer: The Autobiography of a Mafia Hit Man* (Pocket Books edition, 1974), pp. 121–23.
58. "So why am I": Dennis Eisenberg, Uri Dan, Eli Landau, *Meyer Lansky: Mogul of the Mob* (1979), p. 81.
58. Lansky net worth: Joey, *Killer*, p. 123.
58. Linsey and gangsters: *Wall Street Journal*, July 25, 1967; CCT, p. 945; Dorman, *Payoff*, pp. 249–250.
58. "When Prohibition": Vincent Teresa with Thomas C. Renner, *My Life in the Mafia* (1973), pp. 74–75.
59. Linsey testimonial: *Boston Herald*, May 27, 1966.
59. "We have a way": *New York Times*, March 21, 1973.
59. Dalitz and associates: IOC 10:908–9.
59. "I have been": IOC 10:923.
59. "silent syndicate": Hank Messick, *The Silent Syndicate* (1967).
59. "sportsman and race track owner": *New York Times*, January 27, 1926.
59. Undercover gossip: Emory Buckner to Lincoln C. Andrews, November 11, 1926, box 600, John Marshall Harlan Papers.
59. Dwyer after Prohibition: Fred J. Cook, *The Secret Rulers* (1966), p. 73; Mark H. Haller in *Gambling in America* (Commission on the Review of the National Policy Toward Gambling, Appendix 1, 1976), p. 130; Craig Thompson and Allen Raymond, *Gang Rule in New York* (1940), p. 98.
59. Dwyer case: *New York Times*, October 22, 1938, May 26, 1939.
60. "I've never had": Gloria Swanson, *Swanson on Swanson* (1980), p. 373.
60. "It really wasn't": Eisenberg et al., *Lansky*, pp. 108–9.
60. "This was": Rose Fitzgerald Kennedy, *Times to Remember* (1974), p. 192.
61. "The only thing": David E. Koskoff, *Joseph P. Kennedy: A Life and Times* (1974), p. 371.

61. Kennedy, 1932: *The Fruitful Bough,* ed. Edward M. Kennedy (1965), pp. 62–63; Roy Howard to Newton D. Baker, July 12, 1932, box 122, Newton D. Baker Papers.

61. "I'm the one": Kennedy, *Times,* p. 196.

61. "Joe, I know": Raymond Moley, *After Seven Years* (1939), p. 288.

61. "I prefer": *Harvard College Class of 1912: Twenty-fifth Anniversary Report* (1937), p. 401.

63. "We didn't consider": Joseph Bonanno with Sergio Lalli, *A Man of Honor* (1983), p. 223.

63. "The law works": Richard Gambino, *Blood of My Blood: The Dilemma of the Italian-Americans* (1974), p. 53.

63. Mafia in Sicily: Francis A. J. Ianni with Elizabeth Reuss-Ianni, *A Family Business: Kinship and Social Control in Organized Crime* (1972), pp. 27, 40.

63. "courage, strength": Gambino, *Blood,* p. 268.

63. Mafia as culture to U.S.: Frederic D. Homer, *Guns and Garlic: Myths and Realities of Organized Crime* (1974), p. 37.

64. "It was a byword": IOC 5:369.

64. New Orleans: Herbert Asbury, *The French Quarter* (1936), pp. 406–11; David Leon Chandler, *Brothers in Blood* (1975), pp. 73, 96–97.

64. Pittston: IIA 32:12255; MAR, p. 327.

65. New York: Howard Abadinsky, *Organized Crime* (1981), p. 45; Thomas Monroe Pitkin, *The Black Hand: A Chapter in Ethnic Crime* (1977), pp. 130, 210.

65. "The city is confronted": Pitkin, *Black Hand,* p. 54.

65. "I was here": IOC 5:410.

65. Jack Dragna: Justice Department case 23-8-142, Record Group 60, National Archives.

65. "the top man": Bonanno, *Man,* p. 298.

65. Morelli and Becker-Rosenthal: Herbert B. Ehrmann, *The Untried Case* (1960 edition), p. 72.

65. "These two suckers": Teresa, *My Life,* p. 46; and see Ehrmann, *Untried Case;* Joseph Morelli to Morris Ernst, January 19, 1939, file 3-11, Herbert B. Ehrmann Papers; Morris Ernst, *The Best Is Yet* (1940); Ernst to Herbert B. Ehrmann, May 19, 1966, file 12-3, Ehrmann Papers; William Young and David E. Kaiser, *Postmortem: New Evidence in the Case of Sacco and Vanzetti* (1985), pp. 141–52.

65. Cleveland: Messick, *Syndicate,* p. 10; OCN 4:1049; Humbert S. Nelli, *The Business of Crime: Italians and Syndicate Crime in the United States* (1976), pp. 171–72.

66. Pueblo: OCV, p. 380; IIA 46:16600–602; James E. Hansen in *Colorado Magazine,* winter 1973.

66. Springfield: IIA 46:16590–91.
66. Unione Siciliana: Chandler, *Brothers,* p. 135; Ianni and Reuss-Ianni, *Family,* p. 58; John Kobler, *Capone* (1971), pp. 232–33.
67. Cleveland meeting: *Cleveland Press,* December 6, 7, 1928; *Cleveland Plain Dealer,* December 6, 17, 1928; materials in box 207, Roscoe Pound Papers.
67. "to expand": IOC 7:746, 749.
67. Castellammarese War: OCN 1:180.
67. "In exchange": Bonanno, *Man,* p. 107; next quotation, ibid., p. 163.
68. Commission: ibid., pp. 141, 159–61.
68. "After a time": Peter Maas, *The Valachi Papers* (1968), pp. 94–97.
69. "When you become": OSS 3:818.
70. Mafia rules: Bonanno, *Man,* p. 154; Maas, *Valachi,* p. 196.
70. Schematic diagrams: e.g., facing OCN 2:410.
70. Handshakes: WFC, p. 377.
70. "a willingness": Bonanno, *Man,* p. 123.
71. "Just kill": OCN 1:116.
71. "I know": IAP 5:423–24.
71. "The two groups": George Wolf with Joseph DiMona, *Frank Costello: Prime Minister of the Underworld* (1974), p. 11.
71. Luciano and Lansky, 1931: Bonanno, *Man,* p. 127.
71. "Anywhere where": OCN 1:159.
71. Guzik: CHI, pp. 161–62.
71. Linsey: see above, pp. 58–59.
71. Rockman: IRC, pp. 579–80; PCH 2:49; Angelo Lonardo testimony, April 15, 1988, before Nunn committee, on Cable News Network.
72. Rosen: IOC 11:72; OCN 4:960–61.
72. "She was": IOC 11:86.
72. Rosen as boss: J. Richard (Dixie) Davis in *Collier's,* August 19, 1939; IOC 11:28, 18:69; Mark Haller in *Law, Alcohol, and Disorder,* ed. David E. Kyvig (1985), p. 148.
72. Hoff death: *New York Times,* April 28, 1941.
72. Zwillman: Mark A. Stuart, *Gangster #2: Longy Zwillman, the Man Who Invented Organized Crime* (1985), pp. 65–66; IOC 12:588–628.
72. "Now I don't": Mickey Cohen as told to John Peer Nugent, *In My Own Words* (1975), p. 42; next three quotations, ibid., pp. 17, 19, 35.
73. Bernstein later: *New York Times,* March 9, 1968.
73. Gordon later: Irey, *Tax Dodgers,* p. 145; Davis in *Collier's,* August 5, 1939; OCN 3:788.
73. Wallace and Walsh murders: *Boston Herald,* January 24, 1932.

73. "We've knocked off": *Boston Herald,* July 30, 1932.

74. Carroll later: see below, p. 263.

74. Touhy later: Roger Touhy with Ray Brennan, *The Stolen Years* (1959), pp. 71, 77–78, 81, 96, 228–29, 254–55.

74. "even Owney": Herman Klurfeld, *Winchell* (1976), p. 41.

74. "These legitimate": Denis Tilden Lynch, *Criminals and Politicians* (1932), p. 84.

74. Madden in Hot Springs: Haller in *Gambling in America*, p. 129; Art Cohn, *The Joker Is Wild* (1955), p. 211; and see below, pp. 226–27.

75. Lansky and Italian masters: Teresa, *My Life,* p. 216.

75. "Jews, outsiders": Michael Hellerman with Thomas C. Renner, *Wall Street Swindler* (1977), pp. 142, 221.

75. Italians and killing: Kwitny, *Vicious Circles,* p. 65.

75. "If you're not": SDC 4:371–72.

CHAPTER THREE

age

78. "In the end": Nils Thor Granlund with Sid Feder and Ralph Hancock, *Blondes, Brunettes, and Bullets* (1957), pp. 137–38.

78. "Hoods got in": Ronald L. Morris, *Wait Until Dark: Jazz and the Underworld, 1880–1940* (1980), p. 118.

78. Madden and partners: Walter Winchell, *Winchell Exclusive* (1975), p. 49.

79. "a quiet man": Willie the Lion Smith with George Hoefer, *Music on My Mind* (1964), p. 194.

79. New York clubs: Smith, *Music,* p. 193; John Scarne, *The Odds Against Me* (1966), p. 114; Herbert Asbury, *The Great Illusion: An Informal History of Prohibition* (1950), p. 206.

79. "21": John Kobler, *Ardent Spirits: The Rise and Fall of Prohibition* (1973), pp. 212–18; Smith, *Music,* p. 205.

79. El Morocco: Robert Sylvester, *No Cover Charge* (1956), pp. 94–100; Robert Sylvester, *Notes of a Guilty Bystander* (1970), pp. 132–33.

79. Billingsleys: Lowell S. Hawley and Ralph Bushnell Potts, *Counsel for the Damned: A Biography of George Francis Vanderveer* (1953), pp. 159–70, 197–99; Norman H. Clark, *The Dry Years: Prohibition and Social Change in Washington* (1965), pp. 131–32; Larry Engelmann, *Intemperance: The Lost War Against Liquor* (1979), pp. 37–38.

80. Billingsley in Leavenworth: George H. White to Westbrook Pegler, January 15, 1948, box 36, Westbrook Pegler Papers.

80. "a real estate developer": *New York Times,* August 5, 1963.

80. Billingsley selling booze: Sylvester, *Notes,* p. 202.

80. "It was": *Current Biography* (1946), p. 43.

80. "dressed like": Eddie Condon, *We Called It Music* (1947), p. 219.

80. Zwillman clubs: Mark A. Stuart, *Gangster #2: Longy Zwillman, the Man Who Invented Organized Crime* (1985), p. 138.

80. Mounds Club: *Jimmy the Greek by Himself,* with Mickey Herskowitz and Steve Perkins (1975), pp. 216–17.

80. Hoff club: *New York Times,* November 16, 1928.

81. "It struck me": Milton "Mezz" Mezzrow and Bernard Wolfe, *Really the Blues* (1946), p. 92.

81. Capone clubs: *Hear Me Talkin' to Ya,* ed. Nat Shapiro and Nat Hentoff (1955), p. 130.

81. "They sat": Mezzrow, *Really,* p. 63.

81. Rex Cafe: Fred D. Pasley, *Muscling In* (1931), pp. 102–3.

81. "and the South Side": *My Life in Crime: The Autobiography of a Professional Criminal,* reported by John Bartlow Martin (1952), p. 138.

82. "Maxine's was": Gene Fowler, *Schnozzola: The Story of Jimmy Durante* (1951), p. 25.

82. "little more than": Granlund, *Blondes,* p. 153.

82. "Lou Clayton was": Eddie Cantor with Jane Kesner Ardmore, *Take My Life* (1957), p. 56.

82. Clayton and Rothstein: Lewis Yablonsky, *George Raft* (1974), p. 32.

82. Gordon and Durante: Fowler, *Schnozzola,* p. 162.

82. "I always got along": Dean Jennings, *We Only Kill Each Other: The Life and Bad Times of Bugsy Siegel* (1967), p. 162.

82. Cohen and Durante: Mickey Cohen as told to John Peer Nugent, *In My Own Words* (1975), p. 165.

82. "I don't go": Hank Messick, *The Beauties and the Beasts: The Mob in Show Business* (1973), p. 140.

82. "I never liked": Norman Katkov, *The Fabulous Fanny* (1953), pp. 335–36; next three quotations, ibid., pp. 149, 231.

83. "Broadway during": Billy Rose, *Wine, Women and Words* (1948), p. 83.

83. Backstage Club: ibid., p. 84; Earl Conrad, *Billy Rose: Manhattan Primitive* (1968), pp. 68–70.

83. "Billy could": Conrad, *Rose,* pp. 78–79.

83. Casino de Paree: Rose, *Wine,* pp. 90–91; Polly Rose Gottlieb, *The Nine Lives of Billy Rose* (1968), pp. 89–90; Conrad, *Rose,* pp. 75–76.

83. "Why the hell": John Kobler, *Capone* (1971), p. 148.

84. Capone offer: Art Cohn, *The Joker Is Wild* (1955), pp. 90–92.

84. Lewis and mob: Messick, *Beauties,* pp. 34–35.

84. "Sometimes I wondered": Milton Berle with Haskel Frankel, *An Autobiography* (1974), p. 256; next five quotations, ibid., pp. 257, 130, 182, 183, 160.

85. "I came up": Smith, *Music*, p. 29.

85. "Back then": *Pops Foster* as told to Tom Stoddard (1971), pp. 65, 32–33.

85. "It's got guts": Condon, *We Called*, p. 125.

85. Waller and Capone: Maurice Waller and Anthony Calabrese, *Fats Waller* (1977), pp. 62–63.

85. "I knew a lot": Earl Hines in *Ebony*, September 1949.

85. "That was one": Stanley Dance, *The World of Duke Ellington* (1970), p. 67.

86. "My very youth": Lena Horne and Richard Schickel, *Lena* (1965), p. 48.

86. Payne and Moten: Stanley Dance, *The World of Count Basie* (1980), pp. 266, 321; *Hear Me*, ed. Shapiro and Hentoff, p. 297.

86. "For twenty-five": Dance, *Basie*, pp. 12–13.

86. Reno Club: Ross Russell, *Jazz Style in Kansas City and the Southwest* (1971), pp. 22–23; Ross Russell, *Bird Lives!* (1973), pp. 49–55.

86. "That whole band": Dance, *Basie*, p. 268.

86. Ellington and Cotton Club: Mercer Ellington with Stanley Dance, *Duke Ellington in Person* (1978), p. 41.

86. Armstrong managers: James Lincoln Collier, *Louis Armstrong* (1983), pp. 204, 224–26.

86. Glaser and Capones: Teddy Brenner as told to Barney Nagler, *Only the Ring Was Square* (1981), p. 2.

87. "He talked tough": Collier, *Armstrong*, p. 270.

87. "Speak to Papa": Dizzy Gillespie with Al Fraser, *to BE, or not . . . to BOP: Memoirs* (1979), p. 296.

87. "In all the years": Granlund, *Blondes*, p. 140.

87. Horne's stepfather: Hines in *Ebony*, September 1949.

87. "The underworld really": Dicky Wells as told to Stanley Dance, *The Night People* (1971), p. 28.

87. "I keep hearing": Morris, *Wait*, p. 2.

87. "He asked me,": Timothy Sullivan with John Kobler in *Sports Illustrated*, November 6, 1972.

89. Big Tim Sullivan: Steven A. Riess in *Sport in America*, ed. Donald Spivey (1985), pp. 96–102.

89. "When money comes": Randy Roberts, *Papa Jack: Jack Johnson and the Era of White Hopes* (1983), pp. 41–42.

89. Three cities: Jack "Doc" Kearns with Oscar Fraley, *The Million Dollar Gate* (1966), p. 68.

89. "The fight game": Nat Fleischer, *50 Years at Ringside* (1958), p. 45.

89. "It will probably": Mark Sullivan, *Our Times: The United States, 1900–1925* (1937), 4:562.

89. "They are all": Roberts, *Johnson,* p. 82.

89. "Many said": Jack Dempsey with Barbara Piatelli Dempsey, *Dempsey* (1977), pp. 46, 50.

90. Kearns record: PBX 2:981.

90. Kearns claimed: Jack "Doc" Kearns with Oscar Fraley in *Sports Illustrated,* January 13, 1964.

90. "They were nice": Peter Heller, *"In This Corner . . ."* (1973), p. 70.

90. "The bootleggers did it": PBX 3:1297.

90. "I got completely": Cohen, *My Own,* p. 12.

91. Billy Gibson: Riess in *Sport,* p. 109.

91. "It got so": Bob Burrill, *Who's Who in Boxing* (1974), p. 81.

91. "I made a hurried": Gene Tunney, *A Man Must Fight* (1932), p. 225.

91. Hoff suit: *New York Times,* December 7, 1927, January 14, 1931.

91. "one of my number": Dempsey, *Dempsey,* p. 136.

91. Capone and Dempsey rumors: ibid., pp. 217, 254.

91. "I was more": ibid., p. 136.

92. "I quit because": Cohn, *Joker,* p. 74.

92. "He was always": transcript of *U.S.* v. *James Rutkin,* Newark, October 10, 1950, et seq., p. 512, in box 1:28, Estes Kefauver Papers.

92. Dempsey hotel: Alan Block, *East Side—West Side: Organizing Crime in New York, 1930–1950* (Transaction edition, 1983), p. 138; *New York Times,* November 16, 1936.

92. Madden's champs: Cohn, *Joker,* p. 210.

92. Carnera: Stanley Walker, *The Night Club Era* (1933), p. 111.

92. "every once in a while": *New York Times,* June 30, 1967.

93. "He didn't seem": Joe Louis with Edna and Art Rust, Jr., *Joe Louis: My Life* (1978), p. 29; next three quotations, ibid., pp. 30–31.

93. Trafton's and underworld: Berle, *Autobiography,* p. 159.

93. "He was friendly": Louis, *Louis,* p. 34; next quotation, ibid., p. 49.

94. Mike Jacobs: Budd Schulberg in *Collier's,* April 22, 1950.

94. "With Uncle Mike": Schulberg in *Collier's,* April 29, 1950.

94. "Mike's relations": Schulberg in *Collier's,* May 13, 1950.

95. "We're gonna take": Louis, *Louis,* pp. 106–7.

95. Jacobs and Gould: ibid., p. 107.

95. "He was a": Sugar Ray Robinson with Dave Anderson, *Sugar Ray* (1970), p. 106.

95. Robinson and Jacobs: ibid., p. 100.

95. "Maybe he had": Schulberg in *Collier's,* April 15, 1950.

96. "The newspapers": IIA 32:12476.

97. "I never worked": IOC 5:34.

97. "A lot of Jews": Cohen, *My Own*, p. 34.

97. "just to make": IMW, p. 152.

97. "I was dark": IOC 11:98.

99. "This element has": John A. Hennessy in *Harper's Weekly*, March 25, 1893.

99. Racing ca. 1900: *Harper's Weekly*, November 25, 1893; L. A. Wilkinson in *North American Review*, September 1930.

99. "Racing lowers": Leroy Scott in *World's Work*, August 1906.

99. "At the New York": William Maxwell in *Collier's*, September 9, 1916.

100. Tracks shut down: Mark H. Haller in *Gambling in America* (Commission on the Review of the National Policy Toward Gambling, appendix 1, 1976), p. 107.

100. "I run tracks": IOC 6:194; and see *New York Times*, August 13, 1929.

100. Pendergast track: William M. Reddig, *Tom's Town: Kansas City and the Pendergast Legend* (1947), p. 165.

100. Capone betting: Edward D. Sullivan, *Rattling the Cup on Chicago Crime* (1929), p. 106.

100. O'Hare: Kobler, *Capone*, pp. 244–45.

100. Tropical Park: Haller in *Gambling*, p. 130; interview with John Patton, December 1, 1950, in box 5, George S. Robinson Papers; E. J. Kahn, Jr., *The World of Swope* (1965), p. 422.

101. Rockingham: Craig Thompson and Allen Raymond, *Gang Rule in New York* (1940), p. 98.

101. Suffolk Downs: OCS 1:204–5; *Boston Globe*, May 12, 1955.

101. Wonderland: Hank Messick, *Secret File* (1969), pp. 116–17.

101. Tanforan: Drew Pearson, *Diaries, 1949–1959* (1974), p. 66.

101. Zwillman: Mark Haller in *Law, Alcohol, and Disorder*, ed. David E. Kyvig (1985), p. 148.

101. Kennedy and Hialeah: *Boston Traveler*, May 14, 1943; *The Fruitful Bough*, ed. Edward M. Kennedy (1965), p. 119.

101. "He was positive": ibid., p. 247.

101. Horse doping, 1934: *Popular Mechanics*, January 1935.

101. "We found": Harry J. Anslinger and Will Oursler, *The Murderers: The Story of the Narcotic Gangs* (1961), p. 247.

101. "I don't know": IOC 5:620.

102. "Gambling is not": *Christian Century*, September 2, 1936.

102. Annenberg publications: F. B. Warren in *Nation*, August 6, 1938.

103. Nationwide: Elmer R. Irey as told to William J. Slocum, *The Tax Dodgers: The Inside Story of the T-men's War with America's Political and Underworld Hoodlums* (1948), p. 215.

103. $50 million: Warren in *Nation,* August 6, 1938.

103. "Our position": Moses L. Annenberg to L. Stanley Kahn, May 11, 1936, enclosed with E. C. Crouter to Sewall Key, July 20, 1939, box 58, Frank Murphy Papers.

103. Wire service and betting: GOC, p. 375; IOC 2:219.

104. Reformers, 1905: Haller in *Gambling,* p. 107; *New York Times,* July 11, September 14, 1905; John Landesco, *Organized Crime in Chicago* (1968 edition), p. 51; re Helen M. Gould: *New York Times,* December 21, 1938.

104. Mont Tennes: Haller in *Gambling,* p. 107; Landesco, *Organized,* pp. 45–52; *New York Times,* August 7, 1941; Pasley, *Muscling,* p. 86.

104. "Why, I haven't": Landesco, *Organized,* p. 68.

104. Annenberg: John Cooney, *The Annenbergs* (1982); John T. Flynn in *Collier's,* January 13, 1940.

105. Circulation wars: George Murray, *The Madhouse on Madison Street* (1965), pp. 42–48.

105. "I was a hungry": Flynn in *Collier's,* January 13, 1940.

105. "a mixture": Emile Gauvreau, *My Last Million Readers* (1941), p. 378; next quotation, ibid., p. 379.

105. "Up to this time": John Francis Neylan to Joseph A. Moore, October 22, 1921, box 63, John Francis Neylan Papers.

106. "His world became": Cooney, *Annenbergs,* p. 59.

106. Annenberg and Lynch: Flynn in *Collier's,* January 27, 1940.

106. Annenberg holdings: Irey, *Tax Dodgers,* p. 217; Gauvreau, *My Last,* p. 421.

106. One reporter: Flynn in *Collier's,* January 20, 1940.

106. "That was repeated": ibid.

107. Ragen: Justice Department case 5-23-1205, Record Group 60, National Archives.

107. Ragen and gangsters: Stuart, *Zwillman,* p. 115; Cooney, *Annenbergs,* pp. 83–84; Brien McMahon to Frank Murphy, May 12, 1939, box 58, Murphy Papers.

107. "He is no better": Mrs. Charles J. Tennes to Frank Murphy, April 27, 1939, in case 5-23-1205.

107. Payments to Capones: Gaeton Fonzi, *Annenberg: A Biography of Power* (1970), p. 78; J. David Stern, *Memoirs of a Maverick Publisher* (1962), p. 239; Cooney, *Annenbergs,* pp. 98–99; James V. Bennett, *I Chose Prison* (1970), p. 101.

107. "a murderer": Cooney, *Annenbergs,* p. 141.

108. "Give him": Kahn, *Swope,* p. 63; next quotation, ibid., p. 26.

108. "If you started": "The Reminiscences of Eddie Dowling" (Columbia Oral History Collection, 1964), p. 332.

108. "It seemed": Kahn, *Swope*, pp. 113–14.

108. Swope and Kennedy: ibid., p. 378.

109. "give him a good": interview with Arthur Krock, May 10, 1964, p. 2, John F. Kennedy Presidential Library.

109. JFK applying to Harvard: application, April 23, 1935, box 2, John F. Kennedy Personal Papers, Kennedy Library.

109. "My whole capital": Kahn, *Swope*, p. 51; next quotation, ibid., p. 120.

109. Swope gambling: ibid., pp. 68, 304, 307; John Francis Neylan to Swope, October 23, 1936, and Swope to Neylan, October 21, 22, 23, 1936, box 90, Neylan Papers.

109. "Those guys' stakes": Harpo Marx with Rowland Barber, *Harpo Speaks!* (1961), p. 200.

109. "The feature": Carolyn Rothstein, *Now I'll Tell* (1934), pp. 22–23.

110. "While he is": Kahn, *Swope*, p. 118; next quotation, ibid.

110. Swope helped quash: Donald Henderson Clarke, *In the Reign of Rothstein* (1929), pp. 52–53.

110. Swope warned commissioner: note by Farley, 1926, in box 37, James A. Farley Papers.

110. "Members of the staff": Kahn, *Swope*, p. 153.

111. Hearst crusades: Gauvreau, *Last*, pp. 144–45; Edwin P. Hoyt, *A Gentleman of Broadway* (1964), pp. 254–55; Hearst newspapers, May 14–29, 1933; Harry J. Anslinger to William Randolph Hearst, November 23, 1933, box 3, Harry J. Anslinger Papers.

111. "The master": Cohen, *My Own*, p. 247.

111. Spiro: IOC 7:871.

111. Gross: section 3 of Sam Giancana file, FBI FOIPA Preprocessed Files, FBI Building, Washington, D.C.

111. "Many of our": Gauvreau, *My Last*, p. 261; next quotation, ibid.

111. "the highest-paid editor": *Current Opinion*, May 1924; next quotation, ibid.

112. Lunchtime dice game: Oliver Carlson, *Brisbane: A Candid Biography* (1937), p. 257.

112. "I have given": ibid., pp. 300–301; next quotation, ibid, p. 302.

112. "those infernal": Arthur Brisbane to John Francis Neylan, June 26, 1933, box 190, Neylan Papers.

112. Winchell salary: John Francis Neylan to William Randolph Hearst, October 28, 1935, box 191, Neylan Papers.

112. "Prohibition has made": John B. Kennedy in *Collier's*, October 5, 1929.

113. "Everything in those": Ed Weiner, *Let's Go to Press: A Biography of Walter Winchell* (1955), p. 55.

113. "I have no": Walter Winchell, *Winchell Exclusive* (1975), p. 74.

113. "Meet Mr. Costello": Herman Klurfeld, *Winchell* (1976), p. 82.

113. Winchell bodyguards: St. Clair McKelway, *Gossip: The Life and Times of Walter Winchell* (1940), pp. 20, 123.

113. "a passionate": Henry F. Pringle in *American Mercury*, February 1937.

114. "a man as emotionally": Tom Clark, *The World of Damon Runyon* (1978), p. 79.

114. "Of course it is": Damon Runyon, *Guys and Dolls: Three Volumes in One* (n.d.; ca. 1946), p. 42.

115. "It was just": Hoyt, *Gentleman*, pp. 230–231.

115. "Damon would sit": Dempsey, *Dempsey*, p. 103.

115. "This Black Mike": Runyon, *Guys*, p. 106; next two quotations, ibid., pp. 467, 305.

116. "Coppers always": *A Treasury of Damon Runyon*, ed. Clark Kinnaird (1958), p. 137.

116. "The way I figure": Runyon, *Guys*, p. 203; next quotation, ibid., p. 225.

116. "While snatching is": *Treasury of Runyon*, p. 96; next quotation, ibid., p. 230.

117. "I had softened": Clark, *Runyon*, p. 101.

117. "The 'mob' ruled": Gauvreau, *My Last*, p. 154.

117. "I've done a lot": Cohen, *My Own*, p. 1.

118. "He was always": J. Richard (Dixie) Davis in *Collier's*, July 29, 1939.

118. "There is a twisted": Anslinger, *Murderers*, pp. 5–6.

118. "One of the": Joseph Bonanno with Sergio Lalli, *A Man of Honor* (1983), p. 156.

118. Reporters and gangsters: Kenneth Allsop, *The Bootleggers: The Story of Chicago's Prohibition Era* (1968 edition), p. 347; *The Chicago Crime Book,* ed. Albert Harper (1967), p. 86.

118. "If there is": Willie Sutton with Edward Linn, *Where the Money Was* (1976), p. 250.

119. "Never should have": Robert St. John, *This Was My World* (1953), pp. 193–94.

119. Loss of immunity: G. Robert Blakey and Richard N. Billings, *The Plot to Kill the President* (1981), p. 376; Nicholas Gage, *The Mafia Is Not an Equal Opportunity Employer* (1971), p. 16.

119. Lingle: Edward Dean Sullivan, *Chicago Surrenders* (1930), pp. 9–11, 21–24, 42.

119. "You guys ain't": Eliot Ness with Oscar Fraley, *The Untouchables* (1957), p. 130.

119. Buckley: *New York Times*, July 24, 25, 1930, June 25, 1931; *New Republic,* August 13, 1930.

119. "I can't be under": Winchell, *Winchell*, p. 85; Winchell to Alexander Woollcott, July 14, 1940, Alexander Woollcott Papers.
120. Berle estimate: Berle, *Autobiography*, p. 316.
120. "I was as hooked": ibid., pp. 155–56.
120. Swope at tracks: Kahn, *Swope*, p. 419.
120. Swope resignation: memo, Martin F. Fay to Estes Kefauver, n.d., box 1:30, Kefauver Papers.

CHAPTER FOUR

age 131. Loesch: *National Cyclopedia of American Biography*, 32 (1945), pp. 24–25.
131. "to lift Chicago": *New York Times*, June 24, 1928; next quotation, ibid.
131. "to remonstrate": NJW, p. 145; next quotation, ibid., p. 146.
132. "but they'll only": ibid., p. 262; next six quotations, ibid., pp. 145, 262, 145, 143, 147, 148.
133. Public enemies by 1933: *New York Times*, October 8, 1933.
133. "It is the hand": NJW, p. 214.
133. "largely unassimilable": *New York Times*, December 20, 1932.
133. "The American people": *New York Times*, March 23, 1930.
133. "The real Americans": *New York Times*, July 1, 1930.
134. "We live in": Louther S. Horne in *New York Times Magazine*, April 10, 1938.
134. Seabury: Herbert Mitgang, *The Man Who Rode the Tiger: The Life and Times of Judge Samuel Seabury* (1963).
134. "He was a little": ibid., p. 67.
135. "We have labored": *Review of Reviews*, July 1932.
135. Rumors re Rothstein: Gene Fowler, *Beau James: The Life & Times of Jimmy Walker* (1949), pp. 208, 222.
136. Crater: Mitgang, *Seabury*, pp. 167–68; Virgil W. Peterson, *The Mob: 200 Years of Organized Crime in New York* (1983), p. 169.
136. "That is the way": Mitgang, *Seabury*, p. 195.
137. Bookmaking cases, 1929: Alan Block, *East Side—West Side: Organizing Crime in New York, 1930–1950* (Transaction edition, 1983), p. 33.
137. Corrigan role: Lewis J. Valentine, *Honest Cop* (1939), p. 142.
137. Prostitution racket: Peterson, *Mob*, p. 171.
138. Flynn: Block, *East Side*, p. 46.
138. McQuade: William B. Northrop and John B. Northrop, *The Insolence of Office: The Story of the Seabury Investigations* (1932), p. 165.

138. "money that I borrowed": Peterson, *Mob,* p. 176; next quotation, ibid.

138. "moneys that I saved": Walter Chambers, *Samuel Seabury: A Challenge* (1932), p. 331.

138. "Kind of a magic": Northrop and Northrop, *Insolence,* p. 164; next quotation, ibid., p. 226.

139. Sherwood accounts: Block, *East Side,* pp. 54–57.

139. "I just work along": *New Yorker,* March 31, 1945.

139. Anslinger: *Current Biography* (1948), pp. 20–22; Douglas Clark Kinder in *Pacific Historical Review,* May 1981; John C. McWilliams, "The Protectors: Harry J. Anslinger and the Federal Bureau of Narcotics, 1930–1962" (Ph.D. thesis, Pennsylvania State University, 1986).

139. "I was brought up": "Serenity Through Prayer," box 1, Harry J. Anslinger Papers.

140. "I never forgot": Harry J. Anslinger and Will Oursler, *The Murderers: The Story of the Narcotic Gangs* (1961), p. 8.

140. Different versions: ibid., pp. 9–10; MS, [1949], chap. 6, Anslinger Papers.

140. "Such was my": Anslinger and Oursler, *Murderers,* p. 10.

140. "I was frozen": Anslinger to Lincoln C. Andrews, July 11, 1944, box 2, Anslinger Papers.

140. "I firmly believe": Anslinger to Secretary of State, April 20, 1926, box 3, Anslinger Papers.

141. "The world belongs": Anslinger to R. W. Kauffman, March 19, 1945, box 3, Anslinger Papers.

141. "it gives you": Jay Richard Kennedy in *This Week,* March 7, 1948.

141. "Getting an informer": Anslinger and Oursler, *Murderers,* p. 142.

141. "This morning": Harry V. Williamson to Anslinger, October 19, 1931, box 3, Anslinger Papers.

141. "There goes": OCN 1:351.

141. Undercover agents: Andrew Tully, *Treasury Agent* (1958), p. 62.

142. "the old douche bag": Anslinger to James E. Hamilton, March 17, 1952, box 2, Anslinger Papers.

142. "Your bureau's work": Kennedy in *This Week,* March 7, 1948.

142. George White: Joachim Joesten, "Dewey, Luciano, and I," MS, November 1955, p. 79, in box 1:24, Estes Kefauver Papers; Malachi L. Harney and John C. Cross, *The Narcotic Officer's Handbook* (2nd edition, 1973), p. 194.

142. "George was": Harry J. Anslinger with J. Dennis Gregory, *The Protectors* (1964), p. 79.

142. White and Japanese spy: Joesten, "Dewey," p. 81.

142. "George would just": Warren Olney III, "Law Enforcement and Judicial Administration in the Earl Warren Era" (Earl Warren Oral History Project, Bancroft Library, 1981), p. 279.

142. Chinese tongs: Anslinger and Oursler, *Murderers*, pp. 20–21.

142. "the undisputed narcotics boss": Anslinger, *Protectors*, p. 53.

142. Jewish dope dealers: IOC 2:89, 14:382; OCN 4:891; Frederic Sondern, Jr., *Brotherhood of Evil: The Mafia* (1959), p. 94; Anslinger to Assistant Secretary Gibbons, February 6, 1936, and B. M. Martin to Anslinger, December 21, 1934, box 3, Anslinger Papers.

142. "At that occasion": George White to Westbrook Pegler, November 20, 1943, box 79, Westbrook Pegler Papers.

143. Mafia and narcotics: David Leon Chandler, *Brothers in Blood* (1975), pp. 209–10; OCN 4:891, 919; IOC 7:1086–90; "The Kansas City Investigation," Treasury Intelligence Unit report, April 1, 1943, p. 151, in box 58, Pegler Papers.

143. Sicilian informer: Harney and Cross, *Informer*, pp. 107–8.

143. "We knew that": Sondern, *Brotherhood*, p. 94.

143. "I made a vow": Charles Siragusa as told to Robert Wiedrich, *The Trail of the Poppy: Behind the Mask of the Mafia* (1966), p. x.

143. "I have a lot": Sondern, *Brotherhood*, p. 137.

143. "I would like": CLP, p. 215.

143. "There are so many": Sondern, *Brotherhood*, p. 132.

144. Kansas City informer: MS, [1949], chap. 6.

144. Antinori-Lopiparo conversation: IOC 4:84–87.

146. "For many years": Bureau of Narcotics memo, March 7, 1947, box 16, Herlands file, Thomas E. Dewey Papers.

147. Copeland: *National Cyclopedia of American Biography*, 15 (1916), pp. 358–59; *Dictionary of American Biography*, supplement 2 (1958), pp. 120–22.

147. "At Washington everybody": Ray Tucker in *Collier's*, July 14, 1934.

148. Runyon series: Hearst newspapers, May 14–29, 1933.

148. "to destroy this growing evil": *New York Times*, May 9, 1933.

148. Startling to learn: *Brooklyn Eagle*, June 26, 1933, scrapbook 13, Royal S. Copeland Papers.

148. "Alien criminals": *Washington Star*, August 13, 1933, ibid.

148. "It is inconceivable": *New York Times*, June 27, 1933.

148. "There is a growing": ISR, pp. 1–2; next nine quotations, ibid., pp. 437, 59, 251, 134, 83, 52, 49, 52–53, 45.

149. Lewis Lawes: *Current Biography* (1941), pp. 496–98.

150. Copeland bills after hearings: *New York Times*, December 17, 1933, January 12, 1934.

150. FDR crime package: Kenneth O'Reilly in *Journal of American History*, December 1982.

150. "the most intelligent": G. Edward White, *Earl Warren: A Public Life* (1982), p. 25.

150. "He was devoted": Earl Warren, *Memoirs* (1977), p. 22; next quotation, ibid., p. 17.

151. "He has a strong": Oliver Carlson in *American Mercury*, May 1948.

151. "that I could not": Warren, *Memoirs*, p. 72; next quotation, ibid., p. 104.

151. Oakland whorehouses: ibid., pp. 140–41.

152. Recounted forty years later: Donald R. Cressey, *Theft of the Nation: The Structure and Operations of Organized Crime in America* (1969), pp. 61–62.

152. Alameda: Jack Harrison Pollack, *Earl Warren: The Judge Who Changed America* (1979), p. 51.

152. Oakland: Warren, *Memoirs*, p. 68.

152. Emeryville: Roger Dionne in *Sports Illustrated*, June 3, 1985.

152. "You take care": Warren, *Memoirs*, p. 86; next three quotations, ibid., pp. 101, 87, 103.

153. Emeryville to present day: Dionne in *Sports Illustrated*, June 3, 1985.

153. "I never heard": Irving Stone in *Life*, May 10, 1948.

154. "I could give": Warren, *Memoirs*, p. 106.

154. Warren activities in state: ibid., pp. 106–8, 119.

155. Jerome later: "Conversations with Earl Warren on California Government" (Earl Warren Oral History Project, Bancroft Library, 1982), pp. 115–16.

155. "Do you think": Warren, *Memoirs*, p. 131: next quotation, ibid., p. 143.

155. "When the snow": IOC 10:172.

155. Dragna arrest, 1931: Justice Department case 23-8-142, Record Group 60, National Archives.

155. Dragna assertion: Warren Olney III in "Proceedings of the Attorney General's Conference . . . on Organized Crime," Austin, Texas, March 30–31, 1951, p. 84, in box 1:27, Kefauver Papers; article by Sid Hughes and Herb Stinson, 1950, in box 1:29, Kefauver Papers.

155. "Jack wasn't pulling": Mickey Cohen as told to John Peer Nugent, *In My Own Words*, p. 41; next quotation, ibid., p. 62.

156. Siegel in Hollywood: Florabel Muir, *Headline Happy* (1950), pp. 162–64; Burton B. Turkus and Sid Feder, *Murder, Inc.: The Story of "the Syndicate"* (1951), p. 269; John Scarne, *The Odds Against Me* (1966), p. 360; J. Richard (Dixie) Davis in *Collier's*, August 19, 1939.

156. "The most fascinating": Anita Loos, *A Girl Like I* (1966), p. 205.

156. Greenberg murder and Siegel: PBX 1:105.

156. "I dont owe": Tony Cornero to Joseph Lawrence, June 17, 1936, in Justice Department case 23-11-869, Record Group 60, National Archives.

157. Dragna arrest, 1930: IOC 2:217–18.

157. *Rex* ownership: Bugsy Siegel statement, August 16, 1940, in box 7, Murder Inc. Papers; Warren, *Memoirs*, p. 132; Muir, *Headline*, p. 164.

157. "With things like": Olney, "Law Enforcement," p. 173.

157. Olney in library: interview with Scott Elder, March 9, 1986.

158. "I won't give up": *Los Angeles Times*, August 4, 1939.

158. Cornero launched: Earl Warren to Harry S Truman, August 6, 1946, OF 1578, Harry S Truman Presidential Library; Warren, *Memoirs*, p. 137.

158. "It was assumed": "The Reminiscences of Thomas E. Dewey" (Columbia Oral History Collection, 1973), p. 73; next quotation, ibid., p. 53.

158. "Our home": Thomas E. Dewey, *Twenty Against the Underworld* (1974), p. 32; next quotation, ibid., p. 43.

159. "I'd heard": Dewey, "Reminiscences," p. 220; next quotation, ibid., p. 206.

159. "We were seeing": Dewey, *Twenty*, p. 77; next five quotations, ibid., pp. 335, 345, 336, 339, 444.

160. "Dewey was the perfectionist": Elmer R. Irey as told to William J. Slocum, *The Tax Dodgers: The Inside Story of the T-men's War with America's Political and Underworld Hoodlums* (1948), p. 135.

160. Gordon case: Dewey, *Twenty*, pp. 119–20.

161. "His courtroom technique": Irey, *Tax Dodgers*, p. 137.

161. "There's something": *New York Times*, December 1, 1933.

161. "astounding": *New York Times*, December 2, 1933.

161. "We were just": *Kansas City Star*, February 21, 1938.

162. "You know": Richard Norton Smith, *Thomas E. Dewey and His Times* (1982), p. 157.

162. "We were all young": Dewey, *Twenty*, p. 169; next quotation, ibid., p. 168.

163. "It was a fact": Jenna Weissman Joselit, *Our Gang: Jewish Crime and the New York Jewish Community* (1983), p. 169.

163. "our real law man": Dewey, *Twenty*, p. 164; next quotation, ibid., p. 165.

163. Hire some Catholics: Smith, *Dewey*, p. 343.

163. "He could quell": Dewey, *Twenty*, p. 168; next two quotations, ibid., pp. 364, 368.

164. "Gentlemen, a verdict": *Boston Herald,* August 2, 1935.

164. "For months thereafter": Davis in *Collier's,* August 5,1939.

164. "It is wrong": Davis in *Collier's,* July 22, 1939.

164. "The audacity": Joseph Bonanno with Sergio Lalli, *A Man of Honor* (1983), pp. 156–57.

165. Schultz murder: Turkus and Feder, *Murder,* pp. 138–40; memo re Schultz murder, March 7, 1941, box 7, Murder Inc. Papers.

165. "My knees trembled": Davis in *Collier's,* August 19, 1939.

165. Carter and Harlem ring: Rupert Hughes, *Attorney for the People: The Story of Thomas E. Dewey* (1940), p. 80.

166. "We just locked": Dewey, "Reminiscences," p. 379.

166. "Petillo is of greater": Anthony E. Mancuso to Lt. Dowd, February 17, 1936, box 27, Luciano files, Manhattan District Attorney Papers.

166. "We were always": Dewey, "Reminiscences," p. 249.

166. "As you know": Thomas E. Dewey to Edward G. McLean, April 2, 1936, box 12, Luciano files, Manhattan District Attorney Papers.

167. "Listen, you fellows": digest of Sam Warner testimony, April 22, 1936, box 5, Luciano files, ibid.

167. Luciano complained: summary of case, n.d., box 6, Luciano files, ibid.

167. Spiller as witness: memo by Sol Gelb, July 10, 1936, box 35, Luciano files, ibid.

167. "What were you": Dewey, *Twenty,* p. 242.

168. "I could not break": Dewey summation, June 4, 1936, p. 23, box 1:90:5, Thomas E. Dewey Papers.

168. "I have been in many": report, 1946, by Dr. Harry L. Freedman in box 21, Herlands file, Dewey Papers.

168. Luciano always insisted: *Reprieve: The Testament of John Resko* (1956), p. 206.

168. Bendix confided: Joesten, "Dewey," pp. 92–95; and see Thomas Plate, *Crime Pays!* (1975), p. 98.

168. "I was astonished": Polly Adler, *A House Is Not a Home* (1953), pp. 294–97.

169. Runyon story: Hughes, *Dewey,* p. 155.

169. "Today there is not": Dewey, *Twenty,* p. 402.

169. Luciano in prison: James D. Horan, *The Mob's Man* (1959), p. 85.

169. "He practically ran": Sondern, *Brotherhood,* p. 109.

170. "The fact stands out": ISR, p. 448.

170. "It broke": Peter L. Berger, *The Sacred Canopy* (1967), p. 112.

171. "Protestantism is not": Michael Novak, *The Rise of the Unmeltable Ethnics: Politics and Culture in the Seventies* (1972), p. 173.

171. "Being an": Cohen, *My Own,* p. 257; next quotation, ibid., p. 18.

171. "It wasn't that": *My Life in Crime: The Autobiography of a Professional Criminal,* reported by John Bartlow Martin (1952), p. 16.

172. "I never met": Robert Sylvester, *Notes of a Guilty Bystander* (1970), p. 239.

172. "Pop always said": Francis A. J. Ianni with Elizabeth Reuss-Ianni, *A Family Business: Kinship and Social Control in Organized Crime* (1972), p. 72.

172. O'Hare and son: John Kobler, *Capone* (1971), p. 244.

172. "the most important": Frank J. Wilson and Beth Day, *Special Agent* (1965), p. 32.

173. Threat against O'Hare, 1937: *New York Times,* November 14, 1939.

173. "Though he engaged": John Cooney, *The Annenbergs* (1982), p. 71; next quotation, ibid., p. 330.

CHAPTER FIVE

age 175. Benny Fein: Jenna Weissman Joselit, *Our Gang: Jewish Crime and the New York Jewish Community, 1900–1940* (1983), pp. 107–9.

175. "a use of gangsters": Virgil W. Peterson, *The Mob: 200 Years of Organized Crime in New York* (1983), p. 122.

175. Lanza: Fred D. Pasley, *Muscling In* (1931), pp. 170–72; Craig Thompson and Allen Raymond, *Gang Rule in New York* (1940), pp. 264–65; Burton B. Turkus and Sid Feder, *Murder, Inc.: The Story of "the Syndicate"* (1951), p. 209.

176. "The Business Agent": Gordon L. Hostetter and Thomas Quinn Beesley, *It's a Racket!* (1929), pp. 82–83; next four quotations, ibid., pp. 84–85, 39–40.

177. "Our shops had been": *Chicago Tribune,* March 20, 1943; next quotation, ibid.

178. Chicago rackets: Hostetter, *Racket,* p. 16; Pasley, *Muscling,* pp. 12–17, 27–28, 58.

178. "antagonistic to": Victor Olander to John H. Walker, February 12, 1926, box 2, Victor Olander Papers.

178. Loesch asserted: NJW, pp. 212–13.

178. "Maliciously untrue": ibid., pp. 260–62.

179. "in order to sustain": statement, September 2, 1932, to Illinois State Federation of Labor, box 57, Olander Papers; and see statement, January 9, 1933, box 62, ibid.

179. "subjected to the racketeer": ISR, p. 269; next two quotations, ibid., pp. 798, 416–17.

180. Sumner fortified: *New York Times,* August 29, 1932.

180. Gangsters picked on: Garth L. Mangum, *The Operating Engineers* (1964), pp. 191–92.

181. Laborers: Arch A. Mercey, *The Laborers' Story, 1903–1953* (1954).

181. Carozzo: *Chicago News*, April 14, 1943, and other clippings in Hod Carriers file, box 86, Westbrook Pegler Papers; IIA 33:12542.

181. "the gunman from Chicago": ISR, p. 80; next two quotations, ibid., pp. 79–80.

182. New York construction site: ibid., pp. 801–2.

182. Stirone: *Pittsburgh Post-Gazette*, August 31, 1944, June 23, 1943; *Pittsburgh Press*, February 12, 1941, April 16, 1944, and other clippings in Hod Carriers file, box 86, Pegler Papers.

182. LaRocca: MAR, p. 330.

183. "Finis Written": *Pittsburgh Post-Gazette*, August 31, 1944.

183. Stirone convicted of extortion: *New York Times*, October 7, 1961, November 27, 1962.

183. Fay: *New York Times*, August 11, 1972.

183. "There were fights": IIA 20:8086.

183. Zwillman and Fay: Mark A. Stuart, *Gangster #2: Longy Zwillman, the Man Who Invented Organized Crime* (1985), p. 130.

184. Hague and Fay: Mangum, *Engineers*, pp. 183–84.

184. "one of the real": John Hutchinson, *The Imperfect Union: A History of Corruption in American Trade Unions* (1970), p. 46.

184. Fay gambling: Harold Seidman, *Labor Czars: A History of Labor Racketeering* (1938), p. 163.

184. "Fay was not": Max Block with Ron Kenner, *Max the Butcher* (1982), p. 193.

184. "When he came over": IIA 20:7925–26.

184. Fay stole millions: Hutchinson, *Imperfect*, p. 191.

184. Maloney: IIA 20:8304–5, 8156; Hutchinson, *Imperfect*, p. 190.

184. Zeigler: Pauline Zeigler Christianson to John L. McClellan, January 30, 1958, file 24-D, John L. McClellan Papers.

185. "You son of a bitch": IIA 20:8257; next three quotations, ibid., 8255–56.

186. Zeigler murder: *New York Times*, February 25, 1933.

186. "What hurt the most": Christianson to McClellan, January 30, 1958.

186. "If this strike": *New York Times*, February 21, 1937.

186. Redwood murder: *New York Times*, February 28, October 7, 1937.

186. Fay and Bove: Hutchinson, *Imperfect*, pp. 46–47.

187. "This local has been": Charles P. Larrowe, *Harry Bridges: The Rise and Fall of Radical Labor in the United States* (1972), p. 53.

187. "the way they sweat": Walter Galenson, *The CIO Challenge to the AFL* (1960), p. 440.

187. "If there is brought": Seidman, *Czars*, p. 242.

188. "Recourse to": ISR, p. 74.

188. 40 percent of CIO unions: Herbert Harris, *Labor's Civil War* (1940), p. 135.

188. "Industry should not": Arthur M. Schlesinger, Jr., *The Coming of the New Deal* (1959), p. 419.

188. "the Irish bartenders' union": Matthew Josephson, *Union House Union Bar: The History of the Hotel and Restaurant Employees and Bartenders International Union AFL-CIO* (1956), p. 68.

189. Schultz gang: ibid., pp. 218–22; J. Richard (Dixie) Davis in *Collier's*, July 22, 1939; *New Republic*, November 27, 1935; Jay Rubin and M. J. Obermeier, *Growth of a Union: The Life and Times of Edward Flore* (1943), pp. 234–36.

189. "I'll do for your union": Seidman, *Czars*, p. 203.

189. HRE New York locals: Bert Cochran, *Labor and Communism: The Conflict That Shaped American Unions* (1977), pp. 57–58; Irving Bernstein, *Turbulent Years* (1970), p. 125.

190. Maddox: IIA 33:12531–33.

190. Romano: IIA 33:12543–44.

190. "Give us the names": IIA 33:12540.

190. "I said I was afraid": *Chicago Tribune*, March 24, 1943; next quotation, ibid.

191. Nitti cited: IIA 33:12542.

191. "Either I would": Josephson, *Union*, p. 245.

191. 1938 convention: ibid., pp. 248, 254.

191. Capones dumped McLane: IMW, p. 154.

192. "No other union": *Fortune*, May 1941.

192. Shape-up: Hutchinson, *Imperfect*, pp. 96–97.

192. Hoboken and Jersey City: Mary Heaton Vorse in *Harper's*, April 1952.

192. Public loading: Malcolm Johnson, *Crime on the Labor Front* (1950), pp. 118–19.

193. Longshoremen: Philip Taft, *Corruption and Racketeering in the Labor Movement* (2nd edition, 1970), pp. 13–14.

193. "The work was hard": Maud Russell, *Men Along the Shore* (1966), p. 92.

193. "I went up through": WFI, p. 448.

193. "Since it was all": Willie Sutton with Edward Linn, *Where the Money Was* (1976), p. 14.

194. Eighteen bosses murdered: Pasley, *Muscling*, pp. 180–84.

194. "No one was ever": Sutton, *Money*, p. 14.

194. Strollo: IIA 32:12239–41.

194. Clemente: WCC, p. 175.

194. Camarda: Daniel Bell, *The End of Ideology* (Collier edition, 1962), p. 192; Joseph Bonanno with Sergio Lalli, *A Man of Honor* (1983), p. 169.

194. Anastasias: Russell, *Men*, pp. 258–61.

194. "all longshoremen are hoodlums": ibid., p. 267.

194. Tough Tony a capo: chart facing OCN 1:294.

195. Camarda locals: Johnson, *Crime*, pp. 192–93.

195. "I wish you'd stop": *New York Times*, October 31, 1945.

195. Panto murder: *New York Times*, December 19, 1952; Burton Turkus to William O'Dwyer, April 8, 1952, box 12, Murder Inc. Papers.

195. "Panto wasn't": Charles P. Larrowe, *Shape-up and Hiring Hall* (1955), p. 37n.

195. Ryan named brother-in-law: WCC, p. 173.

195. Irish gangs on West Side: Johnson, *Crime*, p. 97; WCC, p. 175.

195. "In 1936 me and George": Johnson, *Crime*, p. 167.

196. Varick Enterprises: Bell, *End*, pp. 184–85; Johnson, *Crime*, pp. 122–23; IIA 37:13971–75.

196. "We got a police": Johnson, *Crime*, pp. 160–61; next three quotations, ibid.

196. "Because a man's": Larrowe, *Shape-up*, p. 20.

196. "They dump them": Johnson, *Crime*, p. 160; next quotation, ibid., p. 154.

196. "We call Ryan": Larrowe, *Shape-up*, p. 64.

197. Ryan would make phone call: Lester Velie in *Collier's*, February 9, 1952.

197. McCormack: Velie in *Collier's*, February 9, 16, 1952.

197. "a capacity for": Joseph Ryan to Westbrook Pegler, October 4, 1951, box 91, Pegler Papers.

197. "This may sound": Hutchinson, *Imperfect*, pp. 98–99.

197. "I liked to do": Johnson, *Crime*, p. 96.

197. "We as workers": Schlesinger, *Coming*, p. 390.

198. "I found them": Larrowe, *Bridges*, p. 183.

198. "to fight Communism": Larrowe, *Shape-up*, p. 18.

198. "Clear out of California": Russell, *Men*, p. 130.

198. "Here lies": Larrowe, *Shape-up*, p. 112.

198. "The crookedest": *Fortune*, May 1941; next quotation, ibid.

199. "They are not college": IAI, p. 205.

200. Tobin: *Biographical Dictionary of American Labor Leaders*, ed. Gary M. Fink et al. (1974), p. 354.

200. "were kicked around": *Fortune*, May 1941.

200. "My losses": Nathan W. Shefferman with Dale Kramer, *The Man in the Middle* (1961), p. 16.

200. "Dan Tobin drank": Ralph C. James and Estelle Dinerstein James, *Hoffa and the Teamsters: A Study of Union Power* (1965), p. 51.

200. Tobin consulted Beck: ibid., p. 18.

200. "While Tobin was not": John D. McCallum, *Dave Beck* (1978), p. 76; next quotation, ibid., p. 102.

200. "Our cars were bombed": James and James, *Hoffa*, p. 86.

201. Fratianno and Teamsters: Ovid Demaris, *The Last Mafioso: The Treacherous World of Jimmy Fratianno* (1981), p. 9.

201. "I went down there": IRC, p. 358.

201. Triscaro and Local 436: IIA 40:15131.

201. "Mob guys had": James R. Hoffa as told to Oscar Fraley, *Hoffa: The Real Story* (1975), p. 92; next quotation, ibid., p. 93.

201. Hoffa tried to arrange: IIA 36:13681–82.

202. "I am surprised": Walter Chambers, *Labor Unions and the Public* (1936), p. 142.

202. Sasso of Local 863: *New York Times*, December 3, 1940.

202. Minneapolis: IRM, pp. 199–200.

202. Glimco and Aiuppa: IIA 34:13104–5, 13121, 49:17731–32, 17749, 17770.

202. Philadelphia: IIA 36:13565, 13631.

202. "I'm putting you": Johnson, *Crime*, p. 73.

202. "one or two so-called": *Fortune*, May 1941.

202. "He said he": *Chicago Tribune*, March 22, 1943; next two quotations, ibid.

203. Minneapolis: Galenson, *CIO Challenge*, pp. 482–86; Hutchinson, *Imperfect*, pp. 254–55.

204. Bennett: Harry Bennett as told to Paul Marcus, *We Never Called Him Henry* (1951).

204. "the little guy": Josephine Fellows Gomon, "The Poor Mr. Ford," MS in box 10, Josephine Fellows Gomon Papers; next quotation, ibid.

204. Bennett and Ford: Robert Lacey, *Ford: The Men and the Machine* (1986), p. 379; David L. Lewis in *Detroit Magazine*, January 20, 1974; Bennett, *We Never*, p. 38.

205. "What I like": Allan Nevins and Frank Ernest Hill, *Ford* (1963), 3:114.

205. Edsel Ford and Bennett: ibid., 2:591; Heber Blankenhorn memo, May 18, 1950, box 3-30, Heber Blankenhorn Papers.

205. "I supervised anything": IOC 9:81; next quotation, ibid.

205. "They're a lot": John McCarten in *American Mercury*, May 1940.

205. "They never looked": Charles E. Sorensen with Samuel T. Williamson, *My Forty Years With Ford* (1956), p. 256.

205. "The army": Edmund Wilson, *The American Earthquake* (Anchor edition, 1964), pp. 245–46.

206. "I don't know": hearings transcript, p. 989, box 1-20, Homer Ferguson Papers.

206. "You can have": transcript, p. 840, box 1-19, Ferguson Papers.

206. Bennett and GOP conventions: Gomon, "Poor Mr. Ford."

206. "I talked to": IOC 9:92.

206. "On numerous occasions": Lacey, *Ford*, p. 163.

207. Bennett solved murder: Gomon, "Poor Mr. Ford."

207. Protected witness: O'Brien in *Forum*, February 1938.

207. "He won't bother": McCarten in *American Mercury*, June 1940.

207. "Mr. Ford heard": IOC 9:83.

207. "I am the king": Lewis in *Detroit Magazine*, January 20, 1974.

207. La Mare was given: Keith Sward, *The Legend of Henry Ford* (1948), p. 300.

207. "didn't know a banana": IOC 9:84.

207. D'Anna and Hancock: IOC 9:20–26.

208. D'Anna's agency and contract: IOC 9:28–29, 31, 89; executive session transcript, p. 6326, box 1:28, Estes Kefauver Papers.

208. Bennett and Adonis: IOC 7:298–99, 316; 9:98, 12:762–64; Fred J. Cook, *The Secret Rulers* (1966), p. 122; Sward, *Legend*, p. 300.

208. Bennett and Licavoli: IOC 9:74–78; Agnes S. Wolf, "Draft of Committee Report on Infiltration of Organized Crime into Legitimate Enterprises," March 22, 1951, p. 94, in box 1:25, Kefauver Papers.

208. UAW factions: Galenson, *CIO Challenge*, p. 150.

208. Hunger March: Sward, *Legend*, pp. 235–38.

208. "They got a small": ibid., p. 395.

209. "There stood two": Victor G. Reuther, *The Brothers Reuther and the Story of the UAW* (1976), pp. 206–7.

209. Reuther paid an informer: ibid., pp. 208–9.

209. Reuther was told: IIA 25:10060, 10115; Blankenhorn memo, May 18, 1950.

209. "a great victory": Sward, *Legend*, p. 417.

210. Patriarca fired at Reuther: OCS 2:768 (date given as 1938).

210. Schenck: *The Education of Carey McWilliams* (1979), p. 91; *New York Times*, October 23, 1961.

210. "Whatever Joe": Arthur H. Samish and Bob Thomas, *The Secret Boss of California* (1971), p. 50.

211. Schenck and Farley: "The Reminiscences of Eddie Dowling" (Columbia Oral History Collection, 1964), pp. 553–54; notes on March 7, September 6, 21, October 21, December 6, 1938, box 43, James A. Farley Papers.

211. "I am quite sure": Joseph Schenck to John Francis Neylan, February 2, 1936, box 10, John Francis Neylan Papers; and see Neylan to William Randolph Hearst, July 12, 1927, October 2, 1931, box 65, and Neylan to Hearst, August 7, 1925, box 64, Neylan Papers.

211. "He came to know": Anita Loos, *A Girl Like I* (1966), pp. 187–88.

211. Schenck arranged: ibid., p. 189.

211. Bioff: *New York Times*, October 28, 1941.

211. "I was a youngster": Florabel Muir, *Headline Happy* (1950), p. 85.

211. Stagehands and gangsters: Taft, *Corruption*, p. 48; Seidman, *Czars*, pp. 177–84; Stuart, *Zwillman*, pp. 115, 130; anonymous to Westbrook Pegler, April 25, 1940, and clippings in IATSE file, box 87, Pegler Papers.

211. "Our theatres": James Edwards, Jr., to Franklin D. Roosevelt, May 12, 1933, in Justice Department case 60-6-30-5, Record Group 60, National Archives.

212. Maloy: Edward Dean Sullivan, *This Labor Union Racket* (1936), pp. 21, 61–62; John H. Lyle, *The Dry and Lawless Years* (1960), pp. 250–53; anonymous to Westbrook Pegler, May 28, 1941, IATSE file, box 87, Pegler Papers.

212. Bioff and Browne: *Chicago Tribune*, March 18, 1943; Elmer R. Irey as told to William J. Slocum, *The Tax Dodgers: The Inside Story of the T-men's War with America's Political and Underworld Hoodlums* (1948), p. 273.

212. Riverside meeting: *New York Times*, October 7, 1943.

212. "and many other heads": excerpt of Nitti transcript dictated by Boris Kostelanetz, March 20, 1951, box 1:30, Kefauver Papers.

213. Roselli and Siegel: IOC 5:394–96; Turkus and Feder, *Murder*, p. 269.

213. Costello: Leonard Katz, *Uncle Frank: The Biography of Frank Costello* (1973), pp. 140, 250.

213. "The guy's all right": Mickey Cohen as told to John Peer Nugent, *In My Own Words* (1975), p. 83.

213. Foy: IOC 5:373–75.

213. "on anything": Jim Bishop, *The Mark Hellinger Story* (1952), p. 125; and see ibid., pp. 95, 111–12, 244, 284, 361.

213. Bioff and producers: *New York Times*, October 10, 15, 17, 1941.

213. Money bought privileges: *Education of McWilliams*, p. 89; Johnson, *Crime*, pp. 25–28; *New York Times*, December 1, 1943; Muir, *Headline*, pp. 79, 88–89; Carey McWilliams to Westbrook Pegler, January 9, 1940, IATSE file, box 87, Pegler Papers.

214. "good business": *New York Times*, October 22, 1941.

214. "We have had less": Hutchinson, *Imperfect*, p. 133.

214. "My wife is nuts": Florabel Muir in *Saturday Evening Post,* January 27, 1940; next quotation, ibid.

214. "We had about": Irey, *Tax Dodgers*, p. 271.

214. Dissidents in Local 37: Carey McWilliams in *New Republic,* October 27, 1941.

214. Pegler on case: Pegler columns, November 24, 28, 1939, et seq.

215. FDR's most influential: Galenson, *CIO Challenge*, p. 292.

215. Hillman: Matthew Josephson, *Sidney Hillman* (1952).

215. Hillman fought Communists: Harvey A. Levenstein, *Communism, Anticommunism, and the CIO* (1981), pp. 80–81.

215. "One is more likely": Joseph Gollomb in *Atlantic,* July 1938.

216. "should have turned out": Joselit, *Our Gang*, p. 122.

216. Lepke: *New York Times,* March 5, 1944; Turkus and Feder, *Murder,* pp. 331–33.

216. "His eyes were": *My Life in Crime: The Autobiography of a Professional Criminal,* reported by John Bartlow Martin (1952), p. 209.

216. "He was a pleasant": Al Hirshberg and Sammy Aaronson, *As High as My Heart: The Sammy Aaronson Story* (1957), p. 59.

216. "We thought Lepke": Harry J. Anslinger with J. Dennis Gregory, *The Protectors* (1964), p. 47.

216. "Everybody knew": memo, n.d., of information from Seymour Magoon, box 4, Murder Inc. Papers.

217. "We had to go": memo, n.d., re Goldstein and Strauss as told by Abe Reles, box 4, Murder Inc. Papers.

217. Lepke rackets: Hutchinson, *Imperfect*, p. 72; Turkus and Feder, *Murder,* p. 346.

217. "They were all through"; IOC 18:647.

217. "the curse of underworldism": *New York Times,* July 1, 1931.

217. Hoodlums in Local 4: Josephson, *Hillman*, pp. 328–29.

217. "They both dealt": "The Reminiscences of Thomas E. Dewey" (Columbia Oral History Collection, 1973), p. 495.

217. Hillman and Lepke: memo, n.d., re Sidney Hillman from Albert Tannenbaum, in Parisi file, box 4, Murder Inc. Papers; and see Turkus and Feder, *Murder,* p. 85; Harry J. Anslinger and Will Oursler, *The Murderers: The Story of the Narcotic Gangs* (1961), pp. 51–52; Joselit, *Our Gang,* p. 126.

218. Weinstein role: memo re Hillman from Tannenbaum.

218. "Tannenbaum did 'slugging' work": ibid.

218. Special occasions: Anslinger and Oursler, *Murderers,* p. 52; Turkus and Feder, *Murder,* p. 341.

218. "a piece of the action": Bonanno, *Man,* p. 151.

219. "Listen, Mr. Hillman": statement by Morris Blustein, June 27, 1941, box 8, Murder Inc. Papers.

219. Lepke on lam: Anslinger and Oursler, *Murderers,* p. 52; memo, n.d., of information from Albert Tannenbaum, box 7, Murder Inc. Papers.

219. Ferreri murder: *New York Times,* August 1, 1931, March 3, 1944; George H. White to Westbrook Pegler, November 20, 1943, box 79, Pegler Papers.

219. "The facts fitted": Anslinger and Oursler, *Murderers,* p. 53.

220. "He is a big shot": statement by Max Rubin, December 16, 1937, box 1, Murder Inc. Papers.

220. "Clear it with Sidney": Josephson, *Hillman,* p. 618.

CHAPTER SIX

age 222. "the wickedest city": Frederick L. Collins in *Liberty,* July 22, 1939.

222. Hot Springs history: Dee Brown, *The American Spa: Hot Springs, Arkansas* (1982), pp. 50–62.

223. McLaughlin: interview with James L. Dowds, July 24, 1980, in "The Life and Times of Leo P. McLaughlin," oral history project, Tri-Lakes Regional Library, Hot Springs, Arkansas.

223. "His love for his mother": interview with Vern Ledgerwood, August 7, 1980, ibid.

223. "All the good people": Nancy Russ, "The Life and Times of Leo P. McLaughlin," in *Record* of Garland County Historical Society (1983).

223. "We had an airtight": Ledgerwood interview.

224. "I don't know how": Russ, "McLaughlin."

224. "If you don't want": Collins in *Liberty,* July 29, 1939.

224. "He is a large": Walter Davenport in *Collier's,* August 8, 1931.

224. Jacobs casinos: Frank Buckley, "Report of the Prohibition Situation in Arkansas," Treasury Department, 1930, in box 207:3, Roscoe Pound Papers.

224. "We, on our side": Davenport in *Collier's,* August 8, 1931; next quotation, ibid.

225. Gangster resort: Vivian Lynn to Estes Kefauver, October 27, 1950, box 1:29, Estes Kefauver Papers.

225. "a chronic ailment": *New York Times,* December 1, 1933.

225. Capone liked to stroll: Russ, "McLaughlin."

225. "the remarkable civic health": Davenport in *Collier's,* August 8, 1931.

225. Akers and Dickson: Collins in *Liberty,* July 22, 1939.

225. "The whole crowd": Thomas E. Dewey to Edward G. McLean,

April 2, 1936, box 12, Luciano files, Manhattan District Attorney Papers.

226. "We put him out": Ledgerwood interview.

226. Madden controlled: section 3 of Sam Giancana file, FBI FOIPA Preprocessed Files, FBI Building, Washington, D.C.; GOC, pp. 559–66; interview with Maxine Temple Jones, October 20, 1985.

226. "Owney was really": Mickey Cohen as told to John Peer Nugent, *In My Own Words* (1975), p. 13.

226. Madden parole: *New York Times,* July 12, 13, August 3, 1934.

226. Cash from Lansky's man: Craig Thompson and Allen Raymond, *Gang Rule in New York* (1940), p. 384.

226. Costello claimed: *Washington Post,* November 29, 1949.

226. "He was a pretty nice": interview with Nathan L. Schoenfeld, September 25, 1980, McLaughlin oral history project.

226. Madden trips to New York: *New York Times,* May 4, 1940, July 29, 1947.

227. "Mr. Madden said": Hank Messick with Joseph L. Nellis, *The Private Lives of Public Enemies* (1973), p. 99.

227. "I'm the governor": IOC 10:753.

227. Samish: Arthur H. Samish and Bob Thomas, *The Secret Boss of California* (1971).

228. Samish description: *Our Sovereign State,* ed. Robert S. Allen (1949), pp. 396–97.

228. "My staff and I": Samish and Thomas, *Boss,* p. 8; next two quotations, ibid., pp. 81, 80.

228. "I've got the damndest": Lester Velie in *Collier's,* August 20, 1949; next quotation, ibid.; and see Elmer R. Rusco, "Machine Politics, California Style: Arthur H. Samish and the Alcoholic Beverage Industry" (Ph.D. thesis, University of California at Berkeley, 1960), p. 237.

229. "I've always been known": *Sovereign,* ed. Allen, p. 389.

229. "I'm always looking": IOC 10:1218.

229. "I always kept": Samish and Thomas, *Boss,* p. 106.

229. Co-authored racing bill: Rusco, "Machine Politics," p. 193.

229. Racetrack clients: IOC 10:752-53; Velie in *Collier's,* August 13, 1949.

229. "and I put that money": Samish and Thomas, *Boss,* p. 65.

230. Samish and Rosenstiel: ibid., p. 93; Herbert Solow in *Fortune,* April 1954.

230. "I didn't hear": Samish and Thomas, *Boss,* p. 96.

230. Rosenstiel paid Samish: IOC 10:1203–4.

230. "the damndest political machine": Velie in *Collier's,* August 13, 1949.

230. "Every branch": *Sovereign*, ed. Allen, p. 399; next quotation, ibid., p. 390.

230. Party organizations: Carey McWilliams in *Nation*, July 9, 1949.

231. "Procedure is the secret": Velie in *Collier's*, August 20, 1949.

231. Seeman and Samish: *Sovereign*, ed. Allen, pp. 409–10.

231. Murphy and Samish: *Reports of the Special Crime Study Commission on Organized Crime*, Sacramento, third report, January 31, 1950, pp. 19–20.

231. Cohen and Samish: IOC 10:274; George Redston with Kendell F. Crosson, *The Conspiracy of Death* (1965), p. 215.

231. "See, if I had": Cohen, *My Own*, p. 3.

231. "Yes, I would say": IOC 7:1664.

231. "just for the baths": *Sovereign*, ed. Allen, p. 400.

231. "You are down there": IOC 10:1218–19.

231. "I don't know anything": IOC 10:1219.

231. "Some of these guys": *Sovereign*, ed. Allen, p. 400.

231. "a powerful—if secretive": IOC 10:754–55.

232. "I have been": IOC 10:1165; next four quotations, ibid., pp. 1199, 1203.

232. "A national reputation": Herbert Solow in *Fortune*, April 1954.

233. "On this night": *Detroit News*, January 20, 1944; next quotation, ibid.

233. "We have only three": *Detroit News*, August 10, 1939.

233. Detroit Citizens League: see William P. Lovett to Homer Ferguson, January 12, 1944, box 1:8, Homer Ferguson Papers.

233. Ferguson: *Current Biography* (1943), pp. 202–4; interviews with Myrtle Ferguson and Amy Ferguson Beltz, September 14, 1985.

233. "In the 1880s": statement for *Who's Who*, February 1973, box 1:1, Ferguson Papers.

234. "My old Dad": *Time*, June 1, 1942.

234. Grand jury process: "Personal History," MS in box 1:1, Ferguson Papers; interviews with Ferguson and Beltz.

234. Worried about threats: interview with Homer Ferguson, November 8, 1944, box 1:8, Ferguson Papers.

234. Former FBI agent: interview with Ferguson, January 31, 1973, ibid.

234. Shooting range and nightmares: interviews with Ferguson and Beltz.

235. Consulted Dewey: interview with Ferguson, January 31, 1973.

235. "You come": "Recordings of Statements Taken for Wayne County Graft Grand Jury" (thirty-four discs in a green box, Ferguson Papers), disc 10; other quotations re Block from discs 26, 9, 8, 2, 8, 21, 22.

236. Colburn and McCrea: *Detroit News*, April 29, 1941; testimony, pp. 58–68, box 1:14, Ferguson Papers.

236. "Looks like": disc 30; other quotations re Boettcher from discs 30, 37, 42, 45, 50, 51, 53, 55.

237. "Ryan was the class": *Detroit News*, January 6, 1944.

238. Boettcher's bag work: *Detroit News*, January 3, 6, 10, 14, 1944.

238. Purples and Italians split: Jack Carlisle in *Gambling in America* (Commission on the Review of the National Policy Toward Gambling), appendix 1 (1976), p. 147.

238. Payoffs before Reading: *Detroit News*, January 5, 8, 1944; statement by Josephine Fellows Gomon, pp. 93–94, box 10, Josephine Fellows Gomon Papers.

238. "People say": *Time*, June 1, 1942.

238. "I decide": John McCarten in *New Yorker*, February 12, 1938.

238. Richard Reading: *New York Times*, November 3, 1937, December 10, 1952.

239. "Politics is a business": George Creel in *Collier's*, October 10, 1936; next two quotations, ibid.

240. "I was what folks": Dayton David McKean, *The Boss: The Hague Machine in Action* (1940), p. 24.

240. Brothers in Red Tigers: Thomas A. Repetto, *The Blue Parade* (1978), p. 136.

240. "You didn't do": Sutherland Denlinger in *Forum*, March 1938.

240. McLaughlin: Alfred Steinberg, *The Bosses* (1972), pp. 12–13.

240. Hague rise: Repetto, *Blue Parade*, pp. 137–38.

241. Hague personality: McKean, *Boss*, pp. 8–10.

241. "Probably nobody": McCarten in *New Yorker*, February 12, 1938.

241. "the most moralest": Steinberg, *Bosses*, p. 48.

241. Hague gambling: ibid., p. 37; McKean, *Boss*, p. 12.

241. Goode and Morarity: Thomas F. X. Smith, *The Powerticians* (1982), pp. 140–41.

241. Payoff system: Thomas J. Fleming in *Saturday Evening Post*, January 6, 1962.

241. "You pay only": Reinhard H. Luthin, *American Demagogues* (1954), p. 144.

241. Horse Bourse: Fleming in *American Heritage*, June 1969; McKean, *Boss*, p. 220.

241. "I've cleaned up": Creel in *Collier's*, October 10, 1936.

241. "It's all a goddam": McCarten in *New Yorker*, February 12, 1938.

242. $2 million: J. H. Sterling to Estes Kefauver, March 24, 1951, box 1:24, Kefauver Papers.

242. Bootleggers: Mabel Walker Willebrandt to A. T. Mason, January 31, 1951, box 83, Harlan Fiske Stone Papers; WFI, pp. 243–44.

242. Hague and Zwillman: Lester Velie in *Collier's,* April 25, 1951.

242. "gangsters and labor racketeers": Richard J. Connors, *A Cycle of Power: The Career of Jersey City Mayor Frank Hague* (1971), p. 131.

242. "I found that four gangsters": McKean, *Boss,* p. 191.

242. Mob unions: Garth L. Mangum, *The Operating Engineers* (1964), pp. 183–84; Connors, *Cycle,* p. 98; Malcolm Johnson, *Crime on the Labor Front* (1950) pp. 208–10; WFI, pp. 202–41.

242. Moore: *National Cyclopedia of American Biography,* E (1938), p. 372; Luthin, *Demogagues,* p. 137.

242. "I do not have": Lyle W. Dorsett, *Franklin D. Roosevelt and the City Bosses* (1977), p. 102.

243. Norton: *Notable American Women* (1980), 4:511–12; Steinberg, *Bosses,* p. 34.

243. "An ample figure": Maxine Davis in *Ladies' Home Journal,* May 1933.

243. "I never have had": *Newsweek,* June 26, 1937.

243. "He has never asked": *Current Biography* (1944), p. 502.

243. Catholics: McKean, *Boss,* pp. 160–62.

243. Protestant clergy: ibid., pp. 159–60.

244. "The Republican Party": Connor, *Cycle,* pp. 95–96; next quotation, ibid., p. 94.

244. Lieutenant at Western Union: Fleming in *American Heritage,* June 1969.

244. "Animal spirits": Steinberg, *Bosses,* p. 41.

244. "Whenever I hear": McKean, *Boss,* p. 228.

244. *Journal* episode: Jack Alexander in *Saturday Evening Post,* October 26, 1940.

245. "Sure, he had": Smith, *Powerticians,* p. 139.

245. Acknowledged $8 million: Fleming in *American Heritage,* June 1969.

245. Payroll and taxes: Steinberg, *Bosses,* p. 42; *New Republic,* February 2, 1938.

246. "Nobody can beat": McCarten in *New Yorker,* February 12, 1938.

246. "I'm not bragging": Maurice M. Milligan, *Missouri Waltz: The Inside Story of the Pendergast Machine by the Man Who Smashed It* (1948), p. 79.

246. Mansion: *Kansas City Star,* September 30, 1928.

246. "all immaculate": Carroll K. Shackelford to William Jeremiah Burke, March 4, 1947, box 223, William Jeremiah Burke Papers.

246. "We're very close": Jerome Beatty in *American Magazine,* February 1933.

246. Pendergast office: Steinberg, *Bosses,* pp. 330–31; William M.

Reddig, *Tom's Town: Kansas City and the Pendergast Legend* (1947), pp. 131–32; Ralph Coghlan in *Forum,* February 1937.

247. "He seems to be about": ibid.

247. "His strength beamed": Beatty in *American Magazine,* February 1933.

247. "They were large": Milligan, *Missouri,* p. 220.

247. "No politics": Coghlan in *Forum,* February 1937.

247. "My concrete": *Omaha World-Herald,* February 27, 1938.

247. Triumvirate: Richard Lawrence Miller, *Truman: The Rise to Power* (1986), p. 247.

247. Pendergast youth: Milligan, *Missouri,* pp. 27–41; Lyle W. Dorsett, *The Pendergast Machine* (1968), pp. 3–5.

248. "Old Turkey Neck": Henry C. Haskell, Jr., and Richard B. Fowler, *City of the Future* (1950), pp. 137–39.

248. "Tom and I": Steinberg, *Bosses,* p. 322.

248. Truman position: Miller, *Truman,* p. 168.

248. "I had to compromise": Andrew J. Dunar, *The Truman Scandals and the Politics of Morality* (1984), pp. 9–10; next quotation, ibid., p. 10, and Miller, *Truman,* p. 223.

249. " 'The Boss' says": Dunar, *Scandals,* p. 11.

249. "I think maybe": Miller, *Truman,* p. 247.

249. Pendergast spoke only once: ibid., p. 263.

249. "The fanatic": Miller, *Truman,* pp. 357–58.

250. "I used to go": IOC 4:353.

250. Lazia gang: "The Kansas City Investigation," Treasury Intelligence Unit report, April 1, 1943, p. 7, in box 58, Westbrook Pegler Papers; Samuel S. Mayerberg, *Chronicle of an American Crusader* (1944), pp. 114–17; Blackie Audett, *Rap Sheet: My Life Story* (1954), pp. 120–22, 148–49.

250. Open town: Ross Russell, *Jazz Style in Kansas City and the Southwest* (1971), p. 8; Nathan W. Pearson, Jr., *Goin' to Kansas City* (1987), pp. 92–106.

250. "This town was fast": Morris (Red) Rudensky and Don Riley, *The Gonif* (1970), p. 82.

250. "Most of the night spots": *Hear Me Talkin' to Ya,* ed. Nat Shapiro and Nat Hentoff (1955), p. 288.

250. Lazia convicted: Justice Department case 5-43-100, Record Group 60, National Archives.

250. "Now, Jim": *St. Louis Post-Dispatch,* November 30, 1934; next quotation, ibid.

251. "Democratic Leader Slain": *New York Times,* July 11, 1934.

251. Murder of Gregory: Lear B. Reed, *Human Wolves* (1941), pp. 31–33.

251.   Pendergast floral offering: *St. Louis Post-Dispatch,* January 9, 1950.

251.   Arrangements with Carollo: "Kansas City Investigation," pp. 92–93.

251.   "We have turned": Beatty in *American Magazine,* February 1933.

252.   Illegal tax breaks: Dorsett, *Roosevelt and Bosses,* p. 14.

252.   "People were actually told": Mayerberg, *Chronicle,* p. 111.

252.   Mayerberg crusade: ibid., pp. 118–40.

253.   "One of my hardest": ibid., p. 131.

253.   "Where the hell": Elmer R. Irey as told to William J. Slocum, *The Tax Dodgers: The Inside Story of the T-men's War with America's Political and Underworld Hoodlums* (1948), pp. 226–27.

253.   Riverside Park: Reddig, *Tom's Town,* p. 165; Coghlan in *Forum,* February 1937.

253.   "T. J.'s penthouse": Steinberg, *Bosses,* p. 350.

254.   Pendergast betting: Milligan, *Missouri,* p. 80; Reddig, *Tom's Town,* pp. 278, 324.

254.   Bribe of $750,000: statement of facts, May 22, 1939, Maurice M. Milligan Collection.

254.   "I never desert": *Newsweek,* April 17, 1939.

254.   "I want you to know": James V. Bennett, *I Chose Prison* (1970), p. 144.

254.   Reformers took over: Stanley High in *National Municipal Review,* October 1941.

254.   "The terrible things": Miller, *Truman,* p. 315.

255.   "To be a real mayor": Roger Biles, *Big City Boss in Depression and War: Mayor Edward J. Kelly of Chicago* (1984), p. 49.

255.   "The visitor": John T. Flynn in *Collier's,* July 13, 1940.

255.   Nitti and Accardo: CHI, p. 163.

255.   "great native intelligence": Paul H. Douglas, *In the Fullness of Time* (1972), p. 90.

255.   Kelly: Victor Rubin in *Collier's,* August 25, 1945.

256.   "We have purged": Flynn in *Collier's,* July 13, 1940.

256.   Kelly youth: *Dictionary of American Biography,* supplement 4 (1974), pp. 450–51; Biles, *Kelly.*

256.   Threw rocks at troops: Douglas, *Fullness,* p. 90.

256.   Income 1919–29: Biles, *Kelly,* p. 29.

256.   Nash and Kelly: ibid., pp. 13–14, 47.

256.   "When I first came": *Life,* July 17, 1944.

256.   "He turned": Biles, *Kelly,* p. 41.

257.   Stolen votes: ibid., p. 39.

257.   Tribute from gambling: ibid., p. 107.

257.   Listed $50,000: *The Secret Diary of Harold L. Ickes* (1954), 2:561.

257.   "It was commonly known": Douglas, *Fullness,* p. 90.

257. "Everybody knows": Biles, *Kelly,* p. 113.
257. One hundred joints protected: Flynn in *Collier's,* July 13, 1940.
257. "Gambling isn't": Rubin in *Collier's,* August 25, 1945.
257. "The mayor is part": Biles, *Kelly,* p. 69.
257. Joints shut down: J. B. Martin in *American Mercury,* June 1949.
258. Policy games: St. Clair Drake and Horace R. Cayton, *Black Metropolis* (1961 edition), pp. 470, 481, 486.
258. Jones brothers: William Brashler, *The Don: The Life and Death of Sam Giancana* (1977), pp. 86–87.
258. "They may come": Drake and Cayton, *Metropolis,* p. 489; next quotation, ibid., p. 484.
258. Dawson: James Q. Wilson, *Negro Politics: The Search for Leadership* (1960), p. 50; Ovid Demaris, *Captive City* (1969), p. 172.
258. "Betting is a": John Madigan in *Reporter,* August 9, 1956.
259. Capones took over: Mark H. Haller in *Gambling in America,* p. 121.
259. Guzik and Dawson: Virgil W. Peterson to George S. Robinson, October 18, 1950, box 1:29, Kefauver Papers.
259. Defending crooked Teamsters: IRM, pp. 44, 57; IRC, pp. 359, 432–33, 1004.
259. Dealt in favors: Edward T. Clayton, *The Negro Politician* (1964), pp. 82–83.
259. "I have never been": Madigan in *Reporter,* August 9, 1956.
260. FDR and bosses: Edward T. Flynn, *You're the Boss* (1947), pp. 91–92.
260. "But keep this": Dorsett, *Roosevelt and Bosses,* p. 103.
260. "I am not overlooking": *Secret Diary of Ickes,* 3:122.
260. Kelly led movement: Biles, *Kelly,* pp. 84–85, 94–97.
260. 1940 convention: James A. Farley, *Jim Farley's Story* (1948), pp. 280–81.
260. Kelly suggested Hannegan: Flynn, *Boss,* p. 178.
260. 1944 convention: ibid., p. 183.

CHAPTER SEVEN

Page 261. Effect of war: Ralph Salerno and John S. Tompkins, *The Crime Confederation* (1969), pp. 284–86; Mickey Cohen as told to John Peer Nugent, *In My Own Words* (1975), p. 66; Peter Maas, *The Valachi Papers* (1968), pp. 185–90.
262. "There were so many": OCN 1:109.
262. "The members of this": *My Life in Crime: The Autobiography of a Professional Criminal,* reported by John Bartlow Martin (1952), pp. 235–36.

262. Bushnell: *National Cyclopedia of American Biography*, 39 (1954), p. 283.

262. Bushnell youth: *Boston Globe,* June 10, 1940.

263. 1919 commencement: *New York Times*, June 18, 1919.

263. Returned $144,000: *Boston Herald*, January 12, 1930.

263. "a vast subterranean": *Boston Herald,* December 8, 1930.

263. "All rackets are controlled": memo, John C. Bresnahan to Edward W. Fallon, July 30, 1936, box 44.18, Henry Lee Shattuck Papers; and see anonymous to Elmer Irey, May 15, 1944, box 44.17, ibid.

264. Pinetree stable: Vincent Teresa with Thomas C. Renner, *My Life in the Mafia* (1973), pp. 24–25.

264. Hotze: *Boston Globe*, March 16, 1935, January 25, 1940; testimony in box 27.19, Shattuck Papers.

264. Coleman: *Boston Herald,* May 17, 1944; Watch & Ward report, January 19, 1944, box 5, New England Watch & Ward Society Papers.

264. Knocko McCormack: note in Coleman file, n.d., and report to Wall, October 4, 1940, Timilty file, box 2, Sidney A. Aisner Papers.

264. Sagansky: *Report of the Attorney General* (1945), in Massachusetts State Library, Boston, pp. 31–33.

264. "This defendant": Robert Robinson in case 4666 (1923), Superior Criminal Court, Boston.

264. Sagansky holdings: *Boston Herald,* January 14, 1943.

265. $100,000 a year: interview with Matthew McGrath, Jr., January 13, 1984.

265. Timilty and Kennedys: *Lynn Telegram*, October 17, 1943; Hank Searls, *The Lost Prince* (1969), p. 93.

265. "If it wasn't for Curley": summary of Timilty testimony, February 10, 1943, box 44.19, Shattuck Papers.

266. Diamond Jim Timilty: *Boston Globe,* July 7, 1921.

266. $3 million in contracts: James Michael Curley, *I'd Do It Again* (1957), p. 346.

266. Timiltys indicted, 1926: case 6199 (1927), Superior Criminal Court, Boston.

266. "I sought to do": *Boston Globe,* June 9, 1938.

266. Curley and Timilty: *Boston Globe,* November 26, 1936; *Boston Herald*, November 26, 1936.

266. "I'm going to clean up": *Boston Herald,* December 1, 1936.

266. "Such men are used": *Boston Sunday Advertiser,* March 21, 1937.

266. "We can never": *Boston Sunday Advertiser,* December 12, 1937.

266. "Quack doctors": Robert T. Bushnell in *North American Review,* April 1930.

267. "We have come": Watch & Ward annual message, March 1936, box 5, Watch & Ward Papers.

267. Watch & Ward tracked: reports, April 30, 1938, May 27, September 26, 1939, May 22, September 25, November 13, 1940, box 5, Watch & Ward Papers.

267. "The commissioner advanced": report, March 7, 1941, box 5, Watch & Ward Papers.

267. "Morality has gone haywire": *Boston Post*, June 28, 1942.

268. "I'm not a crusader": *Boston Globe*, March 23, 1941.

268. "It is not my disposition": *Report of Attorney General* (1945), pp. 18–19.

268. "I do not believe": report by James V. Crowley, June 20, 1941, Timilty file, Aisner Papers.

268. Section secretly deleted: Claflin testimony, February 18, 1943, pp. 28–31, 51, box 44.19, Shattuck Papers.

268. Memo from *Herald: Report of Attorney General* (1945), pp. 20–22.

269. Cocoanut Grove: ibid., pp. 12–13; Paul Benzaquin, *Fire in Boston's Cocoanut Grove* (1967 edition), pp. 36–37.

269. "In all the time": Edward Keyes, *Cocoanut Grove* (1984), p. 204.

269. "You won't have to get": Benzaquin, *Fire*, p. 201.

270. Curley life insurance policy: *Boston Globe*, January 14, 1943.

270. Movies of Boston cops: stills after p. 34, *Report of Attorney General* (1945).

270. Timilty and safe-deposit box: *Boston Globe*, February 10, 1943.

270. "because if that money was discovered": summary of Timilty testimony, February 8, 1943, box 44.19, Shattuck Papers.

271. "all in a fog-like": ibid., February 10, 1943.

271. Removed four drawers: report by William F. Hayes, May 22, 1943, Timilty file, Aisner Papers.

271. "absolute knack": Jacob Lewiton to Robert F. Bradford, November 25, 1944, box 6, Robert F. Bradford Papers.

271. Called press conference: *Boston Herald*, January 20, 1943; interview with Jacob Lewiton, May 4, 1984.

271. "I have never had": *New Bedford Standard-Times*, February 17, 1944.

271. Bushnell and Irish Catholic judge: interview with George Leary, December 20, 1983.

272. "wanted for questioning": *Boston Herald*, August 19, 1943.

272. "I have tried press conferences": *Boston Traveler*, August 30, 1943.

272. Dismissal of Timilty indictment: *Boston Herald*, July 3, 1943.

272. Timilty with Kennedys: *Boston Herald*, November 1, 14, 1943.

272. "The hypocrisy and arrogance": *Boston Herald*, November 27, 1943.

272. Sagansky later: *Boston Globe,* June 14, 1987; March 1, 1989.

273. Death of Bushnell: *New York Times,* October 24, 1949.

273. Humphrey: Carl Solberg, *Hubert Humphrey: A Biography* (1984).

273. "the plain and unambiguous": Hubert Humphrey to Erskine Johnson, November 12, 1947, box 5, Mayoralty General Correspondence, Hubert Humphrey Papers.

273. "It is not enough": Humphrey to Mr. and Mrs. Donald Fredericks, February 23, 1945, box 1, ibid.

273. "If I run": interview with Arthur Naftalin, November 25, 1969, box 2, Autobiography files, Humphrey Papers.

274. Banks and Cann: Hubert H. Humphrey, *The Education of a Public Man* (1976), p. 78; Justice Department case 5-39-166, Record Group 60, National Archives; *Minneapolis Star,* June 26, 1959, December 13, 1976, June 21, 1981; *Minneapolis Star and Tribune,* September 12, 1985; Paul Fishman Maccabee in *Mpls. St. Paul,* January 1982.

274. LaPompadour: report, ca. 1936, in file 23.L.Z.9B, Humphrey Papers.

274. Guilford murder: *New York Times,* September 7, 1934.

274. Liggett murder: *Editor and Publisher,* December 14–28, 1935, February 15, 1936.

274. "Sure I've done": *Minneapolis Times,* December 12, 1935.

274. "Criminals, racketeers": *Modern Monthly,* January 1936.

274. Cann and Schuldberg claimed: *Minneapolis Times,* December 10, 1935.

275. Soltau claimed three thousand: Henry J. Soltau to Humphrey, January 26, 1945, box 1, Mayoralty General Correspondence, Humphrey Papers.

275. "be honest": Soltau to Humphrey, April 15, 1947, box 20, Mayoralty file, ibid.

275. "I was dedicated": interview with Bradshaw Mintener, May 13, 1980, in Carl Solberg Papers.

275. "this white-haired guy": interview with Ed Ryan, p. 5, box 1, Autobiography files, Humphrey Papers.

275. "I'm disgusted": Ryan interview, p. 6.

276. "What a tragedy": *Minneapolis Star Journal,* May 21, 1943.

276. Underworld and police control: Ryan interview, p. 8.

276. "I am no blue-nose": Humphrey to John Cowles, February 14, 1945, box 1, Mayoralty General Correspondence, Humphrey Papers.

276. Kasherman murder: *New York Times,* January 24, 1945.

276. "He was a shakedown": interview with Marvin Kline, May 13, 1969, p. 43, box 1, Autobiography files, Humphrey Papers.

276. "open flaunting": *Minneapolis Star Journal,* November 3, 1944.

276. Operators started removing: *Minneapolis Tribune,* July 3, 1945.

277. "Well, here's another": Ryan interview, p. 8.

277. "He could swear": ibid., p. 18.

277. Law Enforcement Committee: Humphrey to Mintener, August 15, 1945, and Mintener to Humphrey, August 13, 1945, box 2, Mayoralty General Correspondence, Humphrey Papers.

277. Discussion of "14": minutes of Law Enforcement Committee, October 19, 1945, ibid.

277. "This is quite": Humphrey to Earl Latham, September 4, 1945, ibid.

277. "When you see": *Minneapolis Times,* November 3, 1945.

277. "I understand": Humphrey to Ryan, November 12, 1945, box 2, Mayoralty General Correspondence, Humphrey Papers.

277. "Crack down": Humphrey to Ryan, October 8, 1945, ibid.

278. "We hope this shameful": Henry J. Soltau to Ed Ryan, August 25, 1945, ibid.

278. "For the first time": Mintener speech, April 15, 1946, box 17, Mayoralty files, Humphrey Papers.

278. MacLean more regular: interview with Bradshaw Mintener, November 11, 1985.

278. MacLean defended: MacLean to Humphrey, January 13, 1947, box 20, Mayoralty files, Humphrey Papers.

278. "It was just": *Minneapolis Tribune,* January 13, 1947.

278. Humphrey absolved MacLean: Humphrey to MacLean, January 16, 1947, box 19, Mayoralty files, Humphrey Papers; and see Mintener to Humphrey, January 20, 1947, box 5, Mayoralty General Correspondence, Humphrey Papers.

278. Banks and Cann and licenses: Solberg, *Humphrey,* p. 104.

278. "I never tried to have": Humphrey interview, n.d., p. 12, file 35, box 2, Autobiography files, Humphrey Papers.

279. "I am going to leave": Humphrey to Bill Simms, December 4, 1946, box 17, Mayoralty files, Humphrey Papers.

279. "You don't": Ryan interview, p. 18.

279. Bingo relegalized: *Minneapolis Tribune,* December 1, 1947.

279. "meddling with petty": *Minneapolis Star,* September 10, 11, 1947.

279. Teamsters and 1945 election: Humphrey to Harold Purvis, November 26, 1945, box 2, Mayoralty General Correspondence, Humphrey Papers.

279. "I never got along": Humphrey interview, September 1969, p. 2, box 2, Autobiography files, Humphrey Papers.

279. Brennan crooked: *New York Times,* March 21, 1956.

279. "for all that you are doing": Humphrey to Sid Brennan, July 17, 1947, box 5, Mayoralty General Correspondence, Humphrey Papers.

279. Gates: Solberg, *Humphrey*, p. 101.

279. "all of them": Mintener interview, November 11, 1985.

279. "He knew everything": Humphrey interview, n.d., pp. 254–55, file 48, box 2, Autobiography files, Humphrey Papers.

280. Gates as associate: Gates file, box 2, Personal and Family Papers, Humphrey Papers.

280. Urged to get rid of Gates: Humphrey, *Education*, p. 93; Glenn MacLean to Humphrey, September 9, 1948, box 17, Personal and Family Papers, Humphrey Papers.

280. Peterson: interview with Virgil W. Peterson, September 23, 1985.

280. "I had a lot": ibid.

281. Peterson and Purvis: Peterson to author, January 23, 1985.

281. "When I was there": Peterson interview.

281. "From the very beginning": Peterson to author, March 27, 1985.

281. "the most honorable": Peterson interview; next quotation, ibid.

282. "Those who belong": *Walther League Messenger*, September 1961.

282. "I always assumed": Peterson interview.

282. Beverly Club: *Washington Post*, November 28, 1949.

282. Costello at Roosevelt Hotel: IOC 7:1012.

282. "I have had": IOC 8:380.

282. "What should I have": *Donahue*, syndicated October 18, 1986.

283. Colonial Inn: IOC 7:300.

283. $5,000 to Runyon fund: Harold Conrad, *Dear Muffo* (1982), pp. 9–12.

283. Sullivan lost $36,000: note of call from Sterling Noel, July 16, 1947, box 73, Westbrook Pegler Papers.

283. Capones in Miami: Daniel P. Sullivan to Estes Kefauver, October 24, 1950, box 1:29, Estes Kefauver Papers.

283. "We wrote the Chicago Crime Commission": "Proceedings of the Attorney General's Conference . . . on Organized Crime," Austin, Texas, March 30–31, 1951, pp. 97–98, in box 1:27, Kefauver Papers.

283. Cornero nightclub, 1932: Justice Department case 23-11-869, Record Group 60, National Archives.

284. First Las Vegas casinos: Dean Jennings, *We Only Kill Each Other: The Life and Bad Times of Bugsy Siegel* (1967), pp. 150–51; Mark Haller in *Law, Alcohol, and Disorder*, ed. David E. Kyvig (1985), p. 151; IOC 6:196–97; 10:54–58, 912.

284. Later casinos: Ed Reid, *The Grim Reapers: The Anatomy of Organized Crime in America* (1969), p. 218; Ed Reid and Ovid Demaris, *The*

Green Felt Jungle (1963), p. 107; Hank Messick, *The Beauties and the Beasts: The Mob in Show Business* (1973), pp. 161–63; Ovid Demaris, *The Last Mafioso: The Treacherous World of Jimmy Fratianno* (1981), p. 106.

284. Cornero death: *Los Angeles Times,* August 1, 1955.

284. "The people who ran": *Jimmy the Greek by Himself,* with Mickey Herskowitz and Steve Perkins (1975), p. 221.

284. "They had to have": Robert W. Greene, *The Sting Man: Inside Abscam* (1981), pp. 222–23.

284. "He knows": Demaris, *Fratianno,* p. 69.

285. "the most capable": CHI, p. 163.

285. Mollenhoff and Fratto: Clark R. Mollenhoff, *Strike Force: Organized Crime and the Government* (1972), pp. 35–37.

285. Capones and Sheltons: Mark H. Haller in *Gambling in America* (Commission on the Review of the National Policy Toward Gambling, 1976), appendix 1, pp. 126–27; Martin, *My Life,* p. 227.

285. "the clique from Chicago": Martin, *My Life,* p. 211.

285. Capones in Dallas: IIA 33:12519–26; 34:13032–34; notes by George Butler, fall 1946, box 1:29, Kefauver Papers; transcript of discussion, November 1, 1946, ibid.

285. "We have told Steve": transcript of discussion, November 7, 1946, ibid., p. 1; next quotation, ibid., pp. 5, 9.

286. Capones arrested: Estes Kefauver, *Crime in America* (1951), p. 81.

286. Jack Ruby: Anthony Summers, *Conspiracy* (1980), pp. 457–59.

286. "an almost puritanical": Sidney Shalett in *Saturday Evening Post,* March 19, 1955.

286. Olney: *National Cyclopedia of American Biography,* 28 (1940), pp. 24–25; interviews with Elizabeth Olney, Elizabeth Olney Anderson, Margaret Olney, and Scott Elder, March 9, 1986.

287. "to housebreak myself": Shalett in *Post,* March 19, 1955.

287. Olney and Warren: G. Edward White, *Earl Warren: A Public Life* (1982), pp. 97–98.

287. "He is as much": Shalett in *Post,* March 19, 1955.

287. "We found it": IOC 2:219.

287. "He was exactly": interview with Elder, March 9, 1986.

288. "When he made up": interview with Elizabeth Olney, March 9, 1986.

288. "We kept hearing": IOC 2:219; next quotation, ibid.

288. "Bookmaking has nothing": "Conversations with Earl Warren on California Government" (Earl Warren Oral History Project, Bancroft Library, 1982), p. 30.

288. "we felt that we had": IOC 2:221.

289. "I got him elected": Elmer R. Rusco, "Machine Politics, California Model: Arthur H. Samish and the Alcoholic Beverage Industry" (Ph.D. thesis, University of California at Berkeley, 1960), p. 155.

289. Howser and Samish: interview with Arthur Sherry, March 9, 1986.

289. "The word was out": Earl Warren, *Memoirs* (1977), pp. 198–99; next quotation, ibid., p. 199.

289. Howser held up $7,500: interview with Elizabeth Olney, March 9, 1986.

289. "He said anybody": interview with Elizabeth Olney Anderson, March 9, 1986.

290. "The problem was": Arthur H. Sherry, "The Alameda County District Attorney's Office and the California Crime Commission" (Earl Warren Oral History Project, Bancroft Library, 1976), p. 114.

290. "It became": Warren Olney III, "Law Enforcement and Judicial Administration in the Earl Warren Era" (Earl Warren Oral History Project, Bancroft Library, 1981), p. 275.

290. Wire service after Annenberg: IMW, p. 359; IOC 10:186–87; Florabel Muir, *Headline Happy* (1950), pp. 189–90; FBI Director to T. L. Caudle, December 3, 1946, in Justice Department case 5-23-1205, Record Group 60, National Archives; abstract of testimony of Thomas F. Kelly, n.d., box 5, George S. Robinson Papers; memo by Daniel P. Sullivan re Continental Press, May 2, 1950, box 1:22, Kefauver Papers; chart of competing wire services and Samuel Klaus to Estes Kefauver, May 5, 1951, box 1:25, ibid.; IIA 33:12525; GOC, pp. 371–77.

290. "Naturally I missed": Cohen, *My Own,* p. 81.

290. "From evidence furnished": *Reports of the Special Crime Study Commission on Organized Crime,* Sacramento, second report, March 7, 1949, pp. 15–16.

290. "The organization of bookmakers": *Reports of Commission,* final report, November 15, 1950, pp. 28–29.

291. Howser bodyguard for Cohen: Sherry, "Alameda," pp. 129–30.

291. Dragna and Rochester: Olney, "Law Enforcement," pp. 288–90.

291. Howser scheme: Sherry, "Alameda," pp. 103–4; *Reports of Commission,* final report, pp. 10–18.

291. "They said they were": ibid., p. 19.

291. "a tumorous growth": *Our Sovereign State,* ed. Robert S. Allen (1949), p. 407; and see Olney, "Law Enforcement," pp. 282–84.

291. Howser and dope case: George H. White to Kefauver, February 15, 1951, box 1:26, Kefauver Papers; IOC 2:90–91.

292. "The thing that made us": Sherry, "Alameda," p. 112.

292. Samish and Cohen: *Reports of Commission,* third report, January 31, 1950, pp. 18–20.

292. "Our policy was never": Sherry, "Alameda," p. 117.

292. Olney and Samish tax case: Shalett in *Post,* March 19, 1955.

292. "Has Artie Samish": Herbert Bayard Swope to John Francis Neylan, December 13, 1954, box 53, John Francis Neylan Papers.

292. "He started away back": Neylan to Swope, December 23, 1954, ibid.

293. "It is the best thing": Mrs. J. Jackson to Charles W. Tobey, March 16, 1951, box 105, Charles W. Tobey Papers.

293. Kefauver: *National Cyclopedia of American Biography,* 52 (1970), pp. 393–94; Jay Walz in *New York Times Magazine,* July 30, 1950.

293. Reports by crime commissions: Jack Anderson and Fred Blumenthal, *The Kefauver Story* (1956), pp. 140–41; and see M. H. Goldschein to Kefauver, November 10, 1949, box 1:25, Kefauver Papers.

294. "We are not naive": IOC 5:135.

294. Tobey: autobiography, November 1947, box 62, Tobey Papers; Tobey to Barry Bingham, March 1, 1951, box 101, Tobey Papers; Frank Gervasi in *Collier's,* August 2, 1947.

294. "There is no place": Charles W. Tobey, *The Return to Morality* (1952), p. 74; next three quotations, ibid., pp. 88, 58.

294. "Do you feel": executive session transcript, Kansas City, p. 834, box 1:31, Kefauver Papers.

294. "Some of our good": IOC 10:729; and see 10:1083–84.

294. Committee and crime commissions: William Howard Moore, *The Kefauver Committee and the Politics of Crime, 1950–1952* (1974), pp. 39, 87; interview with Peterson, September 23, 1985.

295. "For convenience": IOC 2:127; next quotation, ibid., p. 202.

296. Hoover and organized crime: Richard Gid Powers, *Secrecy and Power: The Life of J. Edgar Hoover* (1987), pp. 332–34.

296. "They're just a bunch": William C. Sullivan with Bill Brown, *The Bureau: My Thirty Years in Hoover's FBI* (1979), p. 117.

296. Hoover played horses: ibid., p. 89; Ovid Demaris, *The Director: An Oral Biography of J. Edgar Hoover* (1975), pp. 10, 36.

296. Tips from Winchell: Herman Klurfeld, *Winchell* (1976), p. 82.

296. "I regret to advise": Hoover to Kefauver, September 27, 1950, box 1:29, Kefauver Papers.

297. "The federal government": IOC 12:526; next quotation, ibid., p. 538.

297. White was assigned: George H. White to Kefauver, February 15, 1951, box 1:26, ibid.

297. "I would say": IOC 2:95.

297. "They are far more": IOC 10:171.

297. Intrigued by Mafia: Kefauver, *Crime,* p. 19.

297. Bureau of Narcotics and Mafia: see above, pp. 142–46.

297. "the little-known": *Reports of Commission,* third report, p. 25.

298. "almost fictional": Moore, *Kefauver,* p. 127; and see Daniel P. Sullivan to Kefauver, November 18, 1950, box 1:29, Kefauver Papers.

298. "They have no": IOC 6:236; and see Edward J. Allen to Kefauver, April 4, 1951, box 1:30, Kefauver Papers.

298. "Sort of a loose-knit": IOC 10:494; next two quotations, ibid., pp. 495, 501.

298. "Do you know what": IOC 7:264; next quotation, ibid., pp. 748–49.

299. Anslinger trying to nail Costello: Harry J. Anslinger with J. Dennis Gregory, *The Protectors* (1964), p. 71.

299. "A complete gentleman": Cohen, *My Own,* p. 81; next quotation, ibid., p. 58.

299. "Believe me": Leonard Katz, *Uncle Frank: The Biography of Frank Costello* (1973), p. 193.

299. Mafia Commission: Joseph Bonanno with Sergio Lalli, *A Man of Honor* (1983), pp. 170–73.

299. Costello urged others: Maas, *Valachi,* pp. 231–32.

299. "Throughout my long": George Wolf with Joseph DiMona, *Frank Costello: Prime Minister of the Underworld* (1974), p. 146.

299. Costello investments: IOC 7:935–36, 941–42, 1625, 1629, 1635.

300. Costello and politics: Katz, *Costello,* pp. 111–13; IOC 7:1597; Wolf, *Costello,* p. 96; *New York Times,* March 18, 1951.

300. "How can you analyze": IOC 7:1536.

300. Gauvreau visit: Emile Gauvreau, *My Last Million Readers* (1941), pp. 169–70.

300. "I am tied up": transcript of tapped call, July 29, 1943, box 1:30, Kefauver Papers.

300. "Good morning, Francesco": *Time,* November 28, 1949.

301. "He is the real": Herbert Asbury in *Collier's,* April 12, 1947.

301. November 1949: *Time,* November 28, 1949; *Newsweek,* November 21, 1949; *Washington Post,* November 27–December 1, 1949.

301. "It was a mistake": James A. Bell in *American Mercury,* August 1950.

301. "We talked about": Igor Cassini with Jeanne Molli, *I'd Do It All Over Again* (1977), pp. 116–17.

301. Costello read widely: Katz, *Costello,* p. 227.

301. Big words: IOC 7:946, 966, 1000, 1662.

301. "All I know": *Washington Post,* November 29, 1949.

302. "What I saw": Katz, *Costello,* p. 244.

302. "To me he is": *Washington Post,* November 30, 1949.

302. Yearning for good name: Wolf, *Costello,* p. 196.

302. "the most influential": IOC 2:158.

302. TV viewers: Kefauver, *Crime,* p. 283; Gregory C. Lisby in *Journalism Quarterly,* summer 1985.

302. "I am not expecting": IOC 7:895; next five quotations, ibid., pp. 1179, 1668, 1670, 1596, 1676.

303. Wagering Stamp Act unenforceable: GOC, pp. 9–10, 121, 140–41.

303. Adonis sold to Chiri: Frederic Sondern, Jr., *Brotherhood of Evil: The Mafia* (1959), p. 11.

303. "Very bad": IOC 10:487–88.

304. 24 of 559: FEA 1:9–10.

304. 874 tax convictions: Kefauver to George Hatcher, April 29, 1960, box 1:19, Kefauver Papers.

304. "If there had been": Lester Velie in *Collier's,* May 19, 1951.

304. "It's a criminal": *U.S. News & World Report,* April 20, 1951; and see Moore, *Kefauver,* pp. 114–34.

304. "In this city": IOC 8:13; and see deLesseps Morrison to Kefauver, March 29, 1950, box 1:21, Kefauver Papers, and Morrison to Hubert Humphrey, October 10, 1946, box 4, Mayoralty General Correspondence, Humphrey Papers.

304. Morrison payoffs from local gamblers: Morrison file in box 1:30, Kefauver Papers; and see IOC 8:306–9 and GOC, pp. 510, 524, 538–40.

304. Kefauver attended races: letters, 1942–50, in box 4C:5, Kefauver Papers.

305. "What's so bad": Dennis Eisenberg, Uri Dan, Eli Landau, *Meyer Lansky: Mogul of the Mob* (1979), p. 306.

305. "He never knew": David L. Lewis in *Detroit Magazine,* January 27, 1974.

305. Kefauver vulnerably broke: Bobby Baker with Larry L. King, *Wheeling and Dealing: Confessions of a Capitol Hill Operator* (1978), pp. 47–48.

305. Checking account: checkbooks and canceled checks in box 9:6, Kefauver Papers.

305. Signed book contract: *New York Times,* March 21, 1951.

305. Brodys: letters between Kefauver and Brodys in boxes 4B:1 and 5D:4, Kefauver Papers.

305. Brody arrest: *Knoxville News-Sentinel,* March 2, 1951; *New York Times,* March 8, 1951; and see Flora Brody to Kefauver, [February 2, 1951], box 4B:1, and R. L. Summitt to Kefauver, January 8,

1951, and Kefauver to Summitt, January 15, 1951, box 4B:1, Kefauver Papers; *Knoxville News-Sentinel,* January 8, July 13, 1951, November 24, 1970.

305. Rumor of $5,000: WIBK to Kefauver, March 29, 1951, and Kefauver to WIBK, March 29, 1951, box 4B:1, Kefauver Papers.

305. "I can't go on": *Knoxville News-Sentinel,* March 23, 1951; for the official version, see Kefauver, *Crime,* p. 319.

305. "Jeez, everything": IOC 7:334.

CHAPTER EIGHT

age 306. "We saw pieces": Kenneth P. O'Donnell and David F. Powers with Joe McCarthy, *"Johnny, We Hardly Knew Ye"* (1972), pp. 27–28.

307. Witnesses and knoll: Tip O'Neill with William Novak, *Man of the House* (1987), p. 178; Anthony Summers, *Conspiracy* (1980), pp. 55–61.

307. Ruby: ibid., pp. 456–59; David E. Scheim, *Contract on America: The Mafia Murders of John and Robert Kennedy* (1983), pp. 65–110.

307. "The sins": *The Merchant of Venice,* act III, scene 5, line 1.

308. "Time after time": *The Fruitful Bough,* ed. Edward M. Kennedy (1965), p. 210; next quotation, ibid., p. 263.

308. "one of the most evil": Ralph G. Martin, *A Hero for Our Time* (1983), p. 24.

308. "Dishonorable": John Cooney, *The Annenbergs* (1982), p. 263.

308. "A tough customer": Joseph Schenck to Sam Goldwyn, October 24, 1939, confidential source.

308. "As big a crook": Merle Miller, *Plain Speaking: An Oral Biography of Harry S Truman* (1974), p. 187.

308. "I was surprised": Frank Saunders with James Southwood, *Torn Lace Curtain* (1982), p. 133.

309. Downey and Kennedy: Dan Parker in *Collier's,* August 19, 1944; Collie Small in *Collier's,* March 19, 1949.

309. "I saw more": *Fruitful Bough,* ed. Kennedy, p. 33; next two quotations, ibid., pp. 32, 34.

309. Downey sentence, 1931: *New York Times,* April 30, 1931.

309. Downey and gangster clubs: interview with Morton Downey, Jr., June 27, 1985; *Boston Herald,* April 17, 1941; Nils Thor Granlund with Sid Feder and Ralph Hancock, *Blondes, Brunettes, and Bullets* (1957), p. 151; Stanley Walker, *The Night Club Era* (1933), p. 98.

309. Downey and Billingsley: Robert Sylvester, *Notes of a Guilty Bystander* (1970), p. 138.

309. AGVA: see AGV; file 44D, John L. McClellan Papers.

309. Downey and Tropicana: Ed Reid and Ovid Demaris, *The Green Felt Jungle* (1963), p. 85; interview with Downey, Jr.

309. Cornero funeral: Warren Olney III, "Law Enforcement and Judicial Administration in the Earl Warren Era" (Earl Warren Oral History Project, Bancroft Library, 1981), pp. 313–14.

310. Lewis: *New York Times,* June 5, 1971.

310. "He's a real smart": *Boston Herald,* September 24, 1965.

310. Kennedy sent three cases: Art Cohn, *The Joker Is Wild* (1955), p. 260.

310. Lewis and mob: Hank Messick, *The Beauties and the Beasts: The Mob in Show Business* (1973), pp. 34–35; Antoinette Giancana and Thomas C. Renner, *Mafia Princess* (1984), pp. 232–33.

310. Kennedy at Copa: *Boston Herald,* September 23, 1965.

310. Timilty as police commissioner: see above, pp. 265–72.

311. Kennedys called him Commish: cf. John F. Kennedy to Joseph Timilty, July 6, 1956, box 957, Prepresidential papers, John F. Kennedy Papers.

311. Reporter telephoned news: *Boston Globe,* May 14, 1948.

311. "He hasn't talked": *Boston Globe,* May 28, 1948.

311. Timilty after Dallas: *Boston Herald,* November 25, 1963.

311. "I was not": *Fruitful Bough,* ed. Kennedy, p. 109.

311. Rosenbloom and Kennedys: Harry Wismer, *The Public Calls It Sport* (1965), p. 85; and see Carroll Rosenbloom to Robert F. Kennedy, [December 1955], box 18, Preadministration Personal files, Robert F. Kennedy Papers.

311. "Maybe because": *Fruitful Bough,* ed. Kennedy, pp. 109–10.

312. Rosenbloom: *New York Times,* April 3, 1979; Robert H. Boyle in *Sports Illustrated,* December 13, 1965; David Harris, *The League* (1986), pp. 43–49.

312. Rosenbloom and gamblers: Bernie Parrish, *They Call It a Game* (1971), pp. 196–99; Wismer, *Public,* p. 52.

312. Bet on Colts: Joey with Dave Fisher, *Killer: Autobiography of a Mafia Hit Man* (Pocket Books edition, 1974), pp. 159–60; Parrish, *They Call,* pp. 200–203.

312. Scalped tickets: *Sports Illustrated,* June 30, 1986.

312. Rosenbloom death: Robert Blair Kaiser in *New York Times Magazine,* December 23, 1979; *New York Times,* January 15, 1983.

312. "I want you": Herbert Bayard Swope to Eugene Meyer, August 9, 1934, box 42, Eugene Meyer Papers.

312. "He is very able": Hearst to Neylan, February 17, 1937, box 200, Neylan Papers.

312. Kennedy and Davies: Saunders, *Torn,* p. 37.

312. "She was a woman": ibid., p. 88.

312. Sinatra and mob: Nicholas Gage, *The Mafia Is Not an Equal Opportunity Employer* (1971), pp. 84–85; OCS 2:752.

312. Sinatra background: Kitty Kelley, *His Way: The Unauthorized Biography of Frank Sinatra* (Bantam paperback edition, 1987), pp. 1, 16, 25, 172–73, 244.

313. "Some of them": Hank Messick with Joseph L. Nellis, *The Private Lives of Public Enemies* (1973), p. 223.

313. "I'd rather be": Kelley, *His Way*, p. 289.

313. Sinatra brought women: Saunders, *Torn*, pp. 83–84.

313. Kennedy bet up to $10,000: Peter Collier and David Horowitz, *The Kennedys* (1984), p. 212.

313. Kennedy private bookmaker: Edward Linn, *Big Julie of Vegas* (1974), p. 95.

314. "I got a friend": Harold Conrad, *Dear Muffo* (1982), p. 12; Harold Conrad to author, September 24, 1983.

314. "Kennedy is getting": Conrad, *Muffo*, pp. 12–13.

314. "Everybody used to": Messick, *Private Lives,* p. 258.

314. "Some mob business": Max Block with Ron Kenner, *Max the Butcher* (1982), p. 131; next quotation, ibid., p. 273.

314. Cal-Neva: Ovid Demaris, *The Last Mafioso: The Treacherous World of Jimmy Fratianno* (1981), p. 101; Olney, "Law Enforcement," p. 254; section 15 of Sam Giancana file, FBI FOIPA Preprocessed Files, FBI Building, Washington, D.C.; Giancana, *Princess*, p. 222; IOC 2:189–90; Dean Jennings, *We Only Kill Each Other: The Life and Bad Times of Bugsy Siegel* (1967), p. 225.

315. Sinatra tried to kill himself: Kelley, *His Way*, p. 185.

315. Kennedy at Cal-Neva: Anthony Summers, *Goddess: The Secret Lives of Marilyn Monroe* (1985), p. 231; *Fruitful Bough*, ed. Kennedy, pp. 141, 216; Margaret Kemper to Robert F. Kennedy, June 11, 1958, box 46, Preadministration Personal files, Robert Kennedy Papers.

315. "He may be old": Walter Winchell, *Winchell Exclusive* (1975), p. 281.

315. "visited by many gangsters": Kelley, *His Way*, p. 304.

315. FBI's 343 files: Athan G. Theoharis and John Stuart Cox, *The Boss: J. Edgar Hoover and the Great American Inquisition* (1988), p. 338.

315. Kennedy sold interests: Richard J. Whalen, *The Founding Father: The Story of Joseph P. Kennedy* (1964), pp. 380–81.

315. "The way he talked": Leonard Katz, *Uncle Frank: The Biography of Frank Costello* (1973), pp. 68–69.

315. Cassara: IOC 2:172, 6:360, 13:214; Daniel P. Sullivan statement, November 19, 1949, box 1:22, Estes Kefauver Papers.

315. "Cassara when he first": IOC 5:607; next quotation, ibid., p. 595.

316. Kennedy sold business: *New York Times*, September 28, 1946.

316. "that Joe Kennedy": Judith Exner as told to Ovid Demaris, *My Story* (Grove Press edition, 1978), pp. 189–90.

316. "Business, even his own": *Fruitful Bough*, ed. Kennedy, p. 215.

316. "just another businessman": *Boston Herald*, May 20, 1948.

316. "When they talked": interview with Charles Spalding, March 22, 1969, p. 70, Kennedy Library.

317. "while we sat": *Fruitful Bough*, ed. Kennedy, p. 219.

317. "Although you could not": Paul B. Fay, Jr., *The Pleasure of His Company* (1966), p. 9.

317. "He could be tough": *Fruitful Bough*, ed. Kennedy, p. 56; next two quotations, ibid., p. 211.

317. Rose and servants: Rita Dallas with Jeanira Ratcliffe, *The Kennedy Case* (1973), p. 65.

317. "Mrs. Kennedy would be": interview with Dinah Bridge, October 30, 1966, p. 7, Kennedy Library.

317. Rose and children: Rose Fitzgerald Kennedy, *Times to Remember* (1974), p. 148; interview with Ruth Young Watt, 1981, p. 185, Kennedy Library.

317. "Winning is what": Marcia Chellis, *Living With the Kennedys: The Joan Kennedy Story* (1985), p. 34.

318. "We did well": *Fruitful Bough*, ed. Kennedy, p. 217.

318. Kathleen cheating at tennis: confidential interview with her opponent.

318. "You must remember": Collier and Horowitz, *Kennedys*, p. 150.

318. Letters to children: Doris Kearns Goodwin, *The Fitzgeralds and the Kennedys* (1987), p. 351.

318. "One rule always": Charles P. Larrowe, *Harry Bridges: The Rise and Fall of Radical Labor in the United States* (1972), p. 219.

318. "I used to think": *Fruitful Bough*, ed. Kennedy, p. 233.

318. Kennedy office and children: Mary Barelli Gallagher, *My Life with Jacqueline Kennedy* (1969), pp. 104–5; Fay, *Pleasure*, p. 10; materials in Preadministration Personal files, Robert Kennedy Papers.

318. Jack's check for $3,000: M. G. Woodward to Mary W. Davis, November 11, 1948, and Davis to Woodward, November 17, 1948, box 5, Prepresidential files, John Kennedy Papers.

318. "Joe Kennedy was": Goodwin, *Fitzgeralds*, p. 713.

319. "I can feel Pappy's": Fay, *Pleasure*, p. 152.

319. *American* never mentioned: O'Neill, *Man*, p. 76.

319. "The essential campaign": interview with Mark Dalton, August 4, 1964, pp. 6, 9, Kennedy Library.

319. Joe in 1952: *Fruitful Bough,* ed. Kennedy, pp. 219, 237; Kennedy, *Times,* p. 321; interview with Clement A. Norton, November 24, 1963, p. 20, Kennedy Library.

319. "The father was": Ralph G. Martin and Ed Plaut, *Front Runner, Dark Horse* (1960), p. 161.

319. "And boy!": interview with Jean McGonigle Mannix, March 6, 1966, p. 8, Kennedy Library.

319. Joe bought *Post:* Goodwin, *Fitzgeralds,* p. 765; *Boston Herald,* June 27, 1958; Ralph Lowell diary, June 5, 1952, Ralph Lowell Papers.

319. "We had to buy": Herbert S. Parmet, *Jack: The Struggles of John F. Kennedy* (1980), p. 511.

319. "the First Kennedy Bank": John Hay Whitney to Henry Cabot Lodge, November 11, 1952, box 16, Henry Cabot Lodge II Papers.

319. Bobby and Investigations Subcommittee: O'Donnell and Powers, *"Johnny,"* p. 98.

319. "But I kept picturing": Goodwin, *Fitzgeralds,* p. 790.

320. Sons resented suggestion: Theodore C. Sorensen to James MacGregor Burns, October 6, 1959, box 6, Theodore C. Sorensen Papers.

320. "They are entitled": *Boston Sunday Herald,* April 7, 1957.

320. "The problem is": Exner, *Story,* p. 189.

320. Family hubris: Goodwin, *Fitzgeralds,* p. 153.

320. "You watched these people": Collier and Horowitz, *Kennedys,* p. 113.

320. "Men who wanted": Saunders, *Torn,* p. 88.

320. "It means that": Collier and Horowitz, *Kennedys,* p. 356.

321. Argument between Joe and Bobby: Arthur M. Schlesinger, Jr., *Robert Kennedy and His Times* (1978), p. 142.

321. "The old man saw": Collier and Horowitz, *Kennedys,* p. 220.

321. "I simply do not": Karl Mundt to John L. McClellan, December 28, 1957, file 22A, McClellan Papers; and see Mundt to Gregory Burns, Jr., August 30, 1960, box 544, Karl Mundt Papers.

321. "Frankly, I am getting": Barry Goldwater to McClellan, December 24, 1957, file 22A, McClellan Papers.

321. "He is tops": McClellan to Kirk Railsback, March 14, 1958, file 24D, ibid.

322. McClellan and Hot Springs gamblers: interview with Maxine Temple Jones, October 20, 1985.

322. McClellan: *Current Biography* (1950), pp. 363–65; John L. McClellan, *Crime Without Punishment* (1962), pp. 11, 19.

322. "McClellan has": Cabell Phillips in *New York Times Magazine,* March 17, 1957.

322. "There are two": McClellan to Sid McMath, July 29, 1958, file 45C, McClellan Papers.

323. "We should rid": IIA 32:12357; next quotation, ibid., p. 123–58.

323. McClellan in rough going: Phillips in *Times Magazine*, March 17, 1957.

324. Re Teamsters: IIA 13:5268–72, 14:5707–10.

324. Half took Fifth: IIA 40:15290.

324. "This has become": IIA 36:13635.

324. "I think many": IIA 10:3593.

324. Committee as present-minded: Richard Smith to McClellan, April 24, 1958, file 51A, McClellan Papers.

324. "The source": IIA 40:15290.

325. "He promised me": IIA 13:5157.

325. "There is a misunderstanding": IIA 12:4416.

326. "Is there any organization": IIA 17:6744.

326. Apalachin: IIA 32:12194–201, 12353.

326. Fifty others fled: Peter Maas, *The Valachi Papers* (1968), p. 248.

326. Five later placed: ibid., p. 249; Joseph Bonanno with Sergio Lalli, *A Man of Honor* (1983), p. 215; Giancana, *Princess*, pp. 155–56; OCN 2:441, 589.

326. "Well, I hope": Bill Davidson in *Saturday Evening Post*, November 9, 1963; William Brashler, *The Don: The Life and Death of Sam Giancana* (1977), p. 172.

327. Commission since 1931: Bonanno, *Man*, pp. 209, 211, 227.

327. Since 1956 meeting: Gay Talese, *Honor Thy Father* (1971), p. 69; Bonanno, *Man*, pp. 160–61, 172–73, 207; OCN 1:388–89.

327. "It was just": Mickey Cohen as told to John Peer Nugent, *In My Own Words* (1975), p. 81.

327. Costello invited assassin: George Wolf with Joseph DiMona, *Frank Costello: Prime Minister of the Underworld* (1974), p. 257.

327. "I am a dress": IIA 32:12473.

327. Evidence of Genovese wealth: IIA 32:12397–402.

327. "He was the only one": interview with Ruth Young Watt, p. 183.

327. Montana: IIA 32:12293–96; OCN 2:591–92.

328. "I don't understand": IIA 32:12301.

328. Montana and Magaddinos: OCN 2:589.

328. Montana at 1931 meeting: Bonanno, *Man*, p. 127.

328. Montana explained: IIA 32:12297–302.

328. Montana demoted: OCN 1:196.

328. *Times* obit of Montana: *New York Times*, March 19, 1964.

328. Apalachin 58: chart facing IIA 32:12496.

328. "The testimony we have heard": IIA 32:12487.

328. Ninety-six witnesses convicted: Donald F. O'Donnell to McClellan, October 1, 1964, file 33D, McClellan Papers.

329. Zwillman killed self: *New York Times*, February 27, 1959.

329. Newport and Covington: GOC, pp. 110–11; McClellan, *Crime*, p. 253.

329. "We learned that": Harry J. Anslinger with J. Dennis Gregory, *The Protectors* (1964), pp. 213–14.

329. Joe suggested: Joseph P. Kennedy to Robert F. Kennedy, [1957], box 42, Preadministration Personal files, Robert Kennedy Papers.

329. Joe ordered him back: O'Donnell and Powers, *"Johnny,"* p. 138.

329. "You knew when": interview with Ruth Young Watt, p. 186.

329. Bobby delved into conspiracy: Robert Kennedy to John Cort, May 28, 1959, box 47, Preadministration Personal files, Robert Kennedy Papers.

329. O'Rourke: IOC 2:181, 10:252; Cohen, *My Own*, pp. 153–54; Bonanno, *Man*, p. 207.

330. O'Rourke interrogation: IIA 12:4682–97.

330. Rumor passed around town: Murray Kempton to Robert Kennedy, [1957], box 40, Preadministration Personal files, Robert Kennedy Papers; Kempton to author, September 14, 1983; and see Robert F. Kennedy, *The Enemy Within* (1960), pp. 81–82, and Walter Sheridan, *The Fall and Rise of Jimmy Hoffa* (1972), p. 379.

330. "I take my orders": Kennedy, *Enemy*, p. 187.

330. "I don't apologize": Schlesinger, *Robert Kennedy*, p. 161.

330. "To hear Kennedy": James R. Hoffa as told to Oscar Fraley, *Hoffa: The Real Story* (1975), p. 121.

330. "Senator Kennedy is": transcript of *College News Conference*, ABC-TV, December 7, 1958, box 957, Prepresidential files, John Kennedy Papers.

331. "I'm not against": O'Donnell and Powers, *"Johnny,"* p. 151.

331. "Jack, I'm willing": Fay, *Pleasure*, p. 9.

331. "He knew instinctively": Collier and Horowitz, *Kennedys*, p. 238.

331. "He firmly believed": O'Donnell and Powers, *"Johnny,"* pp. 82–83.

331. Buckley: *New York Times*, January 23, 1967; O'Neill, *Man*, pp. 143–44.

332. Crotty became the first: *New York Times*, April 7, 1960.

332. "the Buckley-Crotty crowd": Arthur M. Schlesinger, Jr., to John F. Kennedy, November 13, 1959, box W-10, Arthur M. Schlesinger, Jr., Papers.

332. Green acquitted: *New York Times*, December 22, 1963.

332. "I tried to get": John Kennedy to Arthur Schlesinger, June 29, 1959, box W-10, Schlesinger Papers.

332. Lawrence twice acquitted: *New York Times*, November 22, 1966.

332. "Nobody was there": interview with David L. Lawrence, January 26, 1966, p. 7, Kennedy Library.

332. Daley and Joe Kennedy, 1954: Eugene Kennedy, *Himself!* (1978), p. 154.

332. "the long, tough talks": Harris Wofford, *Of Kennedys and Kings* (1980), p. 38.

333. "We got caught up": Sammy Davis, Jr., *Hollywood in a Suitcase* (1980), p. 84.

333. Sinatra pulled strings: Kelley, *His Way*, p. 294.

333. "I hardly hear": Collier and Horowitz, *Kennedys*, p. 246.

333. Campbell and Kennedy: Exner, *Story*, pp. 86, 102–3, 116.

333. "When I think of it": ibid., p. 235.

333. Campbell set up meetings: Kitty Kelley in *People*, February 29, 1988.

333. Sinatra and Cal-Neva: Michael Hellerman with Thomas C. Renner, *Wall Street Swindler* (1977), pp. 78, 105.

333. D'Amato: IOC 18:605–6; Arthur Marx, *Everybody Loves Somebody Sometime (Especially Himself)* (1974), p. 49; Eddie Fisher, *Eddie: My Life, My Loves* (1981), p. 238.

334. D'Amato and Joe: Hellerman, *Swindler*, pp. 105–6; Ovid Demaris, *The Boardwalk Jungle* (1986), p. 33.

334. Melandra: Kelley, *His Way*, p. 581.

334. First meeting between Giancana and Kennedy: Kelley in *People*, February 29, 1988.

334. "I don't think": Theodore C. Sorensen, *Kennedy* (Bantam edition, 1966), p. 159.

334. Joe stopped in Nevada: Goodwin, *Fitzgeralds*, pp. 800–801; *Fruitful Bough*, ed. Kennedy, p. 253.

334. "You mean to see": interview with Charles Bartlett, February 20, 1965, pp. 115–16, Kennedy Library; next quotation, ibid., p. 51.

334. Ted bet $25,000: *Jimmy the Greek by Himself*, with Mickey Herskowitz and Steve Perkins (1975), p. 162.

334. "Get me a network": Kennedy, *Himself!*, pp. 181–82.

335. Chicago mob wards: CHI, p. 56; Giancana, *Princess*, p. 42.

335. Chicago black wards: Edward S. Clayton, *The Negro Politician* (1964), p. 73.

335. Chicago votes: *Chicago Tribune*, November 10, 1960.

335. "He's really had less": Martin, *Hero*, p. 213.

335. "I read the papers": *Boston Herald*, September 4, 1960.

335. "Listen, honey": Exner, *Story*, p. 194.

335. "Frank won Kennedy": Kelley, *His Way*, p. 307.

335. "I thought nepotism": interview with Robert Kennedy, February 29, 1974, p. 21, Kennedy Library; next three quotations, ibid., pp.

22–23, 284; and see *Boston Advertiser,* January 8, 1961, and interview with Bartlett, p. 68.

336. Kennedy as attorney general: Robert Kennedy to John Kennedy, December 28, 1961, and January 10, 1963, box 80, President's Office files, John Kennedy Papers.

336. Indictments and convictions: Edwin Guthman, *We Band of Brothers* (1971), p. 252.

336. "There was no": interview with Robert Kennedy, December 4, 1964, p. 634, Kennedy Library.

336. "Many law enforcement": Anslinger, *Protectors,* p. 214; next two quotations, ibid., pp. 215, 216.

337. Two agents induced: Anthony Villano with Gerald Astor, *Brick Agent* (1977), p. 40.

337. "to determine": Neil J. Welch and David W. Marston, *Inside Hoover's FBI: The Top Field Chief Reports* (1984), p. 82.

337. "The FBI didn't know": interview with Robert Kennedy, December 4, 1964, p. 626.

337. Two-volume study: William C. Sullivan with Bill Brown, *The Bureau: My Thirty Years in Hoover's FBI* (1979), p. 118.

337. "They started to get": interview with Robert Kennedy, December 4, 1964, p. 627.

337. FBI measures: FBI to Attorney General, January 13, 1961, Sam Giancana file, section 5, FBI FOIPA Preprocessed files, FBI Building.

337. Taps and bugs: G. Robert Blakey and Richard N. Billings, *The Plot to Kill the President* (1981), pp. 85, 209; interview with William G. Hundley, February 17, 1971, pp. 35–38, Kennedy Library; Ovid Demaris, *The Director: An Oral Biography of J. Edgar Hoover* (1975), p. 144.

337. "I need to get": SDC 1:11.

338. Joe and Sinatra, 1961: *Boston Herald,* August 2, 3, 1961.

338. Nineteen-page report: Gage, *Mafia,* pp. 84–85.

338. Sinatra and landing pad: O'Donnell and Powers, *"Johnny,"* p. 380.

338. "Would you tell": IIA 53:18681.

338. "Between you and I": Kelley, *His Way,* pp. 320–22.

339. "He's got it": Blakey and Billings, *Plot,* pp. 376–77; SAC Chicago to FBI Director, December 9, 1961, Giancana file, section 12.

339. "They used him": Vincent Teresa with Thomas C. Renner, *My Life in the Mafia* (1973), p. 124.

339. "Sam did a lot": Kelley, *His Way,* p. 583.

339. D'Amato reminded Joe: Hellerman, *Swindler,* p. 106.

339. New Orleans family: Blakey and Billings, *Plot,* pp. 235–36.

339. Marcello: IAP 9:61–92; GOC, pp. 508–11; Marcello file, box

1:30, Estes Kefauver Papers; IOC 12:583; David Leon Chandler, *Brothers in Blood* (1975), pp. 174–82; John H. Davis, *Mafia Kingfish* (1988).

340. "He is head": IIA 53:18555.

340. "Bobby was pissed": Michael Dorman, *Payoff: The Role of Organized Crime in American Politics* (1972), p. 109.

340. "They dumped": Blakey and Billings, *Plot*, p. 244.

340. Marcello asked Giancana: ibid., p. 242.

340. Kennedy after stroke: Benjamin C. Bradlee, *Conversations with Kennedy* (1975), pp. 136–37, 167–68.

341. "Sometimes he could squeak": Saunders, *Torn*, p. 134.

341. "He's the one": O'Donnell and Powers, *"Johnny,"* p. 39.

341. CIA-Mafia plots: IAP 10:147–95; Wofford, *Kennedys*, p. 392; Donald L. Barlett and James R. Steele, *Empire: The Life, Legend, and Madness of Howard Hughes* (1979), p. 283; Robert Pack, *Edward Bennett Williams for the Defense* (1983), p. 181.

341. "Don't worry": Kelley in *People,* February 29, 1988.

341. Kennedys and Mafia plots: Collier and Horowitz, *Kennedys,* p. 294; C. A. Evans to Belmont, August 16, 1963, Giancana file, section 19; Wofford, *Kennedys,* p. 400.

341. "Here I am": Hellerman, *Swindler,* p. 86.

341. "Take the stone": Ed Reid, *The Grim Reapers: The Anatomy of Organized Crime in America* (1969), p. 158.

341. "Mark my word": Summers, *Conspiracy,* p. 284.

342. "See what Kennedy": IAP 5:443; next three quotations, ibid., pp. 446, 448.

342. Valachi: OCN 1:78–80; Maas, *Valachi,* pp. 48, 50.

342. "Before you knew": Dan E. Moldea, *The Hoffa Wars* (1978), p. 138.

343. "that Bobby Kennedy": Teresa, *My Life,* p. 322.

343. McClellan visited Valachi: Maas, *Valachi,* p. 46.

343. White House announced: Summers, *Conspiracy,* p. 422.

343. Ruby: IAP 9:125–1169; Summers, *Conspiracy,* pp. 456–59; Scheim, *Contract,* pp. 60–71.

343. "Jack Ruby at that time": Scheim, *Contract,* p. 75.

343. "Jack Ruby would sit": Summers, *Conspiracy,* p. 458.

344. "Whenever I wanted": Henry Hurt, *Reasonable Doubt: An Investigation into the Assassination of John F. Kennedy* (1985), pp. 173–74.

344. Ruby, fall 1963: Scheim, *Contract,* pp. 85, 94–95, 212–13, 225; Blakey and Billings, *Plot,* pp. 303–7; Summers, *Conspiracy,* p. 474.

344. Oswald seen with Ruby: Scheim, *Contract,* pp. 240–44.

344. Oswald and Murret: IAP 9:95–99; Summers, *Conspiracy,* pp. 292–93, 339–41.

344. Set up some nut: Blakey and Billings, *Plot,* pp. 244–45.
344. Bobby on November 22: ibid., p. xi.
344. Ruby on November 22: Scheim, *Contract,* pp. 260–61.
345. Oswald description on radio: Summers, *Conspiracy,* p. 83.
345. Ruby corrected him: Hurt, *Reasonable,* p. 186.
345. "So I testified": O'Neill, *Man,* p. 178.
346. Bobby and investigation: Schlesinger, *Robert Kennedy,* p. 614; Garry Wills, *The Kennedy Imprisonment* (1982), p. 37; interview with Frank Mankiewicz, October 2, 1969, p. 69, Kennedy Library; interview with Wes Barthelmes, June 2, 1969, p. 83, Kennedy Library.
346. "Even those of us": Dallas, *Kennedy,* p. 273.
346. Bobby never again met: Blakey and Billings, *Plot,* p. 199.
346. "the day of the": interview with Robert Kennedy, April 13, 1964, p. 187; next three quotations, ibid., pp. 188, 189, 191.

CHAPTER NINE

age 347. "We got to retrench": Ralph Salerno and John S. Tompkins, *The Crime Confederation* (1969), p. 174.
347. Justice over next five years: MRO, p. 117.
348. "Almost nobody": Nicholas Pileggi, *Wiseguy* (1985), p. 58; next quotation, ibid., p. 76.
348. "Our principal problem": OCN 1:14.
349. Numbers game: Mark H. Haller in *Gambling in America* (Commission on the Review of the National Policy Toward Gambling, 1976), appendix 1, pp. 102–43; Francis A. J. Ianni, *Black Mafia: Ethnic Succession in Organized Crime* (1974), pp. 110–12.
349. "The Negroes owned": Willie the Lion Smith with George Hoefer, *Music on My Mind* (1964), p. 175.
349. New York, early 1930s: affidavit by J. Richard Davis, February 27, 1935, box 1:89:2, Thomas E. Dewey Papers.
349. Chicago: Ianni, *Black,* p. 113.
349. Coppola and Salerno: *The American Way of Crime: A Documentary History,* ed. Wayne Moquin and Charles Van Doren (1976), pp. 350–51; James D. Horan, *The Mob's Man* (1959), pp. 52–53.
349. Italians and Jews: Peter Maas, *The Valachi Papers* (1968), p. 133; IOC 11:232.
350. "If you do happen": IOC 11:53–54.
350. Johnny White: OCN 2:413–14.
350. Cheating methods: GOC, pp. 285–87.
351. "Hell, you know": Hank Messick with Joseph L. Nellis, *The Private Lives of Public Enemies* (1973), p. 141.

351. Payments by Cohen: Bob Sylvester to Westbrook Pegler, [late 1940s], box 36, Westbrook Pegler Papers.

351. Massachusetts racetracks: *Time,* April 26, June 7, 1954.

352. NFL owners: Harry Wismer, *The Public Calls It Sport* (1965), pp. 17, 22; Bernie Parrish, *They Call It a Game* (1971), pp. 118, 207; Hank Messick, *The Silent Syndicate* (1967), p. 10; and see above, pp. 311–12.

352. Football players: Wismer, *Public,* p. 32; Parrish, *They,* p. 186.

352. Jacobs: John Underwood and Morton Sharnik in *Sports Illustrated,* May 29, 1972.

352. "Jacobs money meant": ibid.

353. Veeck and Jacobs: OCS 1:327–28, 343.

353. "I associated": Bill Veeck with Ed Linn, *Veeck—as in Wreck* (1962), p. 97; next two quotations, ibid., p. 204.

353. Veeck testified: OCS 1:328.

353. Jacobs and gangsters: Underwood and Sharnik in *Sports Illustrated,* May 29, 1972; OCS 1:118, 3:1123–24, 4:1438.

353. "Anytime you want": Underwood and Sharnik in *Sports Illustrated,* May 29, 1972.

353. "tell Sportservice to OK": OCS 4:1564.

354. Carbo suspected: PBX 1:105; Burton B. Turkus and Sid Feder, *Murder, Inc.: The Story of "the Syndicate"* (1951), p. 282; *New York Herald-Tribune,* April 27, 1958; Ovid Demaris, *The Last Mafioso: The Treacherous World of Jimmy Fratianno* (1981), p. 46.

354. "He did know": PBX 2:703.

354. "Everybody was scared": PBX 3:1450.

354. Carbo and Palermo: Barney Nagler, *James Norris and the Decline of Boxing* (1964), pp. 26–27; IOC 11:147, 228; PBX 1:46.

354. "I seen him watching": PBX 2:469.

354. LaMotta dumped fight: Nagler, *Norris,* pp. 28–33; PBX 1:7–17, 40.

355. "I didn't know": Peter Heller, *"In This Corner . . ."* (1973), p. 269; next quotation, ibid., p. 272.

355. Williams told story: PBX 2:668–78.

355. "As far as bribes": Rocky Graziano with Rowland Barber, *Somebody Up There Likes Me* (1955), p. 320.

355. "When the man": Sugar Ray Robinson with Dave Anderson, *Sugar Ray* (1970), p. 180.

355. Robinson and Mafia boss: ibid., pp. 214–15.

355. "I never considered it": ibid., pp. 104–5.

356. "My father": PBX 2:589; next three quotations, ibid., pp. 559, 615, 570.

356. Key promoters and Carbo: PBX 2:285–95; Raymond Cole to Paul

Rand Dixon, September 3, 1959, box 1:94, Estes Kefauver Papers.

356. "Carbo and Norris had": Angelo Dundee with Mike Winters, *I Only Talk Winning* (1985), p. 128.

356. Arcel episode: ibid., p. 128; confidential to Estes Kefauver, June 16, 1957, box 1:94, Kefauver Papers.

356. "They used": PBX 3:1498.

357. Bocchicchio: IOC 11:148–49; Teddy Brenner as told to Barney Nagler, *Only the Ring Was Square* (1981), p. 29; PBX 2:286.

357. "I was lucky": PBX 3:1274.

357. "a boxing politician": Brenner, *Only*, p. 22; and see IIA 36:13482.

357. "He's very close": PBX 3:1493.

357. Marciano later confided: Howard W. Chappell to George H. White, November 27, 1946, box 4, Harry J. Anslinger Papers.

357. Patterson and Salerno: PBX 2:357–63.

357. Liston: PBX 2:644–45, 762–64; Messick, *Private*, pp. 172–73.

357. Liston management: PBX 2:392, 634–35, 650.

357. Lepera heard: Patsy Anthony Lepera and Walter Goodman, *Memoirs of a Scam Man* (1974), p. 80.

358. "This guy didn't": ibid., p. 81.

358. "Gambling is the standby": OSS 3:813–14.

358. "You find": Francis A. J. Ianni and Elizabeth Reuss-Ianni, *A Family Business: Kinship and Social Control in Organized Crime* (1972), p. 97.

358. Loan sharking: *Columbia Journal of Law and Social Problems*, April 1969; Donald R. Cressey, *Theft of the Nation: The Structure and Operations of Organized Crime in America* (1969), pp. 80–85; Salerno and Tompkins, *Crime*, pp. 228–29.

359. "I have never heard": CSB 2:4.

359. Loan sharking history: Mark H. Haller and John V. Alviti in *American Journal of Legal History*, April 1977; *Organized Crime*, ed. Howard Abadinsky (1981), p. 148.

359. "Shark" as term: CSB 2:94.

359. Dewey arrests: Haller and Alviti in *American Journal of Legal History*, April 1977.

360. "only disreputable": CSB 2:97.

360. DeStefano: Haller and Alviti in *American Journal of Legal History*, April 1977.

360. Murder of Jackson: CSB 2:94–95.

360. 121 sharks in New York: Fred J. Cook in *New York Times Magazine*, January 28, 1968.

360. Forlano and Stein: Salerno and Tompkins, *Crime*, p. 228.

360. "although he does not": OCN 1:312.

360. "I knew some": Pileggi, *Wiseguy,* pp. 108–9.

361. "The only thing": SFA 1:38.

361. "There is one thing": Vincent Teresa with Thomas C. Renner, *Vinnie Teresa's Mafia* (1975), p. 154.

361. Bowdach dealt mainly: SFA 1:37.

361. "You won't find": Cressey, *Theft,* pp. 86–90.

362. Lawmen were guessing: *Columbia Journal of Law and Social Problems,* April 1969; CSB 2:129; MRO, p. 1.

363. Jewish gangsters and drugs: IOC 2:89, 14:382; OCN 4:918–19; Frederic Sondern, Jr., *Brotherhood of Evil: The Mafia* (1959), p. 94, 96–97, 226; *Boston Herald,* January 9, 1952, August 23, 1965.

363. Mafia controlled: IOC 7:1086–90; OCN 3:772–88; PCD, pp. 106–7.

363. Dewey told story: Thomas E. Dewey, *Twenty Against the Underworld* (1974), p. 269.

363. "You go up": testimony of Joseph Lanza, April 30, 1954, pp. 51–52, box 18, Herlands file, Dewey Papers.

363. Luciano stories: Bureau of Narcotics report by Sal Vizzini, September 30, 1959, box 2, Anslinger Papers; Sal Vizzini with Oscar Fraley and Marshall Smith, *Vizzini* (1972), pp. 82–83; Leonard Katz, *Uncle Frank: The Biography of Frank Costello* (1973), p. 147; Charles Siragusa to Harry J. Anslinger, July 24, 1952, box 2, Anslinger Papers.

364. Luciano drug history: Harry J. Anslinger and Will Oursler, *The Murderers: The Story of the Narcotic Gangs* (1961), pp. 102–3; Bureau of Narcotics memo, March 7, 1947, box 16, Herlands file, Dewey Papers.

364. Luciano mediated: OCN 4:891, 912, 1033; Vizzini, *Vizzini,* p. 90; Charles Siragusa as told to Robert Wiedrich, *The Trail of the Poppy: Behind the Mask of the Mafia* (1966), p. 96.

364. "Luciano is uncannily": Anslinger and Oursler, *Murderers,* p. 109.

364. Luciano in Havana: Garland H. Williams to Anslinger, February 24, 1947, box 2, Anslinger Papers.

364. "That son of a bitch": Vizzini report, September 30, 1959.

364. "I hope you dont": Salvatore Lucania to Thomas E. Dewey, January 20, 1953, box 20.2, Herlands file, Dewey Papers.

365. "Just six months": Vizzini report, September 30, 1959.

365. Costello ordered his men: OCN 1:90.

365. "You are in": OCN 1:319–20.

365. Chicago and drugs: ibid., pp. 320–22; CHI, p. 163.

365. Tampa and Kansas City: David Leon Chandler, *Brothers in Blood* (1975), p. 214; "The Kansas City Investigation,"

Treasury Intelligence Unit report, April 1, 1943, p. 151, box 58, Pegler Papers.

365. Priziola: IIA 48:17455.

365. Gambino family: PCI, pp. 329–31; OCA 1:207.

365. Generational issue: testimony of Angelo Lonardo before Nunn committee, April 15, 1988, on Cable News Network.

366. "It was too": PCI, p. 329.

366. Gordon begged: Vizzini, *Vizzini*, p. 23.

366. "I wouldn't put": Ianni and Reuss-Ianni, *Family,* p. 99.

366. "I hear he's talking": G. Robert Blakey and Richard N. Billings, *The Plot to Kill the President* (1981), p. 240.

366. FBI received call: FBI Director to James J. P. McShane, October 4, 1963, box 2, James J. P. McShane Papers; interview with William G. Hundley, February 22, 1971, p. 52, John F. Kennedy Presidential Library.

366. "Vito should have killed": Blakey and Billings, *Plot,* p. 240.

366. Contract on Valachi: Maas, *Valachi,* p. 48; Joey with Dave Fisher, *Killer: Autobiography of a Mafia Hit Man* (Pocket Books edition, 1974), p. 62.

367. "To destroy": OCN 1:119; next two quotations, ibid., pp. 110, 301.

367. Giancana observed: SAC Chicago to FBI Director, October 11, 1963, Sam Giancana file, section 19, FBI FOIPA Preprocessed Files, FBI Building, Washington, D.C.

367. *Times* and Mafia: Dwight C. Smith, Jr., *The Mafia Mystique* (1975), p. 292.

367. Commission, 1967: *The Crime Society,* ed. Francis A. J. Ianni and Elizabeth Reuss-Ianni (1976), pp. 13–22.

367. "Organized crime": Virgil W. Peterson, *The Mob: 200 Years of Organized Crime in New York* (1983), p. 418.

368. Salerno and Cressey: Salerno and Tompkins, *Crime;* Cressey, *Theft.*

368. "There is no longer": *Time,* August 22, 1969.

368. Pressure to stop Maas book: Peter Maas in *New York Times Book Review,* October 12, 1986.

368. Rooney criticism: interview with Hundley, pp. 50–54.

368. "I'm not talking": Peter Maas in *Saturday Evening Post,* November 23, 1963.

368. "I would like": OCN 2:590.

368. Buffalo chart: facing OCN 2:580.

369. "The pretext was": Maas in *Book Review,* October 12, 1986.

369. Sales of *Valachi Papers: Publishers Weekly,* October 24, 1986.

369. Valachi later: Vincent Teresa with Thomas C. Renner, *My Life in the Mafia* (1973), pp. 320–22.

369. "coarse, vulgar": Mario Puzo, *The Godfather Papers and Other Confessions* (1972), p. 13; next two quotations, ibid., pp. 27, 24.

370. "Stories about crime": Tom Buckley in *Harper's,* August 1971.

370. "I felt": Puzo, *Papers,* p. 39; next quotation, ibid., p. 41.

370. Younger member in Brooklyn: Ianni and Reuss-Ianni, *Family,* p. 113.

370. Hell's Angels: OCA 1:409.

370. Young gangster claimed: WFC, p. 372.

370. Son of Adonis: OCA 1:231.

370. Testa: OCA 1:544.

370. "I think it was": OCS 4:1494.

371. "In plain English": Vincent Teresa in *Saturday Review of Society,* February 1973.

371. Talese implied: Gay Talese, *Honor Thy Father* (1971), pp. 27, 73; and see Jonathan Kwitny, *Vicious Circles: The Mafia in the Marketplace* (1979), pp. 106–7.

371. "the responsibilities he felt": Talese, *Honor,* p. 27; next quotation, ibid., p. 43.

371. "Without question": Nicholas Pileggi in *Saturday Evening Post,* November 30,1968.

372. "It was the thing": *Mafia, U.S.A.,* ed. Nicholas Gage (1972), p. 256.

372. "He was the brightest": *Time,* April 17, 1972.

372. "He'd sit around": *Mafia,* ed. Gage, p. 266.

372. "When he asked": *Time,* April 17, 1972; next quotation, ibid.

372. "They'd rather you": Peter Diapoulos with Steven Linakis, *The Sixth Family* (1976), p. 222.

372. "I never see": Frank Costello to Westbrook Pegler, September 12, 1966, box 36, Pegler Papers.

373. "My most difficult": *New York Times,* February 27, 1973.

373. "there is a secret": Ianni and Reuss-Ianni, *Family,* p. 194.

373. "We say there is": Buckley in *Harper's,* August 1971.

373. Colombo: *Time,* July 12, 1971.

374. "He's got the most": Buckley in *Harper's,* August 1971; next quotation, ibid.

374. Colombo as gangster: chart facing OCN 1:308; *Congressional Record,* 91 Cong. 1 Sess., p. 23441; Salerno and Tompkins, *Crime,* pp. 141–42; SDC 3:69, 4:26; *Life,* September 8, 1967.

374. "Is it *possible*": Buckley in *Harper's,* August 1971; next three quotations, ibid.

375. *Godfather* use of Mafia: Smith, *Mafia,* p. 274.

375. Three sons pleaded guilty: *Boston Globe,* June 15, 1986.

376. "Without courageous": John Scarne, *The Mafia Conspiracy* (1976), pp. 279–82.

376. "For one brief": Luciano J. Iorizzo and Salvatore Mondello, *The Italian Americans* (revised edition, 1980), p. 204.

376. Other Italian leaders: Eugene Ruffini in *Nation,* November 22, 1971.

376. Simplified version: see Sondern, *Brotherhood;* Ed Reid, *The Grim Reapers: The Anatomy of Organized Crime in America* (1969).

377. Kempton: Murray Kempton in *New Republic,* October 12, 1963, and in *New York Review of Books,* September 11, 1969.

377. "The logic of capitalism": William J. Chambliss, *On the Take: From Petty Crooks to Presidents* (1978), p. 181.

377. "There is no Mafia": Giovanni Schiavo, *The Truth About the Mafia and Organized Crime in America* (1962), p. 39; next quotation, ibid., p. 75.

377. "These officials": Scarne, *Mafia,* p. 208.

377. Bell: Daniel Bell in *Antioch Review,* summer 1953, and in *New Leader,* December 23, 1963.

378. *Public Interest* articles: Hawkins, winter 1969; Reuter and Rubinstein, fall 1978; Ianni, winter 1971.

378. "a structural-functional": Joseph L. Albini, *The American Mafia: Genesis of a Legend* (1971), p. 11; next five quotations, ibid., pp. 154, 255, 323, 247, 252.

379. "We believe": Ianni and Reuss-Ianni, *Family,* p. 161; next quotation, ibid., p. 173.

380. "We hoped that": Francis A. J. Ianni and Elizabeth Reuss-Ianni in *Psychology Today,* December 1975.

380. "if it was that": Smith, *Mafia,* p. 162; next two quotations ibid., pp. 235, 335.

381. "theory of illicit enterprise": *Contemporary Authors,* 77–80 (1979), p. 505; and see Smith in *International Journal of Criminology and Penology,* May 1978.

381. "ethnic succession": see Ianni, *Black Mafia.*

381. Pistone: Joseph D. Pistone with Richard Woodley, *Donnie Brasco: My Undercover Life in the Mafia* (1988).

382. Teresas: Teresa, *My Life,* pp. 14–16; *Boston Globe,* December 9, 1984.

382. Motives for choosing underworld: see Peter A. Lupsha in *The American Self: Myth, Ideology, and Popular Culture,* ed. Sam B. Girgus (1981), pp. 144–54; Lupsha in *Criminology,* May 1981.

382. "These people": OCV, p. 195.

382. "dependable, ubiquitous": Pileggi in *Post,* November 30, 1968.

382. "The romantic notion": *Publishers Weekly,* February 7, 1986; next two quotations, ibid.

CHAPTER TEN

Page 392. "acids of modernity": Ronald Steel, *Walter Lippmann and the American Century* (1980),p. 262.

393. Sullivan fed information: Daniel P. Sullivan to Estes Kefauver, August 31, October 24, November 18, 1950, box 1:29, Estes Kefauver Papers.

393. "I cannot too highly": CAO, p. 376.

393. "His Italian was": IAP 9:20n.

393. *Times* declared: IAP 5:378.

393. "Unfortunately in the United States": IAP 5:466; next quotation, ibid., p. 470.

394. Kohn: interview with Aaron M. Kohn, April 23, 1988.

394. "The front line": FEP, p. 4; next quotation, ibid., p. 17.

394. "My life has been": Kohn interview.

395. Kohn budgets: ibid.

395. "upon whose toes": FEP, p. 6.

395. Kohn contended: GOC, pp. 538–40; Kohn to John L. McClellan, April 20, 1959, file 25B, John L. McClellan Papers: OCC, pp. 412–17.

395. "He is the most powerful": GOC, p. 509.

395. A few victories: FEP, pp. 6–11.

395. "I guess": G. Robert Blakey to author, February 26, 1988.

396. "I'm an American": interview with G. Robert Blakey, March 23, 1988.

396. "We needed to start": *Boston Globe,* November 23, 1987.

396. Reports from Patriarca office: CCT, pp. 942–54.

396. "Nothing in the": CCT, p. 939; next quotation, ibid., p. 955.

397. McClellan and 1970 bill: interview with Blakey.

397. "The public is demanding": OCC, p. 95; and see interview with John L. McClellan, July 29, 1970, file 58B, McClellan Papers.

398. Agencies shifted slowly: PCH 7:189–90.

398. "A principal problem": CHI, p. 75; next quotation, ibid., p. 78.

398. Giuliani: Michael Winerip in *New York Times Magazine,* June 9, 1985.

398. "During the Fifties": *Time,* February 10, 1986; next quotation, ibid.

399. "There was one": Linda Brandi Cateura, *Growing Up Italian* (1987), p. 232.

399. "Organized crime figures": Winerip in *Times Magazine,* June 9, 1985.

399. Giuliani pushed prosecutors: PCH 6:572; OCA 2:135–39.

399. "It's like stuffing": Winerip in *Times Magazine,* June 9, 1985.

399. "I don't think": Cateura, *Growing,* p. 239.

399. "My view is": Winerip in *Times Magazine,* June 9, 1985.

400. FBI planting bugs in North End: *Boston Globe,* April 5, 1987.

400. description of Office: *Boston Globe,* July 10, 1985.

401. "The best crooking": Noel Behn, *Big Stick-up at Brink's!* (1977), p. 157.

401. Angiulo family: OCS 4:1472; *Boston Globe,* September 21, 1983.

401. "She was the": Vincent Teresa with Thomas C. Renner, *My Life in the Mafia* (1973), pp. 49–50.

401. Angiulo yearbook photograph: *Boston Globe,* April 6, 1987.

402. Angiulo and Patriarca: Teresa, *My Life,* pp. 51–52; OCS 2:767.

402. "Jerry Angiulo bought": OCS 2:751.

402. "They never did": *Boston Globe,* August 20, 1985.

402. Bought $10 million worth: OCS 2:761.

402. Feds knew of $45 million: confidential source, August 14, 1984.

402. Quinn: *Boston Globe,* April 5, 1987.

402. "He is somewhat": *Boston Globe,* December 1, 1983.

403. Video camera: *Boston Globe,* April 7, 1987.

403. "They got two": transcript of Angiulo bugs, February 2, 1981, confidential source.

403. "We could use": ibid., February 4, 1981.

404. "That's why all Irishmen": ibid.

404. "They're saying": ibid., March 13, 1981.

404. "Tell him to take": ibid., March 19, 1981.

404. "I think that's": ibid., March 26, 1981.

405. Zannino describing murders: ibid., April 3, 1981.

405. "we may not survive": ibid., April 21, 1981.

405. "we had to do it": ibid., April 30, 1981.

405. "I wouldn't be in": ibid., April 27, 1981.

405. "They don't have": *Boston Globe,* April 9, 1987.

405. "This could be": *New York Times,* November 7, 1983.

406. "Families, they're no longer": *Boston Globe,* November 23, 1987.

406. "The thing that frustrates": MAR, pp. 286–87.

406. "Union corruption is": CHI, p. 61; and see LMR, pp. 36–38.

406. Four most bemobbed unions: CHI, p. 69.

406. 45 percent of 930 indictments: PCH 6:8–9.

406. "We got our money": Vincent Cafaro testimony to Nunn committee, April 29, 1988, on Cable News Network.

407. Conviction of Hoffa and 115 others: Victor S. Navasky, *Kennedy Justice* (1971), p. 396.

407. Teamsters: PCE, pp. 89–143; PCH 1:109.

407. Mafia families picked successor: *Washington Post,* November 6, 1985; Angelo Lonardo testimony, April 15, 1988, on Cable News Network; PCH 2:70–71.

407. "They was here": PCEA, p. 101.

407. Mob and garbage: see WDI.

407. "We're gonna knock": PCH 6:560.

407. Corallo made $200,000: ibid., pp. 568–69.

407. Loans to Dalitz and Shenker: HRE 2:59.

407. Pritzker family: Ovid Demaris, *The Boardwalk Jungle* (1986), pp. 268–72.

407. "You are making": ibid., p. 277.

408. Longshoremen: PCE, pp. 33–70.

408. "I've lost": Allen Raymond, *Waterfront Priest* (1955), p. 260.

408. Clemente and Field: WFC, pp. 184, 255.

408. Gleason: ibid., pp. 130–31, 456–57.

408. "Teddy is number": ibid., p. 187.

408. Gambinos and Genoveses: ibid., pp. 21–22, 103, 177, 191, 199–201.

408. Fiumara: OCA 1:232; WFC, p. 418.

408. "Tino's good points": WFC, pp. 271–73.

409. Federal investigation of Longshoremen: WFC, pp. 9–11, 297–314.

409. "It would be lovely": WFC, p. 30; and see PCE, p. 65; WFC, p. 132; CHI, p. 70.

409. Laborers: PCE, pp. 145–66.

409. Capones picked Foscos: HRE 3:35.

409. Mafia families and Laborers: GLR, pp. 493–94; PCE, p. 149; MAR, p. 219; CHI, p. 61; PCH 6:75.

409. Most of Laborers members: PCH 6:105.

409. "that the Italians had": PCH 6:107.

409. "Powell, you're dead": PCH 6:109.

409. Medina episode: PCH 6:11, 104, 121.

409. "I remember when all": PCH 6:119.

410. Nunn's five hearings: HRE 1–5.

410. Capones and Hanley: PCE, pp. 71, 73, 83; CHI, pp. 82–83.

410. "I watched their": HRE 2:61.

410. HRE Local 54: PCH 7:243; OCA 1:143–44.

410. Atlantic City long wide open: Elmer R. Irey as told to William J. Slocum, *The Tax Dodgers: The Inside Story of the T-men's War with America's Political and Underworld Hoodlums* (1948), pp. 245–70; IOC 18:10–11, 69, 79, 190–217.

410. Six years after legalization: Ovid Demaris in *Parade*, May 11, 1986; OCA 1:143.

411. Gerace: Demaris, *Boardwalk*, pp. 337–39, 358.

411. "The days of James Cagney": PCH 7:466–67.

412. Motorcycle gangs: OCA 1:336; GLR, pp. 212–13, 569–70.

412. Typical biker: *Washington Post*, April 3, 1982; MAR, pp. 162–69.

412. *Godfather* effect: OCA 1:337.

412. "I joined because": OCA 1:436.

412. Synthetic drugs: MAR, p. 140; OCA 1:369.

412. Probation period: MAR, p. 55; OCA 1:414–15.

412. Tattoo might be cut: OCA 1:425–26.

413. Four main gangs: OCA 1:338, 393–96.

413. Bikers and Mafia: MAR, pp. 19, 64, 112, 151–54; OCA 1:368, 397–404, 411.

413. "Organized crime figures": MAR, p. 105.

413. Lack of traditional code: OCV, p. 93; GLR, p. 99; MAR, pp. 119, 183.

413. Blacks as Mafia employees: Francis A. J. Ianni, *Black Mafia: Ethnic Succession in Organized Crime* (1974), p. 119; OCA 2:254–55.

413. Buffalo and Newark: *Time*, August 22, 1969.

413. "Everybody wants his turn": Ianni, *Black*, p. 96.

414. "The blacks use": Donald Goddard, *Easy Money* (1978), p. 51.

414. Green: PCD, p. 127.

414. Matthews: Goddard, *Easy*, pp. 121–23.

414. Barnes: PCH 5:218; Goddard, *Easy*, pp. 106–7; Fred Ferretti in *New York Times Magazine*, June 5, 1977.

414. Council: PCD, pp. 127–28.

414. "We weren't subjected": PCH 5:213; next quotation, ibid., pp. 205–6.

414. Papa D's Family: PCH 5:220–60.

414. "Every time": ibid., p. 241.

415. Coffin with heroin: ibid., pp. 222–23.

415. Young Boys: GLR, pp. 178–83; PCH 1:53–56.

415. Black succession: Ianni, *Black.*

415. "There was no": PCH 5:195; next quotation, ibid., pp. 210–11.

416. Cuban gangsters: CAO, p. 26; SFA 3:762–63.

416. Battle: PCH 7:104–8.

416. Corporation: PCH 7:103, 110–11, 133–40.

416. Payoffs to Mafia: PCH 7:144.

417. Colombians: *Rolling Stone,* September 20, 1979; *Organized Crime,* ed. Howard Abadinsky (second edition, 1985), pp. 160–63; OCV, p. 474; PCD, pp. 77–78.

417. A dozen gangs: PCH 1:47–48.

417. "I wish we were": FID, p. 27.

417. Wholesale price: PCH 4:684.

417. Chinese population: *New York Times,* January 13, 1985.

417. Tongs and gangs: PCH 3:74–76, 90–93, 95–127; OCA 2:259–60; and see Gerald L. Posner, *Warlords of Crime: Chinese Secret Societies—The New Mafia* (1988).

417. FOB and ABC: PCH 3:80.

417. San Francisco massacre: ibid., pp. 81–84.

418. Ky's group and organized crime: PCH 3:328–42.

418. Vietnamese and Chinese feuds: *Boston Globe,* March 24, 1986, January 5, 6, 27, 1987.

418. Posses: *Time,* March 14, 1988: *Boston Globe,* March 1, 2, 1987.

418. Operation Rum Punch: *Boston Globe,* October 21, 1987.

418. Zips: OCA 2:113; Joseph D. Pistone with Richard Woodley, *Donnie Brasco: My Undercover Life in the Mafia* (1988), pp. 114–15.

418. Bonventre: *Time,* October 15, 1984.

419. $1.65 billion in heroin: PCD, pp. 130–31; Shana Alexander, *The Pizza Connection: Lawyers, Money, Drugs, Mafia* (1988).

419. "You can't trust": Pistone, *Brasco,* p. 132; next two quotations, ibid., pp. 316, 356.

419. "Anyone who deals": transcript of Angiulo bugs, April 23, 1981.

419. "People don't train": Peter McCabe in *Playboy,* July 1987.

419. Younger Mafiosi bound only: PCI, p. 50.

419. "My Tradition": Joseph Bonanno with Sergio Lalli, *A Man of Honor* (1983), p. 404; and see Vincent Siciliano, *Unless They Kill Me First* (1970), p. 57; Teresa, *My Life,* p. 354; Patsy Anthony Lepera and Walter Goodman, *Memoirs of a Scam Man* (1974), pp. 3–4; Vincent Teresa with Thomas C. Renner, *Vinnie Teresa's Mafia* (1975), p. 95; Robert W. Greene, *The Sting Man: Inside Abscam* (1981), p. 82: Vincent Cafaro testimony, April 29, 1988.

420. Hopeful observers: Nicholas Pileggi in *Life,* March 3, 1972; David Leon Chandler, *Brothers in Blood* (1975), pp. 205–6; Peter Reuter, *Disorganized Crime: The Economics of the Visible Hand* (1983), pp. 185–87; GLR, p. 13; PCH 3:8.

420. Italians and national norms: Richard D. Alba, *Italian Americans: Into the Twilight of Ethnicity* (1985), pp. 120–27; Stephen S. Hall in *New York Times Magazine,* May 15, 1983.

420. Mafia remained: PCH 1:22–24.

420. Rising stars: *Wall Street Journal,* April 19, 1984; *Boston Globe,* April 17, 1988; Edward Barnes and William Shebar in *Life,* December 1987.

420. "Their children": testimony of Joseph Pistone to Nunn committee, April 22, 1988, Cable News Network.

420. "He is very": PCI, p. 316.

420. "As a wiseguy": Pistone, *Brasco,* p. 330; and see Nicholas Pileggi, *Wiseguy* (1985), p. 242.

INDEX